Essential MODERN WORLD HISTORY

STEVEN WAUGH

Editorial and ICT consultant: Aaron Wilkes

First published in 2001 by:
Nelson Thornes Ltd
Delta Place
27 Bath Road
Cheltenham GL53 7TH
United Kingdom

01 02 03 04 05 / 10 9 8 7 6 5 4 3 2 1

A catalogue record for this book is available from the British Library.

ISBN 0-7487-6006-7

Printed and bound in Italy by Canale

Page layout by Multiplex Techniques Ltd
Illustrated by Multiplex Techniques Ltd and Angela Lumley
Picture research by Christina Morgan

Contents

Acknowledgements

With thanks to the following for permission to reproduce photographs and other copyright material in this book:

t = top; b = bottom; r = right, l = left.

Advertising Archives 464

AKG, London 145, 243r, 269, 270r, 350t, 354t, 373br, 383

Archiv Gerstenberg 385

Art Archive 50b, 90, 169, 173, 177, 200t, 373bl, 392

Associated Newspapers 188

Bildarchiv Preussischer Kulturbesitz 346, 378b

British Library Newspaper 34

Camera Press 589, 613, *Fackelman* 317

Centre for the Study of Cartoons and Caricatures 338, 368, *Nicholas Garland* 308b, *David Low* 139, 141t, 156, 565

Corbis 85, 120, 140, 180t, 228, 230, 238, 253t, 261t, 263b, 270l, 286, 291, 298, 302, 304, 305, 310, 313, 315, 391r, 463, 469t, 475, 486, 487b, 489, 496, 497, 539, 561, 592, 600, 620, 623

Daily Mail 251, 263t

Daily Telegraph 247b

David King Collection 233, 236, 237, 239r, 245, 398, 402, 405b, 406, 408, 409l, 415, 417, 422, 425r, 429, 435, 439, 442t, 448, 453, 455, 568

Franklin D Roosevelt Library 493, 506

John Frost 21b, 63, 166, 170, 191t, 278, 300, 548t, 549

Gateshead Central Library 560

Guardian/*Andre Krauze* 326

Hulton Getty 121b, 253b, 273, 431, 478, 521t, 536, 554, 564, 594

Imperial War Museum 37, 74, 94, 106, 107, 109, 180b, 185, 200b, 201, 204, 210, 213

Kobal Collection 372r, 418

Magnum *Koudelka* 310, *Marc Ribourd* 607

Mary Evans Picture Library 7, 14, 17, 24, 27, 45, 59, 60, 71, 86, 103, 121t, 122, 124, 135, 152, 165, 194, 202r, 252, 337, 354b, 357, 370, 373t, 468, 469b, 477, 482, 523, 528, 531, 532t, 537, 542, 544b, 547, 548m, 548b, 556, 562

Museum of London 532b

Peter Newark's Pictures 101, 189, 216, 220, 234, 242, 290, 473, 483, 487t, 491, 498, 505

Novosti, London 187, 258b, 259, 264m, 264b, 319, 442b

Popperfoto 153, 202l, 212, 231, 255, 272t, 275, 292, 411t, 584, 602

Portsmouth Museum Department 191b

Public Record Office 205

Punch 527, 550, 574, 575r

Rex Features 254l, 268t, 308t, 311, 324, 325, 617

Philip Sauvain 4t, 6, 8, 10, 13, 19, 22, 23, 36, 39, 41, 42, 43, 44, 50t, 51, 52, 53, 56, 62, 67, 76, 77, 89, 95, 100, 102, 105, 111, 112, 128t, 129, 133, 141b, 149, 332, 333, 343, 345, 347, 348, 350b, 356, 358, 364, 369, 374, 376, 378t, 387, 397, 399, 400, 401, 403, 405t, 407, 409r, 411b, 412, 414, 425l, 432, 433, 436, 437, 441, 443, 446, 449, 465, 517, 519, 521b, 526, 530, 534, 535, 543, 544t, 566

School of Slavonic and Eastern European Studies 247t

Science and Society Picture Library 258t

Suddeutscher Verlag Bilderdienst 352, 359, 591

Topham Picturepoint 154, 209, 261b, 274, 285, 293, 570, 587

Ullstein Bildersteinst 148, 334, 342

Wiener Library 353, 372l, 379, 381

Xinhua News Agency 610

Random House Group for Wilfred Owen's 'Dulce et Decorum Est', page 46, Source L
© Copyright Siegfried Sassoon by kind permission of George Sassoon, page 46, Source M.

Every effort has been made to contact copyright holders. The publishers apologise to anyone whose rights have been inadvertently overlooked, and will be happy to rectify any errors or omissions.

1 The Causes of the First World War

UNDERSTANDING THE CAUSES OF THE FIRST WORLD WAR

The following definitions and explanations should help you understand this chapter.

Alliance	An agreement between two or more countries in which they agree to help each other. This could mean military help in a war.
Armaments	Weapons of war.
Assassinated	Killed violently.
Balkans	The area of south-west Europe which had been controlled by the Turks – including Serbia, Romania and Bulgaria.
Colonies	Territories taken over by countries in Europe. These were mainly in Africa.
Conscription	Making it compulsory for young people of a certain age to spend usually one or two years in the armed services.
Dreadnought	Battleship launched by Britain which made all previous battleships out of date.
Empire	A group of countries, colonies or states ruled over and owned by another country.
Entente	Agreement between two or more countries to settle any problems or differences.
Heir	Next in line to a position.
Imperialism	The policy of building up an empire.
Isolated	Without friends or allies.
Militarism	Settling a problem or dispute through war.
Mobilisation	Getting soldiers and guns ready to do battle.
Nationalism	A strong love of your nation/the thought that your country is better than others.
Neutral	Not becoming involved or staying out of a war. Not taking sides.
The 'Scrap of Paper'	The Treaty of London of 1839 by which the Great Powers guaranteed the neutrality of Belgium.
Terrorist	A person who uses violent methods.
Ultimatum	A final demand from one country to another.

The Causes of the First World War

In 1914 war broke out between the Great Powers. This was the name for the leading powers in Europe – Britain, France, Russia, Germany and Austria-Hungary. The war was caused by long-term rivalries between these powers. These were worsened by a series of crises between 1905 and 1913 culminating in the immediate event that sparked off war, the assassination of Archduke Franz-Ferdinand in June 1914.

EUROPE AND THE GREAT POWERS IN 1900

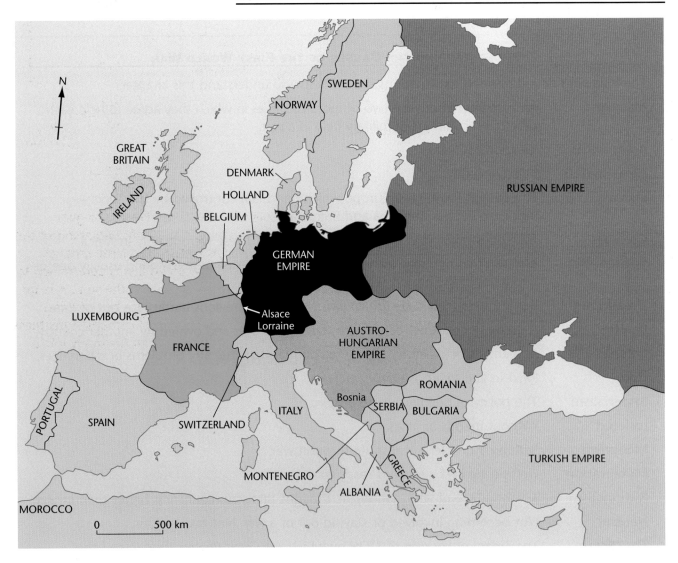

There were several causes building up over a long period of time.

Colonial rivalry

The European colonial empires in 1900

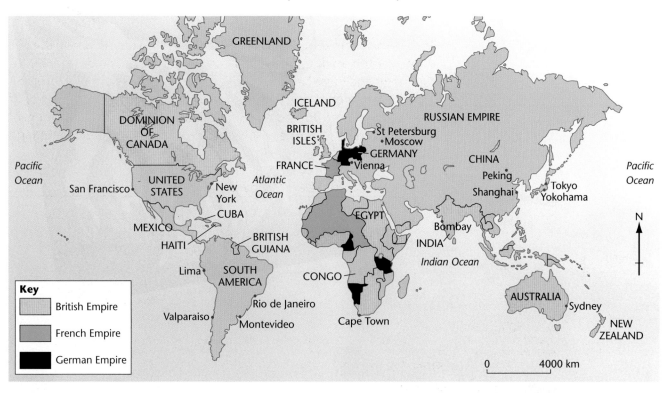

Key
- British Empire
- French Empire
- German Empire

This refers to competition between the Great Powers to gain colonies or areas to build up their empires. By the beginning of the twentieth century Britain and France already had large empires compared to that of Germany. Kaiser Wilhelm II was determined to build up the German Empire and gain 'a place in the sun'. A large empire would provide Germany with a market for her growing industries. It was also a status symbol showing Germany's greatness and gaining it respect. In particular, this brought Germany into rivalry with France in Morocco in North Africa.

SOURCE A

German view of Britain's Empire

HONNI SOIT QUI MAL Y PENSE

SOURCE B

A British view of the Kaiser and his attempt to build up an empire

THE WORLD IS MINE

THE DREAM

Balkan nationalism
The Balkans in 1914

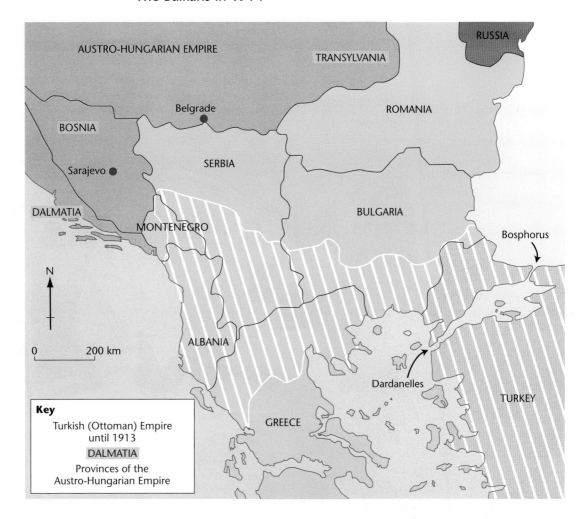

The Balkans is the area of south-west Europe (see map). This area had once been part of the Turkish Empire. It was inhabited by Slav peoples such as the Serbs, Bosnians, Bulgarians and Romanians who were now able to rule themselves.

Russia regarded herself as the protector of these Slavs. Many of these nationalities were part of the Austro-Hungarian Empire. Serbia, in particular, wanted to unite all Serbs within a greater Serbia. This brought rivalry with Austria-Hungary who feared losing not only the Serbs but also other Balkan nationals. In order to preserve its own empire, Austria-Hungary wanted to take over the states of this area. The Balkans was the powder-keg or trouble spot of Europe. It brought increasing rivalry between Russia, Serbia's protector, and Austria-Hungary.

Servia means Serbia. The big bear represents Russia.

PUNCH, OR THE LONDON CHARIVARI.—JULY 29, 1914.

THE POWER BEHIND.

AUSTRIA (*at the ultimatum stage*). "I DON'T QUITE LIKE HIS ATTITUDE. SOMEBODY MUST BE BACKING HIM."

Nationalities of the Austro-Hungarian Empire

AUSTRIA	%
Germans	35.6
Czechs	23.0
Poles	17.8
Ruthenians	12.6
Serbo-Croats	2.6
Romanians	1.0
Other	7.4

LANDS OF THE HUNGARIAN CROWN, INCLUDING CROATIA-SLAVONIA	%
Magyars	48.1
Germans	9.8
Slovaks	9.4
Romanians	14.1
Ruthenians	2.3
Croats	8.8
Serbs	5.3
Other	2.2

BOSNIA-HERZEGOVINA	%
Croats	21
Serbs	42
Mohammedans	34
Other	3

Source D

SOURCE D

From a French magazine of 1893. The French members of parliament argue while the angel (representing France) points to the danger from the soldiers of Germany.

Alsace-Lorraine

Between 1870 and 1871 France fought against Prussia (later the leading state in Germany). The French were defeated and forced to accept a humiliating peace treaty in which they lost the two provinces of Alsace-Lorraine, rich in coal and iron ore, to the new Germany. This created even greater rivalry between France and Germany. Many in France, known as the Revanchists, wanted revenge on Germany and more especially pressed for the return of the 'lost provinces'.

The Arms Race

This means the rivalry between the Great Powers to build up the size of their armed forces. Every major power in Europe except Britain had trained a huge army of conscripts – meaning young men forced by law to become soldiers for a year or so.

These armies could be mobilised (called-up) at a moment's notice. In the period 1900–1914 the main European powers more than doubled their spending on their armies.

Krupps armaments works in Essen

ARMAMENTS SPENDING 1872–1912

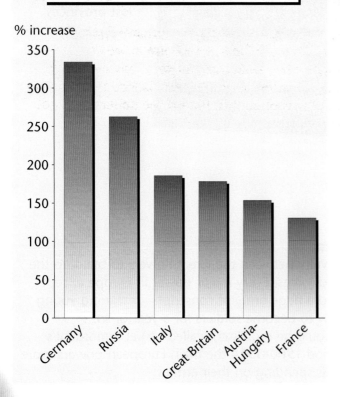

% increase

Guns, shells, bullets and other weapons had been stockpiled in case of war. Ever more destructive weapons were being developed and improved, such as the machine-gun and huge field guns. The Arms Race brought war nearer because:

• It increased tension between the Great Powers. It had a rolling 'snowball' effect. When one power increased its army, another would follow suit.

• It made war more likely. As each country increased its army and weapons it became more confident of success in a future war and more willing to test out their armed forces.

The Anglo-German Naval Race

This was another aspect of the Arms Race. Although Britain only had a small professional army, her Royal Navy was the most powerful in the world. It outgunned and outnumbered all other navies. The navy was vital to Britain for two major reasons:

- It protected the Empire and trade.

- It prevented invasion.

Germany already had the world's best army. In 1898 it began to build a fleet of battleships to rival the British Navy:

- Kaiser Wilhelm, the German ruler, had always had more interest in the navy than the army.

- It would protect and help to build up German trade and colonies.

At first this was not of major concern to Britain. The Royal Navy was far superior and it would take Germany many years to catch up. All this changed with the launch of the super-battleship *Dreadnought* in 1906. This made all previous battleships obsolete or out of date. It was faster, bigger and had a much greater firing range than existing battleships. Worse still it meant Britain was only one new battleship ahead of Germany. A race developed between the two countries to see who could build the most. In 1909 Britain had eight Dreadnoughts to Germany's seven.

This naval race, more than anything else, poisoned relations between the two countries. Britain feared German world domination if the Kaiser had both the strongest navy and army. Germany resisted British attempts in the years before 1914 to slow down the building of Dreadnoughts. Indeed the Kaiser could not understand British concerns.

HMS *Dreadnought*

Focus on

The Dreadnought

The 'Dreadnought' class battleship had an eleven-inch armour plating for protection. Compare this with a battleship built only a year earlier.

HMS *Dominion* built in 1905. 16,350 tons; length 457 feet; 4 twelve-inch guns, 4 nine-inch guns, 5 torpedo tubes; armour 9 inches thick; top speed 18.2 knots.

HMS *Dreadnought* built 1906. 17,900 tons; length 526 feet; 10 twelve-inch guns, 18 four-inch guns, 5 torpedo tubes; armour 11 inches thick; top speed 21.6 knots.

SOURCE I

The *Daily Mail*, 1909

Germany is deliberately preparing to destroy the British Empire. All of Europe is to be taken over by Germany. We are all to be drilled and schooled and uniformed by German officials. Emperor William II is to rule with a rod of iron. Britain alone stands in the way of Germany's path to world domination.

Kaiser Wilhelm II and German militarism

The Kaiser, Wilhelm II, has often been blamed for causing the First World War. He certainly increased tension with other powers through his actions. In particular, he upset the British by deciding to build up the German Empire and navy.

Germany, itself, had a tradition of militarism – of settling problems through war. Many German commanders were convinced by 1904 that the situation in Europe was so bad that war was inevitable. Russia was already modernising and would soon be a major threat. The French wanted revenge for the defeat in 1871.

The Germans feared an attack on two fronts – from Russia in the east and France in the west. By 1905 they had finalised a war plan devised by General von Schlieffen. The plan (p. 32) was to defeat France quickly in a future war by invading through Belgium and then dealing with Russia. This brought the possibility of war closer because:

- If Germany invaded Belgium it might lead to war with Britain (p. 12).

- The very presence of the plan made Germany more willing to go to war.

The Alliance System

By 1907 Europe was divided into two armed camps or rival gangs.

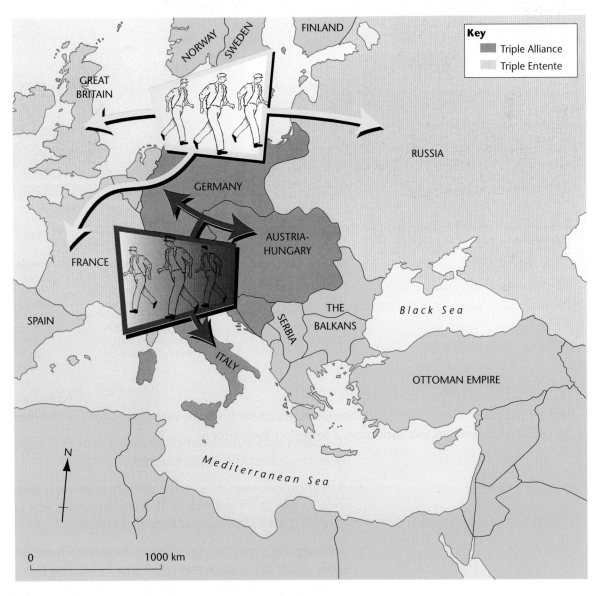

This system of alliances had started under Otto von Bismarck, the Chancellor of Germany between 1871 and 1890. He feared the French desire for revenge after the loss of Alsace-Lorraine and wanted to keep the French isolated from the other Great Powers.

GREAT BRITAIN

1 was angered by German support of Boers during the Boer War (1899–1902)
2 feared German rivalry in
 a industry and trade
 b naval power
 c empire
3 abandoned its policy of 'splendid isolation' and began to build 'ententes' (friendly agreements).

GERMANY

1 was a new nation (since 1871) anxious about its security
2 felt particularly threatened by France and Russia
3 wanted colonies as Kaiser Wilhelm II was jealous of Britain's empire
4 was building the Berlin-Baghdad Railway through the Balkans.

RUSSIA

1 needed an outlet to the sea and therefore wanted a weak or friendly power in control of the Dardanelles
2 opposed Austrian or German influence in the Balkans
3 saw the Berlin-Baghdad Railway as a threat to its position in the Balkans
4 wished to protect other Slav peoples:
 a hostile to Germany which ruled Polish Slavs
 b supported Serbs and Bulgars.

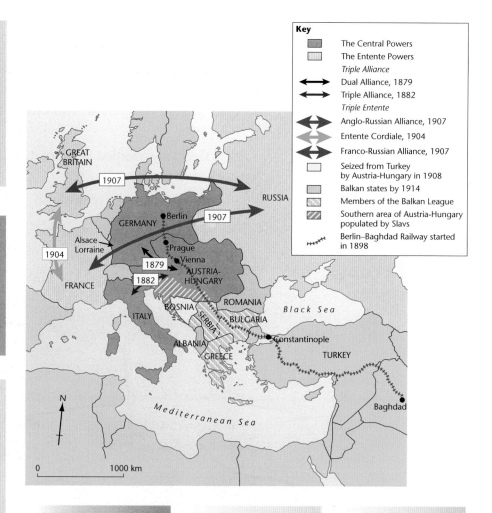

Key

	The Central Powers
	The Entente Powers
	Triple Alliance
←→	Dual Alliance, 1879
←→	Triple Alliance, 1882
	Triple Entente
←→	Anglo-Russian Alliance, 1907
←→	Entente Cordiale, 1904
←→	Franco-Russian Alliance, 1907
	Seized from Turkey by Austria-Hungary in 1908
	Balkan states by 1914
	Members of the Balkan League
	Southern area of Austria-Hungary populated by Slavs
	Berlin–Baghdad Railway started in 1898

FRANCE

1 was angered by the loss of Alsace-Lorraine to Germany after Franco-Prussian War (1870)
2 featured further German aggression
3 wanted to protect its empire, especially in North Africa.

AUSTRIA-HUNGARY

1 was an empire of many nationalities
2 was worried by national groups which might want to rule themselves, especially Slav peoples in the south who looked to Serbia for leadership.

SERBIA

1 was a new nation formed in 1878 after breaking away from the Turkish Empire
2 nationalists planned to create Yugoslavia (Southern Slavia) by bringing into Serbia all Slavs living in the south of Austria-Hungary.

The Alliance System brought war nearer for several reasons:

- It created two armed camps or rival gangs in Europe – the Triple Alliance against the Triple Entente.

- A dispute between one of the members of each camp could well involve the other members. This would turn a war between two countries into a major war between all six.

- Although only an Entente, relations between France and Britain drew much closer between 1904 and 1914. The two countries even planned together how to fight a future war against Germany.

SOURCE J

The four countries linking hands are France, Russia, Britain and Japan. In 1902 Britain signed an alliance with Japan.

Activity

Draw flags representing each of the following countries in 1912:

France, Britain, Germany, Austria-Hungary and Russia.

Write on each flag a sentence explaining for each power:

- Who were their allies (friends) and why.

- With which country or countries they felt tension and rivalry and why.

Questions

1 Write down the links or connections between the long-term causes of the First World War – for example, between the Arms Race and the alliance system: Britain felt threatened by the German navy and drew closer to France.

2 What differences are there between Sources **A** and **B** in their views of the empires of Germany and Britain? Why are the views so different?

3 Explain the importance of the following in increasing rivalry between the Great Powers:
   a the *Dreadnought*.
   b Serbia.
   c Kaiser Wilhelm II.

4 What point is the cartoonist trying to make in Source **C**?

5 How useful is Source **D** to a historian studying rivalry between France and Germany at the end of the nineteenth century?

6 What do Sources **F** and **G** tell you about German motives for building up its navy?

7 Do you agree with comments of the *Daily Mail* in Source **I**? Give reasons for your answer.

There were crises in Morocco and the Balkans. These increased the rivalry between the Great Powers and brought war closer.

The First Moroccan Crisis 1905–6

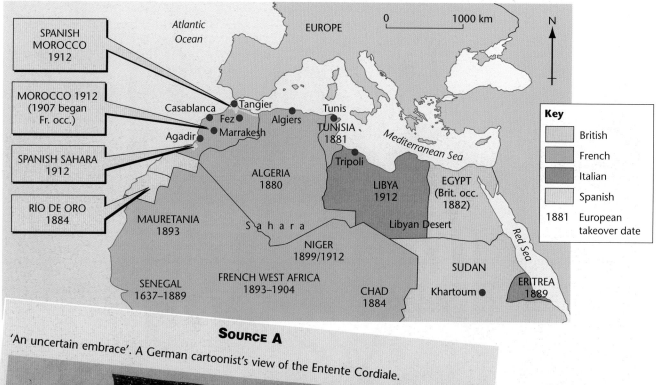

Key	
	British
	French
	Italian
	Spanish
1881	European takeover date

Map labels:
- SPANISH MOROCCO 1912
- MOROCCO 1912 (1907 began Fr. occ.)
- SPANISH SAHARA 1912
- RIO DE ORO 1884
- Atlantic Ocean
- EUROPE
- 0   1000 km
- N
- Casablanca
- Tangier
- Tunis
- Fez
- Algiers
- TUNISIA 1881
- Agadir
- Marrakesh
- Mediterranean Sea
- ALGERIA 1880
- Tripoli
- LIBYA 1912
- EGYPT (Brit. occ. 1882)
- MAURETANIA 1893
- Sahara
- Libyan Desert
- Red Sea
- NIGER 1899/1912
- SUDAN
- SENEGAL 1637–1889
- FRENCH WEST AFRICA 1893–1904
- CHAD 1884
- Khartoum
- ERITREA 1889

SOURCE A

'An uncertain embrace'. A German cartoonist's view of the Entente Cordiale.

Die französisch-englische Parlamentarier-Verbrüderung (Avers und Revers)

France wanted Morocco to complete her empire in North Africa. In 1904 Britain and France agreed the Entente Cordiale (Anglo-French Entente). This Entente gave France a free hand in Morocco. The Kaiser, however, decided to interfere in Morocco:

- He wanted to test the strength of the Entente and believed he could split the agreement. He did not believe Britain would stand by France over Morocco.

- He did not want to see France extend her North African Empire.

In 1905 the Kaiser paid a visit to the Moroccan port of Tangiers. There he made a speech in which he declared that Morocco should remain independent of France. This sparked off a crisis. France, backed by Britain, refused to back down but did agree to the Kaiser's demand for an international meeting or conference to discuss the future of Morocco.

Kaiser Wilhelm II riding through Tangiers in 1905

The conference took place at Algeciras at Spain. It was a disaster for the Kaiser. Only Austria-Hungary backed his demands for Moroccan independence. Britain supported the French. This crisis increased tension because:

- France was more or less given a free hand in Morocco. The Kaiser had suffered an embarrassing defeat.

- He blamed this defeat on the British and their support for France.

- Wilhelm II's actions had achieved the opposite of what he had hoped. They had strengthened the Entente Cordiale.

The Bosnian crisis 1908–9

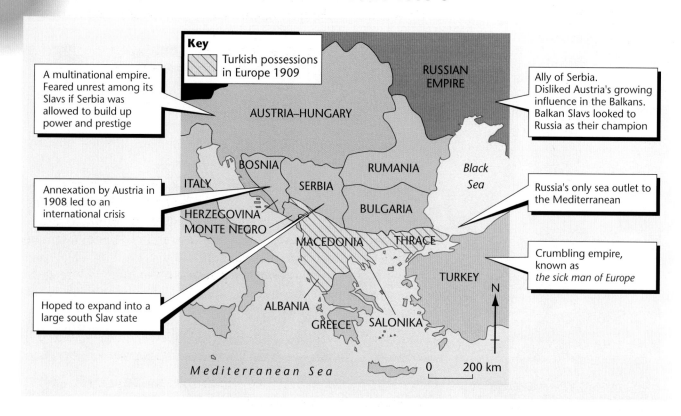

Key
Turkish possessions in Europe 1909

A multinational empire. Feared unrest among its Slavs if Serbia was allowed to build up power and prestige

Ally of Serbia. Disliked Austria's growing influence in the Balkans. Balkan Slavs looked to Russia as their champion

Annexation by Austria in 1908 led to an international crisis

Russia's only sea outlet to the Mediterranean

Crumbling empire, known as *the sick man of Europe*

Hoped to expand into a large south Slav state

In 1908 Austria-Hungary added Bosnia-Herzegovina to its empire. This created a second international crisis. The Serbians were furious because they had hoped to make Bosnia part of a 'greater Serbian' state. They appealed to Russia for help. Russia's answer was to call for an international conference to discuss Austria's action. Austria refused to attend and was backed by Germany.

Germany demanded that Russia accept the Austrian seizure of Bosnia-Herzegovina. Russia had little choice but to back down. Russia's armies were no match for the German forces. This crisis again increased tension:

- Serbia was furious with Austria and wanted revenge and the return of Bosnia.

- Russia was humiliated but was unlikely to back down in another crisis.

- Germany was now fully committed to supporting Austrian policy in the Balkans, even if it led to war.

- Russia drew even closer to France and Britain.

The second Moroccan or Agadir crisis, 1911

In 1911 there was a second crisis in Morocco. Early in 1911 the Sultan, the ruler of Morocco, asked the French for help in crushing a revolt led by rebel tribesmen. Germany was certain that this would be followed by a French takeover. As soon as the French occupied Fez, in Morocco, the Kaiser sent a gunboat, *Panther*, to the Moroccan port of Agadir.

SOURCE C

The German Chancellor, Bulow, in 1908

Our position would, indeed, be dangerous if Austria lost confidence in us and turned away. In the present situation we must be careful to keep Austria as a 'true partner'.

SOURCE D

L. Seaman, a British historian, writing in 1955

The dispatch of the Panther showed German policy. They did not really want trading rights in Morocco or compensation from the French in Central Africa. They simply wanted everyone to go on being frightened of them.

As in 1905, the Kaiser was trying to break the Entente Cordiale. He was also seeking compensation from France in the form of the whole of the French Congo in Central Africa.

Once again Germany's action misfired. Britain was even more determined to support France and oppose Germany:

- The British believed that Germany was trying to set up a naval base in Morocco.

- It seemed to be another attempt by the Kaiser to break up the Entente.

The British Chancellor of the Exchequer, David Lloyd George, someone who was known to be against war, warned Germany that Britain would fight rather than see France pushed around in this way. Britain's fleet was even prepared for war. In the end, Germany backed down rather than risk war.

Another crisis had brought the powers to the brink of war and increased tension:

The Agadir crisis:

- Drew Britain and France closer together. France was again very pleased to have Britain's support against Germany.

- Again humiliated the Kaiser who blamed the British. He was unlikely to back down again.

SOURCE E

A British cartoon on the Agadir Crisis from *Punch*, 2 August 1911

PUNCH, OR THE LONDON CHARIVARI.—August 2, 1911.

SOLID.

GERMANY. "DONNERWETTER! IT'S ROCK. I THOUGHT IT WAS GOING TO BE PAPER."

SOURCE F

Von Moltke, the German Chief of Army Staff, speaking in 1911

I am thoroughly fed up with this wretched Morocco affair. If once again we crawl out of this affair with our tail between our legs I despair of the future of the German Empire. In that case I shall quit.

The Balkan Wars, 1912–13

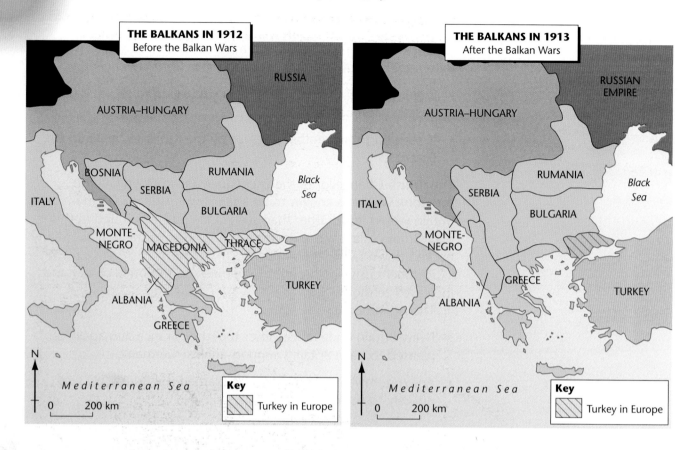

Ever since the Bosnian disaster of 1908–9 (see p. 16) Russia had tried to get the Balkan states to form an alliance. In this way Russia hoped to block an Austrian takeover of the Balkans. In 1912 Serbia, Greece, Bulgaria and Montenegro formed a group called the Balkan League. In October the armies of this League attacked the Turks to drive them out of the small area they still controlled. They were very successful and drove Turkey out of Europe.

This alarmed Austria, particularly because Serbia had emerged as the strongest Balkan state. The Austrian generals now wanted a quick war to crush Serbia once and for all. Fearing this could well trigger off a major European war, the Great Powers stepped in and forced a peace settlement on the victorious Balkan states. At the peace conference of 1913:

- Serbia gained much territory because the Turkish lands were shared out among the Balkan League.

- The Austrians, however, managed to defeat Serbia's plans to gain a coastline by having a new country, Albania, placed between Serbia and the Adriatic Sea.

Within a month the Balkan League had fallen out and there was a second Balkan war. Bulgaria quarrelled with Serbia and Greece. In June 1913, the Bulgarians attacked their former allies. They were, however, quickly defeated. In the peace settlement that followed, Bulgaria surrendered nearly all the lands it had won in the first war to Greece and Serbia. Serbia gained even more land.

The Balkan Wars brought war one step nearer because:

- Serbia became almost twice as large. It was now even more determined to unite with the Serbs in the Austrian Empire.

- Serbia was now a much greater threat to Austria. Austria, in turn, was more determined than ever to crush the Serbians. On the other hand, Russia was more determined than ever to support this bigger Slav state.

- The Germans had restrained Austria during this period but knew, in another crisis, they would have to support Austrian action.

- Bulgaria was determined to gain revenge on Serbia and Greece.

SOURCE G

A British cartoon published in *Punch* magazine during the Balkan crisis, October 1912. The figures in the pot represent the five Great Powers.

PUNCH, OR THE LONDON CHARIVARI.—October 2, 1912.

BALKAN TROUBLES

THE BOILING POINT.

SOURCE H

Secret meeting between the Kaiser and his top commanders, December 1912

The German Kaiser predicted that if the Austrians did not face up to the Serbian menace, they would have considerable trouble from the Slav peoples within the Austro-Hungarian empire. The fleet must now look upon England as the enemy. Moltke, the Army Chief, believed war was bound to happen and said 'The sooner, the better'. Tirpitz, the Navy Chief, wanted another eighteen months to get the navy ready for war.

Activity

1. Compare the two maps of the Balkans before and after the Balkan Wars and answer the following questions:

   a. What happened to the Turkish Empire?

   b. Which Balkan state increased in size the most as a result of these wars?

   c. What important geographical advantage would Serbia have gained if Albania had been included in its borders?

2. Sketch the chart below

Great Powers and the Crisis, 1905–13

Crises	Which powers involved	How it increased rivalry
1905 Morocco		
1908 Bosnia		
1911 Agadir		
1912–13 Balkans		

In the box next to each crisis write:

a. Which powers were involved in that crisis.

b. How it increased rivalry between those powers.

Questions

1. What do Sources **C** and **H** show about Germany's attitude to:
   a. Austria?
   b. war?

2. What point is the cartoonist making in Source **E**?

3. Why did the two Moroccan crises increase rivalry between Germany and Britain?

4. Is Source **D** a reliable view of the Agadir crisis of 1911?

5. How useful is Source **H** to an historian studying the Balkan wars of 1912–13?

6. Why was war more likely in 1913 than in 1904? Give reasons for your answer.

THE IMMEDIATE CAUSE OF WAR

General war was eventually caused by events in the Balkans and the murder of a member of the Austrian royal family.

The Assassination of Franz-Ferdinand

Profile on

Franz-Ferdinand

The Archduke Franz-Ferdinand had fallen out with the Emperor of Austria-Hungary, Franz Josef, over his plans to marry the beautiful Countess Sophie von Chotkowa und Wognin. She was not of royal blood and was seen as a commoner. The two eloped and married secretly on 28 June 1900. Then they returned to Austria. Franz Josef was so annoyed that he refused to allow them to be seen in public together. Sophie was continually insulted by the Emperor and other members of the royal family. Franz-Ferdinand, however, was able to get over his father's ban on joint public appearances. He was Field Marshal of the army and could appear with a commoner as his wife in public. It was in this role that he visited Sarajevo in 1914.

Archduke Franz-Ferdinand was heir to the throne of Austria. On 28 June 1914 the Archduke and his wife, Sophie, paid a state visit to Sarajevo, the capital of Bosnia.

Focus on

Gavrilo Princip and the Black Hand Movement

Gavrilo Princip was only 20 years of age when he killed the Archduke. Princip was a printer, born in Herzegovina, whose real name was Nedjeliko Gabrinovitch. He was a member of the Black Hand, a secret society in Serbia. The Black Hand was organised by Colonel Dimitrievitch. Its aim was to unite all Serbs, including those of the Austrian empire, into an enlarged Serbia. It would achieve this through a campaign of violence. Dimitrievitch had trained some of its members to carry out the murder in Sarajevo. Waiting for Franz-Ferdinand were six young men armed with pistols and guns supplied by the Black Hand.

HEIR TO AUSTRIA'S THRONE IS SLAIN WITH HIS WIFE BY A BOSNIAN YOUTH TO AVENGE SEIZURE OF HIS COUNTRY

Francis Ferdinand Shot During State Visit to Sarajevo.

TWO ATTACKS IN A DAY

Archduke Saves His Life First Time by Knocking Aside a Bomb Hurled at Auto.

SLAIN IN SECOND ATTEMPT

Lad Dashes at Car as the Royal Couple Return from Town Hall and Kills Both of Them.

LAID TO A SERVIAN PLOT

Heir Warned Not to Go to Bosnia, Where Populace Met Him with Servian Flags.

AGED EMPEROR IS STRICKEN

Shock of Tragedy Prostrates Francis Joseph—Young Assassin Proud of His Crime.

Special Cable to THE NEW YORK TIMES.
SARAJEVO, Bosnia, June 28, (By courtesy of the Vienna Neue Freie Presse.)—Archduke Francis Ferdinand, heir to the throne of Austria-Hungary, and his wife, the Duchess of Hohenberg, were shot and killed by a Bosnian student here today. The fatal shooting was the second attempt upon the lives of the couple during

Archduke Francis Ferdinand and his Consort the Duchess of Hohenberg

Slain by Assassin's Bullets.

could only certify they were both dead.

The authors of both attacks upon the Archduke are born Bosnians. Gabrinovics is a compositor, and worked for a few weeks in the Government printing works at Belgrade. He returned to Sarajevo a Servian chauvinist, and made no concealment of his sympathies with the King of Servia. Both he and the actual murderer of the Archduke and the Duchess expressed themselves to the police in the most cynical fashion about their crimes.

ARCHDUKE IGNORED WARNING

Servian Minister Feared Trouble if Heir Went to Bosnia.

Special Cable to THE NEW YORK TIMES.
[Dispatch to The London Daily Mail.]
VIENNA, June 28.—When the news of the assassination of the Archduke

by splinters from the bomb. Several persons on the pavement were very seriously hurt by the explosion of the bomb, which was thrown by a young man named Tabrinovitch. (Gabrinovics,) who is a typist from Trebenje in Herzegovina, and is of Servian nationality. He was arrested some twenty minutes later.

The Archduke and his wife left the Town Hall, intending to visit those who had been injured by the bomb, when a schoolboy 19 years old, named Prinzip, who came from Grahovo, fired a shot at the Archduke's head. The boy fired from the shelter of a projecting house.

Were Bullet-Proof Coat.

The boy must have been carefully instructed in his part, for it was a well-guarded secret that the Archduke always wore a coat of silk strands which were woven obliquely, so that no weapon or bullet could pierce it. I once saw a strip of this fabric used for a motor-car tire, and it was

it is feared that it will lead to serious complications with that unruly kingdom, and may have far-reaching results. The future of the empire is a subject of general discussion. It is felt that the Servians have been treated too leniently, and some hard words are being said about the present foreign policy.

All the public buildings are draped in long black streamers and the flags are all at half-mast.

BRAVERY OF ARCHDUKE.

Gave First Aid to Those Wounded by the Bomb.

SARAJEVO, Bosnia, June 28.—Archduke Francis Ferdinand, heir to the Austro-Hungarian throne, and the Duchess of Hohenberg, his morganatic wife, were shot dead in the main street of the Bosnian capital by a student today while they were making an apparently triumphant progress through the city on their annual visit to the annexed provinces of Bosnia and Herzegovina.

The Archduke was hit full in the face

MURDER IN SARAJEVO!

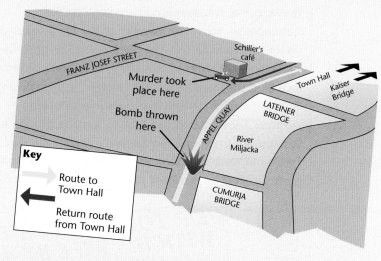

Schiller's café

FRANZ JOSEF STREET

Murder took place here

Bomb thrown here

Town Hall

Kaiser Bridge

LATEINER BRIDGE

APPEL QUAY

River Miljacka

CUMURJA BRIDGE

Key

→ Route to Town Hall

← Return route from Town Hall

The Archduke Franz-Ferdinand and his wife Sophie were spending their wedding anniversary on a visit to Sarajevo. They received a very warm welcome and the glorious weather enabled them to drive through the streets in an open-topped car. The Archduke wore a bright blue tunic, trimmed with gold and red.

Six big cars drove through the streets. Everyone stopped to look. Cabrinovic, young Bosnian terrorist and member of the Black Hand organisation, threw a small bomb at the Archduke's car. Everyone was shouting and running and twenty people were hurt. The Archduke and his wife were not injured.

Officials now decided to cut short his visit and changed the route home. The driver of the first vehicle, however, did not follow the new instructions and made a right turn back along the original route. The second car, containing Franz-Ferdinand and Sophie, followed suit. Officials shouted out instructions to stop and turn back. As the driver of the car tried in vain to find reverse gear another Bosnian terrorist, Gavrilo Princip, stepped forward.

He took out his revolver and fired at point blank range. The first bullet went through the side of the car. It hit the Duchess and she died immediately. The second bullet hit the Archduke in the neck. It cut the jugular vein. The Archduke died within minutes.

The Archduke and his wife about to drive away from the Town Hall

SOURCE A

A sketch of the assassination of Franz-Ferdinand and his wife

SOURCE B

The arrest of Gavrilo Princip after his assassination of Franz-Ferdinand

SOURCE C

Gavrilo Princip at his trial

I did not know whether I shot him. I didn't even know how many shots I fired. I wanted to kill myself and I raised my arm but the policeman grabbed me and beat me. Then bloody as I was they took me to the police station. They beat me again. They wanted revenge.

SOURCE D

A student eyewitness

At last Detective Spahovic grabbed Princip and, with the help of another policeman, dragged him away. Princip was vomiting because he had taken poison and had cuts from his fight with the crowd.

The countdown to war

The news of the assassination shocked the world and set off a chain of events which culminated in a major war. Austria was furious and blamed the Serbs but did nothing for nearly a month. The Austrians needed to be certain of German support. If they invaded Serbia it might well lead to war with Russia. On 5 July the Kaiser met the Austrian ambassador and told him to go ahead.

Focus on

Was the assassination a set-up?

There is much evidence to suggest that Franz-Ferdinand was set up to be assassinated to provide Austria with an excuse to invade Serbia.

The Austrian army wanted to destroy the Black Hand by attacking Serbia. Between January 1913 and June 1914 the Austrian army chief-of-staff recommended war with Serbia 25 times.

> **SOURCE E**
>
> The Kaiser to the Austrian ambassador
>
> *It is now or never. Deal with the Serbs. Straight away. The Tsar is unlikely to intervene. If he does, Germany will stand at Austria's side.*

- The Archduke could not have chosen a worse day to visit Sarajevo. It was Serbia's National Day – the anniversary of the battle, in 1389, when Serbia had been conquered by the Turkish Empire. On the same day a Serb hero, Milos Obilic, assassinated the Turkish Sultan.

- Austrian spies in Serbia had reported that there was going to be an assassination attempt.

- Pasic, the Prime Minister of Serbia, had also told the Austrian government that there was going to be trouble.

- Only 120 policemen were on duty in Sarajevo. There was no extra security.

> **SOURCE F**
>
> Serb reactions to the assassination
>
> *The accounts of eyewitnesses say that people fell into each other's arms in delight. Remarks were heard such as: 'It serves him right. We have been expecting this for a long time.'*

- The Archduke and his wife travelled in an open-topped car. An easy target for an assassin.

- The assassins were allowed to cross the border from Serbia into Bosnia.

Activity

Do a series of newspaper headlines in the following countries showing how each reacted to news of the murder:

Serbia
Russia
Germany
Austria-Hungary

WAR

31 JULY
Germany gave Russia a threatening ultimatum.

30 JULY
The Kaiser warned the Tsar of Russia to stop mobilising.

29 JULY
Russia mobilised the armed forces in support of Serbia.

28 JULY
Austria declared war on Serbia. Serbia appealed to Russia for help.

23 JULY
The Austrians delivered an ultimatum which they knew the Serbians would reject. The Austrian Foreign Minister deliberately phrased it so 'that it would be wholly impossible for Serbia to accept'. It included ten demands which would mean the virtual end of Serbian independence. Surprisingly, the Serbs accepted all but one. The Kaiser, who by now had cold feet, said, 'Now there can be no object in going to war'. But the Austrians, seeking revenge, went ahead anyway.

The German Chancellor, Bethmann-Hollweg

Just for a word – 'neutrality' – a word which has so often been ignored in wartime. Just for a scrap of paper Great Britain is going to make war on a fellow nation who desires nothing better than to be friends with her.

Why did Britain go to war?
Britain went to war in August 1914 for several reasons:

1 Rivalry with Germany, especially the Naval Race.

2 Britain was closely allied to France and to a lesser extent to Russia. The British felt morally bound to come to the aid of a friend or friends.

3 The consequences of not intervening would be bad for Britain. If Germany defeated France then the Kaiser would dominate Europe and be a greater threat to Britain. If France won, the French would no longer trust Britain who would be left isolated.

SOURCE G
From *The Sunday Times*, 2 August

Britain has no written alliance with France. But it has an obligation to honour. We have a vital interest in seeing that France is not overwhelmed by Germany.

4 The British sympathised with 'little' Serbia being invaded by the large Austro-Hungarian empire.

5 Belgium and the 'Scrap of Paper'. This was the immediate reason for British entry. In 1839 Britain and the other Great Powers signed the Treaty of London. This guaranteed the neutrality of Belgium in a future war. This was the 'Scrap of Paper'. Britain did not want a major country to occupy Belgium and use it as a base to invade Britain. The German Schlieffen Plan, however, meant that Germany would have to invade France through Belgium. The Germans gambled that either Britain would not go to war over Belgium or, if they did, they would arrive in France too late to make any difference to the outcome. The German invasion of Belgium really annoyed the British people and the vast majority supported the British declaration of war.

SOURCE I
A cartoon showing Britain's attitude to the German invasion of Belgium, from *Punch*, August 1914

PUNCH, OR THE LONDON CHARIVARI.—August 12, 1914.

NO THOROUGHFARE

F. H. Townsend Aug. 1914

BRAVO, BELGIUM!

Questions

1 How did the following long-term causes contribute to the murder at Sarajevo and the countdown to war:
   a the Alliance system?
   b the Arms Race?
   c rivalry in the Balkans?
   d German militarism and the attitude of Kaiser Wilhelm II?

2 Using the following table, decide how far each of the following countries was responsible for the outbreak of war in 1914: Austria-Hungary, Germany, France, Britain, Belgium, Serbia and Russia. Explain your decision for each country.

	Greatly responsible	Partly responsible	Little responsibility	No responsibility
Austria-Hungary				
Germany				
France				
Britain				
Belgium				
Serbia				
Russia				

3 Which country do you think had the greatest responsibility for causing the war and why?

4 Describe in your own words the assassination of Archduke Franz-Ferdinand.

5 Do you think it was set up by the Austrian government? Give reasons for your answer.

6 Which source, **A** or **B**, would be the most useful to an historian studying the assassination at Sarajevo?

7 What message is the cartoonist trying to put across in Source **I**?

8 What was the 'Scrap of Paper'?

Summary and Revision

LONG-TERM CAUSES OF THE WAR

For this section, you will need to understand:

- Colonial rivalry – competition for even bigger empires.

- Balkan nationalism – the desire for the Slav peoples of this area to join with those in the empire of Austria-Hungary.

- Alsace-Lorraine – the French desire for its return from Germany.

- The Arms Race – competition for bigger armed forces and more armaments.

- The Naval Race – between Britain and Germany.

- Wilhelm II and German militarism.

- The Alliance system – the Triple Alliance and the Triple Entente.

Revision questions

1   Name the Great Powers in Europe in 1900.
2   Why did the Kaiser want a 'place in the sun'?
3   Explain the rivalry between Serbia and Austria-Hungary. Who was the protector of Serbia?
4   Who were the 'Revanchists' in France?
5   How did the Arms Race increase rivalry between the Great Powers?
6   Why was the *Dreadnought* so important in the Naval Race?
7   In what ways did Kaiser Wilhelm II increase rivalry between the Great Powers?
8   Who were the members of the Triple Entente and Triple Alliance?

THE CRISES 1905–14

This section includes:

- The Moroccan Crisis of 1905–6.

- The Bosnian Crisis 1908–9.

- The Agadir Crisis of 1911.

- The Balkan Wars, 1912–13.

Revision questions

1   Why did the Kaiser become involved in Morocco in 1905?
2   How did the first Moroccan crisis worsen relations between:
    a   France and Germany?
    b   Germany and Britain?
3   Russia failed in the Bosnian Crisis of 1908–9. Why? What effects did this crisis have on relations between Austria and Serbia?

4   Explain the significance of the *Panther* in the crisis of 1911.
5   What was the Balkan League of 1912? Explain the results of the First Balkan War of 1912–13? Why was there a second Balkan War in 1913?
6   Why, by 1913, was the Balkans the powder-keg of Europe?

THE IMMEDIATE CAUSE OF WAR

You will need to understand:

- The murder of Archduke Franz-Ferdinand at Sarajevo.

- Austrian reaction and German support.

- The declarations of war, late July to early August.

- Why Britain decided to go to war.

Revision questions

1   What part did the following play in the assassination of Franz-Ferdinand:
    a   Gavrilo Princip?
    b   the Black Hand?
2   How did Austria and Germany react to the murder?
3   Explain what took place on the following dates in 1914:

    23 July   28 July   30 July   1 August   4 August.

4   Explain at least three reasons why Britain went to war.

2
The First World War

UNDERSTANDING THE FIRST WORLD WAR

The following definitions and explanations should give you a better understanding of this chapter.

Armistice	Agreement to stop fighting.
Attrition	Wearing down. It was the word used to describe Haig's tactics on the Western Front.
Barrage balloon	Barrier made of gas-filled balloons.
Chaperone	Person who accompanies a woman in public.
Conscription	Forcing people to join the army.
Howitzers	Field guns.
Infantry	The foot soldiers.
Jerry	Nickname for German soldiers (also Hun and Boche).
Munitions	Military equipment – ammunition, bullets, shells.
Mutinies	Rebellions against superior officers.
Neutral	Not supporting either side.
Offensive	An attack.
Pacifist	Someone who objects to killing.
Reconnaissance	Surveying the enemy positions.
Shrapnel	Piece from a shell.
Stalemate	Neither side is able to win.
Synchronise	Time to operate together.
Tommies	Nickname for British soldiers.
U-boat	German submarine – *unterseeboot*.

The First World War

Although the war was fought across the world, the main area of war was the Western Front between France, Belgium and Germany. The failure of the Schlieffen Plan in 1914 saw the emergence of trench warfare in which neither side could break through for over three years.

THE EVENTS OF 1914

The plan had been devised by General von Schlieffen in 1905. Germany assumed they would have to fight a war on two fronts, against Russia in the east and France in the west. Schlieffen thought that Britain would not get involved. Germany was determined to avoid having to split their armed forces and fight both countries at the same time.

How the Schlieffen Plan was supposed to work

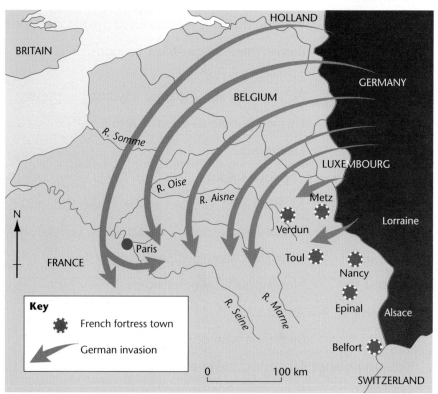

Focus on

What the Schlieffen Plan assumed

- Belgium would not resist and would allow the Germans to march through quickly and unopposed.

- The British would not enter the war. If they did, their army would not arrive until after the defeat of France.

- The Russians would be slow to mobilise and Germany would only need a small army in the east.

- German armies would reach Paris and encircle it before the French arrived.

- French armies would collapse in the face of the German advance.

The plan was to concentrate on knocking France out of the war quickly with just a small force in the east facing Russia. The main French armies would be expecting a German attack through Alsace-Lorraine. Instead the Germans intended to invade through Holland, Belgium and Luxembourg, take Paris and encircle the French armies. With France defeated in six weeks, the Germans would transfer their troops to the east and fight Russia.

THE EVENTS OF AUGUST

Schlieffen was dead by the time war broke out and the German armies were led by General von Moltke.

3 August An army of over one million German soldiers marched into Belgium. The Belgians were not swept aside as easily as the Germans had expected. Deep concrete forts protecting cities like Antwerp, Liège and Namur, seriously delayed the Germans. Heavy guns had to be called up to pound the defences to rubble. Antwerp did not surrender until 10 October.

18 August The British Expeditionary Force (BEF), 100,000 professional soldiers under the command of Sir John French, began to arrive in France.

19 August General von Moltke had to transfer troops from the Eastern Front to face the BEF.

23 August The BEF stumbled into the Germans near the mining town of Mons. The BEF was small but it was excellently trained – the British rifle fire, for example, was so fast and accurate that the Germans believed they were facing machine-guns. The BEF were heavily outnumbered and had to retreat. They had, however, further delayed the German advance.

26 August A further battle at Le Cateau. Again the BEF retreated but delayed the German advance.

Key

- ⚙ Allied fortress town
- ← German invasion
- ← French advance
- → British advance

0   100 km

SOURCE A
A BEF soldier recalls the retreat

We were walking corpses... we were dead men falling to bits... We looked like it and smelled like it.

SOURCE B

A German officer writing on 2 September 1914

Our soldiers stagger forward, their faces coated with dust, their uniforms in rags. They look like living scarecrows.

The Battle of the Marne 5–19 September

By 5 September the German armies had reached the river Marne, just to the north-east of Paris but had gone to the east rather than west of Paris. The two most advanced German armies, under Generals von Kluck and von Bulow, had split. The French, meanwhile, had realised the German trap and had moved their armies northwards to the Marne to protect Paris. French troops from Alsace-Lorraine had marched until they were exhausted. Between the French armies stood the British, pushed back from Belgium but still intact. Their armies were further reinforced with every available soldier from Paris, transported by taxis and buses.

BEF reconnaissance balloons spotted the gap between the two German armies. Cautiously the BEF advanced into the gap. The battle lasted for over a week across a front 200 kilometres wide. Finally, the exhausted Germans fell back to a safe position 60 kilometres north at the River Aisne in order to avoid a permanent split between their two armies. The battle ended on 19 September and Paris was saved.

Source D

Newspaper headlines on Marne

The Schlieffen Plan was in ruins. General von Kluck said to the Kaiser, 'We have lost the war'. The failure of the German plan meant there would be no quick end to the war. In fact the war dragged on for over another four years. After the Battle of the Marne, the Germans dug trenches to protect their soldiers, and the opposing allies did the same.

Belgian resistance

The Germans expected to march through Belgium unopposed. The Belgians, using their forts, resisted and slowed down the German advance. This gave the BEF time to arrive.

The BEF

The Kaiser dismissed the BEF as a 'contemptible little army'. The British arrived much more quickly than expected, slowed down the Germans at Mons and Le Cateau and played a crucial role at the Marne.

WHY THE SCHLIEFFEN PLAN FAILED

French resistance

The delays by the BEF and Belgians gave the French armies the time to march north and defend Paris.

German exhaustion

The German soldiers were exhausted by the end of August. They had been on the move since 3 August and had faced stiff resistance from the Belgians and British.

Changes to the Plan

- In 1913 Schlieffen's dying words are said to have been 'keep the right wing strong'. He urged that the right wing of the German army should be six times stronger than any other. Von Moltke ignored this advice and the army was not strong enough to carry out the plan.

- The German armies which invaded Belgium were 100,000 less than was required because more troops were sent to hold back the Russians on the Eastern Front.

- The original plan involved a wide sweep through Holland, Luxembourg and Belgium. This was changed to a narrower attack through Belgium.

- German armies were supposed to encircle Paris. This was abandoned in early September and they moved to the east of Paris with a split between the armies of von Kluck and von Bulow.

German cartoon against French and British soldiers, 1914

Race to the sea October–November, 1914

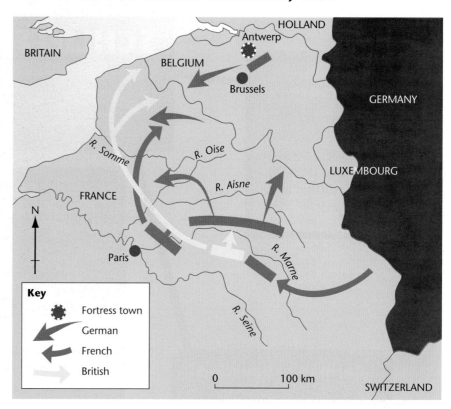

Despite their retreat from the River Marne, the Germans were not defeated. They still occupied most of north-east France and Belgium. The Germans now tried to outflank, or move around the sides of, and surround the British and French armies by sweeping north. Wherever they pushed, they found the French also moving in the same position.

The Germans now tried to capture the Channel ports of Dunkirk, Calais and Boulogne. This would cut off the BEF from supplies and reinforcements from Britain.

The BEF made a hasty march north to protect the ports. They arrived just in time as the Germans tried one last curve round northwards behind the Allies. The British and Germans met in a bloody battle at the town of Ypres. The Germans attacked the British but suffered very heavy casualties. After a month the fighting ended. About 20,000 of Germany's finest troops were killed and another 80,000 wounded. Britain had lost 8000 but the ports were saved.

The situation at the end of 1914

The fighting at Ypres ended on 22 November, well into winter. The 'war of movement' was now over. Both sides dug themselves in for the winter. An unbroken line of trenches soon stretched from the English Channel to the Swiss border in the south.

SOURCE F

German troops preparing their first trenches, 1914

Britain's professional army, the BEF, was more or less wiped out in 1914. It would now have to depend on a mainly volunteer army.

Activity

You are a German soldier who took part in the Schlieffen Plan. Describe your reactions to the following:

- The invasion of Belgium.

- The march through Belgium and the opposition of the Belgian forts.

- The quick arrival of the BEF and the battle of Mons.

- The Marne and the retreat to the River Aisne.

- The battle of Ypres.

- Christmas 1914.

Focus on

Christmas 1914

Christmas 1914 came – the time when soldiers on both sides expected to come home victorious. On Christmas Day itself an extraordinary thing happened at many points along the front line. An unofficial truce began and the shooting died away. German soldiers sang carols, and from their trenches the British responded. They shouted greetings to each other. In some places men from both sides climbed out of their trenches and walked into the area between known as No-Man's-Land. Here they swopped cigarettes and played football. Two days later, however, the shooting started again.

Questions

1. Explain in your own words what part the following played in the failure of the Schlieffen Plan:
   a. von Moltke
   b. BEF
   c. the Belgians
   d. Battle of the Marne.
2. Why did the Germans try to capture the Channel Ports?
3. Why was the battle of Ypres, October–November, so important?
4. What message are the Germans trying to get across in Source **E**? How do they achieve this?
5. How useful are the headlines in Source **D** to an historian studying the battle of the River Marne?

TRENCH WARFARE

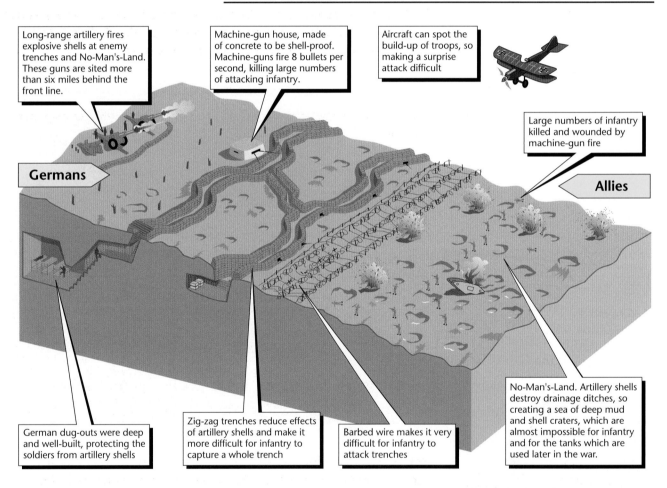

Long-range artillery fires explosive shells at enemy trenches and No-Man's-Land. These guns are sited more than six miles behind the front line.

Machine-gun house, made of concrete to be shell-proof. Machine-guns fire 8 bullets per second, killing large numbers of attacking infantry.

Aircraft can spot the build-up of troops, so making a surprise attack difficult

Large numbers of infantry killed and wounded by machine-gun fire

Germans

Allies

German dug-outs were deep and well-built, protecting the soldiers from artillery shells

Zig-zag trenches reduce effects of artillery shells and make it more difficult for infantry to capture a whole trench

Barbed wire makes it very difficult for infantry to attack trenches

No-Man's-Land. Artillery shells destroy drainage ditches, so creating a sea of deep mud and shell craters, which are almost impossible for infantry and for the tanks which are used later in the war.

The trenches built in 1914 were simply to house the soldiers of both sides during the winter of 1914–15. They were to remain until well into 1918.

The trench system

The trench system became more complex and stronger defensively. A front line of trenches was backed up by two more, the support and reserve lines. The front line faced the enemy, who might be between 200 and 800 metres away. The space in between was called No-Man's-Land.

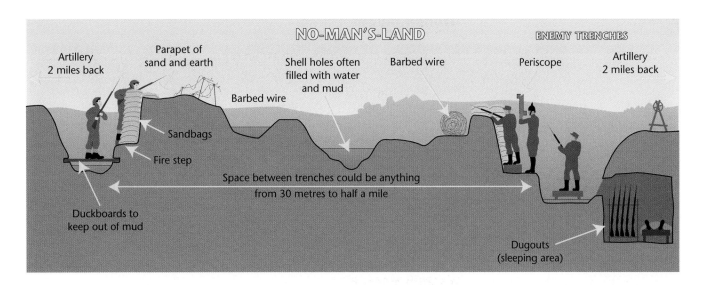

NO-MAN'S-LAND | ENEMY TRENCHES

Artillery 2 miles back

Parapet of sand and earth

Shell holes often filled with water and mud

Barbed wire

Periscope

Artillery 2 miles back

Barbed wire

Sandbags

Fire step

Space between trenches could be anything from 30 metres to half a mile

Duckboards to keep out of mud

Dugouts (sleeping area)

Each side protected itself with rows of barbed wire, secretly erected at night. No-Man's-Land became a deserted strip of devastated battleground, full of shell holes and muddy from rain.

SOURCE A

Using very thick barbed wire a German engineer party set up a barbed-wire entanglement in front of a trench

SOURCE B

A German soldier wrote

Part of our trench went through a cemetery. We cleared out the contents of the family vaults and used them to shelter ourselves from artillery fire. Hits from heavy shells would hurl the coffins and semi-rotted corpses high into the air.

Behind the front line were the 'reserve trenches'. These were a second line of defence in battle, in case the front line should be captured. They were also used as a resting place for front-line troops. Sometimes the reserve trenches were known as the second line or 'support trenches'. There were even parts of a third line in places.

Running across these lines were the 'communication trenches'. They led back to safety sometimes for a kilometre or more. Everything going up to the front had to use these communication trenches – fresh troops, food, water, mail, ammunition and all other supplies.

Trench layout

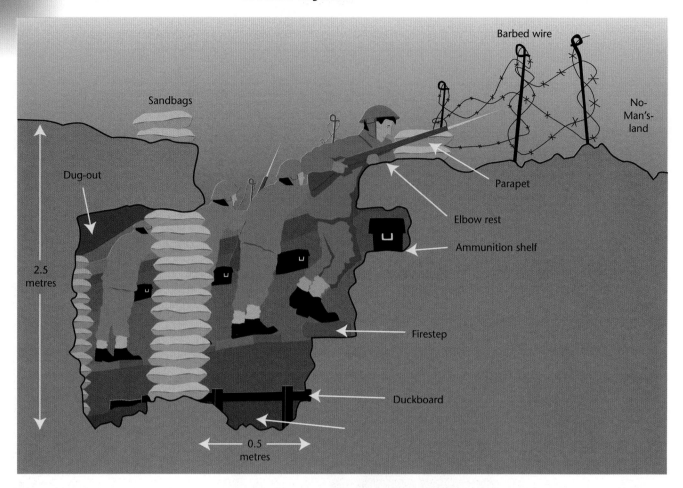

Sandbags

Barbed wire

No-Man's-land

Dug-out

Parapet

Elbow rest

Ammunition shelf

2.5 metres

Firestep

Duckboard

0.5 metres

Most trenches were deep enough for a man to walk without his head being seen and wide enough for a man to rest while others went by. The soil dug out of a trench was usually heaped in front to form a 'parapet' that gave extra protection from bullets. This was usually reinforced with sandbags. The trench would also have a 'firing step' to enable the men to see over the parapet. It was dangerous to show your head over the top. It was likely to be shot at by an enemy sniper. The soldiers generally used periscopes to watch the enemy.

In a trench at Ovillers: on the look-out while other soldiers rest

The back walls of a trench were sometimes strengthened with railway sleepers, corrugated iron, or specially made sections of woven-basket fencing. They stopped the soil from slipping down into the trench.

Wherever possible, trenches were dug in a zig-zag line. This lessened the blast from shells and prevented attackers from shooting right along a straight trench. Barbed-wire doors were placed at intervals along many trenches. When open, the doors fitted into recesses in the trench wall. In battle they were closed in the hope of slowing down the enemy if they got into the trench. Most trenches had 'firing bays' which pushed a few extra metres into No-Man's-Land, allowing the men to fire into the sides of the enemy as they attacked the trench.

Rain quickly made most trenches very muddy, so 'duckboards' were laid along the bottom. These were flat planks of wood nailed together like a ladder. The troops lived in dug-outs – holes dug out of the sides of the walls. Often two or three men slept above each other, as if on bunks.

Officers also lived in the trenches, but in better dug-outs deeper in the ground. This was more like a small room sometimes with iron beds. Some officers even managed to rig up an electric light. German trenches and dug-outs were often better than those of Britain and France. Some of them had concrete defences, and most German dug-outs were deeper than British ones. Even ordinary German soldiers might live in a strong barrack-room six or nine metres underground. Some German dug-outs even had wallpaper!

SOURCE D

A view in an officer's quarters of a dug-out

Questions

1 What were the following:
   a No-Man's-Land?
   b reserve line?
   c communication trenches?
   d parapet?
   e dug-outs?
2 Using Sources **C** and **D**, explain the differences between the dug-outs for men and officers.
3 Which of these sources, **C** or **D**, gives a more reliable view of the trenches?

Activity

You are a reporter for a British newspaper who visits a British trench. Write an article describing the trench system and trench layout. You could include a diagram.

Life in the trenches

Most days were very monotonous and boring and seemed to pass very slowly. People were killed, but there were few great battles. Troops did not often go hungry but there was little variety in their diet. There was usually tinned 'bully' or corned beef and a loaf of bread, which had to be shared among up to ten men. There was jam, but it was nearly always Tickler's plum and apple variety and the men soon tired of it. If nothing else was available there were always emergency supplies of hard biscuits but these were like concrete.

Cooking facilities were basic. Some troops had no hot meals for weeks on end. Where hot meals could be prepared, there were few cooking utensils, so all the food was cooked in the same few pots, making it all taste the same. Water was a problem. Normally it was brought in petrol cans to the front, where chloride of lime was added to kill off the germs. This made it taste awful. In winter snow and ice were melted to make tea.

Hygiene was another big problem. Each day there was a medical check. Diseases were common in the trenches, where men crowded together in unhygienic conditions. Everyone had lice – in his hair, on his body, and thriving in every part of his clothing. Occasionally men were deloused behind the lines, but the lack of washing facilities meant that the lice reappeared after a few days. Rats also ran everywhere, feeding on rotting bodies and horse carcasses. They even nibbled the troops as they slept. Many men

Source A

Private George Coppard, who served in the trenches, remembers the food

Wrapping loose rations such as tea, cheese and meat was not considered necessary. They were all tipped into a sandbag, a ghastly mix-up resulting. In wet weather their condition was unbelievable. Maconochie, a 'dinner in a tin', was my favourite. I could polish one off very quickly, but the usual share-out was one tin for four men.

Source B

A British officer writes about rats in the trenches

There are millions. Some are huge fellows, nearly as big as cats. Several of our men were woken up to find a rat snuggling down under the blanket alongside them.

Source D

George Coppard remembers

The lice lay in the seams of trousers, in the deep furrows of woolly pants. A lighted candle applied where they were thickest made them pop like Chinese crackers. After a session of this my face would be covered with small blood spots, from extra big fellows who had popped too much.

Source C

The result of 15 minutes' chase in the trenches

I have been talking to one of my stretcher-bearers. He has a foot swollen to three times its normal size. It looks like a great helpless pink lump. I shall be surprised if he does not lose that foot.

felt a rat run over them as they slept in their dug-out.

One of the most common diseases suffered by soldiers in the trenches was known as trench foot, which was caused by standing for long periods in mud and water. The feet would swell and go completely numb for a few days. Then they would become extremely painful and begin to rot. Sometimes the feet had to be amputated. Foot inspections were carried out to try to detect the disease and soldiers were advised to wash their feet daily and rub them with whale oil.

Much more serious were the epidemics. Germs in food and water led to typhus, cholera and dysentery. These killed thousands of men.

Much of the day was boring. Men sat around reading or smoking or playing chess. Some wrote letters home. These were checked by a censor before being posted. Anything that might help the enemy was crossed out with a blue pencil.

Finally, the soldiers in the trenches had to put up with the extremes of weather. From snow and frost in the winter to rain on a regular basis, especially in Flanders in Belgium. The bottom of the trenches was frequently under at least a foot of water.

SOURCE F

Robert Graves from his memoir *Goodbye to All That*, 1957

The familiar trench smell still haunts my nostrils. The mixed smell of mud, latrine buckets, chloride of lime, unburied or half-buried corpses, rotting sandbags, stale human sweat. Sometimes it was sweetened by cigarette smoke and the scent of bacon frying over wood fires.

SOURCE G

A flooded trench

Dangers in the trenches

There were many dangers apart from disease and rats:

- Enemy marksmen known as snipers would wait for the soldier who popped his head over the parapet. Many unsuspecting new arrivals were killed this way. Even a lighted match could be fatal and soldiers never lit more than two cigarettes from one match before quickly putting it out. The reason was that on the first cigarette the sniper spotted the light of the match, on the second cigarette he took aim and on the third cigarette he fired.

- Enemy bombardment, which happened most days, could lead to injury or death from flying splinters or ricochets.

- Poisonous gas, first used by the Germans in 1915 (p. 49), brought a slow, horrible death to many.

- Some soldiers suffered from shell shock caused by the constant strain of living under shellfire. The constant fear of being hit tore at their minds and reduced some men to nervous wrecks. From then on, any sudden noise might trigger their fear, causing them to take shelter or tremble or weep in terror. Early in this war this mental illness was not understood by the Army. Many men who suffered from shell shock were accused of cowardice and shot.

Many men envied those wounded soldiers who were sent home to Britain, or 'Blighty'. Later in the war, some deliberately shot themselves, perhaps through the foot or hand, hoping that this would make them unfit for further duty and that they would be sent home.

The War Poets

The experiences in the trenches led to bitterness amongst some of those who served on the Western Front. This was expressed in songs, paintings or poems. The early war poems were often optimistic, describing men bravely going off to fight, with great hopes for the future.

Later poems show how bitter the soldiers became, once they knew what the trenches were like. The optimism had gone. War had hardened them. Then, finally, came the protest poems and demands that there should never be anything like it again. Two of the more famous poets were Siegfried Sassoon and Wilfred Owen.

Profile on

Siegfried Sassoon

Sassoon was an officer on the Western Front for three years. He was wounded twice and decorated for his bravery. In 1917 he wrote a number of poems in which he accused the generals of being out of touch. In July 1917, while recovering from wounds, he wrote his 'soldier's declaration' which was read out in the House of Commons. He said that it had been a war 'of conquest and aggression' and wanted no further part in the 'sufferings of the troops'. The government responded by sending Sassoon for psychiatric treatment in a hospital for victims of shell shock. Sassoon later withdrew his 'soldier's declaration'. He said it was due to a nervous breakdown. He returned to France in 1918.

SOURCE J

First World War song 'Sing a Song of Wartime', sang to the tune of 'Sing a Song of Sixpence a pocket full of rice'

Sing a Song of War-time

Sing a song of War-time
Soldiers marching by,
Crowds of people standing,
Waving them 'Goodbye'.
When the crowds are over,
Here we go to tea,
Bread and margarine to eat
War economy!

If I ask for cake, or
Jam of any sort,
Nurse says 'What! In War-time?
Archie, cert'nly not!'
Life's not very funny
Now, for little boys,
Haven't any money,
Can't buy any toys.

Mummie does the housework,
Can't get any maid,
Gone to make munitions,
Cause they're better paid.
Nurse is very busy,
Never time to play
Sewing shirts for soldiers,
Nearly ev'ry day.
Ev'ry body's doing
Something for the War,
Girls are doing things
They've never done before,
Go as 'bus conductors,
Drive a car or van,
All the world is topsy-turvey
Since the War began.

SOURCE K

From 'The Soldier' by Rupert Brooke

'If I should die, think only this of me:
That there's some corner of a foreign field
That is forever England. There shall be
In that rich earth and richer dust concealed;
A dust whom England bore, shaped, made aware,
Gave, once, her flowers to love, her ways to roam,
A body of England's breathing English air,
Washed by the rivers, blest by the suns of home.'

SOURCE L

From 'Dulce et Decorum Est' by Wilfred Owen

'Bent double, like old beggars under sacks,
Knock-kneed, coughing like hags, we cursed through sludge,
Till on the haunting flares we turned our backs
And towards our distant rest began to trudge...

...Gas! GAS! Quick, boys! — An ecstasy of fumbling,
Fitting the clumsy helmets just in time;
But someone still was yelling out and stumbling,
A flound'ring like a man in fire or lime...
Dim, through the misty panes and thick green light,
As under a green sea, I saw him drowning.

In all my dreams, before my helpless sight,
He plunges at me, guttering, choking, drowning.

If in some smothering dreams you too could pace
Behind the wagon that we flung him in,
And watch the white eyes writhing in his face,
His hanging face, like a devil's sick of sin;
If you could hear, at every jolt, the blood
Come gargling from the froth-corrupted lungs,
Obscene as cancer, bitter as the cud
Of vile, incurable sores on innocent tongues, —
My friend, you would not tell with such high zest
To children ardent for some desperate glory,
The old Lie: dulce et decorum est
Pro patria mori.'

('Dulce et decorum est pro patria mori' means 'It is sweet and noble to die for your country'.)

SOURCE M

From 'The General', written by Siegfried Sassoon in 1917

'Good-morning; good-morning!' the General said
When we met him last week on our way to the line.
Now the soldiers he smiled at are most of 'em dead,
And we're cursing his staff for incompetent swine.
'He's a cheery old card', grunted Harry to Jack
As they slogged up to Arras with rifle and pack.

But he did for them both by his plan of attack.

Questions

1   In your own words explain what the following sources, **A** to **E**, tell you about life in the trenches.

2   Source **F** is an extract from a memoir. How useful are such extracts to an historian studying life in the trenches?

3   Does Source **G** give a reliable view of life in the trenches?

4   What were the main dangers in the trenches?

5   What differences are there between the poems, Sources **K** and **L**, in their view of war?

6   Which poem do you think was the first and why?

From the end of 1914 to 1918 there was a stalemate on the Western Front. This meant that despite numerous attacks neither side was able to break through and secure victory.

THE MACHINE-GUN

These were ideal defensive weapons. They could fire up to 600 rounds per minute and were able to cut down the lines of attackers, causing huge casualties. The German Maxim gun accounted for 90% of Allied victims in the Battle of the Somme.

SOURCE A

A German machine-gunner describes a British attack

The officers were in front. I noticed one of them calmly carrying a walking stick. When we started firing we just had to load and re-load. They went down in their hundreds. You didn't have to aim, we just fired into them.

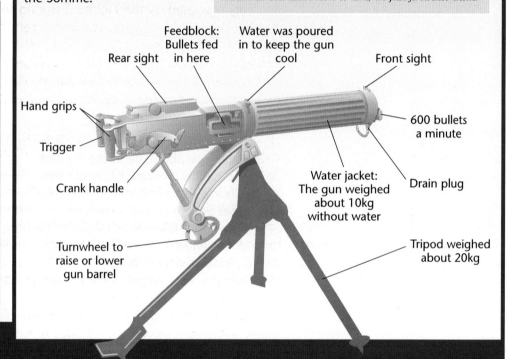

Feedblock: Bullets fed in here

Water was poured in to keep the gun cool

Rear sight

Front sight

Hand grips

600 bullets a minute

Trigger

Crank handle

Water jacket: The gun weighed about 10kg without water

Drain plug

Turnwheel to raise or lower gun barrel

Tripod weighed about 20kg

THE TRENCH SYSTEM

In the First World War foot soldiers or infantrymen were supposed to attack quickly through gaps in the enemy defences. This proved impossible against trenches which were defended by barbed wire and sandbags.

As men crossed No-Man's-Land they could be picked off by enemy machine-guns.

WHY STALEMATE?

THE COMMANDERS

The commanders on both sides had little or no idea about trench warfare and the tactics necessary to break the stalemate. Many of the British senior generals had very out-of-date ideas. Lord Kitchener, the Minister of War, said that four machine-guns per battalion would be enough. Meanwhile the Germans had sixteen per battalion. They still believed that cavalry would win wars. General Haig even said 'cavalry will have a greater use in future wars'. Most commanders agreed with him. France and Germany each had over 100,000 cavalry, which they believed would be vital for winning battles. In fact they were hardly ever used. The French commander, Field Marshall Joffre, believed that the 'spirit' of the French soldiers would see them across No-Man's-Land. The commanders on both sides failed to make use of the many new weapons developed. They persisted for over three years with the belief that weight of numbers of infantry soldiers would achieve a breakthrough against machine-guns and barbed wire.

FAILURE OF NEW WEAPONS (p. 49)

Several new weapons were developed, including the use of poison gas, flame-throwers and the tanks. None were successful in achieving a breakthrough until the tank in 1918.

New weapons and methods

In the course of the war, both sides developed new weapons and methods of fighting to try to break the stalemate.

The flame-thrower

This consisted of a can of petrol that a soldier carried on his back, connected to a hose through which he squirted the liquid towards the enemy. The hose had a trigger and a sparking mechanism, so when the soldier fired, the petrol was set on fire and a stream of burning liquid sailed through the air at the enemy. It was mainly used against machine-gun posts. The Germans used this weapon quite a lot, especially at Verdun, where it caused great panic among the French. But it did not help to shorten the war or even win battles. In fact it was quite likely to explode and kill the soldier using it.

Gas

This was first used by the Germans during the Second Battle of Ypres in April 1915. It appeared as a greenish-yellow cloud that gradually changed into a bluish-white mist, drifting with the wind towards the Allied trenches. Here it created utter terror. Some young officers advised their men to urinate into their handkerchiefs and hold them to their noses as a primitive disinfectant. Not surprisingly, this did not work.

To begin with, gases were mainly lung irritants such as chlorine or phosgene. They were released from cylinders when the wind was blowing in the right direction and allowed to drift towards the enemy. Later, gas shells were introduced. Other gases attacked the nervous system or caused paralysis and these were more lethal. Then in 1917 there appeared 'mustard gas'. This was like an acid. It burnt the skin and caused blisters, but it also formed a foam in the lungs which could be fatal. The normal gas mask gave no protection and 'mustard gas' was difficult to spot because it was colourless and had no smell.

Gas, for all the terror it caused, did not kill as many men as might have been expected. Gas was unsuccessful for several reasons:

- Both sides developed gas masks. These offered protection, at least against the earlier forms of poisonous gas.

- The wind in France generally blew towards the Germans, which prevented them using it very often.

- As the war went on, the Germans began to run out of chemicals and did not have enough gas at any one time to win a battle.

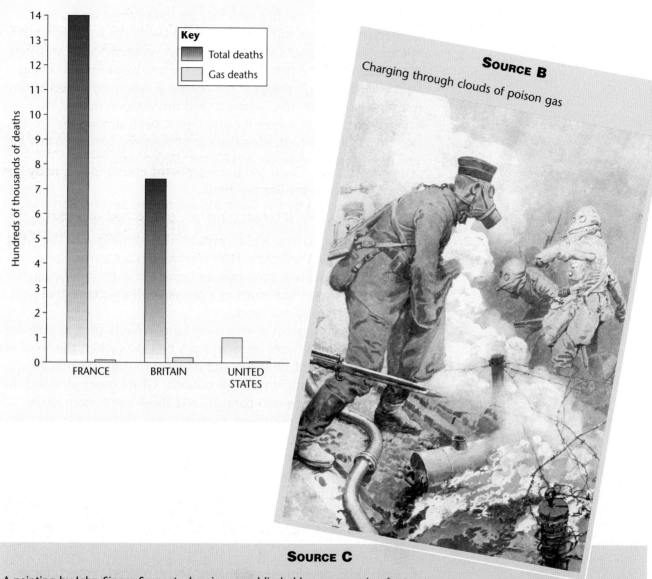

Charging through clouds of poison gas

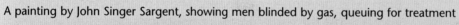

SOURCE C

A painting by John Singer Sargent, showing men blinded by gas, queuing for treatment

Artillery

This means the use of heavy field guns to bombard the enemy trenches. Heavy artillery (howitzer) guns fired a heavy shell a short distance; lighter guns fired over further ranges. Almost all the artillery guns were located behind the front lines. Such bombardments were supposed to destroy the trenches and allow for an easy crossing of No-Man's-Land. At one stage the Germans had over 20,000 guns. However, this did not prove effective:

- The artillery attack simply warned the enemy of a possible attack.

- In the case of the Germans they took refuge in their dug-outs 30 feet below the ground. These could not be destroyed by the bombardment. Once the bombardment ended they quickly got back to their front-line positions.

- The bombardment failed to destroy the barbed wire and churned up No-Man's-Land, leaving it pitted with huge craters, making it even more difficult to cross.

SOURCE E

Heavy British howitzer (field gun) bombarding the German trenches

SOURCE F

A French gunner describes the effects of an artillery bombardment

You have no idea of the number of Germans blown to bits. What a horrible sight in the woods in which not a single tree had been spared. Human remains, arms and legs, knapsacks, blankets etc. hung on the spruces. We watched Germans flying in the air as much as three or four hundred feet.

The creeping barrage

During the Battle of the Somme, in September 1916, the British tried a new tactic called the creeping barrage. This was to try to stop the fatal gap between the artillery bombardment and the infantry attack which enabled the German defenders to shelter and then return to their trenches. The artillery would fire in front of soldiers as they crossed No-Man's-Land. Such a tactic required extreme accuracy and there were many examples of men killed by their own artillery. Nevertheless this tactic was to prove very successful in 1918.

Tanks

The tank was easily the most original invention of the war. It was invented by Ernest Swinton, an army officer and engineer and was based on the pre-war caterpillar tractor, widely used on muddy farms. Swinton suggested adding a few guns and armour plating round it. His idea was eagerly taken up by Winston Churchill, the First Lord of the Admiralty. The Navy spent £75,000 on improving the design. Early tanks were called water carriers to deceive the Germans but the name was changed as the committee responsible for its development did not like the abbreviation – the WC Committee.

The war minister, Lord Kitchener, was not enthusiastic about the use of tanks: 'A pretty mechanical toy, but the war will never be won by such machines'. The British commander on the Western Front, Sir Douglas Haig, was sufficiently impressed to order further development of the weapon. The first prototype, nicknamed 'Big Willie' after the Kaiser, could travel at 4 mph (6 kph), turn sharply, reverse, climb a 1:1 slope of at least 5 feet, cross a gap of 8 feet and keep going for at least 20 miles. It carried a crew of 20 men.

SOURCE G

Tanks in action on the Western Front

The tank, however, did not prove to be a war-winning weapon until 1918 when it spearheaded the devastating breakthrough which brought an end to the war:

- Tanks were used for the first time in September during the Battle of the Somme. They were a disastrous failure. There were only 40 of them, most of which broke down. Fortunately, the Germans did not take them seriously and did little to develop their own tanks.
- They were unreliable, frequently breaking down in battle. Sometimes the caterpillar tracks came off, or the engine stopped. Often they ran out of petrol or were damaged by artillery fire.
- They were not used correctly until 1918, as a battering ram to open the way for the infantry. At Cambrai in 1917 (p. 68) 378 tanks broke through the German lines but had to return due to the lack of infantry support.

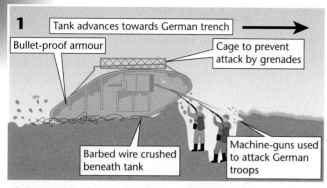

1
- Tank advances towards German trench →
- Bullet-proof armour
- Cage to prevent attack by grenades
- Barbed wire crushed beneath tank
- Machine-guns used to attack German troops

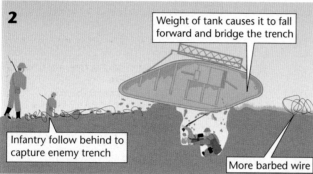

2
- Weight of tank causes it to fall forward and bridge the trench
- Infantry follow behind to capture enemy trench
- More barbed wire

3
- Weight of tank enables caterpillar tracks to grip and so it can move forward
- Troops capture enemy trench

4
- Troops build parapet and reinforce trench against enemy counter-attack
- Tank moves on to attack next line of defence

Tanks did have a devastating effect on the Germans.

Activity

Make a copy of the following table and write in the advantages and disadvantages of the new weapons and tactics.

Weapon	Advantages	Disadvantages
Gas		
Tanks		
Flame-thrower		
Artillery		
Creeping barrage		

Questions

1. What is meant by stalemate? Explain two reasons for the stalemate on the Western Front.
2. What do Sources **B** and **D** show you about the limitations of the use of gas?
3. Is Source **C** a useful source to an historian studying the effects of a gas attack?
4. Using Sources **H** and **I**, explain why tanks were very effective on the Western Front.
5. How reliable is Source **H** as a view of the effectiveness of tanks on the Western Front?

Tank production, 1916–18

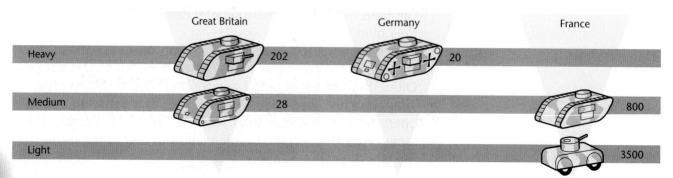

	Great Britain	Germany	France
Heavy	202	20	
Medium	28		800
Light			3500

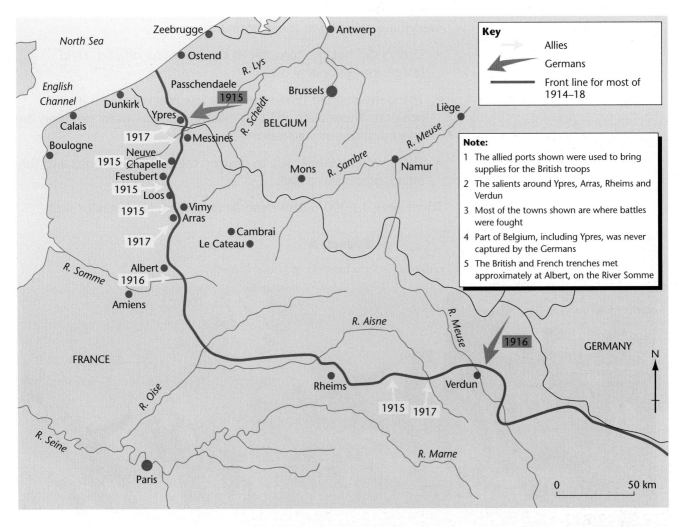

There were several major attempts to break through during the period 1915 to 1916. Most were by the Allies because the Germans were content to remain mainly on the defensive:

- They held most of Belgium and much of France. The Allies had to drive them out.

- The Germans were the first to build trenches and had generally picked the higher ground. This made them difficult to attack.

Faced by the strong German defences the Allied generals decided on a war of attrition or wearing down the German defenders. This would be achieved by regular attacks across No-Man's-Land that would grind down the German army until there was nothing left, even if only a handful of Allied troops also survived.

The battles of 1915

This was the first year of trench warfare. In January the French attacked the Germans in Champagne and were stopped by German machine-guns. Well over 100,000 French soldiers died or were wounded for a gain of no more than eight kilometres.

In March the British launched at an attack at Neuve Chapelle. The British actually broke through the German lines but then everything stopped at the moment of success.

- Orders did not get through to the front-line officers. Field telephones did not work.

- The Germans had time to move a few machine-guns into position. There were still only twelve machine-guns stopping the entire British army advancing any further.

- There were no shells left to destroy these machine-guns and the attack ground to a halt.

There were 13,000 British dead or wounded. No breakthrough.

SOURCE A

The capture of German trenches at Neuve Chapelle

In April the Germans attacked the British at Ypres and used poison gas for the first time. This caused panic but did not create a breakthrough for the Germans. In the following month the British attacked at Aubers Ridge. As the troops advanced they were mown down by German machine-gunners. The attack was a complete failure. Once again there were not enough shells to destroy the machine-gunners.

In September the French again attacked in Champagne. They drove the Germans back little more than three kilometres. The cavalry, waiting to charge through the expected gap in the German lines, was never used. In the same month the British attacked at

Loos and once again frontal attacks made no progress against machine-guns. Twenty Scottish regiments took part in the battle. Because of their kilts, the Germans nicknamed them the 'Ladies from Hell'.

At the end of 1915 there was still stalemate.

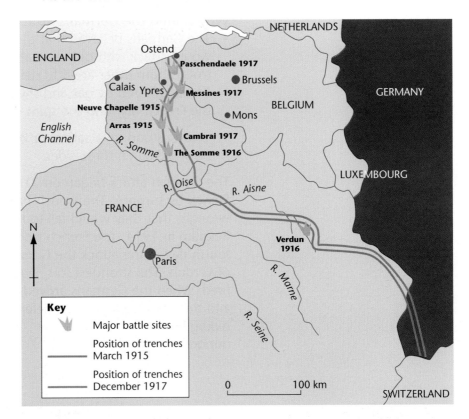

The Battle of Verdun, 1916

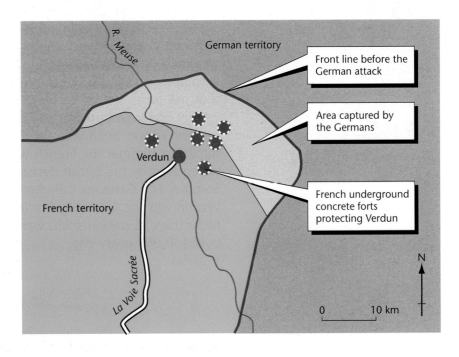

In February 1916 the Germans launched an offensive (attack) on the French fortress of Verdun. This was the strongest part of the French defences, with a ring of fortresses surrounding Verdun itself. It was the symbol of their defiance against the Germans. Verdun had never been captured, even during the first invasion of 1914.

Why should the Germans attack such a strong position?

- The Germans believed that the city was like a huge trap. They would attack with only a small army and the French would pull troops from other areas to defend Verdun. These troops would be slaughtered by gas and shellfire. The Germans would 'bleed the French dry' and the spirit of the French army would collapse.

- Verdun stood on a salient or bulge on the River Meuse. It could be attacked on three sides.

The German attack began on 21 February 1916 and took the French by surprise. The French had abandoned their forts believing, wrongly, that they would fall to the Germans just as those of Belgium in 1914. The French troops were in flimsy trenches. On the fourth day of the attack the Germans captured the outer defences of Verdun. The strongest fort, Douamont, fell without a shot being fired. When the Germans arrived they found the drawbridge down and the few veteran French defenders hiding in the dungeons.

SOURCE B

A.J.P. Taylor, British historian

The French commander, Joffre, refused to take the attack seriously. He would not allow it to interfere with his preparations for his own attack on the Somme.

A new commander, General Pétain, was sent to the city. He was an expert on defensive fighting. He held on to the main fortress of Verdun by issuing his famous orders 'Ils ne passeront pas' (They shall not pass) and by ensuring that the one road leading into Verdun was kept open for supplies and reinforcements. This became known as La Voie Sacrée (the Sacred Road). As the spring turned to summer the French were still clinging on. The French were saved by the British decision to attack the Germans on the Somme. The Germans called off the offensive.

Verdun was the first really horrifying battle of the First World War. More than 23 million shells were fired by both sides – over 150,000 every day.

SOURCE C

A French writer, Heuze, explains La Voie Sacrée

Check points along the road have established that it was used by as many as 6,000 vehicles a day. An average of one every fourteen seconds. At one time vehicles even passed at the rate of one every five seconds, and this for hours in a row.

French and German losses at Verdun

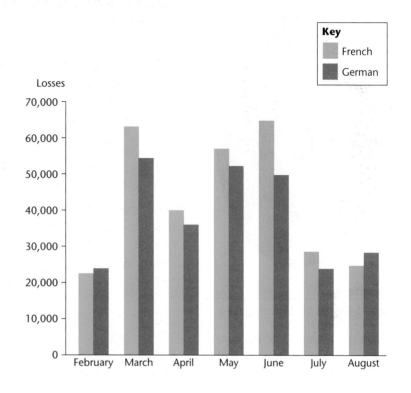

Key
French
German

Losses

70,000
60,000
50,000
40,000
30,000
20,000
10,000
0

February | March | April | May | June | July | August

SOURCE D

A cartoon by Louis Raemakers shows Crown Prince Wilhelm, who led the German forces at Verdun, standing on a pile of dead German soldiers and saying: 'We must have a higher pile to see Verdun'.

The Somme, 1916

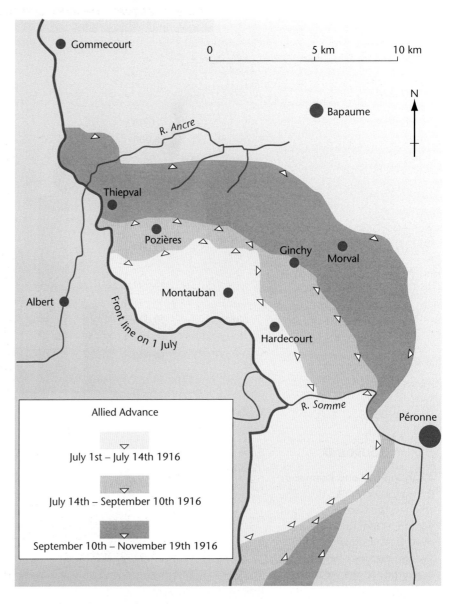

Profile on

Field Marshal Sir Douglas Haig

There is still much debate over
the part played by Haig in the
First World War. Born in 1861,
the son of an Edinburgh distiller,
Haig took up a career in the
army and gained wide
experience serving as an officer
in the 17th Lancers. He served
as a military adviser to the
Liberal Minister of War, Lord
Haldane, between 1906 and
1908. In 1914 he was made
commander of I Corps of the
BEF and showed sound
leadership qualities in the
defence of Ypres, October to
November 1914. He became
very critical of Sir John French,
the commander of the British
forces on the Western Front,
1914–15. In December 1915 he
replaced Sir John French as
overall commander, remaining
in that position to the end of
the war. He believed strongly in
'attrition' and seemed to be
lacking in new ideas on how to
win the war. His leadership was,
however, successful in 1918.

The Battle of the Somme began on 1 July 1916. It was a combined
British and French offensive that had been planned since 1915.
There were several reasons for the attack:

1   Lord Kitchener, the Minister of War, had recruited over a
    million volunteers for the British army between 1914 and the
    beginning of 1916. These fit young men were keen to go into
    battle.

2   Both Joffre, the French commander, and Haig, the British
    commander, believed in a policy of attrition. They wanted to
    attack constantly until they wore down the German defenders.
    Haig also hoped to split the German armies in two and trap
    them.

3   The most immediate reason was to take the pressure off the
    French at Verdun.

The French and British planned to attack at the point where the two armies met, the River Somme.

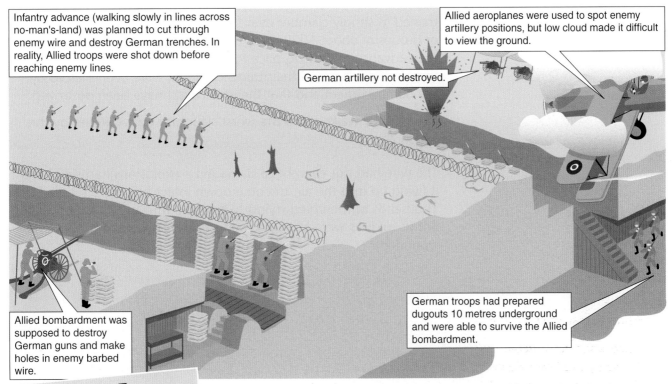

Infantry advance (walking slowly in lines across no-man's-land) was planned to cut through enemy wire and destroy German trenches. In reality, Allied troops were shot down before reaching enemy lines.

Allied aeroplanes were used to spot enemy artillery positions, but low cloud made it difficult to view the ground.

German artillery not destroyed.

Allied bombardment was supposed to destroy German guns and make holes in enemy barbed wire.

German troops had prepared dugouts 10 metres underground and were able to survive the Allied bombardment.

Source E

Haig after the battle

The German defences consisted of several lines of deep trenches, well-provided with bomb-proof shelters and protected by wire entanglements forty yards wide, built of iron stakes interlaced with barbed wire. The woods and the villages between the trenches had been turned into veritable fortresses.

The attack was doomed from the start:

- The Somme area was the strongest part of the German defences.

- There was no secrecy. Long before the attack started the Germans knew all about it. Their spotter planes watched the preparations. Their tunnellers overheard British messages as signallers shouted into field telephones. The Germans further strengthened their barbed wire and made their dug-outs even deeper.

- The Allied bombardment during the last week of June gave the Germans the final indication of when the attack would start. 1500 guns shelled the German lines continuously. The sound of the barrage was so loud it could even be heard across the Channel in Kent. Even so, there were not enough guns to do the job and the shells they fired were not powerful enough to destroy the German dug-outs.

- German signallers intercepted a 'good luck' message from General Rawlinson, commander of the coming attack, and any last chance of a surprise had gone.

- When the shelling ended, the Germans, who had been sheltering in deep dug-outs, knew what to expect and lay ready in waiting.

1 July 1916

The first men went 'over the top' at 7.30 a.m. on 1 July. It was a beautiful sunny morning. As untried civilian volunteers, they were trained to simply clamber over the trench parapet and form 'waves' or groups of about 1000 men, two paces between each man, and then advance at walking pace towards the Germans. They were told that the Germans and their trenches would have been blasted by the bombardment and that the wire would have been destroyed.

In fact, they walked into the worst slaughter ever suffered by the British army.

The wire had not even been damaged – explosions had simply sent it flying up into the air, to come down intact but more tangled. Thousands of men died trying to struggle through it. About 20,000 British soldiers were killed on the first day. More than 40,000 were wounded.

Source F

By Sergeant Cook of the 1st Somerset Regiment

The 1st Rifle Brigade advanced in perfect order. Everything was working smoothly, not a shot being fired. The first line had nearly reached the German front line, when all at once machine-guns opened up all along our front with a murderous fire. We were caught in the open, with no shelter. Men were falling like ninepins. I tripped over dead bodies, fell headlong into shell holes. My clothes were torn to ribbons by barbed wire.

Source G

The British front line of attack walking towards the German defences on 1 July

BRITISH ADVANCE.

16 MILES OF GERMAN FRONT TRENCHES STORMED.

"THE DAY GOES WELL" FOR OUR HEROIC TROOPS.

Special Telegrams to the "News of the World."

British Headquarters, July 1.—Attack launched north of River Somme this morning at 7.30 a.m., in conjunction with French.

British troops have broken into German forward system of defences on front of 16 miles.

Fighting is continuing.

French attack on our immediate right proceeding equally satisfactorily.

On remainder of British front raiding parties again succeeded in penetrating enemy's defences at many points, inflicting loss on enemy and taking some prisoners.

FRENCH OFFICIAL.

Paris, July 1. The following communique was issued this afternoon:—

On both banks of the Meuse the enemy yesterday evening and in the course of the night launched repeated and violent offensive actions.

On the left bank, in the whole of the eastern district, and to the west of Hill 304 the struggle was especially keen.

The Somme campaign

The soldiers were ordered into battle on the following day and every day thereafter for the next 20 weeks. Despite the losses of the first day, Haig refused to call off the offensive. He was under great pressure from the French to continue fighting on the Somme, since the Battle of Verdun was still being fought. In September tanks were used for the first time (p. 52). The villages of Beaumont Hamel and Beaucourt were captured using the tactic of the creeping barrage. Bad weather finally brought an end to the battle in November. The Germans had been pushed back a little but there was no breakthrough.

SOURCE I

Haig

By the third week in November the three main objects with which we had commenced our offensive had already been achieved. Verdun had been relieved, the German forces had been held on the Western Front and the enemy's strength had been considerably worn down.

SOURCE J

The British *Official History of the War*

For this disastrous loss of the finest men there was only a small gain of ground to show. Never again was the spirit or the quality of the officers and men so high. The losses were heavy and could not be replaced.

SOURCE K

Lloyd George in the 1930s. Lloyd George was an opponent of Haig and the policy of attrition.

The Battle of the Somme was not responsible for the failure of the German effort to capture Verdun. The French Commander-in-Chief (Joffre) said in May that the Germans had already been beaten at Verdun. It is claimed that the battle of the Somme destroyed the old German Army by killing its best officers and men. It killed off far more of our best and of the French best.

French, British and German losses at the Somme

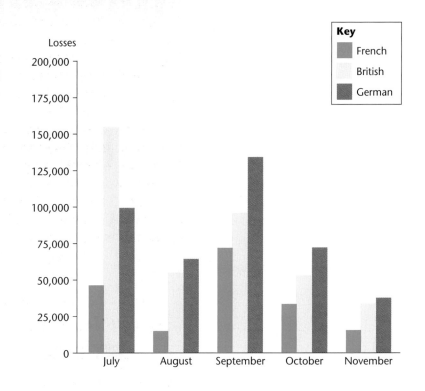

Losses

Key
- French
- British
- German

Questions

1 How reliable is Source **A** as a view of the attack at Neuve Chapelle in 1915?
2 Explain at least two reasons why the Allies failed to break through in 1915.
3 Why did the Germans decide to attack Verdun?
4 What message is the cartoonist trying to get across in Source **D**?
5 Why was it a mistake to launch an offensive on the Somme?
6 What differences are there between Sources **I** and **K** in their views of the Somme?
7 Why do you think they differ?

Activities

1 Read the newspaper headlines of the first day of the Somme, Source **H**.

   a Do the headlines give an accurate account of what took place?
   b Why do you think they give a misleading account of what took place?
   c Write your own headlines and article describing what really happened on 1 July.

2 The Battle of the Somme has been described as a total failure and disaster for the British. Copy the table below and, using the information and sources from the section on the Somme, note down the successes and failures of the battle.

Balance sheet on the Somme	
Successes	**Failures**

Do you agree it was a total failure?

The Germans, exhausted after Verdun and the Somme, did not launch any offensives in 1917. For Britain, it was the busiest year of the war, so far, on the Western Front.

April – the Nivelle offensive

General Nivelle replaced General Joffre as overall commander of the French army. He planned a new offensive in the valley of the River Aisne. It was a complete failure. The French troops were mown down by German machine-gun fire as they clambered uphill against the uncut barbed wire. The Germans had used the winter of 1916–17 to build an even stronger defence system with four lines of trenches. They called it the Hindenburg Line. The British nicknamed it the Siegfried Line. The French lost 200,000 men and there was no breakthrough.

Worse was to follow. For about six weeks in 1917, from the end of April to June, many French troops simply refused to obey orders. They had suffered enough. Troops on leave rioted at railway stations and refused to return to the fighting area. General Nivelle was sacked and replaced by Pétain, the hero of Verdun. He saved the day by:

- Executing 55 ringleaders of the mutiny.

- Promising that there would be no more French attacks in 1917.

- Improving pay, conditions and leave.

Fortunately, the Germans never learned of the mutiny. They did not believe their spies until too late. It meant the British would have to lead the way for the rest of the year.

Vimy Ridge, April

The British had already taken part in an attack at Vimy Ridge. This was to act as a diversion for the Nivelle offensive. Vimy Ridge was a German-held hill near the town of Arras. On 9 April the troops, mainly Canadian from the British Empire, went 'over the top' in heavy sleet and snow at 5.30 a.m. By midday the British and Canadian troops were on top of the ridge. This attack was a success because:

- They used the creeping barrage (see p. 52).

- The artillery bombardment beforehand was very accurate.

- The attack was kept a secret with thousands of troops hidden in cellars and caves all over the town of Arras.

Messines Ridge, June 1917

This attack was another success for the British. For a year miners had been digging 22 tunnels under Messines Ridge, a German-held hill that overlooked many British trenches around Ypres. Once the tunnels were under the German front-line trenches they were packed with dynamite. At 3.10 a.m. on 7 June one million pounds of high explosive blew up right under the feet of the Germans.

The effect was shattering. Nineteen of the tunnels exploded with a noise that could be heard in London, 208 kilometres away. About 10,000 Germans were killed instantly, buried alive by falling earth, or thrown high into the air like rag dolls. British, Australian and New Zealand troops charged and by midday the entire ridge was captured.

The Third Battle of Ypres – Passchendaele

Messines was a diversion from the main offensive, to the north on the flat land of Flanders. Haig had several reasons for launching this offensive:

- Once again, he needed to take pressure off the French by diverting the Germans.

- He still believed in attrition. Haig was convinced that the Germans were exhausted after so many tough battles and ready to collapse.

- Finally he believed that the British could break through at Ypres, advance north, and capture the Belgian ports of Zeebrugge and Ostende. These were important bases for German submarines, which were sinking a great number of British ships in 1917 (p. 69).

The first attack took place on 31 July but, once again, there was no breakthrough and the British suffered heavy casualties. They lost 30,000 men in the first week. The figure reached 67,000 by the end of the first month, by which time only 5 kilometres of swampland had been won. By October the fighting had reached the ruins of the village of Passchendaele, about 11 kilometres from the starting point. On 6 November the Canadians finally captured Passchendaele.

The Third Battle of Ypres failed to achieve a breakthrough for several reasons:

1 The offensive was delayed for six weeks after Messines Ridge. There was no secrecy and the Germans had plenty time to strengthen their defences.

2 During the British attacks the Germans used mustard gas for the first time. Gas masks provided no protection from this nerve gas (p. 49).

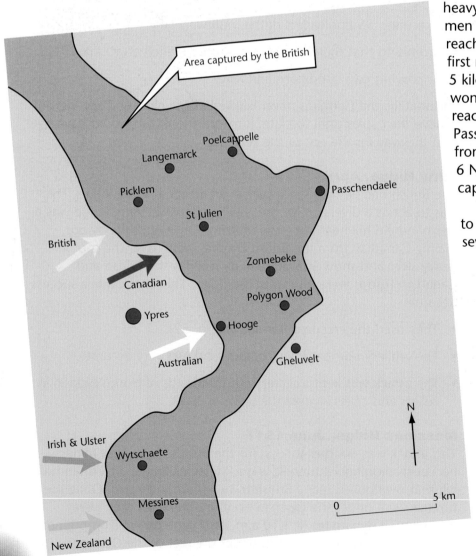

Area captured by the British

Poelcappelle
Langemarck
Picklem
St Julien
Passchendaele
British
Canadian
Zonnebeke
Ypres
Polygon Wood
Hooge
Australian
Gheluvelt
N
Irish & Ulster
Wytschaete
Messines
0   5 km
New Zealand

3   The main reason, however, was the weather. The ground here was flat and soggy from recent rain. The whole battlefield turned into a sea of mud, making it impossible for horses, tanks, guns or supplies to advance.

4   The ground conditions made it totally unsuitable for tanks.

Source A

Canadian soldiers using shell holes for machine-gun nests

Source B

Hugh Quigley, *A Diary of 1917*, published in 1928

The country resembles a sewage-heap more than anything else, pitted with shell holes, and filled with green, slimy water. Above them a blackened arm or leg might stick up. It becomes a matter of great skill picking a way across a network of death-traps. Drowning is almost certain in one of them.

Source C

The German General Ludendorff later wrote about the Third Battle of Ypres

Enormous masses of ammunition were hurled upon men who spent a miserable existence scattered about in mud-filled shell holes. It was no longer life at all. It was mere unspeakable suffering.

Was the battle a total failure?

SUCCESSES
- It took the pressure off the French and gave them time to recover from the mutinies of May.
- The Germans lost about 200,000 men.

FAILURES
- The British lost about 250,000 men.
- They gained 11 kilometres of mud with no breakthrough.
- For the first time since the start of the war, the spirits of the British army fell sharply.

Cambrai

Cambrai was part of the Hindenburg Line. The Germans did not expect an attack on this heavily fortified stretch of trenches. At 6.20 a.m. on 20 November 378 tanks supported by 289 aircraft smashed through the German trenches. By 4 p.m. the British tanks had punched a hole 10 kilometres wide and 6 kilometres deep through the German lines. At first the attack was a success because it had been kept secret and the tanks were used on firm ground.

Unfortunately, many of the tanks broke down due to lack of petrol or engine failure. The rest had to turn back to the British trenches as there was not enough infantry to take advantage of the German infantry. There were few troops to spare after the heavy losses of Ypres. Nevertheless, tanks had shown that, if used properly, they could be a war-winning weapon.

SOURCE D

George Coppard, *With a Machine Gun to Cambrai*, 1969

We saw the tanks coming, looking like giant toads at the top of the slope. The big guns stopped firing. Down swept the tanks. At zero plus one we moved forward. Rushed forward behind the tanks. The tanks had taken all fighting for an hour. We ran across no-man's-land. The German wire had been dragged about like old curtains. There wasn't a German in sight.

The situation at the end of 1917

By the end of 1917 there was stalemate on the Western Front. However, there had been two major changes on the Allied side with the loss of Russia and the entry of the USA.

The Bolshevik Revolution in Russia in 1917 (p. 416) led to the withdrawal of Russia from the war. Only days after coming to power Lenin announced that Russia would make peace with Germany. In March 1918, the two sides signed the Treaty of Brest-Litovsk (p. 420).

On 6 April 1917 the USA declared war on Germany. Britain had hoped that the Americans would join the war earlier. The Americans thought differently. To them, when it first broke out the war in Europe was a distant quarrel they had not helped to make and which had nothing to do with them. Indeed the USA continued to trade with Germany, as well as the Allies, during the period 1914 to 1917. There were two main reasons for the entry of the USA:

1   American ships in the Atlantic Ocean were being attacked by German U-boats. Americans had already suffered when the liner *Lusitania* was torpedoed in May 1915, killing 128 of the American passengers on board. Many Americans now demanded that the USA should go to war with Germany. The Germans cut back their U-boat attacks for over a year. In February 1917, however, the German U-boats once again began sinking any ships coming in or out of the UK. This included American merchant ships. Within eight weeks they had sunk eight American ships. America made strong protests but the U-boats continued their sinkings.

2   America's patience finally ran out when news of the Zimmerman Telegram was printed in the newspapers. Arthur Zimmerman, Germany's foreign minister, sent a telegram to one of his agents in Mexico. It suggested that Mexico should make an alliance with Germany if America joined the war. The Mexicans would then attack America's southern states such as Texas and Arizona. This was the last straw. President Woodrow Wilson had no choice but to go to war.

SOURCE E

The American government's ultimatum to Germany, April 1917

Unless the Imperial Government should now abandon submarine warfare against passenger and freight carrying vessels, the government of the US can have no choice but to break off diplomatic relations with the Central Powers (Germany and Austria) altogether.

SOURCE F

Extract from the Zimmerman Telegram, January 1917

If America joins the war we make a proposal of alliance to Mexico. Mexico is to reconquer lost territory in Mexico, New Mexico and Arizona.

America's arrival in the war was a great boost to the Allies. By 1917 the USA was the wealthiest country in the world. The Americans had vast gold reserves and industrial resources now available to help the Allied war effort. The American army was not very big and would not be able to join the fighting at once. Weapons had to be made, men recruited and ships built to take them across the Atlantic to Europe. This would all take months. Nevertheless, in the long term the Americans would be able to raise a very large army which could well swing the balance on the Western Front in favour of the Allies.

1   Do a balance sheet for the Allies at the end of 1917. Copy and use the following chart.

Allied successes/gains	Allied failures/losses

Include in your balance sheet:

- The different offensives of 1917.

- Developments with Russia and the USA.

2   You are a soldier serving in the British army on the Western Front in 1917 in the Ypres/Flanders area. You keep a diary. Write out some of the important extracts of your diary from June–November 1917. This could include your views/reactions:

- News of the American entry.

- Messines Ridge.

- The mud of Ypres.

- The use of tanks at Cambrai.

- Russian withdrawal from the war.

Questions

1   Why were the Canadian forces able to successfully capture the ridges at Vimy and Messines?
2   What do Sources **A**, **B** and **C** tell you about conditions during the Third Battle of Ypres?
3   Why did the USA declare war on Germany in April 1917? How did this help the Allies?

THE EVENTS OF 1918

The stalemate ended in 1918 with Allied victory in November. This was partly due to the failure of German attempts to break through in the spring.

Ludendorff's offensives

In March 1918 the German commander on the Western Front, General Ludendorff, decided on one major offensive. This was a gamble, an attempt to win the war quickly before the arrival of the Americans in numbers. Why did Ludendorff decide on this gamble?

Ludendorff's offensive and the German retreat, 1918

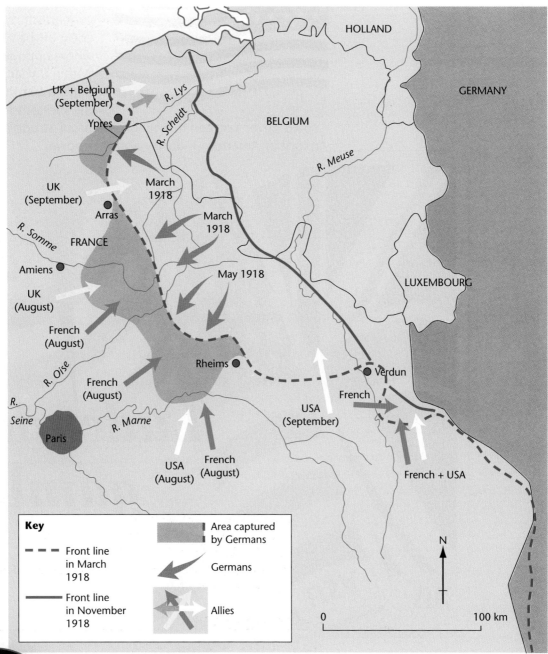

Map labels:
- HOLLAND
- GERMANY
- BELGIUM
- UK + Belgium (September)
- Ypres
- R. Lys
- R. Scheldt
- R. Meuse
- UK (September)
- Arras
- March 1918
- March 1918
- R. Somme
- FRANCE
- May 1918
- LUXEMBOURG
- Amiens
- UK (August)
- French (August)
- Rheims
- R. Oise
- French (August)
- Verdun
- French
- USA (September)
- R. Seine
- R. Marne
- French + USA
- Paris
- USA (August)
- French (August)

Key
- – – – Front line in March 1918
- —— Front line in November 1918
- Area captured by Germans
- Germans (arrow)
- Allies (arrow)

N

0   100 km

Profile on

Erich Ludendorff

He was born in 1865 in Prussia, the son of a family of rural merchants. He entered the army and was quickly promoted. When the war started he impressed with his leadership during the capture of the Belgian fort of Liège in 1914. In the same year he was appointed chief of staff to General Hindenburg and by 1916 had become very much the controller of the German war effort. It was his decision to gamble with all out German attack in the spring of 1918 and Ludendorff was very much responsible for the use of stormtroopers and the adoption of new tactics.

American entry

Ludendorff realised that the entry of the USA changed the whole outlook of the war. Within a year the Allies would outnumber the Germans on the Western Front. Germany could never succeed in a long-drawn-out struggle against the might of American industry and manpower.

Ludendorff's gamble

Failure of the U-boat campaign of 1917

The German navy tried to starve Britain out of the war in 1917 by sinking all ships going in and out of the UK. This failed due to the use of the convoy system (p. 87) and brought the USA into the war.

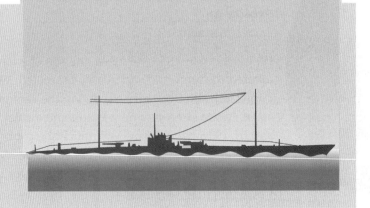

The British naval blockade

The British navy had been blockading the German coast since the start of the war in order to restrict and even stop German seaborne trade. This was much more effective between 1917 and 1918 as:

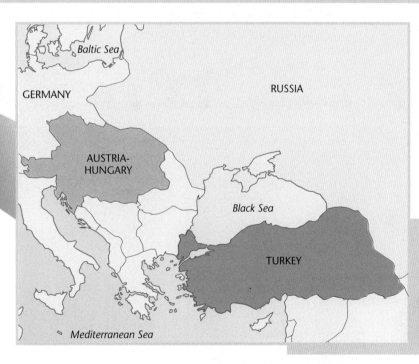

- Sweden agreed to limit its overland exports of iron ore to Germany. This badly affected German production of armaments.

- Denmark reduced its overland exports of dairy produce.

- The USA no longer traded with Germany after April 1917.

By early 1918 Germany was seriously short of food, iron and steel and chemicals. There was serious hunger among the civilian population. Ludendorff realised that a quick victory was needed or Germany would be starved out of the war.

German allies

Turkey and Austria, Germany's allies, were both in trouble and talking of surrender.

Russian withdrawal

This meant Ludendorff could transfer one million German troops from the Eastern to the Western Front. For a short time the Germans outnumbered the Allies.

The German attacks, March–May

Ludendorff deliberately concentrated his first attacks on the British. He believed they had been weakened by the events of 1917. He also felt that, overall, Britain was the stronger of the Allies. Should the British collapse, the French would soon follow.

He realised that the usual frontal attack was doomed to failure. Instead he had developed new tactics based on the use of 'stormtroopers'. They were trained to attack at speed in small groups along the whole of the front line so that the Allies would not be able to mass in one place to hold him back. Then when they found a weak spot they would push right through.

The attack began on 21 March at 4 a.m. in the area between Arras and Amiens. Ludendorff intended to capture Amiens and split the British and French armies. At first the German attack was very successful with the British driven back as much as thirty miles in places. This was because:

- Ludendorff adopted new tactics.

- The attack was kept a secret and took the British by surprise. They had been expecting a German attack further north at Ypres.

- The Germans attacked under the cover of smoke and gas shells which hid the stormtroopers.

SOURCE A

Specially trained German stormtroopers in gas masks attack through thick woods

Despite the early confusion the British forces were not destroyed. A new defence line was hastily formed and troops were rushed from Italy and the Middle East to reinforce the British defences. Haig did not panic but issued his famous 'Backs to the Wall' orders.

Haig's orders

Three weeks ago the enemy began terrific attacks against us. Victory will belong to the side that holds out the longest. Every position must be held to the last man. With our backs to the wall, and believing in the justice of our cause, each one of us must fight on to the end.

The Allies now decided to place all their armies on the Western Front under one commander, the French General Foch. He was able to co-ordinate the Allied defences.

In April the Germans attacked again in the Ypres area, hoping to break through and capture the Channel ports. Again they had early success but the British were not defeated and built new defences. Finally, in May, Ludendorff launched attacks on the French defences near to Verdun. The French retreated nearly 40 miles and the Germans were within sight of Paris. Many Parisians packed their belongings and fled the capital. Resolute French defence, with the help of newly arrived American troops, held the German advance.

Results of German offensives

Ludendorff's gamble had failed. Although the Germans had driven the Allies back as much as 40 miles in places, Germany was much weaker by July 1918:

- The Germans had suffered appalling casualties because they had been attacking. Indeed by July at least 400,000 men had been killed.

- There was no breakthrough and they had a much greater area to defend with a makeshift, hastily assembled trench system. Paris, Ypres, Arras, Amiens and Verdun were still in Allied hands.

- The German troops were exhausted and low in morale. They had been told the Allies were hungry and unhappy but they found huge supplies of food in captured trenches.

- The British blockade continued, causing even greater food shortages and discontent with the German civilians.

- In May the first Americans went into battle, and now every week brought fresh boatloads of fit, keen soldiers from the USA. The Germans had lost their superiority in numbers on the Western Front.

A WASTED LIFE.

Kaiser (to Count Zeppelin). "Tell me, Count, why didn't you invent something useful, like the 'tanks'?"

The Allied drive to victory

On 8 August the Allies hit back against the Germans. General Ludendorff called it the 'black day of the German army'. Canadians, Australians, Americans, Belgians, French and British troops combined to burst through the German defences and force the Germans back. At Amiens an attack in a thick fog by 456 tanks captured about 30,000 Germans and 400 field guns. Eventually about 400,000 Germans were taken prisoner. With losses like this the Germans could not possibly fight on and what remained of Ludendorff's army was driven back steadily.

By late October the coast of Belgium had been liberated. In a single day the Allies advanced 13 kilometres from Ypres, which was more than they had managed in months of bitter fighting the year before.

SOURCE D

Ludendorff later wrote about the events of 8 August

Whole bodies of our men had surrendered to single troopers, or isolated squadrons. The officers in many places had lost their influence and allowed themselves to be swept along with the rest.

Events in Germany itself brought an end to the war on the Western Front. The revolution of late October and early November (p. 78) led to the collapse of the German war effort, and the abdication of the Kaiser, who fled to Holland. On 9 November the new German government asked the allies for an armistice (or ceasefire). The Allies made certain demands.

The Germans had to:

MEMORANDUM

- Withdraw from the rest of Belgium and France.
- Surrender all weapons and release prisoners-of-war.
- Surrender all warships and U-boats.
- Allow Allied troops into Germany.

The Germans agreed and the ceasefire began at 11 a.m. on the morning of 11 November 1918.

SOURCE E

French poster of 1918. 'Victory of the Allies' by Abel Faivre

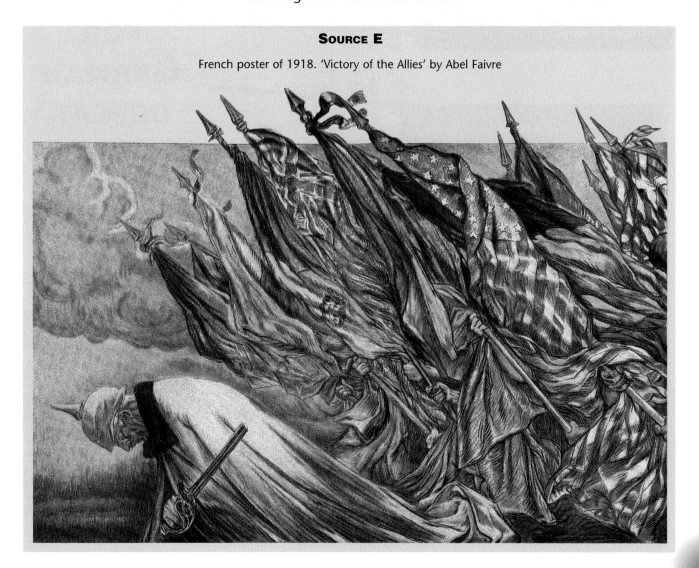

BRITISH BLOCKADE OF GERMANY

This had serious effects on the German war effort. Industry ran short of fuel and chemicals for explosives and gas. In 1915 rationing began in Germany. In 1916 food riots broke out in many German cities as people demanded more bread. By 1918 starvation had hit millions of Germans. About 120,000 died of hunger in 1916 and this figure rose to 290,000 in 1918. By 1918 there were riots and strikes as the civilian population demanded an end to the war.

THE FAILURE OF LUDENDORFF'S GAMBLE

Ludendorff gambled everything on a quick victory in the spring of 1918. There was no breakthrough and the Germans were left much weaker.

REVOLUTION IN GERMANY

Discontent in Germany due to food shortages and a serious flu epidemic which killed thousands led to the abdication of the Kaiser and a new German republic.

REASONS FOR GERMAN DEFEAT

TANKS

These proved a war-winning weapon in 1918. They were used correctly by Haig in early August to force a gap in the German trenches.

DEFEAT OF GERMANY'S ALLIES

Germany's allies collapsed in 1918. Driven back by Serbian and French troops during 1918, the Bulgarian army surrendered on 29 September. A month later, on 30 October, the Turkish forces surrendered to combined British and Arab troops. On 3 November the forces of the Austro-Hungarian Empire surrendered as Czech, Polish and other troops mutinied against the hated Austrians.

THE FAILURE OF THE SCHLIEFFEN PLAN

This meant that there would be no quick end to the war. Germany now had to fight a war on two fronts. It also led to long-drawn-out trench warfare on the Western Front.

AMERICAN ENTRY

This certainly hastened the end of the war. It forced Ludendorff to gamble. It greatly increased the morale of the Allied troops and gave the Allies the benefits of American industry and manpower.

FAILURE OF THE GERMAN U-BOAT CAMPAIGN (P. 86)

The German attempt to break the British blockade and starve Britain out of the war in 1917 failed. It backfired and brought the USA into the war.

Questions

1 Why did Ludendorff decide to gamble by attacking in March 1918?
2 What new tactics did he use?
3 Explain the effects that his attacks had on the German army by July 1918.
4 What point is the cartoonist trying to make in Source **C**?
5 Which would be more useful to an historian studying the events of 1918 on the Western Front, Source **D** or Source **E**?

Activity

Copy the following chart

Reasons for German defeat	Decisive	Important	Quite important	Unimportant
American entry				
U-boat failure				
British blockade				
Tanks				
American entry				
Failure of Ludendorff's attacks				
German revolution				
Loss of German Allies				

1 Decide how important each reason was. Explain your decision.

2 Try to link some of the reasons.
  e.g. The British blockade brought starvation in Germany and led to the German revolution.

3 Which do you think was the most important or fundamental reason for the defeat of Germany? Explain your answer.

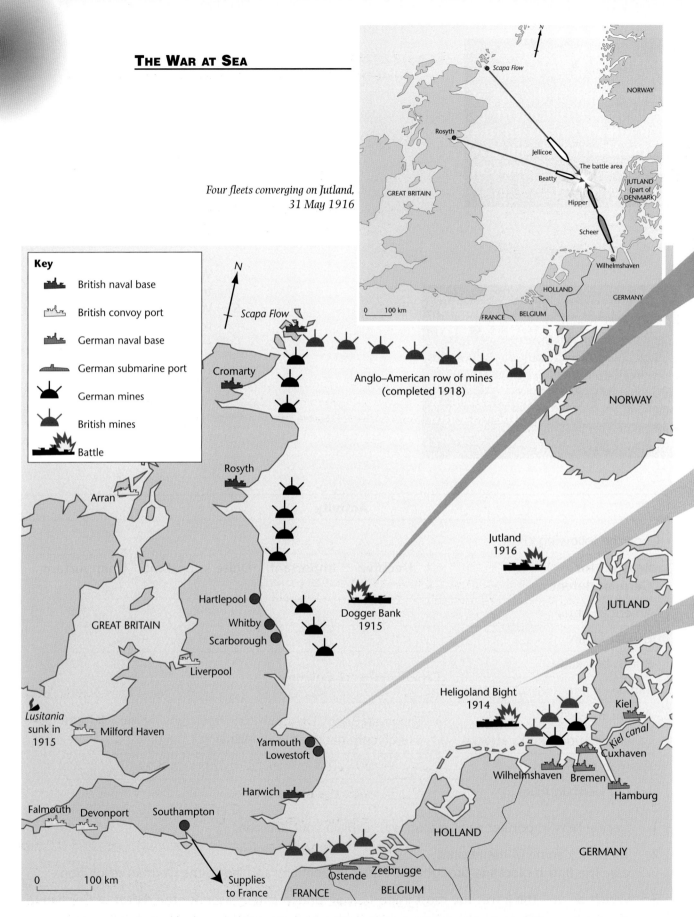

*Four fleets converging on Jutland,
31 May 1916*

Key
- British naval base
- British convoy port
- German naval base
- German submarine port
- German mines
- British mines
- Battle

N

Scapa Flow

Cromarty

Anglo–American row of mines
(completed 1918)

NORWAY

Rosyth

Arran

JUTLAND

Jutland
1916

Hartlepool

Whitby

Scarborough

GREAT BRITAIN

Dogger Bank
1915

Liverpool

Heligoland Bight
1914

Kiel

Lusitania
sunk in
1915

Milford Haven

Kiel canal

Cuxhaven

Yarmouth
Lowestoft

Wilhelmshaven

Bremen

Hamburg

Harwich

Falmouth

Devonport

Southampton

HOLLAND

GERMANY

0   100 km

Supplies
to France

Ostende

Zeebrugge

FRANCE

BELGIUM

This was a conflict between the British Grand Fleet and the German
High Seas Fleet. There was only one major battle, at Jutland in May
1916, because the German Fleet spent most of the war at its base
in Wilhelmshaven, too frightened to face its British rival.

Early events

There were several skirmishes in the early months of the war.

Battle of Dogger Bank

These raids were ended in January 1915 when the British battle-cruiser fleet under Admiral Beatty intercepted the German battle-cruisers near the Dogger Bank. Two German battle-cruisers were destroyed but the British battle-cruiser HMS *Lion* was damaged and had to slow down, allowing the remaining German ships to escape.

German raids

In November–December 1914 the German High Seas Fleet raided the British east coast and caused damage and casualties at Hartlepool, Whitby, Scarborough and Yarmouth.

Heligoland Bight

In late August 1914 the British battle-cruisers enticed out several German warships. Three enemy cruisers and a destroyer were sunk.

The Battle of Jutland

On 31 May 1916, four major fleets headed for the area off Jutland:

- The main British Dreadnought fleet under Admiral Jellicoe, the overall commander of the Navy.

- The British battle-cruisers led by Admiral Beatty.

- The German Dreadnought fleet under Admiral Scheer.

- The German battle-cruisers led by Admiral Hipper.

In a desperate attempt to end the British control of the sea, Admiral Scheer tried to lure the British battle-cruisers into a trap using his own cruiser fleet as bait. The British Admiralty were able to decode German messages and, realising the German plan, sent the Grand Fleet under Jellicoe to intercept the German High Seas Fleet.

Never before had two such mighty fleets sailed into battle. Two hundred and fifty great ships were steaming at great speed into the misty North Sea.

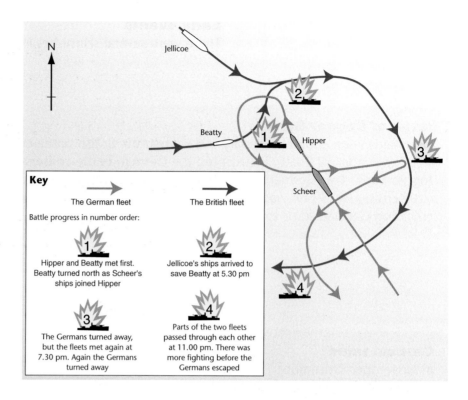

Key

→ The German fleet   → The British fleet

Battle progress in number order:

1 Hipper and Beatty met first. Beatty turned north as Scheer's ships joined Hipper

2 Jellicoe's ships arrived to save Beatty at 5.30 pm

3 The Germans turned away, but the fleets met again at 7.30 pm. Again the Germans turned away

4 Parts of the two fleets passed through each other at 11.00 pm. There was more fighting before the Germans escaped

Beatty's fleet went ahead of the Grand Fleet to meet Hipper's 'bait' squadron. They closed in on each other at great speed. Hipper's ships quickly sank two of Beatty's cruisers and then chased the rest northwards. Hipper did not realise that he was heading straight for the Grand Fleet.

Just before six in the evening the two great battle fleets came into contact off the coast of Jutland in Denmark. Fierce fighting went on all evening. Admiral Scheer, realising he had sailed into a trap, turned his fleet and eventually sailed back to the safety of Germany. Admiral Jellicoe did not try to chase Scheer for he feared that the German submarines and mines were close by. He too turned round and made his way home.

Results of the battle

Both sides claimed victory. German claims were based on the number of ships and casualties suffered during the battle.

Total losses at Jutland

LOSSES	BRITISH	GERMAN
Battle-cruisers	3	1
Armoured cruisers	3	–
Old battleships	–	1
Light cruisers	–	4
Destroyers	8	5
Tonnes lost	110,000	60,000
Sailors killed	6,000	2,500

British newspaper headlines about Jutland

FACTS OF THE SEA BATTLE

ADMIRAL BEATTY FIGHTS THE WHOLE GERMAN FLEET

COMPENSATION FOR OUR HEAVY LOSS:
ADMIRALTY COUNTS 18 GERMAN SHIPS SUNK
AGAINST OUR 14

SOURCE B

American historian, 1964

Jutland gave no cheer to England. If not a defeat, it was a disastrous victory. The German High Seas Fleet had struck down 117,025 tons of British warships. The Grand Fleet had sunk about 61,180 tons of German naval power. German armor had stood up better; German gunnery had shown itself more accurate.

SOURCE E

American newspaper

The German fleet has assaulted its jailor, but it is still in jail.

SOURCE D

An historian

The Kaiser insisted on regarding the battle as a victory. He was quite wrong. Jellicoe had not won a great victory but he had not suffered a defeat. He remained ready to proceed at sea at four hours' notice. The Kaiser was warned that the High Seas Fleet needed a month to make good the damage it had suffered. The German fleet never emerged from port again.

Activity

Write two separate headlines and newspaper reports on the battle of Jutland

- One for a German newspaper.

- The other for a British newspaper.

Questions

1 What happened at Heligoland Bight and Dogger Bank?
2 Why did the four fleets converge on Jutland on 31 May?
3 What does the American newspaper mean by its comment in Source **E**?
4 What differences are there between Sources **B** and **C** in their versions of the Battle of Jutland? Why are they so different?

From the very start of the war the First Lord of the Admiralty, Winston Churchill, ordered a blockade of Germany. This meant stopping all ships heading for German ports and turning back or sinking any found carrying food or supplies such as oil or steel or chemicals. During the course of the war about 12,000 ships were intercepted while fewer than 80 slipped through.

The effects 1914–16

The blockade was not very effective for the first two years of the war:

- Germany was able to import dairy produce overland from Denmark.

- Vital iron ore supplies also came overland from Sweden.

- The USA insisted on trading with Germany and resisted British attempts to stop American ships.

The effects 1917–18

The blockade was far more effective during the final eighteen months of the war:

- Denmark and Sweden agreed to limit their exports to Germany.

- America's entry on the side of the Allies, in April 1917, ended all trade with the Germans.

The importance of the blockade

The blockade played a very important role in the eventual defeat of Germany:

1   It forced Scheer to gamble at Jutland in 1916 in an attempt to end the blockade.

2   When this failed the Germans once again resorted to unrestricted U-boat warfare in 1917 to try to starve out the British before the Germans were likewise starved out of the war. This failed and led directly to American entry into the war.

3   In the spring of 1918 Ludendorff gambled everything on outright victory realising that Germany was close to exhaustion. This gamble also failed.

4   Finally, food shortages contributed greatly to the revolution in Germany in October–November 1918.

SUBMARINE WARFARE

Submarines had been developed before the First World War but the Germans used new tactics. As an island Britain was very vulnerable to attacks from U-boats. British farmers could not produce enough food for the whole population and some crops like tea and sugar cane would not grow in such a cold climate. In addition, Britain lacked oil, rubber and many other important industrial goods. These had to come from abroad, mainly from the British Empire, by ship. Early in the war the Germans realised that if they could sink enough ships, Britain would be forced to surrender from starvation or from lack of war materials.

SOURCE B

German U-boat at Heligoland Harbour

Unrestricted U-boat warfare

At first the German U-boats only sank British and Allied ships. This tactic was known as 'sink on sight'. This did not work well so in February 1915 the Germans created 'war zones' round the entire British Isles. Germany warned the world that from now on, any ship from any country found in these war zones would be sunk. This policy was known as 'unrestricted U-boat warfare'.

In 7 May 1915 the huge transatlantic liner *Lusitania* was torpedoed by submarine U20 off the coast of Ireland. A total of 1198 people were drowned, many of them women and children, including 128 Americans. Germany claimed that the *Lusitania* was carrying war goods which made the ship a fair target. Nevertheless, fearing that America might join the war on Britain's side, the Germans called off 'unrestricted U-boat warfare' at the end of 1915.

SOURCE C

Painting of the sinking of the *Lusitania*

SOURCE D

A report of the sinking of the *Lusitania* in a German newspaper

The sinking of the giant English steamship is a success. With joyful pride we contemplate this latest deed of our navy. It will not be the last.

In February 1917, in a desperate gamble to starve Britain out of the war, Germany resumed unrestricted U-boat warfare. By May it was beginning to work. So many ships were being sunk that Britain was down to six weeks' supply of certain foods. At one point there was only four days' supply of sugar.

Defeating the U-boats

Britain introduced a series of measures to defeat the U-boat threat.

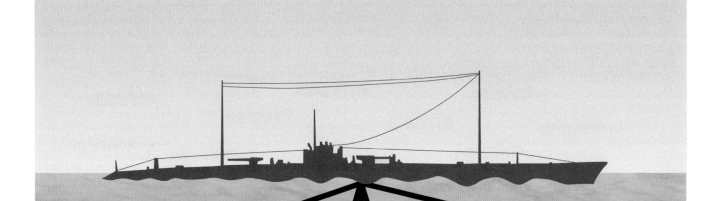

HORNED MINES

These were large round metal containers packed with explosives. Several spikes or 'horns' stuck out – if a ship touched a horn, the mine would explode. By 1918 both the English Channel and the North Sea had been closed off by rows of deadly mines under the surface. However, U-boats would surface at night and sail over these mines. Not until 1918 were searchlights fitted across the Channel.

THE 'Q' SHIP

This was first used in 1915. It looked like a harmless cargo vessel, but it carried powerful guns disguised as freight or even as cabins on deck. When a U-boat surfaced to search the ship (not wanting to waste a torpedo on such an easy target), the crew would wait until the enemy was on deck, making it impossible for the submarine to dive quickly. Then the guns would be revealed and the U-boat sunk. This only worked for a short period. U-boats soon stopped surfacing.

DEPTH CHARGE AND HYDROPHONE

A depth charge was a container about the size of a large oil drum, packed with explosives. It was dropped in the sea above a suspected U-boat and could be set to explode at a certain depth. Some ships were fitted with hydrophones or listening devices. Sounds travel easily under water and an operator with headphones could hear a nearby submarine engine.

RAIDS ON U-BOAT BASES

The British attempted to block off the U-boat bases at Ostend and Zeebrugge using block ships which were sunk at the entrance to the harbours. These two attacks, in early 1918, had limited success and did not completely block off the ports.

THE CONVOY SYSTEM

This proved the most successful idea and was introduced in June 1917. A convoy was a group of ships sailing together and protected by fast warships such as armed trawlers or destroyers fitted with depth charges and hydrophones. From June 1917 to November 1918, 16,539 ships sailed in convoys and only 154 were torpedoed. In addition many more U-boats were sunk whilst attacking the convoys.

SOURCE E

The convoy system

British destroyers and torpedo boats armed with torpedoes and depth charges. Both weapons could sink U-boats. By the end of 1917 one in four U-boats was being sunk.

British naval ships created a smoke-screen so that the convoy was invisible to U-boats when they came to the surface. There was no radar, so sight was the only way to find the convoy.

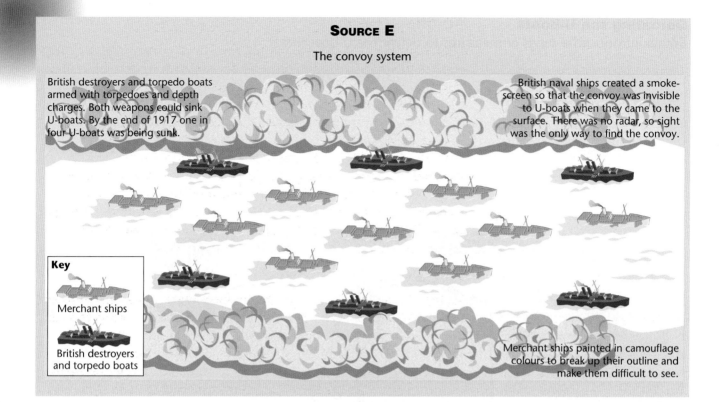

Key

Merchant ships

British destroyers and torpedo boats

Merchant ships painted in camouflage colours to break up their outline and make them difficult to see.

Activity

Assess the importance of each of the anti U-boat measures by copying and using the following table. Write in a reason for each of your choices.

Anti-U-boat measures	Decisive	Important	Quite important	Unimportant
Q-boats Hydrophones Horned mines Raids on bases Convoy system				

Questions

1 Why was the blockade important in the eventual defeat of Germany?
2 What is meant by 'unrestricted U-boat warfare'?
3 Why was Britain vulnerable to U-boat attacks?
4 Compare Sources **C** and **D**. What different views do they give of the sinking of the *Lusitania*? Why are they different?
5 How useful is Source **B** to an historian studying U-boat warfare in the First World War?

Allied commanders underestimated the part that aircraft could play in the fighting. The French commander, General Foch, said aviation was 'good sport but for the army the aeroplane is worthless'. Britain's air force, the Royal Flying Corps, was part of the army until 1918 when it became the Royal Air Force (RAF). Yet aircraft soon proved their value.

In 1914, aircraft were used mainly for reconnaissance. Pilots watched for signs of enemy troops moving up to the front lines. They took photographs of enemy trenches. These helped the artillery to select their targets. A pilot was the first to detect the gap in the German armies as they approached the River Marne in September 1914.

Air fighting

At first, the air war was very gentlemanly: pilots saluted each other as they passed. But soon they were carrying rifles or pistols to shoot each other and were being fitted with machine-guns. It was not easy flying a plane and firing a machine-gun at the same time. In any case there was a risk that you might shoot your own propeller blades to bits. This problem was solved for the Germans by a Dutchman, Anthony Fokker.

He managed to synchronise the machine-gun with the propeller blade. This allowed the pilot to fire between the blades every time. It turned the aircraft into a fighting machine. It made life more dangerous for the pilots. In 1916, the working life of a British pilot averaged just three weeks. German fighter aces, such as Hermann Goering and Baron von Richthofen, did battle with Allied pilots over France.

SOURCE A

Sir John French commenting on the Royal Flying Corps, September 1914

They have furnished me with complete and accurate information which has been of great value in the conduct of operations.

SOURCE B

A wartime painting of a British pilot 'looping the loop' to evade German fighter planes

Bombing

Another development was bombing. Enemy trenches were one target but both British and Germans bombed other targets, including cities. The first German raid on Britain was as early as January 1915. It was the first time that civilians had ever been bombed from the air.

At first, these raids were made by zeppelins. These were huge airships, the length of 2½ football fields, filled with hydrogen gas. Altogether, there were 51 zeppelin raids on Britain during the First World War. They caused about 1900 casualties, including 564 deaths.

New means of attack led to new means of defence. Anti-aircraft guns were improved. Barrage balloons were strung across the sky and searchlights were used to light up a zeppelin, making it an easier target. Explosive bullets were used to set the hydrogen on fire. Once ablaze, they were death traps.

SOURCE C

This painting shows the end of a zeppelin

SOURCE D

Sybil Morrison watched the end of a zeppelin in September 1916. Afterwards she became a pacifist.

To me, it was an awful sight. All the bag part had caught fire. We knew that there were about sixty people in it and that they were being roasted to death. I was appalled to see the kind, good-hearted British people dancing about in the streets – clapping and singing and cheering.

So the Germans switched to using Gotha bombers. In 1918, they killed over 800 people and caused great panic.

SOURCE E

V.S. Pritchett recalled seeing bomber planes over London in *A Cab at the Door*, 1968

It was, for those days, startling. A flight of aircraft had bombed London for the first time by day. I saw the street walls of several houses had been stripped off, carts were overturned and horses lay dead among the crowds. The pubs in Bermondsey had filled with women pouring drink into themselves and their babies as I left.

Meanwhile the British had been attacking German cities.

Aircraft development had been rapid during the war. In August 1914, the Royal Flying Corps had taken just 37 planes to France. In 1918, Britain ended the war with 22,000 planes – the biggest airforce in the world.

Activity

You are one of the people dancing in the street in Source **D**. Write a postcard to a friend describing what you saw and your feelings.

Questions

1   What part did the following play in the war in the air:
    a   Anthony Fokker?
    b   zeppelins?
    c   the Gotha?
2   What does Source **E** tell you about the effects of bombing?
3   Which is the more useful to an historian studying the end of a zeppelin, Source **C** or Source **D**?
4   Why do you think Source **B** was painted?

In October 1914, Turkey joined the war on the side of the Central Powers. In the following year the British launched a campaign on the peninsula of Gallipoli in an attempt to knock the Turks out of the war.

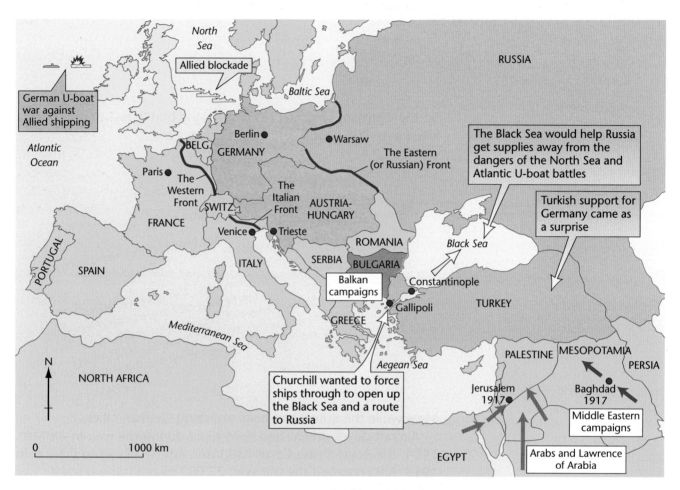

German U-boat war against Allied shipping

Allied blockade

The Black Sea would help Russia get supplies away from the dangers of the North Sea and Atlantic U-boat battles

Turkish support for Germany came as a surprise

The Eastern (or Russian) Front

The Western Front

The Italian Front

Balkan campaigns

Churchill wanted to force ships through to open up the Black Sea and a route to Russia

Middle Eastern campaigns

Arabs and Lawrence of Arabia

Why was the campaign launched?

The plan was the idea of the First Lord of the Admiralty, Winston Churchill.

- By early 1915 Russia desperately needed help from Britain and France. The only real possibility was through a narrow stretch of sea, the Dardanelles, then the Sea of Marmara, both controlled by the Turks, into the Black Sea.

- The British hoped that the Gallipoli campaign would break the stalemate on the Western Front. They would capture Constantinople, the capital of Turkey and knock Turkey out of the war. This, in turn, would encourage the neutral countries close to Turkey, such as Greece, Romania and Bulgaria, to join the Allied side. They would attack and defeat Austria and leave Germany isolated and unable to continue the war.

The Dardanelles campaign

In 1915 Britain could not spare troops for such a plan. The BEF was too busy in France and Lord Kitchener's army of volunteers was not ready. Churchill proposed a naval attack. British and French battleships would sail through the Dardanelles and destroy the Turkish forts and huge guns.

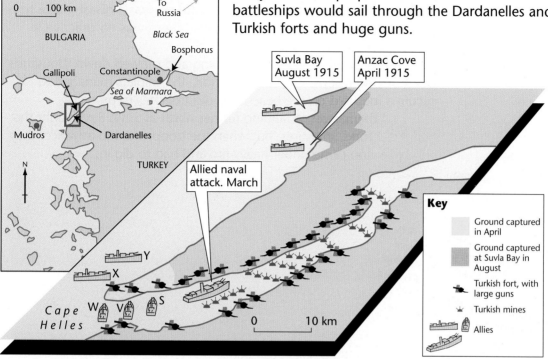

The naval attack began on 18 March 1915 but the Turks had put mines in the water and three battleships were blown up when they sailed into the Dardanelles. The rest of the fleet rapidly retreated. Some forts had been destroyed, but now the Turks had been alerted to the attack plan. Any chance of surprise had gone and the Turks were able to strengthen their position.

The Gallipoli landings

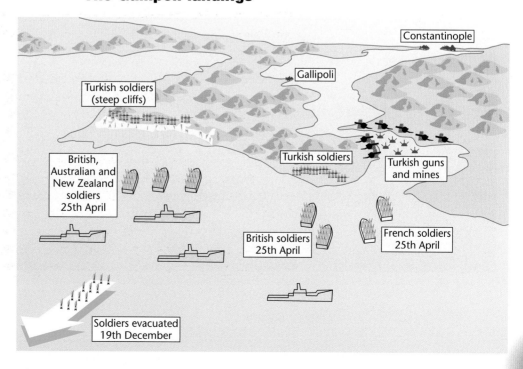

It was decided that troops would now be used to capture the Turkish forts. They would attack the west coast of the Gallipoli peninsula, cross overland, and capture the forts from behind. They would use Australian and New Zealand Arms Corps (or ANZACs), who were diverted from Egypt. The landing was a disaster due to poor planning using out-of-date maps. There was no practice in landing on enemy beaches.

The Turks were ready for the landing and mowed down thousands of advancing troops. With a great effort, the soldiers managed to secure a foothold on the beach and dig trenches to protect themselves. A landing further north at Suvla Bay caught the Turks unawares, but when the troops tried to advance, they too came under heavy fire and had to dig in.

SOURCE A

John Masefield, who took part in the landings, describes the scene

From every rifle and machine-gun began a murderous fire upon the ship and boats. There was no question of their missing. Many were killed in the water, many who were wounded, were swept away and drowned. Others, trying to swim in the fierce current, were drowned by the weight of the equipment. But some reached the shore. These instantly doubled out to cut the wire entanglements, and were killed. Only a handful reached cover.

SOURCE B

Soldiers landing at Anzac Cove

Conditions at Gallipoli

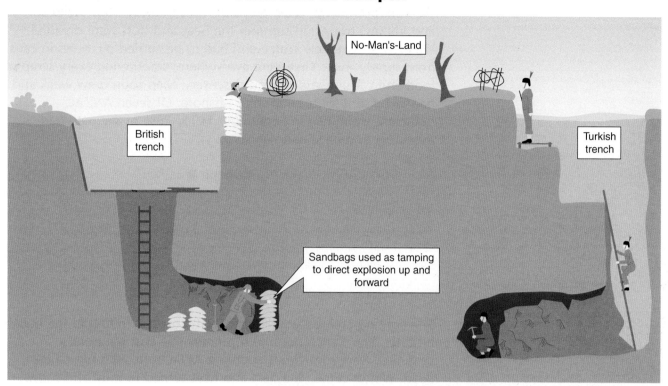

No-Man's-Land

British trench

Turkish trench

Sandbags used as tamping to direct explosion up and forward

SOURCE C

Anzac troops in the trenches at Gallipoli

Life at Gallipoli soon became a struggle for survival. In some places the Turkish trenches were only nine metres away from the British and ANZAC troops. In summer the heat and dust were dreadful. Water was extremely scarce and had to be carried by mules in cans from supply ships. Flies were everywhere, smothering every scrap of food and causing widespread dysentery. Men soon grew weak and had to be sent to hospital ships offshore. Of seven ANZAC battalions examined in September 1915, 78% of the men had dysentery and 64% had skin sores.

> ### SOURCE D
>
> From A. Herbert, *The Great War – I was There*
>
> *We walked from the sea and uphill through a field of tall corn, filled with poppies, through another field, then the fearful smell of death began as we came across scattered bodies. We came over the top of the hill and 4,000 Turkish bodies lay among the thyme and myrtle. It was a nightmare.*

The fighting area became littered with corpses, rotting in the hot weather. The stench became so unbearable that temporary ceasefires were sometimes arranged while both sides buried the dead. Winter came. The dust and heat turned to mud and snow. Water now poured down the hills into Allied trenches. Blizzards swept over men without overcoats, huddled together for warmth, caking them with freezing mud and ice. On 28 November the cold reached its worst. Men simply died where they slept. 15,000 died of exposure.

> ### SOURCE E
>
> From *The War Diary and Letters of Tom Eades, 1915–17*
>
> *At dusk the rifle bullets fell thickly and we laid in our hole listening. The Turks are no more than 180 metres away. The new trenches are too low down. More men get killed on the beaches than tucked up in the cliffs where we are. Salt beef today, hard biscuit and only one pint of tea for drink all day. Kept the bottom half inch for shaving.*

The evacuation

The stalemate lasted until December 1915. It was then decided to call off the attack. The problem was how to evacuate the Allied troops under the noses of the Turks. The evacuation was the only real success of the whole campaign. From 12 December, groups of men were secretly led at night from their trenches to waiting boats and quickly ferried away. Blankets were laid along tracks to deaden the sound of boots. Mules had sacking tied round their hooves. Supplies were destroyed with acid.

Those who remained tried to deceive the Turks by lighting extra cooking fires and firing rifles up and down the deserted trenches. On 21 December the last troops slipped away from Suvla Bay and Anzac Cove. More than 8000 had escaped without a single death.

Turkish defenders

For the Turks this was a Holy War, a struggle to drive out Christian invaders from Muslim Turkey. Time and again the Turks charged downhill on the Allies and were slaughtered by Vickers machine-guns.

Lack of support and enthusiasm

The Gallipoli campaign got little real support from the armed forces. Sir John French refused to release troops from the Western Front. Kitchener believed the war would be won on the Western Front, not in the east.

Lack of surprise

The Turks knew well in advance about the Gallipoli landings and strengthened their defences. It took the British several weeks to organise the landings.

Why did the Gallipoli campaign fail?

Too ambitious

From the beginning the plan had little or no chance of success. It was highly unlikely to achieve its aims of knocking Turkey and then Austria out of the war. There was no serious thought as to what to do once the Allies had captured Gallipoli. How would they take Constantinople?

SOURCE F

Sir Maurice Hankey, a member of Britain's War Council

No one has worked out how many soldiers and guns are needed to take Gallipoli from the Turks. We have just said that we can ship a certain number of soldiers there and that ought to be enough.

Poor organisation

The British did not practice and used out-of-date maps for the landings. During the naval campaign they failed to use proper minesweepers to remove the Turkish mines. The only realistic chance of success was a combined army and navy operation. Instead they were carried out separately.

Results of the campaign

Was it a total failure?

FAILURES

- The naval campaign and landings did not work.

- Turkey was not knocked out of the war.

- Bulgaria joined the war on the side of the Central Powers.

- Churchill resigned due to the failure of the campaign.

- Of the 410,000 British and ANZAC troops who fought in the campaign, 213,980 died, just under three-quarters of them from disease.

SUCCESSES

- The evacuation was carried out successfully.

- The campaign diverted the Turks from Egypt and the Middle East.

- 300,000 Turks died.

- Several British submarines managed to slip through nets and minefields from the Dardanelles into the Sea of Marmora, where they did great damage, destroying one Turkish battleship, a destroyer and five gunboats.

Activity

You are an Australian journalist who has managed to get on board a ship coming home from Gallipoli. Many of the letters from soldiers sent home have been censored. Write the questions you want to ask the returning soldiers, and think of the sort of answers they might give. Your questions could include:

- The landings.

- Life on the beaches.

- The evacuation.

- Thoughts on why it failed.

Questions

1 Why was the Gallipoli campaign carried out?
2 What does Source **A** tell you about the landings at Gallipoli?
3 How reliable is Source **D** as a view of life on the beaches at Gallipoli?
4 Was the campaign a total failure? Explain your answer.

THE HOME FRONT

The First World War was the first in history to affect all the British people, even those that stayed at home.

Changing attitudes

There was great enthusiasm for the war in August 1914. Many people were excited by the prospect of war. It was thought to be a glamorous opportunity for young men to prove their heroism. This was reflected in the flood of volunteers to join the army. About 500,000 enlisted in August alone in what has often been called a 'war fever'.

I adore war. It is like a big picnic. I have never been so well or so happy. Nobody grumbles at one for being dirty. I have only had my boots off once in the last ten days and have only washed twice.

Many men joined up without realising the horrors of trench life in store for them. Newspapers did not mention rats or trench foot. There was also great anger with Germany and sympathy with Belgium. Most were confident of a quick victory with the war over by Christmas 1914. The troops marched off singing cheerful songs like 'Pack up your troubles in your old kit-bag and smile, smile, smile'.

There was even war fever among people who could not join up. When the British government asked for donations to the troops there was a fantastic response. The public sent 232 million cigarettes and 16 million books. Grannies all over Britain knitted four million pairs of socks and two million pairs of mittens. The whole population was caught up in the enthusiasm for the war.

SOURCE B

A First World War soldier commenting on his feelings in 1918

Towards the end of the war we were so fed up we wouldn't even sing 'God Save the King' on church parade. Never mind the bloody king, we used to say: he was safe enough; it should have been 'God save us'.

The reality of war was different and attitudes began to change. At the front, soldiers became less enthusiastic as the promise of an early victory gave way to long campaigns and horrific casualties. By 1916 few soldiers thought the war was glorious or heroic. Instead it was a job to be done and hope that they would survive it. Few soldiers felt the same in 1918 as they had done in 1914. This disillusionment can be seen in the war poems (p. 46).

SOURCE C

This mock advert appeared in *The Somme Times*, a trench newspaper published on 31 July 1916

ARE YOU A VICTIM TO

OPTIMISM?

—o–o–o–o—

YOU DON'T KNOW?

—o–o–o–o—

THEN ASK YOURSELF THE FOLLOWING QUESTIONS.

—o–o–o–o—

1.—DO YOU SUFFER FROM CHEERFULNESS?
2.—DO YOU WAKE UP IN A MORNING FEELING THAT ALL IS GOING WELL FOR THE ALLIES?
3.—DO YOU SOMETIMES THINK THAT THE WAR WILL END WITHIN THE NEXT TWELVE MONTHS?
4.—DO YOU BELIEVE GOOD NEWS IN PREFERENCE TO BAD?
5.—DO YOU CONSIDER OUR LEADERS ARE COMPETENT TO CONDUCT THE WAR TO A SUCCESSFUL ISSUE?

IF YOUR ANSWER IS "YES" TO ANYONE OF THESE QUESTIONS THEN YOU ARE IN THE CLUTCHES OF THAT DREAD DISEASE.

WE CAN CURE YOU.

TWO DAYS SPENT AT OUR ESTABLISHMENT WILL EFFECTUALLY ERADICATE ALL TRACES OF IT FROM YOUR SYSTEM.
DO NOT HESITATE—APPLY FOR TERMS AT ONCE TO:—

Messrs. Walthorpe, Foxley, Nelmes and Co.

TELEPHONE 72, "GRUMBLESTONES." TELEGRAMS: "GROUSE."

Attitudes at home changed too. Women lived in constant fear of hearing that their husband or son had died. News of death trickled

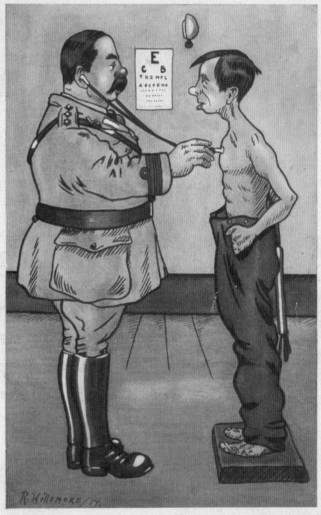

back to civilians in many ways. Letters from wounded men mentioned friends who had been killed. Nurses passed on news of deaths in hospitals. Commanding officers sometimes had time to send a note to families of men killed. Often lists appeared in local papers or shop windows. Eventually the Army would send a telegram confirming what many families had already heard.

After the Somme, almost everyone knew of a family who had lost a loved one. People had to work harder to support the war effort. Some women found it very difficult to do so and raise their children on their own.

SOURCE D

A civilian's comment in 1917

How distant the glory days of August 1914 seem now. No flag-waving crowds, no cheering anymore. Just tired, angry determination to get the war over, to rebuild the world, but most importantly, to rest and recover.

SOURCE E

A British cartoon of 1917

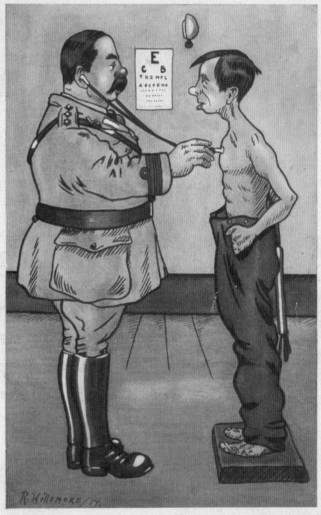

R. Hillsmore/17.

M.O. Have you ever had fits?   M.O. When was that?
Recruit. Yes Sir,—one!   Recruit. When I received my
                                       calling up paper.

Activity

Write two extracts from the letters written by a British mother of three sons in the Army, showing her changing attitude to the war. The first extract could be in August 1914 giving reactions to the start of the war. The second extract in 1917 after the disaster on the Somme.

Questions

1   What differences are there between Sources **A** and **B** and in their attitude to the war?
2   Why are they so different?
3   How useful is Source **C** to an historian studying attitudes to the war in 1916?
4   What attitude to the war is shown in Source **E**?

Censorship and propaganda

One of the first casualties of war is the truth. In 1914, the British government wanted men to fight Germany. At the same time, it wanted neutral countries to stay friendly to Britain. To do this, it used propaganda. This means a plan to spread ideas and beliefs. Its aim is to get everyone to accept these ideas, whether they are true or not. The British did this in various ways:

• They censored the news so that bad news was not published.

• They spread rumours about the enemy.

• They spread lies.

Censorship of the press began in an attempt to keep up morale at home. Newspapers were not allowed to mention the disastrous battles being fought in France or elsewhere. Failures and high casualty rates were played down. Reporters were not allowed into front-line trenches until late in the war.

The government wanted the British people to believe that the Germans were cruel and evil. This would encourage support for the war effort and volunteers for the armed forces. Newspapers went along with this. The Germans were called 'Huns' – the name of the barbarian tribe in the fifth century. Other names included 'vandals' and 'blond brutes'. There were newspaper reports that they crucified enemy soldiers; they raped nuns; they bayoneted babies. Posters depicted the Germans as ugly, cruel brutes. Rumours spread

SOURCE B

'The beastly Hun'. An American propaganda poster.

from Belgian refugees who had fled during the German invasion. They talked of German 'atrocities' and the looting of many towns by greedy soldiers. Newspapers published 'artists' impressions' of women being crucified, children having their arms cut off, unshaven German soldiers and British prisoners being ill-treated. There were never any photographs.

Propaganda also glorified the part played by the British troops. Small successes were exaggerated and given wide publicity. British soldiers were portrayed as brave and merciful.

SOURCE C

A sketch of a British soldier in a newspaper. It reads 'British soldier in a conquered enemy trench: quiet and steadfast in triumph merciful'.

Activity

Design a poster for the British government at the end of 1914.

- It must be simple and eye-catching – make good use of your headline or caption.

- It can either boost morale or turn the public against the Germans.

Questions

1   Why were propaganda and censorship used by the British government during the war?
2   How reliable is Source **B** as a view of the Germans during the First World War?
3   What message is put across by Source **C**?

Volunteers

In August 1914 Britain had a small professional army, the BEF. This was not large enough for the needs of the Western Front while many of its soldiers became casualties of the early battle of 1914. Therefore as soon as the war broke out Lord Kitchener began recruiting for a new army of volunteers to send to France. His original aim was for 100,000 men but from September an average of 125,000 per month volunteered.

Lord Kitchener

Patriotism

A genuine need to fight for Britain against the 'evil Hun' who had invaded 'poor defenceless' Belgium. Patriotism was whipped up by propaganda, public speakers and army bands. It was a chance to 'do your duty' and teach the Germans a lesson.

Why did so many men decide to join up?

Adventure

War seemed to promise adventure. For many it was a chance to escape from poverty and unemployment and to become a hero. Most were confident it would be a short war, over by Christmas 1914.

SOURCE A

Robert Graves, *Goodbye to All That*

I had just finished Charterhouse when England declared war on Germany. A day or two later I decided to enlist. In the first place I believed it would be a short war. In the second place I was outraged to read of Germany's invasion of little Belgium.

Music halls

These were popular places of entertainment in the days before radio and television. Famous variety artists urged young men to join up by singing patriotic songs such as 'Rule Britannia'. Some even offered kisses to any young man who would enlist at a desk behind the stage. Sometimes the enthusiastic audience persuaded men to enlist.

SOURCE D

A gunner explained why he joined up

There was a big show at the Hippodrome. I went with a couple of mates and at the end of the show they put on the film of our boys marching off to France. I think they played 'Land of Hope and Glory'. By the end of the evening tears were running down my face and I knew I had to join up.

Pals' battalions

Many men went to fight in what were called 'Pals' battalions'. Each of these battalions was made up of men who already knew each other. The men who joined these battalions usually trained together and went off to France together. As the war went on they died together too.

The influence of women

In London women handed out white feathers to any man not in uniform. This was a symbol of cowardice. This was particularly cruel, for they sometimes unknowingly picked on men invalided out of the army with shell shock or men who had been prevented, perhaps by bad health, from enlisting.

SOURCE C

A soldier remembers

No one could really refuse because at that time even your parents were ready to call you a coward. We did not have the faintest idea of what we were in for.

Conscience posters

These soon began to appear and were designed to make men feel guilty if they did not volunteer. One typical poster said 'You're proud of your pals in the Army of course! But what will your pals think of YOU?'

SOURCE B

Early conscience poster

"THIS LITTLE PIG STAYED AT HOME"

Conscription

By late 1915 it was clear that even the large numbers of volunteers joining the Army was not going to be enough. The war was spreading to other fighting areas beyond France and more men were needed. Thousands were being killed on the Western Front every day. So, for the first time in British history, conscription began.

This meant the compulsory enlisting of men into the armed forces, even if they did not want to go. Certain men were exempt, particularly those with vital industrial skills, but most men between the ages of 18 and 41 were liable to be 'called up'. The Military Service Act, passed in January 1916, applied to single men only. By May married men were included as well.

RECRUITS FOR THE ARMY AGE LIMIT RAISED 50

We'll Shed the Old
And Don the New
For we're Going to See
This Business through.

Concientious objectors

Some men totally refused to be conscripted. They were called 'conscientious objectors' or 'conchies' because they said their consciences would not allow them to fight. Some refused for religious reasons, quoting the Bible: 'Thou shalt not kill'. Other held strong political views and thought it was wrong to shoot their fellow working-class brothers. Other people called them shirkers and cowards.

Anyone who refused the call-up had to face a special court called a Military Tribunal. Some managed to convince the court of their beliefs. In particular there were the pacifists – people who believed killing was wrong. Some of these were willing to carry out other kinds of army service. They were given ambulance work or drivers' duties. Many were sent to the front as stretcher bearers, where they faced the same risks as all the other troops.

A pacifist
postcard of
1917

Percy Wall failed to enlist and was
sent to a military camp. He
described his time there.

*The attitude of the soldiers at the camp
varied. A very small minority told us they
would like to see us shot. Others wished to
know exactly what we were standing for
and some of them told us they would be
conscientious objectors next time. Another
group seemed to think we were simply
trying to get out of going to the trenches.*

Some conscientious objectors refused to do any form of military
work. These men were known as 'absolutists' and were shown no
sympathy by the Military Tribunals. Almost all of them were sent to
prison or labour camps. Over 6000 were sentenced this way, of
which 71 died due to harsh treatment.

They were given a terrible time in labour camp. They were
beaten, kept in solitary confinement in filthy cells, and given
uncooked food. Men were suspended by their wrists from a rope so
that their feet dangled over the ground. Others were put in wooden
cages like animals. Some were thrown naked into sewage ponds.

Even when the war was over they were still treated badly. Few
stood a chance of getting a job. Workmates, girlfriends, people in
the same street and even
families would have nothing to
do with them. Strangely
enough many soldiers in the
trenches admired the 'conchies'
and realised it was, in many
ways, braver to stand up for
their beliefs and go against the
view of the vast majority.

The Commander of the Military Detention Barracks at
Wandsworth explained his way of dealing with
conscientious objectors in a letter to the *Daily Express*

*I had them placed in special rooms, nude, but with their full army
kit for them to put on as soon as they wished. There were no
blankets left in the rooms which were quite bare. Several of the
men held out naked for several hours but they gradually accepted
the inevitable. Forty of the conscientious objectors who passed
through my hands are now quite willing soldiers.*

Either

You are one of the many who volunteered to join the army in 1914. You are trying to persuade your best friend to do the same. Write down what arguments/reasons you would use

Or

You are a conscientious objector in 1916 who refuses to enlist and serve in the army. Write an account of your experiences 1916 to 1919, including:

* Why you refused to enlist.

* Your hearing with the Military Tribunal.

* Your experiences in labour camp.

* How friends and family reacted.

* What happened to you when the war ended.

Questions

1   How useful is Source **B** to an historian studying methods of recruitment in 1914?
2   Does Source **E** give a reliable view of attitudes to conscription?
3   Why did the government decide on conscription in 1916?
4   What were conscientious objectors? Do you agree with:
    a   their actions?
    b   the way they were treated?
    Give reasons for your answer.
5   What point is the cartoonist trying to make in Source **F**?

DORA

From the very start of the war the government increased its own powers in order to organise Britain for the war effort. In August 1914 the Defence of the Realm Act (DORA) was passed. This allowed the government to make any regulations considered necessary for the safety of the country – even if they seemed very harsh and limited people's freedom. From then on a series of regulations appeared which greatly changed many aspects of everyday life:

* Railways and docks were now under military law.

* Special constables were appointed to help maintain law and order.

* Later in the war air raid precautions were brought in. All windows had to be blackened so that lights would not show at night.

* The 'Direction of Labour' meant that a man could be ordered to stop doing an unimportant job, and move to a different factory where his skills could be better used.

* Certain workers, such as miners, farmers and machine-tool operators, were not allowed to join the Army because their skills were considered too important to waste.

* Strikes in certain vital industries were made illegal under the Munitions Act.

* Censorship of the press was brought in.

Rationing

This was another example of greater government powers. Britain depended heavily for some foods on imports, particularly from the Empire. All sugar, chocolate and cocoa, and most cheese, wheat, fruit and butter came by ship from overseas. 40% of Britain's meat and even 36% of the country's vegetables also had to be imported. German submarine attacks greatly reduced the amount of food getting into Britain but while reserves lasted there were no real shortages in Britain. By 1916, however, the effects of U-boat sinkings of merchant ships was starting to be felt. In February the Germans resumed unrestricted U-boat warfare. This meant they would sink any ships going in and out of Britain. In April 1917 Admiral Jellicoe claimed that there were only six weeks' food supply left in Britain. Allied shipping losses reached 881,000 tons in April 1917.

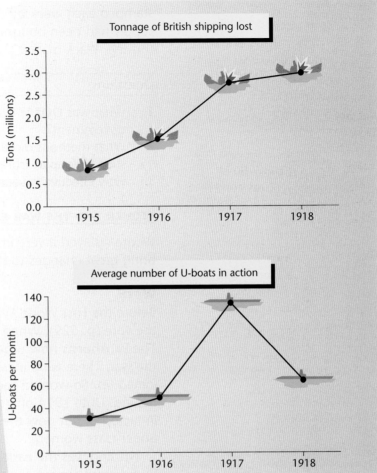

Tonnage of British shipping lost

Average number of U-boats in action

SOURCE A

A government poster encouraging people to save on bread

Food queues appeared for the first time. The shortage of grain led to the introduction of a new bread made from real flour mixed with powdered potatoes or beans. This was called 'standard bread' and was grey in colour. Margarine became a substitute for butter. The government tried various methods of solving the problem of food shortages.

- They used posters to put across slogans such as 'Save the Wheat and Help the Fleet – Eat less Bread'.

- A great effort was made to grow more food in Britain itself. Hillsides and public parks were ploughed up. Wasteland around towns and cities was rented out in small sections as allotments on condition that vegetables were grown. British Summer Time was introduced to create longer daylight working hours for farm-workers.

These measures were not enough and eventually some foods had to rationed. It began with sugar in December 1917. Meat and butter were added in early 1918, followed by products which contained sugar, such as jam, marmalade and chocolate biscuits.

Many other foods were in short supply and queues appeared at many markets.

People received Ration Cards for foods like meat and sugar. These stated the shop where the holder could buy that item. It was stamped each week by the shopkeeper to show that the week's supply had been bought. This worked well, although there was a thriving 'black market' for more food for those who could pay for it.

Questions

1   What was DORA? What changes did it make to the powers of the government?
2   What methods did the government use to deal with food shortages apart from rationing?
3   How effective is Source **A** in getting across its message?

WOMEN AND THE WAR EFFORT

Women played a very important part in the war effort. This was to bring great changes to their position in society.

Work

Before the First World War, women had been campaigning to get the vote (p. 529). When war started, they stopped their protests. The Pankhursts now urged women to find work helping Britain win the war. There were increasing shortages of workers as more men joined up. So women took over the jobs that the men had left behind. Until 1914 only working-class women had worked, mostly in factories, but now they were joined by many middle-class and upper-class women.

Nursing was the easiest way to find work, but women soon found employment as secretaries, shop assistants, bus conductresses, taxi drivers, police, telephone operators, office cleaners and in many jobs usually done by men at that time. They also had to adapt to new ways – short hair or trousers, for example. Women now also appeared in uniform, from railway porters to ambulance drivers.

About 60% of all workers making shells were women. They worked 12-hour shifts, seven days a week, packing explosives and cordite charges into bullets and shells. Sometimes they developed lead poisoning, or diseases from the chemicals which caused their hair to fall out and turned their skin yellow. This earned them the nickname 'canaries'. Some were killed when munitions factories blew up. In 1917 a fire in Silvertown munitions works in East London caused an explosion which killed 69 people and injured 400.

I was doing some crochet work in my tea time when I heard an alarm. In my hurry to get to the fire I ran over an allotment and fell into a ditch. We had to push through a crowd of men who shouted at us not to go near. The exploding cartridges were making a fearful noise. Most of us were struck by bullets but only bruised. There was not much power in the hits.

Nevertheless most women in munitions factories were better paid than in their previous work, which, for many, was probably in domestic service. They were looked after by women welfare supervisors, and there were separate toilets in factories, nutritious food in the canteens and, in many places, government-provided nurseries.

Over 100,000 women also responded to the government's appeal to work on the land by joining the 'Women's Land Army'. These 'Land Girls' replaced the farm labourers who had joined the forces and kept the country supplied with food.

Women's armed forces

Other women wanted to play a more direct role in the war. Many of these volunteered for Voluntary Aid Detachments (VADs) run partly by the Red Cross. They served behind the lines tending to the casualties on the Western Front. Many women even joined the newly created women's armed forces – the WRENs (the Women's Royal Naval Service) or WAACs (the Women's Army Auxiliary Corps). They were not allowed to fight but undertook other duties such as office work, driving, cleaning and cooking.

An example of the work that women did in the armed forces

Social change

The war also brought other changes to women's lives. They gained much greater freedom. With fewer men around, chaperones for wealthier girls became less common. Full wage-packets meant that women had money to spend. They now smoked, went to the cinema or on bicycle trips, or shopping in town unsupervised. Women drank in pubs and smoked in public. Older people were scandalised and troops returning home from France were amazed.

Effects

Did the war improve the position of women? Copy the chart below.

EFFECTS OF WAR ON THE POSITION OF WOMEN	
Progress	*Lack of progress*

Using the information in this section and the following sources complete the table.

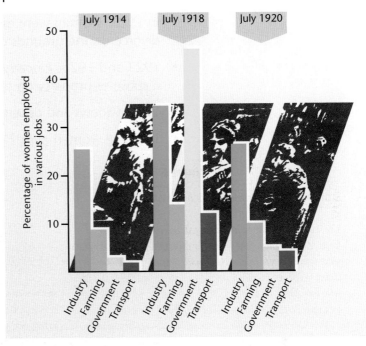

July 1914   July 1918   July 1920

Percentage of women employed in various jobs

Industry Farming Government Transport

Source D

A.J.P. Taylor, *British History 1914–45*, 1965

Women became more independent. Women munitions workers paid for their round of drinks at the pub. Fashion changed for practical reasons. Never again did skirts sweep the ground. The petticoat disappeared, though not for good. Women's hats became neater. A few women cut their hair. Not all the changes in work lasted after the war, but some did. The male clerk with his quill pen and copperplate handwriting was gone for good, replaced by the female shorthand typist.

Source E

Article in the *Daily Mail*, September 1915

The wartime business girl is to be seen at night dining out in restaurants in London. Before she would never have had her evening meal in town unless in the company of a man friend. But now, with money and without men she is dining out more and more. The meal of course is accompanied by the customary cigarette.

After the War

1   Women were expected to give way to men returning from the forces and return to pre-war 'women's work'.

2   The assumption that 'a woman's place is in the home' returned.

3   The percentage of women at work returned to pre-war levels.

4   More women than before worked in offices.

5 Shorter skirts and hair became fashionable.

6 Women went out with men without a chaperone.

7 Women smoked and wore make-up in public for the first time.

Other changes soon followed:

- In 1919: being female or married was no longer allowed to disqualify someone from holding a job in the professions or civil service.

- In 1923: women were given the same right as men to seek divorce on the grounds of adultery.

- 1923 and 1925: *Property Acts* allow married women to hold and dispose of property on the same terms as their husbands.

- 1925: widows and dependant children entitled to pension benefits.

- 1928: all women over 21 allowed to vote.

SOURCE F

From Arthur Marwick, *Women at War*, 1977

The world and women had changed. Some of the sillier ideas about women had gone. For determined women there were totally new professional opportunities. The war also changed the way women thought about themselves. Women who went back to domestic service and shop work insisted on much better conditions than they had before the war.

SOURCE G

'The New Woman' from the *Sphere*, May 1918

She has entered practically all the professions. She will get the vote next month. You meet her at every turn. A postwoman brings you letters and a girl brings the milk for your morning tea. There are girls, uniformed or not, at the wheels of half the cars that pass. If you go by train, women will handle your luggage. If you choose a bus or tram, the conductress in her smart uniform has long become a familiar figure. Familiar too are the blue-overalled window-cleaner with her ladder and the khaki-clad members of the WAAC, besides the great number of Government clerical workers. You can even be shaved by a woman.

Activity

You are a soldier who went off to war in August 1914. You return to Britain in 1917 on extended leave and write a letter to a friend on the Western Front. Explain to him the changes that have taken place in the position of women. You could include:

- Work they do.

- Their appearance and attitude.

- Social activities.

- Your views on these changes – do you agree with them?

Questions

1 Why did the government need to employ women?

2 What were:
   a the Women's Land Army?
   b VADs?
   c WAAC?

3 What do Sources **A**, **B** and **C** tell you about women's work during the war?

4 Which source is the more useful to an historian studying the work of women in munitions factories, Source **A** or **B**?

Summary and Revision

THE EVENTS OF 1914

In this section you will need to understand:

- The Schlieffen Plan.

- The Marne and its significance.

- The reasons why the plan failed.

- The race for the Channel ports.

- The situation at the end of 1914.

Revision questions

1 What did the Schlieffen Plan need to ensure its success?
2 Explain at least three reasons for the failure of the Schlieffen Plan.
3 Why did the Germans try to capture the Channel ports?
4 Describe the First Battle of Ypres and its results.
5 Why were there trenches stretching from the North Sea to Switzerland by the end of 1914?

THE TRENCHES

This section examines:

- The three lines of trenches and a cross-section.

- Why they were difficult to capture.

- Food, health, weather, boredom and dangers in the trenches.

- Why neither side could break through – poor commanders, strong defences and out-of-date tactics.

- The development of new weapons – gas, tanks, flame-thrower, artillery and creeping barrage.

Revision questions

1 Explain the three lines of trenches and describe a typical trench.
2 What were the following:
    a No-Man's-Land?   b dug-outs?
3 Why were the trenches so difficult to capture?
4 Describe the following conditions in the trenches:
    a trench foot   b shell shock   c food.
5 Why did the following not achieve a breakthrough in the period 1915–17:
    a gas?   b tanks?   c artillery?

THE MAIN OFFENSIVES 1915–17

For this section, you need to include:

- The attacks of 1915, including Neuve Chapelle, the Second Battle of Ypres and Loos.

- 1916 Verdun – why the Germans attack and the events of the battle.

- 1916 The Somme – Why it was launched, the events of the first day and what results it had.
- 1917 The main offensives.
- The situation at the end of 1917 – the withdrawal of Russia and the entry of the USA.

Revision questions

1 Why did the Allied offensives of 1915 fail to achieve a breakthrough?
2 Why did the Germans attack the French at Verdun? How did Pétain save the day?
3 Give three reasons for the Somme offensive. What happened on 1 July?
4 Was the battle a total failure?
5 Why was there no British breakthrough in the Third Battle of Ypres?
6 Give two reasons for the American entry into the war. How did this help the Allied war effort?

THE EVENTS OF 1918

This section includes:

- Ludendorff's offensives in March and May.
- Why the attacks failed and the effects on the German war effort.
- Allied counter-attacks from August to October.
- Revolution in Germany and the armistice.
- Reasons for the German defeat.

Revision questions

1 Was the arrival of American troops the only reason for Ludendorff's gamble?
2 Describe the German attacks. What were Haig's 'backs to the wall' orders?
3 Why were the Germans weaker by mid-1918?
4 Describe the allied attacks of August–September. Why did the Germans agree to an armistice in November?
5 Explain three important reasons for Germany's defeat.

THE WAR AT SEA

In this section, you need to include:

- The early battles in the North Sea – Heligoland Bight and Dogger Bank.
- The Battle of Jutland and its results.
- The importance of the British blockade of Germany.
- The effects of the German U-boat campaign 1915–17.
- Anti U-boat measures, especially the convoy system.

Revision questions

1   Explain what happened at Heligoland Bight (1914) and Dogger Bank (1915)?
2   Describe the events leading to all four fleets converging on Jutland in May 1916.
3   Why did both sides claim victory? What were the key results of the battle?
4   Explain the importance of the British blockade of Germany.
5   Describe three anti U-boat measures.
6   Why was the convoy system so effective in the period 1917–18?

THE WAR IN THE AIR

This section has the following topics:

- Early reconnaissance uses.

- Fighter planes and their development.

- The use of the zeppelins.

- German bomber raids.

Revision questions

1   Explain the use of planes for reconnaissance purposes.
2   How were fighter planes improved in 1915?
3   What measures were taken against zeppelin attacks? Were they effective?
4   What effects did bomber raids have on Britain?

THE GALLIPOLI CAMPAIGN

This section includes:

- Reasons for the campaign.

- The naval campaign of March 1915 and why it failed.

- The landings in April and why there was no breakthrough.

- Conditions on the beaches of Gallipoli.

- The organisation and success of the evacuation.

- The results of the campaign and why it failed.

Revision questions

1   Give three reasons for the launching of the campaign.
2   Why were the landings at Gallipoli a failure?
3   Describe conditions on the beaches for the troops.
4   The troops were evacuated in December 1915? Why was this a success?
5   Did the campaign fail because of the strength of the Turkish defences?
6   Was it a total failure?

THE HOME FRONT

For this section, you need to know the following:

- Changing attitudes to the war – reasons for early enthusiasm and later disillusionment.
- Reasons for and methods of propaganda and censorship.
- Early methods of recruitment.
- Conscription – why introduced and conscientious objectors.
- Greater government control, especially DORA.
- The impact of the U-boat campaign.
- Government methods of dealing with food shortages, especially rationing.

Revision questions

1   Why was there so much enthusiasm for the war in 1914? How and why had this attitude changed amongst most civilians and soldiers by 1916?
2   Why was the government so keen on propaganda and censorship? Describe two examples of propaganda.
3   Explain the methods used in 1914 to encourage men to volunteer.
4   Why did the government introduce conscription in 1916?
5   What was a conscientious objector? How were they treated?
6   What was DORA? Give examples of greater government control.
7   What effects did the German U-boat campaigns have on Britain by 1917?
8   What was rationed and how was it organised?

WOMEN AND THE WAR

This section examines:

- Why women were needed in industry during the war?
- The various jobs they did, especially in munitions.
- The Women's Land Army, armed forces and VADs.
- Changes in the lifestyle and social activities of women.
- The impact of the war on the position of women.

Revision questions

1   Explain the different jobs carried by women during the war.
2   What was munitions work and why was it so important?
3   What were VADs, WAACs and WRENs?
4   What changes took place in the appearance of women and their social activities?
5   Overall, what gains did women make from the war?

3
International Relations 1918–39

UNDERSTANDING INTERNATIONAL RELATIONS 1918–39

The following definitions and explanations should help you to understand this chapter.

Anschluss	The union of Germany and Austria.
Aggression	An unprovoked attack by one country on another.
Appeasement	The name given to British and French policies towards the dictators in the later 1930s. It means to make concessions to avoid war.
Collective security	The principle by which countries join together in an organisation to provide for each other's security from attack by another.
Demilitarise	To remove armed forces from an area.
Disarmament	To reduce the size of your armed forces.
Lebensraum	'Living space'. This refers to Hitler's aim to expand eastwards.
Plebiscite	When a decision is put directly to the people for them to choose.
Reparations	Payments made by one country to another after a war. Compensation for damage done during a war.
Refugees	People who have lost their homes and their homeland, usually due to war or natural disaster.
Self-determination	The right of a nation or people to decide its own form of government without outside interference.
Veto	When one vote can stop something from happening.

International Relations 1918–39

During this period the powers tried to avoid the possibility of another war. The victorious countries met at Versailles and forced a series of treaties on the defeated nations. The League of Nations was set up to try to maintain international law and order. The emergence of the dictators, however, especially Hitler and Mussolini, brought a series of crises in the 1930s that ultimately led to war in 1939.

THE VERSAILLES PEACE TREATIES, 1918–20

In January 1919 leaders from the Allied countries met in Paris to decide on the peace terms they would offer to the Central Powers. Twenty-seven victorious Allied powers were present, but the meetings were dominated by the 'Big Three'. Russia was not present as she was not trusted after the Bolshevik Revolution of November 1917 and had already made peace with Germany. The defeated powers were not consulted about the peace terms.

The 'Big Three'

George Clemenceau, Prime Minister of France, President Woodrow Wilson of the USA and David Lloyd George, Prime Minister of Great Britain, were the 'Big Three'. Although they agreed that their task was to make sure that a terrible war never happened again, each had very different ideas about what should be done to achieve this.

Clemenceau

He was nicknamed the 'Tiger' because he was determined that France should not be defeated during the war. He had the strong backing of the French people. He wanted the peace treaties to protect France in the future and to compensate the French for their suffering. Most of the fighting had been done on French soil. It had killed 1.4 million French soldiers and wounded more than twice as many. Huge areas of farmland had been destroyed, together with factories and homes.

To sum up, Clemenceau's aims were:

- To have revenge on Germany for French suffering.

- To make Germany pay for the cost of damage.

- To ensure Germany would never be able to attack France again: take away German land; weaken her industries; reduce her armed forces.

Wilson

Wilson was greatly influenced by his belief in idealism – finding perfect solutions to problems. In 1918 he had proposed Fourteen Points as a basis for the peace talks and future peace. He hoped the countries at the Peace Conference would agree to these points.

Focus on

The Fourteen Points

The most important of these points was self-determination – people of different national groups to have the right to rule themselves. The USA had not joined the war until 1917 and American soldiers did not reach Europe until late 1917. America could take a more detached view. They had not suffered as much as Europe. Wilson wanted:

◆ to prevent Germany from becoming aggressive again

◆ to punish Germany for her aggression but avoid forcing her to pay very heavy damages

◆ to base the peace treaties on the Fourteen Points.

Lloyd George

Lloyd George was a clever politician. He realised he could not ignore British public opinion. Britain had also suffered badly during the war, with 750,000 killed and 1.5 million wounded. The British public, which had just re-elected his government, wanted to 'Hang the Kaiser' and 'Make Germany Pay'.

Lloyd George wanted to protect British interests. His aims were:

• to end the German threat to the British navy and Empire

• to make Germany a non-aggressive country without colonies

• to prevent Germany becoming so weak that a revival of European industry and trade was hindered

• to prevent Germans becoming so poor that they would turn to Communism

• to avoid humiliating Germans so they would not want revenge

• to help secure France against Germany but ensure France did not become too powerful.

There were major differences between these three and much disagreement during the six months of negotiations.

SOURCE A

At an election meeting in 1918 Sir Eric Geddes, a top British politician, promised:

If I am returned to office Germany is going to pay. I personally have no doubt that we will get everything that you can squeeze out of a lemon and more.

SOURCE B

Frances Stevenson, secretary to Lloyd George. 'David' is Lloyd George.

March 14 1919. President Wilson arrived. He has started to annoy David already by talking of matters that have already been settled. Clemenceau can not tolerate him at any price.

March 28 1919. A most unpleasant scene between Wilson and Clemenceau.

The peace treaties that were eventually agreed were a compromise between the different aims of the 'Big Three'.

Questions

1   What does Geddes mean by the second sentence in Source **A**?
2   Are any of his views different from the aims of Lloyd George?
3   What similarities were there in the aims of the 'Big Three'?
4   What differences were there?

The terms of the Treaty of Versailles

On 28 June 1919 the German delegates were summoned to Versailles. There, in the Hall of Mirrors in the famous palace of Louis XIV, they signed the Treaty of Versailles.

SOURCE A

Lloyd George signing the Treaty of Versailles

Territorial changes

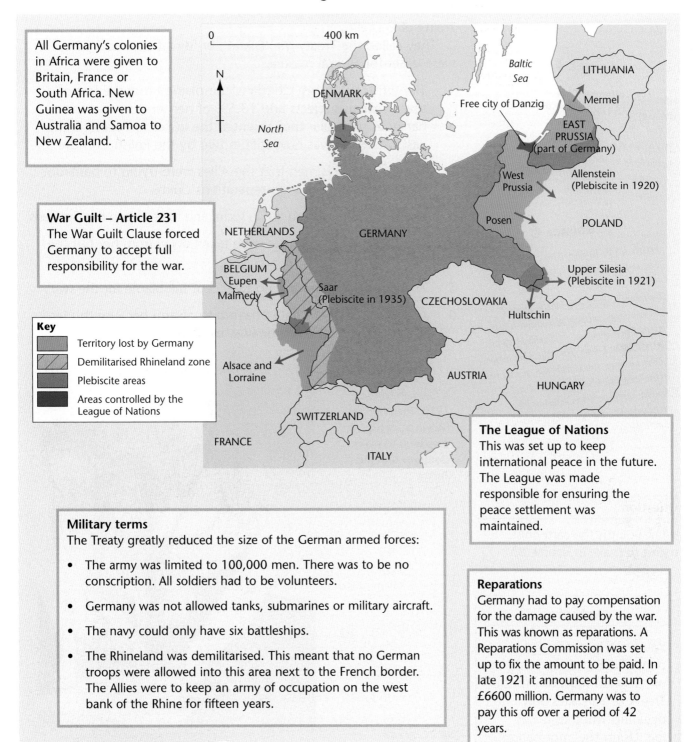

All Germany's colonies in Africa were given to Britain, France or South Africa. New Guinea was given to Australia and Samoa to New Zealand.

War Guilt – Article 231
The War Guilt Clause forced Germany to accept full responsibility for the war.

Key
- Territory lost by Germany
- Demilitarised Rhineland zone
- Plebiscite areas
- Areas controlled by the League of Nations

Map labels:
- DENMARK
- North Sea
- Baltic Sea
- LITHUANIA
- Mermel
- Free city of Danzig
- EAST PRUSSIA (part of Germany)
- West Prussia
- Allenstein (Plebiscite in 1920)
- NETHERLANDS
- GERMANY
- Posen
- POLAND
- BELGIUM
- Eupen
- Malmedy
- Saar (Plebiscite in 1935)
- CZECHOSLOVAKIA
- Upper Silesia (Plebiscite in 1921)
- Hultschin
- Alsace and Lorraine
- AUSTRIA
- HUNGARY
- SWITZERLAND
- FRANCE
- ITALY
- 0   400 km

The League of Nations
This was set up to keep international peace in the future. The League was made responsible for ensuring the peace settlement was maintained.

Military terms
The Treaty greatly reduced the size of the German armed forces:

- The army was limited to 100,000 men. There was to be no conscription. All soldiers had to be volunteers.

- Germany was not allowed tanks, submarines or military aircraft.

- The navy could only have six battleships.

- The Rhineland was demilitarised. This meant that no German troops were allowed into this area next to the French border. The Allies were to keep an army of occupation on the west bank of the Rhine for fifteen years.

Reparations
Germany had to pay compensation for the damage caused by the war. This was known as reparations. A Reparations Commission was set up to fix the amount to be paid. In late 1921 it announced the sum of £6600 million. Germany was to pay this off over a period of 42 years.

SOURCE B

The War Guilt Clause

The Allied governments affirm, and Germany accepts, the responsibility of Germany and her allies for causing all the loss and damage to which the Allied governments and their peoples have been subjected as a result of the war.

Question

Explain in your own words what Germany had to accept in terms of:
a   loss of territory
b   reduction in armed forces
c   war guilt.

German reactions

Germans were horrified when they discovered the terms of the Treaty of Versailles.

They called the Treaty the 'Diktat', or 'dictated peace'. They were upset for several reasons:

1   The territorial losses. Germans complained that the loss of seven million subjects and 13.5% of her territory was too harsh. In particular they resented the losses to Poland in the east. Germany was now split in two by the Polish Corridor.

2   The Germans claimed that the Allies were trying to bankrupt Germany with their high reparations claims.

3   The terms were worked out in secret and forced upon the Germans.

4   All of Germany's colonies were taken away from her but the Allies kept theirs.

5   The Germans hated having to accept full blame for the war.

6   Above all, Germans hated having to disarm because this left the country defenceless against neighbouring states.

SOURCE A

Herr Schneidermann, speaking in the German National Assembly

The Allies are driving the knife into the living body of the German people. The proposed peace means the miserable enslavement of children.

SOURCE C

From A.J.P. Taylor, *The Origins of the Second World War, 1969*

Germany remained by far the greatest power on the continent of Europe. It was greatest in population – 65 million against 40 million in France, the only other major power. German superiority was greater still in the economic resources of coal and steel. Nothing could prevent Germany from overshadowing Europe, even if they did not plan to do so.

SOURCE B

A German cartoon, 1919. The Allies are shown as devils preparing to make Germany sign the Treaty.

Question

What point is the cartoonist trying to make in Source **B**?

Activity

You are a journalist for a neutral country reporting on German reactions to the Treaty of Versailles and deciding whether it was fair. Using the information above write your article. You should include:

- A headline on German reactions.

- Why Germany resented the terms of the Treaty.

- Was it a fair treaty?

Was the Treaty fair?

On the other hand people at the time and historians since have argued that the Treaty was fair on Germany:

1   The Treaty did not weaken Germany anywhere near as much as the Germans complained. By 1925 German steel production was twice that of Britain.

2   Germany had forced an even worse treaty on Russia in March 1918 (see pp. 420–21).

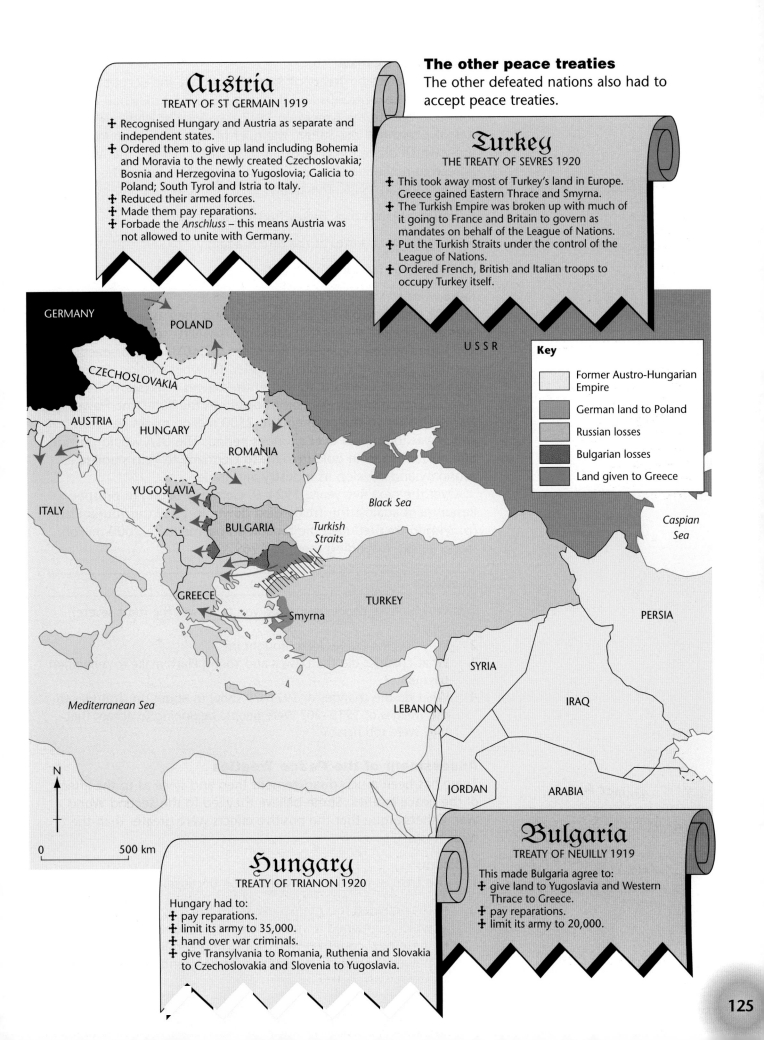

Austria
TREATY OF ST GERMAIN 1919

✚ Recognised Hungary and Austria as separate and independent states.
✚ Ordered them to give up land including Bohemia and Moravia to the newly created Czechoslovakia; Bosnia and Herzegovina to Yugoslovia; Galicia to Poland; South Tyrol and Istria to Italy.
✚ Reduced their armed forces.
✚ Made them pay reparations.
✚ Forbade the *Anschluss* – this means Austria was not allowed to unite with Germany.

The other peace treaties
The other defeated nations also had to accept peace treaties.

Turkey
THE TREATY OF SEVRES 1920

✚ This took away most of Turkey's land in Europe. Greece gained Eastern Thrace and Smyrna.
✚ The Turkish Empire was broken up with much of it going to France and Britain to govern as mandates on behalf of the League of Nations.
✚ Put the Turkish Straits under the control of the League of Nations.
✚ Ordered French, British and Italian troops to occupy Turkey itself.

GERMANY
POLAND
CZECHOSLOVAKIA
AUSTRIA
HUNGARY
ROMANIA
YUGOSLAVIA
ITALY
BULGARIA
GREECE
Smyrna
USSR
Black Sea
Turkish Straits
TURKEY
Caspian Sea
PERSIA
SYRIA
LEBANON
IRAQ
Mediterranean Sea
JORDAN
ARABIA

Key	
	Former Austro-Hungarian Empire
	German land to Poland
	Russian losses
	Bulgarian losses
	Land given to Greece

N

0   500 km

Hungary
TREATY OF TRIANON 1920

Hungary had to:
✚ pay reparations.
✚ limit its army to 35,000.
✚ hand over war criminals.
✚ give Transylvania to Romania, Ruthenia and Slovakia to Czechoslovakia and Slovenia to Yugoslavia.

Bulgaria
TREATY OF NEUILLY 1919

This made Bulgaria agree to:
✚ give land to Yugoslavia and Western Thrace to Greece.
✚ pay reparations.
✚ limit its army to 20,000.

Changes 1921–29

The Turks hated the Treaty of Sèvres, especially the occupation of Turkey by foreign troops and the amount of land they had been forced to give to the Greeks. In 1921 a nationalist leader, Mustapha Kemal, overthrew the Sultan, the ruler of Turkey. He then led an army which drove the Greeks out of Smyrna. In 1922 the Allies agreed to renegotiate the peace settlement. This led to the Treaty of Lausanne, in 1923. This treaty:

- Returned lands that Turkey had lost to Greece.

- Gave Turkey control of the Straits again.

- Ordered all foreign troops to leave.

Reparations

In 1922 Germany paid a small amount and then asked for a two-year delay before the next instalment. The Allies refused and in 1923 the French invaded the Ruhr (see p. 340). This worsened Germany's economic problems and led to hyperinflation. Eventually the French and Germans agreed to the Dawes Plan (see p. 344) and the French withdrew their troops from the Ruhr. The Dawes Plan scaled down the payments to 2500 million marks per year, which was to be paid over a longer period. The USA would provide 800 million marks in gold in loans to Germany to help stabilise its economy and develop its industry and trade.

Over the next five years, 1924–9, Germany began to prosper. Resentment against the Treaty died down. In 1929 the Young Plan (p. 344) further reduced the reparation payments to 2000 million marks a year, extending them to 1969.

Questions

1   Which of the peace treaties do you think was the most severe? Why?
2   Why was the Dawes Plan brought in?
3   What changes did the Dawes and Young Plans make to reparation payments?
4   What do the changes of 1921–29 show us about the attitudes to the Treaties of 1919–20? Were people beginning to accept that they were too harsh?

Assessment of the Peace Treaties

There has been much disagreement then and since as to the effects of the peace treaties. Some believe they led to the Second World War. Others argue that the positive effects were greater than the weaknesses.

Criticisms

1   The Treaties failed in Central Europe because:

- they created too many new states, such as Yugoslavia, which contained unhappy minority nationalities.
- these new countries were not strong enough against powerful neighbours such as Germany and Russia.

Source A

Lloyd George

In many respects terrible terms to force upon a country. We shall have to fight another war all over again in twenty-five years at three times the cost.

2 Turkey was treated very unfairly in order to satisfy the aims of France, Britain and Greece.

3 Many of the terms of the treaties did not work and did not last. The Treaty of Sèvres only lasted three years. Reparation payments were changed on two occasions.

4 The treaties left the defeated countries very bitter and determined to get revenge or overturn the terms of the treaties. This was particularly true in Germany where extremists such as Hitler got support because of the 'stab in the back' theory (p. 337) and by promising to overthrow the Treaty.

Achievements

Questions

1 How useful is Source **A** as evidence of the effects of the Treaty of Versailles?

2 Read Sources **C**, **D**, **E** and **F**. In your own words, explain their views on the peace treaties.

3 Overall, do you think the peace treaties were a failure?

The League of Nations was set up after the First World War in a genuine attempt to prevent future wars. Unfortunately, it failed to prevent aggression, especially in the 1930s.

Origins

Support for such an organisation grew out of the horror and devastation of the First World War. By 1915 many people belonged to League of Nations societies in Britain, France and the USA. However, President Wilson played the key role.

Aims

The League was set up to try to keep the peace. Every member promised:

1   That if it quarrelled with another member it would go to the League and try to settle the problem through talks rather than using force.

2   To help any member that was attacked in defiance of this agreement. This could be through:

- Condemning the aggressor – making them feel so guilty that the country backed down.
- Imposing economic sanctions on the aggressor (cutting off trade with the nation).
- If necessary joining forces with other members to take military action against the aggressor. This method of keeping the peace was known as collective security.

Profile of

Woodrow Wilson

Wilson was horrified by the thought of war. He was aware of the horrors of the American Civil War. He only brought the USA into the Great War as a crusade 'to make the world safe for democracy'. By 1919 he was losing popularity and support in the USA and he was defeated in the next Presidential election.

SOURCE A

An optimistic view of the League of Nations, published in the *Daily Graphic*, June 1920

ORGANISATION OF THE LEAGUE

SOURCE B

Ramsay MacDonald, British Prime Minister, 1924

The League of Nations grows in moral courage. Its frowns will soon be more dreaded than a nation's arms, and when that happens you and I shall have security and peace.

THE ASSEMBLY

The Assembly met annually and each member country had one vote. The Assembly could:

- *recommend actions to the council*
- *fix the League's budget*
- *elect non-permanent members to the council.*

THE COUNCIL

Consisted of four permanent members (Britain, France, Italy and Japan) and non-permanent members (chosen by the Assembly). On average, it met five times a year to deal with emergencies. A unanimous vote was needed for all decisions.

THE INTERNATIONAL COURT OF JUSTICE

Set up in 1921 at the Hague in the Netherlands. 15 judges from 15 different member states dealt with legal disputes between countries (but only when requested to by the countries involved).

THE SECRETARIAT

The Secretariat ensured that all administrative work of the League was carried out efficiently. The Secretariat consisted of a Secretary-General and civil servants. They prepared reports, kept records and translated documents.

AGENCIES AND COMMISSIONS

A wide range of agencies and commissions were formed to deal with a variety of problems. The International Labour Organisation (ILO), the Mandates Commission and the Minorities Commission were among the most important.

SOURCE C

The League of Nations in Session, November 1920

Weaknesses of the League

The League had several weaknesses from the very start:

Membership

The League had 42 members when it was set up and this number increased over the years. However, certain key countries were not members. These included:

- The defeated nations, such as Germany and Austria, who were not invited to join.

- The USSR, which was still distrusted because it was ruled by a Communist government.

- The USA. Woodrow Wilson confidently expected the USA to join the League but many Americans hated the idea. Many had been against US involvement in the war and they certainly did not want the USA dragged into European affairs after 1919. Also within the USA there were millions of recent immigrants from many European countries, including Germany and Austria-Hungary. Congress voted against membership. This deprived the League of the support of the most powerful nation in the world.

- The main members were France and Britain. Both countries were determined to avoid war almost at any cost. Britain simply saw the League as a talking shop. France, on the other hand, wanted the League to enforce the terms of the peace treaties. They rarely worked together, especially in the 1920s when they disagreed over the treatment of Germany. Britain felt Germany had been treated too harshly. The French felt the Treaty of Versailles had not gone far enough.

SOURCE D

The leader of Russia, Lenin's view of the League

The League is a robber's den to safeguard the unjust spoils of Versailles.

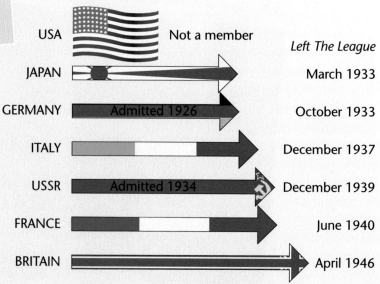

		Left The League
USA	Not a member	
JAPAN		March 1933
GERMANY	Admitted 1926	October 1933
ITALY		December 1937
USSR	Admitted 1934	December 1939
FRANCE		June 1940
BRITAIN		April 1946

Security issues

The League was often successful in forcing smaller nations to give way. The real test came when it had to deal with aggression from the bigger countries. In theory, the Council could raise armed forces from member states, but in practice countries were reluctant to do this. The League was only as strong as its members and nations often looked to the League to solve problems that they would not deal with themselves.

Idealism

The League was an idealistic attempt to try to avoid another horrible war. However, this idealism was also a weakness. All member states, large and small, had equal voting rights. All decisions in both the Assembly and Council had to be unanimous, that is agreed by all members. This was fine when members agreed with each other, but not when they disagreed.

Activity

You are a publicist for the League of Nations in 1920. Draw up a poster that will be sent out:

- Explaining the League.

- Advertising the advantages of joining the League.

Questions

1   What part did the following play in the organisation of the League:
    a   the Assembly?
    b   the Council?
    c   the International Court of Justice?
2   Why did the USA not join?
3   What point is the cartoonist trying to make in Source **A**?
4   How reliable is Source **D** as evidence of the aims of the League?

The League in the 1920s

The League had mixed fortunes in the 1920s.

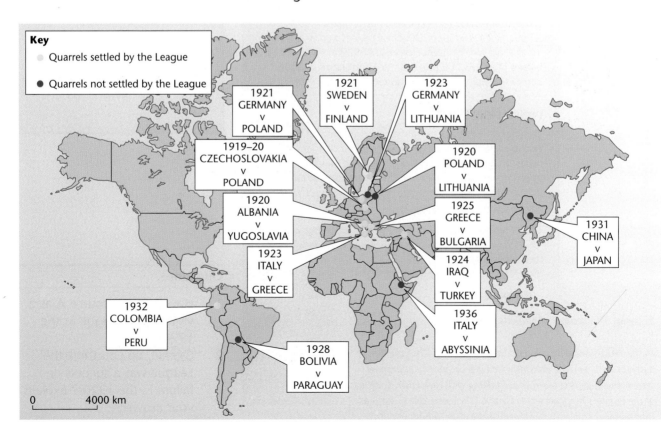

Key

⚪ Quarrels settled by the League

⚫ Quarrels not settled by the League

1921 GERMANY v POLAND

1921 SWEDEN v FINLAND

1923 GERMANY v LITHUANIA

1919–20 CZECHOSLOVAKIA v POLAND

1920 POLAND v LITHUANIA

1920 ALBANIA v YUGOSLAVIA

1925 GREECE v BULGARIA

1931 CHINA v JAPAN

1923 ITALY v GREECE

1924 IRAQ v TURKEY

1932 COLOMBIA v PERU

1936 ITALY v ABYSSINIA

1928 BOLIVIA v PARAGUAY

0   4000 km

SUCCESSES

THE AALAND ISLANDS, 1920

These islands belonged to Finland but were claimed by Sweden. Most islanders wanted to be ruled by Sweden. The two countries referred their dispute to the League which decided that Finland should keep the islands, but that the islanders' Swedish way of life should be protected. Both countries accepted the decision.

UPPER SILESIA, 1921

Upper Silesia was an area which, according to the Treaty of Versailles, could vote on which country should own the territory. In the plebiscite, organised by the League in March 1921, 700,000 voted in favour of Germany, 480,000 for Poland. The League decided to share the area. Germany received over half the land and population. The Poles had most of the industry. This caused bitterness in Germany, but both countries accepted the decision.

THE GREEK–BULGARIAN WAR, 1925

Fighting broke out on the border between Greece and Bulgaria. The Greek army invaded Bulgaria which appealed to the League. The League Council ordered both sides to stop fighting and withdraw, and threatened sanctions when the Greeks appeared reluctant to obey. A League enquiry found the Greeks to be at fault and imposed a fine. Both sides obeyed the League's orders and accepted the enquiry's findings.

REFUGEE COMMITTEE

Led by the Norwegian explorer Fridjtof Nansen, it raised money, found transport, designed houses and provided medical aid for refugees. From April 1920 to April 1922 it helped over 425,000 prisoners to return home. It found homes for 600,000 Greek refugees fleeing from the Turks.

DRUGS COMMITTEE

This persuaded states to tighten up customs and postal controls and to educate people about the dangers of drugs. It investigated the drugs trade and tried to control poppy growing, the main source of the drug, opium.

DISARMAMENT COMMISSION

This organised the Washington Naval Conference of 1921. The naval powers agreed to reduce the number of their warships.

FAILURES

VILNA, 1920

Both the new states of Poland and Lithuania claimed this town. It had been the capital of Lithuania but was now mainly inhabited by Poles. The Polish army seized the town. The League asked the Poles to withdraw to allow the people of Vilna to vote on its future. The Poles refused. The Conference of Ambassadors awarded Vilna to the Poles. The League had been ignored and by-passed.

CORFU, 1923

In August 1923, five Italian surveyors who were working for the League of Nations in mapping the border between Greece and Albania were killed on the Greek side of the border. Mussolini, the new Italian dictator, demanded compensation from the Greek government. The Greeks refused. Mussolini now bombarded and occupied the Greek island of Corfu. The Council of the League wanted to condemn Italy's aggressive actions but France and Britain did not want to upset Mussolini and would not permit it. Instead they put pressure on the Greeks to accept Mussolini's demands. Only when the Greeks had apologised and paid up did Mussolini withdraw his forces from Corfu. This was a disaster for the League, which had failed against a great power.

SOURCE A

S. Lang, *The League of Nations*, 1990

In the 1920s everything seemed to run smoothly. The League's agencies were working extremely well and the world's statesmen were actually getting together and talking with each other. They met at the League's headquarters in Geneva. They were able to sort out international problems over brandy and a cigar in front of a fire.

Questions

1   How useful is Source **A** as a view of the League in the 1920s?
2   Overall, do you think the League was a success or failure in the 1920s? Explain your answer.

STEPS TOWARDS WORLD PEACE IN THE 1920s

The 1920s was a decade of peace for several reasons:

The work of the League
Membership of the League increased from 48 nations in 1920 to 54 nations by 1929. In 1926 Germany was, at last, admitted to the League.

The Washington Conference 1921
This was an important conference because Britain agreed that other countries could develop large navies of their own, providing Britain's was still the largest overall.

The Locarno Treaties 1925
Germany signed these with Britain, France, Italy and Belgium. All agreed not to go to war over disputes. The Germans agreed:

- To accept the western borders given to them in 1919.

- That changes to the borders with Poland and Czechoslovakia would not take place by war, only by negotiation.

The Kellogg–Briand Pact, 1928
This was signed by 45 nations, including Germany. They agreed never to go to war again.

SOURCE A

Aristide Briand, French Foreign Secretary

The international co-operation of the 1920s did not last. The decade that followed saw increasing tension, rivalry and aggression.

Aggression
The leaders of Japan, Italy and Germany tried to improve conditions at home by being aggressive towards other countries. By taking over other lands they aimed to:

- gain land and resources.
- increase national pride.

The Great Depression
The collapse of the American stock market in 1929 (p. 482) led to:

- the collapse of international trade.
- the closure of banks, factories and businesses.
- 25 million people out of work worldwide.
- economic rivalry instead of co-operation. The USA raised customs duties on foreign imports. This meant that countries trading with the USA had to pay an extra tax. Britain also introduced higher duties.
- mass unemployment and poverty.

Failure of the League of Nations
The League failed to stop aggression in Manchuria and Abyssinia.

Italy, Japan and Germany left the League in the 1930s.

RIVALRY TENSION AGGRESSION

Isolation of the USA
They still refused to join the League and avoided involvement in Europe.

Failure of disarmament
The Disarmament Conference of 1932–3. This was organised by the League of Nations. Representatives of more than 60 countries came to discuss ways in which their countries might disarm and so reduce the chances of war. Unfortunately the conference did not achieve anything. Germany wanted everyone to disarm to her own low level. France, still fearful of Germany, refused. Hitler withdrew from the conference and from the League of Nations and began to rearm.

The rise of the dictators
In many countries people blamed their governments for their poverty and lack of work. They gave their support to political parties offering to put things right. Many of these were led by dictators. More than 20 countries became dictatorships after 1929.

SOURCE B

Hitler speaks to the Reichstag, May 1933

Germany is at any time willing to undertake further disarmament ... if all the other nations are ready to do the same. Germany would be willing to disband her entire military forces and destroy the small amount of arms remaining if all other nations would do the same.

SOURCE C

A cartoon showing the League's problems around 1930

MORAL SUASION.

THE RABBIT. "MY OFFENSIVE EQUIPMENT BEING PRACTICALLY *NIL*, IT REMAINS FOR ME TO FASCINATE HIM WITH THE POWER OF MY EYE."

Activity

Draw up a table with the following columns

Decisive contribution
Important contribution
Little contribution

Decide what contribution the following made to world peace in the 1920s by writing them in the relevant column with a brief explanation of your reason(s):

- the League of Nations
- the Locarno Treaties
- the Kellogg–Briand Pact
- the Dawes Plan
- the Young Plan

Questions

1 What were the main terms of the following agreements:
   a the Locarno Treaties?
   b the Kellogg–Briand Pact?
2 Explain at least three reasons for the collapse of international co-operation in the 1930s.
3 Which do you think was the most important reason? Why?
4 What is the purpose of Source **C**?

The first major failure of the League, in the 1930s, was over the Japanese invasion of Manchuria.

Why did Japan invade?

Japan had been badly hit by the Depression. Her industrial strength depended on exports. These fell by 50% between 1929 and 1931. Without exports she could not afford to buy the imports she needed. The country was also overcrowded. The military leaders believed that Japan should expand for more living space and raw materials. Japan chose Manchuria because:

- It belonged to China which was very weak at this time. It was split in two by civil war between Nationalists and Communists.

- Japan argued that Manchuria would act as a buffer against the USSR and Communism.

- Japan already claimed special interests in Manchuria. They ran the South Manchuria Railway and controlled some of the cities along its route.

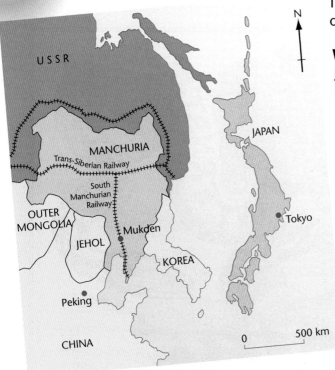

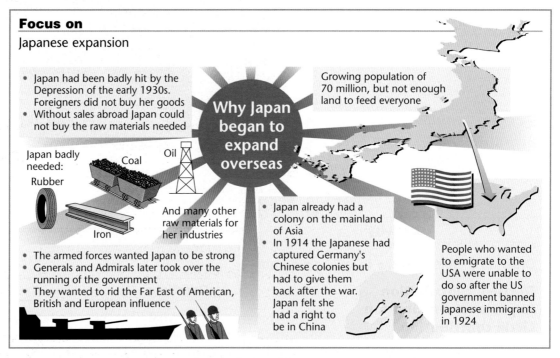

Focus on

Japanese expansion

- Japan had been badly hit by the Depression of the early 1930s. Foreigners did not buy her goods
- Without sales abroad Japan could not buy the raw materials needed

Japan badly needed:
Rubber
Coal
Oil
Iron
And many other raw materials for her industries

- The armed forces wanted Japan to be strong
- Generals and Admirals later took over the running of the government
- They wanted to rid the Far East of American, British and European influence

Why Japan began to expand overseas

Growing population of 70 million, but not enough land to feed everyone

- Japan already had a colony on the mainland of Asia
- In 1914 the Japanese had captured Germany's Chinese colonies but had to give them back after the war. Japan felt she had a right to be in China

People who wanted to emigrate to the USA were unable to do so after the US government banned Japanese immigrants in 1924

The Mukden incident

In September the Japanese army staged the Mukden incident. On the night of 18 September, there was an explosion on the South Manchurian Railway just outside the city of Mukden. The Japanese claimed this was an act of sabotage by the Chinese. The Chinese denied this, claiming that all their soldiers in the area were in barracks at the time. This gave the Japanese the ideal excuse to take over Manchuria. The invasion was a great success. In 1932 Manchuria was renamed Manchukuo. The last Chinese Emperor, Pu Yi, who had been overthrown in 1911, was made the Japanese puppet ruler.

At 10 o'clock last night, Japanese railway guards picked a quarrel by blowing up a section of the railway at Huankutun, and then accused the Chinese government of having done this. The Japanese immediately staged a surprise attack upon Peitaying. Many houses were burnt and many people shot dead.

SOURCE B

Japanese government statement, 24 September 1931

A detachment of Chinese troops destroyed the track of the South Manchurian Railway near to Mukden and attacked our railway guards at midnight on September 18. A clash between Japanese and Chinese troops then took place. To prevent a disaster, the Japanese army had to act swiftly. The Japanese government does not wish to take over the territory of Manchuria.

Questions

1 What interests did Japan already have in Manchuria?
2 Give two reasons why they invaded.
3 Why do Sources **A** and **B** give different versions of the Mukden incident?

What did the League of Nations do?

Most countries were horrified at what Japan had done. China asked the League of Nations for help. The League:

- Condemned Japan's actions and ordered the withdrawal of Japanese troops. The Japanese government agreed but their army refused.

- Appointed the Lytton Commission to investigate the crisis. This took over a year to report, by which time the invasion and occupation was complete. The Commission found Japan guilty of forcibly seizing part of China's territory.

- Accepted the Lytton Report and instructed all of its members not to recognise Manchukuo. It invited Japan to hand Manchuria back to China.

The Japanese government kept Manchuria and then left the League in 1933. The League did not stop Japanese aggression. Indeed Japan went on to occupy the Chinese city of Jehol.

SOURCE C

A cartoon published in Germany in 1931

'Wait a minute! I am going to tell the League of Nations'

Why did the League fail?

The League failed for several reasons:

1 Members were unwilling to impose economic sanctions on Japan because the Depression had already damaged world trade and this would damage it further.

2 The Great Powers were unwilling to take military action. Britain, especially, feared Japanese attacks on its colonies in the Far East.

3 The USA was the most powerful country with interests in the Far East. It sent a representative to join the Lytton Commission but was not prepared to take any further action.

Results of the crisis

This had several results:

- It was the first major failure of the League. It showed that it was weak in the face of a great power.

- The world learnt that it paid to be aggressive. It encouraged further acts of aggression such as Italy in Abyssinia.

- Japan continued its aggression. It took over more provinces in north China between 1933 and 1936.

- The Japanese withdrew from the League and eventually drew closer to dictators such as Mussolini and Hitler. It formed the Anti-Comintern Pact with Germany and Italy, between 1936 and 1937.

SOURCE D

John Robottom, *Modern China*, 1967

Manchuria showed that the League was toothless. The failure of the League to stop aggression in Manchuria had grave consequences in Europe too. The lesson was obvious; there was no power in the world to stop a determined aggressor.

SOURCE E

'The Doormat'. A cartoon published by David Low in the British press in 1932.

THE DOORMAT.

Activity

You live in Britain in 1932 and object strongly to Japanese action in Manchuria. Write a letter to your local newspaper explaining:

- Your objections to Japanese aggression.

- Criticisms of the reactions of Britain and the League.

- What you think they should have done.

Questions

1 Why did the League fail to stop Japan?
2 Could the League have done more?
3 According to Source **D**, what were the results of the crisis?
4 What point is the cartoonist making in Source **E**?

THE ABYSSINIAN CRISIS 1935–36

This was the second major crisis in the 1930s. In 1935 Italy invaded Abyssinia. Once again, the League failed to stop aggression.

Why did Italy invade?

In the 1930s, Abyssinia (now Ethiopia) was the only independent black African state. It was ruled by Emperor Haile Selassie.

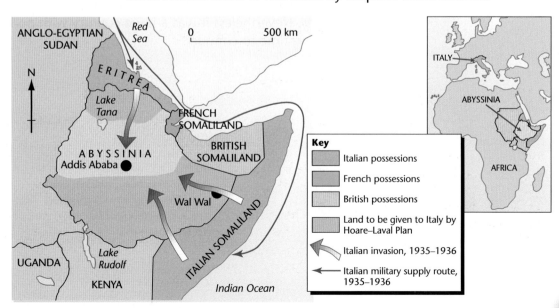

Mussolini, the Italian dictator, invaded for several reasons:

1   Italy had suffered from the Great Depression and unemployment rose. Mussolini turned to foreign conquest to distract the attention of the Italian people.

2   Italy already had an empire in north-east Africa, the colonies of Eritrea and Italian Somaliland which were on the borders of Abyssinia.

3   The Italians had tried to take Abyssinia in 1896. They had been defeated at the battle of Adowa. This was the chance for revenge.

4   Mussolini was jealous of Hitler's rearmament in Germany. He wanted to show that he was still the main dictator in Europe.

Profile on
Benito Mussolini

Mussolini was a journalist before the First World War. He fought and was wounded in the war and was angry at how little Italy gained in the peace treaties. He set up his own party, known as the Fascists, and in 1922 organised a march in Rome which made him prime minister. He soon made himself dictator of Italy and wanted success abroad to boost his popularity.

SOURCE A

Mussolini explains why he invaded Abyssinia

It is not only our army which marches into Abyssinia. 44 million Italians march with that army, all united and alert. When, in 1915, Italy joined with the Allies against the Central Powers, how many promises were made? Italy lost 670,000 dead and 480,000 disabled and more than a million wounded. When we went to the peace negotiations we were only given crumbs.

The invasion

In December 1934 Italian troops provoked a clash with Abyssinians at Wal Wal as an excuse for war. In October 1935 Italy invaded. The Abyssinian forces stood little chance against the modern Italian army. Nevertheless it was a huge country with poor roads and took a long time to conquer.

SOURCE B

An Italian pilot describes the Italian use of bombing

The bombing was magnificent sport. One group of Abyssinian horsemen gave me the impression of a budding rose unfolding as the bomb fell amongst them and blew them up.

What did the League do?

December 1934   The League offered to arbitrate (act as a judge) in the dispute. Rejected by Italy.

October 1935   Emperor Haile Selassie appealed to the League for help. The League:

SOURCE C

Cartoon by Low, on Mussolini's invasion of Abyssinia

THE LEAGUE? PAH! THE LEAGUE IS CONTEMPTIBLE! THE LEAGUE CAN DO NOTHING!

BUT AREN'T *YOU* THE LEAGUE?

MAP OF THE WESTERN FRONT

RIGHTS AND WRONGS OF ABYSSINIA

SELF-PORTRAIT

- Condemned the Italian invasion of Abyssinia.

- Imposed economic sanctions on Italy but these did not include oil, coal and iron. Non League members such as the USA and Germany continued to trade with Italy. Mussolini later admitted that if they had not it would have stopped the invasion in a week.

December 1935   The Hoare–Laval Pact. This was drawn up by the foreign secretaries of Britain and France, Samuel Hoare and Pierre Laval. Large areas of Abyssinia were to be given to Mussolini in return for troop withdrawal. Abyssinia would be reduced to half its original size. Almost immediately details were leaked to the press, causing a public outcry. The plan was abandoned.

March 1936   Threatened oil embargo on Italy. This had no impact. The Italians conquered Abyssinia and united it with Eritrea and Somaliland.

June 1936   Haile Selassie addressed the Assembly calling for League assistance against Italian aggression. No additional League action.

July 1936   Sanctions against Italy abandoned.

SOURCE D

Emperor Haile Selassie on the front cover of *Weekly Illustrated Magazine*, June 1935

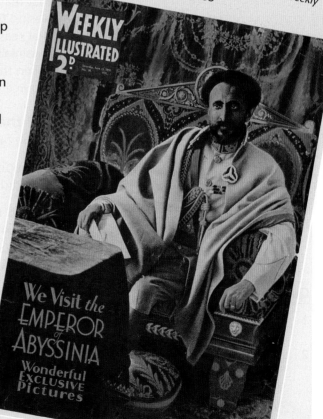

WEEKLY ILLUSTRATED 2^D

We Visit the EMPEROR of ABYSSINIA Wonderful EXCLUSIVE Pictures

Why did the League fail in Abyssinia?

Successful action against Italy was dependent on Britain and France. They were unwilling to take strong measures because:

- They were frightened that if they imposed full sanctions it would lead to war with Italy. They were not ready for a war.

- They wanted to keep Mussolini as an ally. They did not want to upset him as this might drive him to ally with Hitler and Germany.

- Their attempt at a compromise, the Hoare–Laval Pact, showed Mussolini how weak they were. He therefore continued the invasion.

Results of the crisis

Once again, it showed the weakness of the League. Countries lost faith in the League and its ideals. Several countries, including Britain and France, moved away from their policy of collective security and began to rearm.

The actions of the League and Britain and France upset Mussolini. He did not expect them to oppose his invasion. He moved closer to Hitler and in 1936 signed the Rome–Berlin Axis. Once again aggression had been shown to work. Hitler took note of this lesson. In 1937 Italy left the League.

Questions

1   What reason does Mussolini give in Source **A** for the Italian invasion (see p. 140)?
2   What reason is suggested in Source **B** for Italian success in Abyssinia?
3   Explain the Hoare–Laval Pact. Why did it fail?
4   Is Source **C** for or against Mussolini? Explain your answer.

SOURCE A

Mussolini

The League is alright when sparrows quarrel; it fails when eagles fall out.

Questions

1   What is the meaning of what Mussolini says in Source **A**?
2   Which do you think was the most important reason for the failure of the League? Why?
3   Do you think the League was a total failure?

Why did the League of Nations fail?

The League failed for several reasons:

- The organisation of the League contained weaknesses. The League did not meet frequently so there were delays.

- Important nations were absent. The USA never joined. Germany did not join until 1926 and left in 1933. Japan left in 1933 and Italy in 1937. The Soviet Union did not join until 1934 and was expelled in 1939.

- Sanctions were ineffective, especially without the USA as a member.

- The League did not have its own military forces to use against an aggressor.

- Countries were often reluctant to act unless their own interests were at stake and sometimes even acted against League decisions. The Hoare–Laval Pact in Abyssinia is one such example.

In 1933 Hitler became Chancellor of Germany (p. 361). His policies abroad caused a series of crises which led to war in September 1939.

Hitler's aims
Hitler had several aims in his foreign policy:

Reversal of the Treaty of Versailles
Hitler had never accepted the Treaty of Versailles and was determined to restore German pride. He intended to retrieve the lands lost in 1919 and to build up the German armed forces.

Unite all German-speaking peoples
He wanted to create a 'Greater Germany' by uniting all Germans into one homeland. The Treaty of Versailles had denied Germany national self-determination. There were Germans in the Sudetenland in Czechosolovakia. The Treaty also stopped the *Anschluss* with Austria.

Lebensraum, or living space
'Greater Germany' would have a population of 85 million. Their lands would not provide sufficient food and raw materials. To obtain these Germany would have to expand in the east and take over Poland and the west of the USSR. In any case Hitler hated these countries because:

- the Poles and Russians were Slavs whom Hitler saw as an inferior race suitable only as slaves.

- the USSR was ruled by Communism.

Germany gains more land 1933–9

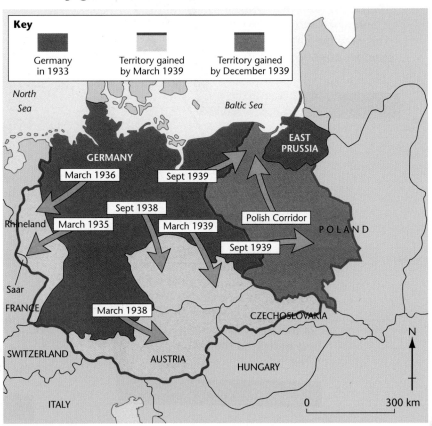

German rearmament

Hitler was determined to build up his armed forces in order to carry out his aims.

SOURCE A

Extract from *Berlin Diary* by William L. Shirer, an American journalist living in Berlin in the 1930s

Germany gets a U-boat tonnage equal to Britain's. Why the British have agreed to this is beyond me. German submarines almost beat them in the last war, and may in the next.

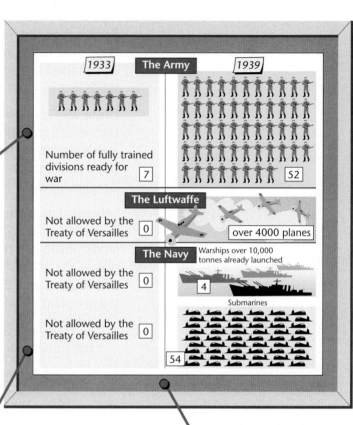

DISARMAMENT CONFERENCE 1933

Hitler asked the other powers to disarm to his level. When they refused he withdrew from the Conference and the League. This now put him in a stronger position to rearm.

ANGLO-GERMAN NAVAL TREATY 1935

This allowed Germany to build a fleet one third the size of Britain's and have the same number of submarines. Britain was accepting Hitler's breach of the Treaty of Versailles. It also destroyed the Stresa Front.

GERMAN ARMED FORCES

Hitler announced in 1933 that the German peacetime army was to be increased to 300,000. A new Air Ministry was to train pilots and build 1,000 aircraft. Two years later Hitler introduced conscription and announced an increase in the army to 550,000. Representatives from France, Britain and Italy met in a town called Stresa where they agreed to work together to preserve the peace in Europe. They condemned German rearmament. This became known as the Stresa Front against German aggression, but it did not last long.

Successes 1935–36

Hitler achieved further success in this period because:

- The League was seen as weak after its failures in Manchuria and Abyssinia.

- He was able to exploit British sympathy with Germany. Britain still felt guilty over the harsh peace terms of 1919.

- French weakness. They were unwilling to go it alone against Germany.

- Britain and France were preoccupied with Mussolini and Abyssinia.

SOURCE B

The German infantry enters Cologne in the Rhineland, March 1936

The Saar

Under the Treaty of Versailles the Saar, a rich coal-mining area, had been taken from Germany and placed under League of Nations control for 15 years. In 1935 a plebiscite or vote was taken among the people of the Saar. They were asked to choose between union with Germany, union with France or remaining under League control. Over 90% voted to return to Germany. This was a great boost for Hitler.

The reoccupation of the Rhineland

In March 1936, Hitler ordered his troops to cross the bridges over the Rhine and occupy the Rhineland. It was a daring move, being against the Treaty of Versailles. Hitler's generals had advised against the move. They felt the French would resist and that the German army was still too weak to fight back.

When the German troops moved into the Rhineland they had strict orders to withdraw if they met any opposition. In fact the invasion went smoothly. The German people in the area welcomed the troops. Later over 98% of them voted in favour of the reoccupation.

Hitler's gamble paid off. The French were unwilling to fight and the British could do nothing without the French. In any case the British felt that Hitler was only reclaiming what rightfully belonged to Germany. For Hitler the message was clear. France and Britain both lacked the nerve and will to fight. As soon as the time was right he would move again.

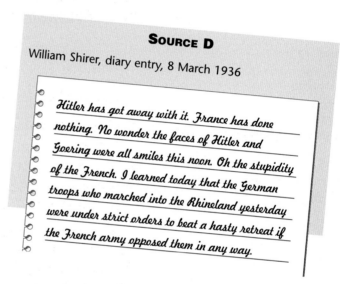

Questions

1   What was meant by *Lebensraum*? Explain at least one other aim of Hitler's foreign policies.
2   What effects did the Anglo-German Naval Treaty of 1935 have?
3   Why does Shirer, in Source **A**, believe it was a disaster?
4   According to Sources **C** and **D**, could Hitler have been stopped in 1936?
5   Explain the reasons for German success 1935–6.

The *Anschluss*, union with Austria

Hitler wanted to unite with Austria for several reasons:

- He had been born in Austria.

- Both countries spoke German. Indeed 96% of Austrians were German-speaking.

- Austria had been seriously reduced in size by the Treaty of St Germain (p. 125) and had experienced economic problems. Austrians might welcome the union.

- It was part of Hitler's aim of creating a 'Greater Germany'.

- There was already a strong Nazi Party in Austria.

Dollfuss 1934

As early as 1934 Hitler had tried to take over Austria. He used the Austrian Nazi Party to put pressure on the Austrian Chancellor, Dollfuss. However, he was determined to keep his country independent of Germany. He outlawed the Nazi Party.

In July 1934 the Austrian Nazi Party struck back by assassinating Dollfuss and trying to seize power. The uprising was not successful due mainly to Mussolini. He was not, as yet, close to Hitler and did not want a powerful Germany on his border. Mussolini sent 100,000 troops to the Austrian frontier in case Hitler decided to invade. Hitler was surprised by this. He denied all knowledge of the assassination.

The *Anschluss* of 1938

By 1938 Hitler was in a much more powerful position:

- He had already achieved successes in the Rhineland.

- Hitler had built up his armed forces.

- Mussolini and Hitler had signed the Rome–Berlin Axis in 1936.

- Hitler had seen the weaknesses and failures of the League of Nations.

- The new Austrian Chancellor, Schuschnigg, had appointed Nazis into his government. In return Germany had agreed to respect Austria's independence.

Hitler began to step up his campaign in early 1938. He ordered the Austrian Nazis to bomb public buildings and stage mass parades. Then, in February, he summoned Schuschnigg to Germany. For two hours Hitler ranted and raved and threatened the Austrian Chancellor. Finally Schuschnigg agreed to give the Austrian Nazis more power. On his return to Austria he changed his mind. On 8 March Schuschnigg ordered a plebiscite (vote) to be held. Austrians would decide whether they wanted to remain independent of or unite with Germany.

Hitler was furious and ordered invasion plans to be drawn up. At the same time he forced Schuschnigg to withdraw the plebiscite and resign. He was replaced by the Austrian Nazi leader, Seyss-Inquart. The new leader asked Germany to send troops to restore law and order. On 11 March German troops invaded Austria. Two days later Austria was made a province of Germany. A month later the Nazis claimed that 99% of the Austrian people had voted in favour of the *Anschluss* in a plebiscite held on 10 April.

SOURCE A

A report from Germany published in *The Times* on Monday 14 March, three days after German troops entered Austria

Herr Hitler returned here yesterday, a conquering hero. His triumphant welcome was shared by the army he sent into Austria. Flowers were strewn in the path of the armoured cars. If any Austrians were against him on Friday, they either hid their faces or were completely converted yesterday and today.

Buttonhole for a soldier after the *Anschluss*, March 1938

Activity

You are an adviser to the British government, 1934–38. You must decide what to advise the prime minister to do in reaction to the following:

- German rearmament 1934–5

- the reoccupation of the Rhineland 1936

- the *Anschluss* with Austria 1938.

Your options are to:

1   Allow Hitler to carry out these actions.

2   Ask the League to condemn Germany.

3   Unite with other countries to force Hitler to back down.

4   Declare war on Germany.

SOURCE C

Neville Chamberlain, the British Prime Minister, speaking on 15 March 1938

Throughout these events His Majesty's Government have remained in the closest contact with the French government. Both governments have entered a strong protest to Berlin. It seems to us that the methods used call for the severest disapproval.

Results

This time Mussolini did not protest. Britain, France and the League of Nations did protest but took no other action. Most people in Britain did not object because the majority of Austrians seemed pleased with the union. In any case, they argued, Hitler had been born in Austria. Once again Hitler had got away with breaking the Treaty of Versailles. He would not stop there. After the *Anschluss*, however, it was clear that Czechoslovakia would be the next country to attract Hitler's attention.

Questions

1   Why did Hitler want the *Anschluss*?
2   Explain the events of February–March 1938 leading to the German occupation.
3   Which source, **A** or **B**, would be the more useful to a historian studying the *Anschluss*?

Profile on
Neville Chamberlain

Neville Chamberlain was the British Prime Minister from 1937 to 1940. He was the brother of Austen Chamberlain who had won the Nobel Peace Prize following the Locarno Treaty in 1925. Neville Chamberlain had been Lord Mayor of Birmingham where he introduced many reforms, building council houses, schools and public libraries. Chamberlain had also been Chancellor of the Exchequer. He had a great desire to keep peace in Europe and was prepared to take an active role in foreign affairs. He believed that by meeting the dictators, especially Hitler, he could prevent international aggression and war.

APPEASEMENT

In 1937 Neville Chamberlain became Prime Minister of Great Britain. He wanted to avoid war at all costs. The policy he carried out to try to keep the peace was known as appeasement.

This meant negotiating with Hitler and, if necessary, giving him everything he demanded, in order to avoid another world war. It is a very controversial policy and has caused much disagreement over the years. Some historians believe it was the best policy in the circumstances. Others see it as a disaster. Below are the arguments for and against.

ARGUMENTS FOR

1. Some British people approved of Hitler's policies, especially the way in which he had reduced unemployment in Germany (p. 374). Many British people agreed with Hitler that the Treaty of Versailles was unfair. Hitler was only getting back what rightfully belonged to Germany.

SOURCE A

Harold Nicolson, who was in the British delegation at Versailles in 1919

The treaties of Versailles were neither just nor wise. There is not a single person among the younger people who is not unhappy at the terms.

2. The British people hoped that a strong Germany would stop the spread of Communism. The USSR under Stalin was seen as a much greater threat.

SOURCE B

H.A.L. Fisher, *History of Europe*, 1936

Hitler is a guarantee that Russian Communism will not spread westwards.

ARGUMENTS AGAINST

1. It gave Hitler the advantage. He grew stronger and stronger. When war came it was against a strong Germany. It was fought in Poland, a country too far away for Britain to help.

SOURCE E

A speech by Winston Churchill in 1938

Europe is faced with a programme of aggression. There is only one choice open, not only to us but to other countries. Either to submit like Austria, or to take effective measures while time remains to ward off the danger. Where are we going to be in two years time when the German army will certainly be larger than the French army.

2. It was not right. Britain and France allowed Hitler to break international agreements and especially the Treaty of Versailles. They were also prepared to give away parts of other countries, especially Czechoslovakia, to keep the peace. Appeasement was simply another word for weakness and cowardice.

3 Britain was too weak militarily to stop Hitler. In 1938 the heads of the armed forces told Chamberlain that they were not ready to fight. At the very least appeasement would give Britain time to rearm.

4 The majority of people in Britain still remembered the First World War. They did not want a repeat and were determined to keep the peace. By 1936 the British Peace Pledge Union had 100,000 members who had all promised 'Never again will I support a war'. The British people would not have supported war to help either the Austrians or Czechs.

SOURCE C

Neville Chamberlain in 1938

I am myself a man of peace to the depths of my soul. Armed conflict between nations is a nightmare to me.

5 Chamberlain believed that Hitler could be appeased and trusted. If Britain gave way to Hitler's demands he would eventually be satisfied.

SOURCE D

Chamberlain speaking to the Cabinet in September 1938

Hitler would not deliberately deceive a man he respected. I have established an influence over Hitler who can now be trusted.

3 Chamberlain misjudged Hitler. He believed Hitler was a normal leader who would listen to reason. He did not realise, until it was too late, that appeasement simply encouraged Hitler to believe he could do anything. He would never be satisfied in his demands.

SOURCE F

The Yorkshire Post, December 1939 – three months after the outbreak of the Second World War

By repeatedly surrendering to force, Chamberlain has encouraged aggression. Chamberlain's policy has always been based on a fatal misunderstanding of the minds of the dictators.

4 The appeasers missed excellent opportunities to stop Hitler, especially over the reoccupation of the Rhineland in 1936.

5 The biggest argument against appeasement is that it did not stop war coming in 1939.

Activity

You are a journalist for one of the leading British newspapers. You have to write an article explaining appeasement to the British public in the weeks after the *Anschluss*. In your article explain the arguments for and against, at that time, and whether you agree with the policy.

The Sudetenland Crisis, 1938

After the *Anschluss* Hitler turned his attention to Czechoslovakia and the Sudetenland.

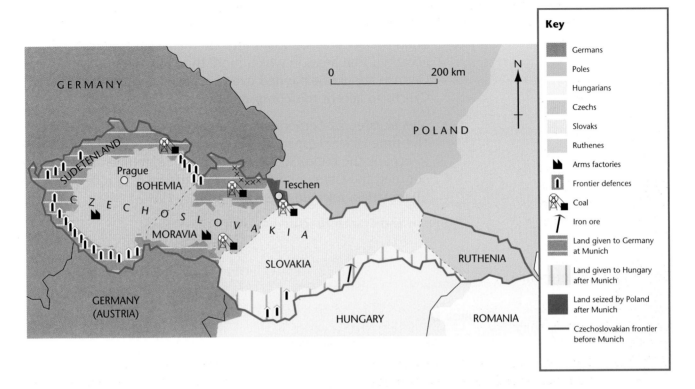

Hitler's aims

Hitler had several reasons for wanting to take over Czechoslovakia:

- A free and hostile Czechoslovakia would make it impossible for Germany to fight a war in the West, as Hitler would then face a war on two fronts which he wanted to avoid.

- He thought that the USSR might invade Germany through Czechoslovakia.

- He hated the Czechs because they were Slavs.

- He wanted their wealth and resources.

The crisis April–September

First Hitler instructed Henlein, the German Sudeten leader, to demand separation from Czechoslovakia. He also staged protests and riots. This gave Hitler the excuse for a military take-over. In the meantime he ordered the German army to prepare to 'smash Czechoslovakia'.

The Czechs knew that to surrender the Sudetenland would make them defenceless against Germany. All their defences against Germany were in this area. They also had an alliance with France and believed the French would support them.

Focus on

The Sudetenland

This was a mainly German-speaking area given to Czechoslovakia on its creation in 1920. It was badly affected by the Great Depression and this led to:

- a resentment of Czech control.

- support for Konrad Henlein, a pro-Nazi Sudeten German. He demanded that the Sudetenland should join with Germany.

Also the Sudetenland contained much of Czechoslovakia's defences. Once absorbed into Germany, the rest of Czechoslovakia lay vulnerable.

Chamberlain, however, did not want war over the Sudetenland. He felt that a peaceful solution could be found. He met Hitler on two occasions, each time flying to Germany for talks:

- On 15 September he met Hitler at Berchtesgaden, the German leader's personal residence. Hitler insisted he would risk war to bring the Sudeten Germans into Germany. Chamberlain accepted that areas in which more than half the population was German should be handed over. He persuaded the French and Czechs to accept this compromise.

- A week later, 22 September, he met Hitler again at Godesberg. This time Hitler stepped up his demands. He wanted Germany to occupy the entire Sudetenland by 28 September. If they were not met, the German army would invade on 1 October. Chamberlain rejected these demands.

Britain and France prepared for war.

The Munich Conference

SOURCE B

A cartoon of Neville Chamberlain travelling to Munich entitled 'Still hope'

STILL HOPE

SOURCE A

Part of a broadcast by Neville Chamberlain to the people of Britain, 27 September 1938

How horrible it is that we should be digging trenches and trying on gas masks here because of a quarrel far away between people we do not know.

With Europe on the brink of war, Chamberlain asked Mussolini to persuade Hitler to agree to an international conference. Hitler agreed and postponed his planned invasion of the Sudetenland.

Four leaders – Chamberlain, Hitler, Mussolini and Prime Minister Daladier of France – met at Munich. Czechoslovakia and the USSR were not invited. It was agreed that the Sudetenland would be transferred to Germany. It was also agreed that Czechoslovakia's new frontiers would be guaranteed by the four powers.

The day after the conference, Chamberlain met Hitler alone and they agreed an Anglo-German Declaration. The two countries promised never to go to war with each other again. They would settle all disputes between the two countries by talks. It was a copy of this agreement that Chamberlain waved to the cheering crowds on his return to Britain.

SOURCE C

Chamberlain's return from Munich. He is waving a copy of the agreement to the crowd.

RESULTS OF MUNICH

Europe had been saved from war.

Britain and France gained time to build up their armed forces – so did Germany.

Czechoslovakia was deserted by her allies, Britain and France. The Czechs lost vital resources and their defences against Germany.

Hitler decided that Britain and France were unlikely ever to oppose him by force. He gained even more popularity at home and became even more determined to pursue his policy of *Lebensraum*. He now turned his attention to the rest of Czechoslovakia.

Stalin, the leader of the USSR, was very upset at being left out of the Munich Conference. He decided that Britain and France would stand back if Hitler moved against Poland and the USSR.

SOURCE D

A Soviet cartoon published shortly after the Munich agreement. It shows Daladier and Chamberlain pointing Germany towards the East.

REACTIONS TO MUNICH

There have been many different reactions to the Munich agreement both at the time and later.

Neville Chamberlain

  ❝ *My good friends, this is the second time in our history that there has come back from Germany to Downing Street peace with honour. I believe it is peace in our time.* ❞

Winston Churchill

❝ *I will begin by saying what everybody would like to ignore or forget. We have experienced a total defeat. Silent, mournful, abandoned, broken Czechoslovakia will be swallowed up in the Nazi regime. And do not suppose this is the end. This is only the beginning.* ❞

Daily Express

Give thanks to your God. The wings of peace settle about us and the peoples of Europe. The prayers of the troubled hearts are answered. It was the war that nobody wanted. Nobody in Germany. Nobody in France. Nobody, above all, in Britain, which had no concern with the issues at stake.

Chicago Tribune

There is little to prevent Hitler from dominating and organising Middle and Eastern Europe.

A British historian G.A. Craig

As late as 1938 a firm stand in support of the Czech government would not have probably caused the kind of war that came a year later. Germany was far from ready to fight a war on two fronts.

Questions

1. Explain Chamberlain's attempts to solve the Sudetenland Crisis in September 1938. Why did they fail?
2. What is the purpose of the cartoon, Source **B**?
3. Is Source **D** a reliable view of the effects of the Munich Conference?
4. Read the effects of the Munich Conference and the different reactions. Copy and complete the following chart:

Advantages of Munich	Disadvantages of Munich

5. Do you think the Munich agreement was worthwhile?

Activity

Write a page of headlines from a variety of British newspapers explaining their reactions to the Munich settlement.

The destruction of Czechoslovakia, March 1939

"EUROPE CAN LOOK FORWARD TO A CHRISTMAS OF PEACE", SAYS HITLER

In March 1939 Hitler took over the remainder of Czechoslovakia. He ordered his armies to occupy Bohemia and Moravia, two parts of Czechoslovakia that had been protected by the Munich agreement. Slovakia became a 'puppet state' under German domination. Czechoslovakia had ceased to exist. On 23 March Hitler also seized the territory of Memel from Lithuania.

Reactions

Britain and France immediately ended their policy of appeasement because:

- Hitler had proved that he could not be trusted to keep a promise.

- Chamberlain was furious at Hitler's betrayal of his trust.

- Hitler's argument that he was bringing Germans into a 'Greater Germany' was no longer justifiable. He was now taking over the lands of non-Germans.

Britain and France agreed that they had to stop further German conquests. They both speeded up rearmament and guaranteed to defend the independence of Poland.

Poland and War

Hitler now turned his attention to Poland. This was to be the immediate cause of the outbreak of war. He demanded, from the Poles, the return of Danzig and the Polish Corridor. He ordered his generals to prepare an invasion. To ensure Mussolini's support Italy and Germany signed the Pact of Steel in which they agreed to help each other in the event of war. Hitler was convinced that Britain and France would not fight for Poland.

SOURCE B

Stalin speaking in a radio broadcast in 1941

We secured peace for our country for one and a half years, as well as an opportunity of preparing our forces for defence if Nazi Germany risked attacking our country. This was a definite gain for Russia and loss for Germany.

SOURCE C

The ultimatum from the British to the German government, 3 September 1939

Unless not later than 11 am British summer time, today 3 September satisfactory assurances have been given by the German government and have reached His Majesty's Government in London, a state of war will exist between the two countries from that hour.

Activity

You are an MP in the House of Commons who believes Britain should go to war in September 1939. Write out your speech. You will need to give reasons for your views.

The Nazi–Soviet Pact, August 1939

Stalin and the USSR were the key to Poland:

- Geographically, the USSR lies just to the east of Poland.

- Hitler was determined to avoid a war on two fronts. He was prepared to make an agreement with Stalin.

- Britain and France also wanted an agreement with Stalin. This might warn off Hitler.

Stalin wanted to avoid a war and buy time to build up his armed forces, which had been weakened by recent purges (p. 452). He had to choose between Britain and France or Germany. He chose Hitler because the USSR would then share in the partition of Poland. Britain and France did not like dealing with Stalin and delayed negotiations. Stalin believed they were going to force a war between the USSR and Germany. He distrusted them because they had left him out of the Munich talks. He wanted a full military alliance with Britain and France so that they would fight together. The Western Powers refused.

The Nazi–Soviet Pact was signed in August 1939. Publicly, it was agreed that the USSR would not object if Germany invaded Poland. Secretly they agreed that once Poland was overrun, the two powers would divide it between them. Thus the USSR would gain the land lost to Poland in 1921.

The pact was the final cause of the war. Hitler had planned to invade Poland. He could now do so without any interference from the USSR. German armies invaded Poland on 1 September 1939. Britain and France did not declare war immediately. They still hoped that there might be a chance to make Hitler change his plans. They knew they could not save Poland. On 3 September the British government sent Hitler an ultimatum. The French did the same. When no reply was received by 11 a.m. Britain declared war on Germany. They had no choice. They had guaranteed Poland's independence.

Why did war break out?

It has usually been taken for granted that Hitler caused the Second World War:

- He planned for war from 1933 and built up his armed forces.

- Hitler took advantage of Germany's genuine dissatisfaction with the Treaty of Versailles.

- He could not justify the occupation of the rest of Czechoslovakia in March 1939 and the invasion of Poland in September of that year. Neither were German-speaking.

- Hitler made alliances and agreements to clear the way for war – the Pact of Steel and the Nazi–Soviet Pact of 1939.

Activity

Create a time line showing the events of 1939 leading to the outbreak of war.

However, Hitler was not entirely responsible. He was greatly assisted by circumstances:

- The attitude of Britain and France encouraged Hitler to demand more and more. Once the principle of agreeing to changes in the Treaty of Versailles was accepted, Hitler was able to take advantage and demand the total destruction of the treaty.

- Hitler was encouraged by Britain and France who saw Germany as a useful barrier to the expansion of Soviet Russia.

- Britain and France stopped working through the League of Nations. Hitler realised this and saw that the League was now useless.

- Hitler was also greatly helped by the isolation of the USA. He knew that he could do what he liked in Europe. America would not interfere.

Questions

1 How useful is Source **A** as a view of Hitler and his ambitions at the end of 1938?
2 Using Source **B**, explain why Stalin decided to sign the Nazi–Soviet Pact.
3 Write out a plan showing the causes of the Second World War. Your plan should include:
   - Long-term causes, such as the Treaty of Versailles.
   - Short-term causes, such as Hitler's invasion of the rest of Czechoslovakia.
   - Immediate causes.
4 What do you think was the most important, fundamental reason for war?

Summary and Revision

For this section you need to know the following key developments.

THE PEACE TREATIES OF VERSAILLES

This includes:
- The aims of the 'Big Three' – Clemenceau, Lloyd George and Wilson.

- The terms of the Treaty of Versailles with Germany.

- German reactions to the treaty.

- The other peace treaties with Austria, Hungary, Turkey and Bulgaria.

- The changes in the peace treaties in the 1920s.

Revision questions

1 What differences were there between the aims of Wilson, Clemenceau and Lloyd George at Versailles?
2 What were the main terms of the Treaty of Versailles in connection with:
    a   territorial changes?
    b   the military?
    c   reparations?
3 Give three reasons why the Germans were unhappy with the Treaty.
4 What were the main terms of the following treaties:
    a   St Germain?
    b   Trianon?
    c   Neuilly?
    d   Sèvres?
5 What changes were made to the original peace treaties by:
    a   the Treaty of Lausanne?
    b   the Dawes Plan?

THE LEAGUE OF NATIONS

This includes:

- The aims and organisation of the League.

- Membership and early weaknesses.

- Successes and failures of the League in the 1920s.

- Other reasons for peace in the 1920s.

- The move away from international co-operation.

- The causes, events and results of the Manchurian and Abyssinian crises.

- Why the League failed.

Revision questions

1   Why was the League set up? What were its early weaknesses?
2   Give examples of League successes and League failures in the 1930s.
3   How did the Locarno Treaties and the Kellogg–Briand Pact help to keep the peace?
4   Explain at least three developments that brought an end to international co-operation in the 1930s.
5   Why and with what results did the League fail to stop Japanese aggression in Manchuria and the Italian invasion of Abyssinia?
6   Explain at least three reasons for the failure of the League.

HITLER AND THE ROAD TO WAR 1933–39

This involves:

- Hitler's aims and ambitions.

- Early rearmament of the Germany navy, army and air force.

- Successes in the Saar and Rhineland, 1935–36.

- The causes, events and results of the occupation of Austria in 1938.

- The meaning of appeasement. Arguments for and against.

- The causes, events and results of the Sudetenland crisis of 1938.

- The Munich Conference – results and effects.

- The German occupation of the rest of Czechoslovakia in 1939.

- Hitler, Poland and the Nazi–Soviet Pact.

- Why did war break out in September 1939?

Revision questions

1   What was meant by *Lebensraum*?
2   Explain Hitler's success in rearmament 1933–35.
3   Describe the German reoccupation of the Rhineland and its results.
4   Explain the causes, events and results of the *Anschluss*.
5   What is meant by appeasement? Give at least three arguments for and three against.
6   Explain the events of the Sudetenland Crisis of 1938.
7   What was agreed at Munich? Why has this agreement been criticised?
8   What happened to the rest of Czechoslovakia in March 1939?
9   Why did Hitler and Stalin agree to sign the Nazi–Soviet Pact of August 1939?
10   Why did Britain and France declare war on Germany on 3 September 1939?

4
The Second World War

UNDERSTANDING THE SECOND WORLD WAR

The following definitions and explanations should help you to understand this chapter.

Blitzkrieg	'Lightning war'. The name given to the German tactics at the start of the war based on the rapid movement of tanks and planes.
Evacuation	Moving people from cities and towns to the countryside.
Evacuees	People evacuated.
Incendiary bomb	A bomb intended to start a fire.
Luftwaffe	The German air force.
Outflank	To go round the side of an opposing army.
Panzers	Units of German tanks.
Pincer movement	Attack from two sides in an attempt to cut off from the remainder.

The Second World War

The Second World War did not repeat the pattern of the First World War in Western Europe. There was no trench warfare nor stalemate. Instead the German armies advanced rapidly and, in the first year, were very successful. At home there were many similarities with the earlier conflict, with the emphasis on rationing, censorship, propaganda and the role of women.

EARLY GERMAN SUCCESS 1939–40

Within a year of the outbreak of war Hitler's armed forces had taken over Poland, Norway, Denmark, Belgium, Holland and France.

Blitzkrieg

This word meant 'lightning war' and was used to describe the tactics successfully used by the Germans early on in the war. Hitler had remembered the lessons of the First World War and was determined to avoid trench warfare. He had also remembered the initial success of Ludendorff's stormtroopers during the Spring offensives of 1918 (p. 74).

Blitzkrieg was based on two weapons – the aeroplane and the tank. It depended on surprise, speed and weight of forces and followed the following pattern:

- Bombers attacked enemy airfields and communication centres. This was to prevent any resistance from enemy aircraft and to slow down enemy reinforcement.

- Parachutists were dropped behind enemy lines to capture bridges and other important targets and further disrupt communications.

- Dive bombers moved ahead of the tanks and attacked enemy strong points.

- Tanks broke through weak points in the enemy lines and travelled fast across country and outflanked the enemy front lines.

- Motorised infantry followed up to mop up resistance.

This proved a very successful tactic because:

- It was a new and unexpected tactic. The Allies, especially Britain and France, believed it would be a war of attrition like that of 1914–18. For this reason they remained on the defensive in the early months of the war.

- It was carried out very quickly and did not give the enemy an opportunity to recover.

SOURCE A

A description of Blitzkrieg by Rommel, one of Germany's leading commanders

The tanks now rolled in a long column through the line of fortifications and on towards the first houses, which had been set alight by our fire. Occasionally an enemy machine gun or anti-tank gun fired, but none of these came anywhere near us. Gradually the speed increased. Before long we were 1000, 2000, 3000 metres into the fortified zone. Engines roared, tank tracks clattered and clanked. We swung north to the main road which was soon reached. On we went, at a steady speed, towards our objective.

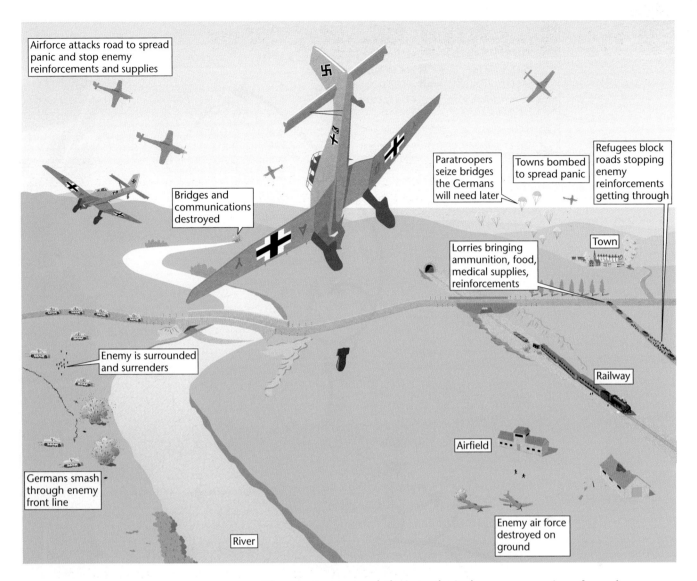

- The Germans used their tanks in large groups in a few places as a spearhead for attacks. Although the British and French had lots of tanks, they divided them into small groups and spread them around their lines.

- The French felt safe from attack by the Germans because of the Maginot Line, a line of fortifications they had built in the 1930s. It stretched along the border of Germany, from Switzerland to Belgium. The French believed it was impossible for any invading army to break through this series of forts, which were linked by underground tunnels.

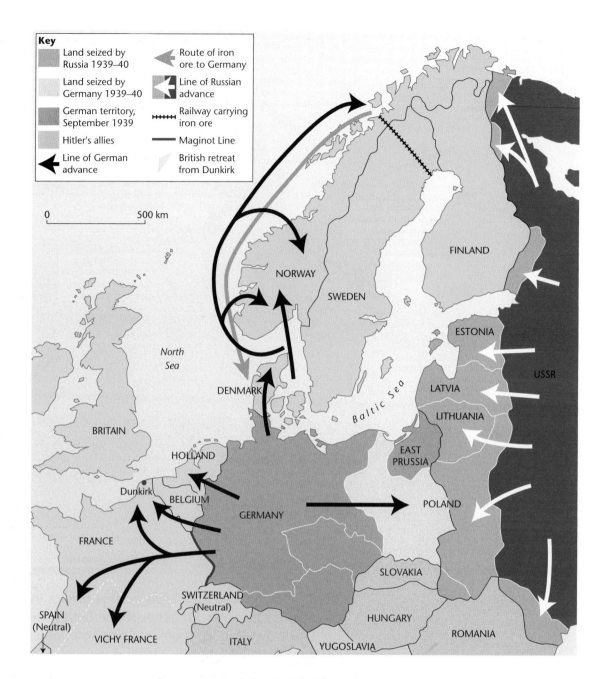

Key

Land seized by Russia 1939–40	Route of iron ore to Germany
Land seized by Germany 1939–40	Line of Russian advance
German territory, September 1939	Railway carrying iron ore
Hitler's allies	Maginot Line
Line of German advance	British retreat from Dunkirk

0   500 km

North Sea

FINLAND

NORWAY

SWEDEN

ESTONIA

USSR

LATVIA

Baltic Sea

LITHUANIA

DENMARK

BRITAIN

EAST PRUSSIA

HOLLAND

Dunkirk

BELGIUM

GERMANY

POLAND

FRANCE

SLOVAKIA

SPAIN (Neutral)

SWITZERLAND (Neutral)

HUNGARY

ROMANIA

VICHY FRANCE

ITALY

YUGOSLAVIA

The defeat of Poland, September 1939

Poland was the first country to experience Blitzkrieg and had no answer. The Germans invaded on 1 September and had completed the defeat of the Polish army by 19 September. Blitzkrieg methods proved very successful across the flat Polish plains and the Polish armed forces and defences were quickly outflanked. Warsaw, the Polish capital, was bombed to force an early Polish surrender. This success was due to several reasons:

1   The Poles had a very large frontier, over 500 miles long, and had to stretch their defences. It was easy for the Germans to attack weak points and force a breakthrough.

2   The time of year assisted Blitzkrieg. It was September and the weather had been dry.

3   The Poles, themselves, were ill-equipped to stop the Germans. The Poles had only one tank brigade against Germany's eleven.

The Polish air force was also small – 210 bombers compared to Germany's 850 – and many of their aircraft were destroyed on the ground anyway.

4 Poland got no help from Britain and France. It was too far away and their allies were slow to mobilise.

The 'Phoney War' 1939–40

From the end of September 1939 to April the following year little progress was made in the war in the west. This became known as the Phoney (or pretend) War in Britain and the *Sitzkrieg* or sitting war in Germany.

Britain and France prepared for war during this period and a British force, again known as the British Expeditionary Force (BEF), was sent to France to support the French. But the military preparations were half-hearted because the French felt safe from

The British and French ignored the lessons of Blitzkrieg in Poland and made no preparations to deal with this new tactic.

Norway April 1940

The British Prime Minister, Neville Chamberlain, still hoped that the Germans would see reason. In April 1940 he announced that 'Hitler had missed the bus' and that the war would not continue. A few days later, however, Hitler launched an attack against Denmark and Norway.

German troops crossed the border into Denmark, which offered no resistance. Hitler then ordered a Blitzkrieg attack by sea, and seized points along the Norwegian coast as far north as Narvik. German paratroopers were dropped to capture places inland, such as bridges and airfields. The British and French were unable to provide sufficient help to prevent Norway being defeated. Britain did send two expeditions but they had to be hastily evacuated due to lack of air cover.

SOURCE D

The French General, Gamelin

We need tanks of course, but you cannot hope to achieve a real breakthrough with tanks. As to the air, it will not play the part you expect. It'll be a flash in the pan.

Key
- German sea forces
- Airborne attacks
- Land attacks
- Counter moves by allies

Narvik

(Iron ore route)

Bodo

Namsos
Steinkjaer
Trondheim
Andalsnes
SWEDEN
Dombas
NORWAY
Lillehammer
Bergen
Oslo
Stavanger
Egersund
Kristiansand
Alborg
Copenhagen

N

0   200 km

SOURCE E

A *Daily Sketch* cartoon, April 1940, shows the German desire for iron ore for use in their arms factories. To get it, they were prepared to invade Denmark.

SOURCE F

The *Chicago Daily News* describes the failure of the British expeditions

They were dumped into Norway's deep snows and quagmires of April slush without a single anti-aircraft gun, without one squadron of supporting airplanes, without a single piece of artillery. A British officer said: 'We have simply been massacred. It is the planes. We were completely at the mercy of the Germans. Their bombers flew low over us at five hundred feet. They scattered us. We were up to our hips in snow.'

Source G

Winston Churchill, *History of the Second World War*

The troops lacked aircraft, anti-aircraft guns, anti-tank guns, transport and training. There were neither snow-shoes nor skis, still less skiers. Thus began this ramshackle campaign.

The Norwegian campaign was important because:

- It provided Hitler with control of the Norwegian port of Narvik. Swedish iron ore, vital for the German war effort, passed through this port to Germany.

- The west coast of Norway provided useful air and naval bases, especially for U-boats, for attacks on Britain.

- In May it led to the resignation of Neville Chamberlain as Prime Minister. He was seen as the man who had failed to stop Hitler between 1937 and 1939 and seemed to have done little to prepare Britain for war between September 1939 and April 1940. The failure to stop Hitler in Norway was the last straw. He was replaced by Winston Churchill who was a much more assertive leader.

Profile on

Winston Churchill

Winston Churchill had much experience before he became Prime Minister in 1940. As early as 1899 he had been a war correspondent during the Boer War when the British fought against the Boer farmers in South Africa. During the First World War he was First Lord of the Admiralty but he resigned in 1915 when the Gallipoli campaign (see p. 92), which had been his idea, failed. He served as Chancellor of the Exchequer in the 1920s. In the later 1930s he was one of the few politicians to speak out against the policy of appeasement (see p. 149). He believed it was wrong and that Britain had to stand up to Hitler. He had important qualities as a wartime leader. He was very determined and was able to inspire the British people through his speeches and leadership. He was ruthless and prepared to make unpopular decisions. Above all else he realised that this was total war. The whole country had to be geared towards the war effort.

Source H

Churchill speaking to the House of Commons, 13 May 1940

I have nothing to offer but blood, toil, tears and sweat. You ask, what is our policy? It is to wage war, by sea, land and air, with all of our might. You ask, what is our aim? I can answer in one word: Victory – victory at all costs, victory, however long and hard the road may be.

Activity

Write a newspaper headline and a short column to describe the main events of:

either
1. The German invasion and defeat of Poland 1939,

or
2. The German invasion and defeat of Norway 1940.

Questions

1. What does Blitzkrieg mean? Why was it so successful in the first year of the war?
2. What do Sources **B** and **C** tell you about the reasons for the defeat of Poland in September 1939?
3. What similarities are there between Sources **F** and **G** in their explanation for the failure of the British expeditions in Norway?
4. Which is the more reliable view? Why do you think this?
5. Explain the results of the Norwegian campaign.
6. What is the purpose of the cartoon in Source **E**?

The defeat of France

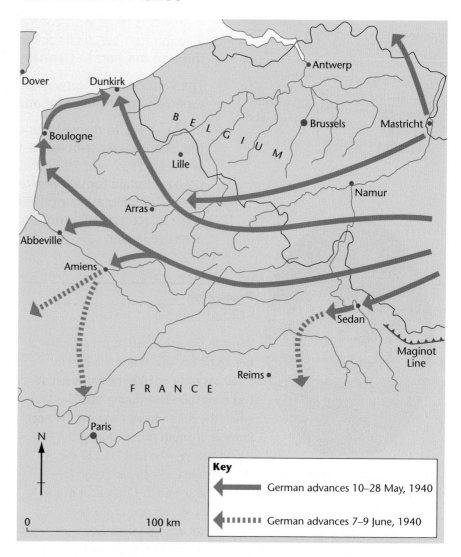

On the same day that Churchill made his speech the Germans launched a Blitzkrieg attack against the Low Countries (Belgium and Holland) and France. It was an outstanding success. German attacks rolled swiftly across Holland and Belgium. Dutch attempts to delay the German advance by opening the dykes and flooding the land were ineffective. The Germans used glider planes to land behind the Belgian line of defences and outflank their defenders. Holland surrendered within five days.

Other troops attacked the French. The French High Command was sure that their expensive line of underground forts on the Maginot Line would stop any German attack. The Germans, however, decided not to attack this Line. Blitzkrieg avoided enemy strong points. Instead the Germans attacked the weakest part of the French defences, the Ardennes. This was a heavily wooded area that seemed unsuitable for tanks. To the astonishment of the French, the Germans did attack this area and quickly broke through to Sedan.

French resistance crumbled as the German tanks raced to the Channel coast where the Germans planned to cut off the retreat of the 150,000-strong BEF. By the tenth day the Germans had reached the Channel. Eight days later Belgium surrendered.

Dunkirk

The BEF had been sent across the Channel, but they and the French, Dutch and Belgians all found it difficult to work together. The British and French troops were sent reeling back towards the Channel port of Dunkirk by the German attack and breakthrough. The Germans planned to race for the Channel ports and seize them. The only hope was to try to evacuate the 380,000 British and French troops before Dunkirk fell into the hands of the Germans.

The British launched 'Operation Dynamo'. Between 27 May and 4 June, as the German air force, the Luftwaffe, pounded the beaches, the Royal Navy evacuated men back to England. Hundreds of small, privately owned boats sailed across the Channel to Dunkirk to rescue as many as possible and transfer them to bigger Royal Navy vessels waiting off-shore.

A painting done at the time by George Cundall, showing troops being rescued from the beaches of Dunkirk

The first day of the evacuation, 27 May, proved disappointing. Only 7,669 troops were brought out by an assortment of destroyers, passenger ferry steamers, self-propelled barges and Dutch shuits. Later a volunteer Armada of some 400 yachts, lifeboats, launches, river tugs, cockle boats, pleasure craft, French and Belgian fishing boats, oyster dredgers... ferried 100,000 men from the beaches on 30 May.

SOURCE C

A British cartoon of 29 May 1940

SOURCE D

From *World War II – Dunkirk* edited by Brigadier Peter Young, 1972

Despite the undoubted setback represented by the allied evacuations from Dunkirk, Hitler had scored a crushing victory. For German losses put at 10,252 killed, 42,523 wounded and 8,467 missing, he announced that 1,212,000 Dutch, Belgian, French and British prisoners had been taken. In addition his armies had captured a lot of equipment: 1,200 field guns, 1,250 anti-aircraft and anti-tank guns, 10,000 machine guns and 75,000 vehicles.

The British government hoped that at least 50,000 men could be rescued. In fact around 340,000 men were rescued. The escape was referred to as a miracle but huge amounts of military equipment had to be abandoned, including 475 tanks, 1,000 heavy guns and 400 anti-tank guns. The BEF had been forced to retreat, leaving the French to fight on alone. Churchill turned the evacuation into a national triumph, playing up the role of the small boats and trying to build up morale and create 'The Dunkirk spirit'.

Why were the British able to carry out the evacuation so successfully?

- RAF pilots did much to protect the soldiers on the beaches by shooting down German dive bombers.

- The Royal Navy and volunteer vessels carried the thousands of troops across the Channel to safety.

- Hitler surprisingly told his tanks and Panzers (top German troops) to stop short of Dunkirk. This may have been to save them for later action against the rest of the French armies. The land around Dunkirk was flooded and unsuitable for tanks. In any case Goering, head of the Luftwaffe, had told Hitler that his planes would finish off the Allied troops on the beaches.

- The BEF left behind a rearguard force who bravely held back the Germans while the troops were evacuated.

Within a month of the Dunkirk evacuation, Paris had been captured and France had surrendered to Germany. Instead of occupying the whole of France, Germany allowed southern France to set up a government at Vichy run by General Pétain. The Vichy government was really controlled by the Germans.

SOURCE E
From Frank Huggett, Cartoonists at War, 1981

What would have been the greatest military defeat in British history was turned into a British victory by British courage and ingenuity, Hitler's caution and Goering's false boast that his Luftwaffe would eliminate the BEF while it waited on the beaches. The British, always at their best when they are staring real disaster firmly in the face, were united in their defence. Not for the first time in their history, Britain stood alone.

REASONS FOR GERMAN SUCCESS IN THE WEST

BLITZKRIEG
French, British, Belgian and Dutch armies were overcome by the speed and weight of the German attack.

GERMAN SUPERIORITY IN EQUIPMENT
- Germany had ten armoured divisions, the Allies only four.
- The Germans had 4000 aircraft to the Allies' 1400.

ALLIED WEAKNESSES
- They did not have one overall commander.
- They went on the defensive in the winter of 1939–40 and made no preparations to deal with Blitzkrieg.
- The Allied commanders wrongly believed it would be a war of attrition.
- They scattered their tanks all over the Western Front instead of concentrating them against the German attack.

GERMAN ADVANTAGES
- They had a commander and a plan of attack.
- Hitler was free to fight on one front only after the defeat of Poland.
- The Germans attacked France through the Ardennes and outflanked the Maginot Line.

SOURCE F

From the memoirs of a British politician, written after the Second World War

Three months before the collapse, I made a tour of the French front. When we reached the ill-fated section of Sedan, the French commander had taken us to the River Meuse and shown us the wooded banks and rushing waters. 'Look at the ground,' he had said to us, 'No German army can get through'.

SOURCE G

From speeches Hitler made to his generals in 1939

Our strength lies in our quickness and brutality. The aim in war is not to reach a certain point, but of completely destroying the enemy. Those poor worms, Chamberlain and Daladier, will be too cowardly to attack. I shall attack France and England at the most favourable and earliest moment.

Activities

1   Copy the table below and, using the information and sources in this section, write in evidence/examples of victory and defeat

    Was Dunkirk a victory or defeat for the British?

Victory	Defeat

    What do you think? Explain your answer

2   Do two radio broadcasts on Dunkirk – one for Germany and one for Britain. In the broadcasts you could include:

    • The lead-up to Dunkirk.
    • The troops on the beaches and German attacks.
    • The evacuation.
    • Whether it was a success or failure, a victory or a defeat.

Questions

1   Describe the German success in the Low Countries and France.
2   What differences are there between the views of Dunkirk given in Sources **D** and **E**?
3   Why are they different?
4   What message is the cartoonist trying to get across in Source **C**? How useful is it to an historian studying the events of May–June 1940?
5   What do Sources **F** and **G** tell you about the reasons for German success in the West in 1940?
6   Germany was successful for several reasons. Which do you think was the most important and why?

For the next year Britain faced Germany alone. The British survived due to the leadership of Churchill, success in the Battle of Britain and the economic support of the USA.

Churchill's leadership

SOURCE A

Churchill on a wartime poster

"LET US GO FORWARD TOGETHER"

Churchill provided the strong leadership needed during this difficult period. He kept up the morale of the British people and made them believe in ultimate victory with speeches and tours of the country. He was said to have 'mobilised the British language'. There was no talk of defeat or surrender.

American assistance

Although the USA was neutral at this time the American president, Franklin Roosevelt, sympathised with Britain. In September 1940 he arranged a deal under which 55-year-old American warships were given to Britain in return for a 99-year lease on certain naval and air bases.

In March 1941 Roosevelt persuaded Congress to agree to 'Lend-Lease' measures. Under these measures the United States lent equipment to Britain for use during the duration of the war. This aid was important because:

- It enabled Britain to get essential supplies from the USA.

- It improved the morale of the British people who no longer felt totally alone.

- Lend-Lease marked the end of American isolationism from European affairs.

The Battle of Britain

At the time of the French collapse the French General Weygand said that 'England will have her neck wrung like a chicken in three weeks'. This might have happened had it not been for the RAF and the British defence system.

Hitler planned to invade Britain but needed control of the Channel and the air space over Britain to protect his seaborne invasion forces. Before the Germans could invade they had to destroy British air power.

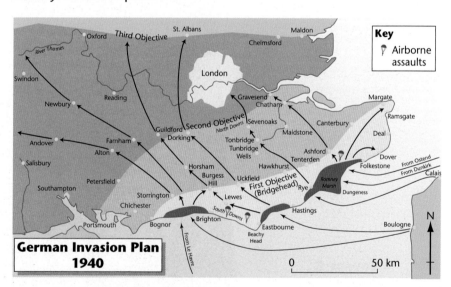

German Invasion Plan 1940

During the summer of 1940 Hitler prepared for 'Operation Sealion', the invasion of Britain. Invasion barges were assembled on the north coast of France. In the meantime the Luftwaffe set about destroying the RAF.

10 July	The Luftwaffe began sending over bombers to destroy Britain's means of defence and force her into submission. At first they bombed convoys of British ships in the channel.
13 August	They switched to full-scale attacks on the south-east of England, targeting sector and radar stations.
18 August	The Germans switched to fighter bases. The position began to look grim for Britain.

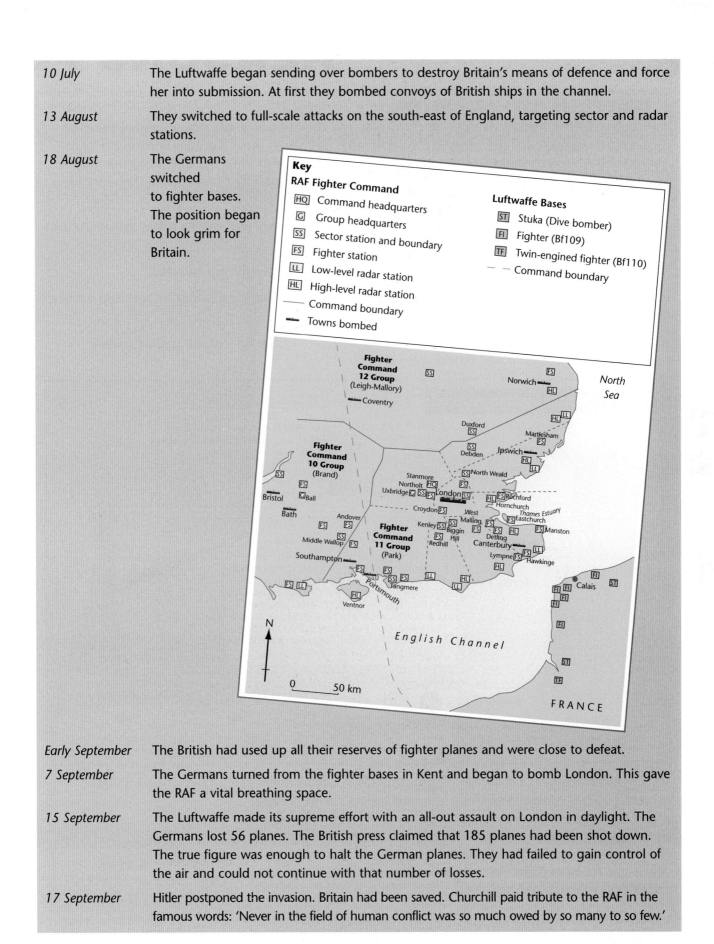

Key

RAF Fighter Command

- HQ Command headquarters
- G Group headquarters
- SS Sector station and boundary
- FS Fighter station
- LL Low-level radar station
- HL High-level radar station
- —— Command boundary
- Towns bombed

Luftwaffe Bases

- ST Stuka (Dive bomber)
- FI Fighter (Bf109)
- TF Twin-engined fighter (Bf110)
- – – Command boundary

Early September	The British had used up all their reserves of fighter planes and were close to defeat.
7 September	The Germans turned from the fighter bases in Kent and began to bomb London. This gave the RAF a vital breathing space.
15 September	The Luftwaffe made its supreme effort with an all-out assault on London in daylight. The Germans lost 56 planes. The British press claimed that 185 planes had been shot down. The true figure was enough to halt the German planes. They had failed to gain control of the air and could not continue with that number of losses.
17 September	Hitler postponed the invasion. Britain had been saved. Churchill paid tribute to the RAF in the famous words: 'Never in the field of human conflict was so much owed by so many to so few.'

In the whole of the Battle of Britain the British lost 857 planes but the Germans twice as many.

BRITISH ADVANTAGES

- The two British fighter planes, the Hurricane and the Spitfire, were a good match for their German counterpart, the Messerschmitt Me109. The other main German fighter, the twin-engined Messerschmitt Me110, was unsuitable for dogfights with the British fighter planes. The Me109 was a very good fighter but lacked the fuel capacity to be able to stay very long over south-east Britain.

- The British were fighting over their own territory. This meant that British pilots that were shot down could be sent back into combat.

- British factories produced an additional 1836 fighter planes in four months.

- The possession of 'Ultra', the key to Germany's radio codes, meant that Britain had advance warning of their plans.

- In the mid-1930s Britain had developed a sophisticated defence system against enemy bombing. This system was based around radar.

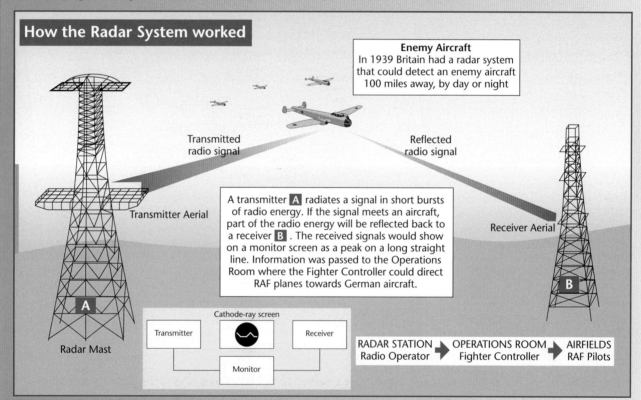

How the Radar System worked

Enemy Aircraft
In 1939 Britain had a radar system that could detect an enemy aircraft 100 miles away, by day or night

Transmitted radio signal

Reflected radio signal

Transmitter Aerial

A transmitter **A** radiates a signal in short bursts of radio energy. If the signal meets an aircraft, part of the radio energy will be reflected back to a receiver **B** . The received signals would show on a monitor screen as a peak on a long straight line. Information was passed to the Operations Room where the Fighter Controller could direct RAF planes towards German aircraft.

Receiver Aerial

A

B

Radar Mast

Cathode-ray screen

Transmitter · Receiver

Monitor

RADAR STATION → OPERATIONS ROOM → AIRFIELDS
Radio Operator · Fighter Controller · RAF Pilots

Having radar prevented the RAF suffering the same fate as the Polish air force when it was attacked by the Luftwaffe before it got into the air. Radar stations made it possible to track approaching enemy planes from their starting points, and so to concentrate the defence just where it was needed. British fighter planes were often in the skies and above the German planes as they arrived over Britain. This gave them the tactical advantage.

Sector stations acted as the nerve centre collecting the information from radar and sending the Spitfires and Hurricanes to intercept the German planes.

Source C

Len Deighton, *Fighter*, 1977

The most common type of attack was a dive out of the sun, pulling out behind, and under the tail of, the enemy, and firing while in his blind spot.

BRITISH VICTORY

GERMAN WEAKNESSES

- Goering was commander of the Luftwaffe. Although he had been a First World War fighter ace he had little understanding of tactics. He underestimated the strength of the RAF, especially the fighter planes.

- Hitler and Goering made the mistake of switching their attacks on 7 September just when the RAF was running out of fighter planes.

- The Germans had to fight over Britain. They lost far more pilots. If a German plane was shot down the pilot was either killed or taken prisoner. The German fighter planes could only carry limited fuel and could not fly over Britain long enough to protect the German bombers. These flew unescorted to bomb London on 15 September.

- The German air force did not have heavy bombers – aeroplanes which could carry large bombs. The medium bomber forces of JU88s, Heinkel 111s and Dornier 17s were no match for the British fighters.

SOURCE D

A comparison of British and German figures for aircraft losses in 1940

Date	RAF Claim in 1940 Diary	RAF Claim post-war	German High Command
15 August	185	76	55
18 August	155	71	49
15 September	185	56	50
27 September	153	55	42
Totals	678	258	196

SOURCE E

Painting of Battle of Britain dogfight

Activity

You are a German pilot who writes to a friend in the German army explaining why the Luftwaffe failed to defeat the RAF during the Battle of Britain.

Questions

1 What do Sources **A** and **B** show you about Churchill's leadership during 1940–1?
2 Why did Hitler have to destroy the RAF?
3 Explain the following reasons for British victory in the Battle of Britain:
 a Radar.
 b German mistakes.
 c British fighter planes.
4 What differences are there between the three sets of figures in Source **D**? Why are they so different?
5 How useful is Source **E** to an historian studying the Battle of Britain?

The Blitz

The Luftwaffe now turned its attention to bombing British towns and cities. This became known as the 'Blitz'. Hitler hoped that Britain would be forced to surrender and that the German people would enjoy revenge for British bombing of their cities. In retaliation, on 25 August 1940 Britain began the night-bombing of German towns.

Between 7 September and 2 November 1940 London was bombed every night. Bombs landed on London Zoo and the papers reported that 'the morale of the monkeys remained unaffected'. The House of Commons building was destroyed and the Commons had to move into the House of Lords. Buckingham Palace was damaged but King George VI was often on the scene soon after a severe raid to cheer and encourage people as they struggled to save those trapped under the debris.

The German bombing raids continued until well into 1941, when most of the Luftwaffe was needed on the Russian Front. London was not the only city to suffer. The Germans also attacked other towns and cities such as Hull, Plymouth, Bristol, Liverpool, Manchester and Birmingham. Perhaps the most famous of these attacks was the raid on Coventry. It was attacked on the night of 14 November 1940 and much of the city, including the cathedral, was destroyed. Yet in spite of this savage raid, the factories in Coventry were back in full production within five days.

178

From the *Daily Herald*, 16 November 1940

COVENTRY

THE bombing of Coventry was as foul a deed as even Hitler has ever ordained. Clearly his airmen were instructed: 'Don't worry if you cannot reach your industrial targets. Bomb and burn the city. Never mind if you fail to hit factories. Hit houses. Have no scruples about military objectives. Kill men, kill women, kill children. Destroy! Destroy! Destroy!

Heil Hitler!   Heil bloodshed!   Heil pain!

THE ORGY

ANTI-AIRCRAFT fire, the Ministry of Home Security's communiqué tells us, hindered accurate bombing of industrial targets.

So the orgy began.

Bombs by the thousand were poured on houses and churches, shops and hotels.

Squadron after squadron dived upon the helpless city.

It was, chortled the Berlin propagandist yesterday afternoon, 'the greatest attack in the history of warfare'.

And what has it achieved?

It has proved once again the calm courage of ordinary British people in this hell of Hitler's making.

It has fortified their resolve to fight him, to smash him, to strive and struggle without pause until the Nazi nightmare is nothing more than a sickening memory.

A broadcast from Berlin radio, 16 November 1940

More than 500 planes took part in the greatest attack in the history of aerial warfare. About 500 tons of high explosive bombs and 30,000 incendiary bombs were dropped. In a short time all large and small factories were set on fire. The German air force struck a violent blow in return for the British raid on the Nazi Party celebrations in Munich on the night of 8 November.

Was the Blitz a success?

Copy the headings below and, using the following sources, list the successes and failures of the Blitz.

SUCCESSES	FAILURES

SOURCE C

Photograph of bomb damage from the *Coventry Evening Telegraph*, 16 November 1940

SOURCE D

From C. Bayne-Jardine, *World War Two*, 1968

It is difficult to assess the damage that they did. Thirty thousand people were killed in the raids and a great number of houses and buildings destroyed. At the same time people suffered from the stresses brought about by lack of sleep and nervous strain. Civilians were in the line of battle in a very real sense.

SOURCE E

From T. Rea and J. Wright, *International Relations 1914–95*, 1997

The bombing of Britain's cities did not break the morale of her citizens. There is evidence to show that it actually made the people even more determined to beat Hitler.

SOURCE F

Wartime slogan chalked on a bombed-out building in London's East End

SOURCE G

Evening Standard, 13 January 1941

Seventeen women and children who were trapped in the basement of a London house damaged by a bomb last night shouted to wardens who went to their rescue: 'We're all right. Look after everybody else'. Then they started singing 'Tipperary' and shouting to the people in the road. 'Are we downhearted? No.'

SOURCE H

German radio, 18 September 1940

The legend of British self-control and coolness under fire is being destroyed. All reports from London agree in stating that the people are seized by fear – hair-raising fear. The 7 million Londoners have completely lost their self-control. They run aimlessly about the streets and are victims of bombs and bursting shells.

SOURCE I

From the diary of a British politician

Everybody is worried about the feeling in the East End, where there is much bitterness. It is said even the King and Queen were booed the other day when they visited the destroyed areas.

SOURCE J

From Hitler's war directive against England, 6 February 1941

The bombing campaign has had the least effect of all, so far as we can see, on the morale and will to resist of the English people. No decisive success can be expected from terror attacks on residential areas.

Activity

Draw two propaganda posters:

- A British poster about the raid on Coventry. Show how the British government wanted people to react to the raid.

- A German poster about the raid on Coventry. Show how the German government wanted people to react to the raid. For example, they wanted people to stop work and demand an end to the war.

Do you think the Blitz was a success? Explain your answer.

Questions

1. What was the Blitz? Which places were bombed?
2. What differences are there between Sources **A** and **B** in their views of the bombing of Coventry? Why are they so different?
3. Which is the more useful to an historian studying the Blitz, Source **G** or Source **H**?
4. Why do you think the Blitz failed to achieve its aims?

Britain was eventually saved by good fortune – Hitler's decision to invade Russia in June 1941.

Operation Barbarossa

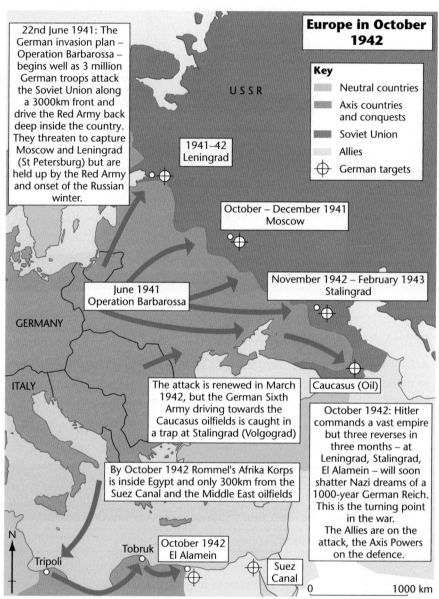

Europe in October 1942

22nd June 1941: The German invasion plan – Operation Barbarossa – begins well as 3 million German troops attack the Soviet Union along a 3000km front and drive the Red Army back deep inside the country. They threaten to capture Moscow and Leningrad (St Petersburg) but are held up by the Red Army and onset of the Russian winter.

Key
- Neutral countries
- Axis countries and conquests
- Soviet Union
- Allies
- ⊕ German targets

U S S R

1941–42 Leningrad

October – December 1941 Moscow

June 1941 Operation Barbarossa

November 1942 – February 1943 Stalingrad

GERMANY

ITALY

Caucasus (Oil)

The attack is renewed in March 1942, but the German Sixth Army driving towards the Caucasus oilfields is caught in a trap at Stalingrad (Volgograd)

October 1942: Hitler commands a vast empire but three reverses in three months – at Leningrad, Stalingrad, El Alamein – will soon shatter Nazi dreams of a 1000-year German Reich. This is the turning point in the war. The Allies are on the attack, the Axis Powers on the defence.

By October 1942 Rommel's Afrika Korps is inside Egypt and only 300km from the Suez Canal and the Middle East oilfields

N

Tripoli   Tobruk   October 1942 El Alamein   Suez Canal

0   1000 km

Hitler knew that Britain would never be able to invade mainland Europe without the aid of at least one powerful ally – either the Soviet Union or the United States.

Hitler had other war aims as well:

- He hated Communism and wanted to destroy it.

- Russia provided valuable *lebensraum* (living space) for the German people.

- Eastern Russia had valuable supplies of wheat and oil, especially the Ukraine and the Caucasus.

On 22 June 1941 the Germans invaded Russia in what was known as 'Operation Barbarossa'. Led by Panzer divisions and Stuka squadrons, the invasion was three-pronged. In the north, the German armies planned to liberate the Baltic states and then advance to Leningrad. In the centre, they intended to press towards Minsk, then Smolensk and on to Moscow. Finally to the south, they hoped to march into the Ukraine and then to the important coalfields in the Caucasus.

At first the German Blitzkrieg was successful. The army group in the north reached Leningrad on 8 September and laid siege to the city. The centre force reached Smolensk by 7 August but had to pause there after severe fighting. The southern strike began in July, encircled 700,000 Russians at Kiev, and reached Rostov on 21 November. Hitler exclaimed: 'Russia is broken! She will never rise again'.

Reasons for early success

The German armies were successful for several reasons:

1   Stalin was not prepared for the German invasion, despite repeated warnings from Churchill. He had seriously weakened the leadership of the Soviet armed forces with his purges in the 1930s (p. 452).

2   The Luftwaffe won control of the air after destroying a large number of Russian planes on the ground.

3   The Russian armies were short of weapons, tanks and motorised transport.

4   In some parts of Russia, the Germans were welcomed. For example, many Ukrainians volunteered to join the German army.

In October Hitler went against the advice of his generals who wanted him to concentrate his attack on one area. He continued to push in all three areas. Moscow and Leningrad, however, remained in Russian hands. By 2 December the German armies had reached the outskirts of Moscow but the onset of winter and fierce resistance prevented its fall.

Leningrad was cut off by the advancing Germans in September 1941. The three million Leningraders refused to surrender and defended their homes for 18 months with great heroism. When faced with starvation the population ate their pets, wild animals, wallpaper and even made soup from carpenter's glue and vaseline.

By the end of 1941 the German advance had halted with Russia still undefeated.

Why did Blitzkrieg fail against the USSR?

This was the first time that Blitzkrieg had failed to achieve its objectives.

FAILURE OF BLITZKRIEG

THE GEOGRAPHY OF RUSSIA

The geography of Russia worked against the German advance. It was too big an area for Blitzkrieg. As the German armies advanced they moved further and further away from their supply bases. Russia's poor roads made advance and supplies even more difficult.

ALLIED AID

Russian resistance was helped by military aid. British convoys risked the U-boats and ice of the Arctic Ocean to reach the ports of Murmansk and Archangel. Supplies also reached Russia overland, by way of Persia.

THE RUSSIAN WEATHER

The terrible rain of November turned the already poor Russian roads into impassable swamps. This was followed by severe cold with temperatures falling below −30 degrees centigrade. Machine-guns and motor engines froze up. When the thaw came, the roads once again turned to mud and, bogged down, men and machines were driven to the limits of their endurance. The Russian troops in the Red Army were used to winter fighting and were equipped with fur-lined boots and clothing and skis.

SOURCE C

German General Blumentritt

It was appallingly difficult country for tank movement – great virgin forests, widespread swamps, terrible roads and bridges not strong enough to bear the weight of tanks. The resistance also became stiffer, and the Russians began to cover their front with minefields. It was easier for them to block the way as there were so few roads.

GERMAN MISTAKES

The Germans made several mistakes:

- Their three-pronged attack was too ambitious. Hitler should have concentrated all his forces on one breakthrough.

SOURCE D

Abandoned German vehicles on the Eastern Front

- Operation Barbarossa was launched too late in the year. Had the Germans invaded in April they could have achieved their objectives before the onset of the Russian winter.

- The German troops were not properly equipped for the winter. They had only overcoats and blankets and suffered terribly from frostbite.

RUSSIAN RESISTANCE

The Russians refused to surrender. Indeed Stalin made sure that most of the Red Army retreated from the advancing German armies and were saved to fight at a later date. As they retreated they carried out a 'scorched earth' policy burning crops, homes and places of shelter. This made the German advance more difficult. Behind the lines Russian partisans – armed men and women – began guerrilla warfare. They attacked German supply, communication and garrison points at every opportunity.

SOURCE E

A German officer recorded his views of the fighting in Russia

The Russians seem to have a never-ending supply of men. They bring in fresh troops from Siberia every day. Every day they bring up new guns and lay mines all over the place. The ice cold, the poor clothing, the heavy losses of men and guns, the poor supplies of fuel are making fighting a torture.

The failure of 'Operation Barbarossa' had important effects on the war:

- It provided Britain with an ally, the USSR. The British were no longer alone.

- Germany now had to fight a war on two fronts. Hitler had tried to avoid this.

- It was the first failure of Blitzkrieg.

Questions

1 According to Sources **A** and **B**, why did Hitler decide to invade Russia in 1941?
2 Account for the early success of the German invasion and its later failure.
3 What do Sources **C**, **D** and **E** tell you about the reasons for the failure of Blitzkrieg in Russia?
4 How useful is Source **C** to an historian studying Operation Barbarossa?

Activity

You are a member of the SS sent to the Eastern Front in December 1941 to find out why the invasion had not achieved its objectives. Write a report addressed to Hitler giving a list of reasons.

Stalingrad

With their advances on Moscow and Leningrad checked, the Germans next concentrated their efforts to the south. Here things had gone well for Hitler. His armies had marched through the Ukraine, crossed the River Donets and poured south towards the Caucasus. In fact, the rapid advance of the German army had greatly extended its lines of communication. The first oil wells they reached had been completely destroyed. Now, with winter approaching, the Germans had to make their position secure.

To do this, they had to take Stalingrad, an industrial city between the Rivers Don and Volga. In late July 1942 von Paulus, commander of the German armies in that part of Russia, made his first moves against Stalingrad. Early in September the Germans reached the River Volga and began to close in on the city.

During the four months that followed, Stalingrad became the scene of the most ferocious battle of the war. The Russians fought for every house in every street. At one stage the Germans held most of the city.

On 19 November, Marshall Zhukov, the Russian commander, mounted a counter-offensive to the north and south of the city. With fresh troops – who were forbidden to retreat or surrender – and 500 new tanks, he was able to take the city in a large pincer movement. The Red Army surrounded the Germans in Stalingrad. Another German army advanced from the west but was beaten back.

SOURCE A

A German lieutenant in October 1942

We have fought for fifteen days for a single house. Already by the third day, fifty-four German corpses lie in the cellars, on the landings and staircases. Ask any soldier what half-an-hour of hand-to-hand struggle means. Then imagine Stalingrad. Eighty days and eighty nights of hand-to-hand struggles. Animals flee this hell. Only men endure.

SOURCE B

A Soviet general's description of the stubborn resistance put up by Soviet troops at Stalingrad

Soviet soldiers had tremendous experience in hand-to-hand fighting. They knew every drain pipe, every manhole cover, every shell-hole, every crater. Nothing short of a direct hit would knock them out.

Source C

A German soldier in January 1943

The ration of bread was reduced to a slice. Water came from melted snow. A kilogram box of potatoes had to make do for fifteen men. There was no meat. We ate our horses at Christmas.

With the position worsening daily, von Paulus asked permission to fight his way out and, if that failed, to surrender. Hitler sent his reply – 'Surrender is forbidden. Army will hold their positions to the last man'. Suffering extreme cold and without food and ammunition, the Germans surrendered on 31 January 1943. Some 200,000 German troops had been killed since November and now a further 91,000 were taken prisoner.

Source D

A Russian soldier prepares to hoist the Red Flag in the centre of Stalingrad towards the end of the battle for the city

Kursk

By the summer of 1943, the Panzers were on the move again. The Germans attacked at Kursk with 3000 tanks. The Battle of Kursk was the biggest tank encounter of the war. The Germans made some limited gains but were finally brought to a standstill. They lost 2000 tanks and 70,000 men were killed. It was the last German offensive on the Eastern Front.

The Germans were now in full retreat. By October 1943, the Red Army was again in Kiev and closing in on the Polish border.

Questions

1   Using Sources **A**, **B** and **C**, explain why the Germans were defeated at Stalingrad?
2   How reliable is Source **B** as a view of the Russian soldiers?
3   What took place at Kursk in the summer of 1943?

Stalingrad marked the turning point in the war and the beginning of the end for Hitler.

The Grand Alliance

By the end of 1941 Hitler was fighting a war against the Grand Alliance of Britain, the USSR and the USA. The USA entered the war in December 1941 after a series of events. On 7 December the Japanese attacked the USA's fleet at Pearl Harbor. On 12 December, Hitler declared war on the USA. Roosevelt had had no intention of becoming involved in the conflict against Germany and was taken by surprise by Hitler's decision.

Preparations for D-Day

The British and Americans began preparations for D-Day (deliverance day) as early as 1942. Stalin was anxious to see the Allies invade Europe and set up a 'Second Front' to relieve the pressure on Russia. Churchill, however, would not invade until the time was right. In mid-August 1942 a limited cross-Channel raid on Dieppe, mainly by Canadians, lost half the force that took part and made no serious impression on the German defences. As a raid it was a disaster. It proved that frontal attacks on heavily defended ports were out of the question. No invasion could take place until some means had been found of supplying a large army over open beaches, and until that army, and craft to land it, were ready.

SOURCE A

A cartoon showing Churchill thinking while the army, navy and air force wait for the date of D-Day

Profile on

Dwight D. Eisenhower

He commanded the American operations in North Africa, 'Operation Torch', in November 1942. Although having little direct military experience, he was very good at making people from different backgrounds and countries work together. He was able to turn the various Allied commanders into a 'team' for D-Day. In later years he became President of the United States.

Eventually the Allies chose June 1944 because the weather would be fine and the tides just right for landing. After several months of research they chose the beaches of Normandy as having beaches suitable for landing a huge army and equipment and an area that was not too heavily defended. The Germans did not expect Allied landings in this area. They believed the Allies would choose the area around Calais and Boulogne.

General Eisenhower was put in charge of the D-Day landings. He was made Supreme Commander over all the Allied soldiers. This was because the majority of equipment and armed forces would come from the USA.

The Allies manufactured a variety of equipment to carry out the invasion and landings. This included:

- Two 'Mulberry' (codename) harbours, comprised of massive hollow reinforced concrete blocks which could be towed across, placed in line, and flooded so that they settled on the bottom.

- 'Gooseberry' shelter piers.

- A pipeline codenamed 'Pluto' to carry petrol direct across the seabed from pumping stations on the English coast.

- Waterproofed tanks and lorries which could creep ashore under their own power from the landing craft.

- Specially designed tanks to deal with the beaches of Normandy.

Men had to be trained in the special techniques of assaulting defended beaches and whole areas on the English south coast were cleared of inhabitants for the purpose. Preparations on this scale could not be hidden from the Germans. However, every means was used to deceive the Germans as to where the landings would take place. The area of Calais was regularly bombed as a decoy measure.

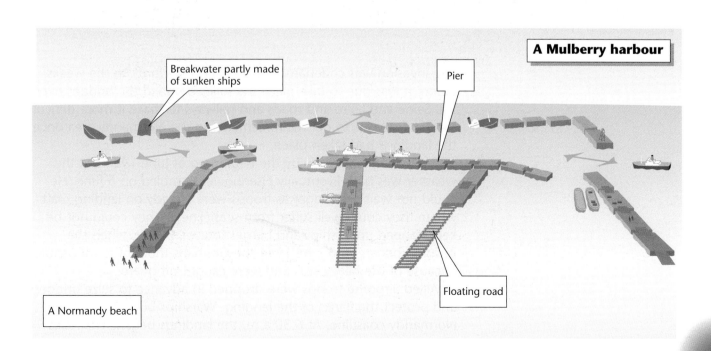

A Mulberry harbour

Breakwater partly made of sunken ships

Pier

Floating road

A Normandy beach

D-Day

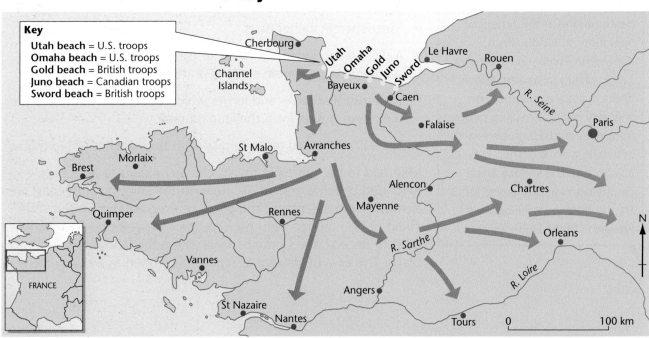

Key
Utah beach = U.S. troops
Omaha beach = U.S. troops
Gold beach = British troops
Juno beach = Canadian troops
Sword beach = British troops

The invasion was codenamed 'Operation Overlord'. In the weeks before it was due to take place the Allies bombed the bridges over the Seine and Loire and roads and railways to make it more difficult for the Germans to get reinforcements to the Normandy area once the landings had taken place.

Everything was ready by the beginning of June 1944 but the weather was bad. Eventually Eisenhower gambled on 6 June. He could not wait any longer as troops were already on landing craft where they could well suffer from seasickness. They could not be kept cooped up in ships and barges forever. In fact, when the invasion began on 6 June 1944 the Germans thought it impossible because of the heavy seas and were caught off guard.

Allied airborne troops were dropped in advance to seize bridges and protect the flanks of the landing. Warships bombarded the Normandy coastline. At 6.30 a.m. the landings began. The Allies landed on five beaches, each of which had a code name. The Americans called their two beaches Utah and Omaha. The British and Canadians called their three beaches Gold, Juno and Sword.

On four of the beaches the landings went well, with limited German resistance. On Omaha beach, however, the Americans came up against a top division of the German army there on a training exercise. There were 3000 American casualties in the first few hours until the beach was secured.

Caught off guard and pinned down by the Allied command of the air, the Germans could not prevent the landings and the establishment of a firm bridgehead large enough to protect the 'harbours' from gunfire.

SOURCE B

US Army report on Omaha landings

As the landing craft reached the beach they faced heavy shelling, machine gun and rifle fire. It came from the cliffs above the beach. Men were hit as they came down the ramps of the landing craft and as they struggled through the defences towards the land. Many others were killed by mines.

SOURCE C

Newspaper headlines for D-Day, 6 June

SOURCE D

The Overlord Embroidery was made in 1968

THE BREAK-OUT

6 June	At the end of the first day the Allies had captured ten kilometres of beach. More and more soldiers poured on to the beaches. Then they moved away and set off inland. The Mulberry harbours and Gooseberry piers were brought across the Channel and put in place. This enabled the Allies to land far more vital supplies and equipment.
27 June	Cherbourg was captured and gave the Allies a port. In the first three months after D-Day the Allies landed four million tons of supplies and nearly half a million vehicles.
8 July	After five weeks of bitter fighting the Allies captured Caen.
15 August	A second invasion was launched in the south of France. It achieved surprise and quickly advanced up the Rhone valley. In less than a month it joined up with the Allied armies in the north.
25 August	Paris was entered.
3 September	Brussels was liberated.

WHY WAS D-DAY A SUCCESS?

ALLIED STRENGTHS

- Thorough preparations since 1942, including training of troops and the build-up of supplies and equipment.

- Leadership of Eisenhower who turned the Allied armies into a 'team'.

- The location of the landings was kept a secret.

- Allied control of the air and sea. This meant the landing craft were free from attack.

- The use of the air force to bomb communications in the Normandy area and slow down German reinforcements to the area.

- The lessons of Dieppe – no attack on defended ports.

GERMAN WEAKNESSES

- The Germans had lost control of the air space over Normandy.

- They had to defend a long French coastline and were bound to be weak in certain areas.

- They were taken in by the Allied bombings of the Calais area and thought the attack would take place here.

- They were slow to send reinforcements to the Normandy area. On the day of the invasions Hitler was still convinced it was a decoy and that the real landings would be near Calais. This gave the Allies precious time to establish a bridgehead and not be driven straight back into the sea.

SOURCE E

German General Rundstedt

I had over 3,000 miles of coastline to cover from the Italian front in the south to the German border in the north. I only had 60 divisions with which to defend it. Most of them were low-grade divisions.

Activity

Using the example of Source **C**, design a front page of a British newspaper for 7 June 1944.

Questions

1 Why did the Allies choose:
a Normandy for the landings on D-Day?
b Eisenhower as overall commander?
2 What point is the cartoonist trying to make in Source **A**?
3 Explain the preparations for D-Day.
4 What does Source **B** tell you about the landings on Omaha beach?
5 How reliable is Source **C** as a view of D-Day?
6 There were several reasons for the success of D-Day. Which do you think was the most important? Give reasons for your answer.
7 Is Source **D** useful to an historian studying the Normandy landings?

VICTORY IN EUROPE 1944–45

The Allied advance towards Germany slowed down in the later months of 1944, for several reasons. Firstly the Allies, as they advanced, moved further away from their supply base at Cherbourg. Although they captured Antwerp in August it could not be used as a port until the German batteries controlling the mouth of the Scheldt estuary were taken at the end of November.

The British and Americans also disagreed about the speed of the advance. Churchill wanted to reach Berlin before Stalin. He feared a Communist take-over of Eastern Europe, but Roosevelt ignored his warnings. The leading British general, Montgomery, suggested a single Allied blitzkrieg through the Low Countries and towards Berlin. This would break through while the Germans were still disorganised. Eisenhower decided instead to keep the Allied armies in line and to close up to the Rhine on a 'broad front'. As a result, progress was slow and this gave the Germans a chance to recover.

The Arnhem operation

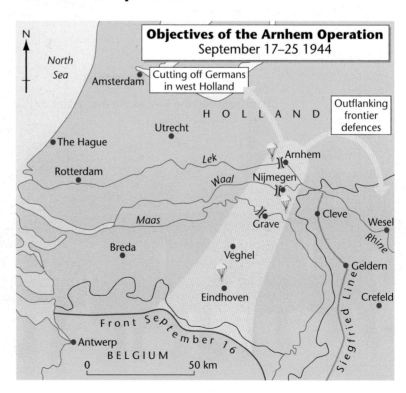

Objectives of the Arnhem Operation
September 17–25 1944

Montgomery was given one opportunity to quicken the advance. The aim was to parachute troops behind the Germans in west Holland and outflank the German Siegfried defences. Thirty-five thousand men with vehicles, guns and equipment were landed from the air on 17 and 18 September at Eindhoven, Nijmegen and Arnhem. They were to seize important bridges over the Maas and Lower Rhine until ground forces arrived.

The ground advance linked up with the Americans at Eindhoven and Nijmegen, but failed by a narrow margin to reach the British at Arnhem. After a week's desperate fighting they had to withdraw with the loss of half their troops.

The general but slow advance towards the Rhine continued, and by the end of November Metz, Strasbourg and Belfort were in Allied hands.

Battle of the bulge
December 16th 1944 to January 18th 1945

B E L G I U M
Aachen
Liége
Monschau
Meuse
Malmédy
Namur
Stavelot
St Vith
Charleroi
Marche
Dinant
Rochefort
Laroche
GERMANY
Houffalize
Bastogne
Vianden
Libramont
Wiltz
Echternach
Trier
N
Arlon
Sedan
Luxembourg
FRANCE
LUXEMBOURG
Montmédy
0   50 km

Key
→ German thrusts
→ Allied counterattacks
— Front December 15th
— Furthest advance

The Battle of the Bulge

This was Hitler's last gamble to avoid defeat. By extending the age-limits of military service to 16 and 50 he raised three-quarters of a million extra troops. He concentrated his limited resources of oil, tanks and aircraft on one last offensive. Hitler wanted to repeat the success of the Ardennes in 1940. This was the junction of the British and American armies. The aim was to break through to Antwerp, separate the Allies and force them to agree to peace.

SOURCE A

Hitler recruited the very young and old for the German army

On 16 December 1944, 30 German divisions attacked the Americans and almost broke through. The Americans were taken by surprise and driven back 40 miles in places. German success was due to:

- Surprise. The Americans were relaxing and did not expect a German attack.

- December mists, which meant that American planes failed to detect the German build-up.

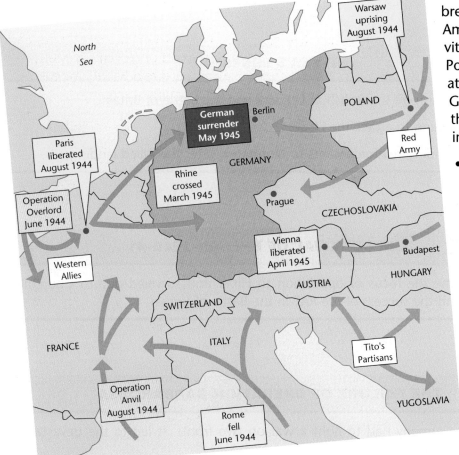

However, there was no German breakthrough to Antwerp. American troops held on to the vital road-centre at Bastogne. Powerful forces were moved up to attack the bulge created by the German offensive. Nevertheless, the Battle of the Bulge had important results:

- It further delayed the Allied advance to Berlin. It took until the end of January to recover the lost land.

- Hitler had used up his last reserves of planes and tanks. They could not be replaced.

- It meant that Russian troops would reach Berlin first.

Crossing the Rhine

Not until March was the Rhine crossed, when the Americans seized a bridge at Remagen. General Patton forced a crossing near Mainz on 22 March and Montgomery one near Wessel the day after. The German armies began to disintegrate.

The Russian Front

The Germans had been on the retreat since the defeat at Stalingrad in January 1943. By the end of 1944 the Russians had cleared the Germans out of the USSR and liberated Poland, Romania, Bulgaria and Yugoslavia. Warsaw was taken in mid-January 1945, Budapest a month later and East Prussia was overrun by early April.

25 April	Russian forces finally encircled Berlin. Eisenhower decided to halt the Allied advance on the line of the River Elbe.
30 April	Hitler shot himself in his underground headquarters in Berlin.
2 May	Berlin fully in the hands of the Red Army.
5 May	German forces in the West surrendered.

STRENGTH OF THE GRAND ALLIANCE

- Britain could be used as a base for the invasion of France and the bombing of Germany.
- The USSR had vast reserves of manpower.
- The USA gave wealth, resources and fighting forces.

Between 1941 and 1945 Hitler faced the two most powerful countries in the world.

HITLER'S MISTAKES

- Failure to finish off the British at Dunkirk and the Battle of Britain.
- Fateful decision to attack the USSR.
- Delay in sending reinforcements to Normandy after the Allied landings.

THE SURVIVAL OF BRITAIN 1940–41

Britain became the focus of opposition to Hitler and survived due to Churchill's leadership and the success of the RAF in the Battle of Britain.

THE FAILURE OF OPERATION BARBAROSSA

This meant Germany had to fight a war on two fronts. It led to the devastating defeat at Stalingrad.

ALLIED AIRPOWER

By 1944 the Allies had total control of the air. This meant they could bomb Germany and protect the Allied landings and advance.

D-DAY LANDINGS

These diverted German forces from the Eastern Front and brought about the liberation of France and the Low Countries.

From a modern history textbook

There was often disagreement between Hitler and his generals. He was always suspicious of them. He refused to delegate authority to them and preferred to play off one against another. There was little agreement between the generals themselves and Hitler preferred to keep it that way.

Activity

Copy the following table and decide the importance of each reason suggested for the German defeat. Give each one a score from 1 (not very important) to 5 (extremely important).

Score	Reasons for German Defeat
	Invasion of Russia
	D-Day
	Grand Alliance
	British survival
	Airpower
	Hitler's mistakes

Which do you think was the most important reason? Explain your answer.

Questions

1 Why was the Allied advance on Germany delayed 1944–5?
2 What effects did the following have on the Allied advance:
  a the Arnhem operation?
  b the Battle of the Bulge?
3 What does Source **B** tell you about the reasons for Germany's defeat?

THE HOME FRONT

Once the war broke out the British government greatly increased its powers by passing the Emergency Powers Act. This gave it almost unlimited power over people's lives in order to run the war. Government involvement in people's lives was deeper and more closely planned than during the First World War.

Recruitment

The government had announced the introduction of conscription after Hitler's invasion of Czechoslovakia in March 1939. It was put into effect when Britain declared war on 3 September. All men between the ages of 18 and 40 were conscripted for military service, beginning with those in their early twenties. Certain occupations, such as coalminers, firemen and doctors, were exempt from military service.

In May 1940 the Local Defence Volunteers, later known as the Home Guard and nicknamed 'Dad's Army', was formed. This was part-time, unpaid volunteer work to help protect the country against invaders. It called for men aged 17 to 65 to volunteer. On the first day 250,000 volunteers were recruited.

In the following year all women aged between 19 and 30 were conscripted. They chose between the Women's Land Army, women's sections of the armed forces and work in factories.

Censorship and propaganda

The Ministry of Information was responsible for propaganda and censorship. It tried to keep in touch with the people through an organisation called Mass Observation whose members carried out surveys and reported on conversations they had heard in shops and pubs.

Propaganda was used in several ways:

- Poster campaigns to encourage people to join the voluntary services and work hard in order to help the war effort.

- Posters were produced that warned people of the dangers of 'careless talk'. There was a fear that German spies could be working in the country so people were told not to discuss the war in public.

- Posters encouraged people to save for the war effort and not to waste. The 'squander bug' became a regular feature of messages to the housewife.

Newspapers were censored by the government during the war. They reported on the bombings but concentrated on the heroism of the rescuers rather than the deaths and injuries in an attempt to keep up morale. The government banned the publication of the *Daily Worker* in 1941 when it claimed that the war was being fought for the benefit of the bosses.

Rationing

At the outbreak of war Britain grew only enough food to feed about one person in every three. Much food was imported but, as during the First World War, these imports were threatened by the activities of the German U-boats.

The government introduced a series of measures to ensure there was an adequate supply of food. Rationing was introduced as early as January 1940. Each person had a ration book filled with coupons which they used to buy the amount of food they were entitled to each week. A points system was introduced later to give people greater choice in what they could buy. The Board of Trade also issued recipes showing people how to make healthy meals using food that was available.

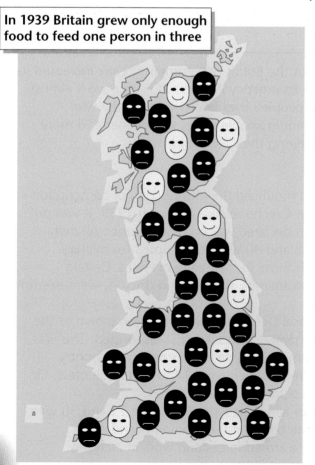

In 1939 Britain grew only enough food to feed one person in three

Focus on	
Wartime recipe	1 cup of breadcrumbs
	½ cup of dried fruit
	1 cup of grated carrot
	1 cup of grated potato
	1 teaspoon of bicarbonate of soda
	2 tablespoons of hot water
This pudding is supposed to taste better than Christmas pudding.	Mix all of this together and put it into a pudding bowl and steam for two hours.

At first only butter, bacon and sugar were rationed. Later this was extended to include tea and most basic foodstuffs, although vegetables were never rationed.

Clothes were rationed from 1941 which led to shorter hemlines and fewer buttons on clothing to save on materials. The government also encouraged people to save by mending their own clothes and to use cheaper, more basic clothes and furniture.

SOURCE B

Menu for a week

	Breakfast	*Lunch*	*Tea*
Monday	Porridge with black treacle, no milk	Jam sandwiches	Corned beef stew with soya bean dumplings followed by bread and peanut butter
Tuesday	Porridge as usual	Potato crisp sandwiches	Whalemeat and carrots and potatoes followed by suet pudding
Wednesday	Porridge as usual	Cheese sandwiches	Dried eggs scrambled followed by stewed apples
Thursday	Porridge as usual	Potato crisp sandwiches	Baked potatoes followed by cake made with dried eggs
Friday	Porridge as usual	Spam sandwiches	Liver, one sausage and potato followed by bread and butter
Saturday	One slice of bacon and a piece of fried bread	Bread and cheese	Dried egg omelette with cabbage and potatoes followed by carrot flan
Sunday	One slice of bacon, fried egg and fried bread	One lamb chop with carrots and potatoes followed by blackberry and apple pie	Potato pie followed by bread and butter and jam

SOURCE C

Cartoon characters were part of the campaign to encourage people to eat healthy food

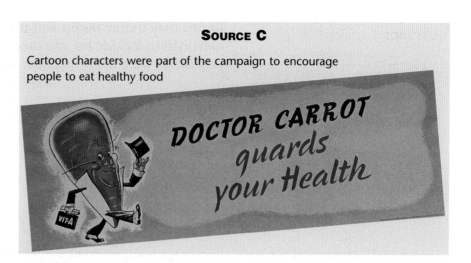

DOCTOR CARROT guards your Health

VIT-A

'Dig for Victory'

People were asked to grow their own food so that less food would have to be imported.

SOURCE D

Poster encouraging people to help the war effort

DIG FOR VICTORY

SOURCE E

The writer George Orwell reported:

Most people are better fed than they used to be. I can't help feeling that people in London look healthier than they used to. There are less fat people. For instance, with the adult milk ration of 3 pints a week, the amount of milk being drunk has actually increased since the war started.

> **Activity**
>
> Using Source **B** as a guide, draw up your own healthy menu guide for a family during the Second World War.

Questions

1 Explain examples of government use of propaganda during the Second World War.
2 How useful are Sources **C** and **D** to an historian studying the Second World War?
3 What was the 'Dig for Victory' campaign?
4 According to Source **E**, did rationing bring any benefits?

Window boxes, lawns, public parks and golf courses were used to grow vegetables to keep the nation fed and healthy. Even the moat of the Tower of London was turned into an area for allotments.

People were also encouraged to keep small animals. Hens and rabbits were the favourites. Goats were kept in large back gardens. Pigs were also popular as everybody loved bacon and ham. Pigs clubs were formed and members shared the cost of buying the pigs and looking after them.

Evacuation

The government expected that the Germans would attack Britain from the air, so it took precautions to protect its civilians from bombings and gas attacks. Children were protected by being moved (evacuated) from the likeliest targets, the cities, to the countryside where they could be safe. The first evacuation was announced on 31 August 1939, the day before Hitler invaded Poland.

Many parents were reluctant to be separated from their children but accepted they would be safer in the country. Parents were told what the children needed to take with them and where they were to assemble for evacuation. The evacuation began on 1 September. Many city schools were closed and many teachers went with the children to the countryside to carry on teaching them.

At their destinations the evacuees gathered in village or school halls where they were chosen by the foster family they were to live with. Homesickness and the 'Phoney War' saw many children drift back to the cities by Christmas 1939. When German bombers starting blitzing London in 1940 a second evacuation from the cities took place, although this was not on the scale of the one in 1939.

SOURCE A

A government poster trying to persuade parents not to bring their children back from the countryside

TAKE THEM BACK! TAKE THEM BACK! TAKE THEM BACK!..

DON'T do it, mother—

LEAVE THE CHILDREN WHERE THEY ARE

Was evacuation a success?

Copy the following chart.

EVIDENCE FOR SUCCESS	EVIDENCE AGAINST

Source B

A Woman's Institute report on evacuees in 1940

Except for a small number the children were filthy. They were unbathed for months. One child was suffering from scabies and the others had dirty septic sores all over their bodies. Their clothing was in a terrible condition. Some of the children were literally sewn into their ragged garments.

Source D

One London child remembers the experience of evacuation

Everything was so clean. We were given towels and tooth brushes. We'd never cleaned our teeth till then. And hot water came from the tap. And there was a lavatory upstairs. And something called an eiderdown. And clean sheets. This was all very odd. And rather scary.

Using the following sources and evidence, complete the chart and decide whether you think evacuation was a success or failure.

Source C

Children being evacuated

Source E

Three very young children being evacuated in September 1939

Types of people evacuated in September 1939

Types of evacuees	Number of evacuated
Schoolchildren	827,000
Mothers and under 5s	524,000
Teachers and helpers	103,000
Pregnant women	13,000
Handicapped people	7,000

SOURCE F

The film actor Michael Caine remembers his evacuation with his brother

Clarence and I used to sleep together and poor Clarence used to wet his bed because he was a nervous kid. She (the foster mother) could never tell who'd done it so she used to bash the daylights out of both of us. So, of course, the more Clarence got hit the more he wet the bed. It was then we started to get locked in the cupboard.

SOURCE H

Beryl Hewitson describes what happened to her when she was evacuated

We were told to sit quietly on the floor while villagers and farmer's wives came to choose which children they wanted. Eventually only my friend Nancy and myself were left – two plain, straight-haired little girls wearing glasses, now rather tearful. A large, happy-looking middle-aged lady rushed in asking: 'Is that all you have left?' A sad, slow nod of the head from our teacher. 'I'll take the poor bairns.' We were led out of the hall and taken to a farm where we spent two years.

SOURCE G

A Gateshead evacuee remembers

I was evacuated from Gateshead because it was thought it would be bombed. It was not. I was sent to Dudley in the Midlands. Dudley was bombed while I was there.

SOURCE I

Ted Cummings, who was evacuated from Manchester to Sandbach in September 1939, describes his experiences

We left feeling sad for our parents and afraid that they would be killed by bombs. When we arrived in Sandbach we were chosen for a variety of reasons. For the extra income they received for us, to help on the farm or with the housework. A few were very lucky because they lived with families who really cared for them. For those, life was like a holiday and they did not want to leave. I was upset because I was separated from my sister. I was glad when I returned home in time for Christmas, but the following September I was evacuated with my school to Blackpool.

SOURCE J

From C. Bayne-Jardine, *World War Two*, 1968

The evacuation of children from danger spots in the towns showed the public that slum conditions still existed in Britain. The result of this was that the government was encouraged to provide better conditions. Cod liver oil, blackcurrant extracts and, later, concentrated orange juice from the United States were given out free of charge at food offices and welfare centres.

SOURCE K

From T. Hewitt, J. McCabe and A. Mendum, *Modern World History*, 1999

The children had mixed experiences. Some were very happy, helping on farms and eating better than they had ever done. Others had a miserable time. Some were seen as a burden by foster families. They also missed their own families, far away in the cities. Many country families, unaware of how town children lived, were in for a shock. They had to deal with children who wet their bed and children who had no experience of using a knife and fork to eat with.

Activity

Imagine that you are an evacuee. Design an advert stating the sorts of things you would like and would not like in your new home. You could include:

- The way you are treated when you finally arrive after your journey.
- The process of being selected.
- Experiences in the foster home.
- Keeping in touch with/returning home.
- Things to remind you of your parents and real home.

Questions

1 Why were children evacuated?
2 How well does Source **A** get its message across? Explain your answer.
3 Source **K** is from a recent textbook. Is it more reliable than Source **F**, from someone who experienced evacuation?
4 How useful is Source **E** to an historian studying evacuation?
5 Why did many children return home by Christmas 1939?

Women and the war

Women were greatly affected by the Second World War:

- They were in much greater danger from bombing raids.

- Many were affected by the evacuation of their children and themselves.

- They had to cope with rationing and food shortages.

- Many of them did civil defence jobs, joined the armed forces and the Women's Land Army.

Industry was short of workers because men were conscripted to serve in the armed forces. At first women volunteered to do the work of men. By 1941 industry was so short of workers that unmarried women were conscripted. Within two years 57% of workers were female. By 1943 nine out of ten single women were doing war work, and so were many married women. Some worked in industry, and those who worked in dangerous conditions, such as in the munitions industry, were well paid. Men were usually better paid for doing the same jobs but, even so, women were earning a lot more than before the war.

SOURCE A

A painting by an official war artist, showing a woman working in an engineering factory

SOURCE B

Clement Attlee, the Deputy Prime Minister, writing about the work women did during the war

This work the women are performing in munitions factories has to be seen to be believed. Precision engineering jobs which a few years ago would have made a skilled turner's hair stand on end are performed with deadly accuracy by girls who had no industrial experience.

The Women's Land Army

SOURCE D

From an interview with Lily Halford, a member of the Women's Land Army

I was called up in 1941. I did not mind being called up. I think all of us were eager to do some kind of war work. I chose the Land Army because I always liked gardening and decided to apply for a job to do with the horticultural side of the Land Army.

On the land there was a shortage of workers because men had joined the armed forces. About 80,000 women joined the Women's Land Army to make up the difference. They were given lodgings in remote areas, sometimes with basic conditions. Many women travelled the country doing everyday farm jobs, such as haymaking, ploughing, harvesting and looking after the animals.

Women's armed forces

The number of women involved in uniformed services	
Auxiliary Territorial Service	198,000
Land Army	30,000
Civil Defence	375,000
Armed Forces	470,000

Women who were conscripted after 1941 could choose one of three organisations:

- ATS – the Auxiliary Territorial Service.

- WAAF – the Women's Auxiliary Air Force.

- WRNS – the Women's Royal Naval Service.

These forces helped the men by doing backroom jobs rather than fighting. They worked alongside men and faced the same dangers, but they did not fire the guns. They operated searchlights or acted as radar controllers. Women pilots were allowed to ferry the planes from the factories to the airfields. Other organisations were the Civil Defence and Women's Voluntary Service.

By 1944 there were 450,000 women working in these three armed services. Many women worked as mechanics, welders, carpenters and even gunners on anti-aircraft guns. However, traditional attitudes towards women remained. Most women in the services worked as cooks, cleaners or secretaries.

Effects on the position of women

Life for many women had been very strict during the 1930s. The clothes shortages led to shorter dresses and skirts. There was a shortage of younger men at home, and there tended to be more freedom in sexual relationships. Some women argued that with all the dangers and worries of wartime they should be allowed to enjoy themselves.

The government did not commit itself to equal pay for women. An Equal Pay Commission was set up in 1943 and reported in 1946. It had no powers to make recommendations. The Ministry of Health refused to set up nurseries, arguing that female employment was only for the duration of the war. By 1944 there were, however, 1,450 nurseries, compared to 104 before the war. These were closed down after the war to help force married women to give up their jobs and go back to their homes.

When the war ended, fewer women wanted to work. Many saw work as a wartime emergency and believed their proper place was in the home. They had delayed having children because of the war and now wanted to start families. The war did, however, bring some change in attitudes towards married women working. In the 1950s some of these women did find work when their children were growing up.

Source F

One woman's memory of married life after the war

After a while we settled to some sort of married life but there were times when I thought it was a hell on earth, I was living it. Many of us felt as though we were going back to prison.

Source E

Mona Marshall, a nursemaid before the war and a steelworker during it

To be honest, the war was the best thing that ever happened to us. I was as green as grass and terrified if anyone spoke to me. I had been brought up not to argue. My generation of women had been taught to do as we were told. At work you did exactly as your boss told you and you went home to do exactly as your husband told you. The war changed all that. The war made me stand on my own two feet.

Activity

Make a comparison between the part played by women in the two world wars. Refer to p. 110 for women in the First World War. Copy and complete the following chart.

	Similarities	Differences
Work		
Armed forces		
Land army		
Social changes		
Gains after war		
How recruited		

Questions

1. Why were women needed during the Second World War?
2. Explain the Women's Land Army and armed services.
3. What attitude is shown by Attlee in Source **B**?
4. Why do you think Source **A** was painted? Is it a reliable view of women's work during the war?
5. What differences are there between Sources **E** and **F** in their view of the effects of the war on women's lives? Why do you think they are different?
6. Did women benefit from the war?

Civil defence

This refers to the defence of Britain against invasion and air attack. At the start of the war, everyone was issued with a gas mask which they had to carry with them wherever they went. Many people volunteered to join vital home defence services such as the ARP (Air Raid Precaution) wardens and the AFS (Auxiliary Fire Service).

There were almost half a million recruits as Air Raid Wardens at the start of the war. They were key figures in the event of a bombing raid, ensuring there was calm, that people knew how the raid was progressing and that people were helped after the raid.

The government also supplied its citizens with air raid shelters. The first shelters were delivered in February 1939. These were Anderson shelters which were sunk in the ground in the back garden. They had enough room for a family and were safer than staying in a house.

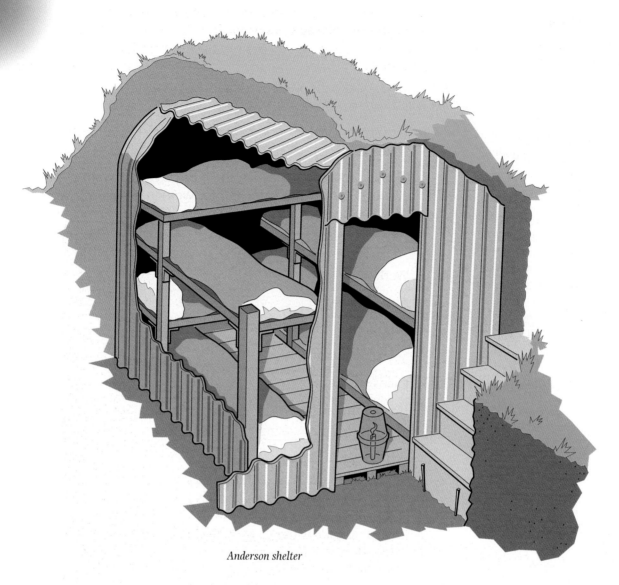

Anderson shelter

Later in 1941, the Morrison shelter was introduced. This could be erected indoors and 500,000 had been distributed by the end of the year.

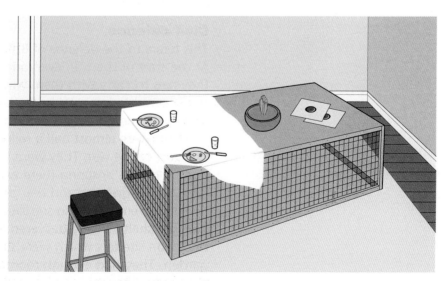

Morrison shelter

At first, people in London were not allowed to use the underground railway stations for fear they would get trapped underground. But public pressure to use them forced the authorities to give way and they became popular places to shelter.

SOURCE A

An extract from an interview with a Londoner remembering the early days of the Blitz

People would rush to get to the tubes, almost knock you down to get to the escalator. We lived like rats underground. People spread newspapers on the floor to show it was their territory. Sometimes you'd get people squaring up and fights.

SOURCE B

Elephant and Castle Underground Station during the Blitz, 11 November 1940

The 'blackout'

The 'blackout' had the most immediate effect on the British people. So that German bombers could not see cities from the air, and therefore bomb more easily, people had to ensure that no light was visible from their homes. Failure to do so meant a visit from the Air Raid Warden.

Streetlights were not lit and cars had to drive without lights. This led to many accidents. In December 1939 over 1500 people were killed on British roads. This was nearly three times the pre-war average of 600 deaths per month. Many people fell into canals or from railway platforms.

Restrictions were eased later in the war, so that civilians could use dimmed torches in the streets and car drivers could use dimmed headlights. To assist pedestrians and drivers, kerbs and roadsides were painted black and white.

IN THE **BLACKOUT**

To hail a bus or tram shine a torch on to your hand

Activity

Write a letter to an American friend in 1940 explaining the changes in civil defence brought about by the war, especially air raid shelters and the 'blackout'.

Questions

1 Why did the government establish air raid shelters and introduce the 'blackout'?

2 Using the two diagrams, explain the differences between the Anderson and Morrison shelters. Which would you have preferred and why?

3 Why did the 'blackout' lead to so many accidents?

4 What point is the poster (Source C) trying to make? How successful is it?

THE BATTLE OF THE ATLANTIC

Winston Churchill admitted that the only thing that worried him during the Second World War was the Battle of the Atlantic. This was the term used to describe the U-boat threat in the Atlantic where 2700 Allied merchant ships and more than a hundred warships were torpedoed.

Germany had almost won the First World War in 1916 and 1917 by cutting off Britain's supplies from the USA. From the start of this war Admiral Doenitz, the German U-boat commander, decided to sink any ships going in and out of the British Isles.

At the outbreak of the Second World War, the British government took control of all merchant ships. Their crews, the Merchant Navy, were civilians and not part of the Royal Navy. All merchant ships had to sail in convoys.

Each convoy had an escort of naval ships. In September 1939 the Germans had 57 U-boats, although only 22 had the range and speed for use in the Atlantic. This was not enough to pose a serious threat. By 1942, however, they had become a serious threat.

SOURCE A

Winston Churchill, *The Second World War*

The Battle of the Atlantic was the key feature of the War. Never for one moment could we forget that everything happening elsewhere on land, sea or in the air depended on its outcome.

SOURCE B

Admiral Doenitz

Britain's ability to maintain her supply lines is the decisive factor for the outcome of the war.

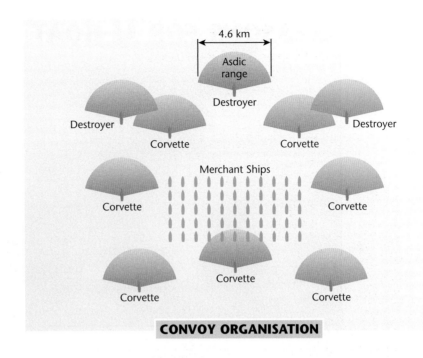

CONVOY ORGANISATION

Reasons for U-boat success, 1939–42

Allied losses reached a peak in 1942. In the first six months 586 ships were sunk by U-boats. With the ships went the vital and costly cargoes of war material and food, and often the merchant seamen, on which the survival of Britain depended.

% of total war losses

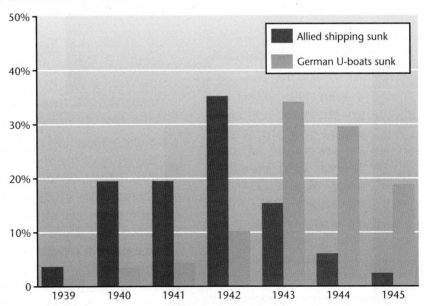

REASONS FOR U-BOAT SUCCESS

U-BOAT BASES

From the middle of 1940 the Germans could use bases along the whole coast of Europe, from northern Norway to the Spanish frontier. This greatly increased the range over which they could operate and the difficulty of intercepting them.

'WOLF-PACK' TACTICS

The U-boat commanders worked out new tactics to bewilder convoy escorts and confuse their direction-finding devices. From the summer of 1941 the German captain sighting a convoy no longer went immediately into a lone attack. Instead, he signalled U-boat headquarters about the position and speed and direction of the convoy, and headquarters moved other U-boats into the same sea-lane. A group of U-boats, nicknamed a 'wolf-pack', gathered and attacked the convoy in numbers. The escort vessels were unable to cope with such attacks.

MID-ATLANTIC GAP

Air cover for convoys proved very effective but Britain did not have aircraft with the range to cover the whole Atlantic, even after the entry of the USA in December 1941. This left an area of the mid-Atlantic known as the 'black gap' where there was no air cover.

AMERICAN ENTRY

In December 1941, the entry of the USA into the war again changed the situation. With the whole of America's eastern seaboard to plunder, the U-boats went on the rampage. The United States was slow to bring in convoys and their ships were often silhouetted at night against the bright lights on shore.

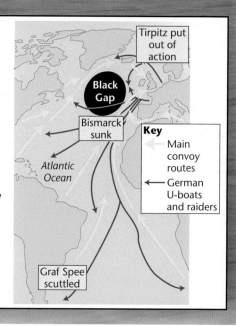

Reasons for Allied success, 1943–45

The turning point in the Battle of the Atlantic came in 1943. By this time the USA was launching far more tonnage than the U-boats could sink. Indeed, the Allies were building four times as many ships as were sunk. The Germans, however, could not replace their increasing number of losses. In the eleven months from June 1943 the average of U-boats sunk was 36. New tactics were introduced in mid-1942, including the convoy system. The British also introduced new 'Hunter-killer' groups of ships that went with the convoys to seek and destroy U-boats, even if this meant leaving the convoy. They also built more destroyers and corvettes to escort the convoys.

Aircraft played an important role. In 1943, 273 U-boats were sunk, many by aircraft. From July 1942 small radar sets began to be fitted in British aircraft, some fitted with searchlights to illuminate the target when found at night. In October the mid-Atlantic gap in Allied air cover was at last closed when Portugal allowed the use of bases in the Azores. The US 'Liberator' aircraft kept watch in the western Atlantic.

SOURCE C

The 'Liberator' played a key role in the defeat of the U-boat menace

Technology proved the key to success in the Battle of the Atlantic. From the beginning of the war British escort vessels had been fitted with ASDIC, a device using sound waves to bounce off U-boats under water, and which were then displayed on board the warship.

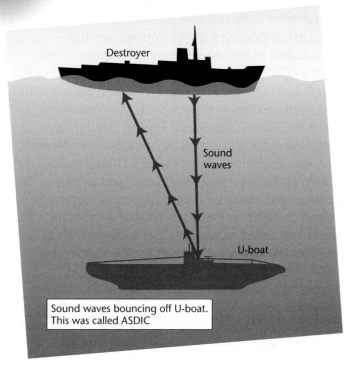

Destroyer

Sound
waves

U-boat

Sound waves bouncing off U-boat.
This was called ASDIC

When the destroyer had found the U-boat, it could drop its depth charges, or, later in the war, a device called the 'Hedgehog' which threw explosive motor shells down onto the submerged U-boat.

The High Frequency Direction Finding system, known as 'Huff Duff', enabled the Allies to pinpoint a U-boat's position from its radio transmissions. Of most importance was the development of 'Ultra', the result of a British system used to decode 'Enigma'. 'Enigma' was a German machine used to transmit secret radio messages in code. The British were able to decode messages between wolf-packs and intercept the U-boats.

The anti-submarine campaign was so successful that the German U-boat fleet was temporarily withdrawn from the North Atlantic in the summer of 1943.

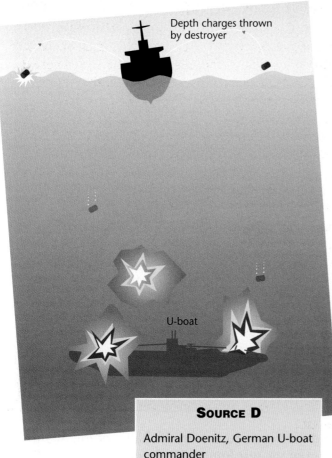

Depth charges thrown
by destroyer

U-boat

SOURCE D

Admiral Doenitz, German U-boat commander

At the present time it is not a victory but the survival of boats and their crews that must come first.

Activity

1   Copy the following chart

Anti-U-boat measures	Rating				
	1	2	3	4	5
ASDIC					
Depth charges					
Huff Duff					
Aircraft					
Radar					
Ultra					
The Azores					

2   Give each measure a rating of importance in the Battle of the Atlantic, with 1 decisive to 5 unimportant.

3   Explain the reasons for your ratings.

4   What was the key measure? Explain your answer.

Questions

1 According to Sources **A** and **B**, how important was the Battle of the Atlantic?
2 Explain at least three reasons for the early success of the German U-boats.
3 Did the entry of the USA help the campaign to defeat the U-boats?
4 What were the following:
   a ASDIC?
   b Huff Duff?
   c Enigma?
   d Ultra?

THE WAR IN THE FAR EAST 1941–45

On 7 December 1941 Japan attacked the US naval base at Pearl Harbor in Hawaii. Eight battleships were destroyed and 2600 Americans killed. This sparked off conflict in the Far East. The following day, President Roosevelt declared war on Japan. At first the Japanese were very successful and conquered huge areas but this was short lived. From 1943 the Japanese armed forces were on the retreat, before finally suffering defeat in 1945.

Reasons for war in the Far East

Japan wanted to create an empire in the Far East. The main obstacle to Japanese expansion was the USA. The attack on Pearl Harbor was an attempt to knock the USA out of the war before it had even started. The military government believed that Japan would have to fight the USA sooner or later and so decided to strike while the USA was unprepared.

The Japanese already occupied large areas of Asia in 1941. In 1931 the Japanese army had invaded Manchuria (p. 136), which was part of China. In July 1937 the Japanese army invaded northern China. Shanghai and other Chinese cities were bombed into submission. Britain and the USA gave large loans to the government of China.

Japan, however, demanded that the British and Western countries should give up supporting China and support the 'new order' in the Far East. The new order was the 'Greater East Asia Co-prosperity Sphere'. In fact, this was to be nothing more than a Japanese Empire to provide living space for Japan's growing population.

Relations with the USA came to a head in July 1941 when Japan invaded the French colony of Indo-China. The Americans responded by cutting off all supplies of oil to Japan. The USA was the main supplier of oil to the Japanese.

SOURCE A

Speech by member of the Japanese government, 5 November 1941

In the first few months of war it is very likely that we would achieve total victory. I am convinced that we should take advantage of this opportunity. We shall use the high morale of the Japanese people and their determination to overcome the crisis facing our country, even at the risk of losing their lives. It would be better to attack now than to sit and wait while the enemy puts more and more pressure upon us.

Pearl Harbor

The attack on Pearl Harbor was a daring raid because it involved the Japanese force sailing more than 3000 miles before launching its attack. US intelligence discovered the force's movements and decoded its messages but failed to warn Pearl Harbor in time. When the Japanese attacked at 8 a.m., they achieved total surprise.

SOURCE B

The *West Virginia* ablaze at Pearl Harbor

The damage inflicted by the Japanese attack on Pearl Harbor

		Destroyed or damaged
Battleships		8
Cruisers and other warships		11
Aircraft		188
Casualties	Dead or missing	3,219
	Wounded	1,272

SOURCE C

Newspaper report on Pearl Harbor, *Honolulu Star – Bulletin*, 7 December 1941

Oahu was attacked at 7.55 this morning by Japanese planes. The 'Rising Sun' sign of Japan was seen on plane wing tips. Wave after wave of bombers streamed through the clouded morning sky from the south-west. They fired their missiles on a city resting on a peaceful Sunday morning. Within 10 minutes the city was in uproar. Bombs fell in many parts of the city and in defence areas. Witnesses said they saw at least 50 planes over Pearl Harbor. Some enemy planes were reported shot down.

Early Japanese success 1941–42

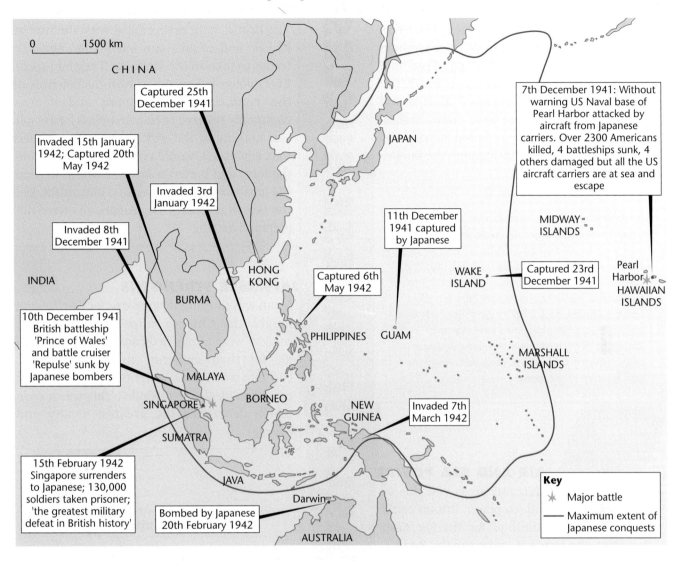

0 — 1500 km

CHINA

Captured 25th December 1941

Invaded 15th January 1942; Captured 20th May 1942

Invaded 3rd January 1942

Invaded 8th December 1941

INDIA

10th December 1941 British battleship 'Prince of Wales' and battle cruiser 'Repulse' sunk by Japanese bombers

BURMA

HONG KONG

Captured 6th May 1942

PHILIPPINES

MALAYA

SINGAPORE

BORNEO

SUMATRA

15th February 1942 Singapore surrenders to Japanese; 130,000 soldiers taken prisoner; 'the greatest military defeat in British history'

JAVA

Bombed by Japanese 20th February 1942

Darwin

AUSTRALIA

JAPAN

11th December 1941 captured by Japanese

GUAM

NEW GUINEA

Invaded 7th March 1942

7th December 1941: Without warning US Naval base of Pearl Harbor attacked by aircraft from Japanese carriers. Over 2300 Americans killed, 4 battleships sunk, 4 others damaged but all the US aircraft carriers are at sea and escape

MIDWAY ISLANDS

WAKE ISLAND

Captured 23rd December 1941

Pearl Harbor

HAWAIIAN ISLANDS

MARSHALL ISLANDS

Key

★ Major battle

— Maximum extent of Japanese conquests

After Pearl Harbor the Japanese forces moved with bewildering speed. By mid-1942 they had successfully taken:

- The American island bases of Guam and Wake.

- The British colonies of Hong Kong, Malaya and Singapore.

- The Philippines, Borneo and Burma.

- The Dutch colonies of Sumatra and Java.

JUNGLE WARFARE

Many of the places where the Pacific war was fought were areas of jungle. This was unfamiliar territory for most Allied troops and the Japanese were far better equipped and trained to fight there than their opponents. The Japanese soldiers who captured Malaya and Singapore, for instance, wore light clothes, carried little equipment, and used bicycles and river boats to move swiftly through the jungle.

SOURCE D

An American general, Eichelberger, described what it was like to fight in jungle areas

The men were more frightened by the jungle than by the Japanese. There is nothing pleasant about sinking into foul-smelling bog up to your knees or lying in a slit trench, half submerged, while a tropical rainstorm turns it into a river. Jungle night noises were strange to Americans. In the moist hot darkness the rustling of small animals in the bush was easily mistaken for the quiet approach of the enemy.

AIR AND SEA POWER

Japanese success over vast areas was due to their superior air and sea power. Britain could only spare two battleships for the Far East. These two, the *Prince of Wales* and the *Repulse*, were sunk by air attack on 10 December 1941. The Japanese used aircraft from aircraft carriers to destroy enemy shipping. Britain did not have aircraft carriers in the Far East.

SOURCE E

A British soldier in Singapore

The Japanese Zero fighters were complete masters of the air over Singapore. They made rings round our Hurricanes, which had recently arrived in crates. They were flown by half-trained pilots. Soon there were no Hurricanes left.

SURPRISE

The swiftness of the Japanese attacks gave the British and Americans little time to prepare.

REASONS FOR EARLY JAPANESE SUCCESS

ALLIED WEAKNESSES AND MISTAKES

The British were preoccupied with the war in Europe and could spare few planes, ships or troops to take on the Japanese. They had spent £60 million before the war on the defences of the peninsula of Singapore and it was commonly believed to be a first-class fortress. It was nothing of the sort. The British assumed that any attack would come from the sea and the forts and batteries faced seaward. Instead the Japanese attacked overland and outflanked the British defences. The Americans were not prepared for war.

JAPANESE STRENGTHS

Japan was thoroughly prepared for war, having fought the Chinese since 1937. Japanese soldiers were totally dedicated and prepared to die for their emperor. To them, Emperor Hirohito was a god. As fighting men they lived up to the ideals of 'bushido'. This was a code which demanded the greatest loyalty and courage.

Activity

Design the front page of the following two newspapers reporting on the attack at Pearl Harbor. Include headlines, reports on damage, eyewitness accounts and reactions of the people in Japan or the USA.

Newspaper in Japan.
Newspaper in the USA.

Questions

1   Using Source **A** and your own knowledge, explain why Japan attacked the American fleet at Pearl Harbor.
2   Which would be more useful to an historian studying the attack of Pearl Harbor, Source **B** or Source **C**?
3   What can you learn from Sources **D** and **E** about the reasons for early Japanese success?

Japanese retreat and defeat 1942–45

The initial Japanese success did not last and from the end of 1942 Japanese forces were being forced back.

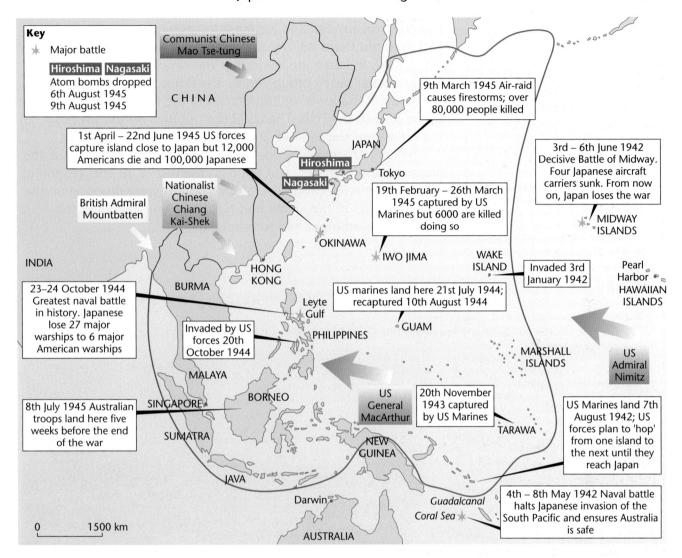

Key
* ✳ Major battle
* Hiroshima | Nagasaki
  Atom bombs dropped
  6th August 1945
  9th August 1945

Communist Chinese Mao Tse-tung

CHINA

9th March 1945 Air-raid causes firestorms; over 80,000 people killed

JAPAN

1st April – 22nd June 1945 US forces capture island close to Japan but 12,000 Americans die and 100,000 Japanese

Hiroshima
Nagasaki
Tokyo

3rd – 6th June 1942 Decisive Battle of Midway. Four Japanese aircraft carriers sunk. From now on, Japan loses the war

Nationalist Chinese Chiang Kai-Shek

British Admiral Mountbatten

19th February – 26th March 1945 captured by US Marines but 6000 are killed doing so

MIDWAY ISLANDS

OKINAWA

IWO JIMA

WAKE ISLAND

Invaded 3rd January 1942

Pearl Harbor
HAWAIIAN ISLANDS

INDIA

23–24 October 1944 Greatest naval battle in history. Japanese lose 27 major warships to 6 major American warships

BURMA

HONG KONG

Leyte Gulf

PHILIPPINES

US marines land here 21st July 1944; recaptured 10th August 1944

GUAM

Invaded by US forces 20th October 1944

MARSHALL ISLANDS

US Admiral Nimitz

8th July 1945 Australian troops land here five weeks before the end of the war

MALAYA

SINGAPORE

BORNEO

SUMATRA

US General MacArthur

20th November 1943 captured by US Marines

TARAWA

US Marines land 7th August 1942; US forces plan to 'hop' from one island to the next until they reach Japan

JAVA

NEW GUINEA

Darwin

Guadalcanal
Coral Sea

4th – 8th May 1942 Naval battle halts Japanese invasion of the South Pacific and ensures Australia is safe

AUSTRALIA

0   1500 km

The turning point was the battle of Midway Island in June 1942. US intelligence was able to break the Japanese military code and knew they intended to occupy Midway Island. Four Japanese aircraft carriers were sunk. This convinced the Japanese High Command that the war would be lost. News of the losses was never published during the war.

'Island-hopping'

The US army developed the strategy of 'island-hopping' as it tried to reoccupy the chain of islands captured by the Japanese. Instead of attempting to invade every island, they left some alone, leaving the Japanese garrison isolated. Even so the US forces suffered very heavy losses.

The war in the Pacific lasted another three years as Japanese forces refused to surrender and fought to the finish on almost every island. On Leyte, in the Philippines, the Japanese garrison of 80,000 fought to the last man. When the first two Japanese islands – Okinawa and Iwo Jima – were attacked, the Japanese defenders cemented themselves into bunkers on the hillsides and refused to come out. Some 28,000 US marines were killed capturing the islands.

By summer 1945 almost all Japanese conquests in the Pacific had been recaptured and Japanese forces were retreating in South-East Asia, but there still remained the prospect of an invasion of Japan itself. In Japan the leadership was divided between the 'war group' and a 'peace group' led by the Prime Minister Suzuki. The government made secret approaches to the USSR to act as a go-between with the USA. The USSR did not pass on this proposal but the Americans learned of it through their intelligence service.

The new American President, Harry Truman, decided to use the atomic bomb as a means of bringing the war to an end as soon as possible. On 6 and 9 August, atomic bombs were dropped on the Japanese cities of Hiroshima and Nagasaki. Within a week the Japanese government had surrendered.

SOURCE A

An account by an American soldier who fought at Guadalcanal, August 1942

We surrounded the Japanese in the valleys. The Japanese were tough fighters. They would never give up. We cut off the remains of a Japanese regiment. After we had surrounded them we used loud-speakers to try to get them to surrender. But they kept fighting. We had to go in the valleys and kill them. They would not surrender.

SOURCE B

John Hersey, a journalist, talked to some of the survivors in Hiroshima soon afterwards. One person he talked to was Rev. Tanimoto, a Methodist minister.

Fearful for his family and church, Tanimoto ran to find them along the Highway. He was the only person making his way into the city. He met hundreds and hundreds who were fleeing. Every one of them seemed to be hurt in some way. The eyebrows of some were burnt off and their skin hung from their faces and hands. Some were vomiting as they walked. Many were naked or in shreds of clothing.

SOURCE D

A Japanese woman, Sadako Moriyama, recalled her experiences in an air raid shelter shortly after the bomb exploded over Nagasaki

I was in the shelter and was petrified with horror when I saw two foul, croaking, lizard-like monsters crawl into the shelter mouth. I was even more terrified when the light revealed them to be human beings. In a pathetic heap on the sand-pit outside were four children who had been chasing dragon-flies a few moments before, now naked and burned, the skin hanging from their fingertips like gloves turned inside out.

SOURCE C

The centre of Hiroshima after the atomic bomb

Should the USA have used the atomic bomb?

ARGUMENTS FOR

◆ The 'war party' in Japan was still in control and had rejected peace terms.

◆ The Americans would suffer huge casualties if they tried to invade Japan. Many Japanese were prepared to fight to the death as a matter of honour. Japan still had four million troops and 4800 kamikaze pilots for suicide missions. Advisers told President Truman that if the war lasted until 1946 there would be at least one million more casualties.

◆ The USA and Britain feared Stalin intended to move into the Far East just as he had moved into Eastern Europe (p. 235). The longer the war against Japan lasted, the more chance he would have. On 8 August Soviet troops attacked the Japanese in Manchuria hoping to share victory with the USA.

◆ Normal bombing of Japanese cities would probably have brought more casualties than the use of the atomic bomb. The American bombing campaign between March and August 1945 had destroyed a quarter of Japanese houses in firebomb attacks.

◆ The Japanese surrendered within a week of the second bomb being dropped.

◆ The cost of the project. The USA had spent millions of dollars developing the bomb. It had been successfully tested in July and was ready for use.

ARGUMENTS AGAINST

◆ The Americans need not have dropped the bombs on mainly civilian cities. They could have attacked a military target or even demonstrated its destructive power on a waste area of Japan. This would have been enough warning to make the Japanese surrender.

◆ The 'peace party' in Japan was known to want to discuss peace terms. The only stumbling block was the Allied refusal to guarantee the position of the Emperor.

◆ Japan had already been defeated using conventional weapons. The atomic bomb made no difference.

◆ The atomic bomb was a terrible weapon to use. It caused appalling casualties both directly and through radiation sickness. When the Americans dropped the atomic bomb on Hiroshima, at the very centre of the explosion the heat was so great that anything caught in it turned from a solid to a gas. Further out, people were burnt alive. The explosion created a wind of 800 kilometres an hour that crushed many people. But in many ways the worst damage was caused by radiation. It caused the flesh to dissolve and hang down in strips. 80,000 were killed, rising to over 138,000 as a result of radiation sickness. In Nagasaki, 40,000 were killed, rising to over 48,000.

◆ The atomic bomb was not dropped to force the surrender of Japan but as a warning to Stalin and stop Soviet expansion in the Far East.

◆ It started a far more destructive Arms Race in the years after 1945.

◆ It was one of the causes of the Cold War – Stalin was very annoyed that the Americans refused to help the USSR to develop its own atomic weapons.

Reasons for Japanese defeat

There were several reasons for the Japanese defeat:

Collapse of the Japanese economy

US submarines sank more than 75% of Japan's merchant ships and US bombing destroyed Japanese homes and factories. By 1945 many people were starving and industrial production had collapsed.

Air- and seapower

At the naval battles of Coral Sea, Midway Island and Leyte Gulf the Americans gained command of the sea and air. This was essential for successful operations in the Pacific Islands. The American bombing campaign of March to August 1945 forced millions to abandon the cities to seek shelter and food in the countryside. This left factories without enough workers and greatly reduced industrial output.

Overstretched resources

Japan's rapid conquests meant that it had too large an area to control and defend. It had no allies.

Superior resources

The USA was able to produce more aircraft, aircraft carriers and weapons than Japan.

New tactics

The British and the Americans gradually trained their troops in jungle tactics. In 1943 the British demonstrated this with Brigadier Wingate's advance deep into Japanese-held territory in Burma. Supplied entirely by air, his columns could travel light and move rapidly. Once air supremacy had been established in early 1944 the British were able to make advances, especially in Burma.

The dropping of the atomic bombs

Although some military commanders wanted to fight to the last, this persuaded the Emperor Hirohito to surrender. He did not know that the Americans had no more atomic bombs.

Activities

1   You are a British reporter arriving in Hiroshima some time after Japan's surrender. Write a broadcast describing what you saw and whether you believe the bomb should have been used.

2   Make a copy of the following table.

Japanese weaknesses	Neither	Allied strengths

Decide which of the reasons given for Japan's defeat belong in which column.

a   Try to link some of the reasons.

For example, American bombing helped to weaken the Japanese economy.

b   What do you think was the most important reason for Japan's defeat? Explain your answer.

Questions

1   What was 'island-hopping'?
2   What can you learn from Source **A** about Japanese resistance?
3   What differences are there between Sources **E** and **F** in their views of the reasons for the dropping of the atomic bombs?
4   Why do you think they have different views?
5   How reliable is Source **G** as a view of the dropping of the atomic bomb?
6   Do you think the Americans were right to drop the atomic bombs in August 1945? Give reasons for your answer.

Summary and Revision

EARLY GERMAN SUCCESS 1939–40

In this section, you will need to understand:
- Blitzkrieg – how it was carried out and why it was so successful.

- Reasons for German success in Poland, September 1939.

- The 'Phoney War' 1939–40.

- The German invasion of Norway, British mistakes April 1940.

- German success in the Low Countries and France May to June 1940.

- Dunkirk – how the evacuation was carried out and whether it was a success.

- The fall of France.

Revision questions

1 Explain the main tactics used in Blitzkrieg.
2 Why was Poland defeated so quickly in 1939?
3 What was the 'Phoney War'?
4 Describe the German invasion of Norway. Why was British aid a failure?
5 What happened in the Ardennes in mid-May 1940?
6 Describe the Dunkirk evacuation. What happened to France in June 1940?

BRITAIN ALONE 1940–41

In this section, you need to know reasons for British survival including:

- The leadership of Churchill.

- American aid, especially Lend-Lease.

- British victory in the Battle of Britain.

- The Blitz and why it failed.

Revision questions

1 What qualities did Churchill have as a wartime leader?
2 How did the USA help Britain in the period 1940–41?
3 Why did Hitler need control of the air over Britain?
4 Explain the following British strengths and German weaknesses in the Battle of Britain:
    a   radar.
    b   British fighter planes.
    c   German bombers.
    d   changes in German attacks.
5 Why did Hitler decide to bomb British cities? Did he achieve his aims?

THE RUSSIAN FRONT 1940–43

This section includes:

- Why Hitler invaded Russia in 1941.

- Early German successes in Operation Barbarossa.

- The German situation by the end of 1941.

- German mistakes in 1942.

- Events at Stalingrad 1942–43 and the German surrender.

Revision questions

1 Explain the early German success in the invasion of Russia. Why did they advance so quickly?
2 By November 1941 the German advance had stopped. Why?
3 What mistakes did the Germans make in the invasion of Russia 1941–42?
4 Describe the German advance on Stalingrad and attempts to capture the city.
5 Why did the German army surrender in January 1943?
6 What effects did the Russian Front have on
   a   Britain's position in 1941?
   b   Germany's position in 1943?

THE INVASION OF FRANCE JUNE 1944

In this section, you will need to understand:

- Why the invasion was delayed 1942–44.

- The preparations and why Normandy was chosen.

- The landings on the five beaches.

- Why the landings were a success.

Revision questions

1 Why was Stalin keen for the Allies to invade France?
2 What lessons were learnt from the failure of the Dieppe raid of 1942?
3 Describe the Allied preparations for D-Day.
4 How successful were the landings on 6 June 1944? Name the five beaches.
5 Why were the Germans unable to stop the landings?

THE ALLIED ADVANCE TO VICTORY 1944–45

This section includes:

- Reasons for slow advance 1944–45.

- The operation at Arnhem and why it failed.

- The Battle of the Bulge and its effects on the Anglo-American advance.

- The Russian advance in the east.

- The crossing of the Rhine and the Russian entry into Berlin.

- Reasons for the German defeat.

Revision questions

1. What slowed down the Allied advance through France and the Low Countries?
2. Describe the Arnhem operation.
3. Why did Hitler attack the Americans in the Ardennes in December 1944?
4. What effects did the Battle of the Bulge have on:
   a the Anglo-American advance?
   b the German war effort?
5. Describe Russian progress in the east 1943–45
6. Why did Russia reach Berlin before the British and Americans?
7. Explain three reasons for Germany's defeat in 1945.

THE HOME FRONT

In this section you will need knowledge and understanding of:

- Recruitment, especially conscription.

- The uses and importance of propaganda and censorship.

- The organisation of rationing and 'Dig for Victory'.

- The organisation of evacuation and whether it was a success.

- The part played by women in the war and its impact on their position.

- Civil defence, especially air raid shelters and the 'blackout'.

Revision questions

1. When was conscription brought in? What was the 'Home Guard' and how was it recruited?
2. How did the government use posters during the war? What was censored and why?
3. What caused food shortages? Explain:
   a how rationing was organised.
   b what was rationed.
4. Why were many children and mothers evacuated?
5. Describe the organisation of evacuation.
6. What effects did evacuation have on:
   a children being evacuated?
   b foster families?
   c the government?
7. How did women help the war effort in:
   a industry?

b armed services?

c farming?

d What gains, if any, were made by women?

8 What air raid shelters were given out by the government? Why did many Londoners shelter in the underground?

9 What was the 'blackout'?

THE WAR AT SEA

In this section, you need to know:

- The threat posed by the U-boats.

- Reasons for early U-boat success, 1939–42.

- Why the U-boat threat was defeated.

Revision questions

1 What was the Battle of the Atlantic?

2 Give three reasons for early U-boat successes.

3 What part did the following play in the defeat of the U-boat threat:

a ASDIC?

b code-breaking?

c new tactics?

THE WAR IN THE FAR EAST

This section includes:

- Reasons for the Japanese attack on Pearl Harbor.

- Why the Japanese were so successful 1941–42.

- Reasons for Allied victory and Japanese defeat 1943–45.

- Why the USA used the atomic bomb and asks whether they were justified.

Revision questions

1 Why did the Japanese attack Pearl Harbor?

2 Give three reasons for the early success of the Japanese in the Far East.

3 What part did the following play in the Japanese defeat:

a new Allied tactics?

b air and seapower?

5
The Early Cold War 1945–50

UNDERSTANDING THE EARLY COLD WAR 1945–50

The following definitions and explanations should give you a greater understanding of the Early Cold War.

Blockade
When a country is blocked in, or surrounded, preventing supplies getting in.

East and West
Terms used to describe the two sides in the Cold War. East for those that followed the Soviet Union and Communism and West for those who followed the USA and capitalism and democracy.

Free elections
Elections that give the people a real choice between candidates and parties. The voting is secret and the results are not 'fixed'.

Ideology
A set of ideas which reflect the beliefs and interests of a country.

Iron Curtain
First used by Winston Churchill in 1946 to describe the guarded border between the Soviet-controlled countries of Eastern Europe and the West.

NATO
North Atlantic Treaty Organisation. Set up by the Western Powers as a defensive alliance against the spread of Communism.

Satellite states
Term used to describe those countries in Eastern Europe controlled by the Soviet Union.

Superpowers
Term used to describe the two most powerful countries in the world after the Second World War: the USSR and the USA.

Western Powers
The Western democracies, especially the USA, Britain and France.

The Early Cold War 1945–50

In the years after the Second World War rivalry developed between the USA and the USSR. This culminated in the Berlin Crisis of 1948–9.

WHAT WAS THE COLD WAR?

The increasing tension that developed between the two superpowers brought a frosty atmosphere that became known as the 'Cold War'. It started in 1945–6 and lasted for well over 40 years. At first it was confined to Europe but during the 1950s and 1960s it spread worldwide, especially into Asia. The Cold War had most of the features of a proper war:

- there were two rival sides – East v West or Capitalism v Communism or USA v USSR

- there was spying and propaganda on both sides

- it encouraged an arms race.

It was not, however, a proper 'hot' war where the two superpowers actually fought against each other.

THE ORIGINS OF THE COLD WAR

SOURCE A

American and Soviet soldiers shake hands in 1945 at the River Elbe, where the two armies met

COMMUNISM

- Usually a one-party state.

- Industry and agriculture owned by the State. People encouraged to work for the common good.

- Classless society with no individual profit-making.

- The government controlled most aspects of people's lives.

- Strong censorship with restrictions on what could be said or written.

CAPITALISM

- Free elections and more than one political party.

- Most industry and agriculture owned by private individuals.

- They employ workers and keep all profits made.

- Limits on government interference in people's lives.

- Freedom of speech and movement.

In 1941 the USA and the USSR allied to fight against Hitler and Nazism. This was out of wartime necessity, not out of genuine friendship. Indeed, during the war there had been tension between the two superpowers and Britain. This was to intensify in 1945 and after, for three major reasons.

1 Ideology
The two superpowers had conflicting systems of government and their societies were organised around very different ideals.

2 Mutual mistrust
This had built up since 1918.

Western mistrust of the USSR	Soviet mistrust of the West
Communism threatened Western values and way of life.	Communists believed the capitalist system was evil since the rich prospered at the expense of the poor.
Dislike of Stalin's dictatorship which had led to many deaths and the purges of the 1930s.	In 1918–19 Western states had helped the Whites fight against Communism in the Civil War. Churchill had been Secretary for War and had sent British troops.
Stalin had signed the Nazi–Soviet Pact in 1939 and divided Poland.	In 1919 the Allies gave Russian lands to other countries, including Poland. In 1942 Stalin was angry that Britain and the USA refused to invade Europe quickly and thus open up a second front v Hitler and take pressure off Russia.

SOURCE B

Stalin speaking to a fellow Communist, Mjilan Djilas, in 1945

Perhaps you think that, because we are allies of the English, we have forgotten who they are and who Churchill is. They find nothing sweeter than to trick their allies.

3 Conflicting aims in Central and Eastern Europe
The Western Allies supported democracy and wanted to hold free elections in all states in Central and Eastern Europe. They wanted to keep Poland's western boundary where it was. They also wanted to help Germany to produce its own goods and food again and to take part in world trade.

The USSR, on the other hand, wanted to create a 'buffer' zone of friendly states between the USSR and Germany. These states would have to set up Soviet-style governments which was unlikely through free elections. Stalin wanted to redraw

Poland's western boundary and keep Germany weak. This would prevent a future German or Western invasion of Russia.

These differences really began to appear at the two peace conferences at Yalta and Potsdam, in 1945.

Questions

1   Explain, in your own words:
    a   the meaning of the Cold War.
    b   the differences between capitalism and Communism.
2   What does Source **B** show about Stalin's attitude towards Britain?

THE YALTA CONFERENCE

In February 1945 Franklin Roosevelt of the USA, Joseph Stalin of the USSR and Winston Churchill met at Yalta in the Soviet Union. The war in Europe was nearing its end and decisions had to be made about how to organise Europe after the war.

Churchill, Roosevelt and Stalin at the Yalta Conference

Decisions
The Allies decided the following:

- Germany was to be defeated and then disarmed. It was to be split into four zones of occupation – the Big Three plus France. Germany would also have to pay reparations.

- In Eastern Europe countries were to be allowed to hold free elections to choose how they would be governed.

- In Poland free elections were to be held. The eastern frontier was to return to the pre-1921 position.

- The USSR was to join the war against Japan three months after Germany's defeat.

- A United Nations Organisation was to be set up.

Profile of

Harry S Truman

As a US Senator Truman had played an important role in organising the country's war effort. He was, however, largely ignorant of foreign affairs and events in Europe. He saw things in black and white with little room for compromise. He believed the Soviet Union was acting like a bully in Europe and should be made to mend its ways. Unlike Roosevelt, Truman had no intention of working closely with Stalin.

Churchill attended the early stages of the conference but Clement Attlee replaced him after the Labour victory in the 1945 General Election.

Tensions

There were already differences between East and West:

- The Western Allies were concerned because the USSR wanted Poland's western frontier moved into Germany and the German population removed.

- They disagreed over how much Germany was to pay in reparations. Stalin wanted to fix a sum that the West thought was too large. The decision was postponed.

THE POTSDAM CONFERENCE

The Allies met again at Potsdam in July 1945. Roosevelt had died suddenly in April, so the USA was represented by its new president Harry S Truman.

Decisions

- In Germany details of the zones of occupation were finalised. The Nazi Party was to be banned and its leaders tried as war criminals.

- For reparations each power was to collect industrial equipment from its own zone. Since its zone was mainly agricultural, the USSR was to receive additional reparations from the other zones.

- Poland's western boundary was to be along a line created by the Oder and Neisse rivers.

- Germans living in Poland, Hungary and Czechoslovakia were to return to Germany.

Tensions

Despite these decisions it soon became apparent that the divisions between East and West were growing:

- The West was suspicious of Soviet intentions in Eastern Europe. In March Stalin had invited non-Communist Polish leaders to Moscow and then imprisoned them. Communists now held key positions in the Polish government.

- Far more Germans were to be expelled from Eastern Europe than the Western Allies had expected.

- Truman did not tell Stalin that the USA intended to drop an atomic bomb on Japan.

- Truman was highly suspicious of Stalin's motives. He was much less willing to trust the Soviet Union than Roosevelt had been. The Red Army was the biggest in the world. Stalin refused to cut down his armed forces. The Soviet Union was trying to catch up with the USA by developing its own atomic bomb. Truman was also suspicious of Stalin's aims in Eastern Europe. He believed the Soviet leader intended to set up buffer states under the control of the USSR.

Design two propaganda posters:

- One to show the advantages/benefits of Communism and disadvantages of capitalism

- The other to advertise the benefits of Capitalism and disadvantages of Communism.

Questions

1   What was agreed in connection with Germany at Yalta and Potsdam?
2   Why were there differences over Poland?
3   Explain why Truman distrusted Stalin.
4   Compare the two conferences at Yalta and Potsdam.
     a   What similarities were there?
     b   What differences were there?

POST-WAR TENSIONS, JULY 1945–6

These tensions soon appeared in the months after the Potsdam Conference.

POINTS OF TENSION

The atomic bomb
Stalin was annoyed with the USA because:

- Truman had not told him before using the atomic bomb.

- The USA refused to share the secret of how to make such a bomb.

- Stalin was convinced that the USA would use the bomb to win worldwide power.

- He ordered his scientists to develop a Soviet bomb. The USA felt threatened by this.

Eastern Europe
Rather than allowing free elections the USSR began to impose Communist rule on the countries it had occupied (see p. 235).

Germany
Disputes soon arose for several reasons:

- The Western Allies accused the USSR of breaking agreements about what could be taken from Germany as reparations. In 1946 the Russians stopped the arrangements, agreed at Potsdam, whereby they gave the USA reparations from their zones.

- The Western Allies wanted to help Germany to recover as quickly as possible. They now realised that a strong Germany would act as a barrier to Communist expansion. The USSR wanted a weak Germany.

- The Western Allies wanted free elections to be held in all the occupied zones. The USSR blocked moves to do this in their zone.

The 'Iron Curtain' speech, March 1946

In March 1946 Winston Churchill made his famous speech at Fulton, Missouri. The speech declared that Europe was divided into two separate halves by Soviet policy. In the West were free, democratic states. In the East, behind an 'iron curtain', were countries under the domination of Communist parties subject to the Soviet Union. This was a clear statement of 'West versus East'. Stalin accused Churchill of trying to stir up war against the Soviet Union.

SOURCE A

An extract from Churchill's speech at Fulton

From Stettin in the Baltic to Trieste in the Adriatic, an iron curtain has descended across the continent. Behind that lie all the capitals of the ancient states of central and eastern Europe – Warsaw, Berlin, Prague, Vienna, Budapest, Bucharest and Sofia. All these famous cities and their populations around them lie in the Soviet sphere and all are subject to a very high and increasing measure of control from Moscow.

SOURCE B

Stalin's response to Churchill's speech, 1946

Mr Churchill now takes the stance of warmonger and he is not alone. He has friends not only in Britain, but in the United States. As a result of the German invasion, the Soviet Union's loss of life has been several times greater than that of Britain and the USA put together. And so what can be surprising about the fact that the Soviet Union, anxious for its future safety, is trying to see that governments loyal to the Soviet Union, should exist in the countries through which the Germans made their invasion. We are not expansionist.

SOURCE C

'Churchill and his predecessors'. Hitler and Goebbels look on approvingly at a warlike Churchill.

233

SOURCE D

A Cold War joke

A Frenchman, an Englishman and a Russian were debating the nationality of Adam and Eve. The Frenchman said that with all the passion they had, they must have been French. The Englishman said that with the fig leaves, Adam was obviously an English gentleman. No, said the Russian, they must have been Russians. Only a Russian could have only a fig leaf and only an apple and yet believe he was in paradise.

Questions

1   Why did the development of the atomic bomb cause tension between East and West?
2   What differences are there between Sources **A** and **B** in their views of Soviet policy in Eastern Europe?
3   Why are these interpretations so different?
4   Which side produced Source **C**? Why have they produced this cartoon?
5   What is the point of the joke in Source **D**?

SOVIET EXPANSION IN EASTERN EUROPE

Having freed much of Eastern Europe from the Nazis, the Red Army remained in occupation and the Soviet Union established Communist governments that were closely controlled from Moscow. These became known as Soviet satellite states.

The same pattern was followed in each country:

- Coalition governments were set up in which the Communists shared power with other political parties.

- Backed by Stalin, the Communists took over the civil service, media, security and defence.

- Opposition leaders were arrested or forced to flee.

- Elections were held but were fixed to ensure support for the Communists.

- 'People's democracies' were set up.

SOURCE A

This shows the Kremlin's (Soviet government) noose tightening round Czechoslovakia

WHEN THE TIME IS RIPE—

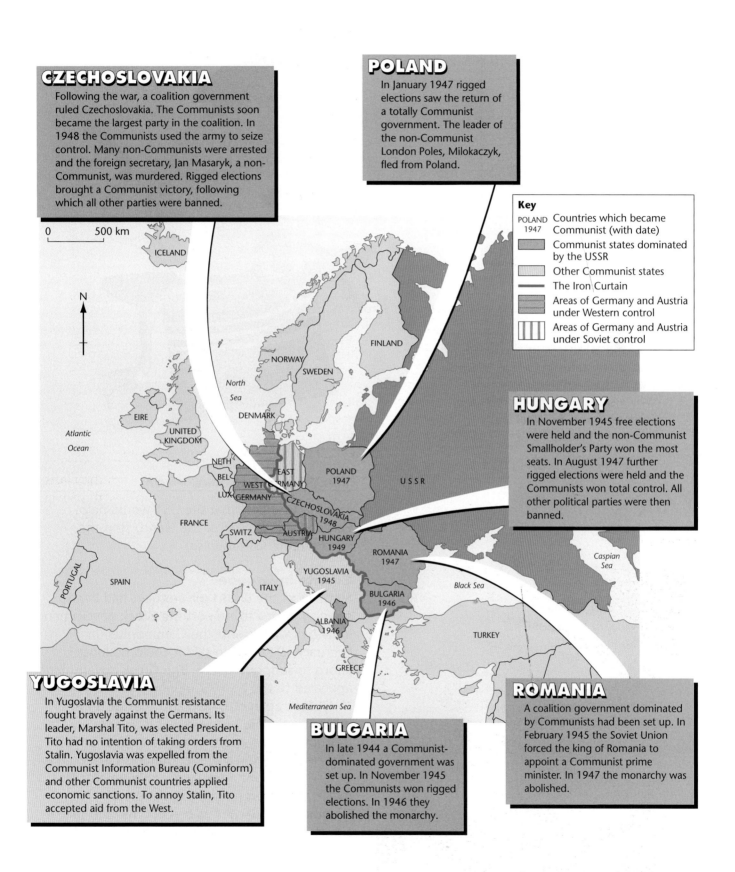

CZECHOSLOVAKIA

Following the war, a coalition government ruled Czechoslovakia. The Communists soon became the largest party in the coalition. In 1948 the Communists used the army to seize control. Many non-Communists were arrested and the foreign secretary, Jan Masaryk, a non-Communist, was murdered. Rigged elections brought a Communist victory, following which all other parties were banned.

POLAND

In January 1947 rigged elections saw the return of a totally Communist government. The leader of the non-Communist London Poles, Milokaczyk, fled from Poland.

Key

POLAND 1947 — Countries which became Communist (with date)

— Communist states dominated by the USSR

— Other Communist states

— The Iron Curtain

— Areas of Germany and Austria under Western control

— Areas of Germany and Austria under Soviet control

HUNGARY

In November 1945 free elections were held and the non-Communist Smallholder's Party won the most seats. In August 1947 further rigged elections were held and the Communists won total control. All other political parties were then banned.

YUGOSLAVIA

In Yugoslavia the Communist resistance fought bravely against the Germans. Its leader, Marshal Tito, was elected President. Tito had no intention of taking orders from Stalin. Yugoslavia was expelled from the Communist Information Bureau (Cominform) and other Communist countries applied economic sanctions. To annoy Stalin, Tito accepted aid from the West.

BULGARIA

In late 1944 a Communist-dominated government was set up. In November 1945 the Communists won rigged elections. In 1946 they abolished the monarchy.

ROMANIA

A coalition government dominated by Communists had been set up. In February 1945 the Soviet Union forced the king of Romania to appoint a Communist prime minister. In 1947 the monarchy was abolished.

Map labels: ICELAND, 0 500 km, N, NORWAY, SWEDEN, FINLAND, North Sea, EIRE, UNITED KINGDOM, DENMARK, Atlantic Ocean, NETH, BEL, LUX, EAST GERMANY, WEST GERMANY, POLAND 1947, U S S R, CZECHOSLOVAKIA 1948, FRANCE, SWITZ, AUSTRIA, HUNGARY 1949, ROMANIA 1947, Caspian Sea, PORTUGAL, SPAIN, ITALY, YUGOSLAVIA 1945, Black Sea, BULGARIA 1946, ALBANIA 1946, TURKEY, GREECE, Mediterranean Sea

Activity

Choose any of the Eastern European countries taken over by the Soviet Union – this could include Poland, Hungary, Bulgaria, Romania or Czechoslovakia.

You live in this country and write to a friend in Britain explaining what has happened in your country since 1945 and your feelings.

Questions

1 How did Stalin ensure the creation of satellite states in Eastern Europe?
2 Was he successful in Yugoslavia?
3 Which side produced the cartoons, Sources **A** and **B**? What is the message of each?

SOURCE B

The central figure is Tito in the hat of the USA

SOURCE A

An extract from Truman's speech

I believe that it must be the policy of the United States to support people who are resisting attempted subjugation by armed minorities or by any outside pressures. I believe that we must help free peoples to work out their own destiny in their own way.

THE TRUMAN DOCTRINE, 1947

This made it clear that the USA would help Europe (and the rest of the world) stop the expansion of Communism.

Events in Greece

Since 1944 the British government had been sending troops to support the Greek government in its civil war against the Communists. In February 1947 Britain said it could no longer afford to support Greece. The Greek government appealed to the USA for money.

Truman agreed to help and provide $400 million in aid. He believed that if one country fell to Communism, those nearby would be at risk. This became known as the 'domino theory'. The USA would adopt a policy of containment. This meant supporting nations in danger of Communist take-over with economic and military aid. He outlined this policy in a speech made in March 1947.

This became known as the 'Truman Doctrine' and was the basis of American policy against Communism for the next forty years.

What were its consequences?

- Greece defeated the Communists.

- The rivalry between the USA and the USSR increased. Truman had publicly stated that the world was divided between two ways of life: the free, non-Communist and the unfree, Communist.

- The USA became committed to the policy of 'containment'.

- Stalin set up the Communist Information Bureau, Cominform, to link Communist parties in Eastern Europe and worldwide, in common action, in 1947.

SOURCE B

A Soviet cartoon shows Europe crushed by the weight of American self-interest

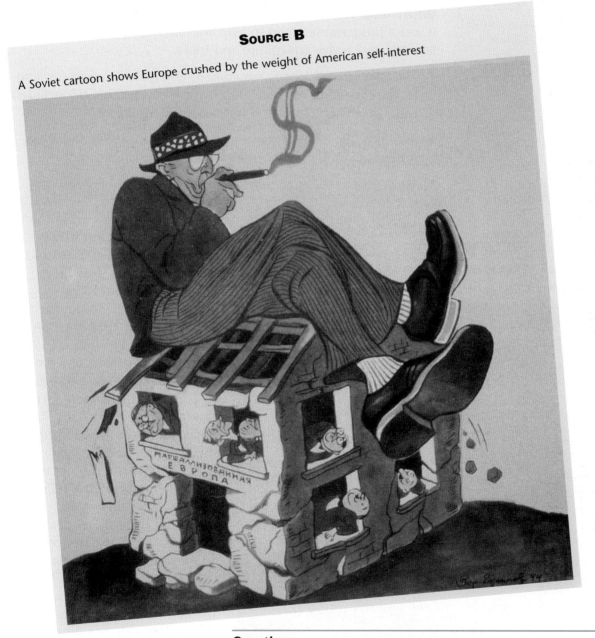

Questions

1   Explain in your own words the 'Truman Doctrine'.
2   What was the Cominform?
3   Is Source **B** for or against the Truman Doctrine?

Truman did not intend to send troops to Europe to fight Communism. Instead he would attack it at its roots. He believed Communism grew in countries where there was poverty. Governments in post-war Europe were struggling to cope with the damage caused by the war. There was still rationing and shortages in many countries. The USA would use its wealth to help Europe recover and prosper. Fewer countries, if any, would be tempted by Communism. The USA realised this policy would also bring their country economic benefits to the USA through encouraging the revival of trade. The plan was announced by the American Secretary of State, General George Marshall, in June 1947.

What was it?

It was a programme of aid to help war-torn Europe to re-equip its factories and revive agriculture and trade.

- The USA offered money, equipment and goods to states willing to work together to create economic recovery. This aid included cash, machinery, food and technological assistance.

- In return, they would agree to buy American goods and allow American companies to invest capital in their industries.

Marshall invited states to meet together and decide how to use American aid.

SOURCE A

General Marshall's view of the purpose of Marshall Aid

The United States should do whatever it is able to do to assist in the return of normal economic health in the world. Without this there can be no political stability and peace. Our policy is directed not against any country or ideal but against poverty, hunger, desperation and chaos. Its purpose should be the revival of a working economy to permit the emergence of conditions in which free institutions can exist.

SOURCE B

Berliners using money from the Marshall Plan to help rebuild buildings destroyed during the war

What were its results?

Sixteen Western European states set up the Organisation for European Economic Co-operation (OEEC) to put the Plan into action. By 1953 the USA had provided $17 billion to help them rebuild their economies and raise their standard of living.

Europe became more firmly divided between East and West. Stalin withdrew the USSR from discussions because he did not trust the USA and did not want to show how weak the USSR really was. He prevented interested Eastern European countries, such as Czechoslovakia and Poland, from becoming involved. He accused the USA of using the plan for their own selfish interests – to dominate Europe and help the American economy.

SOURCE C

The Marshall Plan offers a lifeline to struggling Europe, according to the American cartoonist Fitzpatrick

EUROPE

SOURCE D

The Soviet cartoonist, Krokodil, has the European countries on their knees before the USA, their paymaster

КРОКОДИЛ

Marshall Plan aid to Western Europe

$3.2b UK
$2.7b FRANCE
$1.5b ITALY
$1.4b WEST GERMANY
$1.1b NETHERLANDS
$694m GREECE
$677m AUSTRIA
$556m BELGIUM LUXEMBOURG
$271m DENMARK
$254m NORWAY
$221m TURKEY
$146m IRELAND
$107m SWEDEN
$50m PORTUGAL
$32m TRIESTE
$29m ICELAND

Questions

1 Explain in your own words the reasons for Marshall Aid.
2 Look at Sources **B**, **C**, **D** and the chart above. What does each source show about the effects of the Marshall Plan?
3 Using the evidence from these sources and your knowledge of the Plan, do you agree with Stalin's view that the Plan was set up simply to benefit the USA?

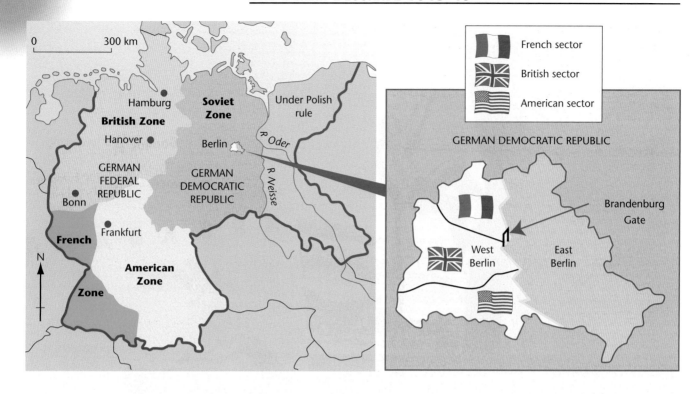

The first major Cold War crisis came in 1948 over Berlin. It had been building up since 1945.

LONG-TERM CAUSES

In 1945 the Allies had agreed to divide Germany into four zones of occupation. These were to be run by a Joint Allied Control Commission. Berlin was also divided into four zones and run jointly. Germany was to be kept as one country and to hold free elections. Soon, however, differences arose over several issues:

Democracy
The USSR gave political authority in its zone to the minority Communists. They tried to force the Socialist majority elected to run Berlin city council to merge with the Communists. The Socialists refused with Western support.

Reconstruction
The war left Germany devastated. Food and fuel were scarce. Thousands were homeless. The USA and Britain wanted to help Germany recover its prosperity as quickly as possible. The USSR, however, objected because it wanted a weak Germany. It refused to allow its zone to trade with the other three.

Berlin
Within the Soviet zone Soviet troops were able to control all access. The Western Allies were allowed access to their sectors by road, rail, canal and air 'corridors'. The USSR believed the Western Allies had no right to be in Berlin. They saw them as a threat because:

- they had a base inside the Soviet zone.
- the capitalist way of life was on show there.

The Western Allies wanted to be there to prevent the USSR controlling the capital. Their presence would also observe Soviet activity behind the Iron Curtain.

SHORT-TERM CAUSES

The Western Allies became increasingly frustrated at the Soviet refusal to help with the economic recovery of Germany, especially in providing much-needed currency. They decided to develop the economy and democracy in their own zones.

The USSR was afraid that a strong, democratic and united Germany would be hostile. They feared that any new 'Western' currency would spread into the Soviet zone. The strong West Berlin currency would undermine that of East Berlin and highlight its relative poverty. This could destroy Soviet control of the economy.

IMMEDIATE EVENTS, 1948

January	The US and British zones merged into one economic unit known as the Bizone.
March	Soviet representatives walked out of the Allied Control Commission complaining that Western attitudes made it unworkable.
1 April	The Western zones were included in the OECC and the Marshall Plan.
April	Soviet troops began to hold up and search road and rail traffic entering Berlin from the Western zones.
1 June	The Western Allies announced plans with France to create a West German State.
18 June	The Allies introduced a new currency in the Western zones.
23 June	The new currency was extended to West Berlin. The USSR introduced its own new currency into the Soviet zone – including Berlin.
24 June	The Soviet Union accused the West of interference in its zone. It cut off all road, rail and canal traffic into the western sectors of Berlin.

STALIN'S MOTIVES

Stalin had several reasons for the blockade. These included:

* To force the Western Allies to pull out of their sectors by starving West Berlin into surrender.
* To make them abandon their plans for separate development of their German zones.

Focus on

Western options

Option	Advantages	Drawbacks	
1 Ignore the Russians and drive through the blockade	• Show the Russians that the West would not bow to blackmail • At the time the Americans possessed the only atomic bombs	• Very high risk of war • Russian forces in Europe far outnumbered those of Western allies	
2 Pull out of Berlin	• Avoid any risk of war • No one would trust the Americans in future to stand firm against Communism	• Loss of prestige for the Western Powers	
3 Supply West Berlin by air	• Less risk of war than option 1 • Risky operation – a daily minimum of 4000 tons of supplies was required	• Enormously costly to supply two million Berliners by air	

HOW TO CLOSE THE GAP?

SOURCE A

American General Lucius D. Clay

If we mean that we are to hold Europe against communism, we must not budge. I believe the future of democracy requires us to stay here until forced out.

The airlift

The Americans and British organised a round-the-clock airlift of essential supplies such as food, fuel and medicines. In 11 months a total of 275,000 flights delivered an average of 4000 tonnes of supplies per day.

As a warning to the USSR, the USA stationed B-29 aircraft capable of carrying atomic bombs in Britain. Despite shortages and hardships, West Berliners supported the Western Allies. They rejected Soviet pressure to become part of one city under a Communist council. On 12 May 1949 the USSR reopened the land routes to Berlin.

Results of the crisis

The Western Powers saw this as a victory. The West had survived and stood up to the Soviet Union. Within a few days the Western Allies announced that their zones would join together to form the Federal German Republic or West Germany.

Stalin's response was to turn the Soviet zone into the German Democratic Republic. Germany was now permanently divided. Relations between East and West had worsened. A state of permanent hostility existed between them. This division was confirmed with the formation of two rival defence organisations – NATO and the Warsaw Pact.

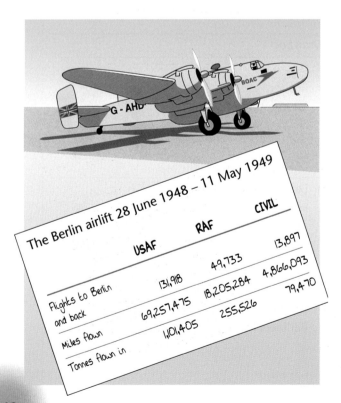

The Berlin airlift 28 June 1948 – 11 May 1949	USAF	RAF	CIVIL
Flights to Berlin and back	131,918	49,733	13,897
Miles flown	69,257,475	18,205,284	4,866,093
Tonnes flown in	1,101,405	255,526	79,470

SOURCE C

A German child's drawing shows the airlift with the words 'We thank the pilots for their work and effort'

SOURCE D

Supplying Berlin from the air

Key

	Areas occupied by the Red Army, May 1945
POLAND 1947	Countries which became Communist (with dates)
	Communist states dominated by the USSR
	Other Communist states
——	The Iron Curtain
◑	Divided cities
	Areas of Germany and Austria under Western control
	Areas of Germany and Austria under Soviet control
– – –	Pre-war boundary of USSR
– – –	Post-war boundary of USSR

SWEDEN

DENMARK

USSR

Berlin

FEDERAL REPUBLIC OF GERMANY

GERMAN DEMOCRATIC REPUBLIC

POLAND 1947

CZECHOSLOVAKIA 1948

Vienna

AUSTRIA

HUNGARY 1949

ROMANIA 1947

YUGOSLAVIA 1945

ITALY

Black Sea

Caspian Sea

BULGARIA 1946

ALBANIA 1946

TURKEY

GREECE

Mediterranean Sea

0   500 km

N

SOURCE E

President Truman

When we refused to be forced out of Berlin, we demonstrated to Europe that we would act when freedom was threatened. This action was a Russian plan to probe the soft spots in the Western Allies' position.

SOURCE F

From a Soviet textbook of 1977

The crisis was planned in Washington, behind a smokescreen of anti-Soviet propaganda. In 1948 there was a danger of war. The conduct of the Western powers risked bloody incidents. The self-blockade of the Western powers hit the West Berlin population with harshness. In the spring of 1949 the USA was forced to give in. Their war plans had come to nothing because of the conduct of the Soviet Union.

Questions

1 Why did the USSR try to force the Allies out of West Berlin?
2 What options did the Allies have to deal with the blockade? Which one did they choose and why?
3 What point is the cartoonist trying to make in Source **B**?
4 How useful is Source **C** as a view of the blockade?
5 What effects did the blockade have on:
   a Germany?
   b the Cold War?
6 Why do Sources **E** and **F** give different interpretations of the Berlin crisis?

Activity

You are a West Berliner who kept a diary during the Berlin Crisis. Write out important extracts from your diary explaining the key events. For example:

• The setting up of the blockade and reactions in West Berlin.

• Conditions in West Berlin due to shortages.

• The Allied airlift.

• The lifting of the blockade.

NATO AND THE WARSAW PACT

The emergence of these two organisations confirmed the Cold War.

NATO

The Western European states feared Soviet aggression. Even joined together they could not match the USSR's power. They needed the support of the USA. The USA was reluctant to be involved in a European military alliance but was persuaded by the Berlin blockade.

NATO was a defensive alliance. It would fight only if attacked. An attack on one member was to be regarded as an attack on all.

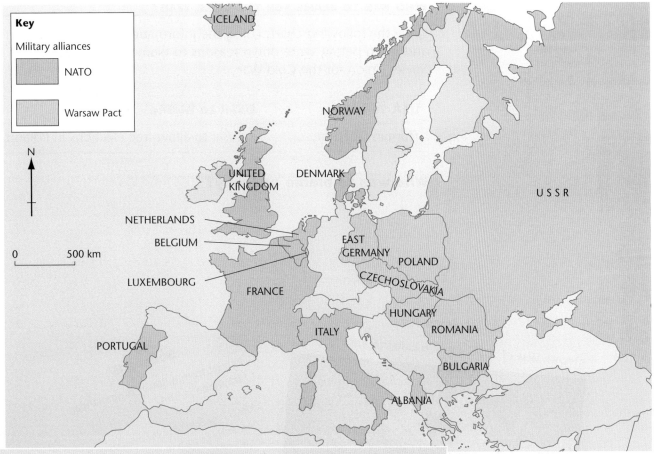

SOURCE A

A Soviet cartoon of NATO generals goose-stepping. Goose-stepping was the German army's method of marching under the Nazi regime.

The Warsaw Pact

The USSR called NATO an 'aggressive' alliance. In response, it set up its own alliance system known as the Warsaw Pact. Members were to support each other if attacked. A joint command structure was set up under the Soviet Supreme Commander.

Questions

1   Using the map above, write down the main members of:
    a   NATO.
    b   the Warsaw Pact.
2   What is the purpose of the Soviet cartoonist in Source A?

Who was to blame for the Cold War?

Copy the following chart. Using the information in this chapter, and given below, write down reasons to blame the USA or the Soviet Union for the Cold War.

USA to blame	USSR to blame
e.g Truman Doctrine	Refusal to allow free elections in Poland

Who was to blame and why?

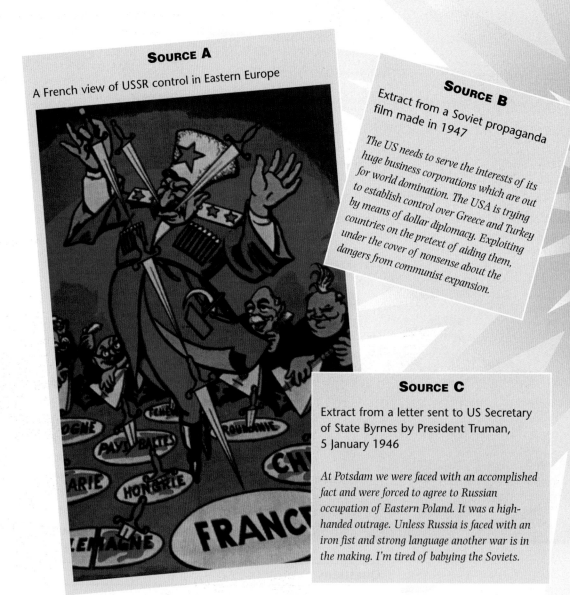

SOURCE A

A French view of USSR control in Eastern Europe

SOURCE B

Extract from a Soviet propaganda film made in 1947

The US needs to serve the interests of its huge business corporations which are out for world domination. The USA is trying to establish control over Greece and Turkey by means of dollar diplomacy. Exploiting countries on the pretext of aiding them, under the cover of nonsense about the dangers from communist expansion.

SOURCE C

Extract from a letter sent to US Secretary of State Byrnes by President Truman, 5 January 1946

At Potsdam we were faced with an accomplished fact and were forced to agree to Russian occupation of Eastern Poland. It was a high-handed outrage. Unless Russia is faced with an iron fist and strong language another war is in the making. I'm tired of babying the Soviets.

SOURCE D

A Soviet cartoon. A fierce dog in a German helmet restrained by a dog lead made of paper. The caption reads 'Do not fear. He is on a chain'.

SOURCE E

Molotov, the Russian Foreign Secretary

Truman decided to surprise us at Potsdam. He took Stalin and me aside and – looking secretive – informed us that they had a secret weapon of a wholly new type, an extraordinary weapon. It's difficult to say what he was thinking, but it seemed to me he wanted to throw us into confusion. The words 'atomic bomb' hadn't been spoken but we immediately guessed what was meant.

SOURCE F

American Senator Arthur Vandenberg, 25 April 1946

I am more than ever convinced that communism is on the march on a worldwide scale, which only America can stop.

SOURCE G

Jan Masaryk, Czechoslovakian non-Communist leader

I went to Moscow as the foreign minister of an independent state.
I returned as a slave of the Soviet Union.

Activity

You are a historian living in the Soviet Union. Write a brief account of the origins of the Cold War. You should use examples from this chapter to suggest it was mainly the actions of the USA that caused the Cold War.

Repeat the above exercise, but this time suppose you are a historian living in the USA.

SOURCE H

Cartoon published in the *Daily Express*, 1949. USA on the left, USSR on the right.

Summary and Revision

This section includes the following:

THE ORIGINS OF THE COLD WAR

- The meaning of the Cold War.
- Long-term differences between East and West, the USA and the USSR.
- The decisions and disagreements at Yalta and Potsdam.

Revision questions

1 What was meant by the Cold War?
2 What were the main differences between Capitalism and Communism?
3 Why did Stalin distrust the other Allied leaders?
4 What were the main decisions reached at Yalta and Potsdam?

POST-WAR TENSION

This includes:
- General reasons for tension.
- Soviet expansion in Eastern Europe 1945–48.
- The Truman Doctrine.
- The Marshall Plan and its consequences.

Revision questions

1 Explain at least three general reasons for East–West tension after 1945.
2 What countries came under Soviet control in the period 1945–48?
3 Why did they fail in Yugoslavia?
4 What was the Truman Doctrine? What was its significance?
5 Describe the Marshall Plan? How did Stalin react to this?

THE BERLIN CRISIS 1948–49

This section includes:
- Long-term differences between East and West over Germany and Berlin, 1945–48.
- The immediate events of 1948 leading to the blockade.
- The Berlin airlift and its effects.
- Results of the crisis on Germany and the Cold War.
- The setting up of NATO and the Warsaw Pact.

Revision questions

1 Explain the differences between the Western Allies and the USSR in:
   a Germany?
   b Berlin?
2 Why did Stalin decide to blockade West Berlin? Why did the blockade fail?
3 What effects did the Berlin crisis have?
4 Why were NATO and the Warsaw Pact set up?

6
The Cold War 1950–63

UNDERSTANDING THE COLD WAR 1950–63

The following explanations and definitions will help you to understand this chapter.

Détente	An easing of tension between two or more countries and a move towards better relations.
ICBM	Inter-Continental Ballistic Missiles. Long-range nuclear missiles.
Peaceful co-existence	Policy carried out by the leader of the USSR in the 1950s. Its aim was to allow the Soviet Union and the USA to live side by side without conflict.
People's Republic of China	The name given to Communist China in 1949.
Sputnik	This is Russian for 'time traveller'. It was the first satellite put in orbit by the USSR in 1957.
Summits	Meetings.
U-2	A Lockheed aircraft used by the Americans to spy on the USSR.
United Nations	This was set up as an international peace-keeping organisation at the end of the Second World War.

The Cold War 1950–63

East–West relations worsened during most of this period. The Cold War spread to Asia with the Korean War and the superpowers came close to a nuclear conflict over the Cuban Missile Crisis of 1962.

THE KOREAN WAR, 1950–53

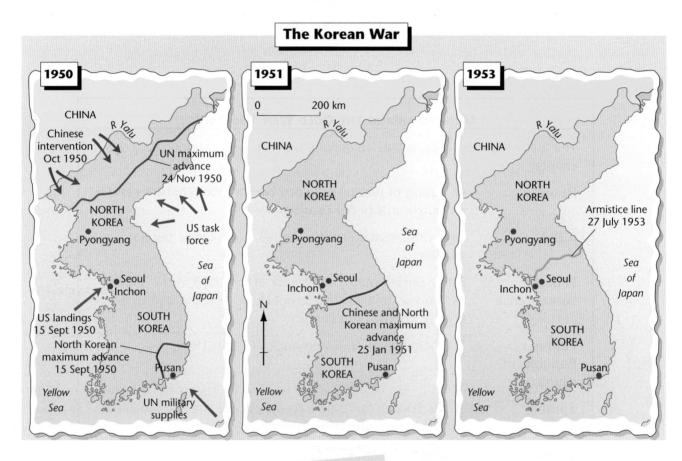

The Korean War

1950

CHINA

Chinese intervention Oct 1950

R Yalu

UN maximum advance 24 Nov 1950

US task force

NORTH KOREA
Pyongyang

Sea of Japan

Seoul
Inchon

US landings 15 Sept 1950

SOUTH KOREA

North Korean maximum advance 15 Sept 1950

Pusan

Yellow Sea

UN military supplies

1951

0   200 km

R Yalu

CHINA

NORTH KOREA

Pyongyang

Sea of Japan

Seoul
Inchon

N

Chinese and North Korean maximum advance 25 Jan 1951

SOUTH KOREA
Pusan

Yellow Sea

1953

R Yalu

CHINA

NORTH KOREA

Armistice line 27 July 1953

Pyongyang

Inchon
Seoul

Sea of Japan

SOUTH KOREA

Pusan

Yellow Sea

On Wednesday 28 June, Americans woke up to headlines telling them that US forces had been ordered to fight in Korea.

Background to the war

In 1945 Japan surrendered to the Allies. Korea, a Japanese colony, was occupied by Soviet troops in the north, American troops in the south. The 38th Parallel (the line of latitude 38 degrees north) divided the two areas of occupation.

In 1947 the United Nations General Assembly decided to hold elections throughout Korea to choose a national government. In the following year the South elected a parliament that in turn set up the Republic of Korea with the capital at Seoul. The USSR set up the People's Democratic Republic of Korea with the capital at Pyongyang. Each government then claimed to rule the whole of Korea. The USA and the USSR withdrew troops but continued to support the two sides with money and weapons.

Meanwhile in 1949 civil war in China had ended with a Communist victory. The Communists set up the People's Republic of China. Stalin and China encouraged the Communist ruler of North Korea, Kim Il Sung, to attack South Korea. They provided aid and military equipment but the Soviets never involved themselves directly. In June 1950, North Korea attacked the South and the Korean War began.

Focus on
_____

The United Nations

The United Nations was set up in 1945 to replace the League of Nations. It had a General Assembly that met every year and a smaller Security Council that met more regularly. The Security Council consisted of the three great powers – the USA, USSR and Great Britain – and elected representatives from the other members of the UN. All decisions taken by the Security Council had to be unanimous. This means that they had to be agreed by the three great powers and the other members. The result was that any one of the great powers could stop any proposal put to the UN that it disliked.

The UN Security Council decided that the North Koreans had broken world peace and called on them to withdraw to the 38th Parallel. The North Koreans ignored this demand. The Security Council met again and called on UN members to help South Korea repel the North Korean attack. It asked the USA to take command of the UN operation.

The USSR was absent from the Security Council in protest against China being represented in the UN by the Chinese Nationalist rather than Communist government. Had it been present it would have vetoed UN involvement. The UN Secretary-General, Trygve Lie, believed North Korea was guilty of planned aggression. He wanted the Security Council to take a strong stand.

The UN response

SOURCE B

Headlines in the *Daily Mail*, 26 June 1950

American involvement

The Americans were frightened of the spread of Communism and the threat to Japan and other non-Communist countries in the Far East. They believed in the 'domino theory' that once one state became Communist, others would soon follow.

Of the sixteen countries who contributed to the UN forces, the USA provided the most: 50% of land forces, 93% of air forces and 86% of naval forces. The UN gave the USA unlimited authority to direct military operations. President Truman appointed General MacArthur as the Commander-in-Chief of UN forces. MacArthur reported to the President and took orders from him.

EVENTS OF THE WAR

June–September 1950	North Korean invasion. The South Koreans were forced back into the area around Pusan.
September–November	MacArthur organised a successful seaborne landing at Inchon that surprised the Communists. UN and South Korean troops drove back the North Koreans. Despite warnings from China not to cross the 38th Parallel, they advanced almost to the Chinese border. MacArthur had disobeyed Truman's orders and approached the Yalu river.
November 1950 to January 1951	The Chinese entered the war. They drove UN forces back again and advanced into South Korea to force them to surrender. MacArthur wanted to use the atomic bomb against China. He was dismissed by Truman.

SOURCE D

This illustration shows Chinese forces in Korea capturing a US tank

1951–53	UN counter-attack in 1951 drove the North Koreans and Chinese back to the 38th Parallel. The two front lines remained roughly along this line until an armistice was signed at Panmunjom in 1953.

MacArthur's dismissal

MacArthur was a popular hero of the Second World War. He enjoyed widespread support in the USA. After a series of secret White House meetings the decision was taken to remove him on 10 April 1951. Truman wanted to limit the war in Korea. He did not want to fight the Chinese. MacArthur had already ignored orders not to approach the Yalu river. Before MacArthur could be told of the decision, the news leaked out in the *Chicago Tribune*. Truman had to call a press conference at one in the morning to make the announcement. MacArthur was furious at the way he had been treated. He returned to the USA to enthusiastic parades wherever he went. Many believed that MacArthur had got 'too big for his britches'.

Results of the Korean War

- In Korea the war led to the death of 1.5 million South Koreans and 3.5 million from the North. Millions more were left homeless and starving. The UN's policy was that Korea should become one country with free elections supervised by the UN. The war did not achieve this. Korea remained divided. The war had, however, stopped North Korean aggression.

- More than 33,000 Americans were killed.

- The UN gained respect because, unlike the League of Nations, it had taken firm action in the face of aggression.

- Many felt that the USA had used the UN in its battle against Communism.

- The Cold War was no longer confined to Europe. It had spread to Asia and now involved China. Mistrust increased between the USSR and the USA when the Americans set up the South East Asian Treaty Organisation (SEATO) as a copy of NATO. It was designed to stop the spread of Communism in Asia.

- The USA saw the Korean War as a success against Communism. It encouraged the Americans to become involved in Vietnam.

SOURCE E

This photo shows a woman and child taking shelter from American heavy bombing of the North

A Soviet cartoon, 1952, shows a bloodied US soldier in Korea and likens him to a Nazi German

Questions

1 According to Source **C**, why did the Americans become involved in the Korean War?
2 Which source, **D** or **E**, would be more useful to an historian studying the events of the war?
3 What effects did the war have on:
   a Korea?
   b the Cold War?
4 What is the purpose of Source **F**?
5 Was Truman right to dismiss MacArthur?

DÉTENTE IN THE 1950s

In the 1950s there seemed to be a thaw in the Cold War. This was known as a period of peaceful co-existence, or détente.

Changes in the USSR

In 1953 Stalin died. After a two-year period Nikita Khrushchev emerged as the new Soviet leader. He was mainly responsible for changes in Soviet policy.

In a speech to the Twentieth Party Congress in 1956 Khrushchev attacked Stalin for his purges and persecution. This had several effects:

- A policy of 'De-Stalinization' began in the USSR and Eastern Europe. This meant removing anything to do with Stalin – such as photos, statues or street names.

Profile on

Nikita Khrushchev

He was born in 1894 in a village in the Ukraine into a very poor family. He served as a political commissar in the Red Army during the Russian Civil War (1918–21). In 1929 his local party sent him to the Stalin Industrial Academy in Moscow. He studied there with Stalin's wife and got to know Stalin. During the purges of the 1930s he rose to the position of second in command of the Moscow party organisation. In 1939 he became a full member of the Politburo. He certainly took part in Stalin's purges (p. 452). Khrushchev had very little education but was a clever politician. Opponents underestimated his cunning which helped him become leader a few years after Stalin's death.

Source A

Crowds pull down a statue of Stalin in Budapest

- In Poland and Hungary this led to violent protest against Soviet rule (see p. 260).

- Western states were encouraged that Soviet leaders recognised the evil of Stalin's government.

- China objected to the speech, especially when Khrushchev said there should be 'different roads to socialism'. The Communist bloc appeared less united.

- Khrushchev changed Communist doctrine by arguing that there need not be a war with the Western Powers. The Communist system would eventually triumph over the capitalist system because it was superior. Meanwhile the two systems could co-exist peacefully. The USSR, however, would continue to compete with the USA.

Results

There was some improvement in East–West relations. It became easier for Western tourists to travel behind the Iron Curtain. In 1959 there was a Summit Conference between Western leaders and Khrushchev. The Soviet leader even visited Britain in 1956 and the United States in 1959.

Despite these improvements in relations, the Cold War continued. East–West suspicions remained. In 1955 the Warsaw Pact was set up. In addition, serious crises continued to flare up such as Hungary (1956) and Cuba (1962).

Questions

1 What was meant by détente?
2 Explain the changes brought about by Khrushchev.

Rivalry between the superpowers increased due to competition in armaments and space exploration.

Why was there a nuclear arms race?

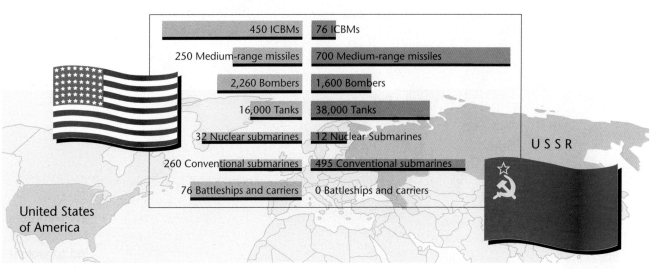

As relations between the USA and the Soviet Union worsened in the years after the Second World War, both sides began to develop their weapons so as to be able to 'outgun' their opponents. This meant:

- developing more powerful weapons.

- trying to build more of each type of weapon than the other side possessed. For example, when the 'Sputnik' was launched, American experts calculated that the USSR would soon have many more missiles than the USA. The USA would then suffer from a 'missile gap'. It therefore poured more money into rocket research.

Both sides developed nuclear weapons for several reasons:

1 They were cheaper than conventional weapons. It was more cost-effective for both sides to build up nuclear weapons than to pay for large armies.

2 Nuclear weapons would act as a deterrent. Each realised that in a nuclear war they would both suffer appalling destruction. Once Inter-Continental Ballistic Missiles (ICBMs) were invented, it was certain that both could retaliate in the event of an attack. The idea was to have so many nuclear weapons that they could not all be destroyed if the other side were to strike first. The enemy would not dare strike first for fear of retaliation. This was known as a situation of MAD – Mutual Assured Destruction.

3 Prestige was also important. Many civilians on both sides saw the Arms Race as a test of the relative strengths of Capitalism and Communism.

1945 USA tests and drops the first atomic (A) bombs.

1949 USSR tests an A bomb.

1952 USA tests its first hydrogen (H) bomb.

1953 USSR tests its first H bomb.

1957 USSR

1 tests an Intercontinental Ballistic Missile (ICBM) capable of carrying an H bomb from the USSR to the USA.

2 puts the space satellite 'Sputnik' into orbit.

1958 USA

1 places Intermediate Range Ballistic Missiles (IRBMs) targeted on USSR in NATO countries. Both sides now capable of direct attacks on each other's cities.

2 launches its own satellite.

1960 USA launches first nuclear-powered submarine capable of firing a Polaris missile with an atomic warhead from underwater.

The failure of disarmament

In 1955 there were high hopes for disarmament. East–West relations had improved. Both Khrushchev and the American President, Eisenhower, wanted to achieve arms reduction to cut defence spending. The USSR proposed:

• a reduction of armed forces.

• the eventual abolition of atomic weapons.

• international inspection to supervise this.

The USA wanted a stronger inspection system. It offered to allow Soviet planes to use aerial photography over the USA to check on weapons' reduction, if the USSR would allow it to do the same. The USSR would not agree to this 'open skies' proposal. The USA rejected the proposals from the USSR.

Attempts again failed at the 1960 Paris Summit due to the U-2 incident (p. 264).

THE SPACE RACE

Khrushchev was keen to take on the USA in the race to explore space. This would increase Soviet prestige and show the superiority of Communist technology. The Soviets launched the first satellite, Sputnik, in 1957. This was a blow to American pride and was the start of a race that was to continue until the 1980s. The effects were worsened by the failure of the Americans to launch their own satellite in the same year.

DAILY HERALD

No. 12992 (D)   Saturday, December 7, 1957   PRICE 2½d

America's Sputnik dies bleeping on the ground

OH, WHAT A FLOPNIK!

Satellite blows up before take-off

By GILBERT CARTER

A MONSTER CLOUD OF FLAME: All that remains of America's bid to launch a satellite.

AMERICA'S much-ballyhooed bid to launch a satellite to join Russia's two Sputniks in space ended yesterday in a huge billow of orange flame—on the ground.

For the tiny 6lb. missile—which will go down in history as the Flopnik—died bleeping a message of failure as its three-stage rocket blew up on the launching ramp.

It happened at Cape Canaveral, Florida, where America's scientific reputation lay at stake because of the world-wide publicity given to this attempt to keep up with the Joneskis.

TEN SECONDS TO DISASTER

The satellite, with its Vanguard launching rockets, was produced in an all-out effort after President Eisenhower ordered a "crash programme" to get some missile, any missile, to orbit the earth.

Yesterday, America's top boffins sheltered in a bunker on the launching site. Thousands of tourists gathered on Florida's sunny beaches staring at the sky. Millions listened on the radio as commentators counted the seconds to zero.

Paul Karpisac, a young propulsion engineer, pressed the firing button that started the rocket engines.

TOPPLED

The Vanguard, its black nose pointing skywards, toppled for a moment but remained on the launching platform.

Belsky's Cartoon

I wonder if I might offer a

...ush by sea | QUIT ORDER TO 50,000 DUTCH

Khrushchev's comments on the success of Communism

The Sputniks prove that communism has won the competition between communist and capitalist countries. The economy, science, culture and the creative genius of people in all areas of life develop better and faster under communism.

The rocket that launched Sputnik was the more immediate threat. A rocket powerful enough to do this could also carry a nuclear weapon to its target. Developments in space technology led to advances in nuclear weapons, in particular ICBMs. By 1960 each side had enough nuclear weapons to destroy the earth.

By the end of the 1950s Khrushchev could argue that the Soviet lead in space proved that Capitalism was not as good as Communism. This seemed reinforced when, in 1961, they put the first man in orbit, Yuri Gagarin.

SOURCE D

Yuri Gagarin, the first man in space

Questions

1 Why did the superpowers decide to develop nuclear weapons?
2 What part did the following play in the Arms Race:
   a Sputnik?
   b ICBMs?
3 How reliable is Khrushchev's view of Communism and Capitalism in Source **C**?

THE HUNGARIAN UPRISING, 1956

In 1956 there was an uprising in Hungary against Soviet control. This was crushed with great brutality by the USSR. The rebellion was encouraged by:

- Khrushchev's 'softer' approach to Communism and Eastern Europe.

- Events in Poland. In 1956 there were demonstrations against the level of food prices in Poland. The Polish government was unable to keep control. Soviet troops were sent to restore order. Khrushchev, however, allowed some reforms that gave the Poles more freedom.

- Khrushchev also ended the dispute between the Soviet Union and Tito's Communist Yugoslavia.

WHY HUNGARIANS OPPOSED SOVIET CONTROL

CENSORSHIP

There was no freedom of expression. The government controlled the press, theatre, art and music.

SECRET POLICE

The hated State Protection Group (AVO), the Hungarian secret police, used terror and torture against opponents of the government, Communism and the USSR.

PATRIOTISM

Hungarians were proud and patriotic. They were aware of their culture, traditions and history. Soviet control of education meant that children were taught a Communist version of history. This ignored Hungary's real past and its traditional links with Western Europe.

RELIGION

Hungarians were strongly Christian but the Communist Government persecuted the Catholic Church. Its leader, Cardinal Minszenty, was put in prison.

SOVIET TROOPS

Hungarians hated the presence of Soviet troops. It reminded them of Soviet control and their loss of freedom.

STANDARD OF LIVING

This was very low under Communism. There were food shortages blamed on the new collective farms. Industrial workers were poorly paid. Many goods were sent to the USSR.

EVENTS IN 1956

July	The hard-line Communist prime minister, Rakosi, was forced to resign. His successor, Erno Gero, another tough Communist, was equally unpopular.
6 October	Thousands of Hungarians turned out to witness the state funeral of Laszlo Rajik. He was a Communist leader who had wanted Hungary to break away from Soviet control. Stalin had him executed. Now it was decided that he should be reburied and have a state funeral.
23 October	Popular demonstrations in Budapest led to fighting with the AVO. Demonstrators wanted the reforming politician, Imre Nagy, as Prime Minister.
24 October	Nagy was named as Prime Minister. Soviet tanks entered Budapest. They were fought by freedom fighters and most of the Hungarian army.

SOURCE A

Demands of demonstrators in Budapest, 23 October 1956

We demand the immediate evacuation of all Soviet troops. The leadership must change. Imre Nagy to the Government.

SOURCE B

A member of the AVO murdered by demonstrators

SOURCE C

Speech by Imre Nagy on Wednesday, 31 October

My dear friends today we have started negotiations for the withdrawal of Soviet troops from our country and for the cancellation of our obligations under the Warsaw Pact. Long live Free Hungary!

27 October	Nagy announced a new government which included members of non-Communist parties. Cardinal Minszenty was freed from prison.
29–31 October	Soviet forces were withdrawn from Budapest.
29 October to 1 November	Nagy announced further reforms. These included the end of one-party rule, the complete evacuation of Soviet troops from Hungary and Hungary's withdrawal from the Warsaw Pact.
4 November	The Red Army invaded Budapest, killing 27,000 Hungarians. Janos Kadar became Prime Minister.

SOURCE E

Soviet tanks in the centre of Budapest, November 1956

SOURCE D

From M. Orr, *Hungary in Revolt*, 1981

Russian tactics were basically simple – to employ the maximum firepower against any target. If it was suspected that a sniper was hiding in the building, tank guns destroyed the building. In the last stages of the battle the Russians used terror tactics. Queues of housewives were shot down by machine guns. Aircraft and artillery destroyed buildings. When the last 30 defenders of the Kilan Barracks surrendered they were shot down as they emerged.

Reasons for Soviet action

Khrushchev acted so harshly for several reasons:

1. Nagy had gone too far in withdrawing Hungary from the Warsaw Pact. Khrushchev was worried that other Eastern European states might want to do the same.

2. China urged him to deal harshly with the Hungarians.

3. Khrushchev needed to secure his own position in the USSR. He could not afford to show any weakness.

4. He knew there was little chance of interference from the West because of the Suez Crisis (see Focus below).

Why did the uprising fail?

One reason was certainly the harsh actions taken by the Soviet Union. The rebels had no chance against the Soviet tanks. The other main reason was the lack of effective support from the West. Public opinion supported the Hungarians and was horrified by Soviet actions in Budapest, but the Western governments were distracted by the Suez Crisis in which French and British troops invaded Egypt in order to protect the Suez Canal.

The UN had no impact on events. Members of the Security Council wanted to call for a withdrawal of Soviet troops but the Soviet Union used its veto to block the resolution. This was in stark contrast to the situation in 1950 when the USSR had been absent from the UN at the outbreak of the Korean War (see p. 251). The USSR refused to allow the UN Secretary-General to visit Budapest.

Focus on

The Suez Crisis 1956

Britain and France had regarded Egypt as their area of influence since the second half of the nineteenth century. Indeed Britain occupied Egypt in 1882 to safeguard the Suez Canal, an important link with the east. In 1949 a new leader, Colonel Nasser, took control in Egypt. He began to open up links with the USSR and then, in 1956, he nationalised the Suez Canal. The majority shareholders of the Canal were British and French. Both countries feared that oil supplies through the Canal would be cut off at will. Britain and France secretly agreed to support Egypt's enemy, Israel, in an invasion to regain control of the Canal. The invasion was a disastrous failure. It annoyed the USA who did not want to upset the Arabs for fear it drove them to support the USSR. Britain and France were preoccupied with the Suez Crisis during the Hungarian uprising.

Results of the uprising

The uprising had effects on Hungary and the Cold War:

- *Hungary.* About 200,000 refugees fled to the West. Nagy was tricked into leaving his refuge in the Yugoslav embassy. In 1958 he was hanged in Moscow. Kadar ruled until 1988. He was loyal to Moscow but did eventually allow some freedom of discussion.

- *East–West relations.* These worsened. The USSR accused the West of supporting Nagy. The West realised that even though Stalin was dead the Soviet Union was determined to keep control of Eastern Europe, by brutal methods if necessary. They became even more determined to resist Soviet expansion in Europe.

- *Eastern Europe.* The other Soviet satellite states now realised that they would not be allowed any independence or the freedom to follow policies different from those of the USSR.

SOURCE H

Headline in the *Daily Mail*, 5 November 1956

Daily Mail

NO. 18,633 TWOPENCE — FOR QUEEN AND COMMONWEALTH — MONDAY NOVEMBER 5 1956

MORNING SPECIAL

A dying nation's last SOS. It reached Vienna from a Hungarian reporter. His full story is in Page 5

good bye we do not forget you — *the russian are too near* — *good bye friends* — *good bye friends.* — *save ou souls*

BUDAPEST CRUSHED—Red troops storm into Parliament

The MURDER OF HUNGARY

Comment

HUNGARIAN TRAGEDY

Nagy marched out at gunpoint

GET OUT! IKE URGES BULGANIN

Coast defences attacked

CYPRUS TROOPS BOARD THE

SOURCE I

Fleeing Hungarian refugees helping one another across the 'Bridge of Freedom' into Austria after the failure of the uprising

Activity

During the Hungarian uprising the Hungarians broadcast an appeal for help from the West. You are responsible for writing the broadcast. Explain:

- Why you dislike Soviet rule.

- What you hope to achieve with your uprising.

- Why you need help from the West.

Questions

1. Why was there opposition in Hungary?
2. How did the Soviet Union respond?
3. What do Sources **D** and **E** tell you about why the uprising failed? What other reasons were there?
4. What differences are there between Sources **F** and **H** in their views of the uprising? Why are they so different?
5. What effects did the uprising have on:
   a. Hungary?
   b. Eastern Europe?

SOURCE A

A picture issued by the USSR at the time of the announcement of the shooting down and arrest of Gary Powers

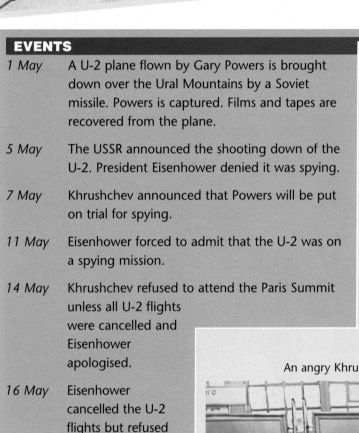

ЛОКХИД U-2
LOCKHEED U-2

THE U-2 CRISIS, 1960

In 1960 another incident brought increased rivalry between East and West – the U-2 incident.

Background to the crisis

The U-2, a Lockheed aircraft developed for the USA's Central Intelligence Agency (CIA), was first used in 1956. It was able to fly at very high altitudes (over 20 kilometres) out of range of Soviet fighters and for very long distances – over 6000 km. It was equipped with powerful cameras and radio receivers enabling it to detect Soviet long-range bomber bases and missile sites. Flights over the USSR were made between US bases in Pakistan and Norway.

EVENTS

1 May	A U-2 plane flown by Gary Powers is brought down over the Ural Mountains by a Soviet missile. Powers is captured. Films and tapes are recovered from the plane.
5 May	The USSR announced the shooting down of the U-2. President Eisenhower denied it was spying.
7 May	Khrushchev announced that Powers will be put on trial for spying.
11 May	Eisenhower forced to admit that the U-2 was on a spying mission.
14 May	Khrushchev refused to attend the Paris Summit unless all U-2 flights were cancelled and Eisenhower apologised.
16 May	Eisenhower cancelled the U-2 flights but refused to apologise. Khrushchev walked out of the Summit.

SOURCE B

Gary Powers

SOURCE C

An angry Khrushchev at a May press conference

Results of the crisis

The U-2 crisis had several effects on the Cold War.

SOURCE D

A Soviet cartoon showing President Eisenhower painting a U-2 spy plane.

- The Paris Summit was abandoned. It was to have been held in May 1960 between the leaders of the USSR, the USA, France and Britain as a major step towards improving East–West relations following Khrushchev's visit to the USA in 1959. The main items for discussion were the future of Germany and nuclear arms reduction. It was unlikely to make much progress over a possible reunification of Germany. In any case Khrushchev was under pressure from the Chinese and his own generals to take a firm line against the West.

- Khrushchev showed the Communist world, especially China, that he could be tough with the West. He may well have played up the U-2 incident in order to do this.

- Gary Powers was tried in Moscow on charges of spying. He was found guilty and sentenced to ten years' imprisonment. After serving seventeen months of his sentence he was sent back to the USA in return for the release of a top Soviet spy from a US prison.

Questions

1. Describe in your own words the U-2 spy incident.
2. Write two sets of newspaper headlines for 1 May 1960 – from an American and a Soviet newspaper – and an article explaining each side's view of the U-2 crisis.
3. What effects did the crisis have on East–West relations?
4. What point is the cartoonist trying to make in Source D?

THE BERLIN WALL

In 1961 the Soviet Union built a wall in Berlin to separate East from West. This, in turn, led to another Cold War crisis.

Background

The building of the Wall was the culmination of years of rivalry between East and West. By 1961 there was a great contrast between the two parts of the city.

- East Berlin was not prosperous and was under strict Communist rule.

- West Berlin was prosperous with the help of US aid. It attracted many visitors from the East due to its cinemas and shops. The USSR saw it as a Capitalist infection in the heart of East Germany. West Berlin also provided an easy escape route from East to West Germany for over 250,000 refugees each year.

Focus on

East German refugees crossing via West Berlin or across the West German border:

1949	129,245		*1957*	261,622
1950	197,788		*1958*	204,092
1951	165,648		*1959*	143,917
1952	182,393		*1960*	199,188
1953	331,390		*1961*	207,026
1954	184,198		*1962*	21,356
1955	252,870		*1963*	42,632
1956	279,189		*1964*	41,876

Western aims	Soviet aims
1 Prevent the USSR from gaining permanent control of East Germany.	1 Maintain control over East Germany.
2 The wartime Allies to sign a peace treaty with a united, democratic Germany.	2 Make the Western Powers recognise it as an independent state.
	3 Stop the flood of refugees from East to West Germany. These refugees were mainly skilled and professional people who were badly needed in East Germany.

Soviet demands in 1958

Khrushchev demanded that the three Western occupying powers should:

- recognise the German Democratic Republic (GDR).

- withdraw their troops from West Berlin.

- hand their access routes over to the East German government.

He said that unless they did so within six months he would sign a separate peace treaty with the GDR and hand East Berlin over to it. The Western Powers refused and Khrushchev backed down.

EVENTS OF THE 1961 CRISIS

June   At the Vienna Summit Khrushchev tried to put pressure on the new American President, John F. Kennedy.

He demanded the withdrawal of the Western forces from West Berlin within six months. Kennedy refused and insisted the USA would protect the freedom of West Berlin.

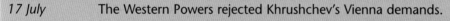

Profile on

John F. Kennedy

John Fitzgerald Kennedy, a member of one of America's richest families, took office as President in January 1961. Like Roosevelt, Kennedy believed strongly in freedom and supported the Black Civil Rights movement. He tried to make life easier for the poor. Kennedy worked hard for peace but was a determined opponent of Communism. He was assassinated while on a presidential visit to Dallas in November 1963.

17 July   The Western Powers rejected Khrushchev's Vienna demands.

23 July   The flow of refugees from East Germany to the West had reached 1000 a day. The East German government tried to reduce the number by introducing travel restrictions.

25 July   Kennedy repeated the USA's support for West Berlin and announced an increase in arms spending.

SOURCE A

Part of a speech made by Kennedy in 1961

We cannot and will not allow the Communists to drive us out of Berlin, either gradually or by force. Our promise to Berlin is essential to the security of West Germany, to the unity of Western Europe and to the faith of the entire free world.

SOURCE B

This German cartoon from 1961 shows President Kennedy arguing with Khrushchev. It also shows the Chinese leader, Mao Zedong, urging Khrushchev to be more firm.

13–22 August On the orders of Khrushchev and the East German government, a barbed wire barrier was put across Berlin, followed by a wall of concrete blocks.

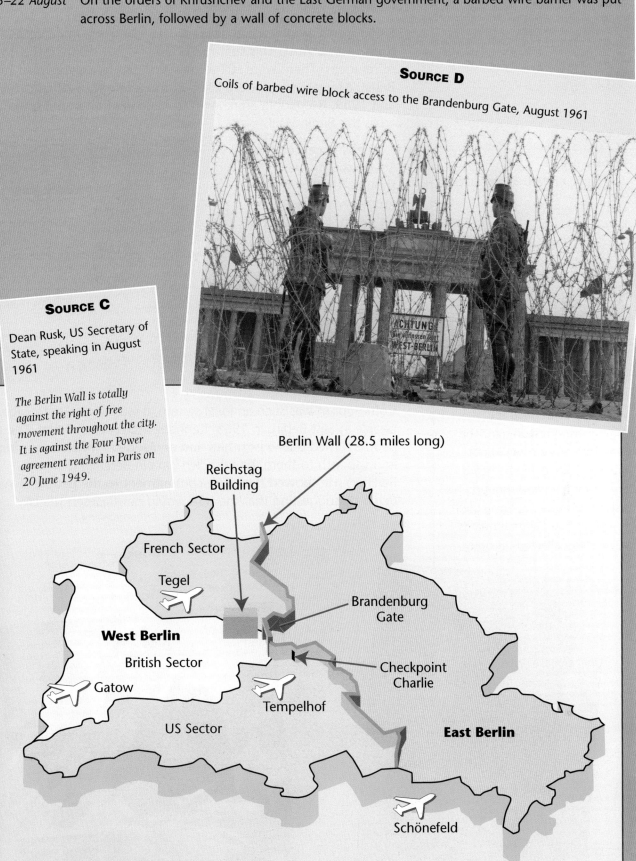

SOURCE D

Coils of barbed wire block access to the Brandenburg Gate, August 1961

SOURCE C

Dean Rusk, US Secretary of State, speaking in August 1961

The Berlin Wall is totally against the right of free movement throughout the city. It is against the Four Power agreement reached in Paris on 20 June 1949.

Berlin Wall (28.5 miles long)

Reichstag Building

French Sector

Tegel

West Berlin

British Sector

Gatow

Tempelhof

US Sector

Brandenburg Gate

Checkpoint Charlie

East Berlin

Schönefeld

Results

The Berlin Wall had significant effects for Berlin, Germany and the Cold War:

- Berlin was now physically divided. The Wall ended free access from East to West. This split many families but stopped the flow of refugees. There were still some who tried to escape from East Berlin. Many of these were killed in the attempt. Between 1961 and 1989, 86 people are known to have died attempting to cross the Berlin Wall.

- Kennedy accepted the Soviet action even though it broke the four-power agreement on Berlin. He refused to use American troops to pull down the Wall, fearing it might lead to war.

- This made Kennedy look weak. The Americans, however, used the Wall for propaganda purposes, asking why, if Communism was such an ideal system, it was necessary to cage people in East Berlin. In 1963, Kennedy visited West Berlin. The people turned out to hear him and applauded him warmly when, in his speech to them, he said, 'Ich bin ein Berliner' (I am a Berliner). He showed the USA's commitment to the people of West Berlin by suggesting that the USA would never desert the city.

Focus on

The death of Peter Fechter

On 17 August 1962 Peter Fechter, an eighteen-year-old bricklayer, tried to cross into West Berlin to join his sister. He was shot by East German border police as he climbed the barbed wire on the eastern side. He fell into the strip between East and West. Fechter was only 300 metres from the West Berlin border post. Crowds on the western side begged the Americans to rescue him. The American officers would not intervene. He could be heard crying for help and shouting his sister's name as he slowly bled to death. East German guards eventually collected his body.

SOURCE E

Colonel Jim Atwood, US military mission, Berlin

Instructions were given to our tank commander that he was to roll up and confront the Soviet tank. This was an identical distance across from Checkpoint Charlie. The tension increased very rapidly for the one reason that this was Americans confronting Russians. It wasn't East Germans. There was live ammunition in both tanks of the Russians and the Americans. It was an unexpected, sudden confrontation that in my opinion was the closest that the Russians and Allies came to going to war in the entire Cold War period.

SOURCE F

26 June 1963. Kennedy speaks to hundreds of thousands of cheering West Berliners.

- Khrushchev lost face by failing to remove the Western Powers from West Berlin. He believed that Kennedy's response showed that he was weak.

Questions

1 Why did Khrushchev decide to build the Berlin Wall?
2 What effect did this have on:
   a   Berlin?
   b   the Cold War?
3 According to Source **E**, how serious was the Berlin Crisis?
4 How useful is Source **B** as evidence of the relations between the USSR and USA in 1961?

THE CUBAN MISSILE CRISIS, 1962

In 1962 a crisis involving the island of Cuba brought the superpowers to the brink of nuclear war.

The USA and Cuba

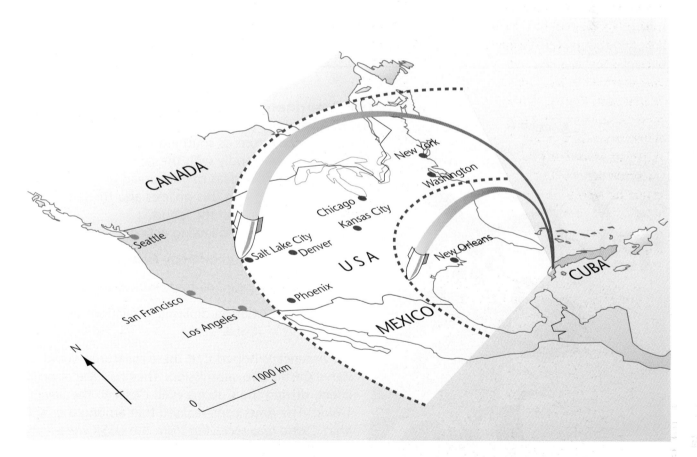

The USA had played an important part in Cuban affairs since the beginning of the twentieth century. They had built a huge naval base at Guantanamo and American companies invested heavily in Cuba, especially in mining and agriculture. In 1934 the Americans helped the Cuban military officer, Fulgencia Batista, to take power. He made himself dictator but his government was not popular. It was corrupt and harsh.

In 1959 Batista was overthrown by Fidel Castro.

Profile on

Fidel Castro

Fidel Castro Ruz was born in Mayari, Cuba, in 1926. The son of middle-class parents, he had a good education and received a law degree from the University of Havana in 1950. In 1953 he was jailed following a failed uprising against Batista. He was sent into exile and lived in Mexico and the USA before returning to Cuba in 1956, when he began a guerrilla campaign against Batista. In 1959 he succeeded in overthrowing the dictator and immediately began to reform Cuba. Because his policies drove many middle-class Cubans into exile, the American government believed that Castro was unpopular. This led the USA to support the Bay of Pigs invasion (see p. 273).

Castro and his followers wanted:

- to improve Cuban prosperity, especially of peasants working on the land and in the sugar mills of American-owned companies.

- to end corruption and terror in Cuban politics.

Castro began appointing Communists to the government. He also signed a trade agreement with the Soviet Union in which Cuban sugar would be swapped for machinery, oil and other economic aid.

SOURCE A

A Soviet cartoon which shows Truman, Eisenhower and Nixon as ravens of war urging Kennedy on against Cuba

The American response

The USA was very concerned to see an island only 150 kilometres away from its southern coast becoming Communist and friendly with the USSR. The Americans feared that Castro's ideas might spread to other countries in the region. His policies also threatened American companies in the island.

The USA took the following actions.

July 1960	Refused to buy Cuban sugar.
October 1960	Ended all trade with Cuba.
January 1961	Cut off diplomatic relations with Cuba.

The Americans hoped that these measures would starve Castro into submission. They had the opposite effect, driving the Cubans even closer to the Soviet Union. The Americans realised that among the 'aid' that Castro was receiving from the USSR were weapons.

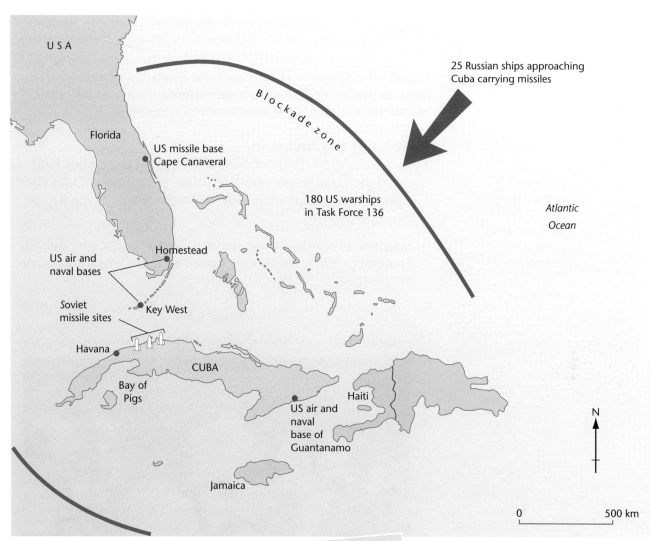

USA

Florida

US missile base
Cape Canaveral

US air and
naval bases

Homestead

*Soviet
missile sites*

Key West

Havana

CUBA

Bay of
Pigs

US air and
naval
base of
Guantanamo

Haiti

Jamaica

Blockade zone

25 Russian ships approaching
Cuba carrying missiles

180 US warships
in Task Force 136

*Atlantic
Ocean*

N

0   500 km

Source B

Happy Cubans celebrate the capture of a landing craft and victory

The Bay of Pigs operation

The USA decided to support Cuban exiles – Cubans who had been forced off the island by Castro – in an attempt to overthrow Castro. The CIA had formed a group of exiled Cuban politicians into a committee in Florida to take over from Castro. In Guatemala, the CIA trained a force of Cuban exiles. In April 1961 the new American President, Kennedy, decided to support an invasion by these exiles. They intended to establish a base in Cuba from which to launch attacks against Castro and were confident that the Cuban people would support them.

SOURCE C

From a biography of Fidel Castro written by a British author in 1981

By nightfall on 18 April it was clear that the attack on the Bay of Pigs was doomed. Earlier attacks by US aircraft had not been successful in grounding the Cuban airforce. The exile troops were surrounded by 20,000 troops with artillery and tanks. The local population had not supported the invaders. The exiles pleaded with the US for more aerial support. Kennedy, reluctant to admit his part in the affair, refused.

The invasion in the Bay of Pigs was a disaster. Fourteen hundred exiles landed, supported by US bombers flown by Cubans. They faced 20,000 Cuban troops. There was no popular uprising to support the invasion. Those exiles not killed were easily taken prisoner. Kennedy denied all involvement in the operation, but it was a humiliation for the new American President.

Results of the invasion

- Castro declared Cuba a Communist state in December 1961. He asked the USSR to provide arms in order to defend Cuba against a possible American attack following the failure of the Bay of Pigs operation.

- Khrushchev agreed to provide arms and announced it publicly in September 1961. He secretly hoped to turn Cuba into a Soviet missile base.

SOURCE D

Fidel Castro of Cuba and Nikita Khrushchev of the USSR embrace in friendship

- In the USA this created even greater fear of the spread of Communism throughout the region. Kennedy said the USA would isolate Cuba and warned the USSR not to put nuclear missiles in Cuba.

Questions

1. Why was Cuba so important to the USA?
2. According to Source **C**, why was the Bay of Pigs invasion a failure?
3. What message is the Soviet cartoonist trying to get across in Source **A**?

Increasing superpower tension 1961–62

The Berlin Crisis and the building of the Wall in 1961 greatly increased the tension between the superpowers. It was followed by an acceleration in the Arms Race.

Why did Khrushchev send missiles to Cuba?

This is unclear. He ran a risk that the USA would discover the missiles but believed they would be in place before this happened. In any case he believed Kennedy would make a weak response. His reasons may have been:

- to defend Cuba following the Bay of Pigs operation.

- to force the USA to bargain to remove their missiles from Turkey.

- to catch up with the USA in the Arms Race by placing missiles as close to the USA as possible.

- to show Soviet strength and force Kennedy to back down.

SOURCE A

Extract from Khrushchev's Memoirs

Everyone agreed that America would not leave Cuba alone unless we did something. We had an obligation to do everything in our power to protect Cuba's existence as a Communist country and as a working example to other countries in Latin America. I want to make one thing absolutely clear. We had no desire to start a war. Only a fool would think that we wanted to invade the American continent from Cuba. Our aim was the opposite. We wanted to keep the Americans from invading Cuba.

THE CRISIS UNFOLDS, 1962

August	US spy planes observed weapons in Cuba.
September	Khrushchev secretly started to send nuclear weapons to Cuba.
4 September	Kennedy warned the USSR not to put nuclear missiles in Cuba.
11 September	The Soviet government assured the USA it would not base nuclear missiles outside the USSR.
14 October	An American U-2 aircraft took a series of reconnaissance photographs twelve miles above the island.
15 October	Defence experts concluded that the site was being prepared for a number of medium-range ballistic missiles. They would soon be ready to fire.

SOURCE B

Aerial photograph of Soviet missile sites in Cuba

16 October — Alarmed by the intelligence reports, Kennedy quickly called a meeting of top-level advisers, including his brother, Robert Kennedy, the Attorney General. This group, which met frequently during the crisis, became known as the Executive Committee (Ex-Comm). One member later recalled that Kennedy was more tense than he had ever seen him. He was 'absolutely determined that the missiles would leave Cuba'.

SOURCE C

'Over the Garden Wall'. This British cartoon from 17 October 1962 shows Kennedy on the left and Khrushchev seated on the right.

19 October — Further reconnaissance photos revealed more missile sites, this time threatening a longer-range strike. The experts said that the Soviets were working non-stop and that the missile sites were nearly ready.

Focus on

Kennedy's options during the Cuban Missile Crisis

Kennedy faced pressure from several groups within his government, including:

The Hawks

These included Dean Acheson, a former Secretary of State.

They wanted swift military action:

◆ A nuclear strike on the sites, but the USSR would almost certainly strike back.

◆ A conventional bombing raid followed by an invasion. This would almost certainly lead to fighting with Soviet troops already in Cuba and a war.

◆ Attack the USSR. This would almost certainly cause a nuclear war.

The Moderates

These were led by Robert McNamara who was Secretary for Defense. They wanted to set up a naval blockade as the first step to getting rid of the missiles. They proposed that the US navy should stop the Soviet ships reaching Cuba. The disadvantage? It might lead to the sinking of Soviet ships and war.

The Doves

Such as Adlai Stevenson, US Ambassador to the United Nations. They advised Kennedy to be cautious. He should talk to the USSR and offer to remove US missiles from Turkey. The disadvantage? The USA would appear weak.

22 October   Kennedy announced a naval blockade of Cuba. All ships carrying weapons to Cuba were to be turned back. The armed forces were placed on the alert. The USSR was told that the USA would retaliate against any missile launched from Cuba against a Western nation. That evening Kennedy went on television to make a live broadcast to the American people. It was probably the most important speech made in the whole period of the Cold War.

SOURCE D

Part of Kennedy's broadcast

Unmistakable evidence has established the fact that a series of offensive missile sites is now in preparation. To halt this offensive build-up, a strict quarantine (blockade) on all military equipment under shipment to Cuba is being introduced... I call upon Chairman Khrushchev to halt and remove this threat to world peace... by withdrawing those weapons from Cuba.

SOURCE E

Headlines in the *Daily Sketch*, 23 October 1962

23 October   The Soviet government insisted that it was simply helping Cuba to defend itself and that the USA was interfering in Cuba's affairs. Khrushchev accused the USA of pushing the world towards nuclear war.

24 October   The blockade was in place. Approximately twenty-five Soviet ships were spread across the Atlantic on their way to Cuba. Then, at 10.25 a.m. Kennedy received the most important message of his political career: a number of ships had stopped dead in the mid-Atlantic. One oil tanker was allowed through unsearched. The rest turned back.

26 October   Khrushchev sent a letter to Kennedy hinting that he was ready to make some sort of agreement. The USSR might withdraw the missiles if Kennedy promised not to invade Cuba. A second message then arrived insisting that the USSR would only remove their missiles from Cuba if the USA removed theirs from Turkey. The Executive Committee advised Kennedy not to give in to Soviet demands 'at the point of a gun'. Khrushchev was obviously coming under pressure from hard-line generals to stand up to the USA. Hence the second message. The crisis seemed to be getting out of hand.

27 October   An American U-2 plane was shot down over Cuba, killing the pilot. Although Castro had acted on his own, Kennedy was stunned. He believed that the Cuban leader was following Soviet orders. Some of Kennedy's more hard-line advisers urged the president to attack Cuba. The world was on the brink of nuclear war. Kennedy had already moved his wife and children to Washington so that they could be in the presidential bunker.

SOURCE F

A young woman recalling her reaction to the crisis

I remember going into a cinema in Sheffield the next evening and wondering 'will I walk out again?'

At this stage Kennedy's attitude softened. A second U-2 flew into Soviet air space. Kennedy apologised. It was at this stage that Robert Kennedy helped to solve the crisis. He suggested that the USA should reply to the first message and ignore the second, more aggressive one. Kennedy's reply to Khrushchev therefore said that the USA would promise not to invade Cuba but would not make a decision on Turkey until they had talked to their NATO allies. In return for the Cuban guarantee, America demanded the withdrawal of the Soviet missiles from Cuba.

28 October — Radio Moscow announced that the nuclear weapons would be removed. Privately, the Americans agreed to remove their missiles from Turkey as long as the USSR kept it a secret.

SOURCE G

Headlines in the USA

New York Mirror

FINAL ★★ 5¢

K BOWS! Will Pull Out Missiles

Khrush:
"The Soviet government, in addition to previously issued instructions for the cessation of further work at the weapons building sites, has issued a new order, for the dismantling of the weapons, which you describe as offensive, their crating and returning to the Soviet Union."

JFK:
"I welcome Chairman Khrushchev's statesmanlike decision to stop building bases in Cuba, dismantling offensive weapons and returning them to the Soviet Union under United Nations verification. This is an important and constructive contribution to peace."

Kennedy Made No Deals

STORIES ON PAGES 2, 3

Results of the crisis

The crisis had important results for the USSR, the USA, Cuba and the Cold War:

Khrushchev claimed that he had achieved the aim of preventing an American invasion of Cuba. He was, however, criticised by China for backing down in the face of American threats. He lost face at home and the crisis probably contributed to his fall from power two years later.

Kennedy increased his reputation at home and worldwide by avoiding a war and forcing Khrushchev to back down.

Cuba remained a Communist country dependent upon Soviet aid and protection.

Khrushchev and Kennedy realised how close they had come to nuclear war. To try to prevent another such crisis they set up a telephone hot line direct from the Kremlin to the White House. They also attempted to improve relations and agreed to a Nuclear Test Ban.

Questions

1 According to Source **A**, why did Khrushchev build Soviet missiles on the island of Cuba?
2 How reliable is Source **A** as a view of Khrushchev's motives?
3 What is the purpose of the cartoon, Source **C**?
4 Using the sources on this page and your own knowledge, do you think the Cuban Crisis was:
   a a victory for the USA?
   b a victory for the USSR?
   c a victory for neither?
Give reasons for your answers.

SOURCE H

Extract from Khrushchev's memoirs, written in the late 1960s

We sent the Americans a note saying that we agreed to remove our missiles and bombers on condition that the President gave us assurances that there would be no invasion of Cuba. Finally Kennedy gave in and agreed to make a statement giving us such an assurance. It was a great victory for us, a spectacular success without having to fire a shot.

SOURCE I

Soviet verdicts. Extracts quoted in BBC2 *Timewatch* special, October 1992.

General: *This was the most humiliating thing for us. The military really resented it.*

Soviet Embassy official in Washington: *It was a humiliation no doubt. And it was well deserved.*

Special Assistant to Khrushchev: *It failed in that the missiles were withdrawn. But it did not fail in that there was a commitment not to attack Cuba. It also led to a better climate between the two leaders and the two countries.*

SOURCE J

Verdict of an American journalist in *Time* magazine, November 1962

Generations to come may well count John Kennedy's determination as one of the decisive moments of the twentieth century.

SOURCE K

The verdicts of America's top officers. From BBC2 *Timewatch* special, October 1992.

Army General: *We'd given Castro too much. And let him off too easy.*

Admiral: *We've been had.*

Air Force General: *It is the greatest defeat in our history, Mr President. We should invade today.*

Summary and Revision

THE KOREAN WAR 1950–53

This section includes the following:

- The background to the war – division north and south.

- Reasons for American involvement.

- Events of the war 1950–53.

- Effects that the war had on the Cold War and Korea.

Revision questions

1 Why was Korea divided into north and south after the Second World War?
2 What was the 'domino theory'?
3 Summarise the main events of the war. Why was MacArthur sacked?
4 What effects did the war in Korea have on:
    a   the people of Korea?
    b   the Cold War?

THE COLD WAR IN THE 1950S

For this you need to know:

- New Soviet policy under Khrushchev.

- Examples of détente in the 1950s.

- The Arms Race and its impact.

- The Space Race and its impact.

Revision questions

1 What changes took place in the USSR as a result of the death of Stalin and emergence of Khrushchev?
2 What is meant by 'détente'? Give two examples from this period.
3 Why did the superpowers decide to build up their nuclear weapons?
4 How important was the Space Race in the Cold War? Who claimed victory in this race by the end of the 1950s?

THE HUNGARIAN UPRISING 1956

For this you need to know:

- Reasons for Hungarian discontent.

- Events in USSR and Poland which encouraged the uprising.

- Events of the uprising.

- Why it failed and its effects on East–West relations.

Revision questions

1 Why did the Hungarians hate Soviet control?
2 How did events in Poland and the USSR encourage the uprising?
3 Summarise the main events during the uprising.
4 Did the uprising fail because of a lack of help from the West?
5 Why did the West not help?
6 What effects did the rebellion have on the Cold War?

THE U-2 AND BERLIN CRISES 1961–62

This includes:

- The American use of U-2 planes.

- The shooting down of the U-2 and its effects.

- Developments in Berlin in the period 1949–61.

- Why Khrushchev decided to build the Wall.

- The effects of the Wall on Berlin, Germany and East–West relations.

Revision questions

1 What was the purpose of the U-2 planes?
2 What effects did the shooting down of the U-2 plane have on the Paris Summit of 1960?
3 Why did many East Germans move from East to West Berlin? Why did this concern the USSR?
4 Why did Khrushchev decide to build the Wall? How did it affect Germany?
5 Why did Kennedy visit Berlin in 1963?

THE CUBAN MISSILE CRISIS 1962

This includes:

- Reasons for American involvement in Cuba.

- The Castro take-over and the changes he introduced.

- Increased Soviet influence in Cuba and US reactions to this.

- The failure of the Bay of Pigs invasion and its results.

- Why Khrushchev decided to build missile sites on Cuba.

- Kennedy's options when he heard of the sites.

- The events of the crisis September–October 1962.

- Robert Kennedy and the ending of the crisis.

- The effects the crisis had on Cuba, Khrushchev, the USA and the Cold War.

Revision questions

1 Why was Cuba so important to the USA?
2 Castro turned to the Soviet Union for support and aid. Why?
3 Why did Kennedy support the Bay of Pigs invasion? It was a disastrous failure.
   a Why?
   b What effects did it have on Castro and his relations with the USSR?
4 How did the USA detect the Soviet missile sites on Cuba?
5 What options faced Kennedy to force the USSR to remove these sites? Which one did he choose and why?
6 How close were the superpowers to nuclear war?
7 Robert Kennedy came up with a solution to the crisis. What was it?

7
The Later Cold War, 1964–91

UNDERSTANDING THE LATER COLD WAR, 1964–91

The following explanations and definitions will help you to understand this chapter.

CIS	The Commonwealth of Independent States. This replaced the USSR in 1991.
Glasnost	Openness. The policy carried out by Gorbachev in the USSR of a more open policy.
Guerrilla warfare	Literally it means 'small war'. Usually used to describe tactics of small armies against powerful opposition – ambush, hit and run, raids. Used by the Vietcong in Vietnam.
Martial law	Using the army to keep the law and reducing people's freedom.
Mujaheddin	Afghan tribesmen who fought against the Soviet invasion.
Napalm	A burning petroleum jelly used by the Americans in Vietnam.
Perestroika	Gorbachev's policy of changing the Soviet economy.
SALT	Strategic Arms Limitation Treaty. Two such treaties were signed by the superpowers in the 1970s. They agreed to limit certain nuclear weapons.
SDI	Strategic Defence Initiative. Anti-missile system devised by the USA in the 1980s. Its nickname was 'Star Wars'.
Solidarity	A movement set up in Poland in 1980 by Lech Walesa to campaign for greater freedom and more workers' rights.
'Star Wars' Project	Nickname for the Strategic Defence Initiative.
START	Strategic Arms Reduction Talks. This replaced SALT in the 1980s.
Vietcong	Communist guerrilla forces who fought against the USA in South Vietnam.
Vietminh	Also known as the National Liberation Front. Set up by Ho Chi Minh in 1960 to reunite North and South Vietnam.
Vietnamisation	President Nixon's policy of withdrawing American troops from Vietnam and supporting the South Vietnamese army against the North.

The Later Cold War 1964–91

Although there were several attempts to improve East–West relations, the Cold War continued. There was American involvement in Vietnam, unpopular Soviet policies in Czechoslovakia and Afghanistan and a movement for greater independence in Poland. Very rapidly, however, the rivalry between the superpowers ended with changes in the USSR and the end of Soviet control over Eastern Europe.

THE WAR IN VIETNAM

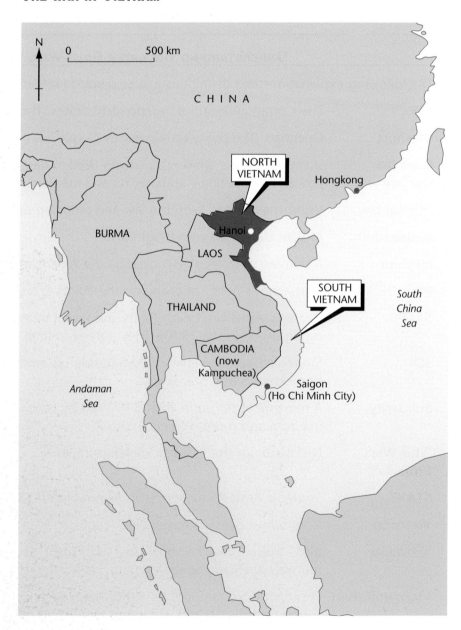

In 1963 the USA became involved in Vietnam. This involvement became greater and greater over the next ten years.

Background

Before the Second World War the French ruled an area called Indo-China. This included Vietnam, Laos and Cambodia. French rule was unpopular and harsh and there had been several uprisings, including one led by the Nationalist Party in 1930. In 1940 Japan invaded and occupied Indo-China. A secret guerrilla organisation, the Vietminh or League for the Independence of Vietnam, was set up to resist the Japanese occupation. This was led by a Communist called Ho Chi Minh.

Profile on

Ho Chi Minh

He was born at Nguyen That Thanh in 1890 in central Vietnam, then a part of French Indo-China. He went to school in Hue and briefly taught before working as a cook aboard a French steamship. He lived in London and Paris before the First World War and helped set up the French Communist Party. He went to China in 1924 where he set up the Indochinese Communist Party. In 1941 he set up the Vietminh to fight against the Japanese occupation of Indo-China. After the Japanese defeat in 1945 he set up the Democratic Republic of North Vietnam and was its first president. He fought against the French, who were defeated in 1954 at Dien Bien Phu. For the next fifteen years Ho led the North Vietnamese battle for reunification with the South. He died in 1969. In 1975 Saigon, the former capital of South Vietnam, was renamed Ho Chi Minh city in his honour.

The Vietminh worked with the allies to get rid of the Japanese. In September 1945, after the defeat of Japan, Ho Chi Minh was able to declare Vietnam independent.

Within three weeks, in 1946, the French had returned and fought the Vietminh who were supplied with weapons from China and the USSR. In May 1954 the French were defeated at Dien Bien Phu and decided to pull out.

In 1954 a conference was held at Geneva. This:

- ended the war in Vietnam.

- gave independence to Laos, Vietnam and Cambodia.

- temporarily divided Vietnam into North Vietnam which was controlled by the Communist Vietminh and South Vietnam which was backed by the USA and France. It was intended that Vietnam would be reunited after elections. The USA, however, refused to allow free elections throughout Vietnam in case they led to a Communist victory.

South Vietnam was ruled by the unpopular Ngo Diem. He was opposed in a civil war by the National Liberation Front (NLF) and the Vietcong, its Communist guerrilla force.

A young Buddhist monk, protesting at Diem's policies, commits suicide in the streets of Saigon

In 1963 Diem was overthrown and replaced by a series of military rulers all of whom were opposed to the Communist North. The Vietcong were backed by the USSR and China. The Chinese supplied weapons, equipment and food. These supplies arrived in South Vietnam down the Ho Chi Minh Trail, a series of supply lines through the jungle that were vital to the Communists and had to be kept open.

The Vietcong took advantage of South Vietnam's problems and became popular in rural areas because it gave land to the peasants and provided schools, postal and banking systems. The Vietcong treated the local people well and won their support.

Vietcong guerrillas described by an American journalist in *Time* magazine, 1961

Every night secret little bands of Communist guerrillas, dressed in black peasant pyjamas or faded khakis, splash through the marshes of the Mekong Delta or dart silently along jungle paths of South Vietnam, pursuing their murderous missions.

American involvement

The USA was involved in Vietnam mainly to stop the spread of Communism and to prevent what Eisenhower called the 'domino theory' (p. 252) coming true. He believed that if Vietnam became Communist, neighbouring countries would each fall in turn.

Until 1954 the USA supported the French against the Vietminh with money and equipment. Between 1954 and 1960 they sent aid, equipment and military advisers to South Vietnam. Between 1960 and 1963 President Kennedy steadily increased the amount of aid and the number of 'military advisers' rose from 900 to 11,000.

Vietnam in 1963

In 1963 the Vietcong managed to take over 40% of the rural areas of South Vietnam. South Vietnamese governments did not last very long. The country had ten different governments within two years of the removal of Diem. The Vietcong appeared to have the upper hand and had over 100,000 active fighters in the South. The very survival of Vietnam was now at stake. Communism seemed on the verge of spreading throughout south-east Asia.

SOURCE C
President Johnson talking in 1963

We fight this war because we must fight if we are to live in a world where every country can decide its own future. And only in such a world will a future be safe. We are in Vietnam because we have a promise to keep. Since 1954 every American president has offered support to the people of South Vietnam. Over many years we have made a national pledge to help South Vietnam defend its independence.

GREATER AMERICAN INVOLVEMENT 1963–5

1963   America continued to send support but no combat troops. As a result the Vietcong lost ground and Ho Chi Minh sent units of the North Vietnamese army to help them.

1964   In August 1964 North Vietnamese torpedo boats attacked US destroyers in the Gulf of Tonkin. This gave Johnson the excuse to attack North Vietnamese naval bases. It also helped him to persuade Congress to give him a free hand in Vietnam.

1965   In 1965 Johnson started to bomb North Vietnam to try to end its support for the Vietcong. He ordered American combat troops into action for the first time because:

- the army of the Vietcong was poorly led and weak.

- he believed that the full commitment of American troops would be a quick and certain way of defeating the Vietcong.

Questions

1   Explain the importance of the following in the background to the war in Vietnam:
    a   Ho Chi Minh.
    b   Dien Bien Phu.
    c   the Geneva agreement.

2   What do the diagram of the 'domino theory' and Source **C** tell you about the reasons for American involvement in Vietnam?

3   Is Source **B** biased against the Vietcong? If so, how do you know?

The war in Vietnam, 1965–1973

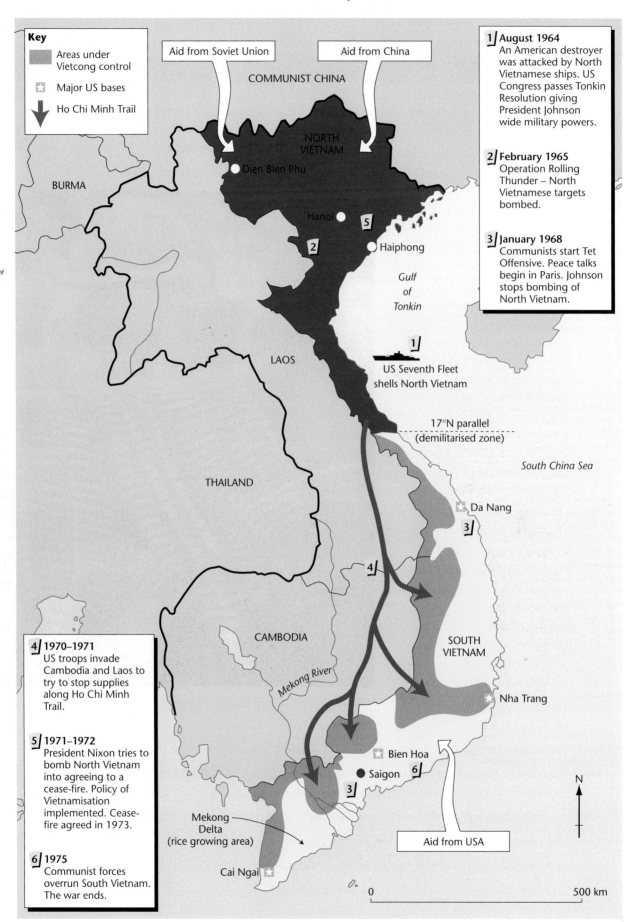

Key
- Areas under Vietcong control
- ★ Major US bases
- ⬇ Ho Chi Minh Trail

Aid from Soviet Union

Aid from China

COMMUNIST CHINA

BURMA

NORTH VIETNAM

Dien Bien Phu

Hanoi ● 5

2

Haiphong

Gulf of Tonkin

1

US Seventh Fleet shells North Vietnam

LAOS

THAILAND

17°N parallel (demilitarised zone)

South China Sea

★ Da Nang

3

4

CAMBODIA

Mekong River

SOUTH VIETNAM

Nha Trang ★

★ Bien Hoa

6

● Saigon

3

Mekong Delta (rice growing area)

Aid from USA

N

Cai Ngai ★

0   500 km

1 | August 1964
An American destroyer was attacked by North Vietnamese ships. US Congress passes Tonkin Resolution giving President Johnson wide military powers.

2 | February 1965
Operation Rolling Thunder – North Vietnamese targets bombed.

3 | January 1968
Communists start Tet Offensive. Peace talks begin in Paris. Johnson stops bombing of North Vietnam.

4 | 1970–1971
US troops invade Cambodia and Laos to try to stop supplies along Ho Chi Minh Trail.

5 | 1971–1972
President Nixon tries to bomb North Vietnam into agreeing to a cease-fire. Policy of Vietnamisation implemented. Cease-fire agreed in 1973.

6 | 1975
Communist forces overrun South Vietnam. The war ends.

1965 *'Operation Rolling Thunder'*
This was a bombing offensive against North Vietnam. The aims were:

- to end North Vietnamese support for the Vietcong by destroying ports, bases and supply lines.
- to do this without committing American troops to the war on the ground. Though this failed, the USA continued to bomb the North heavily throughout the later 1960s. Bombing was also used extensively against the Vietcong in the South. By 1970 the Americans had dropped more bombs on Vietnam than on all previous targets throughout the twentieth century.

1968 *The 'Tet Offensive'*
During the Tet religious festival, the Vietcong made a surprise guerrilla attack on major South Vietnamese towns and American bases. The attack showed that the Vietcong could strike in the heart of American-held territory and had badly affected American military morale. It suggested to the American public that the war could not be won. It increased criticism of American involvement. In the same year Johnson decided to end the bombing of North Vietnam and open peace negotiations with the North.

SOURCE A

The Tet Offensive, 1968

1969 *Vietnamisation*
The new American President, Richard Nixon, decided to start to withdraw American troops from Vietnam and hand over the fighting to the South Vietnamese army. He continued to support the South while US troops were withdrawn.

1970 The US invaded Cambodia to try to destroy North Vietnamese bases there.

1971 The failure of the South Vietnamese Army's attempt to cut the Ho Chi Minh Trail in Laos.

1972 The North attacked the South. Nixon ordered the bombing of the North to check the advance. At the same time there was a breakthrough in the peace negotiations.

1973 A ceasefire was agreed by the USA, the two Vietnams and the Vietcong. The last US troops were withdrawn.

1974 The war continued in Vietnam despite the ceasefire.

1975 Communist troops were victorious in South Vietnam, Laos and Cambodia.

1976 Vietnam was united in a single Socialist Republic.

Criticisms of the War

The Vietnam War was the first televised war because it received so much media coverage. The war became more and more unpopular in the USA for several reasons:

1   *Its high level of casualties.* Over 50,000 US troops were to eventually lose their lives. By 1968 300 were dying each week. Most Americans knew a relative or friend who had died.

SOURCE C

A makeshift first-aid station where wounded marines reach out to each other

2   *The economic cost of the war was high.* By 1968 it was costing $30,000 million each year. This meant cutbacks in spending on social reforms.

3   *The use of horrific weapons,* such as napalm, brought even greater opposition. This burning petroleum jelly was often used against civilians when villages were bombed. It stuck to the skin of its victims and burned them badly. The Americans also sprayed the land with chemical defoliants such as Agent Orange. This destroyed the vegetation and so prevented Vietcong fighters from hiding in the jungle. However, these chemicals polluted the land and also continued to poison human beings well after the end of the war.

SOURCE D

Vietnamese napalm victims

4 There were stories of *drug addiction* within the American forces in Vietnam.

5 *US atrocities against the Vietnamese people* turned many more against the war. One example that shocked the American nation was in the village of My Lai where, in March 1968, 300 people were massacred. The villagers, mainly women and children, were believed to be sheltering members of the Vietcong. They were gunned down by US troops. Lieutenant William Calley was charged with responsibility for the crime but served only three years in prison.

Women and children shot dead by American soldiers lie in the road at the village of My Lai, 1968

Widespread anti-war demonstrations began to occur regularly in US cities. Thousands of young men burnt their 'draft' cards which called them up to fight. Others fled abroad. Many students organised sit-ins and demonstrations at their colleges.

One of the worst incidents took place at Kent State University in Ohio in May 1970. There was a peaceful student demonstration. The Governor of Ohio panicked and sent in the National Guard. Tear gas canisters were thrown among the students who threw them back and also threw stones at the National Guard. The National Guard opened fire and killed four students. An investigation found that these four had not even been part of the anti-war demonstration.

SOURCE F

An extract from the evidence of Paul Meadlo who was a soldier at My Lai

We huddled the villagers up. We made them squat down. I poured about four clips into the group. The mothers were hugging their children. Well, we kept on firing.

Activity

You are a member of a movement in the USA protesting against the war in 1970. You are asked to make a poster advertising your protest to the war. On your poster you could include examples of:

- War crimes.
- Use of chemical weapons.
- Cost to American lives.

Effects on Vietnam

Political
The war turned many of the people of South Vietnam against the Americans and the South Vietnamese government. More and more villagers turned to the Vietcong, partly due to fear of punishment and attack.

Economic
The economy of Vietnam was destroyed by the widespread damage done to fields, animals, crops and forests. The Vietnamese were unable to grow enough to feed the people.

Social
Altogether two million Vietnamese were killed. Civilians suffered brutal treatment, including torture, rape and murder. Villages and communities were destroyed by the fighting.

Effects of the War

Effects on the USA

Political
The war made President Johnson very unpopular. In 1968 he withdrew from the Presidential election.

Economic
The cost led to price rises in the USA and cutbacks in Johnson's 'Great Reform' programme to help the black people of the USA.

Social
It led to a protest movement and draft dodging. This meant trying to avoid being called up to the armed forces.

Why was the USA defeated?

This was due to a combination of American weaknesses and Vietcong strengths:

US WEAKNESSES

They failed to develop an effective response to the guerrilla tactics used by the Vietcong.

American troops were inexperienced and often had low morale. The average age of the American soldiers was just nineteen. They often had no enemy to strike back at. They were frightened in such a hostile country.

The South Vietnamese army was weak.

The USA failed to win the support of the Vietnamese peasants. They generally viewed the Americans as invaders and chose to support the Vietcong who offered to improve their lives.

The Americans also lost support at home when it became clear that the USA could not win the war.

SOURCE G

Stanley Karnow, *Vietnam*, 1983

The US army in Vietnam was a shambles as the war drew to a close in the early 1970s. With President Nixon removing the American troops, nobody wanted to be the last to die for a cause that had clearly lost its meaning.

VIETCONG STRENGTHS

They had high morale because they believed passionately in their cause.

They carried out effective guerrilla tactics.

They were backed by China and the Soviet Union, using the Ho Chi Minh Trail to bring supplies to their bases in South Vietnam.

The Vietcong bases were well hidden. They were frightened of US bombing and built extensive underground bunkers. These contained workshops, kitchens, hospitals and storehouses, all connected by networks of narrow tunnels. These were carefully booby-trapped to kill US soldiers who might discover them. About 300 kilometres of tunnels were built under Vietnam.

SOURCE H

George C. Herring, *America's Longest War: The United States and Vietnam, 1950–75*, written in 1979

American troops fought well, despite the miserable conditions under which the war was fought – dense jungles and deep swamps, fire ants and leeches, booby traps and ambushes, an enemy difficult to find and deadly.

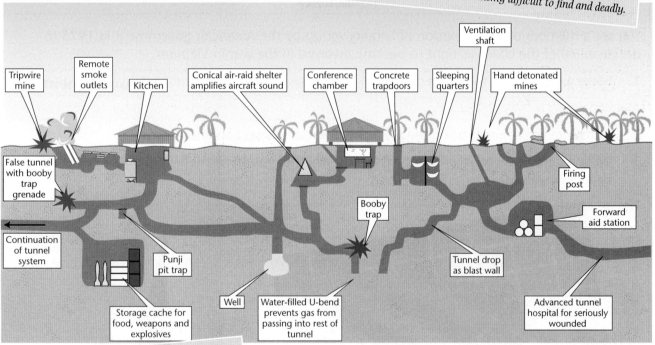

SOURCE I

Captain E.J. Banks, an American marine who fought in Vietnam

You never knew who was enemy and who was friend. They all looked alike. They were all Vietnamese. Some of them were Vietcong. A woman says her husband isn't Vietcong. She watches your men walk down a trail and get killed by a booby-trap. Maybe she planted it herself. The enemy was all around you.

North Vietnamese losses in equipment, raw materials and vehicles were replaced with increased aid from the Soviet Union and China. Total assistance from Russia and China has been estimated at over $2 billion between 1965 and 1968.

Results of the war

- It led to the fall of South Vietnam and the reunification of Vietnam as a Communist country. Twelve million people had lost their homes and relatives in Indo-China. Half a million 'boat people' tried to flee from Vietnam by sea. Many of those died or ended up in camps until they were forced to return to Vietnam.

- Relations between the USA and Vietnam remained hostile. There was no trade between the two countries until 1993.

- There were Communist take-overs in Cambodia and Laos but not Thailand.

- President Nixon announced the end of the Truman Doctrine. Americans had lost confidence in their ability to 'contain' the spread of Communism.

- Some 700,000 veterans suffered psychological effects from fighting in the war.

- Although the war worsened superpower relations for many years, when it ended there was some improvement. Cold War tensions began to ease.

Activity

You are a member of a Commission of Enquiry set up by the American government in 1975 to decide whether the USA was right to become involved in the war in Vietnam.

1 Make a copy of the following chart.

Reasons for	Reasons against

2 Complete the columns using the evidence given in this section and below.

3 Write a conclusion to your report explaining whether you think the USA should have become involved.

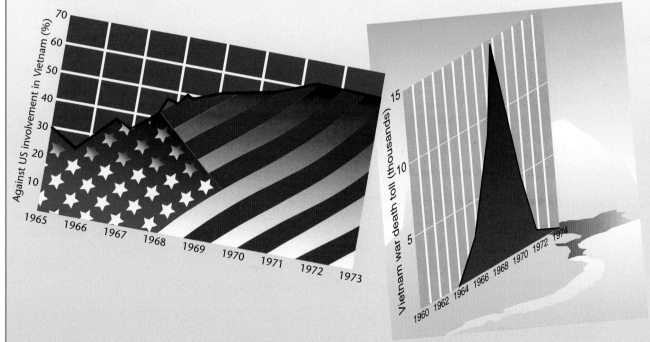

296

SOURCE J

From the *Observer* newspaper, 28 January 1973

By the spring of 1968 American people were convinced that victory in Vietnam was not worth 300 dead and $30,000 million a year.

SOURCE K

Article in *Time* magazine, 24 November 1961

If the USA cannot or will not save South Vietnam from the Communist assault, no Asian nation can ever again feel safe in putting its faith in the USA – and the fall of all of Southeast Asia would only be a matter of time.

SOURCE L

A Soviet cartoon mocks Vietnam's increasing cost in American lives. The first thing President Johnson asked for each morning was the previous day's number of US casualties.

Questions

1. Explain the following events in the war:
   a. 'Operation Rolling Thunder'.
   b. the 'Tet offensive'.
   c. Vietnamisation.
2. Why was there growing opposition in the USA to the Vietnam war?
3. How useful is Source **B** to an historian studying American attitudes to the war in Vietnam?
4. What reasons are suggested in Sources **G**, **H** and **I** for the American defeat?
5. What effects did the war have on Vietnam?
6. Is Source **L** a reliable view of the war in Vietnam?

In 1968 there was another example of firm Soviet action in Eastern Europe – an invasion of Czechoslovakia, which echoed the invasion of Hungary in 1956.

Czech opposition to Soviet control

Czechoslovakia had been a Soviet satellite state since 1948 with its government taking orders from Moscow. However, many Czechs wanted changes including:

- Freedom of expression. They wanted to be free to discuss ideas openly and to express their opinions in the press and on the radio.

- The freedom to set up political parties and to vote freely in elections.

- More influence over the way their factories were run.

- An end to the secret police and their rule of terror.

- An end to Soviet control of the economy. The USSR forced Czech industry to produce those raw materials which the Soviet economy needed, such as steel. It stopped factories from producing consumer goods. As a result the Czechs had a low standard of living.

The 'Prague Spring', 1968

In 1968 the Czechoslovakian Communist Party decided reforms were needed. It removed the unpopular President Novotny who had ruled for more than ten years. Alexander Dubcek became Party Secretary.

Dubcek's aims were to improve the standard of living of the Czech people and give them more freedom. He intended to keep the country Communist, closely allied to the USSR and a member of the Warsaw Pact. He brought in a series of reforms.

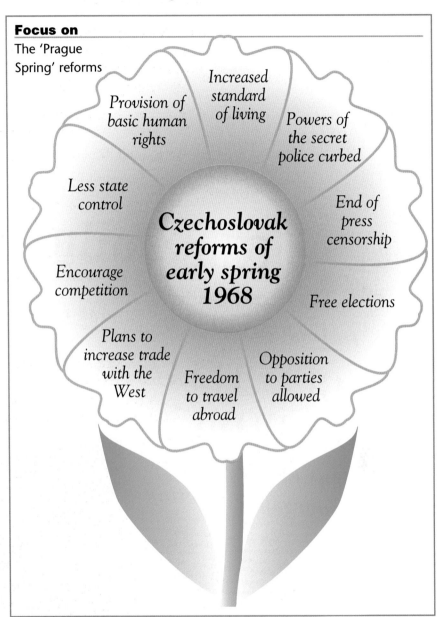

Focus on

The 'Prague Spring' reforms

Provision of basic human rights

Increased standard of living

Powers of the secret police curbed

Less state control

Czechoslovak reforms of early spring 1968

End of press censorship

Encourage competition

Free elections

Plans to increase trade with the West

Freedom to travel abroad

Opposition to parties allowed

The Soviet response

Soviet leaders believed that Dubcek's reforms threatened their control of Eastern Europe. They feared that:

1   There would be further demands for even more freedom in Czechoslovakia. If granted, people in other Eastern European states would demand them too. This, in turn, might destroy the rule of the Communist parties in these countries and Soviet control.

2   The USSR also feared that Czechoslovakia would ally with Yugoslavia, who had refused to join the Warsaw Pact, and Romania, who would no longer attend meetings of the Pact.

1968

June   Soviet tanks remained in Czechoslovakia after Warsaw Pact military exercises.

July   Five of the Warsaw Pact members – USSR, Hungary, East Germany, Poland and Bulgaria – warned Dubcek that his reforms would remove power from the Communist Party.

August   The Warsaw Pact countries invaded Czechoslovakia on 20 August and took control. Dubcek was arrested and taken to Moscow.

SOURCE C

Front page of the *Daily Telegraph*, 22 August 1968

The Daily Telegraph
and Morning Post

Printed in LONDON and MANCHESTER.

Savile Row
the mark of a master shoemaker

Savile Row
Shoemakers Limited
Northampton

Style 330
black calf chelsea

No. 35247. LONDON, THURSDAY, AUGUST 22, 1968.

PLIT.
£264m
E

Dubcek arrested by Soviet troops

PRAGUE TELLS RUSSIANS 'GO HOME'

President on 'free radio': UN emergency meeting

Brothers in arms – two months ago

FIRES raged in Prague last night as the Russian invaders tried to stamp out pockets of Czechoslovak resistance. At least 25 people were killed and hundreds injured throughout the country as Czechs took to the streets, most to shout abuse and to plead with the invaders to leave, but some to fight back with stones and Molotov cocktails.

Mr. Dubcek, President Svoboda and several other liberal Communist leaders were arrested by Soviet troops yesterday. But the tape-recorded voice of Mr. Svoboda was broadcast last night by clandestine radio stations set up after the Russians closed down official stations.

The President said: "We are living through an exceptionally grave moment in the life of our nation." Russian and Warsaw Pact forces had "entered our territory without the consent of the constitutional authorities of our state."

The Prague Government "must achieve the speedy withdrawal of the foreign forces." He had done everything possible to negotiate a settlement and hoped agreement would be reached tomorrow.

"There is no way back," he said, from freedom and democracy.

Mr. Dubcek, Mr. Smrkovsky, President of

We act with U.N., says Stewart

By WALTER FARR
Diplomatic Staff

BRITAIN is joining with other governments in calling for condemnation of Russia's invasion of Czechoslovakia by the United Nations Security Council.

Mr. Stewart, Foreign Secretary, has not yet made a firm decision on whether to attend the Council.

As Russia can veto Council action there are plans for immediate use of the uniting for peace procedure. Under this the General Assembly can be convened when the Security Council has failed to act because there is no unanimity regarding a breach of the peace.

Russian tank crews and Czech soldiers fraternising during Warsaw Pact manœuvres near Prague in June. Withdrawal of Soviet forces at the end of the exercises was delayed because of "abnormal traffic conditions."

U.S. tries to avoid 'crisis'

By DAVID ADAMSON
WASHINGTON, Wednesday.

THE invasion of Czechoslovakia was described as "tragic" today by President Johnson in a sombrely delivered statement at the White House. There was no reference to the effect on relations with Russia, but

SWASTIKAS DRAWN ON TANKS

By DAVID FLOYD
Communist Affairs Correspondent
BRATISLAVA, Wednesday.

COLUMNS of Russian tanks came rolling into this city this evening, which has been

IN a mi for Eng would group in
Its an GEC/A1 biggest industrial country.
Lord Nel English Ele to rejecting statement is said that could "not of the indu the Plessey

CAREFUL
Company's
Lord Nelso advised this posed Plesse the first we This will no amined and English Elect
"The prop control and very broad in of a compan is confined to telephone fiel
"We will statement wh of this situa very carefull been studied.
If English into immedi its mercha Lazards, doe the Plessey battle will r epic which throughout

SHARES R
Terms of t
The Eng price leapt

Source D

Czech radio broadcast, 21 August 1968

Yesterday troops from the Soviet union crossed the frontiers of the Czechoslovak Socialist Republic. This happened without the knowledge of the President of the Republic or the First Secretary of the Czechoslovak Communist Party Central Committee.

September– October	Dubcek agreed to reverse most of his reforms and to allow Soviet troops to be stationed in Czechoslovakia.
1969	The USSR worked with hard-line Communists in Prague to remove Dubcek and his supporters from power. A new government was set up under Gustav Husak.

Source E

Soviet press statement, 21 August 1968

The leaders of the Czechoslovak Socialist Republic have asked the Soviet Union and other allied states to give assistance to the Czechoslovak people, including assistance with armed forces.

Source F

A Czech street poster from 1968. Lenin is shown weeping as the Soviet tanks invade Czechoslovakia.

Results of the Czech crisis

Soviet action in Czechoslovakia had several important effects:

- It temporarily worsened East–West relations. The West protested at Soviet actions. Détente, however, continued after only a slight break.

- Czechoslovakia returned to strict Communist rule. People in Eastern European countries were reminded that the USSR would maintain strict Communist rule and the Warsaw Pact.

- Nevertheless some Communist countries began to move away from Moscow. President Ceaucescu of Romania refused to send troops to join the forces invading Czechoslovakia in 1968. He took a more independent line against Moscow. Albania did likewise and left the Warsaw Pact for good.

- China criticised the invasion. The Chinese disliked the use of force against a fellow Communist nation. They feared that the USSR might do the same against China.

The Brezhnev Doctrine

Brezhnev had eventually succeeded Khrushchev as Soviet leader.

The Soviet leader announced that if forces 'hostile to Socialism' tried to turn a Communist country towards Capitalism it was the duty of Communist countries to intervene. This caused a split in the Communist world. Yugoslavia, Romania, China and Communist parties in the West opposed this doctrine.

Comparison of Hungary (1956) and Czechoslovakia (1968)

Copy the following chart and look for similarities and differences between Czechoslovakia, 1968, and Hungary, 1956.

Comparison of Hungary and Czechoslovakia		
	Hungary 1956	Czechoslovakia 1968
Attitude to free elections		
Attitude to Warsaw Pact		
Help from West		
Reaction of USSR		

Activity

You are an English visitor in Prague at the end of August 1968. Write a letter from Prague, explaining to a friend what has happened.

Questions

1 What reforms were introduced by Dubcek?
2 According to Source **A**, what effect did Dubcek have?
3 Explain why the USSR decided to invade Czechoslovakia.
4 What differences are there between Sources **D** and **E** in their views of the invasion? Why do you think they give different views?
5 What message is the poster, Source **F**, trying to get across? How useful is this source to an historian studying the events of 1968 in Czechoslovakia?
6 What was the 'Brezhnev Doctrine'?

DÉTENTE, 1971–79

The 1970s was another period of détente or thaw in the Cold War, a period when relations between the superpowers improved. It particularly applied to the period between 1971 when the first Nixon–Brezhnev Summit Conference was planned and 1979 when the USSR invaded Afghanistan causing a 'Second Cold War'.

SOVIET REASONS

1   There had been a breakdown of relations with China. This made it even more important to reduce tension with the USA.

2   The USSR had caught up in the Arms Race and felt more confident.

3   In 1969 West Germany had agreed with East Germany not to acquire nuclear weapons. This removed a potential threat.

4   The USSR wanted to increase trade with the West.

REASONS COMMON TO BOTH

1   To reduce the risk of nuclear war.

2   To reduce the ever-growing costs of the Arms Race. Both countries had economic problems in the 1970s. In the USA there was rising inflation. This, together with the cost of the war in Vietnam, was damaging the American economy. The Soviet Union had low living standards and its industry was inefficient.

3   Both superpowers were worried about conflict in the Middle East. Oil supplies from the area were vital to both countries and the Suez Canal was important for sea routes. Communist and non-Communist countries had become involved in the conflict in the area between Arabs and Israelis.

Focus on

nuclear weapons

180 strategic bombers

569 strategic bombers

1054 land-launched ICBMs

1500 land-launched ICBMs

3 anti-ballistic missile sites (9 more planned)

4 anti-ballistic missile sites

656 submarine-launched ICBMs

400 submarine-launched ICBMs

SOURCE B

This American cartoon, about the reasons for the SALT I talks, was published in 1970

SOURCE A

Leonid Brezhnev speaking in May 1975

In the new situation, the leaders of the Capitalist world have also come to realise that the Cold War has outlived itself. There is the need for a new, realistic and sensible policy. The leaders of the West have begun to respond to our calls for peaceful co-existence.

US REASONS

1   After the failure in Vietnam President Nixon changed American policies abroad. He wanted to improve relations with both the USSR and China.

2   There was pressure from the American public to reduce the risks of war.

3   The USSR had caught up in the Arms Race.

4   America was concerned about a possible alliance between China and the USSR.

ACHIEVEMENTS OF DÉTENTE

The 1972 SALT talks

THE EUROPEAN SECURITY CONFERENCE, 1973–75

Representatives from Canada, the USA, the USSR and 32 European countries met in Helsinki. In 1975 they signed the Helsinki Accords (agreements):

- In security they recognised the frontiers of Eastern Europe and Soviet control over the region. West Germany recognised East Germany.
- They agreed to co-operate through trade links, cultural exchanges and the exchange of technological information.
- Finally, they agreed to respect human rights and allow people to travel freely across Europe.

SUMMIT CONFERENCES

Five were held between 1972 and 1979. The first three were between Brezhnev and Nixon. They led to:

- Agreements about procedures to reduce the risk of confrontation and nuclear war.
- A joint space mission in 1975.
- Increased trade links.
- Cultural exchanges.

HUMAN RIGHTS

Many in the West believed that the Helsinki Accords would encourage the USSR to allow human rights. This meant freedom of belief and expression in the Soviet Union and Eastern Europe. The USSR, however, made little effort to improve human rights:

- It stopped the work of Andrei Sakharov, who was a vocal critic of the Soviet government. He wanted an end to the Cold War, the introduction of democracy in the USSR and a worldwide ban on nuclear weapons.
- In Czechoslovakia members of a group called Charter 77 were also suppressed. They were Czechs who wanted better human rights.
- When a US Congressman tried to have a trade agreement linked to the improved treatment of European Jews, Brezhnev cancelled the deal.

ARMS CONTROL

Talks began in 1969 about a Strategic Arms Limitation Treaty (SALT). The superpowers eventually signed two treaties:

- *In SALT 1 (1972) they agreed to reduce their anti-ballistic missile systems and to limit the number of their offensive missiles and bombers.*

- *In SALT II (1979) they agreed further limits on missiles but the talks were less successful than hoped. In 1980 President Carter refused to accept the treaty because of the Soviet invasion of Afghanistan.*

There was little progress on talks to reduce conventional weapons. The USSR refused to reveal the size of Warsaw Pact forces and made it clear that it intended to keep its superiority over NATO forces.

RELATIONS BETWEEN THE USA AND CHINA

These improved in the 1970s. In 1971 the USA agreed that Communist China should be allowed to join the United Nations. The USA table tennis team visited and played matches in Peking (now Beijing). This was given the nickname of 'ping pong diplomacy'.

In 1972 President Nixon visited Peking and met the Chinese leader, Mao Zedong.

SOURCE C

The US table tennis team were among the first Westerners to go to Communist China. They lost matches but won friends.

The failures of détente in the 1970s

Détente reached a peak in the mid-1970s. Overall, however, it proved disappointing. The West became frustrated by the failure of the Soviet Union to improve human rights. They were also suspicious about whether the USSR was keeping to the terms of the SALT I agreement. In fact both superpowers were positioning more missiles against each other. Brezhnev made it clear that détente did not mean an end to the struggle between Communism and Capitalism. Western critics also said that the USSR was only interested in the benefits of détente to itself. Benefits such as trade links and reduced spending on armaments. Superpower rivalry continued in the Arab–Israeli War (1973) and Angola (1974–75).

Activity

Do a balance sheet of the successes and failures of détente in the 1970s.

Successes	Failures

Overall, do you think it was a success or failure?

Questions

1. In Source **A**, what reasons does Brezhnev give for détente?
2. What point is the cartoonist trying to make in Source **B**? Is this a reliable view of the reasons for détente?
3. What part did the following play in détente in the 1970s:
   a. SALT I and SALT II?
   b. the Helsinki Accords?
   c. 'Ping Pong' diplomacy?
4. Explain two reasons why détente disappointed many in the 1970s.

THE WAR IN AFGHANISTAN

Détente came to a sudden halt on Christmas Eve 1979 when Brezhnev sent troops into Afghanistan.

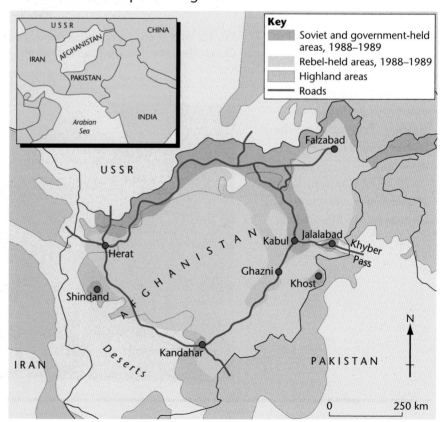

Why did the USSR invade?

Although Afghanistan was poor and mostly barren, it occupied an important position in East–West land routes. It also provided the Soviet Union with a land route to the oil-rich Middle East. The two superpowers had been competing for influence in Afghanistan for some time. Soviet ties with the Afghans were strengthened when, in 1955, Krushchev visited the capital, Kabul, and promised the Afghanistan government aid and equipment. The USA were worried about Soviet influence and also offered aid – but never more than one-third of the Soviet total.

Afghanistan had an unstable government. In 1979 Hafizullah Amin seized power as president. He was a Communist, but was not on good terms with the USSR. Large Muslim groups in the country were opposed to him. The Soviet Union feared that these Muslim groups were planning to take control of the country and set up a Muslim state. This had happened in neighbouring Iran in January 1979. The Soviet Union was also aware that it, too, had a large Muslim population in its areas near the Afghanistan border. This Muslim population might try to break away from the Soviet Union and support the Afghans.

The Soviet invasion

The Soviet troops quickly captured the airport at Kabul and in the next few days 350 Russian aircraft landed with their troops and equipment. Within a week about 50,000 Soviet troops were in Afghanistan. The president's palace at Kabul was captured and President Amin was killed.

On New Year's Day 1980, a new government was set up in Kabul, led by Babrak Karmal. He was an Afghan leader who had been in exile in the Soviet Union.

The Soviet invasion was opposed by rebel Afghan tribesmen known as the Mujaheddin. They were hopelessly outgunned by the Soviet armed forces and retreated to the mountains. They now waged a guerrilla war against the Soviet invaders. This was very effective and tied down over 100,000 Russian soldiers because:

- The Mujaheddin were fighting for a cause – to turn Afghanistan into a Muslim country.

- Their guerrilla tactics were very effective. They successfully attacked Soviet supply routes and shot at Soviet planes and were well hidden in the mountains.

- The new president was seen as a Soviet puppet ruler and was very unpopular.

- The Soviet Union faced hostility from Muslim nations such as Pakistan.

- In 1982 a massive attack against the Mujaheddin in the Panjahir Valley failed.

By 1988 the Mujaheddin controlled over 75% of the country.

SOURCE A

David Halberstam writing in *Time* magazine

The Soviets are learning the big Vietnam lesson. It is easier to go into these countries than it is to get out. They will find out, just as the US did, how amazingly easy it is for a little country to swallow a military machine.

Mujaheddin resistance fighters in Afghanistan

Results of Soviet invasion

1   President Carter said that the invasion had completely changed his view of the USSR. He took several anti-Soviet measures, including:

SOURCE C

Cartoon in the *Daily Telegraph*, 3 January 1980. The figure with the hammer is Brezhnev.

THE HAMMER & CRESCENT

- Refusing to agree to the SALT II agreement.

- Ordering US athletes to boycott the 1980 Olympic Games held in Moscow.

- Starting to rearm.

- Imposing a ban on American grain sales to the USSR.

2 It put an end to superpower détente and was the start of the 'Second Cold War'.

3 The invasion had a devastating effect on Afghanistan:

- Over three million refugees fled to Pakistan or Iran.

- About one million people died.

- Afghans who remained suffered from food shortages because the war had destroyed so much farmland.

4 The invasion proved a failure for the Soviet Union:

- It lost about 20,000 soldiers in the war against the Mujaheddin.

- The war caused great damage to the Soviet economy costing several billion dollars a year.

In 1985 a new Soviet leader, Mikhail Gorbachev, realised that the war could never be won. He started talks in 1987 with the USA and agreement was reached at Geneva in 1988. The last Soviet troops left Afghanistan in February 1989.

Activity

The war in Afghanistan has often been compared to the American involvement in Vietnam (pp. 287–88). Copy the chart below and write in similarities and differences.

	USA in Vietnam	USSR in Afghanistan
Similarities		
Differences		

The following might help your comparison:

- Why each superpower became involved.

- The type of warfare fought.

- The opposition to the Americans and the Russians.

- The effects of the wars on the economies and armies of both superpowers.

- The success or failure of the wars for the superpowers.

- The impact on the Cold War.

Questions

1 Explain the reasons for the Soviet invasion of Afghanistan.

2 Why were the Soviet armed forces unable to defeat the Mujaheddin?

3 Is the cartoon, Source **C**, for or against the Soviet invasion? Give reasons for your answer.

4 What effects did the Afghanistan war have on:
- **a** the USA?
- **b** the USSR?
- **c** Afghanistan?

The Soviet invasion of Afghanistan sparked off further East–West rivalry. There were, however, other reasons.

Reagan's change of policy

In 1980 Ronald Reagan replaced Carter as US President.

Reagan believed that détente had caused the USA to lose ground to the USSR.

He returned to an anti-Soviet policy. This included:

- Expanding the USA's armed forces.

- Developing a new type of bomb – the neutron bomb. This could kill many people without destroying much property. The Americans were also developing the MX missile. This powerful missile could be transported underground and be launched from different underground sites.

- Basing new modern missiles, such as Pershing 2 and Cruise, in those European countries that wished to accept them

- Launching the Strategic Defence Initiative (SDI).

'Star Wars'

This was the nickname for the SDI. It was an expensive programme to develop anti-missile weapons using laser beams. If successful it would mean that the USA could not be the victim of a 'first strike'. The aim was to make it impossible for Soviet missiles to reach US targets by creating a huge laser shield in space.

SOURCE A

Denis Healey, a leading member of the British Labour Party, speaking in the 1980s

When the eighties began, the prospects for world peace seemed worse than at any time since 1945. Brezhnev's invasion of Afghanistan had already led President Carter to break off negotiations with the USSR. He withdrew the SALT II treaty from the Senate and started a massive programme of rearmament.

Questions

1 What was 'Star Wars'?
2 What point is Reagan trying to make in the photo, Source B?

SOURCE B

Reagan makes the case for the 'Star Wars' programme

SDI COULD RUIN A NUCLEAR BOMB'S WHOLE DAY.

The first major threat in the 1980s to Soviet control over Eastern Europe came in Poland with the emergence of the 'Solidarity' movement.

Polish opposition to Soviet control

The Poles disliked Soviet control for several reasons:

1   The Soviet Union had tried to suppress the Polish Catholic Church. Despite this, the Church remained strong and demanded freedom to preach as it wished and to run its own schools.

2   There was a strong feeling of nationalism in Poland. The Poles wanted their country to be free to make its own policies even if it was closely allied to the USSR.

3   There was discontent because of poor living standards. The Poles wanted an end to the shortages of food and other goods.

4   Poles, backed by the Church, wanted a free press and the right to discuss issues openly.

Events in the 1970s

In 1971 Gierek became the Polish Communist Party leader after widespread riots against food prices. He aimed to introduce some reforms while keeping firm control. Economic reforms led to some improvements in living standards. However, Poland went further into debt and food shortages continued.

In 1976 police angered Poles by causing deaths and injuries while cracking down on strikes against proposed price rises.

In 1978 the Polish Cardinal Wojtyla was elected Pope John Paul II. This led to:

- even greater nationalist feeling in Poland.

- greater hatred of the government.

- stronger church opposition to the government.

The 'Solidarity' movement

Shipyard workers led by Lech Walesa in Gdansk (known as Danzig before the Second World War) formed a movement called 'Solidarity'.

Profile on

Lech Walesa

He was an electrician who worked in the shipyards of Gdansk. Within a year, 1979–80, he became the most popular man in Poland. He created Solidarity. The red Solidarity logo, designed by a sign painter at the Gdansk shipyard, became famous as a symbol of opposition to Communism. Like many other Polish workers, Walesa was poorly paid at a time when bread prices were high. He became the spokesman of the Polish workers.

'Solidarity' campaigned for:

Workers to have the right to form trade unions independent of the state

The Polish government to grant Poles more freedom and improve standards of living and working.

SOURCE A

Lech Walesa speaking to a crowd of 4000 shipyard workers in 1980

Shipyard workers! Hull fitters, welders, paint sprayers, plumbers, and you too, members of the intelligensia, listen to me. We demand that prices be brought down, back to their previous levels. And if they're not, then there'll be strikes tomorrow.

SOURCE B

An account written by a Polish woman in 1980

My husband comes home from work and says what they are saying in the District Committee of the Communist Party. They are saying that Lech Walesa, the leader of the strike, has got a criminal record, is a drunkard and a scrounger.

In 1980 there were more food shortages and price rises as the government failed to improve Poland's economy. In protest workers in the shipyards along the Baltic coast went on strike. The government decided to negotiate. It feared that the use of force would upset the whole population and lead to even greater protests.

The agreement

Workers agreed to accept

* The leading role of the Communist Party in Poland.

* The Socialist economic system.

* Poland's links with the USSR and the other East European countries.

The government agreed to

* The right to strike.

* The right to form independent trade unions.

* More open discussion of government policy.

* A relaxation of censorship.

* Improved wages and working conditions.

1981 'Solidarity' threatened Soviet control of Poland. The Soviet government knew that it had to keep control of Poland – otherwise other Communist countries in Eastern Europe might also claim their freedom. The USSR encouraged the Polish armed forces to seize control of the government, ban the trade union and imprison its leaders. The new Polish leader was General Jaruzelski. He introduced martial law and arrested Walesa and other union leaders.

Source C

General Jaruzelski describing the pressure put on him to deal with Solidarity in late 1981

I was summoned three times to the Soviet Union. On the last occasion I was shown army manoeuvres all along the Polish border. The Soviet army leader, Marshal Ustinov, informed me that the USSR would not accept what was happening in Poland.

Source D

Lech Walesa speaking in 1981

I told the gentleman who came to arrest me, 'This is the moment of your defeat. These are the last nails in the coffin of Communism'.

1982 General Jaruzelski banned 'Solidarity' but released Walesa.

1983 He ended martial law but refused to legalise 'Solidarity'.

Source E

Solidarity demonstration in Krakow in 1983

1984–87 The Church and 'Solidarity' led the opposition to the government. The government struggled to improve Poland's economy.

1988   A severe economic crisis led to further strikes.

1989   'Solidarity' triumphed in the elections and the Communists did badly. The leaders of 'Solidarity' refused to join the Communist government. Jaruzelski was forced to appoint a non-Communist prime minister. In return for help from 'Solidarity' in solving the country's economic problems Jaruzelski agreed to:

- legalise 'Solidarity'.
- increase press freedom.
- hold elections while reserving a majority of seats for the Communists.

1990   Walesa elected President of Poland in free elections.

The significance of the Solidarity movement

1   Solidarity had forced a strong Communist government, firmly backed by the Soviet Union, to give way. This had been achieved by:

- the action of industrial workers backed by popular opinion.
- the use of non-violent methods.

2   The movement also showed that a Communist government could not solve Poland's economic problems. The government had lost the confidence of the people and dared not use force against the strikers.

3   The USSR still wanted a one-party Communist government in Poland but had not used force to ensure this – unlike in the cases of Hungary and Czechoslovakia.

Questions

1   According to Source **A**, what were the aims of the Solidarity movement?
2   How reliable is Source **B** as a view of Lech Walesa?
3   Why was the Solidarity movement eventually successful in Poland?

Activity

Write a television speech for General Jaruzelski in 1982 in which he has to tell the Polish people the real reasons he has to ban Solidarity.

Or

Write a speech made by Lech Walesa in 1980 in which he explains the aims of the Solidarity movement.

In the 1980s there were major changes in the Soviet Union, in its policies at home and abroad.

In 1985 Gorbachev became Secretary-General of the Soviet Communist Party. At 54 he was a relatively young Soviet leader committed to carrying out reforms. He inherited many problems in the USSR. The Soviet standard of living was even lower than in most other Eastern European countries. The wealth of the USSR could not keep up with increased military spending. The USSR was suffering severe food shortages and had to import grain from the USA and other Western countries. Standards of health and housing were poor and declining.

Profile on

Mikhail Gorbachev

He was born in 1931 in the village of Privolnoye in Stavropol province. His family were poor farmers and at the age of 13 Mikhail began work on the farm. In the 1950s he studied Law at Moscow University, returning to Stavropol after he graduated. He worked as a Communist Party official and was eventually promoted to become a member of the central committee of the Communist Party with responsibility for agriculture. At the age of only 49 he became a member of the Politburo, the most powerful ruling body of the Communist Party. He served under President Brezhnev and was deputy under President Chernenko. When Chernenko died in 1985 the Politburo made Gorbachev its new leader at the age of 54.

His plan

Gorbachev had several aims:

1   To restructure the Soviet economy. This became known as *perestroika*. This meant allowing more competition and more incentives to produce goods.

2   To listen to public opinion and be more open about government policy. This was known as *glasnost*.

3   To continue to keep real power in the hands of the Communist Party but allow some elections.

4   To reduce party control of the economy.

5   To reduce military spending.

6   To encourage Western firms to invest in the USSR.

Gorbachev did introduce reforms in the Soviet Union. Many people who had been imprisoned for disagreeing with Communist policies were released. Others, such as Andrei Sakharov, were allowed to return from exile. In 1987 changes in economic policy meant that people were allowed to buy and sell at a profit for the first time since Stalin had come to power more than 60 years before.

Détente again 1985–91

This was due to changes in the USSR and in the attitude of Reagan, the American President. At first their aims seemed very different.

Gorbachev's aims

- To withdraw Soviet troops from Afghanistan.

- To reduce Soviet aid worldwide.

- To improve relations with China.

- To seek détente with the USA to reduce defence spending.

- To borrow money from Western banks to pay for imported food, raw materials and equipment.

- To persuade Western firms to build factories in the USSR.

Reagan's aims

- To expand the USA's armed forces.

- To base new missiles – such as Pershing and Cruise – in those European countries that wished to accept them.

- To launch the Strategic Defence Initiative (SDI) – nicknamed 'Star Wars'.

Focus on

REAGAN'S CHOICES

	Action
Refuse détente and refuse to help Gorbachev	He continued to treat the Soviet military threat seriously and follow a strong defence policy. This might force Gorbachev to give way over arms reduction.
Return to détente and help Gorbachev	At the same time he was prepared to work with the USSR over détente. He knew he needed to make cuts in American defence spending.

What was achieved?

There were several achievements:

The Intermediate Nuclear Forces (INF) Treaty 1987
The superpowers agreed to eliminate all intermediate missiles in Europe within three years.

'Genuine friendship'
Reagan and Gorbachev got on very well when they met. They made real progress on the reduction of NATO and Warsaw Pact conventional forces.

SOURCE C

The meeting between Reagan and Gorbachev at Geneva, November 1985

START Treaty 1991
Talks on long-range missiles (formerly the SALT talks) were renamed Strategic Arms Reduction Talks (START). They led to the 1991 Treaty – this agreed significant reductions in weapons.

The collapse of the Soviet Union

Gorbachev's reforms had upset hard-line Communists. They said that he was stirring up trouble and raising the expectations of the Soviet people too much. In some respects, they were right. For example, once freedom of speech was allowed, Gorbachev could not control the media. Many people wanted to get rid of Communism altogether. In fact discontent continued to grow in the USSR:

- The loss of Eastern European countries in 1989–90 (p. 320) made Gorbachev appear weak.

- His economic reforms brought no immediate improvement. There were still food shortages and rising prices.

- Many now wanted to see the collapse of the Communist system, not just Communist reforms.

SOURCE D

A Russian quoted in *The Independent* 20 August 1991

Gorbachev is an idiot. He should never have gone on holiday. They've done for him just like Khrushchev.

- The new President of the Russian Republic, Boris Yeltsin, encouraged the break-up of the Soviet Union.

He was facing more and more criticism from those who thought he had gone too far and from others who believed he had not gone far enough. He could not win.

February 1990	250,000 people demonstrated in Moscow against Communism.
May 1990	At the annual May Day parade in Moscow's Red Square, Gorbachev was booed.
August 1991	Hard-line Communists overthrew Gorbachev. He was made a prisoner in his own country home in the Crimea. Yeltsin led a demonstration against the coup. He insisted that the reform movement had to continue in order to rescue Russia from a slide back to the days of Communist repression. He was seen as a great hero.

SOURCE E

Newspaper headlines in *The Independent*, 20 August 1991

YELTSIN DEFIES COUP 'TERROR'

We won't fire on our own people

Germans lead scramble to pull out their loans

OLD ALLIES SHIVER AS 'ICE AGE' POLITICS RETURN

KOHL WARNS AGAINST FORCE AND 'SPILLING OF BLOOD'

Secret Chinese glee as Mao's maxim lives on

[Mao said 'political power comes from the barrel of a gun']

Experts warn of purges, trials and civil war

YELTSIN WARNS OF A 'REIGN OF TERROR'

WORLD REACTS WITH OUTRAGE AND FEAR

WESTERN STOCK MARKETS TUMBLE

December 1991 Yeltsin disbanded the Communist Party in Russia and formally ended the Soviet Union. Gorbachev resigned as Soviet President. The USSR was replaced by a Commonwealth of Independent States (CIS).

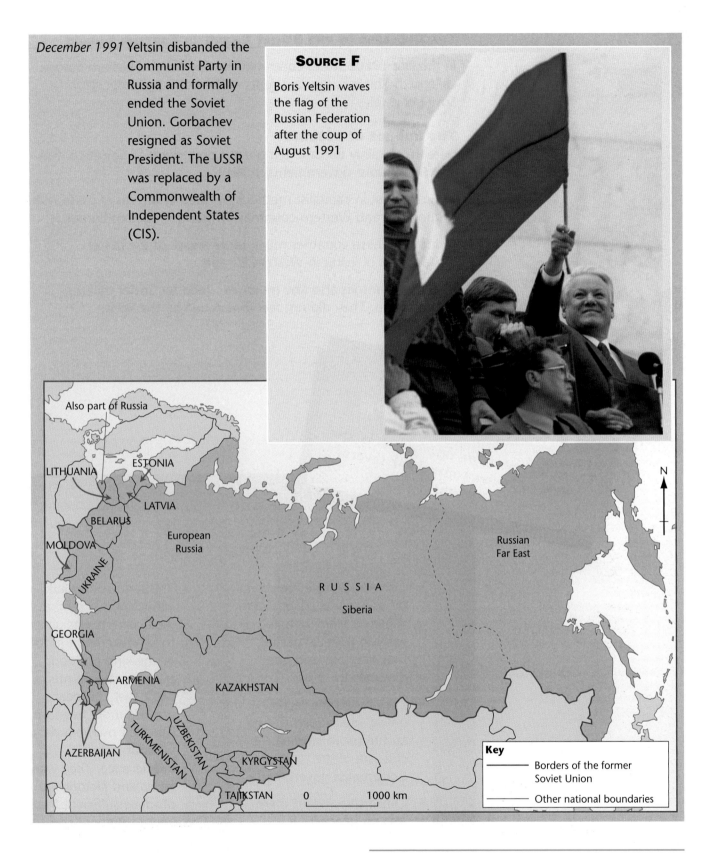

SOURCE F

Boris Yeltsin waves the flag of the Russian Federation after the coup of August 1991

Also part of Russia

LITHUANIA
ESTONIA
LATVIA
BELARUS
MOLDOVA
UKRAINE
GEORGIA
ARMENIA
AZERBAIJAN
TURKMENISTAN
UZBEKISTAN
KYRGYSTAN
TAJIKSTAN
KAZAKHSTAN

European Russia

RUSSIA
Siberia

Russian Far East

N

Key
— Borders of the former Soviet Union
— Other national boundaries

0   1000 km

Activity

You are a hard-line Soviet Communist opposed to Gorbachev's changes. Put together a poster in which you explain why you are against him.

Questions

1 Explain the meaning of glasnost and perestroika.
2 According to Sources **A** and **B**, why was there détente in the 1980s?
3 Why was Gorbachev overthrown in 1991?

THE COLLAPSE OF THE SOVIET EMPIRE IN EASTERN EUROPE

In the late 1980s Soviet control of the countries of Eastern Europe collapsed. This was due to events in the USSR and opposition to Soviet control.

The impact of détente

Détente certainly encouraged greater opposition to Soviet control and Communist governments. It led to:

- An interest in capitalist methods because of increased trade with the West and Western countries investing in Eastern Europe.

- It made these countries much more aware of the better standards of living in Western Europe.

- These countries also saw much less need for Soviet military protection. They did not feel threatened by the West.

GROWING OPPOSITION IN EASTERN EUROPE

There was growing opposition in the 1980s to Soviet control for several reasons.

POLITICAL REASONS

- Communist rule meant no other political parties were allowed. Many people wanted political parties, free elections and free discussion.

- They hated the secret police which used torture and terror to stop all criticism of the Communist governments.

- Censorship meant there was no freedom of expression. The state controlled the press, radio and TV. Many wanted freedom of the press and media.

ECONOMIC REASONS

The state-controlled economy was seen as inefficient. It was unable to produce enough food or the kind of goods people really wanted. Most East Europeans wanted more freedom to run their own businesses without state interference. They wanted farms and factories to produce sufficient food and a variety of consumer goods.

The impact of Gorbachev

His reforms in the Soviet Union certainly did much to encourage change in Eastern Europe. There was a number of popular demands for similar changes from the countries under Soviet control. Gorbachev also changed the relationship between these countries and the USSR. He wanted a more equal relationship. The USSR was no longer prepared to use armed forces to get its way.

This, in turn, created difficulties for the Communist parties and leaders in Eastern Europe. They had to adjust to Gorbachev's declarations that Marxism had proved a failure and that the Party was not always right. They also realised that they could no longer depend on Soviet military aid.

SOURCE A

Gennadi Gerasimov, Soviet government spokesman, October 1989

The Brezhnev Doctrine is dead. You know the Frank Sinatra song 'My Way'? Hungary and Poland are doing it their way. We now have the Sinatra Doctrine.

SOCIAL REASONS

In most East European countries there was a low standard of living. This became worse in the 1980s due to a rise in prices, unemployment, and food and consumer goods shortages. Most were desperate for improved living and working standards.

RELIGIOUS REASONS

Many East European states were strongly religious and wanted freedom of religious belief. The Communist governments persecuted the Churches and their leaders.

NATIONALISM

The Communist Party expected loyalty to Communism and the Soviet Union rather than their own nation. Many East Europeans wanted a nation free from outside control which would act in the interests of its citizens.

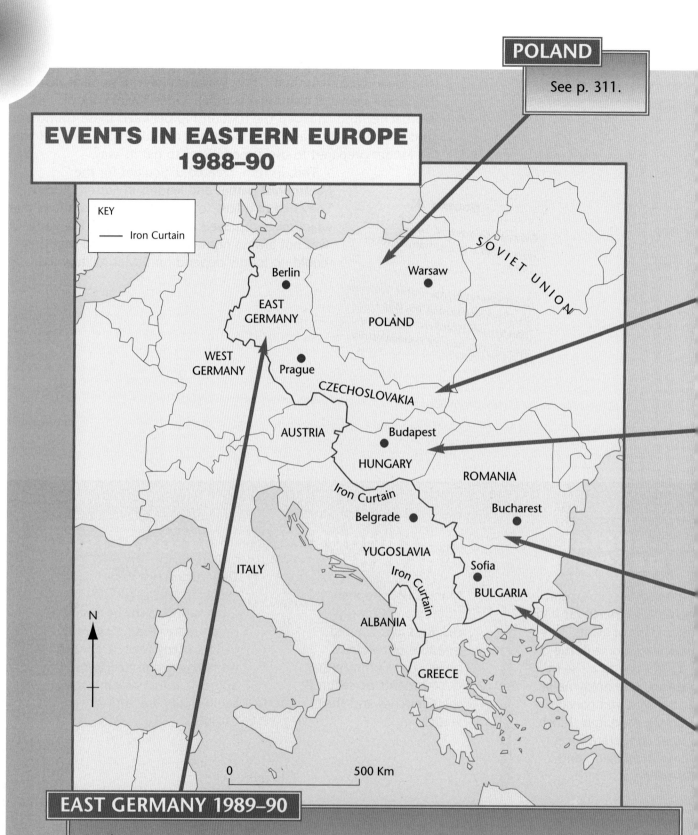

EVENTS IN EASTERN EUROPE 1988–90

POLAND

See p. 311.

KEY

—— Iron Curtain

Berlin

Warsaw

EAST GERMANY

POLAND

SOVIET UNION

WEST GERMANY

Prague

CZECHOSLOVAKIA

AUSTRIA

Budapest

HUNGARY

ROMANIA

Iron Curtain

Belgrade

Bucharest

YUGOSLAVIA

Sofia

ITALY

BULGARIA

Iron Curtain

ALBANIA

GREECE

N

0   500 Km

EAST GERMANY 1989–90

By the autumn of 1989 thousands of people were fleeing East Germany through Austria. Massive demonstrations took place in East German cities when Gorbachev visited the country. Gorbachev told the unpopular East German leader, Erich Honecker, to allow reforms. He refused and ordered his troops to fire on the demonstrators. They refused. Honecker was forced to resign. On 10 November 1989 thousands of East Germans marched to the Berlin Wall, and the guards even joined the demonstrators in pulling it down. In 1990 Communists were defeated in elections. East and West Germany were reunited.

CZECHOSLOVAKIA – THE 'VELVET' REVOLUTION, 1989

In 1987 Gorbachev visited Prague and encouraged many Czechs to demand greater freedom. In January 1989, a crowd of people chanting 'Gorbachev! Gorbachev!' gathered in Prague's Wenceslas Square to commemorate the twentieth anniversary of the death of Jan Palach. The Czech security police broke up the meeting with great brutality. News of changes in Poland and East Germany encouraged the demonstrators to continue. Gorbachev urged the Czechoslovakian government to respond to the people's demands. Non-Communists were brought into the government and free elections were organised. The opposition leader, the author Vaclav Havel, was elected President.

HUNGARY 1988

In 1988 the leader, Kadar, was replaced by a more 'liberal' Communist leader, Imre Pozsgay. In the following year Gorbachev agreed to withdraw Soviet troops. Free travel was allowed to Austria and the West. Pozsgay accepted the need for change and led the moves for reform in Hungary. Other political parties were allowed and, in November 1989, the Communist Party renamed itself as the Socialist Party, promising free elections in 1990. In 1990 a non-Communist government was elected.

ROMANIA

In December 1989 there was a short and bloody revolution in Romania. The hated Communist dictator, Nicolae Ceausescu, and his wife Elena, were murdered. Free elections were held.

BULGARIA

In November 1989 the Communist leader resigned and free elections were held the next year.

SOURCE B

Pulling down the Berlin Wall

SOURCE C

Lothar de Maiziere, the East German Prime Minister, talking in October 1990

We all have reason to be happy and thankful. We are leaving behind a system which called itself democratic but which was not democratic. Unity will of course bring many difficulties, but we have the great advantage of having a partner on our side.

SOURCE D

Headlines in *The Independent* newspaper, 1989

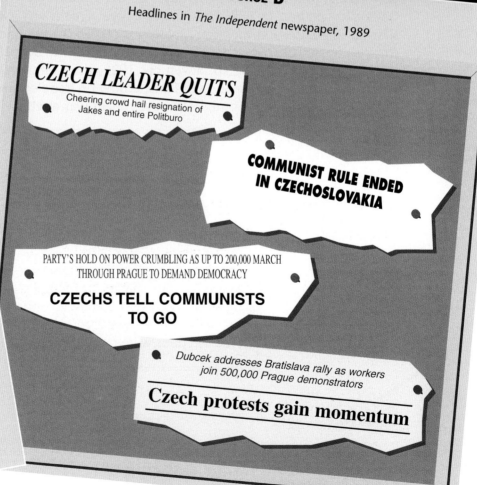

CZECH LEADER QUITS

Cheering crowd hail resignation of Jakes and entire Politburo

COMMUNIST RULE ENDED IN CZECHOSLOVAKIA

PARTY'S HOLD ON POWER CRUMBLING AS UP TO 200,000 MARCH THROUGH PRAGUE TO DEMAND DEMOCRACY

CZECHS TELL COMMUNISTS TO GO

Dubcek addresses Bratislava rally as workers join 500,000 Prague demonstrators

Czech protests gain momentum

SOURCE F

The first chink in the Iron Curtain. Hungarian border guards cut down the barbed wire fence that marked the boundary with Austria.

SOURCE E

Alexander Dubcek speaking in Wenceslas Square, 24 November 1989

We have been too long in darkness. Once already we have been in the light and we want it again. Here today, in front of you citizens and workers of Prague, I declare my support for the new democratic government.

Activity

Using the information and sources given in this section, write a speech for two of the following countries which would have been made at a political meeting explaining why they have decided on independence from the USSR. You could include:

- How that country had been treated in the past by the USSR.

- Why they disliked Soviet control and Communist government.

- The effects of Gorbachev's changes.

Countries: East Germany, Hungary and Czechoslovakia.

Or

Put together a page of newspaper headlines from the three countries summarising their change to independence.

Questions

1 Explain how détente and Gorbachev's reforms encouraged the end of Soviet rule in Eastern Europe.

2 How useful is Source **A** as evidence to an historian studying changes in Soviet policy?

3 Explain the main events that took place 1989–90 in:
   a East Germany.
   b Czechoslovakia.

The Cold War had ended. Communist Eastern Europe had collapsed. The Arms Race was at an end. This, however, did not mean the end of problems in Eastern Europe.

In January 1993 Czechoslovakia split into two separate states – the Czech Republic and Slovakia.

The worst troubles were in the former Yugoslavia where a number of areas tried to win independence after the collapse of Communist control in 1990. The Serbs refused to accept a Croat as leader, and both Slovenia and Croatia declared independence in 1991. This led to civil war and the horrors of ethnic cleansing.

Activity

Look at the following list of reasons for the end of the Cold War and superpower rivalry:

Both the USSR and the USA needed to reduce spending on nuclear weapons.

There was a fear that Europe would be the battleground for a nuclear war.

Both sides realised they had enough weapons to destroy the world several times over.

There was a desire on both sides for international peace.

Gorbachev's reforms in the USSR and Eastern Europe.

Gorbachev and Reagan got on well together.

Reagan and his wife Nancy were keen to see an end to the Arms Race.

The collapse of Soviet rule in Eastern Europe.

The USSR ceased to exist in 1991.

Now make your own rank order list with the most important reason at the top and the least important at the bottom. Write a paragraph explaining your choices.

SOURCE A

A cartoon from *The Guardian* in January 1990. It shows the Communist hammer and sickle in tears.

Perhaps, however, the Cold War had achieved something. Compared with the first half of the twentieth century there was no world war.

SUMMARY AND REVISION

There are several key developments in this period.

THE WAR IN VIETNAM

For this period, you need to understand:

- Background to the war – the French and Indo-china.

- Why the USA became involved.

- The events of the war 1963–75.

- What effects the war had on the USA and Vietnam.

- Why the USA lost the war.

- Results of the war.

Revision questions

1   Explain the significance of the role of Ho Chi Minh in the background to the conflict in Vietnam.
2   Why did the USA become involved in events in Vietnam?
3   What were 'Operation Rolling Thunder' and the 'Tet Offensive'?
4   What effects did the War have on public opinion in the USA?
5   Why and with what success did President Nixon decide on a policy of 'Vietnamisation'?
6   Why did America eventually lose the war?
7   What effects did the war have on Vietnam and the Cold War?

CZECHOSLOVAKIA 1968

You will need to understand the following:

- Why the Czechs were opposed to Soviet control.

- The events of the 'Prague Spring'.

- Why the USSR used force in Czechoslovakia.

- The effects this had on Czechoslovakia and the Cold War.

- Similarities and differences between events in Hungary (1956) and Czechoslovakia (1968).

Revision questions

1   Why did the Czechs want greater freedom from Soviet control?
2   Explain the changes introduced by Dubcek.
3   What was the reaction of the USSR?
4   What effects did the Soviet invasion have on:
    a   Czechoslovakia?
    b   the Cold War?
5   Explain the 'Brezhnev Doctrine'.
6   What similarities are there between the events in Hungary in 1956 and those in Czechoslovakia in 1968?

DÉTENTE 1971–79

This section includes:

- Soviet and American reasons for wanting détente.

- What was achieved, especially SALT talks and agreements.

- Relations between the USA and China.

- Limitations of détente in 1970s.

Revision questions

1   Explain the reasons for détente in the 1970s. What similarities are there between those of the USSR and USA?
2   What were SALT I and SALT II?
3   Was there progress in human rights in the Soviet Union? Explain your answer.
4   Describe attempts to improve relations between the USA and China.

THE WAR IN AFGHANISTAN AND THE SECOND COLD WAR 1979–85

In this section, you will need to understand:

- Why the USSR invaded Afghanistan.

- What effects this had on relations with USA.

- Why the USSR was unable to defeat the Afghan tribesmen, the Mujaheddin.

- Similarities and difference with the war in Vietnam.

- The Second Cold War, especially Reagan's policies.

Revision questions

1   Why did the USSR invade Afghanistan?
2   What similarities are there with the war in Vietnam?
3   What changes took place in relations between the USA and the USSR as a result of the invasion?
4   Why did Reagan return to an anti-Soviet policy?
5   Explain the 'Star Wars' initiative.

POLAND AND SOLIDARITY

This section includes:

- Why the Poles were opposed to Soviet rule.

- Developments in the 1970s under Gierek and the election of Pope John Paul II.

- Lech Walesa and the setting up of Solidarity.

- Events of the 1980s including strikes, arrest of Walesa and the policies of Jaruzelski.

- The success of Solidarity in 1989 and its importance.

Revision questions

1　Explain Polish opposition to the USSR in the late 1970s.
2　What part did the following play in the period 1980–89:
　　a　Lech Walesa?
　　b　Solidarity?
　　c　General Jaruzelski?
3　What was the importance of the Solidarity movement for Poland, USSR and Eastern Europe?

CHANGES IN THE USSR, DÉTENTE AND THE COLLAPSE OF THE SOVIET UNION

For this section, you need to understand:

- The changes brought about by Gorbachev, including glasnost and perestroika.

- The impact on the USSR.

- Gorbachev's aims in the Cold War.

- Other reasons for détente in the late 1980s.

- The achievements of détente, especially the START Treaty.

- Growth of opposition to Gorbachev.

- Events in the Soviet Union 1990–91, including the fall of Gorbachev and the end of the USSR.

Revision questions

1　Explain the key changes that were brought in by Gorbachev in the USSR in the late 1980s.
2　Why was there détente in the same period? What did it achieve?
3　Who opposed Gorbachev in the Soviet Union and for what reasons?
4　Explain the events leading to the break-up of the Soviet Union 1989–91.

THE COLLAPSE OF THE SOVIET EMPIRE IN EASTERN EUROPE 1989–90

This section includes:

- General reasons for the growth of opposition to Soviet control.

- The impact of détente, Gorbachev's policies and Solidarity.

- Events in each of the East European countries, including East Germany, Czechoslovakia, Bulgaria, Hungary and Romania.

- The end of the Cold War and its significance.

Revision questions

1   Why did many East European countries want an end to Soviet control and Communist government?
2   Describe the revolutions that took place in:
    a   Hungary.
    b   East Germany.
    c   Czechoslovakia.
    d   Bulgaria.
    e   Romania.
3   Why were there problems in Yugoslavia in the 1990s?
4   What was the significance of the end of the Cold War?

8
Germany 1918–45

UNDERSTANDING GERMAN HISTORY, 1918–45

The following explanations and definitions will help you to understand this chapter.

Anti-Semitism	This means hatred and persecution of the Jews.
Anschluss	The German term for the union of Austria and Germany. This was forbidden by the Treaty of Versailles.
Aryan	Nazi term for a non-Jewish German, for someone of supposedly 'pure' Germanic stock.
Autobahn	A 'super highway' consisting of four lanes.
Chancellor	The German equivalent of prime minister.
'Diktat'	Dictated peace. This is what most Germans called the Treaty of Versailles.
Freikorps	Group of former army officers and soldiers, set up in 1919 after the First World War. They were anti-Communist, anti-Jewish and nationalistic. Many of the Freikorps went on to join the SA.
Führer	Leader. This was the title adopted by Hitler.
Gestapo	The Nazi secret police.
Hyperinflation	This means a very rapid fall in the value of a country's currency. It happened to the German mark in 1923.
Lebensraum	Living space. Hitler believed the German people needed living space in the east.
'November Criminals'	This was the name given to the German politicians who agreed to the armistice in November 1918.
Passive resistance	This means non-violent disobedience. The German government ordered this of the workers in the Ruhr in the face of the French occupation in 1923.
Proportional representation	The voting system set up in Germany in 1919. Parties won seats in relation to the percentage of the vote they won.
Prussia	The largest state in Germany. It was an independent country but led the way in bringing German states together to form a united Germany in 1871.
Putsch	German word for an attempt to seize power.
Reichstag	The German parliament.
SA	Abbreviation for Sturm Abteilung, Stormtroopers, set up by Hitler in 1921.
SS	Abbreviation for Schutz-Staffel, 'protection squad'. They were originally Hitler's private bodyguard but later became the main instrument of terror in Nazi Germany.
Volk	People, in particular the German people.

Germany 1918–45

Profile on

Kaiser Wilhelm II

Born in 1859 with a badly withered left arm. His mother was an English princess and Queen Victoria was his grandmother. He was intelligent but unable to concentrate for long periods. Wilhelm did not like people to disagree with him. He came to the throne in 1888 but soon quarrelled with his Chancellor, Bismarck, who resigned in 1890. From then on he appointed ministers who did as he wanted. He was ambitious for Germany and keen to build up a strong army and navy. This led to rivalry with other countries such as France, Britain and Russia.

GERMANY 1918–19

In 1918 Germany suffered defeat in the First World War. A revolution in November led to the abdication of the German emperor and the setting up of a new republic. This republic was immediately opposed by a party known as the Spartacists.

Germany before the revolution

Germany was not a democracy. It had an elected parliament but this could be overruled by the Kaiser or Emperor. He had enormous power. He could choose and sack ministers. In 1888 the 29-year-old Wilhelm II became Kaiser.

War broke out in 1914. Germany fought on the side of Austria-Hungary against France, Britain and Russia. The German armies failed to break through the Western Front against Britain and France and by October 1918 were close to defeat.

The revolution of 1918

This was caused mainly by war weariness. The German people had suffered hardship and starvation as a result of the blockade of their ports by the British navy. Many Germans were short of everyday necessities. In Source A, a British secret agent reported on these shortages in September 1918:

SOURCE A

In addition to other hardships, the German public is threatened this winter with an almost complete lack of lights of every description: electric light, gas, lamp oil and candles. The lack of soap and washing powder makes personal cleanliness impossible and helps the spread of disease. Medicines are difficult to obtain.

The revolution began on 30 October in the North Sea port of Kiel when the German navy refused to attack the British navy. Workers and soldiers took over Kiel and nearby ports. Cities throughout Germany joined the revolt.

Profile on

Rosa Luxemburg

Rosa Luxemburg was a revolutionary who had fled from Poland. She came to Germany in 1898 and married a German socialist colleague so she could remain in the country. She was a brilliant speaker and writer and, by 1914, was known as 'Red Rosa'. She disagreed with the war and was put in prison in 1915 for spreading anti-war propaganda. In November 1918 she was released from prison and returned to Berlin to lead the Spartacists.

SOURCE B

This cartoon was drawn in 1918 by the German artist Raemaeker. It shows Kaiser Wilhelm (centre) hand in hand with war (on the left) and starvation (on the right).

On 9 November 1918 the Kaiser abdicated – this means he gave up the throne. On the following day a German republic was set up under Friedrich Ebert, leader of the Social Democratic Party. On 11 November an armistice or ceasefire was signed in a railway carriage at Compiègne, to the north of Paris.

The Spartacists

The Spartacus League (or Spartacists) were a Communist group who wanted Germany to be governed in the same way as Russia after the Bolshevik Revolution of October 1917 with workers' and soldiers' councils in each town. Their leaders, Rosa Luxemburg and Karl Liebknecht, opposed the new German republic and everything that Ebert did.

On the last day of 1918 they renamed themselves the German Communist Party, and made plans to seize power. This alarmed many middle- and upper-class people who feared that a Communist government would take away all banks, factories and land and put them under government control.

SOURCE D

Rosa Luxemburg in late 1918

The rule of the working class means real democracy. It means the use of power to get rid of middle- and upper-class people. It means the smashing of the ruling classes with all the brutality that the working class can develop.

SOURCE E

From an article in a government newspaper, early January 1919

The terrible actions of Liebknecht and Rosa Luxemburg spoil the revolution and threaten all its achievements. The masses must not sit quiet for one minute longer and allow these brutal beasts to force the people into civil war.

The Spartacists tried to seize power on 5 January 1919. They occupied public buildings, organised a general strike and formed a revolutionary committee. The day before the rising, Ebert had created a volunteer force of 4000 soldiers. Known as the Freikorps, they were hard men who hated Communists and liked a fight. After two weeks the revolution was defeated. Many Communists, including Liebknecht and Luxemburg, were shot after they were captured.

Questions on Sources D and E:

1 Explain in your own words the differences between Sources **D** and **E** in their views of the Spartacists.
2 Why do you think they are different?

Importance of the Spartacists

The Spartacist revolution was important for several reasons:

- It showed how unstable the new republic was when a mainly socialist government was attacked by an even more left-wing group.

- It forced the new republic to seek the support of the army in defeating the Communists. In return Ebert promised not to change the army.

- The army remained as it had been under the Kaiser and gave little support to the new republic.

Focus on

German political parties

Party	Supporters	Attitude to Republic
KPD (Communists)	working class	Against
SPD (Social Democrat)	industrial working class and some lower middle class	Supported
DDP (German Democratic)	mostly middle class	Supported
Centre Party	Roman Catholics	Supported
DVP (German People's)	Wealthy middle class	Reluctant supporters
Nationalist Party	Middle and upper class	Against
NSDAP (Nazi Party)	Nationalists, conservatives and lower middle class	Against

---

EARLY PROBLEMS 1919–22

The new republic faced early problems mainly as a result of signing the Treaty of Versailles and weaknesses in the new constitution.

The Weimar Constitution

The new German government was determined to set up a democracy or a system of government where the leaders are voted into office by the people. This was partly because President Wilson of America refused to offer peace to the Germans until it had a government that wanted democracy. However, this meant that some Germans thought that democracy was being forced on Germany by her enemies.

The Spartacist revolt made it impossible for the government to meet in Berlin. Instead it chose the peaceful town of Weimar and drew up a new constitution or set of rules and laws which control how a country is governed. Elections were held and the Socialist, Ebert, became the first ever President of Germany. The chart on p. 336 shows you the new constitution.

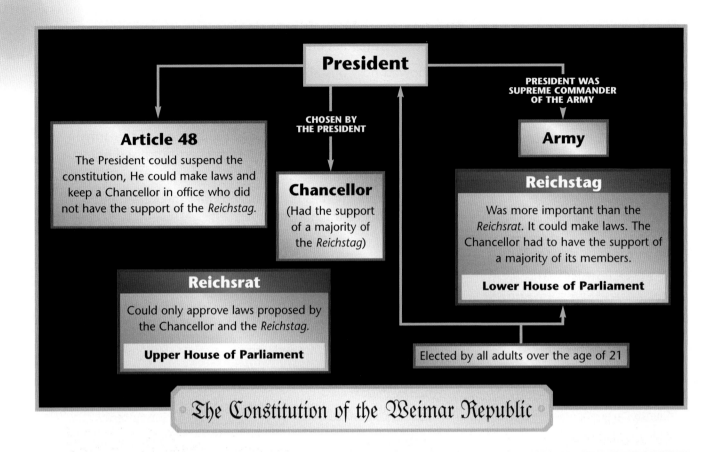

President

PRESIDENT WAS
SUPREME COMMANDER
OF THE ARMY

CHOSEN BY
THE PRESIDENT

Article 48

The President could suspend the constitution, He could make laws and keep a Chancellor in office who did not have the support of the *Reichstag*.

Army

Chancellor

(Had the support of a majority of the *Reichstag*)

Reichstag

Was more important than the *Reichsrat*. It could make laws. The Chancellor had to have the support of a majority of its members.

Lower House of Parliament

Reichsrat

Could only approve laws proposed by the Chancellor and the *Reichstag*.

Upper House of Parliament

Elected by all adults over the age of 21

The Constitution of the Weimar Republic

The new Constitution had both strengths and weaknesses:

Strengths

- All Germans had equal rights, including the right to vote. All women could vote, which made the Constitution even more forward-looking than that of Britain where the right to vote was restricted to women over the age of twenty-eight.

- Proportional representation meant that political parties were given seats in proportion to the number of votes they got. If a party received 5% of the votes it got 5% of the seats in the Reichstag, the German Parliament. This was fair.

- A strong president was necessary to keep control over the government.

- Each state had its own traditions. It was right they should keep some control over their own affairs.

Weaknesses

- In 1919 the Republic had many enemies. Was it sensible to give equal rights to those who wished to destroy it?

- Proportional representation encouraged lots of small parties. No one party could get a majority so governments had to be coalitions where two or more parties joined together. This led to weak governments.

- The president had too much power. Article 48 of the Constitution said that in an emergency the President could abandon democracy and rule by decree. This proved disastrous in the period 1929–33.

- The generals in charge of the army were the same men who had fought the war for the Kaiser. Many of them opposed the Republic. They wanted the Kaiser to return.

- The judges in the new Germany were also the same men who served under the Kaiser. They had sympathy with those who were against the Republic.

Questions

1   Look at the strengths and weaknesses of the Constitution. Do you think the new Constitution weakened the Republic? Give reasons for your answer.
2   Is there any part of the Constitution which you would change to make it fairer or stronger?

The Treaty of Versailles

On 11 November 1918 the armistice was signed. It meant that Germany had agreed to a ceasefire. They were not allowed to take part in the peace negotiations. In June 1919 the terms of the Treaty of Versailles were announced. The German government and people were horrified by the terms (see pp. 122–24).

Why did the German people oppose the Treaty?

The vast majority of Germans thought the Treaty harsh and humiliating. Apart from their objections to the terms of the Treaty they felt bitter about the peace settlement for other reasons:

- Germany was not allowed any say in the making of the Treaty. They called it a dictated peace, or 'Diktat'.

- Germans felt that the military terms had left their country so weak it could easily be invaded by neighbouring states.

- The 'War Guilt Clause' – Article 231 of the Treaty – was seen as very unfair. Most Germans did not feel that they were responsible for causing the First World War. Indeed, they thought they had been fighting a war of defence.

- Germans resented paying vast sums of reparations to countries they believed shared the blame for causing the war.

- Germany signed the armistice believing that the peace would be based on Wilson's 'Fourteen Points', especially the right of national self-determination. This did not happen as Germans now found themselves ruled by Poles, Czechs and Danes.

- Germans had expected to be made full members of the League of Nations. Germany was refused membership.

Was it a fair Treaty?

SOURCE A

German Nationalist poster creates the myth of the 'stab in the back' to explain Germany's defeat in the First World War

SOURCE B

The reaction of the German newspaper, *Deutsche Zeitung*, in June 1919

Vengeance! German nation! Today in the Hall of Mirrors the disgraceful treaty is being signed. Do not forget it. The German people will, with unceasing work, press forward to reconquer the place among nations to which it is entitled. Then will come vengeance for the shame of 1919.

A British historian writing in 1966

The greatest weakness of the Treaty was that it did not end the German 'menace' by means of the punishment clauses. The German empire was left basically intact. Although Germany did lose some territories, by far the major part of her strength (land, population and resources) was untouched.

SOURCE D

A British cartoon published in 1919

DER TAG!

Questions

1 Do Sources **B** and **C** believe the Treaty was fair on Germany?
2 Do you think it was fair? Give reasons for your answer.
3 What is the cartoonist trying to say in Source **D**? How does the cartoonist try to get the point across?

Activity

Produce the front page for a German newspaper reacting to the terms of the Treaty of Versailles. Your front page should include a headline, a brief explanation of the terms and why you think they are unfair on Germany and perhaps the reactions of a few German people you have spoken to. Why not give your newspaper a name?

Results of the Treaty

The German government had no choice but to sign the Treaty. This had several unfortunate results:

- The new Republic got off to a bad start and was immediately associated with the humiliating Treaty.

- Opponents of the Republic, especially the army, blamed the government for signing the armistice that led to the Treaty. They referred to the government as the 'November Criminals', a reference to the signing of the armistice on 11 November. The government was accused of having stabbed the German army in the back. In other words the German army would have won the war if the armistice had not been signed. This, of course, was far from the truth.

- Germany could not afford to pay the reparations. The country had been run down by the war and had lost areas of land that could make money, such as the coalfields of the Saar.

The Kapp Putsch

The Freikorps not only hated Communism. They also hated the Treaty of Versailles and the new government that had signed it. They were also angry because the government had ordered all Freikorps units to disband. They were led by an extreme nationalist, Dr Kapp, who explained what was wrong with Germany in 1919:

SOURCE E

Prices are rising. Hardship is growing. Starvation threatens. The government lacks the authority and is not capable of overcoming the danger. From the east we are threatened with destruction by communism.

In March 1920 a group of Freikorps, led by Dr Kapp, attempted to take power in Berlin. The government fled from the city. Kapp set himself up as head of a new government. His aim was to recover the land taken from Germany by the Versailles Treaty.

The army refused to stop Kapp and his 5000 followers. The putsch – or uprising – was defeated by the people of Berlin. Workers in the city organised a general strike. As a result, Berlin ground to a halt. Kapp thus had to abandon his plans and fled to Sweden. The government returned to Berlin.

The Kapp Putsch showed that the republic had gained much support from the workers of Berlin. It also revealed the lack of support from the army. Army leaders had blamed the republic for the armistice of 1918 and the humiliating peace terms of the following year. Many wanted a return to the Germany of the Kaiser.

The early problems faced by the Weimar Republic came to a head in 1923 with a combined French and Belgian occupation of the Ruhr and massive inflation.

The Ruhr invasion

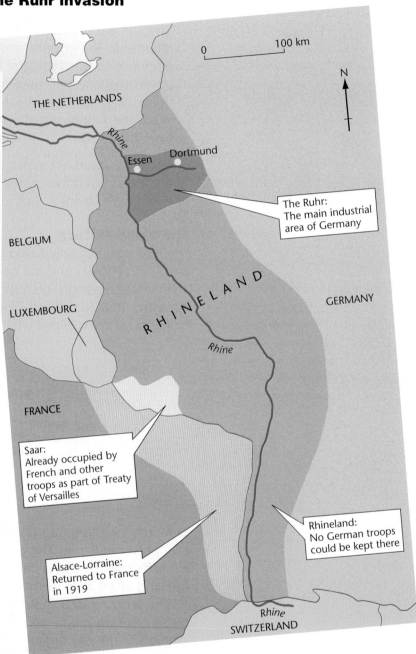

By January 1923 Germany had fallen behind in its reparations payments to Belgium and France. The French were angry because they needed the money to help pay their war debts to the USA. French and Belgian troops marched into the Ruhr, the industrial centre of Germany, to take the goods they needed, rather than waiting for the Germans to send them.

The German government could not use force to oppose the French and Belgians. Instead they chose passive resistance.

German workers in the Ruhr went on strike. Some strikers took more direct action. They sabotaged the pumps in some mines so that they flooded and could not be worked. A number of strikers were shot by the French troops. A German newspaper, *Deutsche Allgemeine Zeitung*, described one incident (Source **B**).

SOURCE B

The children were playing in a field which the invaders had declared out of bounds. When the children wouldn't leave the field, the soldier fired at a seven-year-old boy who was standing laughing six metres away from him. He was shot through the temples. The brave soldier then threw himself upon the corpse and, according to one witness, ate the boy's brains.

Questions

1 Why do you think the German newspaper printed this story?
2 Can you trust the account given in Source **B**? Give reasons for your answer.

Results of the invasion

The invasion had mixed effects:

- It united the German people against the French and Belgians.

- The strikers were seen as heroes to the German people.

- The German government became popular because it backed the strikers and organised passive resistance.

- It had disastrous effects on the German economy. The German government had to print money in order to pay the strikers' wages. This increased inflation.

Hyperinflation

In 1923 the German mark lost all value as a result of hyperinflation. When there is a lot of something, it is worth less. This was the case with the German mark at this time. The government printed so much that it became worthless. Germans continually needed more of this worthless paper to buy even the most basic items.

This situation had come about because from 1921 Germany had to send large quantities of goods to France and Belgium as part of their reparations payments. As a result there were not enough goods in Germany and the prices rose. The German government also printed more money to pay reparations and the workers of the Ruhr. This made inflation worse.

The effects of hyperinflation

Hyperinflation was a disaster for most Germans. Some, however, benefited.

SOURCE C

Children playing with worthless banknotes

SOURCE D

The memories of a German writer

Two women were carrying a laundry basket filled to the top with banknotes. Seeing a crowd standing round a shop window, they put down the basket for a moment to see if there was anything they could buy. When they turned round a few moments later, they found the money there untouched. But the basket was gone?

Focus on

The effects of hyperinflation

THOSE WHO SUFFERED

◆ Old people living on fixed pensions which became worthless.

◆ People who lived on savings which became worthless.

◆ Many of the middle classes who saw their businesses and savings destroyed.

THOSE WHO BENEFITED

◆ Those who had debts or had taken out loans. They could pay the money back at a fraction of the cost.

◆ Many rich businessmen were able to take advantage of the situation by taking over smaller companies which were going bankrupt.

◆ The rise in prices benefited farmers.

◆ Foreigners who were in Germany suddenly found that they had a huge advantage. They could afford things that ordinary Germans could not.

Activity

Study this list of four different people living in Germany in 1923. Explain how you think each of these would have reacted to hyperinflation and its effects:

- an ex-soldier now living on an army pension.

- a wealthy businessman who has borrowed heavily to start up his business and owes a lot of money to the bank.

- an elderly shopkeeper who has saved throughout his working life for his retirement.

- a factory worker living on wages paid daily.

Questions

1   What do Sources **C** and **D** show about the value of the mark in 1923?
2   The Republic faced several problems between 1918–23 including:
- the Spartacist revolt
- the Kapp Putsch
- the French occupation of the Ruhr
- hyperinflation
- the Treaty of Versailles
- the new constitution.
    a How far do you think each of these problems weakened the republic?
    b Which do you think was the most serious problem? Give reasons for your answer.
3   Why was the Weimar Republic able to survive the problems of 1923?

THE RECOVERY OF THE REPUBLIC 1924–29

During this period the Weimar Republic seemed to recover from the problems of its early years. This is often referred to as the 'golden age' of the Weimar Republic.

Why did the Republic recover and prosper?
There were several reasons for the recovery:

The role of Gustav Stresemann
He became the new Chancellor in August 1923. He introduced a new currency, the Rentenmark, to replace the old worthless mark. He ordered the striking workers of the Ruhr back to work and agreed to start to pay reparations. This, at first, made him unpopular with many Germans.

Stresemann became foreign secretary in 1924 and was mainly responsible for negotiating the Dawes Plan and German success abroad. He died in October 1929, on the eve of the Wall Street Crash. He was one of the few Weimar politicians strong enough to appeal to the German people.

Profile on

Gustav Stresemann

Stresemann was born in 1878 and became leader of the National Liberal Party before 1914. This was replaced, after the First World War, by the German People's Party. Stresemann was also its leader. He became Chancellor briefly in 1923 and foreign secretary from 1924–29. As Foreign Secretary he worked closely with his counterparts in France and Britain, Aristide Briand and Austen Chamberlain. He died in October 1929. Many Germans believe he could have saved Germany from the worst effects of the Depression.

343

Economic recovery

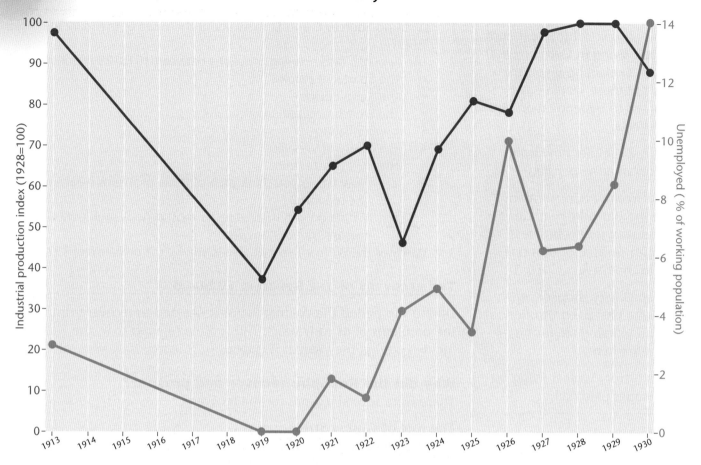

Question

What does the graph show about:

a   Industrial production in the period 1923–29?

b   Unemployment in the period 1923–29?

The recovery was encouraged by:

- The introduction of the Rentenmark which replaced the old worthless mark.

- In return for starting to pay reparations once more, the Germans were rewarded with the introduction of the Dawes Plan in 1924. America agreed to lend Germany 800 million marks. The Germans could use this to build new factories that could produce jobs and goods and could raise the standard of living of the German people.

- In 1925 the French and Belgian troops left the Ruhr.

- In 1929 the Young Plan was introduced. This reduced reparations by over 67%.

- In 1928 industrial production finally improved on pre-First World War levels. By 1930 Germany was one of the leading exporters of manufactured goods.

- In nearly every town new factories and public facilities sprang up. New roads and railways were built and nearly three million new homes.

SOURCE A

'Risen from the Mire.' A 1924 election poster for the German National People's Party shows Germany heading for a better future after being pulled clear of the problems of 1918–24.

Political stability

The period 1924–29 saw more stable governments. After the 1928 election the Social Democrats, for the first time since 1923, joined a government coalition with the other parties who supported the Republic. This showed that the middle-class parties were no longer so suspicious of the socialists. There was less support for extreme parties such as the National Socialist German Workers' Party (the Nazis) who only won 12 seats in the Reichstag in the elections of 1928. The Communists also did less well in 1924 and 1928.

Foreign policy

The foreign secretary, Stresemann, was responsible for several successes in foreign policy.

- In 1925 Germany signed the Locarno Treaties with Britain, France and Italy. These guaranteed Germany's frontiers with France and Belgium.

- In 1926 Stresemann took Germany into the League of Nations. Germany was recognised as a great power and given a permanent seat on the League's council alongside France and Britain.

- In 1928 Germany signed the Kellogg–Briand Pact along with 64 other nations. It was agreed that they would keep their armies for self-defence but 'the solution of all disputes shall only be sought by peaceful means'.

Culture

The 1920s saw a huge cultural revival in Germany. Some believe this was the greatest period in German history for writers and artists to try out new ideas. The key painters of the time, such as George Grosz, used art to criticise society. His painting, *Grey Day* (Source B), was a comment on the boredom experienced by most people in their everyday lives.

Germany also became the centre for new plays and operas. The most famous playwright of the time was Bertolt Brecht whose *Threepenny Opera* was a great success. There was also great progress in the cinema with its best-known director, Fritz Lang, producing epic films such as *Metropolis*, which was the most technically advanced film of the decade.

Literature was dominated by Erich Remarque who wrote the famous anti-war novel, *All Quiet on the Western Front*. This novel described the horrors of the Western Front. Within three months of its publication in 1929, it had sold 500,000 copies. It was later made into a very successful film.

Was this a 'Golden Age'?

Although there was progress in this period, there were also several fundamental problems:

Economic problems

There were still serious problems in the economy:

- It depended on American loans which could be withdrawn at any time.

- Unemployment remained a serious problem. The economy was not growing fast enough for Germany's rising population.

- Farming suffered from depression throughout the 1920s due to a fall in food prices. Income from agriculture went down from 1925 to 1929.

- Growth in industry began to slow down in 1927.

Political instability

The basic problems of the Constitution remained:

- No one party could secure a majority in the Reichstag. There were frequent, short-lived coalition governments.

- Many nationalists opposed Stresemann's policies, especially when he called off passive resistance in the Ruhr in 1923.

- Extremist parties, such as the Nazis and Communists, were determined to overthrow the Weimar Republic.

- In 1925 Hindenburg was elected President. He had been one of Germany's war leaders under the Kaiser and disliked the new Republic.

Question

Using Sources **C** and **D** and page 346, do you think that 1925–29 was a 'Golden Age' for the Weimar Republic? Give reasons for your answer.

Activity

Look again at the list of people on p. 343. How do you think they would react to the republic four years after hyperinflation, in 1928?

Historians also disagree about this period.

SOURCE C

W. Carr, *A History of Germany, 1815–1945*, 1979

By 1930, Germany was once again one of the world's greatest industrial nations. By 1929 iron and steel, coal, chemicals and electrical products had all matched or beaten the 1913 production figures. Up-to-date management techniques and better methods of production brought about a tremendous increase in productivity: blast-furnaces, for example, trebled their output.

SOURCE D

R. Geary, *Hitler and Nazism*, 1993

Germany's recovery was too dependent on foreign loans. Agricultural prices which had been steady after the early 1920s were already falling by 1927. The result was a debt crisis for farmers. Heavy industry (coal, iron and steel) were already experiencing problems making profits even as early as 1927. German steel mills worked at no more than 70% of their capacity.

THE EARLY YEARS OF THE NAZI PARTY 1919–29

The Nazi Party emerged in the years after the First World War and was led by Adolf Hitler.

Adolf Hitler

Hitler was born in the village of Braunau, in Austria, in 1889. In a letter to an admirer, Hitler gave an account of his early life (Source **A**).

SOURCE A

My entire schooling consisted of five years at Primary School and four years of Middle School. I was orphaned, at the age of 17 years and was forced to earn my living as a simple worker. I became a labourer on a building site and during the next two years did every type of casual job. With great effort I was able to teach myself to paint in my spare time. I earned a small living by this work. By the age of 21 I had become an architectural draughtsman and painter and was completely independent.

SOURCE B

Adolf Hitler (centre) while serving in the German army in 1916

Questions

1 What does the letter (Source **A**) tell you about Hitler?
2 Can you trust what Hitler has written?

Hitler moved to Munich, in Germany, and joined the German army in 1914. He fought in the First World War and was awarded the Iron Cross, Germany's highest award for bravery. The end of the war saw Hitler in hospital in Munich recovering from gas poisoning. He was devastated when he heard of the armistice and threw himself, sobbing, on to his hospital bed. He immediately blamed the new Republic for Germany's defeat and for signing the humiliating Treaty of Versailles.

Hitler in a crowd attending a protest meeting against the Treaty of Versailles in 1919

Extract from Hitler's autobiography, *Mein Kampf*

It became impossible for me to sit still one minute more. I tottered and groped my way back to the dormitory, threw myself on my bunk, and dug my burning head into my blanket and pillow.

The Nazi Party 1920–23

In September 1919 Hitler joined the German Workers' Party. It had been set up in Munich, earlier in the year by Anton Drexler. Hitler showed a talent for public speaking and propaganda and rose quickly up the ranks of the party. In February 1920 he was put in charge of propaganda. He bought a newspaper, *The Munich Observer*, and changed the name of the party to the National Socialist German Workers' Party or Nazis.

In 1921 Hitler was strong enough to challenge Drexler and take over the leadership of the Party himself. He now intended to turn the party into a mass movement which would overthrow the Weimar Republic. It had its own emblem, the swastika.

The swastika and colours were deliberately chosen by Hitler. The red represented the socialist part of the party, the white the nationalist and the swastika itself Hitler's racial views. In *Mein Kampf*, Hitler wrote that the swastika represented 'the mission of the struggle for the victory of the Aryan man'.

The swastika. Some flags also have the words 'Germany awake'.

The Party aims

Hitler drew up a 25-point programme which showed the aims of the Nazi Party.

NAZI PARTY

NATIONALISM
- All Germans in a single country
- Destroy Treaty of Versailles
- Rearmament

SOCIALISM
- Workers to share in company profits
- Big companies to be nationalised or taken over by the state
- Land shared out for the benefit of everyone

ANTI-SEMITISM
This meant hatred of the Jews.
- Jews were regarded as the lowest of races
- Hitler blamed Jews for all Germany's problems
- Remove Jews from all positions of leadership in Germany

OTHER AIMS
- Destroy Communism
- Strong central government
- Increase old age pensions
- Educate gifted children at the state's expense

Activity

Make a two-column chart. On the left-hand side list the following:

- an ex-member of the Freikorps

- a factory worker

- a German nationalist who wanted Germany to be great again

- a farmworker

- a pensioner.

On the right-hand side write in the parts of the Nazi programme that would appeal to each of these.

SOURCE F

A pro-Nazi newspaper, the *Kreuzzeitung*, explained Hitler's aims in 1922

Hitler opposes the parliamentary system of the Weimar Republic. Hitler's party wants first of all to set up a dictatorship which will last until Germany's present troubles are ended. The dictator in question is evidently Hitler.

The SA

In August 1921 Hitler set about converting the Nazi Party into a mass movement. He organised a series of armed groups under the title 'Gymnastic and Sports Sections'. In October he changed the name to Sturm Abteilung (SA) or Stormtroopers. The SA attracted many ex-soldiers, especially from the Freikorps, which had been disbanded in 1920. These were men who felt betrayed by the Treaty of Versailles. The SA offered them a new uniform in which to fight for Germany. They would disrupt the meetings of Hitler's opponents, especially the Communists, and often beat up opposition supporters. Their uniform was brown and so they were known as the 'Brownshirts'.

There is no doubt that the SA gave Hitler the confidence to try to seize power in 1923.

SOURCE G

A Nazi poster of 1934. The SA man is shown as a heroic figure, worshipped by children and hated by Jews.

The first leader of the SA was Ernst Röhm.

Profile on

Ernst Röhm

From childhood Röhm had wanted to be a soldier. He was a captain in the German army during the First World War. He was a tough, brutal but very efficient leader. He had a very violent temper. After the war he joined the Freikorps and helped crush the Spartacist uprising. He was a founder member of the German Workers' Party in 1919. He supported Hitler when he took over as Nazi leader in 1921 and he set up and ran the SA for Hitler in 1921. He was a homosexual which was bad publicity for the Nazi Party.

Nazi growth

The Nazi Party was based in Munich but it soon began to spread to other parts of Germany. The Nazis published their own newspaper to spread their ideas. They received support from extreme nationalists and anti-Communists. By 1922 the Nazi Party had 3000 members.

The Munich Putsch 1923

In 1923 Hitler attempted to seize power for the first time. This attempt failed but had important long-term consequences for the Nazi Party.

Why did Hitler attempt the putsch?

Hitler had several reasons for attempting the putsch:

- He wanted to destroy the Weimar Republic.

- Hitler had developed an increasingly close relationship with the former army leader, General Ludendorff, and he believed that if it came to a crisis Ludendorff would be willing and able to persuade the German army to desert the government and side with the Nazis.

- The Bavarian government was right-wing. Its leaders, Gustav von Kahr and General von Lossow, had been plotting against the republic. Hitler felt sure they would support a putsch.

- The Italian leader, Benito Mussolini, had successfully marched on Rome the previous year and taken over the Italian government. Hitler hoped to secure Bavaria and then march on Berlin.

- There was much discontent in Germany in 1923 due to the effects of hyperinflation. Many nationalists were furious when, in September, Stresemann's government called off passive resistance in Ruhr and resumed paying reparations to the French.

The events of the putsch

On 8 November 1923 a meeting being addressed by Gustav von Kahr, the head of the Bavarian government, was suddenly interrupted by a Nazi demonstration. SA men surrounded the hall, and Hitler burst in holding a revolver. He announced that he was taking over the government of Bavaria. He tried to persuade Kahr to support him but the latter said nothing. Kahr was locked in a room, from which he managed to escape sometime during the night.

Hitler tried again the following day, 9 November, with about 3000 supporters, some of whom were SA men. This time he was met by armed police called out by Kahr to break up the march. Sixteen of the marchers were killed when the police opened fire but Hitler stayed in the background and fled the scene. Later he was arrested and put on trial for treason.

Question

What is the significance of the date, 9 November?

SOURCE A

A painting made later by one of Hitler's followers who took part in the putsch. In the foreground the police are opening fire on the Nazis. Hitler stands with his arm raised with Ludendorff on his right.

SOURCE B

Part of Hitler's evidence to the trial

I alone bear responsibility for the putsch but I am not a criminal because of that. There is no such thing as high treason against the traitors of 1918. I only wanted what's best for the German people.

Questions

1   What impression does the painter give of the putsch (Source **A**)?
2   Is this a reliable source of evidence? Give reasons for your answer.

Results of the putsch

The putsch does appear to have been a total failure:

* Hitler failed to win the support of Kahr, the Bavarian army or the police.

* In February 1924 he was put on trial and Kahr appeared as one of the prosecution witnesses.

* Hitler was sentenced to five years in prison.

In many ways, however, it proved a success for Hitler and the Nazis.
   Hitler turned his trial into a propaganda success. He used the occasion to attack the Republic.
   The trial provided Hitler with nationwide publicity. The court was sympathetic to Hitler. Instead of sentencing him to death as it might have done, it gave him the minimum sentence for the offence – five years. The judge also made it clear he could expect an early release.

SOURCE C

A cartoon drawn at the end of Hitler's trial. It shows Ludendorff and Hitler shouting from Munich beer mugs that they are Germany's saviours. The judge below says 'Rubbish. The worst charge we can bring is breaking public entertainment by-laws.'

SOURCE D

Hitler speaking in the mid-1920s

Instead of working to achieve power by armed coup (putsch), we shall have to hold our noses and enter the Reichstag against the opposition deputies. If outvoting them takes longer than outshooting them, at least the results will be guaranteed by their own constitution. Sooner or later we shall have a majority, and after that – Germany.

In fact, Hitler served just nine months of his sentence. He was confined to Landsberg Prison but in special conditions. He was allowed as many visitors as he wished and he spent much of the time dictating the first part of his book, *Mein Kampf* (*My Struggle*).

Most important of all the failure of the putsch made Hitler change his tactics.

This new legal approach was to be important in the years 1929–33.

Questions

1 What point is the cartoonist making in Source C?
2 Was the Munich Putsch a failure? Give reasons for your answer.

Activity

Using the information on these pages make out a balance sheet of successes and failures.

Successes   Failures

The fortunes of the Nazi Party, 1924–29

SOURCE B

Nazi Party membership, 1925–29

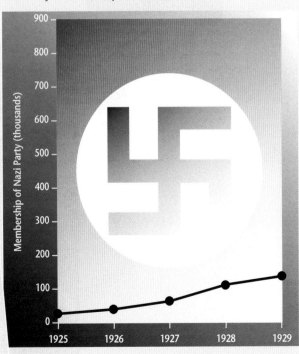

SOURCE A

The Nazi Party's performance in Reichstag elections 1924–28

Date	Nazi seats
1924 (May)	32
1924 (Dec.)	14
1928	12

A Nazi election poster. It says that the sacrifices made by Germany in the First World War were in vain.

From the Nazi newspaper the *Munich Observer*, 31 May 1928 after the Reichstag election

The election results from the rural areas in particular have proved that with a little more money and time better results can be achieved in the big cities.

Hitler refounding the Nazi Party in February 1925, following his release from prison three months earlier

Source F

William Shirer, an American journalist living in Germany, gave this verdict on the Nazis after the elections of 1928

Nazism appears to be a dying cause. It got support because of the country's problems such as hyper-inflation and the French invasion of the Ruhr. Now that the country's outlook is bright it is dying away. One scarcely hears of Hitler except as the butt of jokes.

Focus on

Developments in the Nazi Party, 1924–29

1924 Hitler served prison sentence for Munich Putsch, Nazi Party banned.

1925 In February, the ban on the Nazis was lifted. Hitler relaunched the party.

1926 Nazi organisations were established to try to appeal to certain interest groups:

- The Nazi Student's League
- The Teacher's League
- the Women's League.

A Nazi Party rally was held at Weimar. This began the pattern of military-style parades.

In February Hitler defeated Gregor Strasser in a party leadership contest.

1927 Hitler reorganised the party to make it more efficient:

- He created a national headquarters in Munich and insisted on the central control of finance and membership.
- Branches of the party were set up all over Germany and each regional organisation, or *Gau*, was put under the control of a Party official known as a *Gauleiter*.

This is normally seen as a period of failure for the Nazi Party.

Question

Were the Nazis a failure in this period?

Activity

You are a British journalist in Munich in 1928. You are asked to write an article about the Nazi Party. In your article explain:

- Who the Nazis are
- What they stand for
- Who supports them and why
- Their organisation, especially the SA
- Hitler himself.

From October 1929 Germany was badly affected by an economic depression. This further weakened the Weimar Republic and gave Hitler the opportunity to become Chancellor in January 1933.

Economic crisis

German recovery after the period of hyperinflation in 1923 depended very much upon American loans. In October 1929, disaster struck the New York stock exchange on Wall Street. The value of the shares collapsed following a few days of wild speculation. Many business people were ruined. The Americans had no option but to end their loans to Germany and demand the repayment of existing loans.

This destroyed the whole basis of German recovery. To make matters worse most countries in the world also suffered from depression and so German trade suffered.

Unemployment in Germany (millions)

Year	Numbers unemployed
1928	1.8
1929	2.9
1930	3.2
1931	4.9
1932	6.0

The suffering seemed particularly bad since the German people had so recently experienced a period of prosperity. Many now remembered the hyperinflation of 1923 and felt doubly bitter towards the Weimar Republic. They were more prepared to listen to the promises of extremist parties such as the Nazis and Communists.

Political crisis

The depression brought about a political crisis which led to the downfall of democracy. It showed up the weaknesses in the Constitution. Germany needed a strong government and leader in 1929 to lead them through the economic problems. Stresemann, however, died just before the Wall Street Crash. The two leading parties in the Coalition government, the Centre Party and SPD, fell out with each other. The leader of the SPD, Hermann Muller, refused to agree to cuts in unemployment benefit which the Centre Party, under Heinrich Bruning, believed were necessary.

Bruning and the Centre Party no longer had a majority in the Reichstag. The only way he could continue to rule was to ask the President, Hindenburg, to use Article 48 of the Constitution. This meant that laws could be issued under emergency powers rather than having to go through the Reichstag. Hindenburg agreed and democracy ended in Germany in 1930. Between 1930 and 1932 the Reichstag met less and less and became more and more ineffective.

Profile on

Paul von Hindenburg

He was born in 1847, a member of the Prussian ruling class, and followed a military career. In 1911, at the age of 64, he retired. He was recalled to lead the German armies during the First World War. His popularity increased in the years after the war due to the 'stab in the back' theory and, in 1925, he was elected President. Hindenburg did not belong to any party. He disliked democracy and had little time for the Weimar Republic. He was only too willing to use his emergency powers under Article 48 of the Constitution. In 1932 he was re-elected as President.

Nazi activities 1929–32

During this period Hitler and the Nazis gained increasing support, as shown in the table below. This rise in popularity was for several reasons:

The number of seats in the Reichstag won by the main parties in elections between 1928 and 1932				
	1928	1930	1932 July	1932 Nov
NAZIS	12	107	230	196
GERMAN NATIONALIST PARTY	73	41	37	52
GERMAN PEOPLE'S PARTY	45	30	7	11
CENTRE PARTY	62	68	75	70
GERMAN DEMOCRATIC PARTY	25	20	4	2
SOCIAL DEMOCRATIC PARTY	153	143	133	121
COMMUNISTS	54	77	89	100
OTHER	67	91	33	32
TOTAL	*491*	*577*	*608*	*584*

Nazi propaganda

Josef Goebbels was in charge of propaganda. He used every possible method to get across the Nazi message and carefully trained local groups in propaganda skills. The Nazis knew that their anti-Communist stance was very popular and used propaganda to further whip up fear and hatred of the Communists. They used:

- Posters and pamphlets.
- Eight Nazi-owned newspapers.
- Mobile units to organise entertainment and speeches in different areas.
- Stirring mass rallies using music, lighting and banners as a backdrop to Hitler's speech-making skills. During the 1932 presidential campaign Goebbels chartered planes to fly Hitler all over Germany in order to speak to four or five rallies a day.
- Radio was used for the first time.

The Nazi message was carried to every town and home in Germany.

Profile on

Josef Goebbels

Goebbels was the son of an office worker in a factory. He had not been able to fight in the First World War because he had a crippled foot which caused him to limp. He was very intelligent, well educated and a brilliant public speaker. He joined the Nazi Party in 1922. At first he opposed Hitler's leadership but he soon changed his mind and became a loyal supporter. He was appointed editor of the Nazi newspaper, *People's Freedom* and later put in charge of party propaganda.

The Nazi organisation and programme

The Nazis were very well organised. Many Nazis had been soldiers in the First World War and were experienced in teamwork, obedience and discipline. The Nazi Party had been reorganised in the mid-1920s (see p. 355). The local workers were well trained and motivated. They had skilled leaders at almost every level.

The Nazi programme appealed to many different groups in Germany. Hitler was very flexible. If he found an idea was losing support he would change it. For example, the Nazis spoke in favour of nationalisation (the state taking over control) of industry. When they found how alarmed the industrialists were they quickly dropped the idea. If all else failed the Nazis gave vague promises: 'they would make Germany great again'. However, some promises/slogans brought widespread support:

- By blaming the Jews for Germany's problems Hitler provided people with a scapegoat and united Germans against outsiders.

- To the depressed Germans Hitler offered the possibility of a powerful Germany both at home and abroad.

- To the unemployed Hitler promised work.

- To the employers he offered the prospect of restored profits.

There was something for everyone in the Nazi programme.

Powerful supporters

Hitler persuaded powerful industrialists that he would prevent the Communists from taking power and would restore the German economy. As early as 1929 Alfred Hugenburg, leader of the German Nationalist Party and a wealthy newspaper owner, worked with Hitler in attacking the Young Plan. He gave the Nazis access to his media empire, especially his cinemas. Another industrialist, Fritz Thyssen, explains how he supported the Nazis.

SOURCE B

Industrialist Fritz Thyssen

I have personally given altogether one million marks to the Nazi Party. It was in the period 1929–32 that the big industrial corporations began to make their contributions. In all, the amounts given by heavy industry to the Nazis may be estimated at two million marks a year.

Hitler's qualities

Hitler, himself, did much to win support for the Nazi Party. Posters and rallies built him up as a superman. Hitler developed his speech-making skills still further. He wore spectacles to read but refused to be seen wearing them in public and so his speeches were typed in large print. The campaigns focused around his personality and his skills.

SOURCE C

Otto Strasser, a Nazi who disliked Hitler as a person, wrote about his qualities as a speaker

As the spirit moves him, he is promptly transformed into one of the greatest speakers of the century. Adolf Hitler enters a hall. He sniffs the air. For a minute he gropes, feels his way, senses the atmosphere. Suddenly he bursts forth. His words go like an arrow in their target. He touches each private world in the raw, telling each person what they most want to hear.

Question

How useful is Source **C** as a description of Hitler as a speaker?

The SA and violence

By 1932 the SA numbered 600,000. The SA's violent attacks on rival politicians and political meetings helped the Nazis by:

- disrupting their opponents' meetings.

- attracting many unemployed and unhappy young people who admired the discipline and fighting qualities of the SA.

SOURCE D

The police arrive after a fight between the SA and Communists

Who supported the Nazis?

Hitler and the Nazis won support from many different groups in German society.

Category	% of Nazi Party	% German Society
Working class	28.1	45.9
Middle Class	66.9	35.8
of which:		
White-collar workers	25.6	12.0
Self-employed	20.7	9.0
Civil servants	6.6	4.2
Small farmers	14.0	10.6

In fact the chart generalises the support for the Nazis:

- Those who supported Hitler varied from year to year, and election to election, between 1923 and 1933.

- More of the working class supported the Communists.

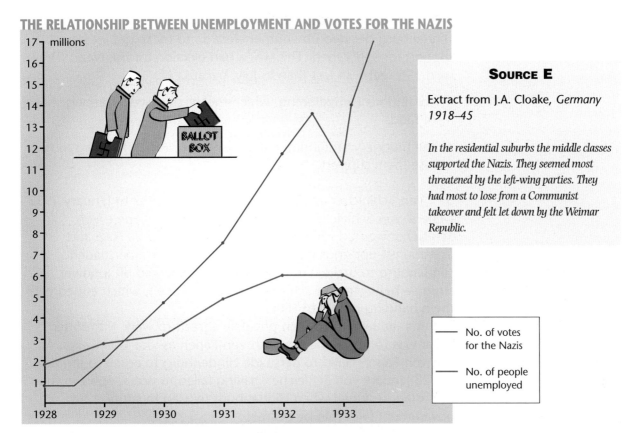

THE RELATIONSHIP BETWEEN UNEMPLOYMENT AND VOTES FOR THE NAZIS

Source E

Extract from J.A. Cloake, *Germany 1918–45*

In the residential suburbs the middle classes supported the Nazis. They seemed most threatened by the left-wing parties. They had most to lose from a Communist takeover and felt let down by the Weimar Republic.

— No. of votes for the Nazis

— No. of people unemployed

Questions

1   According to the chart on p. 360, from which group did the Nazis receive most support?
2   Why was this, according to Source E?

Source F

Hitler and Hindenburg in conversation in August 1932

The President asked Herr Hitler whether he was prepared to enter government under the Chancellorship of Herr von Papen. Herr Hitler replied in the negative. He demanded that the President should make him Chancellor with complete control of the State. The President refused.

Hitler comes to power, 1932–33

On 30 January 1933, Hitler was invited by Hindenburg to become Chancellor. This was due to a series of developments during this period:

1   The Presidential elections in March 1932

Hitler challenged Hindenburg for the presidency. Although Hindenburg won 19.4 million votes, Hitler's own position was strengthened by winning 13.4 million votes. His campaign provided much-needed publicity for Nazi ideas.

2   The fall of Bruning in May 1932

His government could not solve Germany's economic problems – unemployment continued to rise. Bruning, himself, became unpopular as he increased taxes and reduced unemployment benefit. A senior army officer, General von Schleicher, advised Hindenburg to get rid of Bruning. He was sacked and replaced by Franz von Papen who had the support of both Hindenburg and von Schleicher. Von Papen was a rich Catholic nobleman and a favourite of Hindenburg. He had little support in the Reichstag and depended on government by decree.

3   The Reichstag elections in July 1932

Von Papen hoped to win enough seats to strengthen his position in the Reichstag. Instead the elections were a triumph for the Nazis who won 230 seats. They were the largest single party but did not have an overall majority in the Reichstag. Hindenburg refused to appoint Hitler as Chancellor. Hindenburg disliked Hitler, seeing him as a 'trumped up corporal'. He preferred to reappoint von Papen as Chancellor. Hitler refused to co-operate with von Papen.

4 Reichstag elections in November 1932

Hindenburg decided on another election to try to get increased support for von Papen. This was a bad election for the Nazis. They won 196 seats, 34 less than in July, because of:

- continuous campaigning, which meant they were running short of funds.

- the thuggery and intimidation by the SA, which had begun to lose them support.

5 Von Schleicher as Chancellor, December 1932 to January 1933

General von Schleicher stopped supporting von Papen. Von Schleicher warned Hindenburg that there would be Nazi and Communist uprisings if he continued in office. He persuaded Hindenburg to make him Chancellor. This sparked off a power struggle between von Schleicher and von Papen, which ended with them handing power to Hitler.

On 4 January von Papen privately agreed to work with Hitler. Hitler was to be Chancellor with von Papen as vice-Chancellor. At first von Papen failed to persuade Hindenburg to agree to the deal. On 28 January von Schleicher, having failed to win support in the Reichstag, resigned when Hindenburg refused to support his government with rule by decree.

6 30 January 1933 Hitler becomes Chancellor

Hindenburg wanted von Papen to return as Chancellor. Von Papen refused, believing it might trigger a revolution against Hindenburg. He then persuaded Hindenburg to appoint Hitler as Chancellor explaining that:

- refusal might lead to civil war.

- there will be only a few Nazis in the Cabinet.

- Von Papen will be vice-Chancellor.

- they will be able to use Hitler and then get rid of him.

Questions

1. How did the following help Hitler to become Chancellor in January 1933:
   a. the Depression?
   b. Nazi propaganda?
   c. the appeal of Hitler?
   d. the actions of von Papen and Hindenburg?
2. Which was the most important reason? Give reasons for your answer.

Activity

Draw a cartoon sketch representing each of the following people:

- a young, unemployed factory worker

- a young mother of two children

- a leading German Communist

- a retired ex-soldier from the First World War.

Using a bubble above each sketch explain how each might have reacted to the news that Hitler had become Chancellor. See example below.

I think Hitler might help the economy to recover but I'm concerned that he might persecute the Jewish people in Germany.

Hitler was not totally in control when he became Chancellor in January 1933. He did not have a majority in the Reichstag and there were only three Nazis in the Cabinet. Over the next eighteen months he removed the main opposition to his government and laid the foundations of his dictatorship. How he did this is outlined in the following timechart.

The path to dictatorship

1933

30th January	Hindenburg appoints Hitler as Chancellor
27th February	The Reichstag building burns down
28th February	Reichstag Fire decree
5th March	Reichstag election: Nazi Party gains 43.9% of the votes (288 seats), its coalition partners (the Nationalists) take 8%
5th–9th March	Nazis seize power in the Länder (German states)
20th March	Himmler establishes the first concentration camp at Dachau
23rd March	Reichstag passes the Enabling Act
2nd May	Trade unions are dissolved
22nd June	SPD banned; other parties dissolve themselves in the weeks which follow
14th July	Legislation prohibits political parties other than the Nazi Party
12th November	New 'election' to the Reichstag; the Nazi Party gains 92.2% of the vote

1934

30th June	'Night of the Long Knives' – Ernst Röhm and other SA leaders and members of the conservative opposition are arrested and shot without trial
2nd August	President Hindenburg dies. The offices of President and Chancellor are combined. Hitler is now called Führer (leader). The army swears an oath of allegiance to Hitler

The Reichstag Fire

On the night of 27 February 1933 came the sensational news that the Reichstag building had been set on fire. Inside the building the police found a Dutch Communist, Marius van der Lubbe, who was arrested and charged with starting the fire. Van der Lubbe was put on trial and found guilty of starting the fire. Hitler used this as evidence that the Communists were plotting against his government.

- On the night of the fire 4000 leading Communists were arrested and imprisoned.

- The next day Hitler persuaded the President to pass an emergency decree suspending all the articles in the constitution which guaranteed personal liberty – such as freedom of speech and freedom of assembly. It gave the police the powers to search houses, confiscate property and detain people without trial.

Source A

The Reichstag building on fire

Was van der Lubbe guilty?

Activity

Draw two parallel boxes – guilty, not guilty – and use the following evidence to complete each side.

Historians cannot agree on this question. Van der Lubbe appeared to be guilty because:

- He confessed to the crime after his arrest and at his trial.

- He was arrested at the scene of the crime.

- The Communists were arch enemies of the Nazis.

However, there is also evidence to suggest he was not guilty.

- It could well have been the Nazis who set fire to the building and then 'framed' van der Lubbe in order to provide an excuse to persecute the Communists.

- The fire came at a very convenient time for Hitler – just before the March elections.

- The Nazis hated the Reichstag – it was seen as a symbol of the Weimar Republic.

- Van der Lubbe may well have confessed because he was tortured.

SOURCE B

General Halder remembers a conversation with Hitler. Halder was the German army's chief of staff. Hermann Goering, who is mentioned in the extract, was later to be the Nazi Minister of the Interior.

'At a luncheon on the birthday of the Führer (leader) in 1942 the conversation turned to the Reichstag fire. I heard with my own ears when Goering interrupted the conversation and shouted: "The only one who really knows about the Reichstag building is I, because I set it on fire".'

Question

What are your views on the cause of the Reichstag fire? Was van der Lubbe guilty?

The legal revolution

Within a few days of becoming Chancellor Hitler asked the President to dissolve the Reichstag and call an election. Through this election Hitler hoped to gain an overall majority for the Nazi Party and pass the laws he wanted.

The election of March 1933

NAZIS (NSDAP) 288

NATIONAL (DNVP) 52

CENTRE (Z) 74

SOCIAL DEMOCRATS (SPD) 120

COMMUNISTS (KPD) 81

The results of the Reichstag election of 5 March 1933

(number of seats won)

The chart shows the results of the election. Although the Nazis had increased their number of seats, they still had fewer than half of the total. In order to change the Constitution legally, Hitler needed a two-thirds majority. He managed to do this by:

- Using the emergency decree to prevent the Communists from taking up the 81 seats they had won.

- Retaining the support of the National Party, which had 52 seats.

- Gaining the support of the Centre Party (81 seats), by promising to defend the interests of the Catholic Church.

The Enabling Act

With his two-thirds majority Hitler was now able to bring about his first change in the Constitution. In March 1933 he introduced the Enabling Act. This was the legal foundation of his dictatorship because it meant he could now pass laws without the consent of the Reichstag for the next four years.

Bringing Germany into line

Using the powers now given to him by the Enabling Act Hitler removed further opposition to the Nazi government.

1   On 31 March Hitler closed down the state parliaments. They were then reorganised so that the Nazis had a majority in each state parliament. In the following month he appointed state governors who were all Nazis. They had the power to appoint and dismiss state officials and to make state laws. In January 1934 Hitler abolished state parliaments.

2   Next Hitler turned to the trade unions. On 2 May 1933 Nazis broke into trade union offices all over the country and arrested thousands of trade union officials. The unions were then merged into a 'German Labour Front'. These actions meant that the Nazis would not be threatened by strikes or other union activities.

3   Lastly the political parties were brought into line. On 10 May the Nazis occupied the offices of the Social Democratic Party, destroyed its newspapers and confiscated its funds. Two weeks later they confiscated all the property and funds of the Communist Party. By July 1933 only one party was still in existence – the Nazi Party. Hitler made a law stating that the Nazi Party was the only party allowed in the state.

SOURCE C

From a pamphlet written by a banned group of Communists in April 1933

In Berlin alone thousands of Social Democratic and Communist officials were dragged from their beds at night and led away to SA barracks. There they were worked over with boot and whip, beaten with steel rods and rubber truncheons until they collapsed unconscious and blood spurted under their skin. Many were forced to drink castor oil or had urine directed into their mouths.

Questions

1   What view does Source **C** give of Nazi methods in 1933?
2   Source **C** was written by a Communist group. Would it be useful to a historian studying Nazi methods? Explain your answer.

The Night of the Long Knives, June 1934

One of the greatest threats to Hitler's dictatorship came from within his own party – from Röhm and the SA.

Why were Röhm and the SA a threat?

There were several reasons:

- Röhm wanted to merge the SA with the army and take control of the army. Hitler needed the support of the army officers.

- Röhm wanted a second revolution to put Socialist policies into practice. There were two million members of the SA who expected Hitler to take wealth from the rich. Many leading industrialists feared that the SA programme looked far too much like Communism. Hitler did not want to upset these industrialists.

- Hitler no longer needed the SA. He now had the SS, his own personal bodyguard which had been formed in 1925.

- Hitler was embarrassed by the continued violence of the SA.

- Hitler was also encouraged to remove Röhm and the SA by two other leading Nazis who were jealous of Röhm's power – Heinrich Himmler, head of the SS and Herman Goering, Minister of the Interior.

SOURCE A

Röhm speaking to Nazi friends

'Adolf is a swine. He is betraying all of us. Adolf knows exactly what I want. The generals are a lot of old fogeys. I'm the nucleus of the new army.'

SOURCE B

From a letter written by the Minister of the Interior in October 1933

New infringements by the SA have been reported again and again during the past weeks. Above all, SA leaders and men have carried out police actions for which they have no authority. These infringements must cease once and for all.

How the purge was carried out

In the early hours of 30 June 1934 Hitler arrived at a hotel in the Bavarian resort of Bad Wiessee together with Röhm and other leading members of the SA. Using his heavily armed SS, Hitler informed Röhm and the other leaders that they were under arrest. They were taken to Munich where they were shot. Over the next few days other leading members of the SA, such as Gregor Strasser, were also arrested by the SS and shot. Up to 200 people were killed, including politicians such as von Schleicher.

Results of the purge

* Hitler used the purge to tighten his control over Germany.

* He had removed possible rivals to his position – Röhm and Strasser.

* The SS was now established as a separate organisation from the SA. Himmler now took orders only from Hitler.

* In August 1934 the army swore an oath promising to be loyal to Hitler.

SOURCE C

A cartoon in the *Daily Herald*, 3 July 1934

The death of Hindenburg

On 2 August 1934, just weeks after the Night of the Long Knives, President Hindenburg died. Within hours Hitler had declared himself not only Chancellor, but also Head of State and Commander of the Army. His new title was 'Führer and Reich Chancellor'. On the same day every soldier in the German army swore an oath of 'unconditional obedience to Adolf Hitler'. Only eighteen months after becoming Chancellor, Hitler had supreme power in Germany.

Questions

1   What point is the cartoonist making in Source **C**?
2   What effects did Hitler's government have on the following:
    * other political parties?
    * the Reichstag?
    * trade unions?
    * the SA and SS?

NAZI METHODS OF CONTROL

The Nazis attempted to control the German people through terror, using the police state, and by persuasion, employing propaganda.

The police state

Hitler set up a police state in order to remove any opposition to the Nazi government. This means that the police had the power to do whatever they wanted. Hitler developed a number of organisations to carry out this terror.

The SS

The SS had been used to destroy the SA on the Night of the Long Knives. They were led by Heinrich Himmler. They were carefully disciplined and wore black uniforms.

Gradually, the SS was split into three sections:

* The Waffen SS were units who fought alongside the army.

* The SD, or Schutzstaffel, were responsible for state security. In other words they had to search out and deal with enemies of the Nazis.

* The Death's Head Units staffed the concentration camps.

The Gestapo

The Gestapo, or Geheime Staatpolizei, was the secret police. It was set up in Prussia by Hermann Goering in 1933. In 1936 its control was extended to the rest of Germany and it became linked to the SS. The Gestapo was led by Reinhard Heydrich and their job was to search out opponents of the Nazi government. They used informers to uncover any attempts to organise opposition.

Profile on

Heinrich Himmler

Heinrich Himmler was an agricultural graduate and poultry farmer. He fought briefly in the First World War. He was hard-working and very precise. He even recorded in his diary each time he shaved or had a hair cut. He joined the party in 1923 and took part in the Munich Putsch. His early posts were as Gauleiter for various regions. In 1929 he became leader of the SS directly under the control of Röhm.

A member of the Gestapo searching suspects for concealed weapons

SOURCE B

Elspeth Emmerich was eight years old in 1942. She wrote down her memoirs after the war.

It was the Gestapo who came that morning – to arrest grandad. He had been known to them since before the war for his anti-Nazi activities. He had been a member of the Communist Party. They tortured my grandfather at the prison, trying to make him give the names of those who were working against the Nazi regime. It didn't work. They took grandma, mum and two of her sisters to the prison and made them cry out for grandad to hear. That didn't work either.

Question

What do Sources **A** and **B** show about the methods and activities of the Gestapo?

The courts

These were brought under the control of the Nazis. Judges were replaced by Nazi supporters. This meant that opponents of the Nazis could still be punished even if they did get a trial. In 1934 Hitler set up the People's Court. This was to try 'enemies of the state'. By 1939 it had sentenced over 500 people to death and sent many others to concentration camps.

Concentration camps

The SA and SS ran a number of new prisons called concentration camps. The earliest of these was at Dachau near Munich. Others followed, including Buchenwald, Mauthausen and Sachsenhausen. They were places of a harsh, brutal regime against their inmates. Many prisoners died in these camps.

'How is the population of a concentration camp in present-day Germany brought together? In Buchenwald there were 8,000 of us, 2,000 Jews and 6,000 non-Jews.

Our 8,000 prisoners included first of all the 'politicals' (as, for example, the Communist members of the Reichstag), many of whom have been in various concentration camps ever since 1933... In addition to the genuine political prisoners there are many poor devils at Buchenwald accused of having spoken abusively of the sacred person of the Führer...

After the political, the category of the so-called 'work-shy' is the largest. Anyone who imagines that this group has to do with tramps and vagabonds is grossly deceived. An example. A business employee lost his position and applied for employment relief. One fine day he was informed by the Labour Exchange that he could obtain employment as a navvy on the new motor roads. This man, who was looking for a commercial post, turned down the offer. The Labour Exchange then reported him to the Gestapo as being 'work-shy', and he was arrested and sent to a concentration camp.

The next group were the 'Bibelsforscher', a religious sect taking its doctrine from the Bible... but proscribed [banned] by the Gestapo since its members refuse military service.

The fourth category consisted of the households... To charge those it dislikes with this offence is a favourite tactic of the secret police...

The last class of prisoners were the professional criminals...'

Activity

Using the focus on the concentration camps, list the main categories of prisoner.

Question

What changes would the police state have brought to German citizens?

PROPAGANDA

THE PRESS

▶ Non-Nazi newspapers and magazines were closed down.
▶ Goebbels told editors what they could print.

SOURCE A

Orders from the Propaganda Ministry to newspaper 6 April 1935.

Photos showing members of the Reich government at dining tables in front of rows of bottles must not be published in future. This has given the absurd impression that members of the government are living it up.

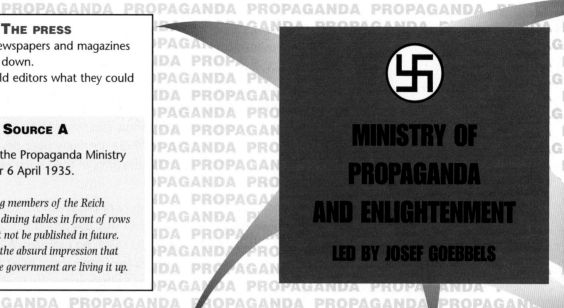

MINISTRY OF PROPAGANDA AND ENLIGHTENMENT

LED BY JOSEF GOEBBELS

RADIO

▶ All radio stations were placed under Nazi control.
▶ Cheap mass-produced radios were sold. Sets were installed in cafés and factories.
▶ Loudspeakers were placed in the streets.

▶ Broadcasts included many speeches by Hitler. Pro-Nazi plays and stories were also common.

SOURCE B

Propaganda Poster which announces that 'All Germany hears the Führer with the People's Receiver'.

SOURCE C

Albert Speer

Through technical devices like the radio... 80 million people were deprived of independent thought. It was therefore possible to subject to the will of one man.

FILMS

The cinema was popular with over 100 German films made each year.

▶ All film plots were shown to Goebbels before going into production.
▶ Political films made. Love stories and thrillers were given pro-Nazi slants.

SOURCE D

A still photograph from the film *Hitlerjunge Quex*. The film tells the story of Heine, who joins the Hitler Youth and is attacked and killed by Communists while giving out Nazi propaganda.

RALLIES

▶ Annual mass rally at Nuremburg.
▶ The 1936 Olympic Games, in Berlin, were used as a propaganda opportunity.
▶ Spectacular parades were held on other special occasions.
▶ Local rallies, marches and fundraising campaigns were led by SA and the Hitler Youth.

SOURCE E

Forty thousand workers being presented to Hitler at a Nuremburg rally.

POSTER CAMPAIGNS

Clever use of posters to put across the Nazi message. Young people were especially targeted.

SOURCE F

A propaganda poster. 'Yes! Leader we will follow you'.

BOOKS, THEATRE, ART AND MUSIC

All carefully censored and controlled to put across the Nazi message.

▶ Many writers, artists and composers persuaded or forced to create works in praise of Hitler and the Third Reich.
▶ Books written by Jews, Communists, and anti-Nazi university professors and journalists were banned. Many were destroyed during public book-burnings in 1933.
▶ Art galleries forced to get rid of 'degenerate' modern art.
▶ Jazz music banned as it originated from black people.

SOURCE G

Students and stormtroopers burning books written by Jews and Communists in Berlin in May 1933

Hitler had realised the importance of propaganda at an early stage. In *Mein Kampf* he set out the best way of doing this. Essentially it was to put across a limited range of ideas time and time again and ensure other ideas gradually disappear. This is known as indoctrination.

In 1933 the Ministry of People's Enlightenment and Propaganda was set up under the control of Josef Goebbels. The Ministry was responsible for the entire organisation of propaganda.

Question

Which of the following methods of propaganda do you think would have had the greatest effect on the German people? Give reasons for your answer.

a the press
b the radio
c the cinema
d rallies
e posters.

Activity

Design your own propaganda poster that could have been used by Goebbels to convert the German people to Nazi ideas.

Nazi Germany was known as the Third Reich, or Empire. The Nazi government resulted in many changes for the German people.

The economy and unemployment

There was a dramatic fall in unemployment under the Nazis. This was due to a variety of policies:

1 The Labour Service Corps

This was a scheme to provide young men with manual labour jobs. From 1935 it was compulsory for all men aged 18–25 to serve in the Corps for six months. Workers lived in camps, wore uniforms, received very low pay and did military drill as well as work.

2 Public works

Unemployed men were used to build government-funded roads, motorways, houses, hospitals, schools and military barracks. By the end of the 1930s Germany had a national motorway or autobahn system.

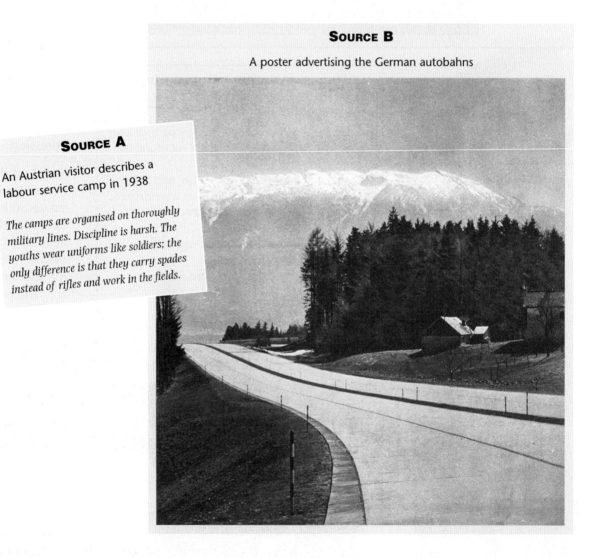

SOURCE B

A poster advertising the German autobahns

SOURCE A

An Austrian visitor describes a labour service camp in 1938

The camps are organised on thoroughly military lines. Discipline is harsh. The youths wear uniforms like soldiers; the only difference is that they carry spades instead of rifles and work in the fields.

3 Conscription and rearmament

From 1935 all men aged 18–25 were compelled to do military service for two years. Rearmament provided thousands of jobs in arms factories making guns, tanks and planes.

Other policies

- Many Jews were driven out of their jobs which then became available for other people.

- Married women were encouraged to give up their jobs and stay at home.

- Neither Jews nor women were registered as unemployed.

- The Nazis created jobs by giving government land to farmers and manufacturers in an effort to make the country self-sufficient in food, raw materials and manufactures.

German unemployment figures compared with British unemployment figures

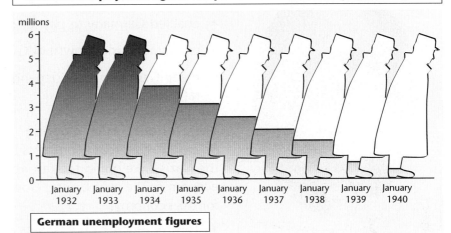

German unemployment figures

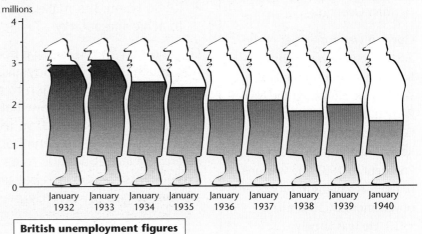

British unemployment figures

Questions

1. Compare the two graphs. Which country seems to have been the more successful in reducing unemployment?

2. Can you think of any problems with Hitler's methods of reducing unemployment?

Autarky

Hitler was determined to make Germany self-sufficient. This was known as autarky.

It meant Hitler wanted to stop Germany being dependent on imports, especially raw materials. Hitler feared that Germany would not be able to depend on imported raw materials should war begin. He remembered how Germany had been starved out of the First World War by the British naval blockade.

The economy under Schacht

In 1934 Hjalmar Schacht was made Economics Minister. He was not a Nazi, having already been head of the Reichsbank, the national bank of Germany. He aimed to improve Germany's level of raw materials by making trade deals with less developed countries. These countries would be paid in German manufactured goods. He also gave priority to those raw materials that were vital to rearmament. Imports of cotton and wool were cut while imports of iron ore increased. Schacht's policies:

- enabled Germany to pay for rearmament.

- encouraged the growth of German industry.

- made Germany more dependent on imported raw materials rather than less.

The economy under Goering

Schacht resigned as Economics Minister in 1937. He believed that the Nazis were going too fast in their efforts to build up a 'war economy'. The year before, Goering had drawn up a Four Year Plan for the economy:

- This set much higher targets for rearmament.

- It also wanted to make sure that Germany moved much closer to achieving autarky.

Goering said 'In the decisive hour it would not be a question of how much butter Germany has but how many guns'.

Experiments were begun to try and produce artificial replacements for those raw materials, such as oil, that could only be obtained from abroad. So the chemical company IG Farben was paid to try to develop a method of extracting oil from coal. Attempts were also made to develop an artificial rubber. These experiments created jobs but did not significantly reduce the amount of goods which Germany imported.

Profile of

Herman Goering

Goering was a member of the aristocracy. He was a famous fighter pilot during the First World War. He joined the Nazi Party during the 1920s. In 1932 he was elected speaker of the Reichstag and then became its President in 1933. He was one of the three Nazis in Hitler's first government of 30 January 1933. He was largely responsible for persuading President Hindenburg to allow the use of Article 48 to declare a state of emergency. As Prime Minister of Prussia he also set up the Gestapo and the first concentration camps.

Did the German people have a better standard of living under the Nazis?

Historians are unable to agree about this.

THE EVIDENCE FOR

In May 1933 the German Labour Front was set up, run by Dr Robert Ley. This looked after workers' interests by improving working conditions instead of fighting for higher pay. To achieve this he set up two organisations:

- The 'Beauty of Labour' organisation which made bosses improve working conditions by installing better lighting and ventilation, providing works canteens serving hot meals, and by planting trees and grassland to create factory gardens.

- The 'Strength through Joy' programme to provide opportunities to improve leisure activities for low-paid workers. It subsidised sea cruises, holidays abroad and at home, built health resorts and spas and ran coach tours. It also provided cheap sports facilities such as sailing and skiing. It even manufactured a 'people's car', the Volkswagen, designed by Ferdinand Porsche.

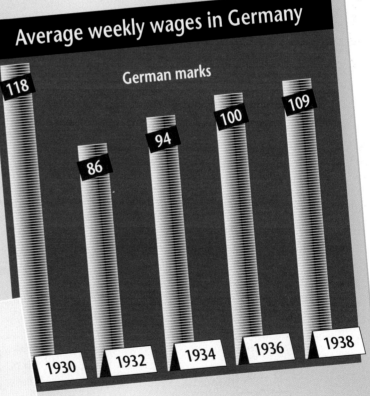

Average weekly wages in Germany

German marks

1930	1932	1934	1936	1938
118	86	94	100	109

Questions

1 What point is the artist trying to make in Source **D**?

2 Do you think that German workers were better off under the Nazis? Give reasons for your answer.

THE EVIDENCE AGAINST

This idea to encourage people to save to buy their own Volkswagen was a con-trick. By the time war broke out in September 1939 not a single customer had taken delivery of a car. The factory was converted for war production and none of the money that the workers had paid in advance was refunded. There was a joke in Germany at the time. It went that a factory worker, unable to afford to buy the car, smuggled parts and pieces of the car out day by day, hoping to put the car together when he had collected all the parts. When that day arrived, he put it together and made a tank!

The cost of living increased during the 1930s. All basic groceries, except fish, cost more in 1939 than they had in 1933. Food items were in short supply partly because it was government policy to reduce agricultural production. This was to keep up the prices for the benefit of farmers.

SOURCE C

A 1938 poster promoting the Volkswagen. It tells people to save five marks per year to buy their own car.

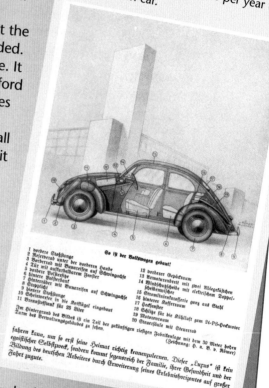

Workers had little freedom under the Nazis. Trade unions were banned in May 1933 (p. 367). Trade unionists and workers who opposed the Nazis were rounded up and sent to concentration camps for 're-education'.

SOURCE D

This painting was produced by the German artist John Heartfield. He was an opponent of the Nazis. The message reads 'Hurrah, the butter is finished'.

SOURCE E

A German remembers Labour Service

We work outdoors in all kinds of weather, shovelling dirt for very low pay. I'm trained as a printer. In the summer of '33 I lost my job. I collected the dole until the spring of '34. That was a lot better than what I'm doing now. At least I was at home, with my family and could pick up odd jobs and work in the garden. Now I only get 10 days' holiday a year.

Average working hours in industry per week

1933	42.9
1939	47.0

Women in the Third Reich

The position of women in society changed under the Nazi government.

Nazi aims

> *'The mission of women is to be beautiful and to bring children into the world'.*

Josef Goebbels 1929

The Nazis had very traditional views about the position of women:

* Women were inferior to men.

* Their job was to raise children and run the household.

* Working women were taking the jobs of men.

Focus on

Women before the Third Reich

* In the 1920s women had made much progress.

* Women over 20 years had the right to vote.

* Many worked in the professions, especially the civil service, law, medicine and teaching.

* Those employed in the civil service were paid the same as men.

* By 1933 there were 100,000 women teachers, 13,000 women musicians and 3000 women doctors. One tenth of the members of the Reichstag were women.

SOURCE A

A Nazi poster from 1937

The Nazis brought in a variety of measures to carry out their aims.

Marriage and children

In 1933 the Law for the Encouragement of Marriage was introduced. This aimed to increase Germany's falling birth-rate by providing loans to help young couples to marry provided the wife left her job. Couples were allowed to keep one quarter of the loan for each child born up to four.

On Hitler's mother's birthday (12 August) medals were awarded to women with large families: bronze for five children; silver for six; and gold for eight or more. Women classed as 'unfit' to bear children because of a physical or mental disability, or having given birth to a weak child, were compulsorily sterilised.

A new national organisation, the German Women's Enterprise, organised classes and radio talks on household topics and the skills of motherhood.

Jobs

Instead of going to work, women were asked to stick to the 'three Ks' – Kinder, Kirche und Kuche, which means 'children, church and kitchen'. Women doctors, civil servants and teachers were forced to leave their jobs. Schoolgirls were trained for work at home. They were discouraged from going on to higher education.

Appearance

Women were encouraged to keep healthy and wear their hair in a bun or plaits. They were discouraged from wearing trousers or make-up, dyeing or styling their hair or slimming as this was seen as bad for childbearing.

How successful were these Nazi policies?

Many women accepted these new policies, especially those who believed in the traditional role of women.

SOURCE C

Population statistics produced by historians

Year	Marriages	Live Births	Deaths
1929	589,600		
1931		1,047,775	734,165
1932	516,793	993,126	707,642
1933	638,573	971,174	737,877
1934	740,165	1,198,350	724,758
1935	651,435	1,263,976	792,018
1936	609,631	1,277,052	795,203
1937	620,265	1,277,046	794,367
1938	645,062	1,348,534	799,220
1939	772,106	1,407,490	853,410

However, not all women were prepared to accept these changes. Women who had progressed during the Weimar years resented these policies. A few women joined opposition groups like the Communists or Social Democrats. Others criticised these policies because they ignored those women who had particular talents for certain types of employment.

SOURCE D

A German cartoon from the 1930s with the caption 'Introducing Frau Mueller who up to now has brought 12 children into the world'

SOURCE E

Views of some German women, 1934

We see our daughters growing up in stupid aimlessness, living only in the vain hope of getting a man and having children. If they do succeed, their lives will be boring.

Questions

1   What image of women do you get from Source **A**?
2   How is Source **D** different to Source **A**?
3   Why were the Nazi policies aimed at increasing population birth-rates not very successful?

By 1939 the economy was set up for war. Large numbers of workers were needed in industry. The Nazis needed women to work in factories, even more so once the war broke out. Many men were needed to fight and as the casualties mounted so more women were needed.

Activity

You are a member of the Nazi propaganda ministry and are asked to promote the ideal German woman. Choose one of the following methods:

a wall display

a poster

a booklet.

Employment of women in Germany (in millions)		
	1933	1939
Agriculture and forestry	4.6	4.9
Industry and crafts	2.7	3.3
Trade and transport	1.9	2.1
Non-domestic services	0.9	1.1
Domestic service	1.2	1.3

Young People in Nazi Germany

Life also changed for the young in Germany as a result of Nazi education and youth policies.

Education

Bernard Rust, the Nazi Minister of Education, said:
'The whole purpose of education is to create Nazis.'

Everyone in Germany had to go to school up to the age of 14. After that schooling was optional. Boys and girls went to separate schools. The Nazis realised that through education they could convert the young to their Nazi ideas:

- Teachers had to swear an oath of loyalty to Hitler and join the Nazi Teachers' League.

- Textbooks were rewritten to fit the Nazi view of history and racial purity.

- PE classes were increased and religious education abandoned.

- Biology lessons taught that Germans, as members of the Aryan race, were superior to all races.

- The education of girls was concerned with turning them into perfect mothers and housewives.

SOURCE A

Typical weekly timetable for a Berlin girl aged 13

Period	Monday	Tuesday	Wednesday	Thursday	Friday	Saturday
8.00–8.45	German	German	German	German	German	German
8.50–9.35	Geography	History	Singing	Geography	History	Singing
9.40–10.25	Race Study	Race Study	Race Study	Race Study	Party Beliefs	Party Beliefs
10.25–11.00	Break	Break	Break	Break	Break	Break
11.00–12.05	Domestic Science with Maths	Domestic Science with Maths	Domestic Science with Maths	Domestic Science with Maths	Domestic Science with Maths	Domestic Science with Maths
12.10–12.55	Eugenics	Health Biology	Eugenics	Health Biology	Eugenics	Health Biology

During break there would be sports and special announcements. There was organised sport every afternoon from 2.00pm – 6.00pm

- Boys were taught military skills.

SOURCE B

From an official statement on the purpose of education for boys

German Language, History, Geography, Chemistry and Mathematics must concentrate on military subjects – the glorification of military service and of German heroes.

A poster encouraging young people to join the Hitler Youth in 1933. It says 'Join us! Be part of the Hitler Youth'.

HER ZU UNS!

Hinein in die Hitler-Jugend

The Hitler Youth

The Nazis also wanted to control the life of young people outside school as well. In 1936 membership of the Hitler Youth Movement was made compulsory. Other youth organisations were banned. Membership rose from two million in 1933, to over seven million in 1939. Boys went camping and hiking with most activities designed to create fit young people who would make good soldiers.

The girls' version, the League of German Girls, also organised camping and hiking, but aimed to make girls fit enough to be strong mothers. The League sometimes had the opposite effect. It allowed girls from small villages and towns to take part in activities that had previously been only for boys.

Hitler Youth		
Organisation	**Age range**	**Typical activities**
DJV German Young People Boys	10–14	Learning Nazi songs and ideas. Athletics. Hiking and camping.
JM League of Young Girls	10–14	As with boys.
HJ Hitler Youth	14–18	Learning Nazi ideas. Athletics, marching, camping. Map reading and military skills.
BDM League of German Maidens	14–18	Learning Nazi ideas. Athletics, marching, camping and learning domestic skills. Preparation for motherhood.

There were mixed reactions to the Hitler Youth.

The memories of a Hitler Youth Leader recorded after the Second World War

What I liked about the Hitler Youth was the comradeship. I can still remember how deeply moved I was when we learned the club mottoes: 'Jungvolk boys are hard, they can keep a secret, they are loyal; Jungvolk boys are comrades'. And then the trips. Is there anything nicer than enjoying the splendours of the homeland in the company of one's comrades?

Memories of another Hitler Youth member

In our troop the Jungvolk activities consisted almost entirely of military drill. Even if sport or shooting was scheduled, we always had to drill first. Endless marching with twelve-year-olds bawling out ten-year-olds and marching them all over the school ground.

Questions

1 What differences are there between Sources **D** and **E** in their views of the Hitler Youth?
2 Why do you think they differ?

Teenage rebels

In the late 1930s there were signs that some young people rejected the Nazi ways. Gangs began to appear on street corners. They played their own music and boys and girls were free to be together. Many gangs went looking for the Hitler Youth and beat them up.

Some gangs considered themselves to be part of a larger movement, the Edelweiss Pirates. They wore a metal badge of the edelweiss flower. They were not only concerned with having fun. They were anti-authority and anti-Nazi. During the Second World War they collected propaganda dropped from Allied aircraft and pushed it through letterboxes.

The Nazis and the Churches

At first the churches and the Nazis seemed to get on:

- The Nazis claimed to approve of Christianity and offered freedom of religious belief.

- The churches supported the Nazis as they believed Germany had become a very immoral country under the Weimar Republic. Most important of all the churches feared the Communists. The Nazis promised to get rid of them.

All this soon changed.

The Catholic Church

This was very strong in the south of Germany. In 1933 Hitler signed a Concordat with the Pope agreeing to allow the Catholic Church to run its churches, schools and newspapers. In return, bishops took an oath of loyalty to Hitler. This co-operation was short-lived:

SOURCE A

A Protestant pastor speaking about his attitude to the Nazis in 1937

We all know that if the Third Reich were to collapse today, Communism would come in its place. Therefore we must show loyalty to the Führer who has saved us from Communism and given us a better future.

- The Nazis disliked the Catholic youth organisation because many Catholic children joined this rather than the Hitler Youth. In 1937 the Catholic Youth was made illegal.

- The Catholics also ran a great number of schools where the children would not hear Nazi ideas. These schools were taken out of church control.

- Many priests opposed this and were sent to concentration camps.

- In 1937, the Pope issued a letter condemning Hitler and the Nazis.

The Protestant Churches

The Protestants were divided. Many Protestants continued to support the Nazis. In 1933 Hitler tried to gain control of them by setting up a single 'Reich Church' under a Nazi bishop. This Church was anti-Christian and promoted Nazi ideas.

Over three-quarters of Protestant pastors, led by Pastor Martin Niemoller, opposed this Church and Nazi persecution of the Jews. They formed the 'Confessional Church'. As a result, many pastors were sent to concentration camps.

Profile of
Pastor Martin Niemoller

Martin Niemoller was a First World War hero – as a U-boat commander he had won Germany's highest decoration for bravery. During the 1930s he became the leader of the Protestants who opposed Nazi policies. He disliked the new German 'Reich Church' and the Nazis. Niemoller was arrested and put in a concentration camp where he spent seven years.

SOURCE B

Comments from police reports in Bavaria in 1937 and 1938

The influence of the Church on the population is so strong that the Nazi spirit cannot penetrate. The local population is ever under the strong influence of the priests. These people prefer to believe what the priests say from the pulpit than the words of the best Nazi speakers.

Question

What does Source **B** suggest about the success of Nazi policies towards the Churches?

Culture in the Third Reich

This was used by the Nazis to put across their ideas, especially of race. There was no freedom of expression. Artists and writers were told what to write or draw. Those who refused were forced abroad or sent to concentration camps.

Art

Hitler hated the style of modern art which had developed under the Weimar Republic.

SOURCE A

Hitler describes modern art

Misformed cripples and cretins, women who inspire only disgust. Men who are more like wild beasts. Children who, were they alive, must be regarded as cursed by God.

He blamed this on the Jews. Art was changed so that it could show Nazi values. Each year exhibitions of German art were held. Paintings showed:

- The Nazi idea of the simple peasant life. Paintings produced in Nazi Germany created a myth of a simple and pleasant peasant life.

- Hard work was shown as heroic.

- Other paintings showed the perfect Aryan. Young German men and women were shown to have perfect bodies.

- Women were shown in the Nazi's preferred role as housewives and mothers.

A painting by Paul Padua called The Führer speaks, *1937*

Question

What is the painter trying to make you think?

Architecture

Hitler had always been interested in architecture and wanted to use it to show the power of the Third Reich. He planned to rebuild much of Berlin by 1950 when the capital would be renamed Germania.

Films

Most of the people who owned the cinemas were Nazi sympathisers. All scripts were checked by the Propaganda Ministry. Directors and actors could not be Jews or opponents of the Nazis.
   Films were used to:

- Put across racial values and ideas and as a powerful weapon in stirring up hatred against Jewish people and Communists.

- To show the great successes of the Nazi regime. The official film of the 1936 Olympics, *Triumph of the Will*, was an impressive propaganda film.

- Provide entertainment. Goebbels realised that films must also entertain. He allowed a great number of films for this purpose.

The Nazi Racial State

Central to Nazi policy was the creation of a pure German state. This meant treating all non-German groups, especially the Jews, as second-class citizens.

The 'Master Race'

The Nazis believed the Germans were a pure race of Aryan descent – from the *Herrenvolk* or 'Master Race'. They were shown in art as blond, blue-eyed, tall, lean and athletic – a people fit to master the world. The Nazis took steps to increase their numbers.

The *Untermenschen*

Jews and Slavs, on the other hand, were *Untermenschen* – or 'subhumans'. Hitler had used the Jews as the scapegoat, the group to blame, for Germany's problems since 1919. They were blamed for German defeat in 1918 and the 'stab in the back'. Nazi propaganda showed the Jews as evil moneylenders. This was not new. Anti-Semitism, or hatred of the Jews, had been common in Europe for many centuries.

Jewish children were made to stand in front of a blackboard slogan – 'The Jew is our greatest enemy'. Even feature films at the cinema were used for anti-Jewish propaganda. Yet the Jews were no real threat to the Nazis. There were no more than half a million Jews in Germany in 1933 – fewer than one person in every hundred.

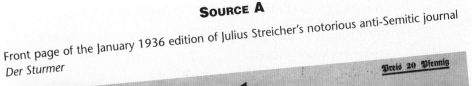

SOURCE A

Front page of the January 1936 edition of Julius Streicher's notorious anti-Semitic journal *Der Sturmer*

The attack on the rights of the Jews 1933–39

This was a gradual process with the aim of removing all Jewish rights. For the first two years of Nazi rule there was little organised persecution of the Jews. Hitler was setting up his dictatorship and using anti-Jewish propaganda to turn the German people in favour of his policies.

1933

- Hitler ordered a boycott of Jewish shops and businesses. The SA painted 'Jude' ('Jew') on windows and tried to persuade the public not to enter.

- A new law excluded Jews from government jobs.

- Thousands of Jewish civil servants, lawyers and university teachers were sacked.

1934

- Anti-Jewish propaganda increased.

- Local councils banned Jews from public spaces such as parks, playing fields and swimming pools.

1935

- The Nazis began to step up their campaign.

- Jews were forbidden to join the army.

- The Nuremburg Laws were passed on 15 September. The Reich Law on Citizenship states that only those of German blood could be German citizens. Jews lost their citizenship, the right to vote and hold government office. The Law for the Protection of German Blood and Honour forbade marriage of sexual relations between Jews and German citizens.

1936

- There was a lull in the anti-Jewish campaign. Germany was hosting the Olympics in Berlin and wanted to give the outside world a good impression.

- Professional activities of Jews banned or restricted – this included vets, dentists, accountants, surveyors, teachers and nurses.

1937

- For the first time in two years Hitler made an outspoken attack on the Jews.

- The Aryanisation of business was stepped up. More Jewish businesses were taken over.

A serious increase in anti-Jewish policies:

- Jews had to register their property, making it easier to confiscate.

- Jewish doctors, dentists and lawyers were forbidden to treat Aryans.

- Jewish children were excluded from German schools and universities.

- Jews with non-Jewish first names had to add and use the name 'Israel' for males or 'Sarah' for females.

- Jews had to have a red letter 'J' stamped on their passports.

1939

- Jews were no longer allowed to run shops or businesses

- Jews were forbidden to own radios or to buy cakes and chocolate.

KRISTALLNACHT, 'CRYSTAL NIGHT', 9 NOVEMBER 1938

Following the murder by a Jew of a German diplomat in Paris, the SA started a three-day campaign to destroy Jewish shops, homes and synagogues throughout Germany. About 90 Jews were killed and a further 20,000 arrested and put into concentration camps. This was known as *Kristallnacht*, or 'Crystal Night' after all the broken glass which littered streets everywhere.

SOURCE B

A German newspaper report of 'Crystal Night', 10 November 1938

The death of a loyal party member by the Jewish murderer has aroused spontaneous anti-Jewish demonstrations throughout the Reich. In many places Jewish shops have been smashed. The synagogues from which teachings hostile to the State and People are spread, have been set on fire.

SOURCE C

The *Daily Telegraph* reports on 'Crystal Night', 12 November 1938

Mob law ruled in Berlin throughout the afternoon and evening as hordes of hooligans took part in an orgy of destruction. I have never seen an anti-Jewish outbreak as sickening as this. I saw fashionably dressed women clapping their hands and screaming with glee while respectable mothers held up their babies to see the 'fun'. No attempt was made by the police to stop the rioters.

Activity

You are a Jewish teenager when Hitler takes over in 1933. You keep a diary of the changes that occur to the Jewish people over the next six years. Write out several extracts from the diary explaining the key changes and how they affected you.

Questions

1 What differences are there between these two versions of 'Crystal Night' (Sources **B** and **C**)?

2 How do you account for these differences?

Opposition to Nazi rule

It was very difficult to oppose the Nazis effectively. Most people who tried to do so were arrested by the Gestapo and sent to concentration camps or executed.

There was, however, some opposition from a variety of groups:

Young people

About one million people failed to join the Hitler Youth. Some joined rival groups such as the Edelweiss Pirates (p. 384).

Intellectuals

Some university teachers, writers and artists opposed the Nazis. Most were forced to emigrate and had to express their opposition abroad.

Conservatives

- Some landowners, diplomats and lawyers disliked Nazi methods from the start.

- Others, including army officers, had at first supported him but later turned against him due to Nazi methods and, later, his failures in the Second World War.

- The most important group of these opponents was known as the Kreisau Circle. Its members planned to restore a democratic government once Hitler had been overthrown. In 1944 the failure of their 'July plot' led to many arrests and executions.

Priests and religious groups

Many individual priests spoke out against the regime. Jehovah's Witnesses refused to co-operate.

The impact of the War on Germany 1939–45

The war had a devastating effect on Germany and also saw the introduction of the 'Final Solution'.

The Home Front

At first the war had little effect on people living in Germany. The long-drawn-out fight against the USSR and the Allies, 1941–45, brought greater hardships. Hitler ordered much greater increases in arms production. The German economy became even more committed to war production. As Minister of Armaments and Munitions Albert Speer took control of the armaments industry using a Central Planning Board.

As more men were called up, the number of industrial workers fell. To solve the labour problems, the government used:

- prisoners of war.

- people from conquered countries who were treated as slaves. Thousands died in appalling conditions.

- women – the Nazis abandoned their previous policy towards women.

SOURCE A

German rations

Civilian life

The War brought shortages. At first some of these were solved by imports from conquered countries – for example, oil from Romania and wheat from Poland. As the war continued food and goods were in ever shorter supply. This led to very low rations.

From 1942 the British launched mass bombing raids on civilian targets. These left thousands of families homeless. Many became refugees.

SOURCE B

The town of Duren, near Cologne, after being bombed by a thousand British aircraft on 30 May 1942

SOURCE C

Extract from the diary of Mathilde Wolff-Monckenberg written in 1943. She was a housewife in Hamburg.

People here don't seem to care any more. On their faces one can read despair and irritation wherever one happens to be; on the tram, in the post office, in the shops. Since the surrender of Stalingrad to the Russians (January 1943) all is grey and still. Shop after shop has closed down.

Question

Using Sources **A**, **B** and **C**, explain the effects that the war had on the German people.

The Final Solution

During the Second World War the Nazis took control of much of Europe and millions of Jews came under their control. Many of them were herded into separate parts of cities known as ghettos. Others were sent to concentration camps.

In 1941 Germany invaded the USSR. Special SS groups, called *Einsatzgruppen*, were formed to follow the German armies. They were ordered to execute all resistance fighters, Communist officials and Jews. Over 800,000 people, mainly Jews, were killed by mass shootings or gassing in vans using carbon monoxide.

In January 1942 the Nazi leaders met at the Wannsee Conference to discuss how to kill all European Jews – the 'final solution'. They decided to evacuate them by rail to five secret 'extermination camps' to be built in remote areas of Poland and equipped with gas chambers.

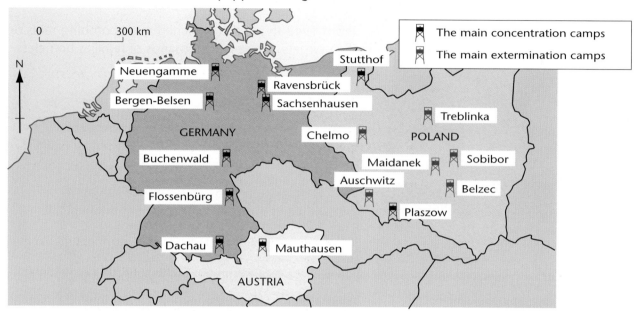

About 4.5 million Jews were killed in the death camps, either by hard labour, starvation or gassing. Altogether the Nazis killed about 6 million European Jews.

Source D

A painting of the scene which greeted the British troops who arrived at the Belsen concentration camps. The painting is by Leslie Cole.

The Germans did not publicise what they did and Himmler, the leader of the SS, ordered that the work should be kept secret. Propaganda films even showed good conditions in the camps. As defeat for Germany loomed an attempt was made to cover up what happened. The Germans pulled up the railway lines used to transport the Jews to the concentration camps.

Summary and Revision

GERMANY 1918–29

For this section you need to know:
- The German Revolution of 1918 and the setting up of the new Republic.
- The new German Constitution – weaknesses and strengths.
- German reactions to the Treaty of Versailles and the 'stab in the back' theory.
- Early opposition to the Republic – the Spartacists and the Kapp Putsch and how it was defeated.
- 1923: the year of crisis – events in the Ruhr and hyperinflation.
- The recovery of the republic 1924–29, especially the work of Stresemann.

Revision questions

1 What weaknesses were there in the new German Constitution?
2 Who were the Spartacists? How was their uprising defeated?
3 Why did the French occupy the Ruhr in 1923? What effects did it have on the German economy?
4 Who suffered as a result of hyperinflation in 1923?
5 What part did the following play in German recovery between 1924 and 1929:
   a Gustav Stresemann   b the Dawes Plan   c the Young Plan?

HITLER AND THE RISE OF THE NAZI PARTY 1919–33

For this section the key developments are:
- The early Nazi Party, 1919–23.
- The causes, events and results of the Munich Putsch, 1923.
- The fortunes of the Nazi Party 1924–29 – reorganisation and tactics.
- The effects of the Great Depression on Germany after 1929.
- The activities of Hitler and the Nazi Party 1929–33 – propaganda, speeches, SA.
- Reasons for increased Nazi support 1929–33.

Revision questions

1 Why did Hitler join the German Workers' Party in 1919?
2 Explain the early aims and organisation of the early Nazi Party.
3 Why did Hitler try to seize power in 1923? Was it a total failure?
4 How did the organisation and tactics of the Nazi Party change between 1924–9?
5 Why was there little support for the party during this period?
6 How and why did the following bring increased support for the Nazis in the period 1929–33?
   a   the Wall Street Crash
   b   Nazi propaganda
   c   growth of Communism
   d   activities of the SA
   e   Hitler's skills.

You will need to know:
- Nazi consolidation in power 1933–4 – the removal of opposition, the Enabling Law and the Night of the Long Knives.
- The Nazi dictatorship – how the Nazis achieved control through the police state.
- The importance of propaganda and its impact on the German people.
- Nazi policies in connection with unemployment and the economy. Were Germans better off during this period?
- The effects of Nazi policies on the young – education and the youth movements. How much opposition was there?
- The changing position of women, especially in relation to marriage and the family.
- Racial policy – Nazi theories of race and the anti-Jewish policies of the period.
- Attitudes towards the Protestant and Catholic Churches.
- Nazi culture – changes in art, films and architecture.
- The impact of the Second World War on the German civilian population.
- The holocaust. Why the Nazis decided on the 'final solution' and how it was carried out.

Revision questions

1 How did the following enable Hitler to establish his dictatorship in the period 1933–4?
   a the Reichstag Fire
   b the Enabling Law
   c The Night of the Long Knives.
2 What methods were used by Goebbels to control and spread propaganda?
3 Explain the part played by the following in the Nazi police state:
   a Gestapo b Law courts c concentration camps.
4 What was 'autarky'? How successfully was it carried out in this period?
5 Explain three methods used by the Nazis to reduce unemployment.
6 Did Germans have a better standard of living under the Nazis?
7 What changes took place in education under the Nazis?
8 How else did they control the lives of the young?
9 What role did women have in the Third Reich? What measures were brought in to encourage this role?
10 Explain Nazi racial theory. Describe the key measures brought in against the Jews during this period.
11 How far did Nazi policies change towards:
   a the Catholic Church?
   b the Protestant Church?
12 What effects did the Second World War have on the German civilian population?

9
Russia 1905–41

UNDERSTANDING RUSSIAN HISTORY

The following definitions and explanations will give you a greater understanding of Russia in this period.

Bolshevik	A member of one of the groups formed after the split in the Social Democratic Party in 1903. This group was led by Lenin.
Capitalist	Owner of the means of creating wealth, such as a factory owner or landowner.
Collectivisation	The setting up of farms operated by groups of people who sell the produce to the state and share the money.
Commissars	Heads of government departments in the Soviet Union.
Duma	Parliament.
Free market economy	An economic system in which buyers and sellers operate without government interference.
Haemophilia	Inherited disease, usually affecting men, in which a person's blood does not clot properly so that they bleed for a long time when injured.
Industrialisation	This refers to the growth of industry – especially heavy industries such as coal, engineering, oil and iron and steel.
Kolkhoz	Russian name for a collective farm.
Kulak	A rich peasant who often owned his own animals and land.
Menshevik	A member of one of the groups formed after the split in the Social Democratic Party in 1903.
Nationalisation	When the state takes over control of an industry.
Nepmen	Russians who made a living out of trading as a result of NEP.
Politburo	The policy-making committee of the Communist Party.
Proletariat	The industrial working class.
Purges	Removal of all those from a political party or organisation who do not agree with the leaders.
Soviet	Elected workers' council.
Tundra	A vast treeless and frozen area of Russia.

Russia 1900–41

RUSSIA IN 1900

Russia at the beginning of the twentieth century was a vast empire covering one-sixth of the world's surface. It was ruled by the Tsar, or emperor, who was said to derive his power directly from God.

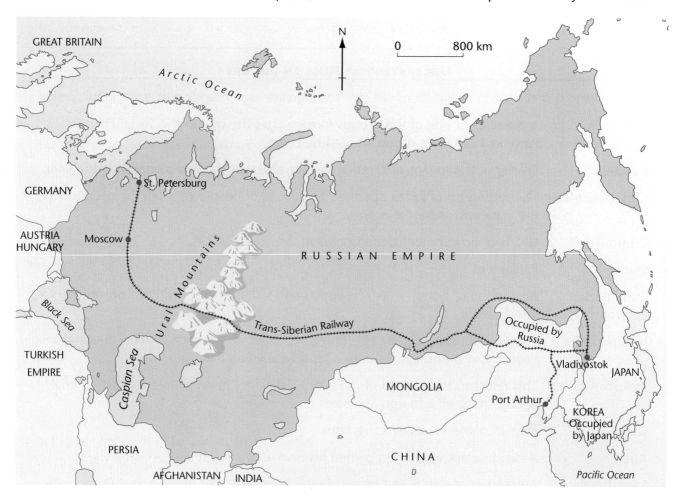

Problems in the Empire

The Tsar faced growing opposition from numerous groups due to the many problems facing the Empire.

A huge Empire

Russia was difficult to rule because of:

- *Its size.* It was almost one hundred times the size of Britain. It stretched from Europe in the west to the Pacific in the east, from the Arctic Ocean in the north to Persia in the south.

- *Poor communications.* Long distances and poor roads made communications slow. In the Arctic circle, frozen coasts and rivers prevented movement by ship for most of the year. In 1900 the Trans-Siberian Railway, which linked St Petersburg, the capital, to Vladivostock in the Far East, was only half finished.

- *Different peoples.* The total population of 125 million was made up of more than 20 different peoples. For six people out of every ten Russian was a foreign language.

Agriculture
The majority of the population, 85%, lived in the countryside. Russian agriculture, however, was poor.

- Extensive tundra, forest and desert meant only about 5% of the land, mainly in the south-west, was used for farming.

- Old-fashioned farming methods led to low food production and frequent famines.

Industry
Russia was rich in oil and minerals but in 1900 it was only in the first stages of industrialisation. Considering its size and resources, its manufacturing output was still very low.

Religion
About 70% of the population belonged to the official Orthodox Church. Large minorities belonged to other churches and religions. For example, 9% were Roman Catholic and 11% Muslim. The Orthodox Church was very important in Russia. In most houses there were holy pictures, or icons, on the walls. Holy men were held in high regard. The Church was very closely linked to the Tsar and supported his way of ruling. It taught that the Tsar was the head of the country and the head of the Church – in other words that he was God's chosen representative on earth.

Russian government
Russia was ruled by a Tsar who was an autocrat, which meant he had total power. He made the laws himself and appointed and dismissed ministers. The Tsar ensured obedience and removed opposition through:

- the secret police, the Okhrana, which was run by the Minister of the Interior. The police arrested suspects and had them tried in special courts.

- the largest peacetime army in the world, an army of 2.6 million men. It helped the police to maintain law and order.

- the Orthodox Church, whose priests taught that it was a sin to oppose the will of the Tsar.

There was growing opposition to the Tsar due to the failure to allow elections and a parliament at national level.

Russian society
The Russian Empire was a land of great contrasts. The vast majority of the people were poor peasants. At the other end of the scale was the aristocracy.

Profile on

Nicholas II

Nicholas was a well-meaning person with a deep affection for his family. He was devoted to his wife, Alexandra, his son, Alexis, and his four daughters. Although kind to those around him, he could be very cruel and merciless. He hated any opposition. At a time when Russia needed a forward-thinking Tsar Nicholas believed, wholeheartedly, in autocracy. He thought that democracy and elections would lead to the collapse of Russia. He was greatly influenced by Alexandra who was deeply religious and believed that the Tsar had been appointed by God and that it was the duty of all Russians to obey him.

The ruling and upper class

This was the royal family and nobility. They owned about 25% of the land and lived a life of luxury. Below them were lesser nobles such as Church leaders, military officers and top civil servants. They also were very wealthy.

The commercial or working class

This was only small in number due to the late development of Russian industry and trade. It consisted of bankers, merchants, factory owners and shopkeepers. Many were becoming very wealthy with the help of government loans and contracts.

The industrial working class

Many were ex-peasants who had moved to the towns and cities to work in the new factories. They were known as the proletariat. They were very poor indeed, with low wages, long hours, bad housing and food shortages. They resented their treatment by their employers. They were not allowed to form or join trade unions.

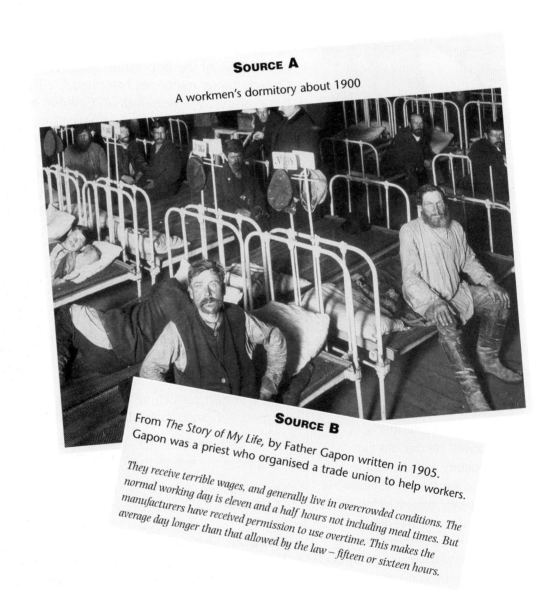

SOURCE A

A workmen's dormitory about 1900

SOURCE B

From *The Story of My Life*, by Father Gapon written in 1905. Gapon was a priest who organised a trade union to help workers.

They receive terrible wages, and generally live in overcrowded conditions. The normal working day is eleven and a half hours not including meal times. The manufacturers have received permission to use overtime. But this makes the average day longer than that allowed by the law – fifteen or sixteen hours.

The peasants

These lived in the country and made their living through farming. They were very poor. Since Emancipation in 1861, when they were given their freedom from the local landowners, they had had to pay for this freedom through 49 yearly instalments. Population increases meant that the land had to support more people. Many were hungry and were leaving the land to find work in the cities.

SOURCE C

A Russian village in about 1900

Questions

1 Why did the size of Russia make it difficult to rule?
2 What do Sources **A**, **B** and **C** show about the living and working conditions of the peasants and industrial workers?
3 How reliable is Source **B** as an account of conditions for town workers?

There was growing discontent in Russia by the beginning of the twentieth century with the emergence of several opposition groups.

Activity

You are a minister in the Tsar's government in 1904 concerned about the problems in Russia and the growth of opposition to the Tsar. Write a report to the Tsar explaining these problems and opposition and your concerns. In your report you could include:

- The plight of the peasants and industrial workers.

- Faults in your government.

- The opposition groups and their aims.

- Your suggestions for change.

The Constitutional Democrats (the Cadets)

This party was set up in 1905 by Paul Milyukov and was known as the Cadets. They wanted to strip the Tsar of virtually all his power and make him a constitutional monarch like that of Britain, in other words to work closely with an elected parliament representing the people. Some even wished to go further and turn Russia into a republic – a country with a president instead of an emperor. They were non-violent and got much support from the middle classes.

The Octobrists

They were more moderate than the Cadets and were satisfied by Nicholas II's October Manifesto of 1905 (see p. 402) which gave very limited reforms. They were also non-violent and received support from the middle classes.

The Social Democratic Party

They were founded in 1898. In 1903 they split into two groups – the Bolsheviks and the Mensheviks. Both groups believed in the ideas of Karl Marx.

The Bolsheviks, meaning majority, were led by Vladimir Lenin. They believed in a small group of professional revolutionaries with total obedience to Lenin.

The Mensheviks, meaning minority, led by Yuly Martov, wanted a party with a broad membership.

Both groups believed in seizing power by revolution and got support from the proletariat.

CAPITALISM

Wealthy people invest money. They employ the workers and keep all the profits.

↓

SOCIALISM

The workers revolt. All land is owned by the government. The government stops the wealthy taking over again.

↓

COMMUNISM

There is now a classless society with everyone working together for the good of everyone.

SOURCE D

Karl Marx, whose ideas were an important part of Communist theory

The Social Revolutionaries

This group was set up in 1901 by Victor Chernov and won support from the peasantry. They wanted Russia to remain a largely agricultural country in which land was not owned privately, but was controlled by each village community. They wanted to seize power by revolution. They also believed in attacking Tsarism by assassinating ministers and officials.

Question

Which class supported each of the following parties and for what reasons:

a the Cadets?
b the Bolsheviks?
c the Social Revolutionaries?

During this period the Tsar survived the first attempt to overthrow him – the 1905 Revolution. This was followed by unsuccessful attempts at reform. In 1914 Russia went to war. This had disastrous consequences for the Russian people in general and Nicholas II in particular.

The 1905 Revolution

This was due partly to the growth of discontent in Russia but there were other more immediate causes.

The Russo-Japanese War 1904–5

In 1904–5 Russia fought Japan for control of Korea and Manchuria. The Tsar expected a quick victory which would silence the opposition groups. Russia, however, suffered a series of defeats on land and sea. Japan destroyed both its Pacific and Baltic fleets.

- The Tsar became more unpopular. His government was shown to be weak and incompetent.

- Conditions for the working people became worse because of increased prices and food shortages. There were factory closures and unemployment.

Bloody Sunday

This was the spark that set off the revolution. In January 1905 about 200,000 unarmed workers marched to the Tsar's Winter Palace in St Petersburg to petition the Tsar. They wanted:

- an end to the war.

- a parliament.

- better working and living conditions.

The march was led by Father Gapon.

Troops guarding the Palace panicked and opened fire on the marchers, killing and injuring hundreds. The Tsar was not there but the massacre:

- destroyed the faith of many who had trusted the Tsar.

- increased support for the revolutionaries.

- sparked off a wave of riots, strikes and murders.

Profile on

Father Gapon

He was an Orthodox Church priest who had been allowed by the authorities to form a union of St Petersburg factory workers. He was actually a police agent. When this was discovered later he was murdered by revolutionaries.

SOURCE A

An extract from the workers' petition of 1905

We people of St Petersburg have come to you, our ruler, in search of justice and protection. We have become beggars. We are treated as slaves. Do not refuse assistance to Your people. End the oppressive behaviour of your officials towards them. Destroy the walls between Yourself and Your people.

EVENTS OF THE REVOLUTION

January	Strikes in St Petersburg. Many government officials were killed.
February	Assassination of Governor-General of Moscow, the Tsar's uncle.
March	Start of peasant uprisings. Landlords murdered. Many non-Russian areas demanded independence.
May	Professional workers such as doctors, lawyers and teachers supported demands for changes in government.
June	Mutiny by the crew of the battleship Potemkin.
July	Strikes and peasant uprisings continued.
September	Treaty of Portsmouth ended war with Japan.
October	General strike brought country to a standstill. The Tsar issued the October Manifesto. This promised:

- freedom of speech and the right to form political parties.
- a Duma, or parliament, elected by all adults.
- to make no new laws without the Duma's approval.

Many strikers returned to work. Liberals welcomed the Manifesto and ended their opposition. Revolutionary groups formed Soviets or workers' councils in major cities.

December	Police and army broke up the St Petersburg and Moscow Soviets.

Why did the 1905 Revolution fail?
The revolution failed for several reasons:

- The end of the war with Japan released troops who remained loyal to the Tsar. They dealt with the disturbances.

- The October Manifesto divided the opposition. It pleased many workers who ended their strikes. It split the Liberals, who wanted the Tsar to set up a parliament, into the Octobrists who supported the manifesto and the Cadets who wanted the Tsar to go further.

- There was no one party which led the revolution and co-ordinated the strikes, Soviets and peasant uprisings.

Activity

Look at the following list of reasons for the failure of the 1905 Revolution. Draw a table of two columns: one headed Strengths of Tsarism and the other Weaknesses of the Opposition and put each of the following reasons in one of the columns:

Liberals split over October Manifesto

Loyalty of the army

No real leadership of strikes, opposition

Middle-class fear of violence of workers

Different aims of opposition

End of the war with Japan

Questions

1 What does Source **A** on p. 401 tell you about discontent in Russia in 1905?
2 Why did the war with Japan increase discontent in Russia?
3 How useful are Sources **A** and **B** to a historian studying the events of Bloody Sunday?
4 Did the 1905 Revolution fail only because of the October Manifesto?

Russia 1906–14

The Tsar did not learn the lessons of 1905. Although there were attempts at reform, these were mostly unsuccessful. There was still discontent when Russia went to war in 1914.

The Dumas

Nicholas had agreed to set up a Duma in his October Manifesto. He had no intention of giving it real power.

SOURCE B

The first meeting of the Duma. Stolypin is reading the Tsar's declaration.

SOURCE A

Nicholas II in 1908

I have created the Duma not to instruct me but to advise me.

This was achieved through:

- the voting system for the Duma which was rigged to give landowners and property owners more influence than peasants and workers.

- the Fundamental Laws of May 1906. These announced that the Tsar remained as an absolute ruler. The Duma had no say in most areas of government and had only limited powers to introduce laws.

- when the first two Dumas (1906 and 1907) demanded reform the Tsar dismissed them.

- further changes to the electoral laws excluded the Socialist Revolutionaries.

The next two Dumas were loyal to the Tsar.

Focus on

The Dumas 1906–14

There were four dumas in the years between the 1905 Revolution and the February Revolution of 1917. The election of deputies to the first two dumas was based on a complicated system of electoral colleges, which were meant to represent the different social classes roughly in proportion to their size. The government imposed a much more restrictive system for the elections to the third and fourth dumas. The four elections produced the following results:

Party or group	First duma 1906	Second duma 1907	Third duma 1907–12	Fourth duma 1912–17
SDs (Mensheviks)	18	47	—	—
SDs (Bolsheviks)	—	—	19	15
SRs	—	37	—	—
Trudoviks•	136	104	13	10
Kadets	182	91	54	53
Octobrists	17	42	154	95
Progressists••	427	28	28	41
Rightists•••	8	10	147	154
National parties	60	93	26	22
Others	—	50	—	42
	448	518	441	432

- • The SRs as a party officially boycotted the elections to the first duma, but stood as Trudoviks (labourists).

- •• The progressists were a party of businessmen who favoured moderate reform.

- ••• The Rightists were not a single party: they represented a range of conservative views from right of centre to extreme reaction.

The rule of Stolypin

In 1906 Nicholas appointed Peter Stolypin as Prime Minister.

Stolypin believed he could achieve stability by:

* suppressing revolutionaries.

* introducing reforms to improve people's lives.

Thousands of revolutionaries were executed, exiled or imprisoned. This led to a reduction in terrorism and revolutionary activity. He also introduced a policy of 'Russification'. This meant that the national groups like the Poles, Ukrainians and Finns had restrictions put on their native languages and were forced to speak Russian and accept Russian customs.

Profile on

Peter Stolypin

Stolypin was born in 1862 and had been a civil servant and a provincial governor. He was known to be clever and strong-minded. He believed in a 'carrot and stick' approach. Reforming to improve conditions was the 'carrot'. The 'stick' was dealing ruthlessly with any opposition. In 1906 1000 people were executed and a further 21,000 sent to prison. Between 1907 and 1911 a further 1800 were hanged and the noose became known as 'Stolypin's necktie'. In 1911 he was assassinated.

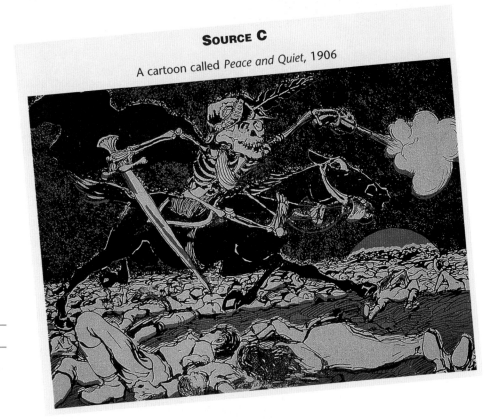

SOURCE C

A cartoon called *Peace and Quiet*, 1906

Question

What point is the cartoonist making in Source **C**?

Reform

Stolypin carried out reforms in the countryside and cities.

In the countryside he abolished the peasants' annual payments for their freedom. He helped the peasants to buy their land and set up their farms. This led to richer peasants called kulaks who ran profitable farms. This, in turn,

- restored loyalty to the Tsar.

- provided more food for the cities.

In the cities he set up health insurance schemes for the workers. There was some improvement for city workers but:

- many remained discontented.

- there were 8000 strikes between 1912 and 1914, especially in the Lena gold field, Siberia, in 1912. This was put down with great brutality by the police, with 270 killed.

SOURCE D

Striking workers killed by the police at the Lena gold field, 1912

Rasputin

In 1905 a previously obscure 'holy man' called Grigory Rasputin, who had travelled around Russia, arrived at the court of Nicholas II. He gained favour with the Tsar and Tsarina through his apparent ability, possibly with the aid of hypnosis, to control the dangerous illness of his son, Alexis, the heir to the throne. Alexis suffered from haemophilia. This was, in those days, an incurable blood disease, making it likely he would die young. Doctors could not cure the disease. His blood did not clot, and whenever he cut himself he was in danger of bleeding to death.

The Tsar and Tsarina became more dependent on advice from Rasputin. Later, during the First World War, Rasputin even gave advice on whom the Tsar should appoint to the government. This would not have mattered had Rasputin been an efficient leader. He was not. Under his influence, corruption grew at court.

Rasputin

Rasputin was a monk and the son of a Siberian peasant. His real name was Grigory Yefimovich, but he gained the nickname Rasputin, meaning 'immoral'. Rasputin was a colourful character. He had sympathy for ordinary Russians and was intelligent enough to predict disaster if ever Russia got involved in a major war. He was also notorious for his orgies and wild living at court and there were even rumours of an affair with the Tsarina. Members of the royal family begged Alexandra to dismiss Rasputin. She refused. In desperation, a group of noblemen led by Prince Yusupov took matters into their own hands. In December 1916 they assassinated Rasputin. It was not an easy job getting rid of him. He was poisoned, shot and finally bound and pushed into an icy river where he drowned.

Rasputin (on the left) surrounded by his court followers

Questions

1 Why were the Dumas not a success?
2 Had Tsar Nicholas II learnt the lessons of 1905?
3 Do you think there would be more or less discontent in Russia in 1914 than in 1905?
4 Why did Rasputin have so much influence over the Tsar and his wife?

Activity

You are a journalist looking for a sensational story to sell your Sunday paper. Do a feature on Rasputin and his influence at the court of Nicholas and Alexandra. Try to include an eye-catching headline.

The impact of the First World War 1914–17

In August 1914 Russia joined Britain and France in fighting the combined forces of Germany, Austria-Hungary and, later, Turkey. At first there was great support and enthusiasm for the war. This did not last long. The war had catastrophic consequences for Russia and was to be the short-term cause of the collapse of Tsardom.

IMPACT OF WAR

• POLITICAL EFFECTS

The war resulted in criticism of both the Tsar and his wife, Alexandra.

- The Tsar was blamed for the military defeats after personally taking command of the army in August 1915. He left behind a weak government under the control of his wife. Nicholas refused to choose new ministers from the Duma.

- The Tsarina Alexandra was inexperienced and incompetent as a ruler. She relied too much on the unpopular advice of Rasputin until his death in December 1916. She dismissed sound ministers and replaced them with officials who were unable to cope with the demands of war. Alexandra was also unpopular because she was a German. Rumours spread that she was working with Rasputin to bring about a German victory.

SOURCE A

An anti-war poster issued by the Bolsheviks during the First World War. It shows the Tsar, the Church, and the Russian nobility riding on the shoulders of ordinary Russians.

ЦАРЬ, ПОП И БОГАЧ
НА ПЛЕЧАХ У ТРУДОВОГО НАРОДА

• MILITARY DEFEAT

The Russian armies were very large but badly led and poorly equipped. They were no match for the Germans and suffered several defeats.

- Within weeks of the outbreak of war Russia was defeated at Tannenberg, where the Germans trapped the Russians in a swampland. About 90,000 Russians were captured and over 100,000 drowned. Just one week later the Germans slaughtered a further 100,000 Russian troops at the battle of Masurian Lakes.

- In the spring of 1915 the Germans and Austrians invaded Russia and advanced 300 miles into Russia. Nicholas dismissed his commander-in-chief and took command himself. This was a serious mistake because the Tsar had little knowledge of military strategy and tactics.

- In 1916 General Brusilov launched an offensive but was forced to retreat yet again. Over one million Russians died in the campaign.

SOURCE B

Report by the Chairman of the Military Commission of the Duma

As early as the beginning of the second year of the war desertions of soldiers at the front became commonplace. The average number of deserters reached 25%. I happen to know of three cases when the train was stopped because there were no passengers on it. All, except the officer in command, had run away.

ECONOMIC EFFECTS

Over 15 million men had to join the army. This left farms and factories without enough workers, causing severe shortages of food and materials. The railway system failed to cope with the additional demands of war causing:

- inadequate supplies to the front.
- food shortages in the towns.
- coal shortages leading to power failures.

Food prices rose so that families could afford less food.

SOURCE C

A queue for bread

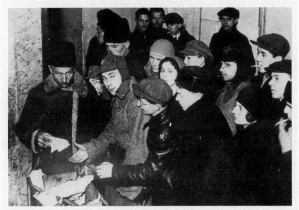

Activity

It is December 1916. You are an opponent of Russian involvement in the war.

Design a poster which will turn the Russian people against the war.

Questions

1. Which of the following do you think was the most important reason for discontent in Russia during the First World War:
   a. the influence of Rasputin?
   b. the military defeats?
   c. the poor transport system?
   d. food and fuel shortages?
2. Does Source **D** give an accurate view of the situation in Petrograd at the beginning of 1917?

SOCIAL EFFECTS

The war brought social change but widespread misery:

- Social changes included the creation of new jobs in the armaments factories and on the railways. The number of town workers increased rapidly as peasants left the countryside to take up new jobs.

- Hunger and discontent due to food shortages and price rises especially among the town workers. St Petersburg, now called Petrograd, experienced a terrible winter, 1916–17, which worsened the problems of food and fuel shortages.

SOURCE D

Workers protest in Petrograd in early 1917

By the beginning of 1917 there was widespread discontent in the armed forces, the cities and towns and in the countryside.

SOURCE E

A telegram sent by Rodzyanko, President of the Duma, to the Tsar in February (March) 1917

The situation is serious. The government is paralysed. The transport system is broken down. The food and fuel supplies are completely disorganised. Discontent is on the increase. There is wild shooting on the streets.

The Russian calendar

In 1918 the Bolshevik government changed the Russian calendar. Before this, Russian dates were two weeks ahead of the rest of Europe. So the revolutions of March and November in Russia took place in February and October in the rest of Europe. All dates in this section will be based on the Russian calendar.

Russia experienced two revolutions in 1917. In March the revolution led to the abdication (resignation) of the Tsar. He was replaced by a temporary government known as the Provisional Government. This made several mistakes and in November was overthrown by Lenin and the Bolsheviks.

The March Revolution

In March 1917 there was a spontaneous revolution which began in Petrograd and spread to Moscow and other major cities. This led to the overthrow of the Tsarist government.

Causes of the revolution

This was due to a combination of long-term, short-term and immediate problems.

- Long-term – including the problems of ruling Russia, the weaknesses of the Tsar and the discontent in the cities and countryside.

- Short-term – Nicholas II's failure to learn from the mistakes of 1905 and to allow the Dumas any power.

- Immediate – the widespread discontent created by Russia's involvement in the First World War.

- An exceptionally cold winter provided the final spark. Trains could not run, causing even greater shortages of food and fuel. The Russian people were suffering from extreme hunger and cold. The Tsar and his wife ignored frequent warnings from the Duma and their own secret police.

SOURCE A

A letter from the Tsarina to Nicholas II, 26 February 1917

This is a hooligan movement. Young people run about and shout that there is no bread, simply to create excitement. If the weather was very cold they would probably stay at home. All this will pass and become calm, if only the Duma will behave itself.

EVENTS OF THE REVOLUTION

7 March	22,000 steelworkers were locked out after pay talks broke down. Other workers went on strike in support.
8 March	International Women's Day. Thousands of women demonstrated in Petrograd calling for bread. More workers came out on strike.
9 March	Large crowds were repeatedly dispersed by police and soldiers.
10 March	250,000 workers, over half the workforce, were on strike. Petrograd was paralysed. The Tsar ordered the army to end the disturbances.
11 March	Troops fired on the crowds killing 40. The President of the Duma advised the Tsar to form a new government urgently. The Tsar ordered the Duma to stop meeting immediately.
12 March	Soldiers mutiny. They refused to fire on the crowds and joined the strikers instead. The Duma set up a Provisional Government. Soldiers, sailors and workers formed the Petrograd Soviet.
13 March	The Tsar set out to return to Petrograd.
14 March	Generals told the Tsar the army no longer supported him.
15 March	Tsar Nicholas abdicated in favour of his brother, Grand Duke Michael.
16 March	Grand Duke Michael refused to become Tsar.

The abdication of Tsar Nicholas II, March 1917

SOURCE C

From a child's textbook written in Communist Russia in 1976

In response to the call of the Bolsheviks the workers of the Petrograd factories went on strike... The Bolshevik Committee met late at night in a small house on the outskirts. 'We can no longer wait and do nothing. The time has come to act openly. We shall begin tomorrow. We must seize the arms stores and disarm the police', the Committee decided.

Profile on

Alexander Kerensky

Kerensky had become involved in revolutionary activities as a young man but he turned to the Social Revolutionary Party rather than the Marxists. He was elected to the Duma in 1912 and became famous for his emotional speeches. It was Kerensky who met the crowds outside the Duma to discuss their demands and then helped persuade the Duma members to form the Provisional Government. He was Minister of Justice in this government, then Minister of War and finally, in July, Prime Minister.

Questions

1   What does Source **A** tell you about the Tsarina's understanding of the situation in Russia at the beginning of 1917?
2   What do you think were the short-term causes of the Tsar's resignation?
3   Why do you think the extract in Source **C** was written?

The Provisional Government

This was set up during the March Revolution. It consisted of twelve members of the Duma. It planned to rule until the people elected a Constituent Assembly to work out a new system of government. The key figure in the government was Alexander Kerensky.

The Provisional Government had several weaknesses and made important mistakes.

The Petrograd Soviet

SOURCE A

Meeting of the Soviet in St Petersburg, March 1917

This was set up during the March Revolution. It was a council of 2500 deputies elected by workers and soldiers whose interests it aimed to protect. It was dominated by the Mensheviks who aimed for a workers' revolution but believed the time was not yet ripe. It recognised the Provisional Government but was determined to influence it and share power.

At first the two worked closely together but gradually they grew apart. The Soviet soon became influenced by the Bolsheviks who opposed the Provisional Government. The Soviet had originally issued Order Number One, stating that it would only obey the government if it thought it was running Russia in the right way.

Weaknesses within the government

The Provisional Government had several weaknesses:

- Its members had no real experience of government.

- It became increasingly dominated by the middle and upper classes. They refused to agree to reforms.

- Because it was temporary its members refused to carry out important reforms until the Constituent Assembly met. Unfortunately, it delayed the elections for the Assembly until the end of 1917. This upset many Russians.

Mistakes of the government

The Provisional Government made at least five important mistakes:

1   It decided to continue the war in order to honour Russia's commitments to France and Britain. These countries threatened to stop loans and supplies. The Russian armies launched an offensive in June. This was a disastrous failure.

SOURCE B

A letter from Guchkov, Minister for War in the Provisional Government, to General Alekseev, at the end of March 1917

The Provisional Government possesses no real power and its orders are executed only in so far as this is permitted by the Soviet of Workers' and Soldiers' Deputies, which holds in its hands the real power – control of troops, railroads, postal and telegraph services.

This led to:

- The collapse of morale and discipline in the armed forces.
- Rising anger at home.
- Increased popularity for the Bolsheviks who demanded peace.

2   It failed to solve the food shortages. The workers were demanding food and would riot if they did not get it. The government's powers were limited as the Petrograd Soviet controlled the food supply system.

3   The Provisional Government did not carry out land reform. Peasants were demanding their own land. The government refused partly because it was controlled by landowners. They promised to bring in reforms later, after the elections for the Constituent Assembly. The peasants were angry at the delay and seized the land for themselves.

4   The Provisional Government needed to control the armed forces. The troops, however, obeyed the Petrograd Soviet's Order Number One. They refused government orders which contradicted those of the Soviet. It was the Soviet which controlled the armed forces.

5   The government needed to stop the spread of support for Socialists aiming to overthrow it, groups such as the Bolsheviks and the Revolutionary Socialists. To create a democratic society, the government:

- allowed free speech.
- allowed a free press.
- released political prisoners.

Although these were very creditable reforms, they meant that government opponents were free to criticise the government and spread their own ideas.

Lenin and the Bolsheviks

Lenin was leader of the Bolshevik Party, which had split from the Mensheviks in 1903. He believed that only a small, secretive, dedicated party could successfully carry out a revolution in Russia. For a long time the Bolsheviks had little hope of success. Several of their leaders, including Lenin, spent many years in prison or in exile in the interior of Russia. Lenin was in Switzerland when the First World War broke out. He totally opposed Russian involvement in the war.

Lenin returned to Russia in April 1917. The German government arranged a special train to take him to Petrograd via Sweden and Finland. The Germans knew that Lenin wanted to stop the war, and they thought that if Lenin caused trouble in Russia, it would disrupt the Russian war effort against Germany. Lenin's activities and leadership over next six months did much to weaken the position of the Provisional Government and prepare the way for a Bolshevik Revolution.

Profile on
Lenin

His real name was Vladimir Ulyanov. He was born in Simbirsk in 1870, the son of a school inspector. He was deeply affected by the execution of his revolutionary brother who had been involved in the assassination of Alexander II. Lenin went to university to study law but was expelled because he took part in demonstrations. He became involved with Marxism and in 1894 joined a Marxist group, changing his name to Lenin. He was sent into exile in London due to his Marxist activities, where he became editor of the Party newspaper *Iskra* (meaning *The Spark*). Lenin believed in a small party of dedicated revolutionaries. In 1903, when the Social Democratic Party split, Lenin led the Bolsheviks. Over the next fourteen years he spent most of the time in exile organising Bolshevik activities.

SOURCE E

A painting showing Lenin returning to Russia

Focus on
Lenin's 'April Theses'

The Provisional Government must be overthrown.
The war must end immediately.
Industry must be nationalised.
Land should be given to the peasants.
All power must be given to the Soviets.

- He issued his 'April Theses' on his return to Petrograd. He turned his ideas into simple slogans such as 'Peace, bread and land' and 'All power to the Soviets'.

- He used shrewd tactics such as persuading the Bolsheviks to work for the overthrow of the Provisional Government and set up a Communist regime. He stopped the close co-operation of the Petrograd Soviet and the government and ensured that more and more Bolsheviks became members.

- Lenin had an excellent sense of timing. He did not want to carry out revolution until the Provisional Government was weak and the Bolsheviks were properly organised.

- He built up the organisation of the Party with the help of money given by the German government. Membership increased from 26,000 to 2,000,000 between April and August. The Party now ran several newspapers such as *Pravda* meaning 'truth'. A central committee ran the Party with local committees in the factories and the army. Finally a private army, the Red Guards, was set up in the Petrograd factories.

The 'July Days'

Angry at the failure of the 'June offensive', workers, soldiers and sailors rioted, demanding government by the Soviets. The Bolsheviks supported but did not lead the riots. The government responded by quelling the riots. They accused the Bolsheviks of working for the Germans. Many leading Bolsheviks were arrested and Lenin fled to Finland.

The Kornilov Revolt

In August General Kornilov, the right-wing Commander-in-Chief of Russia's armed forces, tried to seize power. The Prime Minister, Kerensky, turned to the Bolsheviks to defend Petrograd against Kornilov's troops. He released the Bolshevik leaders and gave weapons to the Red Guards. Bolshevik activists persuaded Kornilov's troops to desert. This had important results for the Bolsheviks who:

- emerged as heroes.

- gained popularity and won a majority in the Petrograd Soviet.

- became a well-armed fighting force.

SOURCE F

Troops fire on demonstrators during the 'July Days'

Activity

You are a member of the Duma in 1917 and have written a diary explaining the events of March–November 1917. Write out several extracts from your diary. This could include some of the following:

- the March Revolution.
- the abdication of the Tsar.
- Lenin's return to Russia.
- the Kornilov rebellion.

Questions

1 What do Sources **B**, **C** and **D** tell you about the weaknesses of the Provisional Government?

2 There were several reasons for the fall of the Provisional Government. Try to make links between the different reasons. For example, you could link the failure to end the war with the continued food shortages. Because the government continued the war food was needed for the armed forces. The food shortages were made worse by the shortage of peasants and farm workers who were called up to fight in the Russian army.

3 Why were the Bolsheviks:
   a weakened by the 'July Days'?
   b strengthened by the Kornilov revolt?

4 Is Source **E** a reliable view of Lenin's return to Russia?

The Bolshevik Revolution, November 1917

In November 1917 the Bolsheviks successfully seized power. This was due to several reasons.

Crisis in Russia

By October 1917 there was once again great discontent in Russia:

- The peasants were killing landlords and taking over land.

- In the army peasant soldiers deserted to go home and claim land. Other soldiers, influenced by Bolshevik agents, refused to fight and killed officers.

- High prices and food shortages caused more hunger in the cities.

SOURCE B

Peasants and army deserters looting and burning a landowner's house

SOURCE A

The situation at the end of the summer, reported by an eyewitness, N. Sukanov

Lynch law, the destruction of homes and shops. Jeering at and attacks on officers. In the country, burnings and destruction of country houses became more frequent. Military discipline collapsed. There were masses of deserters. The soldiers, without leave, went off home in great floods. They filled all the trains, kicked out the passengers and threatened the entire transport system.

Profile on

Trotsky

His real name was Lev Bronstein. He was born, in 1879, in the Ukraine, the son of a rich Jewish peasant. Angry at the persecution of the Jews, he joined a local Marxist group at the age of 16. In 1903 he sided with the Mensheviks and in 1905 returned from exile to join in the revolution of that year. He became Chairman of the St Petersburg Soviet. When the revolution collapsed Trotsky was arrested and sent to Siberia. But he escaped on the way and went to America.

The role of Trotsky

Trotsky had been a Menshevik but joined the Bolsheviks during the 'July Days'. He masterminded the revolution by:

- arranging for it to begin the night before the Second Congress of Soviets met. He wanted to claim that it was done on behalf of the Petrograd Soviet.

- persuading soldiers in the Petrograd garrison and the sailors at Kronstadt naval base to support the uprising and supply the weapons.

- making detailed plans for the military operations, including the seizure of the key buildings in Petrograd and Moscow.

SOURCE C

Writing in November 1918, Stalin praises Trotsky's role in the revolution

All the work of practical organisation of the revolution was carried out under the immediate leadership of the Chairman of the Petrograd Soviet, Trotsky. It is possible to declare with certainty that the swift passing of the garrison to the side of the Soviet and the work of the Military Revolutionary Committee (the group of Bolsheviks organising the Revolution) is owed mainly and above all to comrade Trotsky.

The Government

Kerensky knew of Trotsky's plans but could not take action against him because he had lost the support of many troops in Petrograd. He also did not send enough troops to guard the Provisional Government in the Winter Palace. He left Petrograd to try to raise support but found few generals willing to help.

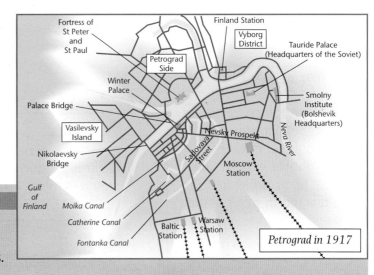

Petrograd in 1917

THE EVENTS OF THE REVOLUTION

6 November	During the night Red Guards started to take over key positions: bridges and telephone exchanges.
7 November	In the morning the Red Guards took over banks, government buildings and railway stations. In the evening the cruiser *Aurora* bombarded the Winter Palace. A Red Guard assault on the Palace met no resistance from defenders which included army cadets and the Women's Battalion. Government ministers were arrested.
8 November	Lenin announced the formation of a new government.

Still from Eisenstein's film *October* showing Lenin standing on an armoured car at the Winter Palace, urging the Red Guards forward

SOURCE E

An extract from *V.I. Lenin – A Short Biography*, by G.D. Obichkin, written in 1976. This is an official Soviet biography of Lenin.

On the 10 October Lenin showed at the Central Committee that the moment was ripe for the seizure of power. Only Kamenev and Zinoviev alone acted as cowards and opposed the resolution. In his guidance of the uprising, Lenin's genius as a leader of the masses, a wise and fearless strategist, who clearly saw what direction the revolution would take, was strikingly revealed.

SOURCE F

From H.E. Salisbury, *Russia in Revolution*. The author was Moscow correspondent to the *New York Times*.

For many years the evidence of Lenin's violent controversy with his colleagues over the uprising was concealed in Party archives. Lenin had the firm support of 15 of the 25 members present. The other 10, led by Kamenev and Zinoviev, felt that the uprising would be a disaster. Bolshevik plans went along in a very casual way. Anger and energy spent, Lenin seemed to become very lethargic. So far as the record goes, he did nothing from 20 to 23 October.

Activity

Draw a cartoon character for each of the following with a speech bubble. In each speech bubble explain how you feel he or she would have reacted to news of the Bolshevik take-over of power:

an industrialist

a rich landowner

a peasant

a factory worker

a Social Revolutionary.

Questions

1   Copy the box below and decide the importance of each person or factor in the success of the Bolshevik Revolution. Write your reason in the box you select.

Decisive	Important	Unimportant
Trotsky Lenin Weaknesses of Provisional Government		

2   Why do you think there was little support for Kerensky and the Provisional Government?

3   How accurate is Source **D** by the Soviet film maker Eisenstein as a view of the events of the Bolshevik Revolution?

4   Sources **E** and **F** have very different views of Lenin's role in the revolution. How do they differ? Why do you think their views differ?

During this period Lenin and the Bolsheviks faced a major struggle to overcome opposition and establish control over Russia. In 1918 Lenin changed the name of his party to the Communist Party.

The first decrees

The Bolsheviks quickly took control of government when the Mensheviks and many Social Revolutionaries walked out of the Second Congress of Soviets. This left the Bolsheviks and their allies with a majority. Lenin then set up a Council of People's Commissars as the new temporary government. He was its chairman and chose its members.

Lenin's new government ruled by decree, which means passing laws without using parliament. It aimed to:

- carry out popular reforms.

- show that it was in charge.

- control opposition.

Land

The land was taken from the Tsars, nobles, Church and other landlords and handed over to the peasants. Lenin abandoned the Bolshevik policy of state ownership of the land. He did not want to upset the peasants.

Factories

All factories were put under the control of elected committees of the workers.

Control

All non-Bolshevik newspapers were banned. A new secret police, the CHEKA, was set up to deal with opponents of the Bolsheviks.

The Constituent Assembly

The Provisional Government had arranged for elections to be held for a Constituent Assembly to set up a new democratic government. The elections were held in November 1917.

THE RESULTS OF THE NOVEMBER 1917 ELECTION

Party	Seats in Constituent Assembly
Socialist Revolutionaries	370
Bolsheviks	175
Left Socialist Revolutionaries (supporters of Bolsheviks)	40
Cadets	17
Mensheviks	16
Others	89

In January 1918, when the Assembly met, Lenin refused to hand over power to the SR majority and ordered it to close. Red Guards carried out his order, killing or wounding over 100 pro-Assembly demonstrators.

Question

Was Lenin really the 'people's hero'?

The Treaty of Brest-Litovsk, March 1918

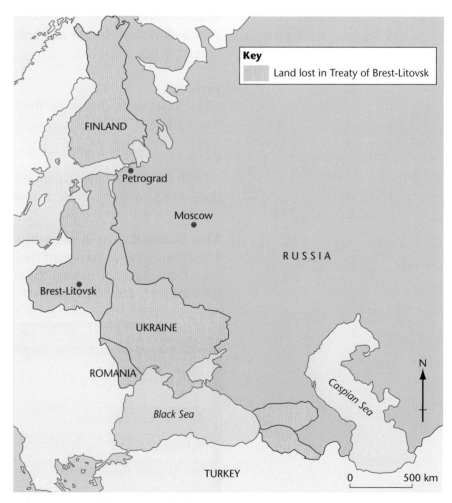

Lenin realised that he must end the war with Germany as soon as possible:

- He had opposed war from the start.

- The effects of the war had brought down the Tsar and the Provisional Government.

- He needed peace in order to win the support of the workers and the peasants and to deal with the enemies of his government.

- He needed to keep the support of the army.

Trotsky, the Commissar (or Minister) for Foreign Affairs, deliberately spun out the negotiations with Germany in the hope that there would be a socialist revolution in Germany. By 1918, however, the Germans threatened Petrograd itself. Lenin decided peace had to be made at any price. The Peace Treaty was signed on 3 March 1918.

The peace terms
Russia lost its richest areas.

26% of its total population.

27% of farmland, including some of the best in Russia.

26% of railways.

74% of iron ore and coal.

Reactions to the peace treaty

Many Russians were upset by the harsh peace terms and wanted Lenin to refuse to sign. Lenin, however, gambled that world revolution was about to break out elsewhere, including Germany, in which case the treaty would not last long. Lenin's gamble did pay off but not for the reasons he believed. Germany was defeated on the Western Front later in 1918 and agreed to an armistice in November.

Communist control

Lenin set up a 'dictatorship of the proletariat' to ensure control of Russia.

The 'Red Terror'

The CHEKA tortured and killed Communist opponents, including the Tsar and his family, to prevent them from becoming the focus of opposition (see p. 428). Terror tactics were used to frighten the population into obedience to the government.

A Communist poster soon after the revolution

Social changes

The Communists brought in a series of changes:

- In education literacy campaigns enabled more people to read and write. The sciences were encouraged and subjects thought to be useless, such as history and ancient languages, were banned.

- The government suppressed religious worship. They banned religious education in schools and persecuted the monks and priests.

- Improvements were brought in for workers. A Labour Law of 1922 gave workers an eight-hour day, two weeks' paid holiday a year and social insurance benefits such as sickness and unemployment pay and old-age pensions.

Question

Why do you think the Communists regarded history as useless?

The Communist Party and the Government

By 1921 Russia had become a one-party state. The leaders of the Mensheviks, Social Revolutionaries and Cadets were arrested and the parties banned. The Communist Party controlled government at every level.

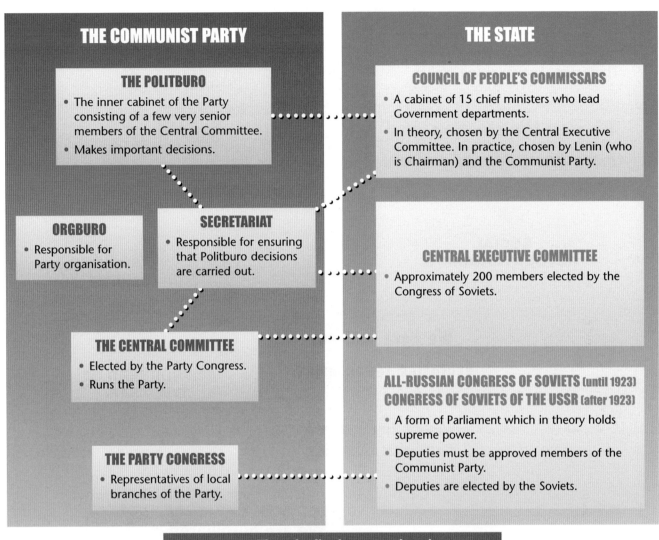

THE COMMUNIST PARTY

THE POLITBURO
- The inner cabinet of the Party consisting of a few very senior members of the Central Committee.
- Makes important decisions.

ORGBURO
- Responsible for Party organisation.

SECRETARIAT
- Responsible for ensuring that Politburo decisions are carried out.

THE CENTRAL COMMITTEE
- Elected by the Party Congress.
- Runs the Party.

THE PARTY CONGRESS
- Representatives of local branches of the Party.

THE STATE

COUNCIL OF PEOPLE'S COMMISSARS
- A cabinet of 15 chief ministers who lead Government departments.
- In theory, chosen by the Central Executive Committee. In practice, chosen by Lenin (who is Chairman) and the Communist Party.

CENTRAL EXECUTIVE COMMITTEE
- Approximately 200 members elected by the Congress of Soviets.

ALL-RUSSIAN CONGRESS OF SOVIETS (until 1923)
CONGRESS OF SOVIETS OF THE USSR (after 1923)
- A form of Parliament which in theory holds supreme power.
- Deputies must be approved members of the Communist Party.
- Deputies are elected by the Soviets.

•••••••••• **These bodies have members in common**

In 1923 Russia became the Union of Soviet Socialist Republics (USSR).

Questions

1 For what reasons did Lenin:
   a abolish the Constituent Assembly?
   b agree to the Treaty of Brest-Litovsk?
   c set up a one-party state?
2 Why do you think many Russians were upset with the terms of the peace treaty?
3 Under the following headings explain Lenin's achievements in the areas of:
   a education
   b land
   c workers.
4 What was the purpose of Source **C**? Do you think it would be a successful poster?

The Civil War 1918–21

Lenin and the Communist Party only survived and established control of Russia through success in the Civil War.

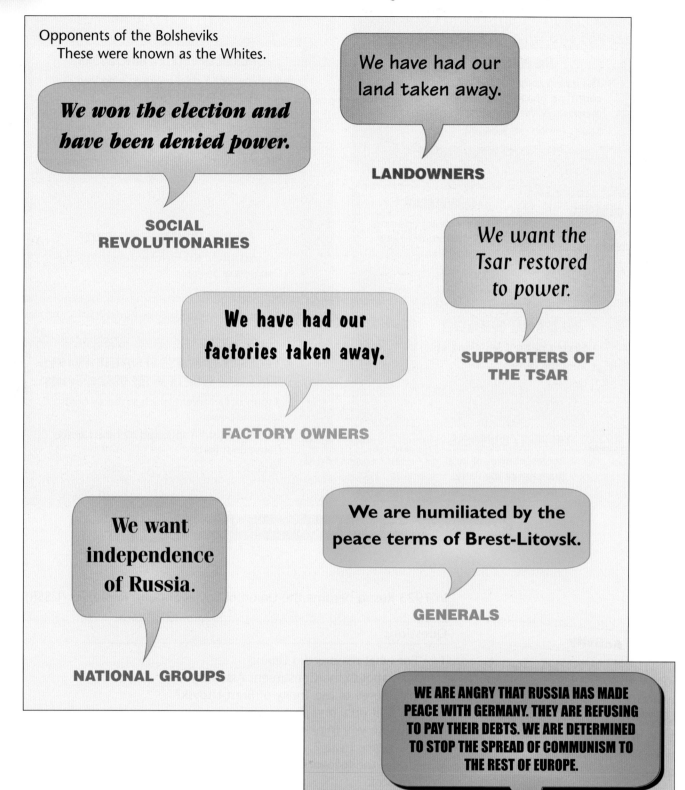

Opponents of the Bolsheviks
These were known as the Whites.

We won the election and have been denied power.

SOCIAL REVOLUTIONARIES

We have had our land taken away.

LANDOWNERS

We have had our factories taken away.

FACTORY OWNERS

We want the Tsar restored to power.

SUPPORTERS OF THE TSAR

We want independence of Russia.

NATIONAL GROUPS

We are humiliated by the peace terms of Brest-Litovsk.

GENERALS

WE ARE ANGRY THAT RUSSIA HAS MADE PEACE WITH GERMANY. THEY ARE REFUSING TO PAY THEIR DEBTS. WE ARE DETERMINED TO STOP THE SPREAD OF COMMUNISM TO THE REST OF EUROPE.

ENEMIES ABROAD
(France, Britain and the USA)

SOURCE A

A *Punch* cartoon, February 1919

PUNCH, OR THE LONDON CHARIVARI.—FEBRUARY 20, 1918.

THE LIBERATORS.

FIRST BOLSHEVIK. "LET ME SEE; WE'VE MADE AN END OF LAW, CREDIT, TREATIES, THE ARMY AND THE NAVY. IS THERE ANYTHING ELSE TO ABOLISH?"
SECOND BOLSHEVIK. "WHAT ABOUT WAR?"
FIRST BOLSHEVIK. "GOOD! AND PEACE, TOO. AWAY WITH BOTH OF 'EM!"

SOURCE C

A Communist poster of 1918 showing the Red Army fighting the Whites, shown as a monster with many heads

SOURCE B

A speech by Lenin in 1919

England, America and France are waging war against Russia. They are avenging themselves on the Soviet Union for having overthrown the landlords and capitalists. They are helping the landowners with money and military supplies. The landlords, in turn, are attacking the Soviet Union from Siberia, the Don and the northern Caucasus in an attempt to restore the Tsar, the capitalists and the landowners.

The Czech Legion
Bolshevik officials quarrelled with Czech ex-prisoners of war on their way to Vladivostock and the sea route home. Angry Czechs took over the Trans-Siberian Railway, formed the Czech Legion and marched on Moscow.

Key

General Miller	White armies and their leaders
British	Foreign armies of intervention
	Land under Bolshevik control, 1919

The Poles took advantage of the Civil War and launched a surprise invasion in 1920, capturing Kiev. A counter-attack by the Red Army drove the Poles back to the outskirts of Warsaw and they agreed to a peace treaty.

N

Arctic Ocean

British, Canadians, French, Italians, Serbs

British, Americans, French

Murmansk

EUROPE

Baltic Sea

General Yudenitch
attacked from the north in the summer of 1919. He threatened Petrograd but by the end of the year he too had been defeated by Trotsky and the Red Army.

Kronstadt

Petrograd

Archangel

General Miller

General Deniken
advanced with the White Army from the Ukraine to within 300 kilometres of Moscow. Again Trotsky organised a counter-attack. Deniken resigned his command and his army was disbanded.

Moscow

French

Kazan

Ekaterinburg

RUSSIA

General Semenov

Americans, Japanese

Black Sea

Samara

British

Caspian Sea

Omsk

Trans-Siberian Railway

Czech Legion

Vladivostok

British

CHINA

0   800 km

Pacific Ocean

Admiral Kolchak
invaded eastern Russia in the Spring of 1919 and advanced as far as Kazan. Trotsky organised a counter-attack against the White forces and drove them back. Kolchak was later captured and executed.

General Wrangel
in June 1920 attacked from the south hoping to link up with the invading Poles. But the Poles made peace and Wrangel's army was forced to withdraw.

WHY WERE THE COMMUNISTS VICTORIOUS?

COMMUNIST STRENGTHS

▶ They were popular because of their reforms. They also used propaganda to turn the Russians against the Whites.

▶ The Communists were fighting for a cause – the revolution. They were fighting for survival. They were united under one leader and army.

▶ The Communists controlled the main cities of Moscow and Petrograd with their factories. They also controlled the railways which allowed them to send supplies and troops where they wished.

▶ War Communism (p. 430) kept the Red Army supplied with food and weapons.

▶ The Bolsheviks also used terror to ensure support. The CHEKA hunted down people who helped the Whites and forced the peasants to hand over food to the government.

▶ They were led by Trotsky. He created the 'Red Army' with the help of professional officers. He enforced strict discipline and used both encouragement and terror to make soldiers fight. He proved an outstanding leader. He was personally very courageous. He had a special train which took him and his army of hand-picked soldiers to the places where the fighting was hardest.

WHITE WEAKNESSES

▶ The Whites were unpopular for several reasons:

  ● they were associated with the Tsar and the landlords.

  ● they were very harsh in their treatment of people in the lands they captured.

For example, at Rostov miners supporting the Bolsheviks were buried alive.

▶ The Whites were not united. They were made up of several different groups and lacked a single leader. Often the commanders were cruel, treated their men with disrespect and set a bad example by drinking and taking drugs. The White generals did not trust each other and would not co-ordinate their attacks. This allowed the Reds to pick off the White armies one by one.

▶ In 1920 they lost outside support when the foreign powers withdrew their armies and supplies.

▶ The Whites were scattered around the central area controlled by the Reds. Often hundreds of miles separated the different armies, so communications were difficult.

SOURCE D

A White poster showing Bolshevik food requisitioning

SOURCE E

Orders to the Red Army from Trotsky, 1918

Every scoundrel who incites anyone to retreat, to desert, or not to fulfil a military order, will be shot.
Every soldier of the Red Army who voluntarily deserts his post will be shot.
Every soldier who throws away his rifle will be shot.

SOURCE F

A White colonel describes the punishment of a village accused of supporting the Reds, in March 1918

The mounted platoon entered the village, met the Bolshevik committee and put the members to death. After the execution, the houses of the culprits were burned and the whole male population under 45 whipped soundly.

The Tsar and his family

The Tsar and his family had been kept prisoner by the Reds in Siberia and then at Ekaterinburg in the Urals. In July 1918 Kolchak's White army was approaching the town, and the Reds were afraid that the Tsar might fall into White hands. He could be a rallying point for opposition to the Bolsheviks. The Red Guards herded the royal family into a cellar, shot them all, and burned their bodies in a nearby mine.

Source G

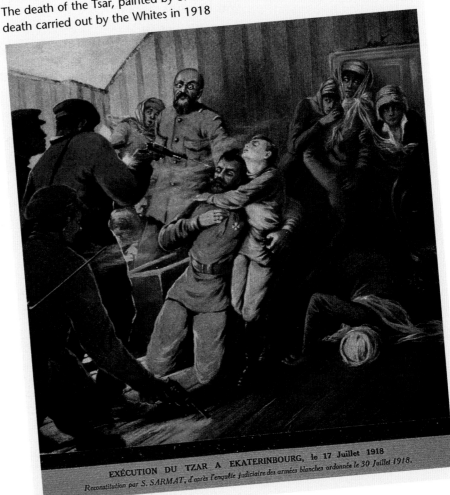

The death of the Tsar, painted by S. Sarmet, based on two investigations of the death carried out by the Whites in 1918

EXÉCUTION DU TZAR A EKATERINBOURG, le 17 Juillet 1918.
Reconstitution par S. SARMAT, d'après l'enquête judiciaire des armées blanches ordonnée le 30 Juillet 1918.

Questions

1 Explain the following advantages that the Reds had over the Whites during the Civil War:

   a   Trotsky and the Red Army.
   b   Control of the centre of Russia.
   c   United in aims and leadership.

2 What further reason is suggested by Source **F**?

3 How useful is Source **D** as evidence of Bolshevik actions during this period?

4 Do you think Source **G** gives an accurate view of the execution of the Tsar and his family? Give reasons for your answer.

Effects of the Civil War

Communist victory ensured the survival of Lenin's government and extended Communist control over a wider area. It also contributed towards famine and industrial collapse.

Activity

Draw a table with the following columns:

Decisive   Important   Quite important   Not important

Put the following reasons for Communist victory in the Civil War in one of the columns with a brief explanation of why you chose that column:

Trotsky's leadership
Communist propaganda
the cruelty of the Whites
the Communist control of communications
lack of one leader of the Whites
the influence of foreign intervention.

429

War Communism 1918–21

This was introduced by Lenin in 1918 to ensure that the Red Army was fed and equipped during the Civil War.

How it worked

- Factories with more than ten workers were taken over by the state.

- A Supreme Council of the National Economy decided what each factory should produce.

- Military discipline was introduced into the factories. Strikes were made illegal. Strikers could be shot.

- Peasants were forced to give up all their surplus produce to the government. They were no longer allowed to sell it for profit.

- Food was rationed in the cities.

- To meet its expenses the government printed masses of paper money. This caused inflation. The government allowed money to lose its value. Many money payments were abolished. In place of money people were told to barter goods.

Results of War Communism

- The government managed to feed and equip an army eventually numbering five million.

- The peasants, however, stopped producing surplus food since they were no longer allowed to sell it for a profit. This, in turn, led to:

Food requisitioning. CHEKA and Red Army units were sent into the countryside to seize the grain. Many peasants burnt their crops and destroyed their livestock rather than letting it fall into the hands of the government.

By 1919–20 there were food shortages. The following year there was a full-scale famine made worse by bad weather and disease. Several million died.

SOURCE A

P.D. Ouspensky, a writer, describes the situation in southern Russia in 1919

The price of all products and necessities has risen by 20, 30, 100 or 600 times. Workmen's wages have risen 20, 50 or even 100 times. But the salary of an ordinary 'brain-worker' – teacher, journalist or doctor – has risen in the best cases no more than three times.

SOURCE B

From Victor Serge, *Memoirs of a Revolutionary*

Parties which were sent into the countryside to obtain grain by requisition might be driven away by the peasants with pitchforks. Savage peasants would slit open a Commissar's belly, pack it with grain and leave him by the roadside as a lesson to all.

SOURCE C

Victims of the famine in Russia in 1921

SOURCE D

An eyewitness account by British refugees from Petrograd who managed to get back to London, 1918

It is a common occurrence when a horse falls down in the street for the people to cut off the flesh of the animal the moment it has breathed its last. Another way of getting food was by buying it at excessive prices from members of the Red Guard who are well fed.

Hunger, low wages and discontent among workers led to a drastic fall in industrial output.

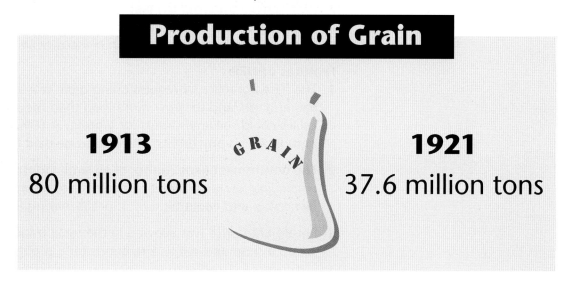

Production of Grain

1913	1921
80 million tons	37.6 million tons

The massive discontent caused by War Communism led to the Kronstadt mutiny.

The Kronstadt Mutiny 1921

In March 1921 Lenin's government faced a mutiny of sailors at the Kronstadt naval base. These sailors had been strong supporters of the November Revolution. They were now unhappy with government policies. They felt that the new government had not kept its promises.

The uprising was such a serious threat to the government that Trotsky was sent with an army of 60,000 men to deal with the sailors. In the fighting that followed thousands of rebels were killed and many more arrested. The victory cost the lives of 10,000 Red Army soldiers.

SOURCE E

Trotsky inspecting an elite regiment of the Red Guard. The Red Guard was used to put down the mutiny.

Activity

You live in a village which has suffered badly due to War Communism. Write a petition to Lenin giving your reasons for being opposed to War Communism and the changes you would like to see.

Questions

1 What were the main features of War Communism?
2 Why was it so unpopular?

New Economic Policy 1921

In 1921 Lenin introduced the New Economic Policy (NEP). This was to try to reduce the discontent in the towns and countryside. He was also desperate to increase production in industry and the countryside.

Features of NEP

1 The hated practice of requisitioning grain was ended. Peasants had enough land to grow more food than they needed and the kulaks could sell any surplus for a profit. A 10% tax was introduced on any profits. This had to be paid in foodstuffs.

2 The government kept control of all large industries, but factories employing less than twenty workers were returned to private ownership and could be run on profit-making lines.

3 Private enterprise was allowed in the retail trade. Anyone could set up a shop and sell or hire goods for a profit.

4 The government tried to stop bartering and encouraged people to use money once again.

A market in Moscow, 1921

Results of NEP

By 1925 food production had returned to pre-war levels and industrial production had risen greatly.

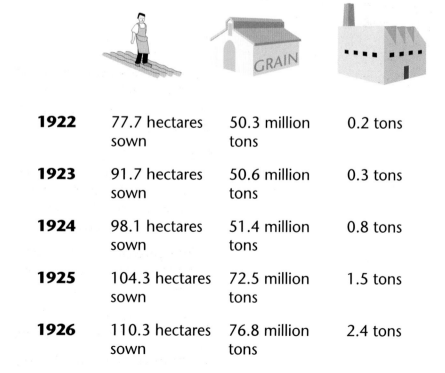

		GRAIN	
1922	77.7 hectares sown	50.3 million tons	0.2 tons
1923	91.7 hectares sown	50.6 million tons	0.3 tons
1924	98.1 hectares sown	51.4 million tons	0.8 tons
1925	104.3 hectares sown	72.5 million tons	1.5 tons
1926	110.3 hectares sown	76.8 million tons	2.4 tons

Nikolai Izachik, Bolshevik Party member, recalling the introduction of NEP in 1921

In 1921 we used to discuss the NEP for hours on end at Party meetings. Most people supported Lenin. Others thought he was wrong. Many even tore up their party cards.

NEP was bitterly opposed by many Communists. They argued that encouraging private enterprise and profit-making went against Communist ideas. It was a retreat to the evils of Capitalism.

Lenin insisted that it was not a permanent retreat from Communism. It was just a temporary measure to revive the economy. Once production increased, NEP would be abandoned.

SOURCE C

Leonid Orlov, Bolshevik supporter, remembering the introduction of NEP, late 1980s

There wasn't a scrap of food in the country. We were down to a quarter of a pound of bread per person. Then suddenly they announced the NEP. Cafes started opening, restaurants. Factories went back into private hands. It was Capitalism. In my eyes what was happening was the very thing I'd struggled against.

Questions

1   Is the author of Source **C** for or against NEP?
2   Using the chart showing the effects of NEP, do you think it was a success?

Activity

You are editor of a newspaper in Petrograd and interview:

- a Communist who is opposed to NEP.

- a kulak or nepman who had benefited from NEP.

Do a two-column article with the views of one on the left-hand side, and the other on the right-hand side.

The death of Lenin, 1924

In the spring of 1922 Lenin suffered a massive stroke. He suffered further strokes in December 1922 and March 1923. Finally, in January 1924, he died. His body lay in state for a week after his death with thousands of mourners queuing in the freezing weather to pay their respects. After the funeral his body was embalmed and put on show in a specially built mausoleum in Moscow.

The 'Lenin cult'

After Lenin's death a 'Lenin cult' developed in Soviet Russia. His image was everywhere – on statues, plaques and posters.
The 'Lenin cult' survived for as long as Soviet Russia itself. In the 1940s a biography of Lenin, written in Russia, described him as 'the greatest genius of all times and of all nations, master of the treasures of human knowledge'.

There have been many different interpretations of Lenin.

SOURCE A

Soviet poster produced on the fifth anniversary of Lenin's death

SOURCE B

From *Lenin and the Bolsheviks* by Adam Ulam, a British historian

Lenin allowed a cult of terror to develop. He allowed mass terror not only to be practised, but to become legitimate and respectable.

SOURCE C

Speech by Winston Churchill, British Secretary of State for War in 1919

Of all the tyrannies of history, the Bolshevik tyranny is the worst, the most destructive, the most degrading. The atrocities committed under Lenin and Trotsky are more hideous and numerous than anything for which the Kaiser is responsible.

SOURCE D

Christopher Hill, a British historian and a supporter of Marxism, writing in 1947

In the Russia of 1918–20 when we recall a very large number of civil servants had deserted their posts or stayed only to spy, it appears almost a miracle that government was able to continue. We are better able to appreciate the sometimes crude methods which Lenin had to use in this period of War Communism.

Questions

1 Are the writers of Sources **B**, **C** and **D** for or against Lenin?
2 Why do Sources **B** and **D** give different interpretations of Lenin's achievements?
3 Copy the headings below and make out a balance sheet of Lenin's successes and failures.

Successes	Failures

4 Overall, do you think Lenin was a success in Russia 1918–24?

Activity

Write an obituary for Lenin in a British newspaper. An obituary means a notice of death which usually includes a short account of the personality, life and achievements of the person who has died.

After Lenin's death in 1924 there was a struggle for power in Russia. By 1928 Stalin had emerged as leader and had begun a dramatic economic transformation of the USSR.

Stalin's rise to power

There were five possible candidates, all members of the Politburo, to succeed Lenin: Stalin, Trotsky, Grigori Zinoviev, Leon Kamenev and Nicolai Bukharin.

Focus on

Stalin's early life and career

Stalin was born in 1879, the son of a Georgian bootmaker. His real name was Joseph Djugashvili. His mother was determined that he would do well and worked hard to pay for his education. He worked well at school but was expelled from college in 1899 for failing to take his exams. He had become interested in the ideas of Karl Marx and wanted to work for a revolution. He became a member of the Bolshevik Party. In the period 1905–8 he took part in over 1000 raids to seize money for the Party. Stalin spent much of the period 1905–17 either in exile in Siberia or on the run from the authorities in Russia. He was freed from exile in 1917 and returned to Petrograd to become editor of the Bolshevik newspaper, *Pravda*. He was not as well known as Trotsky and Lenin and played little part in the November Revolution. In Lenin's government he was made Commissar of Nationalities and crushed a rebellion in his own state of Georgia using great brutality. In 1922 he became General Secretary of the Communist Party.

Profile on
Kamenev

He was an able and modest man and a close associate of Lenin. Like Stalin, he was from Georgia and, like Trotsky, he was Jewish. He greatly angered Lenin in 1917 by opposing the November Revolution. After the Revolution he was made Communist Party boss in Moscow.

Profile on
Zinoviev

He was a founder member of the Bolshevik Party and had worked closely with Lenin between 1903 and 1917. He was a very effective public speaker, but was vain and lacked understanding of the economy. He also was Jewish and opposed the November Revolution. After the Revolution he became Communist Party boss in Petrograd and was head of the Comintern, the organisation through which Soviet Russia tried to bring about Communist revolutions in other countries.

Profile on
Bukharin

Like Lenin he was born into a middle-class family. His parents were Moscow schoolteachers. He first made a name for himself as a left-wing Bolshevik who strongly opposed the Treaty of Brest-Litovsk. He then became a moderate and one of the strongest supporters of NEP.

Stalin seemed to have little chance of success. Lenin had warned against Stalin in his *Testament* written in 1923.

SOURCE A

Lenin's views on Stalin in his *Testament*

Comrade Stalin, having become Secretary, has unlimited authority concentrated in his hands and I am not sure whether he will be capable of using that authority with sufficient caution. Comrade Trotsky, on the other hand, is perhaps the most capable man in the present Committee. Stalin is too rude and this fault is not acceptable in the office of Secretary. Therefore I propose to comrades that they find a way of removing Stalin from his post.

Trotsky had several advantages over Stalin:

- He was Lenin's own choice as successor.

- He had a strong personality and was intelligent.

- He was popular with the army.

- He had played a leading part in the Bolshevik Revolution and the Civil War.

It was Stalin, however, who was successful.

Why did Stalin succeed?

Stalin had several advantages over Trotsky:

- Trotsky was not popular with the Politburo and the old Bolsheviks because he had not joined the party until 1917, having been a Menshevik. Kamenev and Zinoviev disliked Trotsky and disagreed with his political ideas. He also failed to use his popularity in the army to help his cause.

- Trotsky and the other contenders underestimated Stalin because he appeared dull and hardworking.

- As General Secretary Stalin held the key post in the Party. He appointed officials who supported him and built up a power base. He soon commanded the support of most Party officials who owed their position to him.

- Stalin successfully presented himself as Lenin's close follower. For example, he tricked Trotsky so that he did not attend Lenin's funeral. Stalin appeared as the chief mourner. Stalin also used propaganda to show how close he was to Lenin and to criticise Trotsky.

- Stalin also used clever tactics. He played off one group in the Party, Zinoviev, Kamenev and Trotsky against Bukharin in the Politburo.

- Finally, Stalin's ideas for the future proved more popular with the Party. He promoted 'Socialism in One Country'. He felt that the Soviet Union should concentrate on establishing Communism at home, making itself a modern country. Trotsky, on the other hand, believed in 'permanent, or world, revolution'. He felt that Communism would not survive unless the Communist revolution spread to other countries. He believed it was the duty of the USSR to help revolutionary groups in other countries. This did not appeal to many Russians who had experienced four years of war followed by three years of civil war.

SOURCE B

From Ronald Seth, *Leon Trotsky, the Eternal Rebel*, 1967

Trotsky was recovering from an illness when Lenin died. He telephoned Stalin to ask when the funeral was to be. Stalin said: 'On Saturday, you can't get back in time anyway so we advise you to continue with your treatment'. This was a lie, the funeral was not to be until Sunday and Trotsky could have reached Moscow by then.

SOURCE C

A photograph published after Lenin's death in 1924. It shows Stalin (on the right) as the chief mourner at his funeral.

1924 Stalin first had to deal with Lenin's *Testament*. He was saved when the Central Committee decided to keep the letter secret because it might have caused disunity. Kamenev and Zinoviev defended Stalin. They wanted his help in stopping Trotsky from becoming leader.

1925 Stalin ensured that his ideas on 'Socialism in One Country' were popular in the Party. Kamenev and Zinoviev worked with Stalin in the Politburo to dismiss Trotsky as Commissar of War.

1926–27 With three of his allies elected to the Politburo, Stalin had Trotsky, Kamenev and Zinoviev dismissed from the Politburo. Trotsky and Zinoviev were then expelled from the Party.

1929 In the Politburo Stalin now argued against NEP and in favour of expanding industry. When the Right opposed this, Stalin used his majority to vote them down. In 1929 Bukharin was forced to resign.

Activity

A curriculum vitae, or CV, is an outline of a person's qualifications for a job. Trotsky and Stalin are applying for the job of leader as successor to Lenin in 1924. Draw up a CV for each candidate.

Questions

1 What does Source **A** tell you about Lenin's opinion of Stalin?
2 What do Sources **B** and **C** reveal about Stalin's methods of achieving success in the leadership contest?
3 Did Stalin succeed in becoming leader only because of the weakness of Trotsky?

Collectivisation

Stalin was determined to modernise Soviet agriculture and introduced a policy of collectivisation which brought much opposition and suffering.

The problem

Soviet peasants used old-fashioned, inefficient farming methods. Even under NEP they were not producing enough food for the workers in the cities. If the USSR was to industrialise successfully (see p. 444), its farming had to be improved because:

- Even more workers would have to be fed.

- Peasants were needed as industrial workers. Fewer peasants, therefore, would be available to produce the food.

- The government aimed to sell the surplus abroad in order to make the money it needed to spend on developing industry. There had to be a surplus to sell.

Stalin also had other reasons:

- He disliked the richer peasants, the kulaks, who had emerged due to NEP.

- He was determined to get control of the peasants and the countryside.

- Collectivisation fitted in with Communist ideas of common ownership.

SOURCE A

Extracts from speeches made about collectivisation by Stalin in 1928 and 1929

Look at the Kulak farms: their barns and sheds are crammed with grain. They are waiting for prices to rise. So long as there are Kulaks there will be sabotage of our grain needs. The effect will be that our towns and industrial centres, as well as the Red Army, will be threatened with hunger. We cannot allow that. We must break the resistance of this class and deprive it of its existence.

The solution

Stalin decided to collectivise the farms. This meant the peasants had to give up their small plots of land and animals. They were pooled with those of other families to make a farm large enough to use machinery and modern farming methods. The state provided each collective farm or kolkhoz with machinery – in particular, a tractor, other tools and seeds. The government bought the produce of each farm at a low fixed price. The peasants received a small wage.

Was collectivisation a success?

Use the following evidence to decide. Copy the following grid and complete.

Evidence for success	Evidence for failure

Key

▨ Main area collectivised

◆ Area to which 'kulaks' were exiled

Item	1928	1933
Grain (Millions of tonnes)	73	69
Cattle (Millions)	70	38
Pigs (Millions)	26	12
Sheep and goats (Millions)	147	50

SOURCE B

Soviet painting of a celebration on a collective farm

SOURCE C

From *Virgin Soil Upturned*, a novel by Mikhail Sholokhov written in 1934. Sholokhov was living in Russia during collectivisation.

Both those who had joined the Kolkhoz and individual farmers killed their stock. Bulls, sheep, pigs and even cows were slaughtered. The dogs began to drag entrails around the village; cellars and barns were full of meat. Young and old suffered from stomach ache. At dinner times tables groaned under boiled and roasted meat.

SOURCE D

A Russian cartoon illustrating the problem of the peasants on the collectives spending far more time and effort on their own private plots than the collective's land

SOURCE E

Tractors were seen as the key to the introduction of modern agricultural methods

SOURCE F

A Communist Party Official

It took a famine and collectivisation to show the peasantry who the master is.

442

SOURCE G

The 1932 famine

SOURCE H

From Victor Kravchenko's book *I Chose Freedom*. He witnessed collectivisation and the attack on the Kulaks in one village.

A number of women were weeping hysterically and calling the names of their fathers and husbands. In the background, guarded by the OGPU (state police) soldiers with drawn revolvers, stood about twenty peasants, young and old, with bundles on their backs. A few were weeping. The others stood there sad and helpless. So this was 'liquidation of the kulaks as a class'. A lot of simple peasants being torn from their native soil, stripped of all their worldly goods and shipped to some distant labour camps.

SOURCE I

Extract from Nigel Kelly, *Russia and the USSR*, 1996

Yet despite the problems of the early 1930s, collectivisation was ultimately a success at enormous cost to the Soviet people. By 1937 over 90% of peasant farms had been collectivised and the Kulaks had been destroyed. From 1933 Soviet agricultural production improved; by 1937 output was significantly higher.

Question

1 How reliable is Source **B** as evidence of the effects of collectivisation?
2 Overall, was collectivisation a success?

Activity

Write out an interview with a peasant who lives in a village and describes the changes brought about by collectivisation. The interview could:

Describe the village and farming before collectivisation.

Identify changes brought about by collectivisation.

Dicuss the attitude of members of the village to collectivisation.

Explain what happened to the wealthier peasants.

Industrialisation

Stalin was also determined to modernise Soviet industry.

Stalin's motives

Stalin wanted to transform the USSR from a backward agricultural country to a modern industrial one. His main reasons were:

- *Security* He believed the USSR was likely to be attacked by Western capitalist states and that it would be defeated unless it modernised. A modernised industry would enable him to build up the USSR's armed forces.

- *Successful Communism* By creating and sharing wealth among the Soviet people he hoped to create a strong state based on Communist principles.

- *Control* Stalin was determined to achieve total control of Russian industry.

- *Agriculture* Improved industry was essential to collectivisation. It would provide the machinery necessary to modernise farming.

In order to achieve industrialisation Stalin ordered the State Planning Commission to draw up a series of Five Year Plans. Each plan set targets which the workers in various industries had to achieve.

Focus on

The Five Year Plans

The First Plan 1928–32

- This was to enable the USSR to increase its armaments quickly by building up production in heavy industry such as coal and iron and steel.

- All private businesses which had been allowed under Lenin's NEP were closed or taken over by the State.

- In 1929 Stalin decided the Plan should be achieved in four years rather than five.

The Second Plan, 1933–37

- This plan promised to concentrate on consumer goods and better housing for the Soviet people.

- From 1934 the increased threat from Hitler's Germany caused the planners to change their targets in favour of armaments again.

The Third Plan 1937

- This was launched in 1938. It concentrated on the production of household goods and luxuries such as bicycles and radios, in an attempt to provide Soviet citizens with some of the consumer goods common in other industrialised countries.

- The plan was interrupted in 1941 when Nazi Germany invaded the Soviet Union.

The economic results of the Five Year Plans

The Plans had spectacular results:

1 *Output* Although the Plan targets were not all met, every Soviet industry made spectacular advances. By 1940 the USSR was the world's second largest industrial power.

Item	1927 (actual)	1932/3 (plan)	1932/3 (actual)
NATIONAL INCOME (milliard roubles)	24.4	49.7	45.5
GROSS INDUSTRIAL PRODUCTION (milliard roubles)	18.3	43.2	43.3
a) PRODUCER'S GOODS	6.0	18.1	23.1
b) CONSUMER'S GOODS	12.3	25.1	20.2
GROSS AGRICULTURAL PRODUCTION (milliard roubles)	13.1	25.8	16.6
ELECTRICITY (milliard kWh)	5.05	22.0	13.4
COAL (million tons)	35.4	75.0	64.3
OIL (million tons)	11.7	22.0	21.4
PIG IRON (million tons)	3.3	10.0	6.2
STEEL (million tons)	4.0	10.4	5.9
TOTAL EMPLOYED LABOUR FORCE (millions)	11.3	15.8	22.8

FIRST FIVE YEAR PLAN: TARGETS AND ACHIEVEMENTS

2 *New industrial centres* Huge towns and industrial centres, like the Magnitogorsk metalworks, were built from scratch deep inside the USSR where they could be safe from invasion.

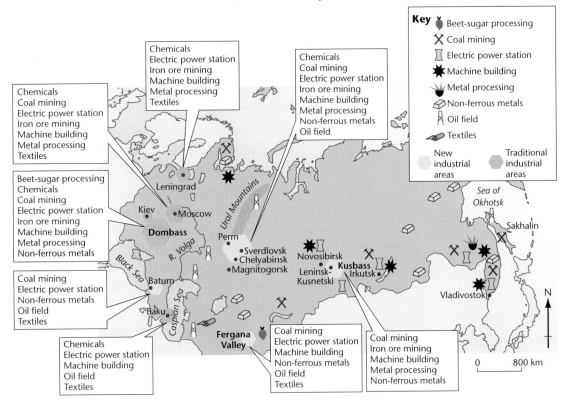

3 *Power and transport* Vast construction projects were completed such as the Dnieper Dam hydroelectric power station and the Belomor Canal.

4 *Urban population* Between 1929 and 1939 the population of the USSR's cities rose by 29 million.

5 *Skills* In 1929 Soviet workers lacked many of the skills needed to carry out industrialisation. Between 1929 and 1937 investment in education and training schemes created a skilled workforce.

SOURCE B

Soviet painting showing industrialisation

The impact of industrialisation on the lives of the Soviet people

Industrialisation had mixed effects on the lives of the Soviet people.

- Women were encouraged to work to help achieve the plans. Facilities such as creches were provided in factories to help them both have children and work.

- A new elite emerged. This was teachers, scientists, engineers, factory managers and skilled workers who were paid far higher wages than ordinary workers. Like many officials they also received extra benefits such as better housing or the right to buy scarce foods. They enjoyed a higher standard of living which went against Communist principles.

- Some of the biggest tasks in the Plans were carried out in appalling conditions by forced labour – prisoners in labour camps. Prisoners built the Belomor Canal and the Moscow Metro.

Source C

An eyewitness account of conditions during the building of the Belomor Canal

At the end of the day there were corpses left on the worksite. Two were frozen back to back leaning against each other. At night sledges went out and collected them. In the summer, bones remained from corpses which had not been removed in time, and together with the shingle they got into the concrete of the last lock at the city of Belomorsk and will be preserved there forever.

> **Profile on**
>
> Alexei Stakhanov
>
> He became a hero of the Soviet Union because, on the night of 30–31 August 1935, it was claimed he shifted 102 tonnes of coal – almost 15 times the normal amount for a single shift. Other workers were encouraged to follow Stakhanov's example and were rewarded with medals, new houses and other benefits. However, the campaign was quietly dropped in the late 1930s after a number of these 'Stakhanovites' were beaten up and killed by their fellow workers. The Stakhanovite story, in any case, was a set-up. He had two helpers who shored up the tunnel and removed the coal while he worked at the coal-face with his pick. It is likely that other Stakhanovites also asked others to help them so that their tremendous achievements could be reported in the newspapers.

Officials often falsified production figures to avoid being punished by the secret police for failing to meet their targets.

Working conditions

In the workplace workers were encouraged to work harder through encouragement and the example of workers such as the miner Stakhanov.

Medals were awarded for those with the best productivity. However, fines were imposed for lateness and bad workmanship. Workers who were absent for more than a day were sacked. Failures were always blamed on saboteurs rather than on the system. The secret police encouraged workers to inform on one another. Anyone blamed for obstructing work could be sent to a labour camp or shot.

Living conditions

There were some improvements in education and health for the workers and their families. All workers' children received free primary education and free health care schemes were extended to cover most of the workforce.

It proved impossible, however, to build enough new houses for the millions of peasants who flooded into the cities. Most families had to live in overcrowded and rundown buildings. Workers were poorly paid. Indeed between 1928 and 1933 the value of their wages fell by 50%. There was a great shortage of consumer goods, including clothes and shoes. Crime, including alcoholism and juvenile delinquency, increased.

Source D

A description of a Moscow apartment by Freda Utley, from *Lost Illusion*, 1949

Badly built, with doors and windows of unseasoned wood which could not be shut properly. Unpapered and thinly whitewashed walls, these two rooms were home. By American and British standards, we were living in a squalid tenement house. But by Soviet Russian standards we were housed almost as Communist aristocrats. We not only had two rooms to live in. We had the luxury of gas for cooking. Best of all we had a bathroom with a lavatory, which we had to share with only one other family.

Activity

Draw up a propaganda poster to encourage Russians to help with the Five Year Plans. You could use the Stakhanovite movement as part of this poster.

Questions

1 Give two reasons why Stalin carried out a policy of industrialisation.
2 What benefits did this have for the economy?
3 Did working conditions improve?
4 Why might the figures for industrial production given on p. 445 not be accurate?
5 Is Source **C** useful as evidence of the effects of industrialisation?

Stalin's dictatorship

By the end of the 1930s Stalin had achieved almost total control of the USSR. This was achieved through a combination of propaganda and terror.

Propaganda

Stalin had much experience of propaganda, having been editor of *Pravda* in 1917. He used propaganda to create the 'cult of Stalin' in which Stalin was worshipped as a leader. Pictures and statues of him were everywhere and places were named after him. People at meetings had to clap when his name was mentioned.

SOURCE A

A poster showing Stalin thanking Soviet youth

Culture and censorship

Writers, artists, film makers and even composers, had to support the government by following the policy of 'Social Realism'. This meant that their work had to:

* deal with the lives of ordinary working people.

* show how Communism was developing.

* give simple, clear, optimistic messages.

Writers had to be members of the Party-controlled Union of Soviet Writers. Books which did not follow the party line were changed or destroyed. History was rewritten to glorify Stalin's part in the November revolution. Photographs were faked to show Stalin next to Lenin. Images of Trotsky, Bukharin, Zinoviev and Kamenev were eventually removed.

SOURCE C

Stalin has been added to this 1922 photo

SOURCE B

From Victor Serge's *Memoirs of a Revolutionary*

Censorship in many forms, mutilated or murdered books. Before sending a manuscript to the publisher, an author would assemble his friends, read his work to them and discuss together whether such-and-such pages would 'pass'. The head of the publishing group would then consult the Gavlit, or Literature Office, which censored manuscripts and proofs.

Education

Children were taught that Stalin was the 'Great Leader'. They learned Stalin's version of history. Stalin chose the subjects and information that children should learn. However, he did ensure that by 1939 the majority of Soviet people could read.

Religion

Religion posed a threat to the 'cult of Stalin'. Stalin continued the attack on religions after the Bolshevik Revolution:

- Christian leaders were imprisoned and churches closed down.

- Muslim mosques and schools were closed and pilgrimages to Mecca banned.

Subject Nationalities

Stalin was a Georgian and from an area which had long wanted self-government and even independence. Unlike Lenin, however, Stalin had no sympathy with these national groups. In the 1930s a policy of 'Russification' attempted to impose Russian culture on the USSR:

- Russian became compulsory in schools.

- Key jobs went to Russians.

- Army recruits were sent away from their homelands and forced to mix with other ethnic groups.

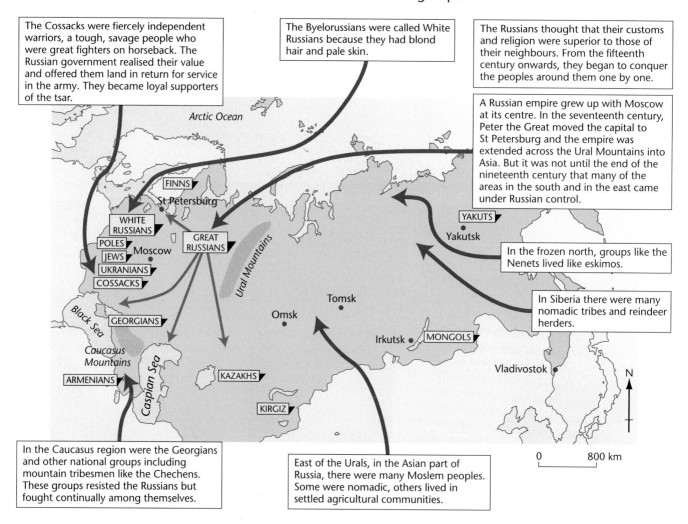

The Cossacks were fiercely independent warriors, a tough, savage people who were great fighters on horseback. The Russian government realised their value and offered them land in return for service in the army. They became loyal supporters of the tsar.

The Byelorussians were called White Russians because they had blond hair and pale skin.

The Russians thought that their customs and religion were superior to those of their neighbours. From the fifteenth century onwards, they began to conquer the peoples around them one by one.

A Russian empire grew up with Moscow at its centre. In the seventeenth century, Peter the Great moved the capital to St Petersburg and the empire was extended across the Ural Mountains into Asia. But it was not until the end of the nineteenth century that many of the areas in the south and in the east came under Russian control.

In the frozen north, groups like the Nenets lived like eskimos.

In Siberia there were many nomadic tribes and reindeer herders.

In the Caucasus region were the Georgians and other national groups including mountain tribesmen like the Chechens. These groups resisted the Russians but fought continually among themselves.

East of the Urals, in the Asian part of Russia, there were many Moslem peoples. Some were nomadic, others lived in settled agricultural communities.

The new constitution of 1936

This was introduced to convince Soviet citizens and the outside world that the people of the USSR lived in a 'free' society. In fact it confirmed Stalin's dictatorship. The USSR now consisted of eleven republics. The Congress of the Soviets of the USSR became the Supreme Soviet of the USSR with two chambers instead of one. Elections were to be held by secret ballot.

The Communist Party kept its close control of both the central government and the government of each republic. Stalin held the posts of General Secretary of the Party, Chairman of the Politburo and Prime Minister.

The secret police

In 1922 the CHEKA became the OGPU and in 1934 it was renamed the NKVD. Stalin increased the size of the secret police and used it to hunt down and destroy his opponents and terrorise ordinary people into obedience. People found guilty of opposition or disobedience were sentenced to death, exile or hard labour.

The labour camps

These were known as gulags and were set up in Siberia and the arctic north. They were run by the secret police. Millions of people were imprisoned and forced to do hard manual work on construction and mining projects. About 13 million died from cold, hunger and ill-treatment.

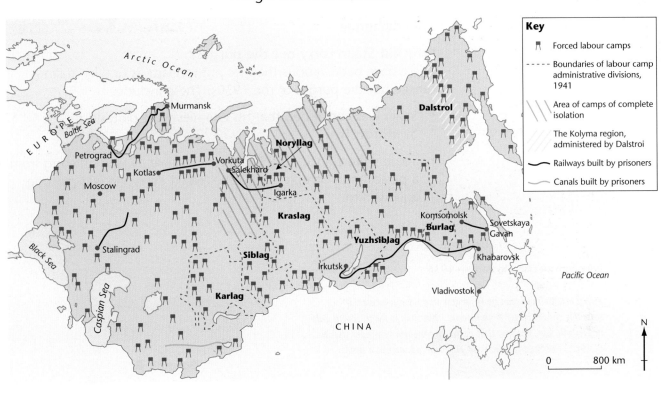

SOURCE D

From the *Gulag Archipelago* by Alexander Solzhenitsyn. He served time in a labour camp.

In 1938 Ivanor Razannik found 140 prisoners in a cell intended for 25 – with toilets so overburdened that prisoners were taken to the toilet only once a day, sometimes at night. He calculated that for weeks at a time there were three persons per square yard of floor space. In this 'kennel' there was neither ventilation nor a window and the prisoners' body heat and breathing raised the temperature to 40 degrees centigrade. Their naked bodies were pressed against one another and they got eczema from one another's sweat. They sat like that for weeks at a time and were given neither fresh air nor water – except for gruel and tea in the morning.

Questions

1 What was the 'cult of Stalin'?
2 How did Stalin use the following to achieve his dictatorship:
   a   censorship?
   b   education?
   c   propaganda?
   d   secret police?
3 What does Source **D** tell you about conditions in labour camps?

The Purges

In the 1930s Stalin used terror in the form of purges to remove all opposition to his dictatorship. He took steps to deal with people who had opposed him in the past or who he suspected might do so in the future.

Why did Stalin carry out the purges?

There have been various theories put forward as to why Stalin carried out the purges of the 1930s. These include:

- Stalin was concerned that his enemies were plotting to overthrow him.

- Some writers, including C.P. Snow, believe he was suffering from a persecution complex – that he feared everyone was plotting against him.

SOURCE A

Bukharin speaking in Paris in 1936

Stalin is convinced that he is greater than everyone else. If someone speaks better than he does, that man is for it. Stalin will not let him live, because that man is a constant reminder that he, Stalin, is not the first and best. He is not a man but a devil.

SOURCE B

From Isaac Deutscher, *Stalin*, 1949

Stalin's real motive was to destroy the men who might form an alternative government.

- Others believe that once the purges started they had a 'snowball' effect and were difficult to stop.

- One theory argues that it was the only way he could get mass forced labour for his industrial projects.

- The purges were also a convenient way of excusing failure and setbacks. For example, failures to achieve targets under the Five Year Plans could be blamed on sabotage rather than faults in the Plan.

- Finally, perhaps he wanted Soviet citizens to feel insecure because this would make them less likely to challenge him.

The purges were carried out in various stages in the 1930s.

The first purges, 1930–33

Stalin purged anyone who held up, criticised or opposed his plans for collectivisation and industrialisation. Most of the accused were deported or imprisoned. Some were shot. The first victims were:

- managers and workers accused of wrecking the Five Year Plans.

- kulaks accused of opposition to collectivisation.

- ordinary party members accused of incorrect attitudes.

1934 Party leaders

Stalin decided that his popular Politburo colleague, Kirov, was a possible rival.

Kirov was murdered, probably on Stalin's orders. Stalin claimed the murder was part of a Leftist plot against him and the Party. NKVD arrested thousands of Kirov's supporters and leaders of the old Left Opposition.

1935 Senior Communists

Senior Communists were arrested: 1108 out of 1966 delegates to the Seventeenth Congress – 98 out of 139 members of the Central Committee. Party branches were told to root out anyone who had supported Trotsky. Thousands were denounced and expelled.

1936 The 'old' Bolsheviks

Zinoviev, Kamenev and other Left Opposition leaders were arrested and confessed to plotting after NKVD torture and brainwashing. They were put on trial in full view of the world in the so-called 'show trials', which were broadcast on radio. Getting confessions was important. Confessions showed that the state and Stalin were right – a conspiracy did exist. The leaders were executed after the trials.

Profile on

Sergei Kirov

Kirov was head of the Communist Party organisation in Leningrad. It was rumoured that the Party wanted Kirov to replace Stalin as leader. At the Congress of leading members in 1934, Kirov showed himself to be more popular than Stalin. He put forward the view that it was time to slow down the drive towards industrialisation and to improve relations with the peasants. He had become a threat to Stalin for several reasons.

SOURCE C

From Evgenia Ginzburg, *Into the Whirlwind*, 1968

They started to work on me again. I was put on the 'conveyor belt'. The interrogators worked in shifts. Seven days without sleep or food. Relaxed and fresh, they passed before me as if in a dream. The object of the 'conveyor' is to wear out nerves, weaken the body, break resistance, and force the prisoner to sign whatever is required.

Ordinary citizens

Neighbours were encouraged to inform on one another's crimes or disloyalty to Stalin. Children were encouraged to inform on their parents. Those denounced were arrested, lost their jobs and were then forced to make confessions. In 1935 one million people in Moscow and Leningrad (formerly Petrograd) alone were executed.

1937 The Red Army

Stalin was determined to remove any possible opposition in the Red Army and ensure total obedience. The Commander-in-Chief, Marshall Tukhachevsky, and seven other generals (all heroes for their part in the Civil War), were arrested and shot.

1938–39 Further 'old' Bolsheviks

Bukharin, Rykov, Tomsky and other old right-wing leaders were arrested, forced to confess to crimes and executed.

All admirals, many naval officers and half the Red Army's officers were executed or imprisoned.

Stalin even purged the secret police. In 1938 Yezhov was removed from his post as head of the secret police. In the following year he was arrested and shot.

In 1940 the supposed architect of the purges, Trotsky, was murdered by one of Stalin's agents in Mexico in 1940.

Effects of the purges

The purges had a devastating effect on the Soviet Union.

They did ensure total control under Stalin with the removal of any potential rivals to his leadership.

The human cost was enormous.

Focus on

Victims of the purges

It is impossible to know exactly how many were killed or imprisoned during the 1930s. However, in 1988 the KGB – the Russian secret police who succeeded the NKVD – allowed some NKVD files to be examined. This revealed the following figures for 1937–38.

Executed	1 million
Died in camps	2 million
In prison, late 1938	1 million
In labour camps, late 1938	8 million

The USSR was seriously weakened, with the loss of most of its senior officers in the army and navy. This almost led to defeat in 1941 when Hitler's armies invaded.

It undermined much of Stalin's earlier work of building up industry. During this period able scientists, administrators and engineers were arrested, executed or imprisoned.

The purges affected every part of Russia. No village, no home could escape, not even Stalin's own family could escape. Cousins and in-laws were victims of the Terror. Even Stalin's closest advisor was arrested and shot. Anyone could receive a knock on the door in the middle of the night and be dragged away by the secret police. No one felt secure. Some people took advantage of the situation by denouncing neighbours or workmates and taking their jobs. All trust disappeared. Eventually the secret police had files on half the urban population in the Soviet Union.

Questions

1   Using the information from Sources **A** and **B**, give at least three reasons why Stalin carried out the purges.
2   Who, if anybody, benefited from the purges?
3   What effects did the purges have on:
    a   the armed forces?
    b   the economy – industry and agriculture?
4   What point is the cartoonist making in Source **D**?

Activity

You work for the BBC radio in Moscow. Do a news report for your listeners on one of the show trials during the purges.

Summary and revision

RUSSIA 1900–17

For this section you need to know:

- Russia in 1900 – size, government, countryside, industry and growth of opposition.

- The causes, events and results of the 1905 Revolution.

- Attempts at reform 1906–14 – the Dumas and Stolypin.

- The economic, political, social and military effects of the First World War on Russia.

Revision questions

1 Why did the following cause problems in Russia in 1900:
   - **a** the position of the Tsar and character of Nicholas II?
   - **b** the size of Russia?
   - **c** the plight of the peasants?
   - **d** the working and living conditions in the cities?
2 Who were the following opposition parties:
   - **a** the Cadets?
   - **b** the Social Revolutionary Party?
   - **c** the Bolsheviks?
3 Why did the Russo-Japanese War increase discontent in Russia?
4 Explain the events of Bloody Sunday.
5 Why did this spark off a revolution?
6 What was the October Manifesto of 1905?
7 Why was the Tsar able to survive the 1905 Revolution?
8 Explain the meaning of Duma. Why were these not a success in the period 1906–14?
9 What effects did the First World War have on the Russian economy?
10 Who was Rasputin? Why did he increase the problems for the Tsar?
11 Why was the Tsar's decision to take command of the Russian armed forces a mistake?

THE EVENTS OF 1917

The key events are:

- The causes, events and results of the March Revolution.

- The mistakes and weaknesses of the Provisional Government.

- The causes, events and results of the Bolshevik Revolution.

Revision questions

1 What were the immediate reasons for the March Revolution?
2 Why did the Tsar decide to abdicate?
3 What was the Provisional Government?
4 Explain at least two weaknesses of this government.

5 What mistakes did the Provisional Government make in connection with:
a the war?
b the land?
6 How did Lenin get back to Russia?
7 Why was he able to increase support for the Bolsheviks over the next few months?
8 Why did the Bolsheviks benefit from the Kornilov Rebellion?
9 Describe the key events of the November Revolution.
10 Explain two reasons for Bolshevik success.

LENIN AND RUSSIA 1918–24

You need to know:

- How Lenin consolidated power – the Constituent Assembly and Treaty of Brest-Litovsk.

- The causes, events and results of the Civil War.

- War Communism and NEP.

Revision questions

1 Why did Lenin dissolve the Constituent Assembly in January 1918?
2 Describe Russian losses in the Treaty of Brest-Litovsk.
3 Why was there opposition to the Treaty of Brest-Litovsk?
4 Who were the Whites? Give examples of groups who opposed Lenin.
5 Explain three advantages that the Reds had over the Whites.
6 Why was War Communism so unpopular by 1921?
7 What were the main features of NEP?
8 Did War Communism improve the Russian economy?

STALIN AND RUSSIA 1924–41

The key developments are:

- Stalin's rise to power 1924–29.

- Collectivisation and its effects.

- Industrialisation – the impact of the Five Year Plans.

- Stalin's dictatorship – especially propaganda, education and the police state.

- Reasons for the purges and their effects.

Revision questions

1 Who were the main rivals to succeed Lenin on his death in 1924?
2 Explain three reasons why Stalin was able to defeat his rivals, 1924–29.
3 Why did Stalin decide on collectivisation?
4 Who were the kulaks? What happened to them under Stalin?
5 Give three criticisms of collectivisation.

6   What were the Five Year Plans?
7   Describe the effects that industrialisation had on:
    a   working conditions.
    b   living conditions.
8   What were gulags?
9   Give three possible reasons for the purges.
10 Who was Kirov? Why was he murdered?
11 Explain the effects of the purges on the Soviet people.
12 Did Stalin benefit from the purges?

10
The USA 1919–41

UNDERSTANDING THE USA 1919–41

The following definitions and explanations should give you a better understanding of this chapter.

Bootlegging	To make, carry or sell illegal alcohol.
Collective bargaining	A group of workers (usually a trade union) who negotiate for better conditions.
Congress	The American parliament consisting of the House of Representatives and the Senate.
Constitution	A set of laws and rules which control how a country is governed.
Consumer	Someone who purchases goods.
Discrimination	Unfair treatment of a person or racial group.
Ghettoes	A slum area of a town or city inhabited by a deprived group.
Immigrants	People coming from abroad to live in a country.
Isolationism	A policy of withdrawing from international affairs. America would concentrate on its own concerns and not get involved in the rest of the world's problems.
Laissez-faire	A policy of non-interference by the government in industry and society.
The Mafia	A secret organisation founded in Sicily and carried to the USA by Italian immigrants where it became a criminal organisation.
Prohibition	The ban on the manufacture and sale of alcohol in the USA, 1920–33.
Rugged individualism	The policy of 'standing on your own two feet' and not relying on government help.
Supreme Court	The highest court in the USA which decides whether laws or policies follow the US Constitution.
Tariff	Tax or duty on goods coming into a country.

The USA 1919–41

This was a period of great extremes in the USA. The boom of the 1920s gave way to depression and high unemployment at the end of the decade. In the 1930s President Roosevelt's New Deal tried to deal with the impact of the Great Depression.

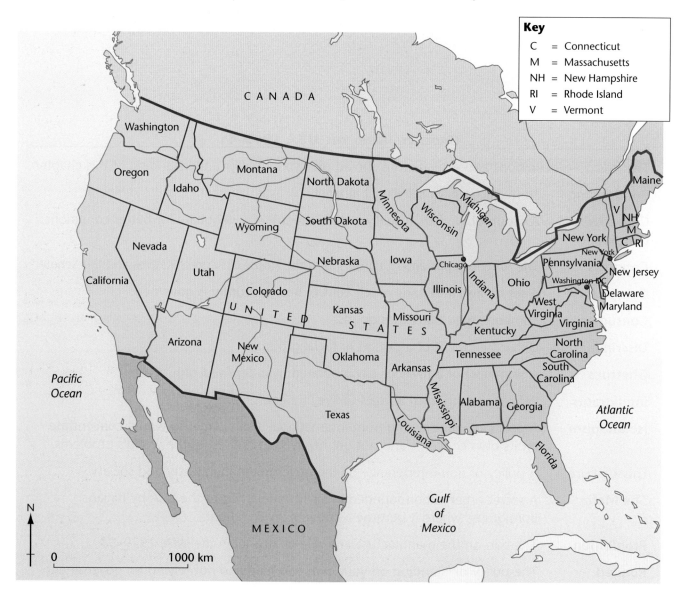

Key

C = Connecticut
M = Massachusetts
NH = New Hampshire
RI = Rhode Island
V = Vermont

THE GROWTH OF ISOLATIONISM, 1919–22

The First World War had a strong effect on many Americans. It forced them to look at their relations with the rest of the world and to look at their own society. The result was a move to isolation. This was seen in:

- The rejection of the League of Nations.
- Changes in immigration policies.
- Trade policies.

US reaction to the end of the First World War

President Wilson led the United States into the First World War in 1917 (p. 68) and later played a leading part in the peace negotiations which followed. His plans for the League of Nations (p. 128) went ahead without him because Congress refused to ratify the Treaty of Versailles and let America join the League. Many Americans were opposed to the idea of joining the League, since it would mean sending American troops to fight in foreign disputes. They wanted the USA to isolate itself from world problems.

This is why many Americans voted for Warren Harding, the Republican candidate for the presidency in 1920. Harding was an isolationist who campaigned with the slogan 'America First'. He talked about a return to 'normalcy', a word he invented, which meant life getting back to what it had been before the war. It is not surprising that Americans voted for Harding as the new President.

Tariffs against foreign goods

Isolation also meant limiting foreign trade. Action was taken to make sure that foreign goods could not compete with home-produced goods on the US market. In 1922 Congress introduced the Ford–McCumber Tariff (tax). A tariff was placed on foreign goods coming into the USA. This made them more expensive than the same American products and so 'protected' American industry. However, foreign governments retaliated by putting high tariffs on American goods exported abroad, which made them harder to sell. The Hawley–Smoot Tariff of 1929 raised import duties even higher.

Restricting immigration

Between 1901 and 1910, over nine million immigrants entered the USA. This number fell by more than half to four million between 1921 and 1930. This was for several reasons:

- Partly the result of war and increased nationalism in the USA.

- There was also an increasing fear that new immigrants, especially from poor countries, would provide cheap labour. This would take jobs from Americans.

- There was a further fear that immigrants might bring with them political ideas, such as Communism, which was against the US spirit of democracy, especially after the Bolshevik Revolution in Russia in 1917.

- Religious prejudice. The majority of Americans were Protestants. New 'immigrants' were often Catholic or Jewish.

- Racial prejudice. White English-speaking Americans looked down on ethnic groups speaking different languages and with different cultures.

Various laws were introduced which kept down the number of immigrants.

1917 Immigration Law

All foreigners wishing to enter the USA had to take a literacy test. They had to prove that they could read a short passage in English before they would be allowed in the country. Many people from poorer countries could not afford to learn English and failed the test.

1921 Immigration Quota Act

This limited the maximum number of immigrants allowed into the USA to 375000 each year. The act also limited the number of people emigrating to the USA from any country to no more than 3% of the people from the same country already living in the USA. This 'quota' system worked in favour of people from western and northern Europe because they had large numbers of immigrant American citizens. It was to ensure that the majority were WASPS – White Anglo-Saxon Protestants.

1924 Johnson–Reed Immigration Act

The quota limit was further reduced to 2% of the population in 1890.

1929 Immigration Act

This limited the number of immigrants each year to 150,000 and stopped any people from Asia.

| | **EFFECTS** | |
Number of immigrants restricted to:	**1921** 3% of 1910 population	**1924** 2% of 1890 population
EUROPE		
UK/Ireland	77,342	62,574
Germany/Austria	75,510	52,012
Eastern Europe	63,191	10,902
Italy	42,957	3,845
Scandinavia	41,859	19,274
Russia	34,284	2,248
Rest of Europe	20,263	10,691
	1,043	1,300
ASIA	122	1,200
AFRICA	424	621
REST OF WORLD		

The Sacco and Vanzetti Case

Most foreigners who entered the USA could only find low-paid jobs. Immigrant ghettoes began to appear where violence and crime were high. This only increased American distrust of foreigners. Sacco and Vanzetti were victims of the anti-immigrant feeling of the time.

The two men were immigrants from Italy who openly said that they hated the American system of government. In 1920 they were arrested and charged with the murder of two guards in an armed robbery. Sixty-one eyewitnesses identified them as the killers. However, these witnesses disagreed on the details of the crime and the description of the killers. The defence produced 107 witnesses who swore to seeing the two men somewhere else at the time of the crime. Some of these witnesses were Italian immigrants.

The jury found the two men guilty of murder. Appeals and petitions were organised but all failed. In 1927 the two men were executed. In 1977, fifty years after their execution, the verdict against the men was declared unjust.

SOURCE B

A painting of Sacco and Vanzetti

Questions

1 Why did many Americans favour isolationism in the 1920s?
2 How did the USA protect its own industry from foreign competition?
3 Explain how the American government tried to encourage emigration from some countries at the expense of others.
4 What does the Sacco and Vanzetti case suggest about American attitudes to immigrants?

Although there was a short slump in 1921, with over 12% of the workforce unemployed, the US economy prospered during most of the 1920s. This period of great prosperity is often called the 'Boom Years' or the 'Roaring Twenties'. The USA was now the richest country in the world.

IMPACT OF THE FIRST WORLD WAR

American manufacturers prospered during the war because:

- There was little competition from British and German manufacturers who were busy making weapons, munitions and uniforms to fight the war instead of exporting goods to America.
- Some US firms made huge profits selling weapons to the Allies.
- America made huge loans to Britain and France to help them buy these weapons.

RAW MATERIALS

The USA was rich in raw materials, including oil, iron ore and coal. This meant that the country did not have to buy these from abroad.

HIRE PURCHASE

If you didn't have the cash you could always borrow the money you needed on hire purchase. Many people began to live on credit, owing money to banks and finance companies. You bought the goods and paid for them in weekly instalments, paying interest on the loan.

NEW TECHNOLOGY

This included:

- The start of radio broadcasting in 1921. This created a demand for radios.
- The widespread availability of electricity supplies which created a demand for electrical goods such as vacuum cleaners and refrigerators.
- The chemical industry created new cheap materials, such as rayon, bakelite and cellophane.
- In 1928 the invention of 'talking pictures' boosted the film industry.

WEAK UNIONS

The Republican governments, like businessmen, did not like trade unions. Employers were allowed to use violence to break strikes, and to refuse to employ union members. Unions were excluded altogether from the car industry until the 1930s. This meant employers were allowed to hold down wages and to keep hours of working long.

REASONS FOR THE BOOM YEARS

ADVERTISING

Demands for goods was stimulated by a flood of advertising. Mail order catalogues, posters, radio and cinema commercials urged customers to buy, buy, buy!

SOURCE A

An advert in the *Saturday Evening Post*, 1929. It shows a woman driver. Advertisers realised that women also bought cars.

GOVERNMENT POLICY

The Republican presidents of the 1920s – Presidents Harding (1920–23) and Coolidge (1923–28) believed in a policy of laissez-faire or not interfering with the economy. Instead they encouraged the growth of industry by low taxes. These encouraged business owners to invest and gave consumers more money to spend. They also protected American industry by introducing tariffs (p. 461).

MASS PRODUCTION

Mass production methods, pioneered by the carmaker Henry Ford, made it cheaper and much easier to manufacture goods than by hand. Ford trained each worker to perform a specific task as a vehicle or engine passed by on an assembly line.

SOURCE B

Henry Ford speaking in 1926 about mass production

The operations are sub-divided so that each man and each machine do only one thing. The thing is to keep everything in motion and take the work to the man, not the man to the work.

THE IMPACT OF THE MOTOR INDUSTRY

The expansion of the motor industry boosted the whole economy. Between 1920 and 1929 the number of Americans owning cars rose from 8 million to 23 million. Annual production rose from 1.6 million to 5.6 million. The motor industry stimulated other industries because:

- The building of vehicles created a demand for products such as steel, rubber and glass.
- Roads had to be built. This created jobs in the construction industry.
- Cars ran on petrol. This boosted the oil industry.
- It employed over half a million workers who, themselves, were consumers.

WAGE RISES AND STABLE PRICES

During the 1920s the average wage of industrial workers doubled. Many people could afford to buy cars, domestic appliances and cinema tickets. At the same time, prices were steady or, in the case of some consumer goods, actually falling due to mass-production methods.

THE CYCLE OF PROSPERITY

The increased production of consumer goods created increased employment. This meant that people had more money to spend on consumer goods, especially as their prices were falling. This in turn created an increased demand for goods and encouraged further production. So the cycle went on.

SHARES

As companies made profits their share prices rose. The system of buying 'on the margin' allowed ordinary people to buy company shares on a hire purchase basis. They hoped that a rise in the share price would mean they could pay for the purchase and also make a profit. Millions of Americans became shareowners and this boosted investment in industry and increased many people's prosperity and willingness to spend on goods.

SOURCE C

Picture postcards from America during the boom years. Oil wells in California (top), iron and steel works in Cleveland, Ohio (middle), small-town bank in New England (bottom).

Profile on

Henry Ford

He was the greatest figure in the car industry. The Ford Motor Company started in 1903. By 1908 Ford had developed the first version of the 'Model T' – the 'universal car' as Ford called it. It was designed to be a car for the masses, not just the privileged few. In 1913 Ford introduced the assembly-line into his factories. Huge numbers of identical, standardised cars could be built more quickly and cheaply than ever before. Ford was able to cut the price of the Model T, so more people could afford one. The original price of $850 fell to just $260 by 1924. Up to 1926 it was the USA's best-selling car. By 1927, when production ended, 15 million had been made.

Activities

Copy the table below. Decide the importance of each factor leading to the boom. Give reasons for your choice.

Causes of boom	Decisive	Important	Quite important	Not important
Car industry				
Advertising				
New technology				
Mass production				
Hire purchase				
Government policy				
Low wages				
First World War				
Shares				

Try to make links between the causes to show how they influenced each other:

For example, advertising helped the car industry by encouraging people to buy more cars.

Which do you think were the most important reasons? Explain your answer.

Questions

1   How reliable is Source **A** as a view of the car industry in the 1920s?
2   What is meant by:
    a   the 'cycle of prosperity'?
    b   buying 'on the margin'?
3   What do the postcards in Source **C** tell you about the boom years?

The economic prosperity of the 1920s brought a change in lifestyle for many people.

Women

Women were freer than ever before to live their own lives. Young fashionable women, known as flappers, drank, smoked, dated and wore outrageous new fashions. In 1920 women gained the right to vote and during the 1920s more and more women went to work. They became financially independent and no longer had to live at home. Being less dependent on men, women could make their own decisions about how to live. The divorce rate rose quickly.

Women looked different. They had their hair cut short in the new 'bobbed' style. They wore make-up, went out on their own without a chaperone and smoked in public. The new fashions were much simpler and freer than before the war, and skirts became much shorter.

However, this was not the case for many women. Most were not flappers and disapproved of these changes. They were too busy at work or raising families to go out. The lives of these women were often more affected by the new labour-saving devices such as washing-machines and vacuum cleaners which began to free them from domestic chores.

Complete a chart like the one below to show changes in the position of American women during this period.

	Women before the war	Women in the 1920s
Work		
Vote		
Fashion		
Behaviour		

SOURCE A

An extract from an article in *Cosmopolitan* magazine written by a female English journalist, 1921

Think of the modern young American girl of this great country. Do they ever think? Do they ever ask whence they have come, whither they are going? It would seem not. Their aim appears to be to attract men and to secure money. What can a man with a mind find to hold him in one of these lovely, brainless, cigarette-smoking creatures of undisciplined sex whom he meets continually?

Work before the war

Women were employed in traditional 'female' areas of work, such as domestic service, textiles, clerical and secretarial work and teaching.

Work during the 1920s

During the war women took over jobs traditionally done by men, such as those in manfacturing and heavy industry. After the war most women went back to traditional jobs, but the number of working women increased by 25% to 10.5 million by 1929. The number of upper- and middle-class women in employment increased, especially in teaching and secretarial work.

The vote before the war

Only one in four states gave women the vote.

1920s

In 1920 all women were given the right to vote.

In July 1920 a fashion-writer reported in the New York Times *that 'the American woman had lifted her skirts far beyond and modest limitation'. This was another way of saying that the hem was now all of nine inches above the ground. The flappers wore thin dresses, short-sleeved and occasionally sleeveless. Many of them were visibly using cosmetics.*

Fashion before the war

Women were expected to have long hair, often worn up, and to wear tight undergarments (including corsets), and full-length dresses.

The 1920s

Many women stopped wearing corsets. Hemlines went up and hair was cut short in bobs.

Behaviour before the war

Women were expected not to smoke or drink in public. They were not to drive cars or play vigorous games. If they were unmarried, they were accompanied by a chaperone when they went out in the company of men.

In the 1920s

Women smoked and drank in public. They began to take part in strenuous sport and dances such as the Charleston. They went out with men unaccompanied by chaperones and drove cars.

SOURCE C

A flapper in the 1920s

The leisure industry

Radio changed everyday life. It brought entertainment into the home. Cinema managers complained that customers were staying at home instead of going to the movies. In 1920 only $2 million worth of radios were purchased but in 1929 the figure was $600 million. Radios, cars and the telephone made people more mobile, making it easier for them to seek their fortunes elsewhere, such as in the cities.

Young people found freedom in a range of leisure activities: jazz, ragtime, dancing, smoking, motoring and cinema. Jazz was a form of music that developed from earlier forms of black music, such as the blues. Famous nightclubs, like the Cotton Club in Harlem, New York, provided opportunities for some of the great performers such as Duke Ellington and Louis Armstrong. Part of the appeal of jazz was the sense of excitement and danger it gave to whites, who, for the first time, were exposed to black music.

One result of the popularity of jazz was the dance crazes. The most famous of these were the Charleston and the Black Bottom.

The cinema

The movie industry had begun before the First World War, but its popularity soared during the 1920s. Audiences more than doubled during the decade. By 1929, 95 million people a week were going to the cinema. Hollywood, in California, was the centre of the film industry. The studios encouraged the 'star system', which made actors like Charlie Chaplin and Mary Pickford into household names. Hollywood stars influenced the way people dressed, the perfume women used, and the way in which men combed their

In 1927 perhaps the most important change in the history of the film industry occurred. Warner Brothers released *The Jazz Singer*, starring Al Jolson. It was the first 'talkie' film.

Motoring

In 1929 4½ million new cars were registered in the USA. Mass ownership of cars had many social effects.

- The growth of suburbs.

- Rural communities were brought into contact with the outside world. Farmers could drive to the nearest towns for supplies and young people could drive into town for entertainment.

- City dwellers could now escape into the country or drive further for holidays.

- Many people in the USA were able to move anywhere to look for work.

SOURCE D

Mae West, one of the stars of the period

SOURCE E

The ten millionth Ford automobile

Focus on

Charles A. Lindbergh

In 1919 a New York businessman offered a prize of $25,000 to whoever flew non-stop from New York to Paris for the first time. On 20 May 1927 Captain Charles A. Lindbergh set out to win the prize. He took off from New York in a small, one-engined plane called the *Spirit of St Louis* with no map or parachute. Some reporters described him as 'The flying fool'. Thirty-three and a half hours later he touched down at Le Bourget, near Paris. Lindbergh arrived back to a 'ticker-tape' welcome in New York and soon became America's greatest hero of the twentieth century. Hundreds of streets were named after him. The whole country mourned five years later when his baby son was kidnapped and brutally murdered.

Sport

Sport also flourished as workers began to enjoy greater prosperity and have more leisure time. Baseball was the most popular sport of the town workers with 'Babe' Ruth the most famous player. Boxing also enjoyed a boom period, with Jack Dempsey the heavyweight champion from 1919–26, the most famous boxer. Many of the wealthier Americans turned to golf as a leisure activity.

Questions

1 Is the author of Source **A** for or against the flapper? Give reasons for your answer.
2 In this period, what changes were there in work opportunities for women?
3 What do Sources **B** and **C** show or tell you about the flapper?
4 Which source would be the more useful to an historian studying the flapper?
5 Why was the cinema so popular?
6 Explain the social effects of motoring.

RELIGIOUS PROBLEMS IN THE 1920s

Religion was particularly strong in the countryside. Country people prided themselves on being god-fearing, church-going Christians. In the cities however, less and less people were attending church.

The revivalists

To try and stop this, a number of revivalist groups were formed. They wanted to restore belief in the Christian faith. The most famous revivalist was Aimee Semple MacPherson, known as Sister Aimee. She was head of the 'Four Square Gospel Alliance'. Sister Aimee often dressed as an angel, led the congregation in hymn singing, beating time with a tambourine. Within five years she had built up a large fortune.

The fundamentalists

More than half the Christians in the USA were Protestant. The Protestants, however, in the 1920s split into two groups – those

Activity

You live in a remote rural area of the USA but visit a major city in which you see the 'new woman' or flapper. Write home:

- describing the flapper.
- giving your views on the changes in the position of women. You can either approve or disapprove.

that agreed and those that disagreed with Charles Darwin's theory of evolution outlined in his book *The Origin of Species*. Darwin argued that human beings had developed gradually from the same origins as animals and had the same ancestors as, say, apes.

This brought opposition especially from Protestants in rural America. They believed that Darwin meant that human beings evolved from monkeys. He seemed to be attacking the Bible which said that God created the universe and everything in it in six days. In 1919 Protestants who believed this Biblical explanation set up 'The World's Christian Fundamentals Association' and became known as Fundamentalists.

In 1924 they set up an Anti-Evolution League to campaign against Darwin's ideas. Six states passed laws making it illegal for teachers to teach the theory of evolution.

The 'Monkey Trial'

One teacher, Johnny Scopes, who lived in Dayton, Tennessee, where the teaching of evolution was illegal, decided to put the law to the test. He taught his class the theory of evolution and was arrested for breaking the law. His subsequent trial attracted press from all over the world. Scopes was defended by a leading lawyer called Clarence Darrow, who argued for the theory of evolution, while a leading Fundamentalist lawyer, William Jennings Bryan, acted as prosecutor. Although Scopes was eventually found guilty of breaking the law and fined $100, Bryan was made a laughing stock when he tried to defend the Bible's version of the creation of man. He argued that Eve was literally created out of Adam's rib. He insisted that Noah had survived the flood in the ark in the year 2348 BC.

ECONOMIC WEAKNESSES IN THE 1920S

Some areas of the American economy did not experience a boom period for several reasons and there were other economic problems.

- In reply to US tariffs foreign countries introduced their own taxes on American goods. This made it harder for American businesses to sell their goods abroad.

- By the late 1920s more goods were being made than there were people who could afford to buy them. As a result, companies lowered their prices, made smaller profits and started to lay off workers.

- Trusts were giant firms that dominated the business world. They took advantage of the freedoms given to businesses by the Republican governments and kept wages low and prices high. In the long term this kept down demand because it meant that people could not afford to buy their goods.

- Unequal distribution of wealth was also a weakness. The richest 5% of the population earned 33% of all the money earned in the USA. This meant that only a small number of Americans could really afford the cars and household goods being made.

Question

Explain the meaning of:

a Revivalists.

b Fundamentalists.

Activity

Write a press report for the 'Monkey Trial'. In your report include:

- Darrow's arguments for the theory of evolution.
- Bryan's arguments against.
- The reactions of the world press.

The older industries

Some major industries, such as coal and textiles, did not expand during the 1920s. Coal lost ground to newer forms of energy – oil, gas and electricity. Many coal mines were closed. Textiles depended on the demand for clothes. The industry was badly hit by the new women's fashion for shorter skirts and dresses. This required less material than before. It also suffered as a result of the demand for new synthetic fibres.

Agriculture

After 1920 the wartime prosperity of American farmers ended because:

- The demand from Europe fell as European farmers started to produce again after the war.

- American farmers, often using modern machinery, overproduced, causing a fall in prices at home.

- With lower incomes many farmers could not afford to make repayments on the money they had borrowed to buy their land and machinery. The banks which had lent them money started to evict them. In 1924 about 600,000 farmers lost their land. By 1929 millions of farmworkers were unemployed.

- The introduction of tariffs made it even more difficult for farmers to sell abroad.

The crisis in agriculture had a 'knock-on' effect on industry. Farmers and farmworkers would not afford to buy goods. Shops in farming areas bought less from the manufacturers and the manufacturers made less profit. They had to lay off workers and with factory workers unemployed the demand for goods fell again.

DID ALL AMERICANS BENEFIT FROM THE BOOM?

The USA became much richer during the 1920s, but it would be wrong to think that this wealth was shared out equally. It has been estimated that, in 1929, 60% of all American families lived below the poverty line. Many of these were in rural areas, but the poor were numerous in big cities too. Throughout the decade the poor remained poor and in the rural areas they became even poorer.

SOURCE A

US government report in 1938

South eastern farms are the smallest in the Nation. Family incomes are very low, the sickness and death rates are unusually high. Even in southern cities from 60 to 88% of the families on low incomes are not spending enough on food to purchase an adequate diet.

Areas of the USA were affected in different ways by the boom. The industrial north and north-west did well but the agricultural south did not benefit. The effects varied even within agricultural areas. Fruit farmers benefited from the growing demand for fresh produce and were quite well-paid. Wheat farmers of the Great Plains, however, suffered a period of low prices caused by falling demand and competition from abroad.

SOURCE B

Monthly earnings 1929

Occupation	Monthly salary $
South Carolina farmer	129
South Carolina town worker	412
New York town worker	881
Californian fruit farmer	1246

Black Americans

The black population suffered discrimination of all kinds but especially in employment. During the First World War many black families had moved from the south to cities in the north, attracted by jobs available in the factories. Once the war finished, competition for jobs increased and many whites resented the black newcomers. During 1919 there were race riots in many cities. The cities of the north were segregated, with Black Americans living mainly in the city slums, such as Harlem in New York City. They were given the lowest paid jobs and, in hard times, were the first to be laid off.

Conditions were even worse in the south where the law was used to enforce racial discrimination. Most worked as agricultural labourers and lived in extreme poverty.

There was extreme racial discrimination in all areas:

Segregation The 'Jim Crow' laws of the southern states meant that black people were segregated from white. This meant that, for example they were forced to go to separate schools, use separate buses and trains and live in separate neighbourhoods.

Education and jobs Black people had the lowest standards of education and the poorest paid jobs.

The vote The laws of many southern states meant that few black people could vote.

SOURCE D

A black family and their home in Virginia in the 1920s

SOURCE C

A poor Black remembers life in the south in the 1920s. From R. Wright, *Black Boy*, 1947.

Whenever I begged for food my mother would pour me a cup of tea. This settled my stomach for a moment or two, but a little later I would feel hunger nudging my ribs, twisting my empty guts until they ached. I would grow dizzy and my vision would dim.

Native Americans

Indians lived in the USA long before the arrival of white people. By the beginning of the twentieth century, most Indians lived in reservations. These were special areas set aside for the Indians by the American government. Reservations mostly had poor soil, so Indians found it difficult to grow crops. The government gave them very little help to survive.

Rich businessman

Black American

Flapper

Immigrant

Native American

Car worker

Housewife

Activity

For each of these characters give their feelings about the 1920s in the USA.

For example, a car worker could be saying how well he is doing because of pay rises, regular employment and lower prices.

Questions

1 What problems were there in the US economy in the 1920s?

2 Why did the older industries and agriculture not enjoy boom conditions?

3 What do Sources **C** and **D** tell you about conditions for black Americans?

4 How reliable is Source **C** as a view of the conditions for black Americans?

THE KU KLUX KLAN

This organisation terrorised black Americans in the south. It started as a terrorist organisation in the years after the American Civil War of 1861–65 with the aim of preserving white supremacy over the newly freed black slaves. The members of this organisation dressed in white robes and wore pointed hoods to hide their identity. In 1915 the Klan was restarted in Georgia by William Simmons. He kept the original Klan's ideas and costume.

Membership and aims

It was open to WASPS and membership reached an all-time high of five million in 1923. It included many police officers, judges and politicians. It benefited from the anti-foreigner atmosphere after the war. It had several aims:

- To defend white superiority against black people and other ethnic minorities.
- To defend Protestant superiority against Catholics and Jews.
- To 'clean up' American society by attacking anyone, such as drunks and gamblers, who threatened moral standards.

SOURCE A

Extracts from the *Kloran*, the Klan's book of rules

Are you a native-born, white, non-Jewish American? Do you believe in the Christian religion? Will you faithfully strive for the eternal maintenance of white supremacy?

Its activities

Although it was a secretive organisation, its members became confident enough to parade openly through many cities, including Washington. Klan members held ceremonies in which they dressed in their robes and hoods and Klansmen spoke to each other in secret codes known as 'Klonversations'.

Torture and violence were used against people who were not 'true Americans', with black people suffering the most. Victims were beaten, whipped, tarred and feathered, or lynched where victims were put to death without a trial. Their homes were set on fire and their property destroyed. In many cases the Klansmen were not punished for these activities. They were often protected by the authorities – the police or judges – who were themselves members of the Klan. Juries made up of white people were reluctant to find people guilty of Klan activities.

SOURCE B

Victims of a Ku Klux Klan lynching in 1930

Membership of the Klan declined after 1925. By the following year it had fallen to 300,000. This was for two main reasons:

- There were some successful prosecutions against the Klan, especially for the most violent activities. The trials were widely reported and brought a reaction against the Klan.

- In 1926 a Klan leader was convicted of rape and murder of a woman on a train in the state of Indiana. This destroyed the image of the Klan.

Questions

1   Why was the Klan popular in the south in the early 1920s?
2   What does Source **A** tell you about the aims of the organisation?
3   Describe the activities it carried out. Why were few Klan members convicted?

PROHIBITION

In January 1920 the USA introduced Prohibition – the making, selling or transporting of alcoholic drink in the USA became illegal. This was made part of the American Constitution in the 18th Amendment. A separate law, the Volstead Act, defined an alcoholic drink as any drink that contained more than 0.5% of alcohol.

Why was Prohibition introduced?

Moral reasons Those who opposed alcohol argued that it caused a variety of social problems, such as violence, crime, and poverty. If alcohol was banned, they believed that the USA would be a better healthier and more moral place in which to live. It also brought increased absence from work.

Existing prohibition By 1918 alcohol was banned in 18 states. Thirteen of these states were totally 'dry' by 1919. The majority of other states had also introduced some kind of control on the sale of alcohol.

Campaigners Many organisations led campaigns against alcohol. The most famous was the Anti-Saloon League of America, set up in 1893. These organisations were very effective because they:

- Launched a strong propaganda campaign and put pressure on politicians to support the cause.

- They were supported by Protestant churches in rural areas where members criticised standards of behaviour in the cities.

- They helped to get supporters of prohibition elected to Congress.

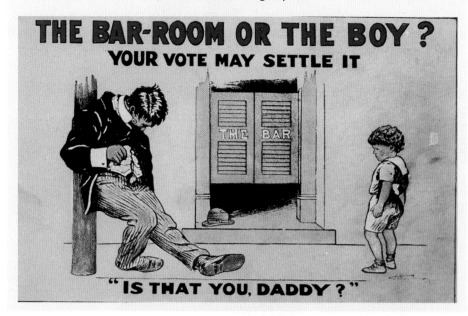

THE BAR-ROOM OR THE BOY ?
YOUR VOTE MAY SETTLE IT

THE BAR

"IS THAT YOU, DADDY ?"

The First World War Many of the USA's brewers were of German descent. When the USA joined the war in 1917, there was a lot of anti-German feeling, and campaigners were able to argue that it would be patriotic to close the brewers down.

The effects of Prohibition

Prohibition had almost the opposite effect from that intended. Once it was banned, alcohol became more attractive and consumption actually increased. In many cities, the law was ignored. Illegal bars, known as 'speakeasies', opened in their thousands. By 1930 there were over 30,000 in New York alone. Illegal alcohol came from several areas:

Moonshine Some people tried to make their own alcohol. This was known as 'moonshine' but could be very poisonous. Several hundred people a year died from this during the 1920s. Government prohibition agents found it impossible to stop the production of moonshine. Thousands of illegal distilleries and breweries were in operation throughout the USA.

Smuggling Much alcohol was smuggled from the West Indies and Canada by famous 'rum-runners' such as William McCoy. In four years McCoy is thought to have smuggled $70 million worth of whiskey.

Gangsters The enormous profits to be made from alcohol soon attracted the attention of gangsters who were able to take control of many cities by bribing local policemen, judges and politicians. This meant the criminal could operate with little fear of arrest.

SOURCE B

From W.E. Leuchtenburg, *The Perils of Prosperity*, 1958

Many people made their own home brew. In large cities, hardware stores openly displayed copper stills along with yeasts, hops and other ingredients. Other people bought their whiskey from bootleggers who claimed they were selling the best imported brands from Canada and Scotland, and sometimes did. More often they passed off inferior products – at worst substances like Jamaica ginger, better known as 'jake', which paralysed thousands of people, Jackass Brandy, which caused internal bleeding or Yack Yack Bourbon from Chicago, which blended iodine and burnt sugar.

SOURCE C

A comment by Al Capone

When I see liquor, it's called bootlegging. When my patrons serve it on silver trays on Lake Shore Drive, it's called hospitality.

In 1925 Al Capone became the boss of the Mafia in Chicago. He was involved in gambling and brothels as well as bootlegging and speakeasies. He also used bribery to control the mayor and the police. He was prepared to use violence and is thought to have ordered the murders of 227 rival gangsters in four years. The violence reached its peak in 1929 with the St Valentine's Day Massacre. Seven members of a rival gang were machine-gunned to death. At the end of the 1920s Capone was earning $100 million a year. In 1931 federal agents managed to have him convicted for tax evasion.

Organised crime

This was the biggest effect of Prohibition. Rival gangs in cities fought to take over the other's 'territory' – and the rackets within it. Gangland murders increased. The most notorious city was Chicago, where Mayor 'Big Bill' Thompson was known to be a close friend of the most famous gangster, Al Capone. In Chicago alone, between 1927 and 1931, over 200 gang members were murdered, with nobody convicted for these crimes.

SOURCE D

The St Valentine's Day Massacre, February 1929

The profits made during the Prohibition period were so vast that the gangsters were able to extend their activities into other areas of criminal activity, such as prostitution, labour rackets and illegal gambling. Organised crime also bought its way into legal business activities and into trade unions.

Why did Prohibition fail?

Prohibition did not work. Drinking illegal alcohol was too popular and too profitable. It could not be controlled without huge numbers of enforcement agents. The Prohibition Bureau employed about 4000 agents to stop bootlegging – the illegal making and selling of alcohol – and close speakeasies for the whole of the USA. While agents like Eliot Ness achieved some success, most were ineffective. Indeed, some were guilty of taking bribes from the criminals who ran the trade – nearly 10% of the agents were sacked for taking bribes. In 1933 there were over 200,000 speakeasies in the USA.

SOURCE E

From D.B. O'Callaghan, *Roosevelt and the United States*, 1966

The result of introducing prohibition was that many Americans began to lose their respect for law and order. In Chicago, for example, the gangster Al Capone, with his private army of gunslingers, had more power than the real mayor.

	1921	1925	1929
Illegal distilleries seized	9,746	12,023	15,794
Gallons of distilled spirits seized	414,000	1,103,000	1,186,000
Number of arrests	34,175	62,747	66,878

Perhaps the most important reason why Prohibition failed was that the vast majority of American people did not agree with it. They were prepared to break the law in order to consume alcohol. The Depression also made an important difference. With millions out of work, it seemed nonsense that the government was spending large amounts of money on enforcing an unpopular and ineffective law. The money could surely be spent more wisely on helping the poor.

Opponents of Prohibition were able to argue that by legalising alcohol an enormous number of jobs would be created and tax revenues could be raised again on its sale.

Many Americans were concerned at the amount of crime encouraged by Prohibition, especially the growth of organised crime.

In 1932 Franklin Roosevelt, who promised to end Prohibition, was elected president. One of his earliest actions, in December 1932, was to introduce the 21st Amendment to the Constitution, repealing prohibition.

Activity

Design a poster either:

Supporting Prohibition

or

Against Prohibition

Questions

1   Why was Prohibition brought in after the First World War?
2   What is the purpose of the poster, Source **A**?
3   How useful is Source **A** to an historian studying the campaign for Prohibition?
4   What were:
    a   speakeasies?
    b   bootlegging?
    c   moonshine?
5   Did Prohibition fail only because it was unpopular?
6   What do the chart and Source **F** tell you about why Prohibition failed?
7   Source **E** is by an historian. Does this make it a reliable view of Prohibition?

AMERICA IN THE DEPRESSION

In 1929 the economic prosperity, which many Americans thought would last forever, suddenly ended with the Wall Street Crash (see p. 482). It gave way to depression. This brought unemployment and suffering to millions of Americans who saw themselves reduced to a state of poverty.

Why did the USA fall into Depression?

CYCLE OF DEPRESSION

FALLING DEMAND FOR GOODS
- People who can afford them already have them.
- The majority of people cannot afford them

TOO MANY GOODS PRODUCED

VERY LOW DEMAND ABROAD
- Other countries have imposed tariffs on USA goods in retaliation for the USA tariffs on their goods.
- This makes American exports too expensive.

LOWER PRICES
- Firms reduce prices to attract buyers.

FURTHER DROP IN DEMAND
- Caused by workers being unemployed or on lower wages.

LOWER PROFITS
- Lower prices and falling sales reduce company profits.

JOB LOSSES AND WAGE CUTS

Firms have to cut costs in order to:
a stay profitable
b reduce prices further.
- They do this by:
a laying off workers
b cutting the wages of those who remain.

OVERPRODUCTION

Mass-production methods meant that goods could be produced quickly and in large amounts. However, the market was soon becoming saturated. Once Americans had bought their cars, radios, vacuum cleaners and other consumer goods, the demand for these items fell. Factories were forced to produce fewer goods. This meant cutting back on their workforces, which meant fewer people could afford to buy consumer goods.

UNEQUAL DISTRIBUTION OF WEALTH

The fall in demand was also due to the unequal distribution of wealth. Many Americans no longer wished to buy new consumer goods, but there were millions more who could not afford to do so. A survey of 1928 showed that 60% of American families earned less than $2000 a year – the minimum needed to survive.

TARIFF POLICY

When the USA put tariffs on foreign goods in the 1920s many foreign governments responded by doing the same to American goods. So American businessmen found it very difficult to sell their goods abroad.

CAUSES OF

SPECULATORS

The confidence that had helped to produce prosperity was now shaken. This led to the collapse of the financial markets. During the 1920s as more and more Americans bought shares on the stock exchange, share prices kept rising. People bought shares on credit expecting to sell them for a profit and settle their debts. This is called 'speculation'. In 1928 share prices did not rise as much as in previous years. Many companies were not selling as many goods, so their profits fell and people were less willing to buy their shares. Some speculators even began to sell their shares before the value fell. When other smaller speculators saw this they began to sell too.

SOURCE A

From Studs Terkel, *Hard Times: An Oral History of the Depression*, 1986

The Crash – it didn't happen in one day. There were a great many warnings. The country was crazy. Everybody was in the stock market, whether he could afford it or not. Shoeshine boys and waiters and capitalists.

Rise and fall in share prices 1925–33

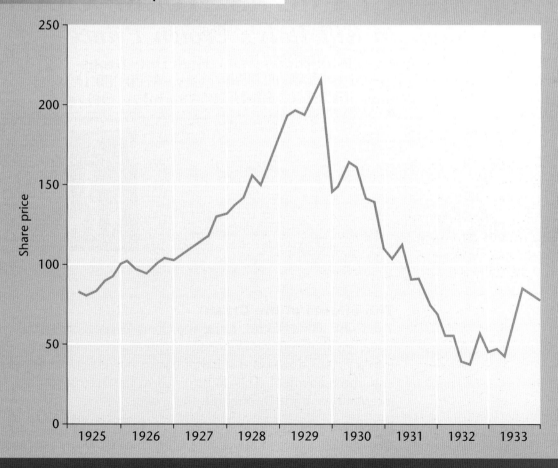

DEPRESSION

This was the immediate cause of the Depression. Prices began to fall quickly as investors tried to sell increasing numbers of shares.

Thursday 24 October   This was known as 'Black Thursday' as 13 million shares were sold. Prices dived as few buyers could be found. A group of bankers spent nearly $250 million buying shares in the hope that this would encourage investors to buy rather than sell shares. It seemed to work and share prices stopped falling.

Monday 28 October   There was renewed panic – over nine million shares were sold at falling prices.

Tuesday 29 October   Over 16 million shares were sold by panic-stricken investors for whatever price they could get. As a result prices tumbled – shareholders lost a total of $8000 million in one day.

Share prices continued to fall for the next few weeks until they stopped falling in mid-November. By then the damage was done.

SOURCE B

Headlines in the *Brooklyn Daily Eagle*, 24 October 1929

BROOKLYN DAILY EAGLE

And Complete Long Island News

LATE NEWS
WALL STREET
1:15 PRICES ★ ★

89th YEAR—No. 295.   ★ NEW YORK CITY, THURSDAY, OCTOBER 24, 1929. ★   32 PAGES   THREE CENTS

WALL ST. IN PANIC AS STOCKS CRASH

Attempt Made to Kill Italy's Crown Prince

STOCKS CRASH IN RUSH TO SELL; BILLIONS LOST

ASSASSIN CAUGHT IN BRUSSELS MOB; PRINCE UNHURT

Hollywood Fire Destroys Films Worth Millions

FEAR 52 PERISHED IN LAKE MICHIGAN; FERRY IS MISSING

PIECE OF PLANE LIKE DITEMAN'S IS FOUND AT SEA

High Duty Group Gave $700,000 to Coolidge Drive

Morgan, Mitchell Buying Stocks in Effort to Check Rush to Unload.

The effects of the Crash
The Crash alone did not cause the Great Depression. It did, however, spark off the Depression. The American economy went into a vicious downward spiral of bankruptcy, falling production and unemployment. This, in turn, led to the destruction of international trade throughout the world.

Economic effects
Demand fell again so many people lost money. Many people lost their jobs when companies closed. Those who had money lost confidence and spent as little as possible which further reduced demand. Companies cut back production and laid off more workers.

A victim of the Crash tries to sell his car for a bargain price, October 1929

$100 WILL BUY THIS CAR. MUST HAVE CASH. LOST ALL ON THE STOCK MARKET

Financial effects

- Many individuals and businesses were ruined.

- Many people who had borrowed money to buy their shares went bankrupt because they could not pay back the loan.

- Some people lost their homes because they could no longer afford the mortgage.

- Banks which had loaned to people so that they could buy shares could not get their money back. Some banks ran out of money and had to close down. In 1929 alone nearly 700 banks collapsed.

- People with savings in the banks lost their money.

- In an attempt to try to recover some of their money banks began to call in loans from companies and ordinary people who had borrowed money from them.

- Companies who could not repay had to close.

- Farmers were evicted when banks tried to get their loans back.

- Thousands of other companies went out of business because their shares were worth so little.

SOURCE D

Arthur A. Robertson, a businessman, remembers the Crash

Suicides, left and right, made a terrific impression on me, of course. People I knew. It was heartbreaking. One day you saw the prices at a hundred, the next day at $20, at $15. On Wall Street, the people walked around like zombies. You saw people who yesterday rode around in Cadillacs lucky now to have the fare for a bus.

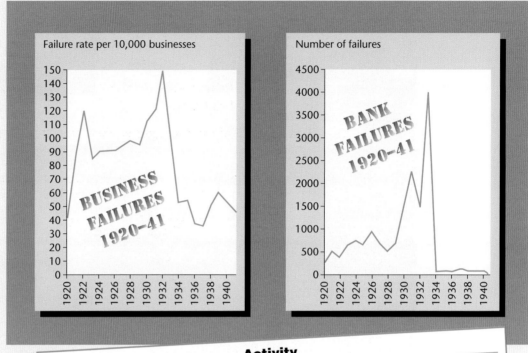

Failure rate per 10,000 businesses — BUSINESS FAILURES 1920–41

Number of failures — BANK FAILURES 1920–41

Activity

You are a businessman who kept a diary in 1929. Write out several extracts from your diary. These could include:

Warnings in early 1929 about over-speculation and falling share prices.

The events of late October.

The effects that the Crash had on your own business and that of friends you know.

Questions

1 Why did the American economy collapse in the 1930s? You must include:
   - Overproduction.
   - Cycle of depression.
   - Speculators.
   - The Wall Street Crash.

2 How useful is Source **A** to an historian studying the reasons for the Wall Street Crash?

3 What were the economic and financial effects of the Wall Street Crash?

4 What do Source **D** and the graphs tell you about the effects of the Crash? Which information would be more useful to an historian?

THE EFFECTS OF THE DEPRESSION ON THE AMERICAN PEOPLE

The Depression had disastrous economic and social effects.

Economic effects

The economy suffered badly between 1929 and 1933.

The value of goods sold in shops fell by 50%.

The total wealth produced by the country, known as the Gross National Product or GNP, fell by just under 50%.

About 10,000 banks stopped trading.

Thousands of companies went out of business. Some 20,000 went bankrupt in 1932 alone.

The number of unemployed workers rose from 1.5 million to 12.8 million.

Farm income and the wages of farmworkers fell by 50%.

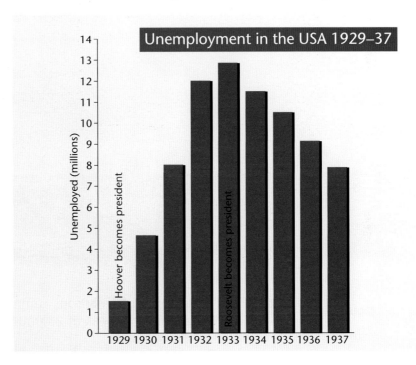

Unemployment in the USA 1929–37

Social effects

Unemployment reached 25% of the workforce by 1933. In the industrial cities of the north, the rate was even higher as factories and businesses cut down on production or shut down completely. In Chicago, for example, nearly half the labour force was unemployed in 1933. For those in work wages were cut by 25%. Some Americans took to travelling from place to place to find work wherever they could. They became tramps or 'hobos'.

Unemployment plunged millions of families into poverty. This was because there was no system of unemployment benefit. Many people relied on hand-outs of bread and soup from soup kitchens run by charities. Most had to sell their possessions to pay back loans or credit taken out during the good years. If they had mortgage payments they could not meet, their homes were repossessed. If they fell behind with their rents, they were evicted. In 1932 alone a quarter of a million Americans lost their homes.

The homeless ended up on the streets, sleeping on park benches or in bus shelters. Some deliberately got themselves arrested so that they could spend the night in jail. Many moved to the edge of towns or to waste grounds in towns. There they built shelters from whatever they could – corrugated iron, scrap metal, old wood. These shanty towns were nicknamed 'Hoovervilles' as an insult to the President, Herbert Hoover.

SOURCE B

A picture of a Hooverville in Central Park, New York. In the background are luxury flats.

SOURCE C

From *Since Yesterday*

One vivid, gruesome moment of those dark days we shall never forget. We saw a crowd of some fifty men fighting over a barrel of garbage outside the backdoor of a restaurant. American citizens fighting for scraps of food like animals.

The number of Americans committing suicide rose during the Depression to a peak of 23,000 in 1932.

Farmers

The Depression made life even more difficult for farmers. Unemployment in the towns meant that farmers sold less of their produce. Prices of farm produce fell so much that it was not profitable to even harvest the crop. Farmers went bankrupt and in 1932 one farmer in every twenty was evicted.

Farmers in the south and Midwest were badly hit by the Dustbowl. In 1930 there was drought. Strong winds and little rainfall turned the top soil to dust. The land became like a desert. Thousands of farmers were ruined. Many left their farms to try to find work elsewhere.

A young mother and her child, migrants from Oklahoma to California due to the effects of the Dustbowl, 1937

SOURCE E

An American journalist writing in 1932

In the state of Washington I was told that forest fires were caused by bankrupt farmers trying to earn a few dollars as fire-fighters. In Oregon I saw apples rotting in orchards. I saw sheep farmers feeding mutton to the buzzards.

The reaction of Hoover

SOURCE F

Hoover speaking to the American people in 1928

One of the oldest hopes has been the abolition of poverty. We Americans are nearer the final triumph over poverty than ever before.

Hoover was unsuccessful in dealing with the effects of the Crash. As a Republican, he believed that governments should stay out of business matters and should not interfere with people's lives. He believed in 'rugged individualism', the idea that people should work hard for themselves and not expect the government to help them. He thought that the American economy was basically strong and would soon recover from the Depression on its own.

Because of this attitude it was some time before Hoover took action to combat the Depression and its effects. Eventually he realised he had to do something. He pleaded with employers to keep their nerve, and not to sack workers or cut their pay.

1930 Hawley–Smoot Tariff This placed even higher taxes on imports. Naturally enough other nations retaliated by doing the same, which made it even harder for the USA to export its surplus production. In the same year he cut taxes by $130 million to try to give people more money to spend.

1931 Money was given to help build river dams such as the Hoover Dam. This was an attempt to create jobs. The government provided over $4000 million for major building projects.

1932 The Reconstruction Finance Commission was set up to give loans to businesses which were in trouble. It provided loans totalling $1500 million.

The Emergency Relief and Reconstruction Act gave over $300 million to the states to help the unemployed.

The Federal Farm Board purchased surplus crops in an attempt to hold up prices.

Despite these measures millions of Americans blamed Hoover for the Depression and all the problems that came with it. 'In Hoover we trusted, now we are busted.' His image was of being heartless and uncaring. This was unfair but he was the wrong man for the task of bringing about recovery.

Focus on

Hoover and the Depression

During the depression, Hoover's name took on a number of new meanings:

Hoovervilles	were shanty towns built on the outskirts of towns where the homeless sheltered.
Hoover Stew	was the thin soup distributed at emergency kitchens.
Hoover Blankets	were old newspapers used for warmth.
Hoover Apples	was the fruit sold by the unemployed on the streets.
Hoover Leather	was the cardboard with which people patched their shoe soles.

Help and protest

The homeless needed help. Some towns and cities decided to run their own public relief programmes which organised temporary homes, food, clothes and even jobs for the unemployed. Private charities were also set up. In some cases wealthy individuals gave help. These charities set up soup kitchens, bread kitchens or cheap food centres to feed the hungry.

By 1932, however, money to help the poor was running out. In June the city of Philadelphia had to cut off all relief funds to 50,000 families. Protests began to increase.

In the state of Iowa farmers organised a strike to try to create food shortages and so drive up prices. They attacked trucks being sent to market and banded together to resist officials carrying out evictions.

A crisis point was reached in the summer of 1932. Under an act passed in 1924 ex-First World War servicemen were promised a bonus payment of $500 but this was not payable until 1945. 25,000 such destitute veterans marched on Washington DC to demonstrate for the payment of the 'bonus' in 1932. In May they gathered in camps round the city. Hoover saw these as a revolutionary threat and refused to meet them.

Congress also voted against paying the bonus and the 'Bonus Army' decided to stay in Washington and continue their protest. They even set up a 'Hooverville' opposite the White House. Eventually Hoover decided that the veterans would have to be evicted. He called in the army who used tanks and tear gas and burnt the tents and shelters. Two veterans were killed and nearly a thousand others were injured. The Bonus Army had been defeated but Hoover became even more unpopular.

SOURCE G

Police and the Bonus Army clashing in Washington in 1932

An eyewitness account of the attack on the Bonus Marchers

The troops came with their gas bombs and their bayonets. They fired the shacks on the edge of the camp. Tanks and soldiers guarded the bridge back into the city so that no refugees could get into Washington. They might disturb the sleep of a few of the Government officials. The jeers and cries of the evicted men and women rose over the crackling of the flames. The flames were mirrored in the drawn bayonets of the infantry as they advanced through the camp. There is no way of knowing whether a few homeless men perished or not.

Hoover tried to explain away his action by claiming that most of the marchers were Communists and criminals and that more than half of them had never been in the armed forces. Between 65 and 70% had served overseas.

Activity

Did Hoover do enough to ease the Depression and help the unemployed?

Copy the chart below and complete the two columns.

Evidence for Hoover	Evidence against Hoover

What is your conclusion?

Questions

1   How differently has the Depression affected those people mentioned in Sources **A** and **C**?
2   How useful is Source **C** to an historian studying the effects of the Depression?
3   Describe the effects of the Depression on the unemployed
4   Why did Hoover do little at first to help the unemployed?
5   What do Sources **D** and **E** reveal about the effects of the Depression on farming?
6   What were:
    a   Hoovervilles?
    b   the Bonus Army?
    c   the Dustbowl?
7   Is Source **H** biased for or against the Bonus Army? Does the eyewitness give a reliable view of the eviction of the veterans?

In 1932 Roosevelt became President of the USA. The new President offered a different approach, called the New Deal, to solve the problems caused by the Depression.

Profile on

Franklin Delano Roosevelt, 1882–1945

Franklin D. Roosevelt was from a wealthy background and did not do particularly well at school or at Harvard University. On leaving university he worked for a law firm but soon became interested in politics. He had the right personality, being friendly, open and optimistic. In 1910 he was elected state senator in New York and within ten years he ran as the Democrats' vice-presidential candidate. He was not successful as the Republican, Harding, was elected President. Then, in 1921, Roosevelt caught polio, which left his legs paralysed. He was never again able to walk without help. He refused to allow his illness to force him out of politics. In 1928 he successfully stood for governor of New York state. As governor he did much to help the unemployed in his state using public money to create employment.

Presidential election

The result was 16 million votes for Hoover and 23 million for Roosevelt. Roosevelt won 42 of the 48 states of the USA. The scale of his victory surprised many Americans. It was the biggest victory in a Presidential election that anyone had known. Why did Roosevelt win?

HOOVER'S WEAKNESSES

- Hoover had taken office shortly before the Crash. Many Americans blamed him for it.

- Others blamed him for not doing enough to deal with the Depression.

- Many feared the country was descending into violence and disliked Hoover's treatment of the Bonus Army.

- In the election campaign all Hoover offered was that the USA had 'turned the corner' back towards prosperity.

- Even in the depths of the Depression Hoover did not regard the capitalist system as his responsibility. So a vote for Hoover would be a vote for doing nothing.

- When Hoover went out campaigning he received a hostile reception. Demonstrators pelted his train with eggs and tomatoes and carried placards saying 'Hang Hoover'.

ROOSEVELT'S STRENGTHS

- He was seen as a fighter, having battled successfully against polio.

- As governor of New York state he had tried to help ordinary people with old age pensions and unemployment relief.

- He believed the power of the government should be used to create a fairer society.

- He promised 'a new deal for the American people'. He outlined policies which would provide jobs and relief for the poor and the unemployed, action to help industry and agriculture and resolve the banking crisis.

- Roosevelt's words gave many Americans hope. Even the middle classes who were still in work saw him as the only hope to save the USA from revolution.

SOURCE A

Roosevelt speaking during the 1932 campaign

I pledge you, I pledge myself, to a New Deal for the American people. This is more than a political campaign. It is a call to arms. Give me your help, not to win votes alone, but to win in this crusade to restore America. I am waging war against Destruction, Delay, Deceit and Despair.

Under the American Constitution, Roosevelt had to wait four months before he could take over from Hoover. During this time, November 1932 to taking office in March 1933, the economic situation got worse:

- Unemployment rose to 15 million.

- Thousands of banks went out of business.

During this period Roosevelt worked out the New Deal in greater detail. It aimed for the 3 Rs:

- *Relief.* Help the unemployed.

- *Recovery.* Rebuild the economy.

- *Reform.* Create a fairer and more just society.

To carry out this programme the government would put money into the economy to provide new jobs. This would give people money to spend and the demand for goods would increase. This in turn would lead to more employment and restore the 'cycle of prosperity'.

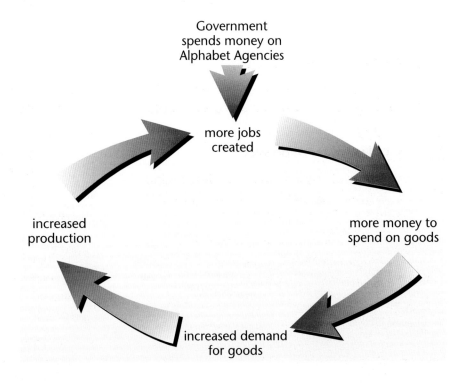

Government spends money on Alphabet Agencies

more jobs created

more money to spend on goods

increased demand for goods

increased production

SOURCE B

A cartoon showing President Roosevelt throwing out the policies of the previous government, March 1933

The Hundred Days

During Roosevelt's first one hundred days in office, March to June 1933, he laid the foundations for his promised New Deal. It required massive state involvement in the economy and the setting up of government-controlled agencies. Roosevelt was given the authority to do this when Congress granted him 'emergency powers' – the sort of powers he would have if the USA had been at war. Roosevelt set up a number of agencies that became known as the 'alphabet agencies' because the people found it easier to remember them by their initials than by their full names.

Roosevelt also realised the need to explain to the American people what he was doing. They needed to have trust and confidence in his measures and in the recovery of the economy. He used the radio to reach a large audience of millions of Americans and to talk directly to them. In his 'fireside chats', in which he sat in a chair by a fire in his office, he explained in simple terms why the USA had fallen into depression and what he proposed to do to end it. The broadcasts were very successful – especially the first one dealing with the banking crisis. Roosevelt was able to relax the American public by telling them about his pet dog. His wife, Eleanor, had her own national newspaper column called 'My Day'.

SOURCE C

Extract from Roosevelt's first radio broadcast, March 1933

The only thing we have to fear is fear itself. This nation asks for action, and action now. Our greatest primary task is to put people to work. This problem can be solved in part by the government creating jobs and treating the task as we would treat the emergency of war.

SOURCE D

Roosevelt's wife, Eleanor, wrote about him.

His voice lent itself remarkable to the radio. It was a natural gift, for in his whole life he never had a lesson in public speaking. His voice definitely helped him to make the people of the country feel that they were an intelligent and understanding part of every government task during his administration.

Activity

Draw two posters for the 1932 presidential election – one promoting Hoover and the other promoting Roosevelt and his policies.

Questions

1 Did Roosevelt win the presidential election of 1932 only because of Hoover's weaknesses? Explain your answer.
2 Is the cartoonist in Source **B** for or against Roosevelt? Give reasons for your answer.
3 What do Sources **C** and **D** tell you about his 'fireside chats'?
4 Source **D** is by Roosevelt's wife. Is it a reliable view of Roosevelt's qualities?

Helping the banks

If the banks stayed closed, the economy would cease to work. Very quickly nobody would have money to spend. If the banks opened, they might collapse. Roosevelt introduced a series of measures to deal with this problem:

Emergency Banking Act, March 1933
This was an attempt to solve the immediate crisis:

- It forced banks to stay closed for four days.

- Those whose finances were completely hopeless were ordered to close permanently.

- The rest were promised the backing of government grants so that the public could regain confidence in them.

- Roosevelt broadcast to the nation, appealing for the panic to end and for people with money to take it back to the banks. It worked, and the banks were saved.

The Securities Act
Roosevelt also wanted to reform the harmful practices that had got the USA into the trouble it now faced. He was determined to bring Wall Street under control in order to prevent another crash. The Securities Act forced companies issuing new shares to provide full information about the company to the public. Directors of companies that failed to do so would be prosecuted.

The Securities and Exchange Commission
This was set up in 1934 and given wide powers to control the activities of the stock market. In future investors could have greater confidence and they would not be swindled out of their money.

Helping agriculture

Agriculture's most serious problem was overproduction. While this continued, prices would remain low, and farmers would be unable to make a decent living. Roosevelt's solution was to pay farmers for not producing.

Agricultural Adjustment Act (AAA)
This legislation:

- Gave the government the power to influence prices by destroying surplus produce.

- Gave farmers compensation for lost produce.

- Helped farmers who were having difficulty in meeting their mortgage payments.

- Reached agreement with farmers on sensible amounts to be produced in future years.

As a result of these measures farmers' income doubled in the period up to 1939. However, it failed to help farmworkers. Many of these were evicted as there was less work for them to do. The AAA had to close because of a ruling by the US Supreme Court (p. 501). Nevertheless, the government continued to find ways of helping farmers. The Resettlement Administration (RA) helped poor farmers by purchasing equipment for them and resettling some of the poorest on land purchased by the RA. It also gave grants to farmers for soil conservation schemes.

SOURCE A

From an interview in 1970 with C.R. Baldwin who had been Assistant to the Secretary of Agriculture in the New Deal

There was a problem with the price of cotton. Prices were down 4 cents a pound and the cost of producing was 20 cents. So the government set up a programme to plough up the cotton. A third of the crop was ploughed up. Cotton prices went up 10 cents, maybe 11.

Helping the unemployed

The key to the success of the New Deal was the creation of jobs to reduce the high level of unemployment which the USA experienced in the Depression. A number of agencies were set up to deal with the problem.

AGENCY	PURPOSE	ACTION
Civilian Conservation Corps (CCC)	To provide conservation work for unemployed young men.	Camps jointly organised by the US Army and US Forestry Service. 18–25-year-old men given six months' work in return for food, shelter, and pocket money.
Federal Emergency Relief Administration (FERA)	To give money to the states to help unemployed and homeless people.	The government gave each state one dollar for every three the state spent on the relief of poverty.
Civil Works Administration (CWA), 1933–34	To provide work for unemployed people.	Unemployed people were found work and paid wages for doing it.
Public Works Administration (PWA)	To organise long-term schemes that would be of lasting value to Americans, such as building roads and bridges.	It set up a number of public works schemes.

A works programme in New York

SUCCESSES

300,000 people joined in 1933. By 1941 2.5 million had taken part. The scheme was popular with those that took part and many found work afterwards. Employers respected the programme. Millions of trees were planted; reservoirs, forest roads, fire look-outs and canals built.

Gave help to people in desperate need. $500 million spent on providing soup kitchens and clothing, and setting up employment schemes.

About two million people a year were given work. Schools, roads and airports were built. Thousands of writers, actors and artists were employed on creative projects. Millions of people earned a small wage rather than nothing. They became purchasers again which helped towards economic recovery.

Over the next few years PWA workers constructed many of the USA's public buildings, including schools, hospitals, city halls and court houses. It brought improvements in sewage and drainage systems.

FAILURES/CRITICISMS

Pay was low and it was described by some as forced labour.

The government was not keen on handouts. They wanted to concentrate on providing paid work.

Many people were put to work on projects of little value. A lot of government (taxpayers') money went into the scheme. It only lasted until the end of the winter of 1933–34.

Generally the jobs created were for skilled workers rather than for the millions who lacked a skill or trade.

SOURCE C

Description of men at work on a Civilian Conservation Corps project. From Arthur Schlesinger, *The Coming of the New Deal*, 1939

They planted trees, made reservoirs and fish ponds, cleared beaches and camping grounds and in many ways protected and improved parks, forests and recreational areas. Their muscles hardened, their bodies filled out, their self-respect returned. They learned trades; more important they learned about America, and they learned about other Americans.

Focus on

The Tennessee Valley Authority (TVA)

The TVA aimed to bring help to the Tennessee Valley which was a very depressed region. Agriculture in the area was badly hit by floods and the soil erosion it caused. Half of the population of the area was dependent on government relief for survival. In 1932 barely 2% of farms in the valley had electricity. The TVA was set up to improve the area by encouraging industry and helping agriculture. Trees were planted and forests created to improve the soil. Twenty-one dams were built to control the river and prevent flooding. Power stations were built at the dams to provide cheap electricity for homes and industry. The dams also created lakes and these were used for water transport which linked into the major river systems of the USA. The cheap source of power and good transport facilities attracted industries to the area. As a result the Tennessee Valley recovered and became a prosperous area.

Helping industry

Roosevelt tried to help both sides of industry – employers and workers – through the National Recovery Administration (NRA). It tried to create a partnership between the government and industry that would do away with employment evils like child labour, long hours and low pay.

- The idea was that each industry would agree an employment code with the government.

- The code would guarantee workers fair wages and conditions in return for fair prices.

- Those employers that agreed a code were allowed to display the NRA logo of a blue eagle.

- The government rewarded those firms by favouring them when contracts were awarded.

Workers were given the right to collective bargaining for wages. This gave an enormous boost to trade unions. The unions could now organise in industries where previously they had been excluded.

SOURCE D

The TVA Water Control System

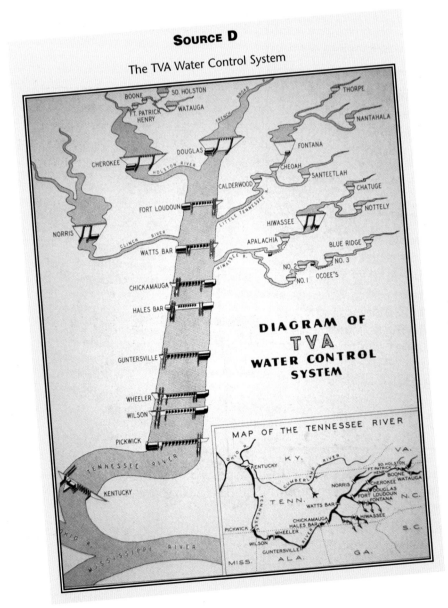

DIAGRAM OF TVA WATER CONTROL SYSTEM

Activities

1 Pick any one of the New Deal Measures. Put together a 'fireside chat' to be given by Roosevelt explaining the measure and what it is hoped it will achieve.

2 Roosevelt's aims for the New Deal were 'Relief, Recovery and Reform'. Draw three columns – headed Relief, Recovery and Reform.

   In the appropriate column, list the measures Roosevelt introduced to achieve these aims.

Other measures of the New Deal

The New Deal introduced a number of measures which tried to help the American people in other ways.

The *Home Owners Loan Corporation (HOLC)* helped people who were having difficulty with their mortgage payments. The government, through the Corporation, lent money to people at low interest rates to prevent them from losing their homes.

The *Social Security Act* was introduced in 1935. It set up a national system of state pensions for people over 65, for widows and for the disabled. It also provided for an unemployment insurance scheme to be run by each state with financial support.

Questions

1   What did the following initials stand for – AAA, FERA, CWA, PWA, CCC and NRA?
2   What did Roosevelt do to help banking and farming?
3   What does Source **A** tell you about the New Deal and farming?
4   How reliable is it as a view of the AAA?
5   Is the writer of Source **C** for or against the New Deal? Give reasons for your answer.

OPPOSITION TO THE NEW DEAL

Roosevelt's enormous popularity earned him victory in the 1936 presidential election. The Republican candidate, Alf Landon, suffered an even heavier defeat than Hoover. Only two states out of the 48 voted against Roosevelt. It seemed as if he had massive support for carrying on the New Deal. Despite this, there was significant opposition to the New Deal.

SOURCE A

The *New York Times*, November 1936

ROOSEVELT SWEEPS THE NATION

POLL SETS RECORD

Americans yesterday gave Franklin Delano Roosevelt the most overwhelming vote of approval in the history of the nation. The President was the choice of an overwhelming majority of the voters in all parts of the country.

SOURCE B

Republican view of the New Deal, *New York Times*, June 1936

The New Deal administration has been guilty of frightful waste and extravagance. It has created a vast number of new offices and sent out swarms of inspectors to harass our people. It has destroyed the morale of many of our people and made them dependent upon the government.

Doing too much

Some critics argued that he was doing too much to help the poor and unemployed. These included:

Republicans They continued to believe in 'rugged individualism' – in individuals helping themselves rather than being helped by the state. The Republicans argued that the New Deal was making people too dependent on the state. They felt that Roosevelt was behaving like a dictator, forcing Americans to do what he wanted. Republicans also objected to the huge cost of the New Deal and felt that people's money was being wasted on worthless jobs.

Businessmen They did not like government interference in their affairs. Many objected to the support for trade unions and the attempts to increase wages. This was the government interfering in business, which was not its job.

States' rights campaigners They argued that some of the Federal (central) Government's New Deal laws clashed with the right of individual states to make their own laws. They objected to schemes, like the TVA, which forced states to co-operate.

Fear of socialism The New Deal was clearly sympathetic in its aims towards the poor, the unemployed and the working class. Roosevelt's opponents believed he was leading the USA along the road to socialism.

SOURCE C

A cartoon published by opponents of the New Deal. It shows Roosevelt using more and more money to 'prime' the New Deal 'pump'.

Not doing enough

Roosevelt was also criticised for not doing enough to help the poor and unemployed. These critics claimed that the effect of the New Deal was not to change American society, but to enable Capitalism to survive.

Father Coughlin Coughlin was known as the 'radio priest'. He broadcast from Detroit and had an enormous national audience. He insisted that the New Deal was not doing enough to help those people whose lives had been shattered by the effects of the Depression. He set up the National Union for Social Justice. At its peak, the National Union had over seven million members.

Dr Francis Townsend He also believed the New Deal did not go far enough and was the author of the 'Townsend Plan'. This was a scheme by which all those over 60 would receive a monthly pension of $200 in return for a promise to retire from work and to spend all the pension each month. 'Townsend Clubs' were organised to campaign for the plan.

Huey Long Long was a serious political opponent to Roosevelt. Until his death in 1935, he was governor of Louisiana. He argued that Roosevelt was too cautious and not doing enough to help those in need. He campaigned for much more extreme reforms, including:

- The 'Share Our Wealth' movement. This would confiscate all fortunes over $3 million and share out the money so that every American family would have between $4,000 and $5,000 and be able to buy a home, car and radio.

- The government would buy up all farming surpluses and sell them as cheap food.

- The state would provide a range of benefits such as free education and old age pensions.

By 1934 Long was preparing himself to be a rival to Roosevelt for the presidency. He was assassinated in 1935 and support for his movement died away.

The Supreme Court

The Supreme Court has the responsibility for deciding if any measure passed by the President and Congress goes against the American Constitution. It can block any such measure and declare it illegal.

It was clear from the start that Roosevelt would have problems with the Supreme Court. Most of the nine judges were Republican and automatically against the policies of the New Deal. In 1935 the Supreme Court found that the National Industrial Recovery Act was against the constitution, so it had to be withdrawn. In the following year the AAA was declared unconstitutional because the Court declared that it was the responsibility of each state, not the central government, to help agriculture. All the help the AAA had given to farmers stopped.

After his re-election in 1936, Roosevelt was determined to change the Supreme Court so that it could no longer block his plans. He wanted to increase the number of judges from nine to fifteen and he, the president, would obviously choose six judges who agreed with the New Deal. This was a mistake because it upset many Americans who disliked Roosevelt's scheme to 'pack' the Court. This seemed to go against the popular belief that politicians should not interfere with the work of the judges. It made him seem like a dictator. It was obvious that Congress would never approve. He was forced to back down and withdraw the plan.

SOURCE D

From a radio broadcast by President Roosevelt, 1937

By bringing into the Supreme Court a steady stream of new and younger blood, I hope to make justice speedier and less costly. Also I intend to bring in younger men who have had personal experience and contact with today's circumstances and know how average men have to live and work.

SOURCE E

The views of the Senate Committee which rejected Roosevelt's plans for the Supreme Court

Roosevelt's proposals would not banish older judges from the courts. They would not reduce expense nor speed decisions. They would place the courts under the control of the President and Congress and would destroy the independence of the courts.

Activity

Write a radio broadcast criticising the New Deal from either:

- those who believed he was doing too much.

- those who believed he was not doing enough.

In one way, however, his scheme did work. It forced the nine judges to accept most of the laws of the New Deal to avoid their number being increased.

Questions

1   Why did the following oppose the New Deal:
    a   Republicans?
    b   businessmen?
    c   Huey Long?
    d   the Supreme Court?
2   What point is the cartoonist trying to make in Source **C**?
3   Is Source **C** a reliable view of the New Deal?
4   What differences are there between Sources **D** and **E** in their views of plans to increase the number of judges in the Supreme Court?
5   Why do you think their views are so different?

HOW SUCCESSFUL WAS THE NEW DEAL?

The New Deal achieved much and helped millions of Americans who had suffered in the years of depression, but there were areas where it was less successful.

SUCCESSES

Unemployment The New Deal reduced unemployment from the very high level of 1933, 12.8 million, to 7.7 million in 1937. Millions of jobs were created.

Welfare Millions of poor people received relief, often food, shelter and clothing. Emergency relief certainly stopped people from starving. Government social security and welfare schemes helped many ordinary people and continued in the future.

Industry Construction work on dams and roads helped the future development of industry.

Workers' rights Workers' rights and conditions were improved. The National Recovery Administration Codes did much to regulate conditions in many industries. When the Supreme Court made this law illegal it was replaced by the Wagner Act. This Act established workers' rights to join unions and to bargain collectively for wages. During the 1930s, union membership increased steadily. During 1937 there were many strikes in the auto and steel industries. Workers used 'sit-down strikes' – occupying their factories to make sure the machinery could not be kept running. Without the backing of the New Deal laws, these workers would have almost certainly been defeated by the employers. In 1937 there were about 4700 strikes with about 80% settled in favour of the workers.

Farmers The New Deal did much to improve the lives of American farmers, especially those with large farms. By the mid-1930s farmers' incomes were rising.

Other effects The New Deal did much to raise the morale and confidence of many Americans. Many began to believe in themselves again. Few turned to extreme Communist or Fascist groups. Roosevelt had increased the role of the Federal (central) government in America. It became much more involved in people's lives. Most Americans now accepted that the Federal government had a role to play in making sure the weaker sections of society – the unemployed, the homeless, the old and the poor – were looked after. Roosevelt's own background of disability meant that he could sympathise with the disadvantaged in American Society. He was determined to help the unemployed, the disabled and the elderly in his policies.

FAILURES

Unemployment This was reduced but not ended. The various schemes had limited impact. Some said they did not provide 'real' jobs and the moment government ceased to pay, the jobs would disappear. Were they just making work for the sake of it? Unemployment was still 9 million in 1936 and rose to over 10 million two years later.

Workers' rights American employers deeply resented this aspect of the New Deal and many large companies hired thugs to beat up union leaders and intimidate workers who were on strike. During a strike by steelworkers in Chicago in 1937, ten demonstrators were shot dead by the police and ninety were wounded.

Farmers Small farmers, farm labourers and sharecroppers saw little benefit from the New Deal. There was still much poverty in rural America, especially in the south. In 1934–5 a long-term drought hit the prairie states, and in many areas the soil was turning to dust. With no rain, previously fertile areas became deserts. These were the 'dustbowl' areas of Kansas, Texas, Oklahoma and Colorado. Many farmers left to seek work in California.

The poor The New Deal did not go far enough in dealing with poverty, or in helping the poorest people in American society. The Social Security Act excluded 20% of the workforce, including five million desperate farmworkers and domestics. Also there was no provision for state-paid medical care. Little was done to share out the country's wealth. In 1941 the richest 20% were earning 49% of the national income. The poorest 20% were earning 4%.

The slump of 1937–8 The limitations of the New Deal were shown in 1937. The economy seemed to be improving and Roosevelt took the opportunity to cut the amount spent on New Deal programmes. The economy went back into depression. Industrial production fell by one-third and unemployment rose by nearly 3 million.

Black Americans The programme did little to improve the position of black Americans. Although around 30% of all black people were dependent on emergency relief for survival, no New Deal laws attempted to assist blacks and improve their civil rights. Roosevelt felt dependent on the support of Democrats from the south, who were determined to deny full rights to blacks.

The Second World War Many argue that it was the rearmament programme and American entry into the Second World War in 1941 that eventually revived the economy and reduced unemployment. Even before American entry, the USA sold goods and food produce to Britain and France which increased the demand for American manufactured goods and food produce. The level of unemployment fell.

Activity

Draw the table and look at the following evidence about the New Deal. Decide which evidence is for, or against the New Deal or neither. Give reasons for your answer.

Views of the New Deal		
Supports	Neither	Against

For example, Source **A** is against the New Deal because it shows that Roosevelt did very little for black Americans.

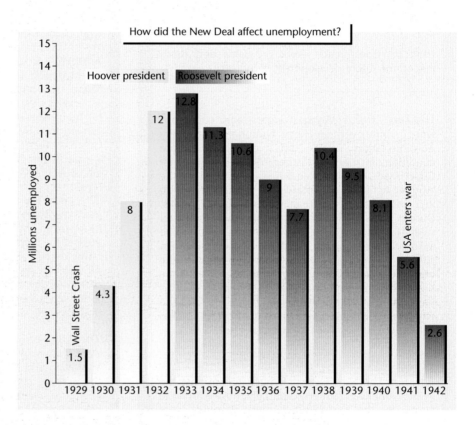

How did the New Deal affect unemployment?

Hoover president   Roosevelt president

SOURCE A

A modern historian

Roosevelt did not attempt to alter the two most obvious methods of keeping down the black citizens of the south: segregation and the lack of the vote. Black Americans could list other grievances. They called the NRA the 'Negro Run Around' because it forced the shutdown of many small black-run businesses and the lay off of black employees. The AAA proved to be an economic disaster for nearly a million black poor farmers.

SOURCE B

Robin Langton, who was a black child during the Depression years. He was interviewed in 1970.

Roosevelt caught the mood of the black community. You did not look on him as being white, black, blue or green. He was President Roosevelt. The WPA and other projects introduced black people to handicrafts and trades, it gave Negroes a chance to have an office to work out with a typewriter. It made us feel there was something we could do.

WORLD'S HIGHEST STANDARD OF LIVING

There's no way like the American Way

Price of wheat per bushel in dollars

1933: 0.74	1934: 0.85	1935: 0.83
1936: 1.03	1937: 0.96	1938: 0.56
1939: 0.69	1940: 0.68	1941: 0.94

SOURCE D

The views of an historian, William Leuchtenburg, writing in 1963

The New Deal left many problems unsolved and created some new ones. As late as 1941 the unemployed still numbered six million and not until the war years of 1943 did the army of jobless finally disappear.

SOURCE F

One of several thousand letters received by Roosevelt every day during the New Deal

Dear Mr President,

This is just to tell you that everything is all right now. The man you sent went down to the bank with us and the mortgage can go on. I wrote about losing the furniture too. Well your man got that back for us. I never heard of a President like you.

A letter sent to
Roosevelt's
wife, Eleanor

I suppose from your point of view the work relief, old age pensions, slum clearance and all the rest seem like a perfect remedy for all the ills of this country but I would like you to see the results, as the other half see them. We have always had a shiftless, never-do-well class of people whose only aim is to live without work. There has never been any need for those able to work in this area being on relief. Many are now eating the bread of charity and living better than ever before. I have had taxpayers tell me that their children came home from school and asked why they couldn't have nice lunches like the children on relief.

SOURCE H

A modern historian

The most damning criticism of Roosevelt's policy was that it failed to cure the depression. Despite some $20 billion poured out in spending and lending, there were still millions of dispirited men unemployed.

SOURCE I

Another modern historian

If the New Deal is judged by economic success alone, then the verdict must be a mixed one. But, generally speaking, the economy had by 1937 recovered to the level reached before the Depression started in 1929. The New Deal also established a far more important role for the Federal government in a whole range of areas. Roosevelt deliberately extended the powers of central government in order to achieve a fairer society and offer its citizens greater security.

Questions

1 How useful are the letters, Sources **F** and **G**, as evidence to an historian of the effects of the New Deal?

2 'Source **H** was written by an historian and must be a reliable view of the New Deal.' Do you agree with this view? Explain your answer.

3 Using the evidence from this section, do you think the New Deal was a success or failure?

Summary and revision

THE GROWTH OF ISOLATION, 1919–22

In this section, you need to understand:

- Reasons for the growth of isolationism.

- Reactions to the League of Nations.

- Tariffs against foreign goods.

- Restricting immigration and the various immigration laws.

- The Sacco and Vanzetti case.

Revision questions

1   How did the following encourage isolationism:
    a the First World War? **b** Warren Harding?
2   What were tariffs and why were they introduced?
3   Explain the Ford–McCumber Tariff.
4   Give three reasons why the USA decided to limit immigration.
5   Describe two measures introduced to achieve this.
6   What was the Sacco and Vanzetti case?

THE BOOM OF THE 1920s

You will need to understand:

- The impact of the First World War on American industry.

- The government policy of laissez-faire.

- Other reasons for the boom, including advertising, mass production, new technology, hire purchase, shares and wage rises.

- The importance of the motor industry.

Revision questions

1   Why was the First World War a long-term cause of the boom?
2   What was laissez-faire and how did it help industry?
3   Explain three other causes of the boom.
4   Why was the car industry so important in the 1920s?

THE BOOM AND THE AMERICAN LIFESTYLE

This section includes:

- Changes in the role of women – the vote, work and behaviour.

- The growth of the leisure industry, including the radio, music and dancing.

- The importance of the cinema and Hollywood stars.

- The growth and impact of motoring.

- Sport, especially baseball and boxing.

Revision questions

1   What changes took place for women in work and behaviour? Were these changes popular with all Americans?
2   Describe the impact of the radio, cinema and jazz music.
3   What changes were brought about by the growth in car ownership?
4   Why did sport flourish?

THE 'OTHER' AMERICA

In this section, you will need to understand:

- Reasons for the decline of old industries, such as coal and textiles.

- Problems in agriculture.

- The plight of black Americans – discrimination in education, the vote and jobs.

- The plight of the Native Americans.

- The Ku Klux Klan – its aims and activities and why it lost support.

- Reasons for the introduction of Prohibition.

- Measures used to try to stop alcohol.

- Speakeasies, bootleggers and the role of gangsters such as Al Capone.

- Why Prohibition failed.

Revision questions

1   Why did the old industries not share in the boom?
2   What problems were there in agriculture?
3   Why were blacks and Native Americans second-class citizens in the 1920s?
4   Explain the aims and activities of the Ku Klux Klan.
5   Why did support for the Klan fall away?
6   Explain two important reasons for Prohibition.
7   What were speakeasies and bootleggers?
8   What part did gangsters play in Prohibition?
9   Why did Prohibition not work?

THE USA IN DEPRESSION, 1929–33

This section includes:

- Reasons for the Depression, including overproduction, tariff policy and speculators.

- The Wall Street Crash – why it happened and its impact on the American economy.

- The effects of the Depression on banks, industry and farming.

- Unemployment, poverty, homelessness and shanty towns.

- The reaction of Hoover – rugged individualism.

- The Bonus Army and the reaction of Hoover.

- Why Hoover became unpopular.

Revision questions

1 What part did the following play in causing the Depression:
   a overproduction? **b** tariff policy? **c** speculators?
2 Why did the stock market collapse in 1929? What were the immediate effects?
3 How were the following affected by the Depression:
   a industry? **b** banks? **c** the unemployed?
4 What were shanty towns?
5 Hoover believed in 'rugged individualism'. What did this mean? What policies did he follow to deal with the Depression?
6 Explain the 'Bonus Army' and Hoover's reaction to it.

ROOSEVELT AND THE NEW DEAL

In this section, you will need to understand:

- Reasons for Roosevelt's election in 1932.

- The aims of the New Deal, the 'Hundred Days' and the 'Alphabet Agencies'.

- Measures to deal with the banks, unemployment, poverty, farming, industry and unions.

- Opposition to the New Deal from Republicans, the Supreme Court and others.

- Roosevelt's policies towards the Supreme Court and their effects.

- The successes and failures of the New Deal.

Revision questions

1 Why did Roosevelt win the presidential election of 1932?
2 What was achieved in the 'Hundred Days'?
3 What were the 'Alphabet Agencies'?
4 Explain the measures taken to help the banks.
5 What were the main agencies set up to help the unemployed? What did they achieve?
6 What was the AAA?
7 Why did union membership increase in the 1930s?
8 **a** Most Republicans and many businessmen opposed the New Deal. Why?
   b Why did the following oppose it:
       i   Father Coughlin?
       ii Huey Long?
9 In what ways did the Supreme Court hinder the New Deal?
10 How did Roosevelt intend to change the Supreme Court? Why did he fail?
11 Explain three important successes and three failures or criticisms of the New Deal.

11
Britain 1905–51

UNDERSTANDING BRITISH HISTORY 1905–51

The following definitions and explanations should help you to understand this chapter.

Affluent	Wealthy. Good standard of living.
Aristocrat	Member of a privileged class usually of high noble birth such as a duke or earl.
Austerity	Reducing luxuries and consumer goods.
Bill	A proposed change in the law which has to be approved by both Houses of Parliament and the monarch.
Borstal	Youth custody centre for juvenile offenders.
Budget	Annual statement of government spending needs and taxes.
Commission	A body of people set up by the government.
Edwardian	Refers to the period 1901–10 when Edward VII was king.
Lock out	When an employer refuses to let the workers into the workplace until they accept his/her conditions.
Militant	A person prepared to use extreme methods to get noticed.
Political levy	Subscriptions raised from trade union members which went to the Labour Party.
Reform	A change, usually for the better.
Socialism	The idea that the government should take more control of the economy and ensure a fairer share out of the country's wealth to reduce the gap between rich and poor.
Subsidy	Help, usually in the form of money, from the government to industry.
Suffrage	The right to vote.
Sweated trades	Industries in which employees worked long hours often for little pay such as tailoring.
Syndicalism	Movement which came from France and the USA which believed in direct action.
Workhouse	A building to house the poor of an area.

Britain 1905–51

During this period there were major changes in British society, including the development of the welfare state and votes for women. There were, however, also major problems such as the General Strike of 1926 and the Depression of the 1930s.

BRITAIN IN 1905

Britain was at the height of its power. It had the largest empire in the world, the strongest navy and was the leading industrial nation.

Politics

Queen Victoria died in 1901 and was succeeded by Edward VII. His reign is often known as the Edwardian period. The Liberals had just taken power from their rivals, the Conservatives, with Henry Campbell-Bannerman as Prime Minister. Indeed in the General Election of the following year, 1906, the Liberals won a landslide victory. The Labour Party, set up in 1900, won only a handful of seats and was still a minor party.

Parliament and government, however, did not represent the majority of the population. Indeed only one adult in three had a vote.

- There was still a property qualification before an adult male could qualify for the vote. Many working class men did not have this qualification.

- All women were denied the vote and were still seen as second-class citizens.

- The rich and wealthy still dominated both houses of Parliament.

The economy

Britain led the world in industry and trade.

- British shipyards produced over half the world's tonnage in shipping.

- Britain's manufacturers were responsible for about one-third of the world's trade.

- Britain's main exports were textiles, coal, machinery, ships and railway engines.

British society

There were great differences between rich and poor in Edwardian society.

The old currency

There was a different currency in 1905 based on pounds, shillings and pence. There were:

20 shillings (s) in a £.
A shilling is 5p today.

12 pennies (d) in a shilling.
1p today is worth about 2.5 old pennies.

There were also halfpennies.

What was money worth in 1905?

You could buy a lot more with far less money.

	1905	Today
A loaf of bread	0.5p	50p
A half pound of butter	1p	90p

BUT

People were paid a lot less

Doctor	£600 a year	£50,000 a year (approx)
Farmworker	£30 a year	£10,000 a year (approx)

A good way of working out the value of money is to multiply the amount in 1905 by 100 to get the present-day equivalent.

Rich

About 2% of all British people earned more than £700 a year. Some were very rich indeed. Many of the upper classes and wealthy businessmen earned more than £5000 a year. The Duke of Portland, for example, had an income of several million pounds a year from the coal mines on his land. Some aristocratic families had over one hundred servants.

Middle class

Still growing in number due to British industry and trade. Industrialists, factory and coal mine owners, shopkeepers, teachers and office managers probably made up about one-quarter of the population and earned at least £500 a year. They could afford at least one servant – a maid.

Working class

This varied from the skilled workers, such as engineers, who earned reasonable wages and lived in relative comfort to the unskilled town and countryside workers who worked long hours for poor pay and often did not have enough money to buy proper food, shelter and clothing. For example, a miner could earn £100 a year, a farmworker's annual salary was about £30 while a housemaid in a rich household earned £20 a year with food and lodging.

Picture of the Thames Embankment from *The Sphere* magazine, August 1905

Questions

1   How useful is Source **A** as evidence of the differences in British society at the beginning of the twentieth century?
2   Do you think *The Sphere* in Source **B** is on the side of the poor? Give reasons for your answer.

Activity
Do a balance sheet of Britain in 1905 using the table below.

Strengths	Weaknesses

The meaning and nature of the welfare state

This came to mean a state which looked after those people who were not able to look after themselves. The state or government provided essential services to ensure that nobody fell below a minimum standard of living. Welfare or security was offered 'from the cradle to the grave'.

During this period the Liberals brought in a series of reforms which laid the foundations of the welfare state.

Despite the country's great wealth, millions of people lived in conditions of desperate poverty. For every thousand babies born in the slums, 33 died before their first birthday. Only four babies in every thousand born to rich parents died before they were one year old.

Two surveys showed the extent of poverty and its causes:

1   In 1884 Charles Booth began an enquiry into the living conditions of people in London. In 1902, he published what he discovered in 17 books. Booth found that nearly 33% of all Londoners did not have enough money to live on because of low wages, unemployment, old age or ill health.

2   In 1899 Seebohm Rowntree, son of the famous chocolate manufacturer, carried out a similar survey of York and came up with much the same conclusion. He worked out that a family of five needed about £1 a week to live on. About 28% of British families had less than this. York was not an industrial city. How much worse must poverty be in centres of industry such as Manchester and Newcastle?

SOURCE A

David Lloyd George, a leading member of the Liberal government

Four spectres haunt the poor – Old Age, Accident, Sickness and Unemployment. We are going to get rid of them. We are going to drive hunger from the home.

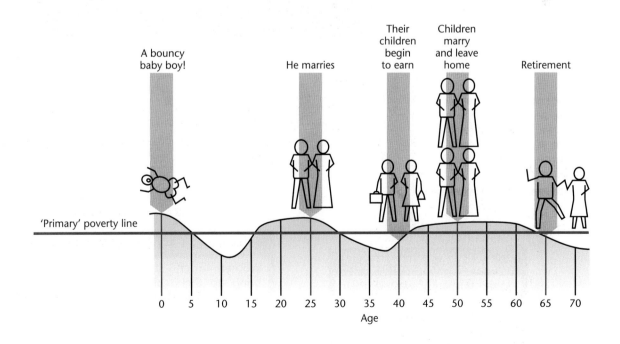

OLD AGE

There were no state pensions. Only skilled workers could afford to pay into private insurance pension schemes. The majority of the working class could not afford to save for old age. When couples were too old to work they often ended up in the local workhouse where they were usually separated.

UNEMPLOYMENT

This was especially serious in:

- seasonal occupations, such as building and farming.
- heavy industries, such as shipbuilding, which suffered from occasional depressions in world trade and a fall off in demand. Men were laid off.

There was a mini-depression in 1904 to 1905 with unemployment reaching over 650,000. Again there was no state unemployment benefit. Only the better off skilled workers could afford to pay into insurance schemes.

LOW WAGES

Many unskilled workers were not paid enough to look after their families. In the so-called 'sweated industries' such as tailoring, there were no trade unions and workers were at the mercy of employers who paid poor piece-rates – by how much the worker produced.

CAUSES OF POVERTY

ILLNESS OR ACCIDENT

Again only the better-off workers could afford sickness insurance schemes. There were no state payments. If the main earner was ill or suffered an accident at work he would lose his income and not get any compensation.

LARGE FAMILIES

Most working-class families had no understanding of birth control. This resulted in large families with even more mouths to feed. There were no maternity allowances, child benefit or family income support.

WASTED EARNINGS

Some husbands wasted their wages on gambling or drink and did not give enough to their wife to run the household.

ONE-PARENT FAMILIES

Women often struggled to bring up their children if the husband had died. There were no widow or one-parent benefits.

SOURCE B

Will Crooks, a Labour MP speaking in Parliament in July 1908

Here in a country rich beyond description there are people poverty-stricken beyond description. If it is necessary to have a strong army and navy to protect the wealth of the nation, do not let us forget that it is the veterans of industry who have created that wealth. Let us bring decency and comfort to our aged men and women.

In most cases poverty was not the fault of the working-class families. Many could survive when the male was working. Any interruption of work through illness, old age or unemployment would lead to poverty.

Liberal motives

It was the Liberals who decided to try to wipe out poverty:

- The reports of Rowntree and Booth had highlighted the extent of poverty.

- The Liberals feared that if they did not bring in change many of the poor would turn to socialism, revolution or vote for the newly formed Labour Party.

- Lloyd George was from a working-class background and understood the need for improvement.

- The Liberals feared that Britain was falling behind Germany who had introduced welfare reforms in the 1880s.

- Britain's military strength depended on a fit population. Two-thirds of recruits for the Boer War, fought between 1899 and 1902, were turned down for medical reasons.

The welfare of children

The Liberals believed it was very important for the children of the poor to be looked after properly.

Profile on
David Lloyd George

David Lloyd George was born in Manchester but brought up in north Wales by his uncle, Lloyd. He became a Liberal MP in the 1880s and made a name for himself during the Boer War, 1899–1902, when he was one of the few people brave enough to stand up in public and criticise the war. This made him very unpopular and he had to leave meetings in disguise to escape the mob. He began as President of the Board of Trade in the Liberal government of 1905 and carried out reforms to improve the position of merchant seamen. He also prevented a serious transport strike. In 1908 he was promoted to the important position of Chancellor of the Exchequer. Lloyd George hated privilege and wealth and was determined to use his position in government to improve the position of the poorer sections of society.

SOURCE C

The Times, October 1906

Let me give you my own experience in a county parish of a little over 2,000 inhabitants. Since 1 January, 1906, we have had 27 deaths. 12 of these have been children aged two years and under. Of the last seven burials, six have been children under eight months and there are more likely to die. The doctors know that the children are for the most part under nourished, but could not swear to this in a court of justice.

SOURCE D

Description by Margaret MacMillan of children in a Bradford school in 1883. She was a pioneer of nursery schools.

Anyone who studies carefully with a magnifying glass will easily detect the matted hair of the girls – although you will not see the vermin. You will see the sore eyes, the open mouths, symptoms of adenoids; the 'tallow candles' hanging from the nostrils of the little children who have probably never heard of handkerchiefs; the evidence of rickets. What you will not be able to see is how many of the children have been sewn into their clothing perhaps with pads of cotton wool underneath, for the whole of the winter months.

They brought in a series of reforms:

1906 School Meals Act

This told local authorities to pay for school meals for the poorest children, for those pupils 'unable, by lack of food, to take advantage of the education provided for them'. By 1914, over 150,000 children a year were eating free school meals.

1908 Children's Charter

This stopped children under 16 buying cigarettes and using pubs. Parents could be taken to court if they were cruel to their children or allowed them to go begging.

1907 School Medical Service

Most children of the poor never saw a doctor. The government told every local authority that it had to have a school medical service. The government paid for school clinics to be set up and run, where treatment was free. Regular health inspections in schools helped doctors treat skin and hair diseases, such as scabies and impetigo.

Infant and juvenile offenders

These were to be separated from adult offenders with the emphasis on trying to reform rather than punish. Juvenile courts were set up and child offenders were sent to Borstal institutions instead of prison.

Old Age Pensions

In 1908 Old Age Pensions were included in the first Budget of Lloyd George, the new Chancellor of the Exchequer. The first pensions were claimed on 1 January 1909.

- Pensions were paid to all old people over the age of 70 who had less than twelve shillings (60p) income. This was over 60% of all people over 70.

- Pensions were paid on a sliding scale of between one (5p) and five shillings (25p) a week (about £5 to £25 a week in present day values), depending on the old person's income.

- The money paid to these pensions came from government funds.

Over 650,000 people applied for a pension in the first year and by the start of the First World War in 1914 there were almost a million pensioners. With the pension the fear of the workhouse almost disappeared. By 1912 the number of people over 70 years old in the workhouses had dropped by 5590.

However, there were some criticisms. The age restriction seemed too high. Not many lived until the age of 70 and 5 shillings was not enough to live on.

Labour Exchanges

To help the unemployed find work the President of the Board of Trade, Winston Churchill, pushed through the Labour Exchanges Act of 1909. The idea was to save unemployed people having to tramp from one factory to another in search of work. Labour Exchanges, nowadays known as Job Centres, would advertise job vacancies. By 1913 there were 430 Labour Exchanges throughout the country.

Health and unemployment insurance

In 1911 the Liberals introduced the National Insurance Act which provided insurance against unemployment and sickness.

Unemployment insurance This, at first, applied to under three million people in trades where workers were regularly laid off, such as the building industry.

- Workers, employers and the state each paid the equivalent of 1p each week into an insurance fund.

- In return workers could claim 7 shillings (35p) a week (about £35 a week in present-day money values) for up to 15 weeks provided they could work and had paid sufficient contributions into the fund.

This was the start of a scheme that was extended to another eight million in 1920. It was criticised because it only applied to three million while members of the Labour Party disliked the fact that often poorly paid workers had to make a weekly contribution.

Health insurance This was an insurance scheme against ill-health:

- It applied to all workers who earned less than £3 a week. This was the majority of the working classes.

- Workers paid 4d (nearly 2p) a week into the scheme, the employer 3d and the state 2d. This led to the slogan '9 pence for 4 pence'.

- In return a worker could claim 'free' medical treatment and could claim 10 shillings (50p or the equivalent of £50 in present-day values) a week for a maximum of 26 weeks if unable to work.

- After that a disability pension of 5 shillings could be awarded.

- A male worker's wife was given a special payment of 30 shillings (£1.50) after the birth of a baby.

The scheme was extended to women workers in 1920. It proved of real benefit to those workers who could not afford to go to the doctor. For many years afterwards, workers off sick said they 'were on the Lloyd George'.

It did bring bitter opposition from doctors who insisted that they would not be paid fairly for their work. The scheme did not apply to the self-employed, wives, farmworkers, domestic servants or women workers. Again 10 shillings a week did not seem enough.

A Liberal poster advertising National Health Insurance. Lloyd George is the 'doctor'.

SOURCE H

A cartoon making fun of the new National Insurance stamps. For each contribution you received a stamp as proof of payment. This was stuck into a book.

Importance of the welfare reforms

These laws introduced by the Liberal government were very important:

- The state was now helping those people – the old, the young, the sick – who could not help themselves.

- They provided the foundations for later improvements.

The Liberals, however, had not introduced a National Health Service.

Activities

1 You are a pensioner who gets his/her first pension in January 1909. You write a letter to Lloyd George praising the pension scheme and explaining how it has helped you.

2 Design a poster criticising one or more of the Liberal reforms.

Questions

1 Using Sources **B**, **C** and **D**, explain why change was needed to help the poor and their children.
2 Copy the following table and write in any criticisms of the Liberal reforms.

Liberal reforms	Criticisms
Child welfare	
OAPs	
Health Insurance	
Unemployment Insurance	

3 What do Sources **E** and **F** tell you about the importance of OAPs?
4 Do they provide reliable evidence?
5 How useful is Source **G** to an historian studying health insurance?
6 What message is the cartoonist trying to get across in Source **H**?

The People's Budget

The Liberal reforms cost money. This money had to be found by the government, on top of the money it needed for the routine running of the country. The problem was made worse because the government also needed money for the building of Dreadnoughts, so it could keep ahead of the German navy (p. 9). The Chancellor of the Exchequer, Lloyd George, reckoned that an extra £16 million would have to be raised by the Budget of 1909.

What did the Budget do?

To pay for the social reforms Lloyd George proposed to tax the rich:

- Income tax raised to 1s 2d (6p) in every pound for people with more than £2,000 a year.

- Income tax of 1s 4½d (7p) in the pound for those with more than £5,000 a year (over 50 times the income of an average worker).

- Death duties doubled. These were taxes on property and wealth handed on when someone died.

- A new tax on the profit gained from selling land.

- A licence fee on cars.

- Increased taxes on tobacco and alcohol.

He called this the 'People's Budget'. It was important because for the first time the government was using taxation to pay for social reforms or taxing the rich to help the poor. It was also important because it led to a clash between the House of Commons and the House of Lords.

SOURCE A

A rich man's opinion of the 'People's Budget'

PUNCH, OR THE LONDON CHARIVARI.—APRIL 28, 1909.

RICH FARE.

THE GIANT LLOYD-GORGIBUSTER: "FEE, FI, FO, FAT,
I SMELL THE BLOOD OF A PLUTOCRAT;
BE HE ALIVE OR BE HE DEAD,
I'LL GRIND HIS BONES TO MAKE MY BREAD."

BERNARD PARTRIDGE.

SOURCE B

Lloyd George speaking at Limehouse, East London, July 1909

We are raising money for the purpose of assisting in the provision for the sick and the widows and orphans. We are providing money to enable us to develop the resources of our land. We are raising money to wage war against poverty.

Questions

1   According to the information in this section, why did Lloyd George bring in these new and extra taxes?
2   What point is the cartoonist trying to make in Source **A**?

This crisis caused major problems for the Liberal government and eventually led to the reform of the Lords.

Why did the Lords need reforming?

Out of place

Many argued that the House of Lords was out of date and out of place in the twentieth century.

The House of Lords

Members of the House of Lords were called peers. They were not elected but there due to birthright – born into wealthy aristocratic families. The House of Lords was one of the two Houses of Parliament – the other being the elected House of Commons. It was there to take away some of the workload of the Commons as well as to keep a check on the elected House and any changes it wanted to bring in. It was known as the 'watchdog of the Constitution'.

Unrepresentative

Opponents of the Lords believed it only represented a small section of society – the rich. This was made worse by the fact that the members inherited their position and were not elected.

Selfish

The House of Lords did not act in its proper role, as a check on the Commons. Instead it used its position to stop any changes in the law which might threaten the wealthy. As long ago as 1832 the Lords had tried to prevent changes in voting and elections because they threatened their influence.

Controlled by the Conservatives

By 1905, the Conservatives had achieved a permanent majority of peers in the Lords. When there was a Conservative government the Lords worked well with the Conservative majority in the Commons and generally passed any measures introduced by the government. With a Liberal government, however, things were different. The Conservative peers often stopped Liberal measures. For example, between 1906 and 1908 they threw out major Liberal measures including Education, Licensing and Plural Voting Bills.

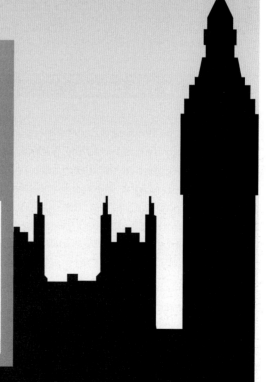

'Mr Balfour's Poodle'

Arthur Balfour, the Conservative leader, was very disappointed with the General Election of 1906 which gave the Liberals a massive majority in the House of Commons – 377 Liberal MPs to 157 Conservative MPs. He decided to use the Lords to stop any Liberal measures which threatened the Conservatives. Lloyd George was nicknamed the Lords 'Mr Balfour's Poodle'.

SOURCE A

Lloyd George in 1910

The real issue is whether the country is to be governed by the King and the Peers or by the King and the People. Should 500 men in the House of Lords be able to turn down the decisions made by people who work to make the wealth of this country? Who made 10,000 people owners of the soil, and the rest of us trespassers in the land of our birth?

Immediate causes of the crisis

By 1908 the Liberal Prime Minister, Campbell-Bannerman, was running out of patience with the peers. He did not believe that it was fair that a government which had been elected with such a majority in the Commons was being handicapped by the Conservative-controlled Lords. Campbell-Bannerman retired in 1908 and was replaced by Herbert Henry Asquith who was prepared to give the Lords one last chance. This came with the peers' reaction to the 'People's Budget'.

Many of the peers were rich and powerful landowners and were naturally against a budget which seemed aimed at the rich. Some believed that Lloyd George was deliberately provoking the House of Lords. In November the Budget, having already successfully passed through the Commons, was vetoed (voted against) by a majority of the peers.

Source B

The reactions of London newspapers to the Budget

MR. LLOYD GEORGE'S FIRST BUDGET AS REFLECTED ON SOME LONDON MORNING NEWSPAPER POSTERS

This infuriated Asquith because:

- The Lords had not rejected a budget for over 200 years.

- The Liberals could not rule the country without the taxes from the Budget.

EVENTS OF THE CRISIS

1910

January Asquith called a general election to see if the country supported the Budget. The election was described as the 'Peers v the People' and was hard fought. The result was that the Liberals and Conservatives won the same number of seats but the Liberals had the support of two other parties, the Irish Nationalists and the Labour Party. Asquith set up a new government.

Focus on

The election results of 1910

	January 1910	December 1910
Liberal Party	275	272
Labour Party	4	42
Conservative Party	273	272
Irish Nationalists	82	84

April The Lords finally passed the Budget of the previous year. Asquith had now decided to try to reduce the powers of the Lords. He introduced a Parliament Bill which:

- would stop the Lords rejecting future budgets.

- only allowed the peers to delay other proposed changes for a maximum of two years.

The Bill passed the Commons but not surprisingly was thrown out by the Lords.

June–November	Edward VII died in May 1911 and was succeeded by George V. The new king arranged a series of meetings over the next four months in an effort to find a solution. When these talks broke down in November Asquith persuaded the king to create an extra 300 new Liberal peers. This would give the Liberals a majority in the Lords and ensure the passage of the Parliament Bill. The king agreed, provided a general election was held to show that the people agreed.
December	The second general election produced an almost identical result to that of January.

1911

August	The Lords passed the Parliament Bill by 131 votes to 114. This was to prevent the creation of 300 new Liberal peers.

A cartoon aimed against the Lords, the small figures

"NOW THEN, OLD BOYS! YOU MUSTN'T STAND IN PEOPLE'S WAY! YOU MUST MOVE ON!"

The Parliament Bill

This brought in several changes:

- All money bills (budgets) passed by the Commons had to be passed by the Lords.

- The House of Lords could delay other bills for two years but then would have to accept the decision of the majority in the Commons.

- MPs were now to be paid for the first time.

- General elections were to take place every five rather than seven years.

Activity

Copy the following table.

Attitude to People's Budget

For	Against	Neither

Using Source **B**, write in the names of the newspapers which are for or against the Budget or neither. Include reasons for your choice.

Questions

1 Explain in your own words why the House of Lords was seen as out of date.
2 What significance did the following events have during the crisis of 1909–11:
a the rejection of the People's Budget?
b the January 1910 General Election?
c the King's promise?
d the December 1910 General Election?
3 What point is the cartoonist in Source **C** trying to make?

WOMEN'S RIGHT TO VOTE

At the beginning of the twentieth century women in Britain were seen as second-class citizens.

- No woman could vote in a British general election. Most people thought that only men should deal with national politics.

- Most men and many women believed that a women's place was in the home supporting her husband and bringing up their children.

- Husbands could get a divorce more easily than their wives and were more likely to get custody of the children.

- Few women went to university or got top jobs such as lawyers, doctors or dentists.

- Where women did the same work as men, they were almost always paid less.

- Employers believed that when a woman married she should leave her job to look after her husband.

SOURCE A

Frederick Ryland speaking in 1896

Why should a person otherwise qualified be refused a vote simply on the grounds of sex? Mrs B's gardener or coachman will probably have a vote, while she is without one.

SOURCE C

Sir Edward Clarke, a lawyer and former Conservative MP, in a speech in 1913

Women are much less educated than men. Studying politics would make a woman a much worse mother and a much less pleasant wife.

SOURCE D

Written by Mrs Wibaut in *Working Women and the Suffrage* published in 1900

The working woman needs the vote in order to obtain better houses, better conditions of living, shorter hours of working, better care for her children.

SOURCE B

A poster issued in 1912 by the National League for Opposing Women's Suffrage

The campaign for the vote

This was stepped up in the years before the outbreak of the First World War for several reasons:

1 In 1901 Queen Victoria died. She had been a fierce opponent of women's rights.

2 Women had been allowed to vote in local elections in 1888. Some women argued that if they were good enough for local then why not general elections.

3 Keir Hardie, the leader of the newly formed Labour Party, and some leading Liberals, including Lloyd George, supported votes for women.

4 Other parts of the British Empire, including New Zealand, had already given the vote to women.

Eventually three different women's societies campaigned for the vote.

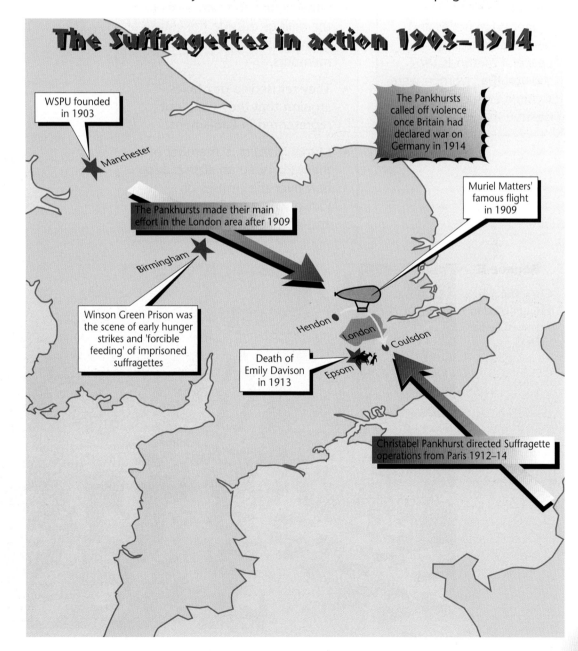

The Suffragettes in action 1903–1914

WSPU founded in 1903

Manchester

The Pankhursts called off violence once Britain had declared war on Germany in 1914

The Pankhursts made their main effort in the London area after 1909

Muriel Matters' famous flight in 1909

Birmingham

Winson Green Prison was the scene of early hunger strikes and 'forcible feeding' of imprisoned suffragettes

Hendon

London

Coulsdon

Death of Emily Davison in 1913

Epsom

Christabel Pankhurst directed Suffragette operations from Paris 1912–14

The Suffragists

The Suffragists believed that women would get the vote eventually. All they had to do was to keep on the right side of the law, and do all they could to persuade the general public and Parliament that women ought to be given the vote. One such group was the National Union of Women's Suffrage Societies (NUWSS) which was set up by Millicent Fawcett in 1897. This organised marches and petitions. By using peaceful methods they showed that women were sensible enough to deserve the vote.

The Women's Freedom League

This was set up by Charlotte Despard who believed the suffragettes had become too violent. However, members were not as peaceful as the suffragists. They were prepared to break the law as long as it did not lead to violence. For example:

- In 1911 members refused to take part in the census, the official population count. They refused to fill in the census form.

- Others chained themselves to the railings outside the House of Commons and picketed the members.

- They refused to pay taxes arguing that they were not represented in Parliament.

- Muriel Matters, a member of the WFL, hired an airship and flew over the Houses of Parliament throwing out carrots and propaganda leaflets.

Suffragettes

In 1903 Mrs Emmeline Pankhurst and her daughters, Christabel and Sylvia, set up the Women's Social and Political Union (WSPU).

SOURCE E

A peaceful march through London organised by the NUWSS

Profile on
Emmeline Pankhurst

Emmeline Goulden was born in Manchester in 1858. In 1879 she married Dr Richard Pankhurst. He was a politician and lawyer who encouraged his wife to work for better rights for women. By 1886 she was joining boldly in the debates about the Married Women's Property Act. By 1895 she was a member of the Board of Guardians responsible for organising help for the poor. After her husband's sudden death she opened a drapery shop in London. The business failed and she returned to Manchester where she got a job as a registrar of births and deaths. She was very beautiful. One lady described her as 'slender, willowy, with the exquisite features of one of the saints'. She became a very good public speaker and a had a great fighting spirit. By 1900 she was determined to fight for votes for women.

THE SUFFRAGETTES

The Suffragettes had had enough of the peaceful methods of the Suffragists, believing that such an approach was ignored by the public and Parliament. One newspaper, the *Daily Mail*, nicknamed them the suffragettes and the name stuck. They were prepared to break the law in order to get votes for women. This would get them publicity and force the government to give way.

Their campaign
At first the suffragettes held meetings and made their protests in a noisy but peaceful fashion. Their extreme methods, known as militancy, began in 1906 when Christabel and Annie Kenney, a cotton worker, were arrested at a public meeting in Manchester and sent to prison after refusing to pay a fine.

- They broke up political meetings, slashed paintings and poured acid into pillar boxes.

- In 1912, they started a massive stone-throwing operation. At 4 pm on 1 March, suffragettes broke hundreds of shop windows. The police arrested 219 suffragettes. They did not mind being arrested because it drew attention to their cause.

- Emily Davison found a terrible way to publicise women's suffrage. On 4 July 1913, which was Derby Day at Epsom, she stood by the rails watching the main race. As the King's horse, Ammer, rounded Tattenham Corner, she threw herself under its hooves, and she later died from her injuries.

- They cut telephone wires, set fire to derelict buildings and frequently attacked and assaulted leading Liberals. The Prime Minister, Asquith, was attacked while playing golf. Acid was poured on golf course greens.

Hunger striking
When they were sent to prison many suffragettes went on hunger strike to get publicity for their cause. The prison authorities were afraid that a suffragette might die in prison, and that this would give them even more publicity. So they began force-feeding prisoners. To force-feed a hunger striker, prison officers pushed a tube down her throat and into her stomach. Then they poured liquid food down a tube. In this way, suffragettes on hunger strike were kept alive.

SOURCE F

From *The Suffrage Movement* written by Sylvia Pankhurst in 1931

Mrs Pankhurst led a small group to see the Prime Minister. They were refused entry at the door of the House of Commons. Mrs Pankhurst then deliberately hit the inspector so that he had to arrest her.

SOURCE G

A suffragette, Mary Richardson, describes being force-fed

There is a wardress holding each shoulder, two at each arm, two at the sides, and these kneel on your ribs until your breathing shows a dangerous shortness. Sheets are flung over you, one over your head and forehead, another wardress holds your head and presses her thumbs in your temple.

The doctor enters and you see his hands at work on the tubes in front of your half-shut eyes. He puts the tube carefully into the nose but then thrust it with violence into the small nasal opening into the throat. This is where the bleeding and swelling occur. Then the tube, a yard long, is run through the nasal passage, down the throat, into the stomach. Medicine or tonic is poured from a glass. Food is run through the tube. Choking and bleeding begin and last during the feedings. Tears stream from the corner of the eyes.

SOURCE H

A suffragette poster showing force-feeding

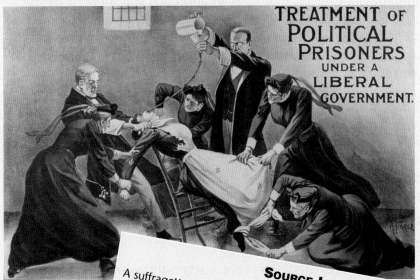

TREATMENT OF POLITICAL PRISONERS UNDER A LIBERAL GOVERNMENT.

This, however, brought bad publicity for the Liberal government. In 1913 they introduced the Temporary Discharge Act. This was nicknamed the 'Cat and Mouse Act'. Prisoners on hunger strike were released when very ill and sent back to prison when they were better. Emmeline Pankhurst went to prison twelve times in as many months and became very weak.

Despite all this activity and publicity when the First World War broke out, in 1914, women still did not have the vote.

SOURCE I

A suffragette view of the Temporary Discharge Act

THE CAT AND MOUSE ACT
PASSED BY THE LIBERAL GOVERNMENT

THE LIBERAL CAT
ELECTORS VOTE AGAINST HIM!
KEEP THE LIBERAL OUT!

BUY AND READ 'THE SUFFRAGETTE' PRICE 1P.

Why didn't women get the vote?
This was for several reasons:

1   Many men and some women were still convinced that women should not have the vote.

2   The two main political parties, the Liberals and Conservatives, were each split over the issue.

The Labour Party was too small to help the WSPU and was divided on the issue

The Conservative Party was wholly against votes for women

The Liberal Party needed to win votes to win the election

3   The Liberal government could not decide which women to give the vote to. They could not give the vote to all women because not all men had the vote. One possibility was to give it to women householders and the wives of householders. But the Liberals feared that these women would vote mainly for the Conservatives.

4   The extreme activities of the suffragettes convinced many men, including members of the government and Parliament, that women were not sensible enough to deserve the vote. Asquith, especially, refused to give way to violent threats as this might encourage other groups to use the same methods.

SOURCE J

A postcard against the Suffragettes

The war and the vote

It was the activities of women during the First World War that finally brought the vote. The outbreak of war brought a truce between the suffragettes and the government. Emmeline Pankhurst rallied the women behind the war effort. In return all existing prison sentences were pardoned. Mrs Pankhurst organised meetings and processions to publicise the part women could play in the war effort.

Women certainly played a vital role (p. 110). In 1917, the Prime Minister, Lloyd George, said that women's work had changed people's opinion of votes for women.

Morton (Source **K**) was right. In 1918 the Representation of the People Act gave the vote to all women over 30 and all men over 21. Nonetheless it still was not fair. Women had to wait until they were 30 to vote simply because Parliament wanted to make sure the majority of voters were male.

Source K

A.C. Morton, in a speech to the House of Commons in 1917

Opinion is changing in favour of giving women a vote due to the excellent work they have done for us and the country during the war.

Source L

Women voting for the first time, 1918

Source M

Charles Graves, writing in 1922

The Vote was won, not by burning churches, slashing pictures or damaging pillarboxes but by women's work during the war. It was not giving way to violence but a reward for patriotic service.

Activities

1   Make a copy of this table:

Sources supporting votes for women	Sources against votes for women

Look at Sources **A** to **D** and write the source label under the appropriate heading in the table. Give brief reasons for your choice.

2   You are eighteen years of age in 1913 and decide to join one of the three societies campaigning for the vote. You write to your parents explaining:

- your reasons for supporting votes for women.
- why you chose this society.
- criticisms of the other two societies.

Questions

1 Explain in your own words the different methods used by
   a the NUWSS.
   b the WFL.
   c the WSPU.
2 What were force-feeding and the 'Cat and Mouse Act'?
3 Was suffragette violence the only reason why women did not have the vote in 1914? Explain your answer.
4 Which Source, **G** or **H**, would be more useful to an historian studying force-feeding?
5 What is the purpose of the postcard, Source **J**?
6 Does Source **J** give a reliable view of the suffragettes?

THE RISE OF THE LABOUR PARTY, 1900–24

The Labour Party was set up in 1900. Twenty-four years later Ramsay MacDonald formed the First Labour government.

Why the Labour Party emerged

The Labour Party emerged for several reasons:

1 Neither of the leading political parties at the beginning of the twentieth century seemed to represent the working man. The Liberals seemed strongly middle class and the Conservatives got much support from the upper classes.

2 Trade unions, which had grown in number in the late nineteenth century, wanted a party in Parliament which would represent their interests.

3 Socialist societies also wanted their own party. In 1884 Henry Hyndman set up the Social Democratic Federation (SDF). This followed the ideas of Karl Marx (p. 529). In the same year a more middle-class group called the Fabian Society was founded. Members of this society, which included George Bernard Shaw, believed in gradually working towards socialism.

4 Keir Hardie played a leading role.

SOURCE A

From a Fabian Society article, 1893

The working class cannot represent themselves in Parliament because of the money problem. They have to earn money in order to live, and MPs are not paid salaries or wages. Working class MPs will depend on the trade unions to raise the money.

SOURCE B

Keir Hardie

VOTE FOR

Home Rule.

Democratic Government.

Justice to Labour

No Monopoly.

No Landlordism

Temperance Reform.

Healthy Homes.

Fair Rents.

Eight-Hour Day.

Work for the Unemployed.

KEIR HARDIE.

Printed and Published by F. W. Scales & Co. [L.S.C.], 151, Barking Road, Canning Town, London, E.

Profile on

Keir Hardie

James Keir Hardie was born in Scotland in 1856, the illegitimate son of Mary Kerr and a miner, William Aitken. He was sent to work underground in a coal mine at the age of eight and had no formal education. He became involved with the local miners' union, eventually rising to the position of Secretary of the Ayrshire and later the Scottish Miners' Federation. In the 1880s he became increasingly convinced of the need for an independent party to represent the working classes. In 1883 he set up the Scottish Labour Party. In 1888 he stood as a Labour candidate for Mid-Lanark and came last. Four years later he won the West Ham seat in London as an Independent Labour candidate. He entered the House of Commons wearing his distinctive working clothes and cap. In 1893 he set up in the Independent Labour Party but this was not successful in elections. Hardie, himself, lost his seat in 1895.

Support for an independent Labour Party grew in the 1890s. Voters elected Independent Labour Party (ILP) members to local councils, school boards and boards of Poor Law Guardians. ILP ideas were spread by special newspapers, like the *Clarion,* and at hundreds of rallies and meetings up and down the country.

The Labour Representative Committee 1900–1906

In February 1900 a Conference took place at the Memorial Hall, Farringdon Street, London. This was attended by representatives from:

- the ILP, including Keir Hardie.

- the socialist societies.

- various trade unions.

They set up the Labour Representative Committee (LRC) which was to sponsor candidates independent of the Liberals and Conservatives.

At first the LRC had little success. It put up 15 candidates in the General Election of 1900, but only two were elected. The Committee lacked money and many trade unions still did not support it. Its fortunes were transformed by three developments over the next three years:

- In 1901 the LRC decided on a political levy. Each member of the LRC would pay the equivalent of 1d (old penny) into a fund used to fight elections.

- The Taff Vale case. In 1901, the Taff Vale Railway Company sued a trade union called the Amalgamated Society of Railway Servants for £23,000. This was because the railway company had lost money when the railway workers were on strike. The court decided that the union had acted illegally, and it had to pay up. This meant that no union could strike because its funds would be threatened. The trade unions swung their weight behind the LRC. Between 1901 and 1902 there were 455,000 members from trade unions. By 1903 this had increased to 847,000.

- In 1903 the LRC made a pact or agreement with the Liberals. They agreed that in certain constituencies either a Liberal or Labour candidate should stand against the Conservatives in the next general election. This would avoid splitting the working-class vote and ensure Labour success in certain constituencies.

In 1906 the LRC won 29 seats and changed its name to the Labour Party.

The Labour Party 1906–14
This period saw mixed fortunes for the Party.

GAINS	LOSSES
The Trades Disputes Act of 1906 changed the law so that unions were not responsible for any money their employers lost during a strike.	The Labour Party made little progress 1910–14 and in every single by-election came second to the Liberal candidate.
1911 payment of MPs with an annual salary of £400 was of benefit to Labour MPs who had few other sources of income.	Many trade union members grew impatient with the slow progress of the Labour Party and once again resorted to strike action. There were a great number of strikes between 1910 and 1912.
Labour won 42 seats in the second general election of 1910.	
The 1913 Trades Disputes Act allowed union funding for the Labour Party. It could now campaign at election time on a more equal footing with the main parties.	

Progress 1914–24
The First World War proved to be very beneficial to the Labour Party:

- Membership of trade unions doubled, which meant more money and support for Labour.

- It became involved in government for the first time, being a member of the wartime coalition governments.

- Its great rival for the working-class vote, the Liberal Party, was seriously split during the war between those who supported Lloyd George and the supporters of Asquith.

In 1918 Labour won 59 seats, becoming the second largest party in the Commons. It had overtaken the Liberals. Four years later it won 142 seats, 25 more than the Liberals. An increase to 191 MPs in the elections of 1923 eventually led to the formation of the first Labour government under Ramsay MacDonald in January 1924.

Activity

Draw up a poster advertising the Labour Representative Committee in 1903. You are trying to win more support for the LRC from:

- the trade unions.
- the working-class voters.

Questions

1 According to Source **A**, what made it difficult for working men to become MPs?
2 What part did the following play in the emergence of the Labour Party:
   a Keir Hardie?
   b the ILP?
   c the LRC?
   d the Taff Vale case?
3 How useful is Source **B** to an historian studying the emergence of the Labour Party?

THE GENERAL STRIKE OF 1926

In 1926 there was a general strike which lasted for nine days. This was due to problems in the coal industry and developments in the trade union movement.

Problems of the coal industry

Before the First World War, individual mine owners fixed what they paid miners. This meant wages varied from pit to pit, even in the same area, and even though miners could be doing the same job. As early as 1889 the miners set up their own trade union, the Miners' Federation of Great Britain and Ireland (MFGB), to campaign for better conditions and a national minimum wage. The miners felt they deserved this due to the great dangers involved in their job. In 1908 they achieved a maximum eight-hour working day underground. Four years later they went on strike for a national minimum wage. Instead they got district minimum wages.

SOURCE A

A miner working at the coal-face in the 1920s

When you are at the pit bottom you have to walk about 3 miles to the coal-face. You then pick up your tools. You crawl down to whatever position you are on the coal-face, usually about 120 yards, dragging your tools with you. You need to crawl because it is two feet high. If anybody has an accident everybody helps. For example, one man got crushed – we were not too far in then, about two miles. There were six of them carrying him out and I was at the side holding his tongue. I had to do this because he kept swallowing it. We had to walk because we were not allowed to ride on the wooden wagons.

SOURCE C

A north-east miner recalls the 1920s

A football team was chosen to play for a colliery, strong young men at the peak of their strength, skill and fitness. Thirteen years later one of then was dead, seven totally disabled, two partially disabled and one was able to perform light duties on the service.

Focus on

Problems in the coal industry

British coal was unable to compete with cheaper coal mined in the USA, Poland and Germany:

◆ British coal was more difficult to mine.

◆ Coal-cutting machinery was standard in the United States but not in British pits.

◆ Britain's 2,500 mines were run by 1,400 small and inefficient businesses. They did not have the cash to make the big improvements that were needed.

◆ Other forms of power were now competing with coal and steam power – electricity, gas and oil.

During the war the government nationalised or took over the coal mines. This benefited the miners because they got:

• a seven-hour day.

• a national minimum wage. In other words the same wages to every miner, no matter which pit he worked in.

Coal mining, however, suffered in the years after the First World War.

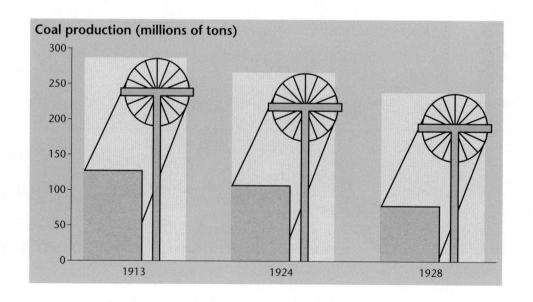

Coal production (millions of tons)

The Graphic, April 1921

American coal is easy to obtain and can be mined cheaply because it is near the surface and in thick, easy to work seams in great quantities. British coal is hard to obtain because it is very deep, often in thin seams, at a great distance from the pit-shaft and therefore expensive to mine.

The miners wanted the government to permanently nationalise the coal industry. In 1919 the Prime Minister, Lloyd George, set up a Royal Commission, the Sankey Commission, to look in to the coal industry. He promised to accept its findings. In 1920 it reported and recommended permanent nationalisation. Lloyd George went back on his word and would not accept this.

SOURCE E

The Sankey Commission, 1919

Even on the evidence already given, the present system of ownership stands condemned and some system must be substituted for it, preferably nationalisation.

SOURCE F

A.J. Cook, Secretary of the Miners' Federation speaking in 1925

We want nationalisation. First, for the sake of economic security. Second, because we want safety. Under private ownership our men are murdered. Safety is not the first consideration but the last. 60% of accidents could be prevented. Explosions ought to be a thing of the past. The men who run the mines run them from London simply for profit, and safety is the last consideration.

When the coal industry began a serious slump in the winter of 1920–21 and began to lose £5 million a month the government handed the industry back to the coal owners. Their solution was to cut the miners' pay and get them to work a longer day.

The trade union movement

The trade union movement grew bigger and stronger in the years before and after the First World War. Between 1910 and 1914 there were a series of official and unofficial strikes that challenged the Liberal government.

- In 1910, railwaymen, boilermakers, miners and cotton workers all went on strike.

- In 1911, a dockers' strike in Liverpool and a national rail strike were both ended by the government using troops. Four men died in street battles between strikers and soldiers.

- In February 1912 there was another miners' strike.

Some trade unions at this time believed that strike action was the most effective way of bringing about changes in society – in particular the trade unions taking over the running of industry. This was influenced by syndicalism, a movement originating in France. Syndicalists believed workers had the right to control industries they worked in. Their ultimate weapon was 'direct action' or strikes culminating in a national or general strike.

The British trade unions moved closer to realising this idea with the formation of the Triple Industrial Alliance in 1913. The three largest unions – the MFGB, the Transport Workers' Federation (mainly dockworkers) and the National Union of Railwaymen – agreed that if one member came out on strike the other two would come out in sympathy. This would effectively lead to a general strike as the country would be paralysed.

The Triple Alliance was stopped during the First World War. Nevertheless unions increased their strength as membership doubled from four to eight million between 1914 and 1920. There was a great number of strikes in the period 1919–20 and the Triple Alliance was revived in February 1919.

SOURCE H

The miners' plea to their fellow workers

Make no mistake. It will be your turn next. The miners are locked out in the great war on wages. Are you going to refuse to support them? Your place is in the firing-line. Your safety, your standards, your wages, depend upon action now.

SOURCE I

From an article about Black Friday published in the *Daily Herald*, 16 April 1921. The *Daily Herald* was a newspaper paid for by the trade unions.

Yesterday was the heaviest defeat that has happened to the Labour Movement. We on this paper have said that if organised workers stand together they will win. They have not stood together and have been beaten. The National Union of Railwaymen and the Transport Workers Federation have called off their strike. The miners are fighting on alone.

'Black Friday', 15 April 1921

There was almost a general strike in 1921. In April 1921 the coal owners announced wage cuts and a longer working day and locked out the miners until they agreed. The longer working day did not make sense. It meant the miners would produce even more coal that could not be sold. The MFGB called upon the transport workers and the railwaymen to support them in a strike against the cut in wages on Friday 15 April.

At the very last moment, however, these two unions pulled out, leaving the miners to fight on alone. This is why the miners called it 'Black Friday'.

This defeat had several effects:

- The Triple Alliance was now known as the 'Cripple Alliance' and collapsed.

- The miners were eventually starved back to work in July 1921 and had to accept pay cuts and an extra half-hour a day.

- The problems of the coal industry continued. There had been no long-term solution.

- The General Council of the Trades Union Congress (TUC) was set up to represent trade unions in future negotiations.

'Red Friday', 31 July 1925

Coal prices continued to fall, leading to the second occasion when there could have been a general strike. The coal owners again announced a longer working day and pay cuts. The miners' leader, A.J. Cook, was furious. His reply, 'Not a penny off the pay! Not a minute on the day!' became the miners' slogan.

The Miners' Leader, A.J. Cook

Prime Minister Stanley Baldwin

The TUC backed the miners and all movement of coal by land or water was to be stopped from 31 July. The Conservative Prime Minister, Stanley Baldwin, was not ready for a general strike. He therefore:

- Gave a subsidy, or money support, to the coal owners to last nine months and prevent a cut in wages.

- In the meantime he set up another Commission led by the Liberal Herbert Samuel to study the problems of the coal industry and come up with a long-term solution.

The unions called their success 'Red Friday'. It was, however, only a breathing space. Everyone knew there would be a showdown if the miners and pit owners did not agree about what was to happen when the government subsidy ended on 1 May 1926.

Meanwhile the government made preparations for a general strike (see p. 546).

Immediate events leading to the General Strike, March–May 1926

The Samuel Commission reported in March 1926 but failed to find a solution that could keep either side happy. It agreed with the owners' plan to cut wages but not to lengthen hours. It also said that the owners should spend money modernising the coal industry. To be fair it was difficult for owners, who were losing money each month, to spend money on modernising their coal mines. Shortly after the Commission report, Baldwin announced that the subsidy would end on 30 April. The owners then set wages lower than even Samuel had proposed. The miners refused to accept this and were again locked out. They called on the other unions to support them by coming out on strike. The TUC agreed to support the miners and to negotiate with the government on their behalf.

SOURCE J

Published in August 1925. The small figure is Baldwin and the large figure the typical British person, John Bull.

A PRETTY PENNY IN THE SLOT.

MASTER STANLEY BALDWIN. "COME ON, UNCLE, FORK OUT; IT'S WELL WORTH IT."
JOHN BULL. "ALL RIGHT, MY BOY, I'LL TAKE YOUR WORD FOR IT. BUT ONLY THIS ONCE, MIND."

A cartoon from the *Trade Union Unity*, a trade union newspaper, 1925

The *Daily Mail* article which the printers refused to print

A General Strike is not an industrial dispute. It is a revolutionary movement intended to inflict suffering upon the great mass of innocent persons in the community and thereby to force the Government to act. It is a movement which can only succeed by destroying the Government and the rights and freedom of the people.

On 30 April 1926 the employers made their final offer – a 13% wage cut and a 'temporary' increase in the working day by one hour. It was rejected by the MFGB. On the following day the TUC voted by a large majority in favour of striking in support of the miners. Talks between the TUC and Baldwin continued to try to find a solution. These were called off by Baldwin on 2 May when he heard that the printers at the offices of the *Daily Mail* had refused to print an article 'For King and Country' (Source L) which criticised the miners. The strike began at midnight on 3 May.

Activity

Who was responsible for the General Strike? Was it the miners, coal owners, trade union movement or government? Look back at the section on the causes of the Strike and the sources and then complete the bubbles on each of the cartoon characters giving reasons why you think they did or did not cause the strike.

Trade Union leader

Miner

Coal owner

Prime Minister

Questions

1 What does Source **D** tell you about the problems of the coal industry?
2 How useful is Source **G** to a historian studying the Triple Industrial Alliance?
3 Why was there not a general strike in 1921 and 1925?
4 How reliable are Sources **F** and **K** as views of the coal owners?
5 What point is the cartoonist trying to get across in Source **J**?
6 Why did Baldwin call off negotiations with the TUC on 2 May 1926?

The events of the Strike, 4–12 May 1926

On 4 May the people in many British cities woke up to silence. Trains and buses were not running. Even the TUC was surprised. Union members had followed their leaders' request and come out on strike. An estimated three million workers backed the miners. At first, only the printing, power and transport workers were called out.

At first the strike seemed successful and in the first few days the numbers on strike actually increased. The strikers were clearly well organised. They allowed essential supplies through and had no intention of bringing out hospital workers or other key workers. There was little trouble and only one person was killed in the first week. However, scenes of violence gradually increased. In Glasgow and Doncaster strikers were arrested, tried and imprisoned. There were police baton charges, incidents of stone-throwing, the attempted derailment of trains driven by volunteers and overturned lorries and buses.

SOURCE A

A bus leaving the garage under police escort

The attitude of both sides hardened as the strike went on. As the strike entered its second week there was even talk of the TUC bringing out its 'second line' of strikers, the electrical workers, which would have cut electric light from the streets of major towns.

Much to the surprise of the miners and most strikers, the TUC did not extend the strike. Instead, on 12 May its leaders went to Downing Street and called off the strike.

GOVERNMENT PROPAGANDA

With the printers on strike the government realised the importance of getting their version of events across to the public. They used two methods:

1. Their own newspaper, the *British Gazette*, was published in the offices of the *Morning Post* with the Chancellor of the Exchequer, Winston Churchill, as editor.

2. Broadcasts on the BBC radio. The chairman of the BBC, Sir John Reith, decided to allow only broadcasts by the government and refused to allow the TUC or the Labour Party leader, Ramsay MacDonald, to broadcast. The government even placed loudspeakers in many streets to ensure more people heard the government version.

The government portrayed the strike as a threat to the British system of government and an attempt by a minority of the people to bully the majority. They insisted that the strike was not working and praised the work of the volunteers.

SOURCE C

The *British Gazette* headlines, 12 May

ORDER AND QUIET THROUGH THE LAND

Growing Dissatisfaction Among Strikers

INCREASING NUMBERS RETURNING TO WORK

SOURCE D

A cartoon showing the government view of the Strike

THE LEVER BREAKS.

GOVERNMENT PREPARATIONS

The government had expected a general strike and had been preparing since 'Red Friday'. In September 1925 they set up the Organisation for the Maintenance of Supplies. This was to use volunteers to ensure that essential supplies such as food, electricity and gas were kept up. Branches were set up all over the country to encourage people to join. By March 1926 the Government had a list of 100,000 volunteers. During the strike the government used the army to escort food convoys and guard the food depot set up in Hyde Park. Special constables were recruited to help keep law and order.

SOURCE E

Food convoy escorted by the army

THE WORK OF VOLUNTEERS

Many middle-class people disagreed with the idea of a general strike and volunteered to help the Government. For some people jobs such as driving buses were 'good fun'. They kept some trains and buses running.

TUC MISTAKES

- Many members of the TUC were unhappy with the idea of a general strike. They feared that if it went on too long it would get out of hand and lead to violence and revolution.

- They refused to call out essential workers in electricity, health, water and sewerage.

- They did not get their message across to most of the public because they were not allowed to broadcast on the BBC. Their own newspaper, *The British Worker*, was not well distributed and did not reach the North-East until 12 May, the last day of the Strike.

- The TUC was looking for a way out. On 10 May it asked the miners' leaders to accept the Samuel Commission's recommendations. When the miners refused the TUC met the Prime Minister and called off the strike.

SOURCE F

The British Worker, 5 May 1926

THE BRITISH WORKER
OFFICIAL STRIKE NEWS BULLETIN
Published by The General Council of the Trades Union Congress

No. 1. WEDNESDAY EVENING, MAY 5, 1926. PRICE ONE PENNY

LONDON AND THE SOUTH

WONDERFUL RESPONSE TO THE CALL

General Council's Message : Stand Firm and Keep Order

SOUTH WALES IS SOLID !

SOURCE G

The British Worker, 8 May 1926

There is as far as the Trade Union Movement is concerned, no 'attack on the community'. There is no 'challenge to the Constitution'. The workers have exercised their legal right to strike in order to protect the miners against a serious lowering of their standard of life.

SOURCE H

Headlines in *The British Worker*, 10 May

Nothing could be more wonderful than the magnificent response of millions of workers to the call of their leaders. Firmer and firmer every day of the Strike.

WHY DID THE GENERAL STRIKE FAIL?

THE PRIME MINISTER, STANLEY BALDWIN

He played an important role. He made a radio broadcast to the nation every day and spoke in a very matter-of-fact, commonsense way. He did not attack the miners. He insisted that he wanted to help them but that a general strike was not the way to get what they wanted. Above all else he refused to talk to the TUC until they called off the strike.

THE ATTITUDE OF THE GENERAL PUBLIC

This was very important. Their support would decide the outcome of the strike. Government propaganda successfully convinced many that the strike was a threat to the government and was wrong.

SOURCE I

Beatrice Webb, a supporter of the Labour Party and trade unions, wrote in her diary, 4 May

Such methods cannot be tolerated by any government. If it succeeded it would mean that a militant minority were starving the majority into giving way to their will. It would be the end of democracy.

Results of the General Strike

The miners were left to fight on alone. Some began to drift back to work in August 1926 and the majority by December. They had to accept the owners' conditions, pay cut and longer working day. The problems of the coal industry had not been solved. Indeed, they were even worse because of the exports lost during the coal strike.

Calling off the General Strike lowered confidence in the TUC. Many workers were penalised when they returned to work. Ringleaders were sacked. Others had to accept inferior terms of employment. Baldwin passed a new law in 1927, the Trades Disputes Act. This made all future general strikes illegal. Workers could no longer come out on strike in sympathy with other workers.

The General Strike was a disaster for the trade union movement. TUC membership fell from 5.5 million in 1925 to 3.75 million in 1930. Nevertheless it was a success for the Labour Party. Many workers now turned away from strike action and began to support the idea of a Labour government to improve their conditions. In 1929 the Labour Party, for the first time, won more seats than either the Liberals or Conservatives.

SOURCE J

A cartoon published in August 1926

THE MAN IN CONTROL.

John Bull (to the Pilot). "YOU'VE GOT US THROUGH THAT FOG SPLENDIDLY."
Mr. Baldwin (sticking quietly to his job). "TELL ME ALL ABOUT THAT WHEN WE'RE PAST THESE ROCKS."

Activity

You are a coal miner who kept a diary of the events of 1926. Write out key entries for several days. You could include:

• Reactions to the Samuel Commission, March 1926.

• Owners' pay cuts April 1926 and being locked out.

• Start of the General Strike 3 May.

• An entry written during the Strike.

• TUC decision to call off the Strike.

• The struggle alone after and the decision to return to work.

Questions

1 The General Strike failed for several reasons. Which do you think were the most important and why?
2 What part did the following play in the Strike:
   a   the BBC?
   b   the OMS?
   c   the *British Gazette*?
3 What differences are there between the headlines in Sources **C** and **H**? Why are they so different?
4 Is Source **D** a reliable a view of the General Strike?
5 How useful is Beatrice Webb's view in Source **I** to an historian studying attitudes to the General Strike?
6 What effects did the failure of the General Strike have on:
   a   the trade union movement?
   b   the coal industry?
7 Which side does the cartoonist in Source **J** support? How do you know?

During this period Britain experienced a serious depression which brought high unemployment in certain parts of the country. On the other hand, for those in work this was certainly a time of affluence or good living standards.

Why was there a depression in Britain?

This was due to long-term problems with the British economy and the more immediate effects of the Wall Street Crash in the USA (see p. 482).

The First World War had a disastrous effect on the British economy. Before the war Britain sold goods like ships, machinery and textiles to countries that had no industries of their own. After the war there was less demand for British goods:

- Japan and the USA had taken some of Britain's customers.

- Many countries started to set up their own industries.

- British goods were too expensive to produce compared with those abroad. There were too many small mills and factories and too many old machines.

Britain had not developed the newer industries as quickly as its rivals such as Germany and the USA – industries such as chemicals, motor vehicles, electrical goods and artificial fibres. Since fewer goods were exported, factories cut back on production and unemployment rose rapidly to about one in every ten members of the population.

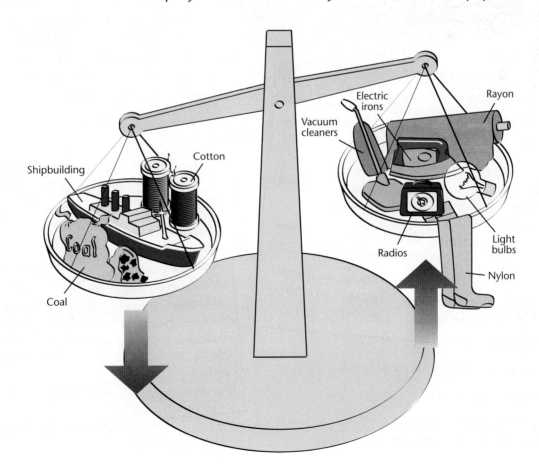

COAL

This could be produced much cheaper abroad (see p. 541). In the mid-1920s coal could be produced in America for 65p a tonne compared to £1.56 a tonne in Britain.

IRON AND STEEL

This suffered due to less demand for ships. It also faced competition from abroad. In the USA and Germany new efficient plants easily produced iron and steel more cheaply than British rivals.

DECLINING INDUSTRIES

SHIPBUILDING

Shipbuilding suffered even more than the rest. Shipbuilding declined rapidly because:

- there was a fall in world trade and less need for merchant ships.

- international disarmament meant a fall in demand for warships.

- foreign countries such as Japan and the USA could produce cheaper ships.

TEXTILES

(especially cotton)
Japanese cotton was much cheaper than that of Britain. Japan's workers were paid one-fifth of their British counterparts and worked in modern, efficient factories. British factories were still using steam-powered machinery. Cotton suffered due to competition from synthetic fibres such as rayon. Shorter skirts became fashionable and these needed less material. Finally Britain had exported cotton goods to India. By the 1920s India not only had its only cotton industry but was competing for Britain's customers.

The effects of the Wall Street Crash

The Wall Street Crash began on 24 October 1929. It brought the American economy to its knees (p. 482). The Americans could no longer afford to lend European countries money to build up their industries or to buy goods and recalled some of their earlier loans. Therefore economic depression soon hit Europe too and millions of workers lost their jobs.

Britain followed the USA into a depression. It was even harder now to sell British goods abroad, such as coal, cloth, steel and pottery. Most of these goods were made in the North. This led to:

- A rise in unemployment. By 1932 nearly one worker in four was out of a job.

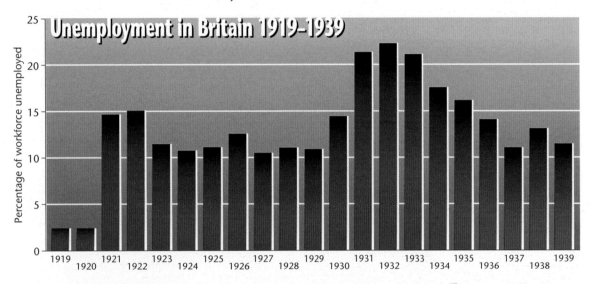

Unemployment in Britain 1919–1939

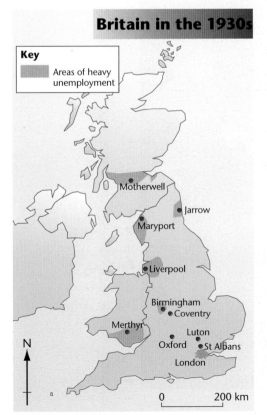

Britain in the 1930s

Key
Areas of heavy unemployment

Motherwell
Jarrow
Maryport
Liverpool
Birmingham
Coventry
Merthyr
Luton
Oxford
St Albans
London

N

0   200 km

- The areas of heavy industry were badly affected. Northern Ireland, South Wales, Clydeside, the north-west and north-east became known as the 'Depressed areas'.

Questions

1 **a** Why were Britain's main industries in decline in the 1920s?
   b Give examples of at least two industries?
2 Explain the effects of the Wall Street Crash on Britain.
3 What were the 'depressed areas'?

'Depressed' Britain

Many in the 'depressed areas' found it difficult to maintain even a minimal standard of living. Areas which depended on shipbuilding or coal mining for employment were particularly badly hit with unemployment, poverty, malnutrition and ill-health.

In 1931 the national unemployment rate was 23%, but this figure hid the real effects of the Depression. By the mid-1930s the worst-hit areas like Jarrow on Tyneside and Merthyr Tydfil in South Wales had over 60% unemployment. In Birmingham and Oxford it was less than 6%. In Jarrow the local coal mine, Hebburn Colliery, closed in 1930. In the following year the

I have not seen nothing like it since the war. There is no escape anywhere from the prevailing misery. One of every two shops appears to be closed. Wherever we went there were men hanging about, not scores of them but hundreds and thousands of them. The men wore the drawn masks of prisoners of war.

steel works. In 1934 the National Shipbuilders' Security, set up to shut down shipyards that were not profitable, closed Palmers, Jarrow's shipyard. This had a devastating effect on the town. Ellen Wilkinson, the local Labour MP, described it as 'the town that was murdered'.

In an area of high unemployment everyone in the community felt the impact. Local shopkeepers were hit hard. In some towns half the shops closed, with the shopkeepers themselves joining the ranks of the unemployed. Jarrow was no exception.

Effects of unemployment

SOURCE B

An unemployed worker on a street corner

Poverty

Several surveys of the 1930s showed the connection between unemployment and poverty:

- Seebohm Rowntree did another survey of poverty in York in 1936 and found that 72.6% of unemployed workers lived below the poverty line.

- This was confirmed by a survey of poverty in Stockton-on-Tees which compared the average weekly income of a family where the wage-earner was out of work and a family where he was in work.

Average weekly income unemployed family £1.46.
Average weekly income for employed family £2.57.

Health

Not surprisingly, the health of the unemployed and their families, especially their children, suffered.

- Several studies showed that the unemployed had an inadequate diet. They ate much bread, margarine, potato, sugar and tea but little meat, fresh fruit and vegetables and milk. The diets of wives and mothers were the most inadequate as they sacrificed their needs for those of their husband and children.

- A much higher infant death rate existed in the depressed areas. In the south-east in 1935 the infant death rate was 42 per 1,000 live births. In Northumberland and Durham it was 76.

- Local medical officers frequently reported on the poor health record of districts in the depressed areas. There were more children with rickets, and more recorded cases of childhood diseases such as tuberculosis, bronchitis, pneumonia, scarlet fever, diphtheria and measles.

Psychological

One common consequence of unemployment was mental suffering. Investigators found a general trend. The first week or so of unemployment was treated as a holiday. They got up early, put on their best clothes and went down to the local labour exchange seeking work. After a few weeks confidence began to go, expectations fell and the unemployed took less interest in personal appearance. Many, used to being the breadwinner, felt guilty and lost all self-respect and self-esteem.

Source C

A story from the *Daily Worker*, 30 January 1933

How an unemployed man's wife literally starved herself to death for her children was told at an inquest on Mrs Minnie Weaving, aged 37, of Elmscott-Road, Downham, S.E. George Henry Weaving, the husband, said his wife had not seen a doctor since July, when she had twins. They had seven children living. Major Whitehouse (the coroner): 'Did she have enough to eat?' 'That is the trouble with us all. I am out of work' replied Mr Weaving. Dr Arthur Davies, pathologist, said Mrs Weaving's body was much wasted. Death due to pneumonia. He added: 'I have no doubt that had she had sufficient food this attack would not have proved fatal. It appears that she deliberately starved herself and gave such food as came into the house to the children. She sacrificed her life.'

Source D

From *Love on the Dole*, a novel by Walter Greenwood written in the 1930s

It got you slowly like a malignant disease. You fell into the habit of slouching, of putting your hands in your pockets and keeping them there. Of glancing at people secretly, ashamed of your secret, until you believed that everyone looked at you suspiciously. You knew that your shabby appearance gave away your secret. You prayed for the winter evenings and the kindly darkness. Pants with the backside patched and re-patched; patches on knees, on elbows. Jesus! All bloody patches.

The Jarrow Crusade

The people of Jarrow decided to fight back. Public meetings were held. The town council decided to draw up a petition demanding the right to work. They organised a march to London to present the petition to the government. Two hundred men were carefully selected by the local medical officer of health for the long journey to London. The men decided to march between 15 and 25 miles a day.

There had been a number of hunger marches but the Jarrow march caught the public imagination. It had been approved by the local council and the marchers were led on their journey by the local MP, Ellen Wilkinson. The marchers were accommodated each night along the route by householders who supported their cause. The press gave them mouth organs so they could play music to march to.

SOURCE E

Jarrow men march on London in October 1936

SOURCE F

The Illustrated London News, November 1936

Everywhere they were met with friendly feeling and were cheered by the music of their own mouth-organ band.

SOURCE G

An account of the life of one of the Jarrow marchers

Amongst the marchers was Robert Winship. He was 42 and worked in Hebburn Colliery from the age of 13 until it closed in 1930. He did not have another job until the war started in 1939. The year the colliery closed his wife was taken to a mental hospital. She died there in 1935. He had to bring up two daughters on an income of 95p a week.

How important was the march?

ACHIEVEMENTS

- It certainly publicised the plight of towns like Jarrow to people in the more prosperous south.
- The police praised the marchers for being well organised and disciplined.
- The men returned back home as heroes.
- A few found work in the Team Valley Trading Estate in nearby Gateshead.

LIMITATIONS

- The government refused to let them present the petition when they got to London.
- They did not get new work for the town.
- When they returned to Jarrow they discovered that their unemployment benefit had been stopped because they had not been available for work while on the march.

Activity

You are a reporter for a national newspaper tipped off about the possibility of a march of the unemployed from Jarrow to London. You go to Jarrow to investigate and end up following the march. At the end of the march you write a newspaper article. In your article you could:

- Include a headline.
- Explain why the men decided to march.
- Describe a typical day on the march.
- Explain what happened when they reached London.
- Suggest what you think the march achieved.

You could also include interviews with some of the marchers.

Questions

1 Look at Sources **B** and **D**. How far do they agree about the image of the unemployed?
2 Does Source **C** give a reliable view of the effects of unemployment?

Government action against the Depression

There is much debate on government action. Did they do enough to help the 'Depressed areas' and the unemployed? In 1931 a National Government was set up to try to reduce unemployment. This was a coalition of the three main parties, Conservatives, Liberals and Labour.

Unemployment benefit

Those out of work could at least claim unemployment benefit or dole money. Unemployment insurance had been set up in 1911 (p. 520) and in 1920 it was extended to anyone earning less than £250 a year, an average working-class wage at that time. Originally payments were only made for the first 15 weeks on the dole. It was expected that an unemployed person would find work in that time.

By 1922, however, there were growing numbers of long-term unemployed. So in November 1922 the government had to extend benefit to all those out of work for an unlimited period.

Between 1929 and 1931 the numbers of unemployed grew rapidly. The government found it was paying out far more in benefits than it was receiving. Ramsay MacDonald's Labour government of 1929 to 1931 had been unable to cope with this increased spending. MacDonald resigned in August, 1931, but within a few days returned as leader of the National Government.

The National Government cut unemployment benefit by 10%. It also introduced the Means Test.

The Means Test

A government officer visits the family at home

The family's total income is added up

If the family has any extra income, e.g. a son working, then the dole is reduced

The officer can also order the family to get more money by selling household goods

Many claimed that the Means Test was more about the government trying to save money than helping the unemployed. It was carried out by officials from the local authorities' Public Assistance Committees (PACs) which had been set up in 1930. The unemployed claiming benefit had to reveal what everyone in their house, including grown-up children, had in savings and earnings. The test even looked at the value of things in the home that could be sold to raise cash.

The Means Test was extremely unpopular:

- It was humiliating for families to have to reveal earnings, savings and the value of things they owned.

- If the officials thought there was enough money in the house they would stop the dole.

- Some local authorities applied the Means Test very harshly. Others, such as those in County Durham, refused to carry it out.

The Means Test was a great strain on family life, especially if one of the older children who had a job was forced to pay more towards the family funds.

SOURCE A

From *The Road to Wigan Pier* by George Orwell, 1937

The means test breaks up families. An old age pensioner would usually live with one of his children. Under the means test, he counts as a 'lodger' and his children's dole will be cut.

SOURCE B

The thoughts of a miner being means tested

My unemployment benefit came to an end in March 1932 when I was disallowed because I had not qualified for the necessary contributory period of thirty weeks. After this I was given a food ticket for 23 shillings a week (£1.15) which continued until January 1933, when it was stopped because of the means test. So now we have to depend on the boys and they have to keep all six of us, including my wife and the two children who are still going to school.

Interest rates
In June 1932 the Government lowered the bank interest rate to only 2%. This is called 'cheap money' because it makes it cheap to take out a loan. It helped industry to borrow money to buy new machinery and encouraged people in work to borrow money from banks to buy homes, cars and domestic appliances. The increased demand for goods created more jobs.

Rearmament
Britain began to build up the armed forces from 1935 due to the threat from Hitler. This further reduced unemployment as it encouraged industries such as shipbuilding, iron and steel, engineering and the manufacture of aircraft.

Import Duties Act
The National Government tried to protect British industry by making the cost of foreign goods more expensive in Britain. They did this by taxing all imports by between 10 and 20%. They hoped this would encourage British industry to produce and sell more goods. The idea was that if more British goods were bought more would have to be produced, and so more people would be employed to produce them. This would mean a fall in unemployment. This benefited British cars and electrical goods in the south but:

- had little effect on areas of high unemployment.

- other countries put taxes on goods coming into their country from Britain. This made it more difficult for British export industries.

Special Areas Act, 1934
The government realised that certain parts of the country were suffering far more than the rest from the Depression. It decided to

give additional help to these 'Special' or 'Depressed' areas. The Special Areas Act appointed two commissioners with a budget of £2 million to try to attract some of the new industries to the old industrial areas. It had limited success. Some industrial estates were established, such as the Team Valley Trading Estate in Gateshead. However, the Act created fewer than 15,000 jobs. Many companies did not want to move to the north. Small industrial estates could not replace the coal mining or shipbuilding industries.

SOURCE C

The Team Valley Trading Estate in Gateshead

Questions

1 What do Sources **A** and **B** tell you about the Means Test?
2 How useful are they to an historian studying the effects of the Depression in the 1930s?
3 Why did many people hate the Means Test?

How effective were these measures?

By the end of the 1930s unemployment had fallen to one million. This was partly due to government policies, but was also due to favourable circumstances such as a world revival in trade which helped Britain's exports.

Activity

Copy the following table and write in each column whether the measure helped, did not help unemployment, or a combination of both.

Government measure	Helped unemployed	No help	Combination
Insurance			
Means Test			
Interest rates			
Rearmament			
Import Duties Act			
Special Areas Act			

The new industries

Overall, despite the Depression, the British economy grew in the period between the wars. In the South East and the Midlands cities such as Coventry thrived because of the growth of new industries. New light industries had developed since the war. These produced, for example, cars, aeroplanes, vacuum cleaners and toasters. Demands for household goods rose sharply in the 1930s as factories became more efficient and prices fell. These new industries were located in the south and Midlands because:

- The greater employment in these areas encouraged the owners and directors of new companies to set up their businesses in locations close to new customers who had the money to buy washing machines and radios, as well as make them.

- Electricity provided the power to run the new washing machines and radios as well as make them. Factories no longer needed to be close to coalfields as in the days of steam power.

- Raw materials no longer had to be close by. Roads and railways could transport what was needed.

Affluent Britain

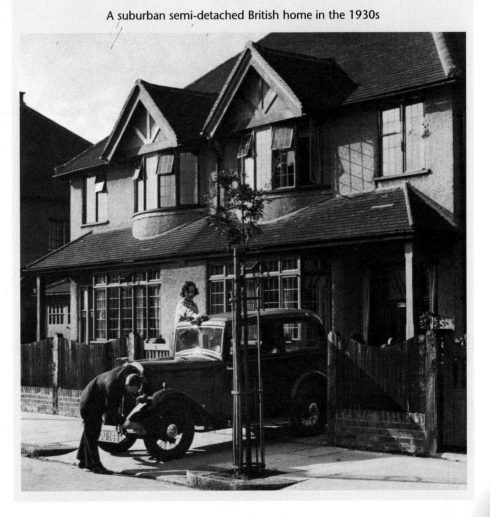

SOURCE B

A suburban semi-detached British home in the 1930s

SOURCE C

Con Dawson remembers what it was like for her in the 1930s

The 1930s were a wonderful time for me. I went to dances and shows and to the cinema with my latest boyfriend. I worked as a secretary at the recording company HMV in their London office and met lots of stars. The Depression never touched us, though I do remember hanging out of my office window to watch one of the hunger marches.

For many in Britain the 1930s was a time of rising standards of living. Even when the Depression was at its worst, 75% of British workers still had a job. Where there were new industries families lived better than before. There was much evidence of this affluence:

- Twelve times as many people were using electricity in 1938 as in 1920.

- Three million new houses were built in the 1930s. This included private and council houses with much better facilities, including inside toilets and, in some cases, gardens.

- People in employment were having smaller families while their wages were increasing. This meant their living standards were rising. This was also helped by a fall in prices.

- Most people worked fewer hours. In 1900, people had worked for around 55 hours a week. In 1935, people who had a job were expected to work around 45 hours a week.

- Most workers had holidays with pay too. The seaside became more popular than ever before. Authorities in Blackpool claimed that the town had more than half a million visitors on the August Bank Holiday, 1937.

- Many people had time and money to spend on going to the cinema, dance halls and theatres.

- Sport became more popular and attracted larger audiences than ever before. A million and more watched Saturday football matches – one shilling (5p) was enough to gain admission. Many towns acquired greyhound tracks.

- Car ownership increased dramatically in the 1930s. In 1929 the industry produced 180,000 cars. By 1938 production had almost doubled to 340,000.

SOURCE D

An advertisement for new housing in south-east England

METRO-LAND

PRICE TWO-PENCE

In the mid-Thirties an electric heater was installed for a water tank. In the late Thirties my mother had a small refrigerator installed in the pantry. We had two live-in servants, a cook and a housemaid.

SOURCE F

From Robert Graves and Alan Hodge, *The Long Weekend*, 1938

Labour-saving devices were introduced. Cereals, eaten with milk, began to challenge bacon and eggs in well off homes. Bottled and tinned goods grew plentiful. By the Thirties almost every kind of domestic and foreign fruit, meat, game, fish, vegetable could be bought. Woolworth's stores were the cheap providers of household utensils and materials. The instalment or 'never-never' system was being applied to all major household purchases; furniture, sewing-machines, vacuum-cleaners, gas-ovens, wireless sets.

Activity

Copy the table below. Look back over this section on Britain 1929–39 and write in the letters of those sources that show:

a Depressed Britain.

b Affluent Britain.

Give a brief explanation for each choice.

Source showing depressed Britain	Sources showing affluent Britain

---

Questions

1 Explain three reasons why new industries were generally located in the south and Midlands.

2 How useful are Sources **D** and **E** as evidence to an historian of life in Britain in the 1930s?

3 Which of the following views of Britain is the more accurate of the 1930s?
   - a decade of depression, hunger and unemployment.
   - a decade of improving standards of living.
   - a combination of the two.
   Explain your answer.

BRITAIN 1944–51

This period saw the completion of the welfare state and several other important reforms, due mainly to the work of the Labour governments of 1945 to 1951.

The impact of the Second World War

The Second World War encouraged further welfare reforms for several reasons:

1 There were great housing shortages due to German bombing and the lack of house building because building materials and labour were diverted to the needs of war.

2 The war itself had done much to unite the different classes and convince many of the need for a more equal society after the war. Few wanted to return to the conditions of the 1930s.

Profile on
William Beveridge

He is often described as the architect of the welfare state. He worked as a civil servant during the Liberal governments of 1905 to 1914 and was mainly responsible for the details behind the introduction of labour exchanges in 1910 and the National Insurance Act of the following year. By 1941 he had a great knowledge of social insurance and the difficulties that faced ordinary people in their lives. He was given sole responsibility for settling the contents of the Beveridge report and signing it. He did, however, work with a team of 11 hand-picked civil servants, all experts in different fields.

3 The evacuation of schoolchildren had highlighted the social problems of many inner cities. Middle-class families were shocked at the condition of some of their working-class evacuees (see pp. 201–203).

The Beveridge Report 1942

In 1941, the Government asked Sir William Beveridge to suggest ways in which it could help the sick, the unemployed, low-paid workers and retired people.

Beveridge produced his report a year later. It was called Social Insurance and Allied Services. He said that he had looked at all the problems, as the government had asked him to do. He had decided that they were all linked together and therefore the solutions should be linked as well. Beveridge identified five giant problems that would have to be overcome to make progress and create a better society.

Want

This was the lack of basic needs of life, especially food. This could be defeated by a new system of national insurance run by the government. It would give:

- benefits to the sick, unemployed and disabled.

- benefits to pregnant women.

- allowances to families with children.

- grants to meet the costs of funerals.

- pensions to old people and widows.

Ignorance

The lack of a proper education for everyone. This would be defeated by the building of new and better schools.

Disease

To create a healthy nation and get rid of unnecessary diseases. This would be achieved by setting up a new health service for the whole nation.

Squalor

To end living in poverty. This would be achieved through a massive programme of house building.

Idleness

This refers to unemployment. This was to be solved by the government helping industry create more jobs for everyone.

Beveridge's scheme was very popular. Over 100,000 copies of his report were sold in the first month it was published. The wartime government had no choice but to act. It set up a Reconstruction Committee that proposed changes in education, housing, health, employment and social insurance.

The General Election, 1945

In July 1945, a general election was held. Winston Churchill, the wartime Prime Minister, was popular but his party, the Conservatives, were associated with the unemployment and depression of the 1930s. The Labour Party, led by Clement Attlee, won a landslide victory. Most of the voters wanted the changes suggested by the Beveridge Report and believed Labour would carry these out.

SOURCE A

Cartoon published in 1942

RIGHT TURN

Clement Attlee on the front cover of *Illustrated* magazine, July 1948

ATTLEE'S FOURTH YEAR

Clement Attlee speaking in 1945

The men and women of this country who have endured great hardships in war are asking what kind of life awaits them in peace. They need good homes, sufficient food, clothing and amenities of life. They also need employment and leisure, and social provision for accident, sickness and old age. For their children they desire an educational system that will give them the chance to develop their full potential.

The attack on want

Labour followed most of the recommendations of the Beveridge report to try to reduce poverty:

Family allowances

To improve the standard of living a family allowance was set up in 1945 and the first payments were made in August 1946. A family received 5 shillings (25p) a week for each child after the first until each child reached the age of 16 or was employed full time. There was no Means Test. All families received the benefit.

National Insurance

The National Insurance Act was introduced in 1946:

- Employers, workers and the government all paid into the scheme.

- It provided benefits to workers who were out of work through sickness, unemployment or pregnancy.

- If someone was sick, there was no limit to how long they could claim sickness benefit for.

- If unemployed, they could only claim unemployment benefit for six months.

National Insurance (Industrial Injuries) Act
This Act of 1946 gave benefits to workers who were injured or disabled while at work and set up tribunals (courts) to decide the amount of compensation to be paid.

National Assistance Act
Two years later Labour brought out the National Assistance Act to provide for those in great need, especially those not covered by the National Insurance Act. It set up a Board whose purpose was to prevent extreme poverty and provide everyone with a minimum income. The *Times* said that the National Assistance Board was now 'the citizen's last defence against extreme poverty'.

The attack on disease
Aneurin Bevan, the Minister of Health, was responsible for improving the nation's health. In 1946 he brought in the National Health Service Act. Under this Act:

- Everyone received free medical, dental, hospital and eye treatment.

- There was no charge for spectacles, false teeth or medicines.

- Most hospitals came under the control of the government as part of the National Health Service (NHS).

- Local councils provided midwives, home nurses, health visitors and ambulances.

- All this was paid for by taxation and National Insurance contributions.

- Doctors were paid under the NHS which encouraged general practitioners (GPs) to practise in poorer areas without fear of not getting paid because people could not afford to.

The NHS brought much opposition from the medical profession. By January 1948, only one in every 100 specialist doctors and surgeons in London was in favour of the scheme. They said they would lose their independence, spend valuable time filling in forms and have their earnings controlled by the government. Bevan had to give way to the British Medical Association (BMA) which represented the doctors. He allowed them to treat private patients and gave them a guaranteed income each year – not just a payment each time they treated a patient. The opposition collapsed and the NHS came into being on 5 July 1948.

A *Daily Mirror* cartoon from May 1946

The importance of the NHS

BENEFITS OF THE NHS

- At first it was the envy of the world.

- It brought immediate improvements in medical care such as a fall in infant death rate.

- Older people got better-fitting false teeth, good quality spectacles and efficient hearing aids.

- Young mothers visited free antenatal clinics and were paid maternity benefit.

- There was a fall in deaths from diseases such as tuberculosis and diphtheria.

- In the first year alone eight and a half million people received dental treatment and five and a quarter million pairs of spectacles were provided.

CRITICISMS OF THE NHS

- The NHS was very expensive to run. It cost £400 million in its first year.

- Others said it encouraged people who wanted something for nothing and that taxpayers' money was being needlessly squandered.

- Some disliked the fact that there was still private practice. This would lead to twin standards – better care for those who could afford to pay.

- In 1951 the Labour government introduced charges for spectacles, false teeth and prescriptions. Bevan resigned in protest, insisting that everything should be free.

The attack on ignorance

This was the work mainly of the wartime coalition government rather than Labour. R.A.B. Butler, the Education Minister, introduced the 1944 Education Act.

* This introduced 'free secondary education for all'.

* Children had to be taught in separate primary schools and secondary schools.

* No one could leave school until they were 15 years old.

* Every child took an examination at the age of 11, known as the 11 plus. How they did in this examination decided the type of school they went to when they left primary school.

* There were three types of secondary school. Grammar schools gave children an academic education: secondary modern schools taught more practical subjects and technical schools taught technical skills. It was hoped that every child would have the sort of secondary education that suited them best.

This Act finally ensured that all children would get schooling from the age of 5 to 15 and it was the responsibility of the state to provide both the primary and secondary schools. The school leaving age was not raised to 15 until 1947. The Act, however, was criticised.

1   The three different types of secondary school were supposed to be of equal status. This did not turn out to be the case. Very few technical schools were set up so most children went to either grammar or secondary modern schools. Grammar schools were seen as the way to better-paid jobs. Children who went to secondary modern schools often saw themselves as failures.

2   The age of eleven was seen as too young to divide children in this way and decide their future education. It ignored those who were late developers.

SOURCE E

A 60-year-old woman remembers how she felt when she got her eleven plus results

Mum and dad woke me up shouting: 'You've passed! You've passed!' I was very excited. I would be going to a grammar school. My joy turned to tears when I got to school. My best friend was going to the local secondary modern school. I was sad because we would be going to different schools.

The attack on squalor

There were serious house shortages due to the effects of the Second World War. Families were housed in temporary accommodation such as 'pre-fabs'. These could be put up in a few hours. The first one went up in April 1944 and before long thousands were built all over Britain. Pre-fabs were meant to last for ten years, but many people were still living in them in the 1990s.

Pre-fabs in York

The Labour government began to build a series of estates of council houses which were built to rent. Over 1.25 million council houses were built in the period 1945 to 1951.

Another wartime report had recommended the building of new towns. This would prevent the further growth of cities such as London and reduce overcrowding. The new towns would be carefully planned to ensure a pleasant environment and a 'Green belt' countryside which could not be built on. The Labour government accepted this idea and the New Towns Act 1946 provided government money to set up new towns close to London and other major cities. Twelve towns were planned in all, eight round London, two in Scotland, one in Wales and one in County Durham.

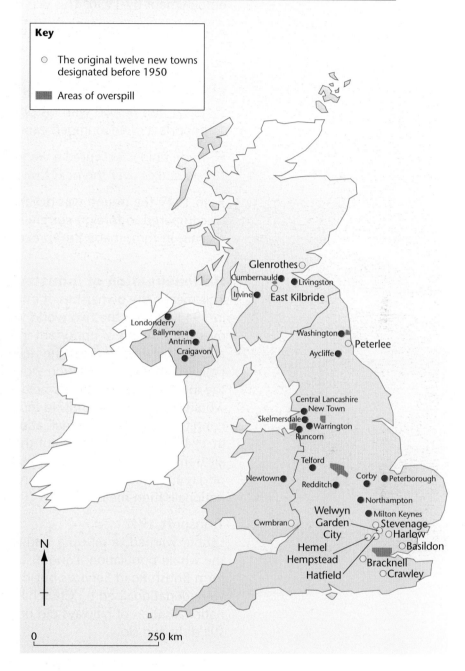

The new towns of Britain in 1980

Key

○ The original twelve new towns designated before 1950

▨ Areas of overspill

Glenrothes ○
Cumbernauld ● ● Livingston
Irvine ●
East Kilbride ●

Londonderry ●
Ballymena ●
Antrim ●
Craigavon ●

Washington ●
Peterlee ○
Aycliffe ●

Central Lancashire New Town ●
Skelmersdale ● ● Warrington
Runcorn ●

Telford ●
Corby ● ● Peterborough
Newtown ●
Redditch ●
Northampton ●

Welwyn Garden City ○
Cwmbran ○
Milton Keynes ●
Stevenage ○
Harlow ○
Basildon ○
Hemel Hempstead
Bracknell ○
Hatfield
Crawley ○

N

0   250 km

The population of each of the new towns was about 50,000 and they were carefully planned in districts, each with their own amenities, within walking distance of the houses. Industry was attracted to the new towns with loans and grants. There, were, however, some mistakes. There were too few parking spaces and garages in the new towns. It was also difficult to build a community spirit as so few of the residents had known each other before moving to the new estates.

The attack on idleness

Beveridge believed that there should be more jobs available than workers. The Labour government managed to achieve virtually full employment by 1950. This was helped by several factors:

- Industry recovered after the war with the help of Marshall Aid (p. 238), the demand for new houses and repairs to wartime damage.

- Stafford Cripps, who became Chancellor of the Exchequer in 1947, also helped with his policy of 'austerity'. He cut down on imports and encouraged exports.

- Trade unions accepted a wage freeze in 1948 and there were few strikes over the next few years.

- In 1949 the pound was devalued. This meant it was worth less compared to foreign currencies such as the American dollar. This, in turn, made British exports cheaper.

Nationalisation of industry

This means the ownership of industry by the state. It was not new in 1945. During the two world wars the government had taken over the running of important industries and services such as coal and the railways to meet the needs of war. The Labour government believed that nationalisation would help the workers. It would put the interests of the workers before profit. Government money would be spent modernising industry and improving working conditions. Several nationalisation policies caused little opposition. In 1946 the nationalisation of the Bank of England and wireless and air transport. In the following year the state took over the running of gas and electricity. There were, however, three controversial nationalisation measures:

Transport 1947

Labour wanted to set up a system of transport that would benefit the whole population. Long-distance hauliers were taken over to form British Road Services but this only lasted until 1953 when they were denationalised by Churchill's Conservative government. The nationalisation of railways did not bring quick benefits. Trains were still dirty and slow.

Coal 1947

The National Coal Board took control of the coal industry on 1 January 1947. Unfortunately, state ownership did not seem to improve the industry:

- The severe winter of 1947 led to a shortage of fuel and many blamed nationalisation.

- The government was not prepared to spend a lot of money on modernising the pits. Mechanisation was very expensive.

Steel

The government wanted to nationalise the iron and steel industry. There was much opposition because it was profitable and efficient.

The Conservatives and the House of Lords delayed the passing of the Steel Bill until 1950. Nationalisation began in 1951 but was ended by the Conservative Government in 1953.

Criticisms of nationalisation

Many were disappointed by nationalisation:

- Some believed that Labour had not gone far enough. These critics believed they should have nationalised all the major industries. They were also disappointed because workers got little or no say in the running of the nationalised industries.

- Others believed it was wrong for the state to run industries. They would only make a profit and be run efficiently in private hands.

- Nationalisation became associated with shortages, such as the coal industry, and inefficiency, in the case of British Rail.

- Labour also possibly made the mistake of nationalising run-down industries such as coal and the railways – the so-called 'lame-ducks'.

SOURCE G

A nurse interviewed on BBC TV in 1990

The great day came for the launch of the NHS. It didn't only uplift us. It was the patients as well. It was just fantastic. It was something that you never believed could have happened. You know when you'd struggled and tried so long.

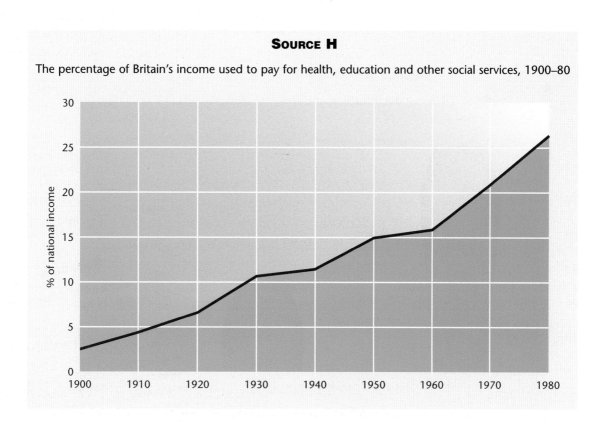

SOURCE H

The percentage of Britain's income used to pay for health, education and other social services, 1900–80

SOURCE J

A cartoonist's view of the welfare state, 1950. The figure in the pram is the typical British person, John Bull. He is being pushed by a nanny who represents the welfare state.

THE WELFARE STATE

SOURCE I

A doctor commenting on the NHS

It's all paperwork. I've got so much of it. Look at these. I'm sending patients to hospital, so I've got to fill these damn things in. It's senseless. And all for sixteen bob a week (80p).

SOURCE K

Deaths of children under the age of one year

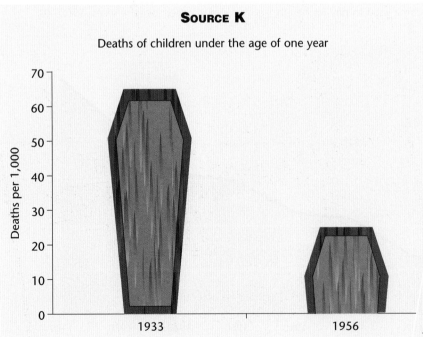

SOURCE L

The wife of a crane-driver, aged 34, speaking in 1949

You can bring the children to the surgery and get attended there free. Sometimes when my little girl, Aggie, was sick, I usedn't to have the money when he came in. It's everything to a mother to know that you can call a doctor even when you haven't the money – you have to count it day by day just how you spend it.

SOURCE M

WIFE, CHILD AND WELFARE STATE TO SUPPORT

SOURCE N

Cartoon of 1945 commenting on 'pre-fabs'

Hollowood

"Well, were you or were you NOT the young couple advertising for a roof to put over their heads?"

SOURCE O

From R.J. Cootes, *The Making of the Welfare State*, 1966

People who thought of council housing as a special service for the poor objected to this. They said it was unfair to give council houses to people whose rent was helped by the state when they could afford to pay the full rent.

Questions

1   Explain briefly the main measures introduced by the governments of 1944–51 to get rid of:
    a   Want.
    b   Ignorance.
    c   Disease.
    d   Squalor.
    e   Idleness.
2   What point is the cartoonist trying to make in Source **A**? How does he get this point across?
3   How useful is Source **E** to an historian studying the effects of the Education Act of 1944?
4   Was nationalisation a good idea? Did it work?
5   What does Source **C** tell you about Labour's aims in 1945? How far do you think they were achieved by 1951?

Summary and Revision

THE LIBERALS AND THE WELFARE STATE 1905–14

In this section, you need to include:

- Why there was a need for reform in 1905.

- Reasons for poverty.

- Liberal reforms to help the young.

- OAPs and Labour Exchanges.

- The National Insurance Act of 1911 – insurance against sickness and unemployment.

- The importance and limitations of these reforms.

Revision questions

1. Explain at least four reasons for poverty at the beginning of the twentieth century.
2. Why did the poverty surveys of Rowntree and Booth encourage welfare reforms?
3. How did the following help children:
   a. school health checks?
   b. the Children Act of 1908?
4. Explain the main terms of the Old Age Pensions. What criticisms were there of this measure?
5. Why did the Liberals introduce Labour Exchanges?
6. How did the National Insurance Act of 1911 help:
   a. the sick?
   b. the unemployed?
7. Did the Liberals lay the foundations of the welfare state?

THE LIBERALS AND THE LORDS

This section includes:

- The main terms of the People's Budget of 1909.

- Why it upset the Lords.

- Long-term reasons for reform of the Lords, especially the Conservative majority.

- The actions of the Lords 1906–8 and 'Mr Balfour's Poodle'.

- The events of 1910, including the two general elections, the Parliament Bill and the King's promise.

- Reform of the Lords in 1911 – the main changes brought by the Parliament Act.

Revision questions

1 Why did Lloyd George need to raise extra money? What new taxes did he bring in?
2 Why did the following force reform of the Lords:
   a Permanent Conservative majority?
   b 'Mr Balfour's Poodle'?
   c rejection of the People's Budget?
3 Explain the following events of 1910:
   a the First election.
   b the King's promise.
   c the Second Election.
4 Why did the Lords eventually back down? How were their powers changed by the Parliament Bill?

WOMEN'S RIGHTS AND THE LABOUR PARTY

This section includes the following:

- Why women did not have the vote in 1900.

- The activities of the three women's societies – the WFL, the WSPU and the NUWSS.

- Suffragette militancy, hunger striking and the 'Cat and Mouse Act'.

- Why women did not have the vote by 1914 and got the vote in 1918.

- Why there was a need for a Labour Party.

- The part played by Keir Hardie and the ILP.

- The LRC and the fortunes of the Party 1900–14.

- Why the Labour Party benefited from the First World War and the immediate aftermath.

Revision questions

1 Give three reasons why women did not have the vote in 1900.
2 Explain the different methods used by the three women's societies:
   a the WFL.
   b the WSPU.
   c the NUWSS.
3 What were the following:
   a hunger striking?
   b force-feeding?
   c the 'Cat and Mouse Act'?
4 Was suffragette violence the only reason women did not have the vote in 1914?
5 Why were many working-class people keen on having their own party?

6 What part did:
   a   Keir Hardie
   b   socialism
   c   trade unions
   play in the emergence of the Labour Party?
7 What were:
   a   the ILP?
   b   the LRC?
   c   the Taff Vale case?
8 How did the First World War help the Labour Party?

THE GENERAL STRIKE 1926

In this section, you need to include:

- Long-term causes of the strike, especially the decline of the coal industry and the growth of trade union power.

- The causes, events and results of 'Black' and 'Red Friday'.

- The immediate causes – the Samuel Commission and the breakdown in negotiations.

- Why the Strike failed, especially government preparations and organisation and TUC mistakes.

- Effects the Strike had on the coal industry and trade union movement.

Revision questions

1 Explain why the coal industry declined after the First World War. How did this affect miners' wages and hours of work?
2 What was the Triple Industrial Alliance? How did this encourage the idea of a general strike?
3 Explain the causes, events and results of:
   a   'Black Friday'.
   b   'Red Friday'.
4 How did the following finally bring about the Strike:
   a   reactions to the Samuel Commission?
   b   the printers of the *Daily Mail*?
5 Explain the following reasons for the failure of the Strike:
   a   government preparations and organisation.
   b   government publicity.
   c   mistakes made by the TUC.
   d   the attitude of the general public.
6 How did the failure of the Strike affect the trade union movement?

BRITAIN 1929–39

This section includes:

- Why there was a depression in the 1930s, especially the problems of the old industries and the impact of the Wall Street Crash.

- The impact on the depressed areas – on health, standard of living and morale.

- The help given by the National Government, especially the Special Areas Act.

- The growth of new industries and why they located in the south and the Midlands.

- Affluent Britain – examples of those who were better off in the 1930s.

Revision questions

1   Why were coal, shipbuilding, cotton and iron and steel in decline between the wars?
2   How did the Wall Street Crash affect Britain?
3   What effects did unemployment have on the standard of living and health of families in the depressed areas?
4   What were the causes and results of the Jarrow March of 1936?
5   Which new industries emerged during this period? Why were they mainly in the south and the Midlands?
6   What is meant by 'affluent Britain'? Give examples.

BRITAIN 1944–51

For this section you need to include:

- How the Second World War, the Beveridge Report and the Labour government encouraged the completion of the Welfare State.

- National Insurance, National Assistance and family allowances.

- The introduction of the NHS – opposition and criticisms.

- The importance of the 1944 Education Act.

- Council housing and new towns.

- The nationalisation of coal, railways and iron and steel.

Revision questions

1   Why was the Beveridge Report so important in the development of the welfare state? What were the five giants it wanted to remove?
2   How did the following help to reduce want:
    a   National Insurance?
    b   Family Allowances?
3   Give the main terms of the NHS Act of 1946. Why did many doctors oppose it?
4   What were the main terms of the New Towns Act of 1946 and the Education Act of 1944?
5   Was the nationalisation of coal, railways and iron and steel a success?

12
China 1911–90

UNDERSTANDING CHINA

The following explanations and definitions should help you to understand this chapter.

Autocracy	A system of government in which one leader holds total power.
Boycott	Combining together to refuse to trade or do business with a country.
Census	An official count of the population.
Dynasty	A ruling family or group.
Manchu	Tribe from Central Asia who conquered China in the seventeenth century.
Mandarin	Ruler of province of China under the emperors, usually chosen from the upper classes.
Missionary	A member of a religious group who goes to a foreign country to try to pass on his/her religion.
Press-gang	To force someone to do something.
Red Guards	Armed members of the Communist Party, trained like soldiers.
Revisionist	Word used by one group of Communists to describe another group of Communists who want to make changes.
Third World	The poorer countries of the world.
Warlord	Someone who rules all or part of a country because he has an army with which to back up his rule.

China 1911–90

China is a very large country with a huge population. Nearly one in every four human beings is Chinese. It underwent frequent and substantial changes during the course of the twentieth century.

CHINA IN 1900

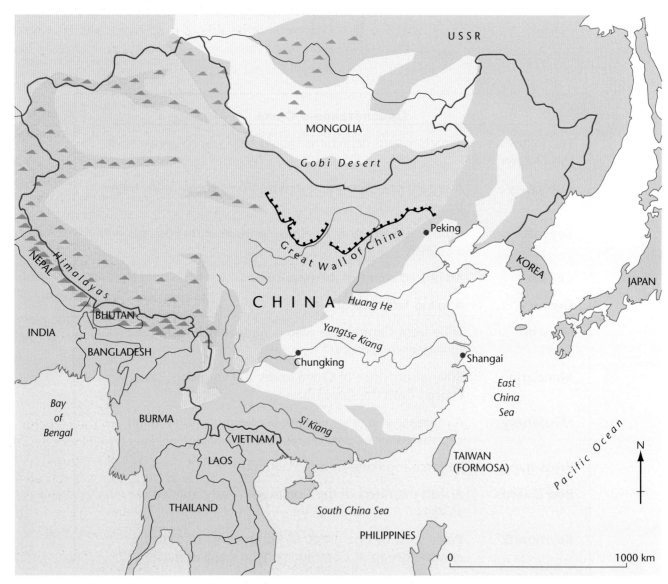

For many centuries China was cut off from the rest of the world. This was partly because China is surrounded by mountains, jungle, deserts or oceans. Except for the Japanese, the Chinese met few other peoples. To them, China was everything. In fact, the word 'China' means 'the earth' or 'the world'. It was visited by few foreigners and largely ignored.

The people

There had been a great increase in the population of China in the eighteenth and nineteenth centuries – from 100 million in 1700 to 400 million in 1900. At the top of Chinese society was a small select group of highly educated officials, large landowners and rich merchants. At the bottom were the poor – the peasants who made up 80% of the population. Most of them lived in villages, owned a little land and kept a pig and a few chickens. For the peasants, life was a constant struggle. In 1930, for example, the average peasant holding was under four acres in size. The rising population made this shortage of land worse.

Half, or even three-quarters, of the crops had to go to the landlord as rent. Then there were taxes to pay. Money-lenders took advantage of the peasants, charging high interest rates. If the crops failed, the peasant would not be able to meet these bills. He would have to sell all he owned, even his wife and children. In a really bad year, millions died.

SOURCE A

A Chinese peasant describes his lifestyle in J. Myrdal, *Report from a Chinese Village*

We have always been farmers. But we do not have our own land. We rented it for three generations from the landlords, Wang. Landlords did not eat as we others did. They ate meat and vegetables every day. He was very hard. People hated the landlords, but there was no way of getting round them. 'As long as we have our daily food we are satisfied', people said. 'We must do what our masters say. They own the land and the oxen'. Everybody owed him money. As long as you owed him money you could not get permission to leave the village in order to look for a better landlord. The landlords ate up people's work. They ate and we worked.

The peasants of China were used to this poverty and did not think of change. They were ruled by custom and tradition. Women were inferior and had no rights. They had to be completely obedient to their fathers or husbands.

The Government

China was ruled by an emperor, living in Peking. Since the seventeenth century, the emperors had all come from the Manchu dynasty. They had conquered China and made every Chinese person wear their hair in a pigtail, Manchu-style, as a sign of conquest.

Under the emperors, the work of governing China was carried out by the Mandarins. These were educated, upper-class Chinese. They also believed in custom and tradition and were against change. They studied the writings of Confucius, who said that in the past everything was good, and that therefore all change is bad. The Mandarins made sure that the laws were obeyed.

Power in China was in the hands of a small group of landlords, Mandarins and the Emperor, which made up about 10% of the population. They resisted change and lived by traditions which were more and more out of date.

The Empress, Tzu Hsi

Foreign influence

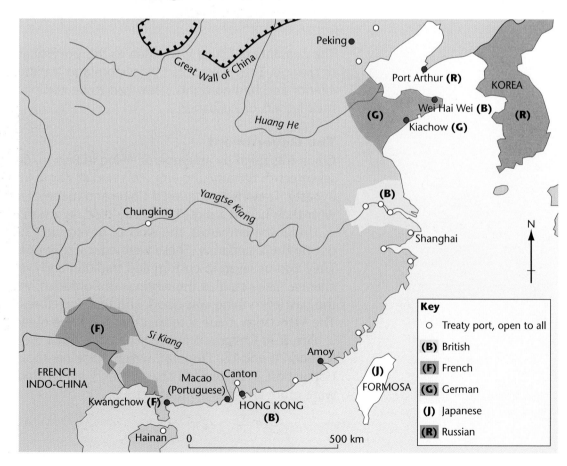

Peking

Great Wall of China

Port Arthur **(R)**

KOREA

Huang He

(G)

Wei Hai Wei **(B)**

Kiachow **(G)**

(R)

(B)

Chungking

Yangtse Kiang

Shanghai

N

(F)

Si Kiang

FRENCH
INDO-CHINA

Amoy

(J)
FORMOSA

Macao
(Portuguese)

Canton

Kwangchow **(F)**

HONG KONG
(B)

Hainan

0   500 km

Key

○ Treaty port, open to all

(B) British

(F) French

(G) German

(J) Japanese

(R) Russian

From the 1840s onwards the European powers took advantage of the weakness of China and started to divide the country among themselves. These countries developed factories and produced goods which the Chinese could not match. European countries wanted to trade with China, and sell them industrial goods. At first the Chinese refused but Britain and then other countries forced the Chinese to trade. By 1900 many parts of China were really controlled by foreigners. These were known as 'Treaty Ports'. Soon the European countries controlled most of China's key industries.

The emperors were powerless to stop them. Their old-fashioned weapons were no match for European guns and warships. China's final humiliation at the hands of foreigners came in 1895 when the emperor was defeated in war by Japan. After this defeat, China could no longer claim to be the strongest power in Asia.

The Boxer Rebellion, 1900

The Chinese, who had thought themselves superior for so long, were angry. In one city controlled by foreigners, there was a sign at the entrance to a park:

'CHINESE AND DOGS NOT ADMITTED'

The foreigners were hated and one of China's many secret societies, the Boxers, organised a rising to get rid of foreigners. The Boxers killed 200 foreign missionaries and 30,000 Chinese. The European powers acted quickly and sent in an international police force which crushed the Boxers.

SOURCE D

A Boxer print. Christians are shown as pigs. The goats represent Westerners.

This setback led to further criticism of the Manchus. For years, educated Chinese had argued that the cause of China's weakness was her outdated government. Now, under pressure, the Empress, Tzu Hsi, decided to introduce various reforms. The education system, the civil service and the army were all improved. There were even plans to set up a parliament. The days for reform had passed. An entirely new system of government seemed the only answer to China's problems.

Questions

1　Explain the following:
　a　Manchu dynasty.
　b　Mandarins.
　c　the growth of foreign influence.
2　What can you learn from Source **A** about peasant grievances?
3　Which is the more useful source to an historian studying the attitude of the Chinese to foreign influence, Source **C** or Source **D**?

CHINA 1911–28

In 1911 the Emperor was overthrown and a republic set up which was controlled by a series of warlords.

SOURCE A

This woodcut, 'The Starving People Seize the Grain', shows hungry peasants attacking a landlord

Sun Yat-sen and the revolution of 1911

This was due to several reasons:

1　Hatred of foreign influence and control.

2　The failure of the emperor and the Mandarins to reform the government of China.

3　The death of the old Empress, Tzu Hsi, in 1908. She was replaced by her nephew, Pu Yi, who was only three years old. This was followed by three years of poor harvests, droughts, floods and rising taxes. There was a wave of peasant riots between 1909 and 1911.

4　The influence of Sun Yat-sen. He was trained as a doctor and had travelled outside China – to Britain, France and the USA. His ideas for the future of China were based on his 'Three Principles':

- *Nationalism* The Manchu emperors and foreigners should be driven out of China.

- *Democracy* China should be ruled by a president and a parliament, elected by the people.

- *Socialism* The government should take over all businesses, all transport and all farms. These should be modernised so that everyone had a good standard of living.

Profile on

Sun Yat-sen, 1866–1925

Sun Yat-sen was the son of a peasant family. He knew what it was like to spend hours in the rice fields trying to grow enough to eat. His life changed when his brother, who had emigrated to Hawaii, invited Sun over to join him. In Hawaii, Sun received an education from English missionaries. He learned all about how England was governed, with a Parliament and laws and compared this with the emperor and mandarins of China. When his education was finished he returned to China and began to criticise the outdated government and society. In 1894 he began to work as a doctor in Canton, a city in southern China. However, he also worked for revolution and when his first attempt failed in 1895 he fled to Tokyo, the capital of Japan.

In 1894 he set up the Revive China Society. During the next few years Sun went abroad and organised a series of unsuccessful attempts to overthrow the Manchus. While abroad he spread his ideas among educated Chinese in speeches and newspapers. Sun even visited China many times under a false name and using a forged Japanese passport.

Sun's supporters were working towards revolution in 1911 when their plans were discovered, but they decided to go ahead anyway. This was known as the 'Double Tenth' as it took place on the tenth day of the tenth month – 10 October 1911. Military headquarters at Wuchang were seized. Within a month, 15 of China's 18 provinces had rebelled in support of the revolution. A republic was declared on 29 December. All over China, people cut off their pigtails, the hated mark of Manchu rule. Sun Yat-sen was in the USA at the time but hurried back to become the first President.

Yuan Shi-kai

Unfortunately, Sun was not supported by the mass of Chinese people, who did not know what was going on. Furthermore the northern provinces, near Peking, had stayed loyal to the Manchus. Sun's supporters were few in number as only a few Chinese were educated. In a final effort to save the dynasty, the Manchus had handed over power to a powerful local general named Yuan Shi-kai. In order to avoid war, Sun offered to give up the presidency to Yuan if Yuan could force the Emperor to give up the throne. Yuan accepted. On 12 February 1912 the Emperor abdicated. Three days later, Yuan became President of the Republic of China.

China's new government was supposed to be a democracy with an elected parliament. It was expected that Sun's old revolutionary party, now named the Kuomintang (or Nationalist Party), would have most of the say. Yuan, however, ignored parliament and terrorised the Kuomintang. In desperation Sun's followers staged a 'second revolution' to overthrow Yuan. It failed and Yuan now ruled as a dictator.

The impact of the First World War

The First World War had a great effect on China and nationalism. This was due to events during and soon after the war.

In 1915 Japan presented China with a list of Twenty-One Demands. These proposed to give Japan control of much of China's industry. China also had to accept Japanese advisers to help run the affairs of the country. The Chinese were shocked. Yuan was able to get some of the demands dropped but had to accept others. Once more China had been humiliated by the foreigners. Yuan was blamed for giving way and had to give up his plans to become emperor. In 1916 he died a 'broken-hearted man'.

Yuan's death was followed by chaos. Real power fell into the hands of the various generals or warlords who ran the provinces and were always fighting each other. Robberies, killings and lootings became everyday events. As a result of these events, in Chinese history the years 1917 to about 1928 are known as the 'warlord era'.

China was shredded by warlord wars. The peasants and labourers paid for these feudal wars in grain levies and very high taxes, for armies had to be paid and fed, and only China's peasantry – 80% of the population – could do it. Armies also need recruits and only the peasantry could supply them. In some areas men were press-ganged while working the fields. In Szechuan provinces taxes were raised seventy years in advance.

When Hu Tsung-nan came, almost everyone left Liu Ling. We went up into the hills. I was in the people's militia (citizen's army) then. We had buried all our possessions and all our corn. Hu Tsung-nan destroyed everything and his troops ate and ate. They discovered our grain stores and they stole cattle.

In 1917 China entered the First World War on the Allied side in the hope that, once peace came, the foreign powers would give up some of their Chinese territories. In 1914 Japan had captured Shantung from Germany. China wanted Japan expelled from Shantung. In 1919, news arrived from Paris that the peace-makers would allow Japan to keep Shantung. To make matters worse, the warlord government in Peking had agreed to Japan's claim as part of a secret deal for a loan.

The May 4th Movement

The First World War and Japanese gains upset many Chinese. A storm of protest known as the May 4th Demonstrations, swept China in 1919. Demonstrations, strikes and boycotts of Japanese goods were held in all the major cities, including Peking. The government was forced to dismiss three 'traitor ministers' and the Chinese representatives in Paris refused to sign the peace treaty.

The May 4th Movement was a turning point in China's history:

- For the first time students, workers, teachers and merchants had combined in a national movement.

- It showed that the Chinese were beginning to care what happened to their country.

- It also showed the even greater resentment of foreign control of their country.

- It gradually brought the Chinese people to think and act together.

SOURCE D

Student slogans of the May 4th Movement

DON'T FORGET OUR NATIONAL HUMILIATION

THROW OUT THE WARLORD TRAITORS

BOYCOTT FOREIGN GOODS

The real trouble is China is not an independent country. She is the victim of foreign countries. If the foreign countries leave us alone, China will have her affairs in shape within six months. The Peking Government could not stand twenty-four hours without the backing it receives from foreign governments.

The Kuomintang (also known as Guomindang)

Meanwhile, the Bolshevik Revolution had taken place in Russia in 1917 (p. 416). Sun Yat-sen had been disappointed that Britain and the USA had failed to support him. He admired the Russian Communists and asked them for advice.

Sun had been working in southern China trying to gain a base from which the Kuomintang could operate, but progress was slow. Twice Sun had set up a government in Canton (1917–18, 1920–22) and twice he had been driven out by local warlords. Sun needed a strong army. Only then could he hope to defeat the warlords and unite China under his control.

Finally, in 1923, Sun turned to Russia for help. Russia agreed:

- They trained Sun's soldiers, setting up a military academy at Whampoa.

- They provided arms, money and supplies.

- They set up a small Chinese Communist Party.

Sun was not a Communist but he worked with them and allowed Communists to join the Kuomintang. This was now reorganised and strengthened and ready to carry out a revolution to overthrow the warlords. Suddenly, in 1925 Sun died. He was succeeded by a young general named Chiang Kai-shek.

Chiang Kai-shek and civil war

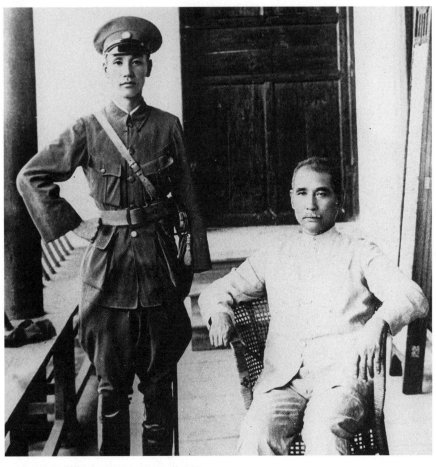

Chiang Kai-shek can be seen here on the left

Chiang Kai-shek was born in 1887 into a rich landowning family. He had been trained as a soldier in Japan, Russia and China, and was not a Communist. His supporters were merchants, landlords and bankers in the Kuomintang. They wanted a modern, up-to-date but Capitalist China. In 1923 Sun appointed him head of the army of the Kuomintang.

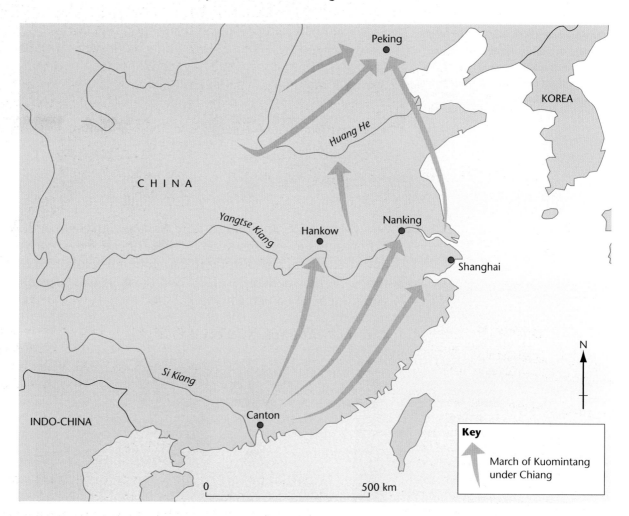

Chiang's first task was to remove the warlords. This was done in the two-year Northern Expedition. In 1926 the Kuomintang forces set out from Canton and reached as far north as Shanghai. By 1928 the rest of China was taken. The Communists helped in the Northern Expedition and worked among the people of the cities as they fell to the Kuomintang. They helped workers organise unions and peasants throw out landlords. In the towns strikes increased as workers demanded higher wages and shorter hours.

This kind of activity worried Chiang. As a wealthy man, he had never trusted the Communists. He was afraid that they would soon rise to overthrow him. So he struck first. In April 1927 he turned on the Communists and ordered the Shanghai Massacres, during which any known Communists were rounded up and killed. Thousands were butchered in Shanghai and other Kuomintang-held cities. One method used to identify Communists was to check the neck of suspects for the red stain left by red scarves worn by Communists in the fighting against the warlords. In wet weather the dye ran.

SOURCE F

Execution in a Chinese street, 1927

SOURCE G

An account by an official at the American consulate of the massacres in Canton in 1927

Many private scores were paid off. Two lots of 500 and 1,000 men each were taken out and machine gunned. Realising that this was a waste of ammunition, the soldiers loaded the victims on boats, took them down the river below the city, and pushed them overboard in lots of ten or twelve tied together. The slaughter continued here for four or five days, during which some 6,000 people, said to be Communists, lost their lives in the city of Canton.

In late 1927 Chiang's armies marched on Peking as the second stage of the Northern Expedition. By the end of 1928 Peking had been captured and the warlords had been defeated. Chiang seemed to have united China under the control of the Kuomintang.

Activity

When famous people die newspapers often write an obituary which means a summary of their life and achievements. Write an obituary in a British newspaper of Sun Yat-sen just after his death in 1925.

Questions

1 Is Source **A** a reliable view of peasant discontent in the period 1909–11?

2 What part did the following play in the history of China during this period:
   a the Kuomintang?
   b the warlords?
   c the Twenty-One Demands?
   d the May 4th Movement?

3 What do Sources **B** and **C** tell you about the warlords?

4 Which Source, **B** or **C**, would be more useful to an historian studying the warlord period?

5 Why did Chiang turn on the Communists?

Profile on

Mao Tse Tung (Mao Zedong)

Mao was born in 1893 into a moderately well-off peasant family in Hunan province. He got on well with his mother but his father was hot-tempered and frequently beat Mao and his brother. When the 1911 revolution overthrew the Manchus, Mao joined the revolutionary army but saw little action. In 1913 he enrolled on a five-year course to train as a teacher in Changsha. From there, he went to Peking to work in the university library. Here he made contact with students and professors and their ideas on how to solve the problems of China. Mao also began to study the writings of Karl Marx and his views on Communism. Marx believed that in an ideal world all property and goods should be shared and no one would be allowed to own property. Such a society appealed to Mao. It seemed much fairer than the China in which he lived, where there was a great gap between the rich few and the poor majority. Mao became a Communist and looked towards Russia, then the only Communist state, for help.

In 1949 China was proclaimed a People's Republic and became a Communist country. This was due mainly to the leadership of Mao Tse Tung, also known as Mao Zedong.

The early Communist Party

In 1920 a Russian agent arrived in Peking to help found a Chinese Communist Party. The following year Mao and 12 others formed the Chinese Communist Party (CCP) in Shanghai. The tiny party worked hard to help workers form unions to improve their miserable wages. In time, it was hoped, the workers would rise up, overthrow their employers and establish a Communist state. In the meantime it seemed a good idea to work with the Kuomintang to drive out the warlords and unite the country. Russia was especially keen on this move. Mao and his followers therefore joined the Kuomintang.

Reorganising the Communists, 1927–34

Many Communists escaped the massacres of 1927. The Central Committee of the Party went underground in Shanghai. The largest group fled to a mountain stronghold on the borders of the Kiangsi and Hunan provinces. This group was headed by Mao. Mao worked hard to govern the countryside. Land was seized from the landlords and given out to the poor peasants. All debts were wiped out. Soviets were organised to govern the countryside. Many peasants joined the Communist Red Army which numbered 11,000 by 1930.

The Red Army was trained in 'hit and run' or guerrilla warfare. This involved ambushing the enemy at its weakest point and then retreating into the countryside. The idea was to avoid taking on the Kuomintang who had more men and were better armed. The Red soldiers were instructed to pay for all their food, to help the peasants wherever they could, and to act as model soldiers. This way they won over the local peasants who were used to soldiers stealing their food and raping their women. The Red army had eight strict rules:

1 Speak politely

2 Pay fairly for what you buy

3 Return anything you borrow

4 Pay for everything you damage

5 Don't hit or swear at the people

6 Don't damage crops

7 Don't take liberties with women

8 Don't ill-treat prisoners

SOURCE A

Mao Tse Tung on Red Army tactics

When the enemy advances, we retreat,
When the enemy halts, we harass,
When the enemy retires, we attack,
When the enemy retreats, we pursue.

SOURCE B

Red Army song

Now listen closely to my song,
Workers and peasants are very poor,
Eating bitterness while the landlords eat meat,
Working while the landlords play
Ah, so hard!
First we must unite and raise the red banner,
Second, sew a badge upon our sleeve,
Third, destroy enemies in the village,
Fourth capture rifles from the landlords.

Karl Marx had written that only industrial workers could lead a revolution. Events in Russia in 1917 seemed to prove this. In China, however, there were few workers. Time and again Communist efforts in the cities failed. Mao realised that in China it had to be the peasants who would lead a Communist rising. His ideas about a peasant rising were not popular in the party at first, and he was dismissed from the Chinese Communist Party Committee in Shanghai. Instead the Red Army of the Central Committee attacked several large cities. These attacks, which took place in 1930, were disasters. The Kuomintang were too strong and few workers rose to support the Communists.

SOURCE C

Mao Tse Tung

In a very short time several hundred million peasants will rise like a hurricane. A force so swift and violent that no power however great will be able to hold it back. They will sweep all the imperialists, warlords, corrupt officials, local tyrants and evil landlords into their grave.

SOURCE D

A peasant recalls first hearing about the Communists

In February 1934, people began whispering about the Red Army, and how it was saying: 'The poor will not have to pay taxes. The poor will not have to pay rent. Poor people's children shall go to school, and landlords will disappear'. Then the landlords said: 'Don't listen to rumours. The Communists are bandits. They want to kill you and take your wives'.

China under the Kuomintang

From 1928 to 1934 Chiang Kai-shek had the chance to carry out Sun's 'Three Principles' and turn China into a powerful and modern state. He only really controlled one part of China – the Lower Yangtse Valley.

- The north-east was occupied from 1931 by the Japanese after the Manchurian invasion (p. 596).

- Warlords remained in control of many provinces.

- Large areas of Kiangsi were under Communist rule from 1931 to 1934. By 1936 they had a new base in Shensi.

Chiang moved his capital from Peking to the more centrally located Nanking. A modernisation programme was begun. New Chinese-owned factories were built. Railways and road communications were improved. More Chinese were educated than ever before. Foreign trade was increased. China also regained control of the customs service.

Yet all these reforms did not make Chiang popular.

- They meant little to the majority of peasants. They remained poor, deeply in debt and having to pay too many taxes. For most tenant farmers, rent alone took between 40% and 60% of the crop.

- No attempt was made to train the people for democracy. Chiang ruled as a dictator and gave positions in the government to his rich friends.

- He made little effort to force the Japanese out of Manchuria.

SOURCE E

Victims of famine, July 1930

SOURCE F

Edgar Snow, an American, was in China during the 1930s

The shocking thing was that in the cities there was grain and food and there had been for months but it could not be shipped to the starving. Why not? Because in the north-west there were generals who wanted to hold all their railways and would release none of them towards the east. In the east there were other Kuomintang generals who would send no railways westwards even to starving people because they feared they would be seized by rivals.

The Long March 1934–35

Chiang was determined to crush Communist rule in Kiangsi province. Between 1930 and 1934 Chiang launched five massive attacks against the Communist base. These all failed. Despite being outnumbered ten to one, the Communists drove back the first four attacks. Their guerrilla tactics proved very successful. In his fifth campaign Chiang changed tactics. He surrounded and blockaded the Red base and tried to starve the Communists to death. Rather than risk being wiped out, the Communists broke out of Kiangsi.

DESCRIPTION

In October 1934 well over 100,000 men, women and children broke through the blockade. Their aim was to march to a Communist base in Northern Shensi at Yenan. In order to give the pursuing Kuomintang troops the slip, a zig-zag course was followed through some of the wildest country in China, through mountains, deserts and swamps. Nevertheless they were attacked by Chiang's modern army and air force most of the way. On their way they fought over a dozen battles, crossed 24 rivers and 18 mountain ranges, covering an average of 24 miles a day. This incredible journey on foot covered 6,000 miles and lasted one year. Fewer than 30,000 survived the journey. The cost was huge.

SOURCE G

Heroic painting of the Red Army crossing the Dadu river on the Long March

SOURCE H

Crossing the grasslands

When we entered the marshlands most men drank the bitter black water and wild grass and vegetables were now plucked. When no green things were to be found the men would gather dried grass and chew the roots. One day someone dug out a kind of plant the size of a green turnip. Those who ate it vomited after half an hour and several died.

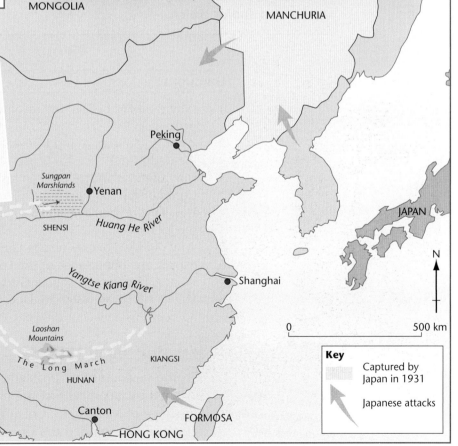

The Long March was important for several reasons:

- It meant that the Communists survived and had a new base.

- It made Mao the new, unchallenged leader of the Communists because he had led the march. It would be his ideas that would be followed in the battle to take control of China.

- Most of all, it was seen as a great Chinese achievement. For many years, the Chinese had had nothing to be proud of. They had been frequently defeated and humiliated. Now a group of Chinese people had done something remarkable and heroic.

- Many Chinese people now saw the Communists as heroes and began to support them.

SOURCE I

From T. Mende, *The Chinese Revolution*, 1961

This unbelievable feat of endurance led across eleven provinces, over remote regions inhabited by suspicious peoples through murderous marshy lands overgrown by grass, and in the face of danger from local and government forces. The basic aim – to save the revolution – was achieved. But the price was high. Of the 130,000 men who left fewer than 30,000 arrived in North Shensi.

Activity

Either

Draw a Communist propaganda poster about the Long March but aiming to win over the Chinese people.

Or

A Communist newspaper account of the March for the same purpose. You could include headlines, a description of the march and a map and/or sketch.

Questions

1. Why did Mao believe the revolution would start with the peasants?
2. What do Sources **A** and **B** reveal about the tactics and methods of the Red Army?
3. How useful is Source **D** to an historian studying support for Communism in China?
4. How far do Sources **E** and **F** explain why Chiang lost support in the 1930s?
5. Why did Mao decide on the Long March?
6. Explain the importance of the Long March.
7. What is the artist of Source **G** trying to make you think?
8. Source **I** is by an historian. Does this make it more accurate than Source **H** as a view of the Long March?

SOURCE A

Chiang Kai-shek

The Japanese are a disease of the skin; it can be cured. The Communists are a disease of the soul; it affects the whole body.

WAR WITH JAPAN 1931–45

Chiang faced another problem. Since 1931, China had been invaded by Japan. At first the Japanese invaded the northern province of Manchuria. Chiang did very little about this because he regarded the Communists as a greater threat.

The Japanese then began to move south into the rest of China. The Communist Chinese in Yenan were not near the Japanese, but they declared war on them. This made the Communists appear more patriotic, because they were fighting for China. Chiang continued to ignore the Japanese. Then, in 1937, Chiang was kidnapped by one of his own generals and made to declare war on Japan. He also agreed to a Communist–Kuomintang united front against the Japanese. For the Communists, this was a major victory. They expected the Kuomintang to exhaust themselves in the coming war with Japan.

The Marco Polo incident

In July 1937 Japan attacked Chinese troops at the Marco Polo bridge near Peking. This was the start of a full-scale war which lasted until 1945. Within eighteen months the Japanese had occupied many of China's great ports and her industrial and commercial centres.

Chiang's forces retreated to Chungking where they remained until the end of the war. His allies, Britain and the USA, supplied him by air and by the famous 'Burma Road'. Chiang's Nationalist forces did not do very well against the Japanese. China was now split into three parts:

- Japanese-occupied China.

- Kuomintang China, centred on Chungking.

- Red China in the north-west of the country.

The Red Army and the Japanese

In the north-west the Communists carried out a highly successful guerrilla war against the Japanese. Small Red Army units struck deep into Japanese-held territory, hit important targets and then retreated back into safety. The Japanese controlled the towns and cities and, by day, the roads. The Communists worked among the peasants and soon controlled the countryside. By night, they used the roads. They never met the Japanese head-on, melting away if attacked. When the Japanese were weak, or caught unawares, they were attacked suddenly.

Source B

Japanese tactics, Quoted in C.P. Fitzgerald and M. Roper, *China – A World So Changed*

The Japanese slogan was 'Kill all, Burn all, Loot all'. As they moved into an area on their mopping-up campaigns, they killed all young men, destroyed or stole all cattle and broke or made off with the farmers' tools and grain. Their aim was to create a no-man's-land in which nothing could live.

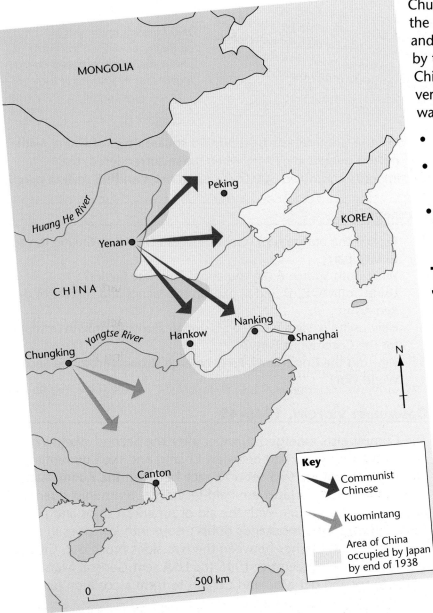

Key

Communist Chinese

Kuomintang

Area of China occupied by Japan by end of 1938

0   500 km

MONGOLIA
Huang He River
Yenan
CHINA
Peking
KOREA
Yangtse River
Hankow
Nanking
Shanghai
Chungking
Canton
N

The Red Army was used to spread Communist ideas. After taking over an area, the Red Army immediately set about winning over the people. To secure peasant support, land rents and interest payments were reduced. Schools were opened and medical care was provided. Where possible the Red Army helped in the fields and around the villages. In these ways the Red troops came to be seen as defenders and friends of the people. By 1945 there were 95 million peasants under Communist rule within 19 freed regions.

The peasant support was also vital to Red Army guerrilla tactics. As Mao said: 'The peasants are the sea, the Red Army the fish who swim in it'. The peasants gave food, shelter and information to them.

SOURCE C

J. Myrdal, *Report from a Chinese Village*

When the Kuomintang fled and the Red Army came, the land was divided up. After that life was better. Having land and not needing to pay the rent to anyone, there was enough for us to eat.

SOURCE D

Agnes Smedley, *Battle Hymn of China*, 1944

Reading, writing, arithmetic were taught by officers to their men. The men sat on the ground tracing characters and figures in the dirt, since there were no paper or pencils. But the most powerful educational method consisted of debate. Not only were battles and campaigns discussed, but the conduct of any commander could be criticised.

SOURCE E

Report from John Paton Davies to the American government, 1944

The Communist government and armies are the first in modern China to have positive and widespread popular support because they are genuinely of the people.

In 1937 the Communists held 30,000 square miles of China, with two million people. By 1945, when Japan surrendered, the Communists controlled 300,000 square miles and 95 million people.

Questions

1 Explain the outbreak of war with Japan. How was Chiang forced to take part?
2 What does Source **B** tell you about Japanese tactics?
3 Using Sources **C**, **D** and **E**, explain the tactics and success of the Red Army.
4 How useful is Source **C** to an historian studying growth in support for the Communist Party?
5 Why did the Communist Party emerge stronger from the Second World War?

COMMUNIST VICTORY, 1945–49

The Communists emerged stronger after the Second World War and within four years had defeated Chiang and the Kuomintang.

Japan's defeat in 1945 set off a race between the Kuomintang and Communists for Japanese-held territory. Communist guerrillas moved into Manchuria. With the aid of American ships and planes, Chiang transported thousands of his troops into key cities in north and east China. Clashes between the two sides broke out. Civil War seemed likely. In December 1945 the USA sent General Marshall to China to try and get Mao and Chiang to form a coalition (joint) government. They agreed to a truce.

Civil War 1946–51

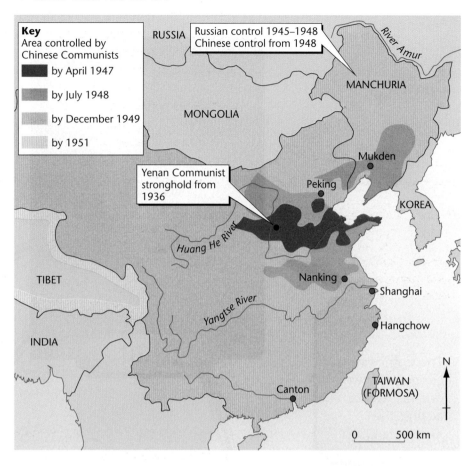

Key
Area controlled by Chinese Communists

- by April 1947
- by July 1948
- by December 1949
- by 1951

RUSSIA

Russian control 1945–1948
Chinese control from 1948

River Amur

MANCHURIA

MONGOLIA

Mukden

Peking

KOREA

Yenan Communist stronghold from 1936

Huang He River

Nanking

Shanghai

TIBET

Yangtse River

Hangchow

INDIA

Canton

TAIWAN (FORMOSA)

N

0   500 km

Source A

Famine riots in Shanghai, Christmas Eve 1948

In July 1946 the truce collapsed. Neither side was willing to trust the other and the civil war began. At first the Kuomintang made spectacular advances into north China and Manchuria. In mid-1947 the Communists counter-attacked. The Kuomintang were forced on the defensive.

In 1948 the Communists took Manchuria and won decisive battles in north China. By the end of the year, the Kuomintang forces were falling apart. In the Kuomintang areas there were serious food shortages. Prices soared and money became almost worthless. Crooked government officials often pocketed money sent from abroad for food and arms.

In January 1949 Tientsin and Peking fell, soon followed by Nanking, Shanghai and Canton. On 1 October 1949 the People's Republic of China was proclaimed. The Kuomintang government fled to Taiwan.

Source B

Rising prices

It was impossible to live on one's wages as money lost its value from hour to hour or even from minute to minute. In 1948 a lunch at the Palace Hotel, Shanghai, cost millions of Chinese dollars. Soup was $800,000 and chicken liver with mushrooms $3,500,000.

Mao

Tactics

The Communists continued their guerrilla tactics against the Kuomintang.

Peasant support

Chiang had always supported the landlords so peasants and Reds continued to work together.

The unpopularity of Chiang and the Kuomintang

As Chiang became older, he became more and more of a dictator. Inflation was high and aid from the USA went into the pockets of Chiang, his family and friends. The Kuomintang had become the party of the landlords. His soldiers, unlike the Red army, treated the areas they went into badly. USA support made Chiang appear to be no more than a puppet of the Americans.

SOURCE C

An American, William Lederer, wrote the following about Chiang's army

As early as 1941, I personally have seen long lines of conscripts chained together on their way from their villages to training camps. Sons of the rich never entered the army. Sons of the poor could never escape.

SOURCE D

Two other American reporters, Theodore White and Annalee Jacoby, wrote

Recruits ate less than the starving soldiers. Sometimes they got no water. Many of them were stripped naked and left to sleep on bare floors. They were whipped. Dead bodies were allowed to lie for days. In some areas less than 20% lived to see the front.

The leadership of Mao

He was very popular due to:

- His leadership during the Long March.

- Successful guerrilla tactics against the Japanese during the Second World War. To many he was seen as a liberator. This won him huge backing from the peasants but also the middle classes who, though not Communist, recognised that Mao was fighting to defend China's national interests.

- Methods used by his Red Army to win over the peasants.

Activity

You are a British journalist in China in 1948. Write two reports home – one from a part of China held by the Kuomintang, the other from a part held by the Communists. In each case you could describe:

- The army and how it treats the people.

- The life and attitude of the people.

Questions

1 How far do Sources **A** and **B** agree about the situation in Kuomintang-held areas?

2 How useful are Sources **C** and **D** to an historian studying Chiang and his army during the Civil War?

3 Do you think Mao's leadership was the most important reason for Communist victory in the civil War? Explain your answer.

COMMUNIST CHINA 1949–58

When Mao took over China in 1949, he took on all of his country's problems:

- It was very poor. Industrial production was 50% down on the best pre-war figure and food production was 25% down.

- Most of the people were peasants who could not read or write.

- There was rapid inflation and hardly any modern industry.

- There had been 40 years of civil war and foreign invasion. Manchuria, China's most industrialised region, had been occupied by the Japanese and looted by Russia.

- The Chinese people did not want change. They mistrusted all modern ideas in farming, industry, education, medicine and women's rights.

- The Communists had to prove they were capable of providing a strong and effective government.

- Opposition to the government had to be removed or brought under control.

- Most of the world refused to recognise the Communists. America continued to recognise the Kuomintang on Taiwan. Only Russia would give aid to help rebuild China.

SOURCE A

A report prepared by the US government, 1967

The economy inherited by the Communists was a shambles. Industry and commerce had almost come to a standstill in major urban centers. Dams, irrigation systems, and canals were badly in need of repair. Railroad lines had been cut and recut by the contending armies. Inflation had ruined confidence in the money system. And, finally, the population had suffered enormous casualties and was half-starved and exhausted.

Setting up government

The Communists had two main advantages. There was little opposition, because Mao had the support of most of the people. Secondly, the Communists were already experienced in government – for years they had ruled large parts of China.

To win the widest possible support, a number of political parties were invited to work with the Communists. In theory this meant that the government was a coalition of parties. In practice it was a single party Communist dictatorship.

601

Communist

Mass media

The Communist Party had complete control of all radio, newspapers, books and cinema. The mass media was used to encourage people to follow the Party line and persuade them to accept it.

Education

Used to ensure the young were brought up to follow the ideas of Mao and Communism.

Campaigns

Many opponents were persuaded to reform their ways and were 're-educated' to Communism. They could be sent to the fields or factories. They had to learn about Communism through manual labour. Large campaigns of 'thought reform' were launched against enemies, usually landowners or businessmen. Mao organised other campaigns to root out various 'evils' in Chinese life.

- *1950* 'Three Mountains' campaign against feudalism, capitalism and imperialism.

- *1951* Against landowners and capitalists. 250,000 were executed.

- *1952* 'Three Antis' against corruption.

SOURCE B

Death of a landlord. A bound landlord awaits a bullet in the back, having been found guilty by a People's Court, 1953.

Dictatorship

Party cadres (organisers)

These controlled the army and various mass groups of peasants, workers, students and children. They persuaded the masses to think and act like true Communists.

Terror

In the early years opponents were hunted out and executed. As many as one million opponents were executed between 1949 and 1951.

'Hundred Flowers' campaign, 1957

In 1957 Mao launched this campaign. The full slogan was:

This invited criticism from anyone. The result was such a wave of criticism that the campaign was stopped. Mao may have used this campaign to flush out criticism of his government. Many of the strongest opponents, especially from the old educated classes, were sent for 're-education'.

LET A HUNDRED
FLOWERS
BLOOM,

LET A HUNDRED
SCHOOLS
OF THOUGHT
CONTEND

Industry

Mao wanted to make China a great industrial power. He moved gradually as regards industry. At first only foreign trade, the banks and heavy industries were nationalised. The rest were left in private hands. When the smaller factories were taken over their former owners were given well-paid jobs as managers so that businesses would benefit from their skills and their experience.

In 1953 the Soviet-style five-year plans (p. 444) were introduced. Like the Russian model, the First Five Year Plan concentrated on heavy industries like steel, coal, electric power and cement. Output was set to double but in fact it increased by 120% and in some cases even more – for example, coal production increased from 63.5 million tons in 1952 to nearly 124 million in 1957. Russia helped out with machinery, equipment and technical assistance. Railways and roads were built.

During this period all remaining private industry was taken over by the government. Any businesses still in Chinese hands were taxed so heavily until their owners gladly handed them over.

Inflation was stopped by insisting on buying and selling at low, fixed prices. These developments, however, did little to improve the standard of living of the Chinese who were desperate for consumer goods such as bicycles.

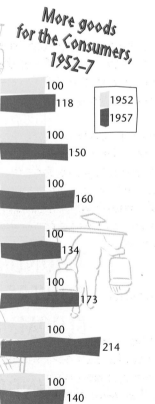

More goods for the Consumers, 1952–7

	1952	1957
Grain	100	118
Edible oils	100	150
Sugar	100	160
Cotton cloth	100	134
Rubber shoes	100	173
Machine-made paper	100	214
Cigarettes	100	140

PRODUCTION TABLE			
(million tonnes)	1952	1957	
		planned	actual
Coal	63.5	113	124
Iron	1.9	4.7	5.86
Steel	1.35	4.12	5.24
Oil	0.44	2.0	1.42
Cement	2.6	6.0	4.65
Power (billion kW)	7.26	15.9	19.1

Agriculture

The main reason why Chinese peasants supported the Communists was because they wanted their own land. Under the Agrarian Reform Law of 1950 land was taken from the landlords and shared out amongst the peasants. Landlords as a class were wiped out. Grain production climbed to a record high by 1952.

Even so the average farm was less than 2.5 acres. Larger farms and more modern methods would be needed if food production was to be increased greatly. This was essential as a census of 1951 showed that China's population was 600 million and rising fast. If famine was to be avoided, something had to be done.

Population growth

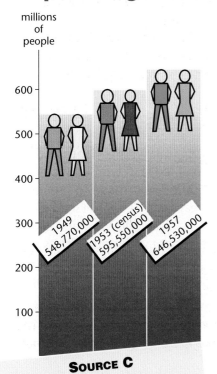

millions of people

600 —
500 —
400 —
300 —
200 —
100 —

1949
548,770,000

1953 (census)
595,550,000

1957
646,530,000

SOURCE C

Mao, introducing a co-operative in 1958

More people mean a greater ferment of ideas, more enthusiasm and more energy. Never before have the masses of the people been so inspired, so militant and so daring as at present.

In 1952 groups of peasant households were encouraged to join together in mutual-aid teams or co-operatives. Under this scheme, farmers kept their own land but shared their animals and labour. By the end of 1952, 40% of all peasants were members of these mutual-aid teams.

In 1953 peasants were called upon to take the second step towards full co-operative or collective farming, as in Russia (p. 440). Mutual-aid teams were joined together and farmed as one unit:

- Profits were shared out among members according to the amount of land, tools and hours of work they had put in.

- Together the co-operatives were able to buy machines and better seeds.

Communist Party workers went round the villages persuading peasants to set up co-operatives. Overall, these co-operatives were well received by the peasants, who grew more food and ate better.

The introduction of higher-grade co-operatives or collectives began in 1955. All land was handed to a collective. Private ownership, except for small garden plots, ceased to exist. Instead farmers became wage earners. Although there was opposition, by 1957 over 90% of the peasants were in collectives.

Education

A massive campaign was organised right from the start to teach the Chinese people to read and write. In 1949, only 20% of the people were literate. By 1980 this had been increased to 90%. Teachers were sent to the villages, teaching the children by day and the adults in the evenings.

Students also received an education in Communism. The books they read from were the works of Marx, Lenin or Mao. They were encouraged to be hard-working, cheerful, loyal to their leaders and helpful to others. Under Mao no one receiving education was allowed to forget the importance of manual work. Pupils worked part-time in factories, students for two months a year in communes and their professors for one month a year.

Health

Disease and lack of hygiene were common in the old China. Mao introduced several improvements:

- Every street set up a committee to tidy up rubbish and litter, arrange the supply of water and keep the area healthy. These helped to reduce greatly the incidence of killer diseases, such as cholera, typhoid and tuberculosis, that were commonplace in 1949.

- China was short of doctors, especially those trained in Western medicine. For this reason, and because the full training of doctors takes so long, 'barefoot doctors' were trained. These were people trained in basic medical skills but not given a full medical training. They were soon ready to go out into the villages to deal with common diseases. More serious cases were sent to fully trained doctors.

- All health care was now free of charge.

- Chinese methods, such as acupuncture, were practised alongside Western skills.

Women

Mao was determined to change old attitudes to women who had been seen as second-class citizens. In the traditional Chinese family, marriages were arranged and women were expected to obey their husbands completely.

The Communist government banned arranged marriages and women were given equal rights. Mao realised that women were a great source of untapped labour. Every effort was made to provide them with workplace nurseries. The Great Leap Forward (see below) introduced compulsory work for mothers. Gradually women came to play a much greater role in Chinese society with equal rights in education and jobs. The government continually used posters and slogans to promote the position of women and overcome resistance.

Activity

You were a well-educated landlord in China before 1949 and fled when the Communists took over. You have now been allowed back. Describe how the village and people have changed under Communist rule and your feelings about these changes.

Questions

1   According to Source **A**, how serious were the problems that Mao faced?
2   How successful were his five-year plans, according to the figures on p. 604?
3   Why was it so important to improve agriculture?
4   Explain the following:
    a   mutual-aid teams.
    b   co-operatives.
    c   collectives.
5   How reliable is Source **C** as a view of the co-operatives?
6   What improvements took place in education and health provision during this period?

THE GREAT LEAP FORWARD

In 1958 Mao decided on a second five-year plan which became known as the Great Leap Forward. This was for several reasons:

1   After nearly ten years of Communism, Mao was worried that China was settling back into old ways. He saw a middle class of 'experts' growing up, running the factories, businesses, hospitals and universities. To Mao they were too much like the old Mandarin class who ruled China under the emperors. He wanted another revolution in order to hand control back to the peasants and workers.

2   Despite the successes of the first five-year plan China's vast source of manpower was not being used efficiently. There was unemployment in the cities and in the countryside most peasants had little to do between harvesting and sowing.

3   Finally, there was a problem of how China could raise enough money to build more industry.

To solve these problems Mao came up with the Great Leap Forward. In the countryside peasants would be fully employed if they were set to work on large irrigation and flood control projects. They could also develop small-scale industries. One result would be more farm produce, which would be taxed to help build industry.

In the cities, industries which required a lot of workers but little money would be set up to solve the unemployment problem. New higher targets for industry and agriculture were set up. Industrial output was again set to double and agricultural output to increase by 35%. Central planning was abandoned in favour of local organisation. China was set the target of overtaking British steel production levels.

Communes

At the same time a new way of organising agricultural life came into being. Collective farms were joined into 24,000 communes, with an average population of 30,000 people. The people in the commune were divided into brigades of workers of about 1,000 to 2,000 and then into teams of workers of 50 to 200 people.

SOURCE A

Chinese propaganda painting showing the hopes of the Great Leap Forward

Communes seemed the ideal way to organise China's vast peasant labour force. They were large enough to tackle large projects such as irrigation works and run their schools, clinics, shops and local citizen army. In addition, each one set up its own local industries. Mao asked communes to mine coal and iron and to set up their own blast furnaces. Millions of people who had never done so before began to operate 'backyard' blast furnaces.

Life in the commune was supposed to be lived communally. Peasants were to eat in mess halls. Nurseries were provided for young children. Family life was cut back. In this way it was hoped that communes would speed up the change to Communism.

The government tried to persuade people to join communes by a tremendous propaganda campaign. By the end of 1958 the whole of China was organised into communes.

SOURCE B

Statements by Mao

During a tour of the country made in 1958 I witnessed the tremendous energy of the people. On this foundation it is possible to succeed at any task whatsoever. It is better to set up People's Communes. Their advantage lies in the fact that they combine industry, agriculture, commerce, education and military affairs. After a number of years, Chinese society will enter into the age of Communism, where the principles from each according to his ability, to each according to his needs will be practised.

The establishment of communes during the Great Leap Forward – percentage of total peasant population	
August 1958 (end)	30.4
September 1958 (early)	48.1
September 1958 (middle)	65.3
September 1958 (end)	98.0
December 1958 (end)	99.1

Focus on

Organisation of commune

PRODUCTION TEAM'S ANNUAL OUTPUT

Costs of production (e.g. seed, fertilizer, repairs)

Savings for

New buildings and machinery

Welfare projects (e.g. clinic)

For distribution to individual peasants (about 2/3 total) based on work-points reckoned according to hours and type of work
Paid spring and autumn in

Payments to Brigade for services (e.g. hospital)

Agricultural tax paid to State

Compulsory purchase of part of crop by State

Cash

Kind, e.g. grain, cotton cloth, meat

Can be added to by:
Growing vegetables or keeping animals on family plots
Side employment (e.g. weaving baskets, making clothes)

Was the Great Leap Forward a success?

The Great Leap tried to do too much too fast, and led to huge mistakes:

Industry

Thousands of small factories proved to be inefficient and wasteful. Much of the 'backyard' iron and steel was of low quality and could not be used. In 1960, after a deterioration in relations between China and the USSR, Russia began to withdraw their technicians and advisers. This deprived the Chinese of much needed expertise and money.

Agriculture

Food production also slumped and too many peasants had been moved from agriculture to industry. By 1961 China was having to buy grain from abroad, and only strict rationing prevented a famine. This situation was not helped by three years of disastrous harvests caused by floods and drought.

The communes

These were not the great success hoped for. Many proved to be too large to be run efficiently. Peasants resented the loss of their private plots and the attacks on family life. The members of the commune were not, at first, allowed to have any private possessions at all. They all received the same wages. Even families were broken up to make certain that all who could work did so.

Activity

The following sources and tables provide different evidence about the effects of the Great Leap Forward. Copy the table headings (p. 611) and write in evidence which shows success of the second five-year plan, evidence of failure and evidence which proves neither.

Source C

From *Eyewitness in China* by Hugo Portisch, a journalist visiting China in this period

There were not enough machines. There was no cement, no mortar and other building materials. Pekingers were summoned to build this dam with their bare hands and feet by voluntary shift work. Hundreds of thousands of inhabitants of Peking, including all the civil servants and university professors, doctors, students etc. They scratched away the earth from the surrounding hills often with no more than their finger nails. They split stones with the most primitive tools. In the next six months the dam was built. It is 2,088 feet high and 38.2 feet wide at its base.

PRODUCTION TABLE	1957	1960	
Grain	185	150	(million tonnes)
Cattle	50	42	(million)
Sheep	52	50	
Pigs	145	82	

Source D

Students building their own university in Ya'an

Source E

Edgar Snow, *The Other Side of the River*, 1963. Snow was an American journalist.

Female engineering students all insisted that they did everything other students did. There was a tendency to give them light work, but they did their turn at the furnaces, the same carrying work, the same risks. They wanted complete equality in work assignments. Did I know who was the first volunteer to carry a cable across the Yellow River rapids at San Men Hsia at the start of the big dam there? A woman engineer.

Source F

An American journalist's report

On September 13, 1961, the American journalist, Joseph Alsop, reported that the average Chinese 'was compelled to live on a diet of no more than 600 calories ' of food intake a day. This was 'a level of nourishment so low that American doctors require patients needing such severe diets to enter hospitals for the purpose'. Mr Alsop went on to report that a person on 600 calories 'can normally expect to lose about 20 pounds a month'. Mr Alsop concluded that the population of China is starving.

Source G

A letter to the *New York Herald Tribune*, written by Sybil Cookson, 1961

Having recently undertaken a three weeks' tour of China – visiting six cities and many country districts – my husband and I were astonished to read Joseph Alsop's recent report from Hong Kong reporting that there is widespread famine in China and even the likelihood of revolt against the present government. It is quite the opposite of our impression formed in China itself last Autumn. We were allowed to travel where we desired – in crowded streets, stores and holiday resorts. We visited communes, schools, colleges, hospitals and homes for old folk. Nowhere did we see any signs of discontent much less of famine despite a disappointing harvest.

Great Leap Forward

SUCCESSES	NEITHER	FAILURES

Do you think it was a success or failure? Explain your answer.

Retreat from the Great Leap Forward

Mao took part of the blame for the failure of the Great Leap and, in late 1958, resigned as China's head of state. China's affairs were now controlled by three leading Communists, President Liu Shao-chi, Prime Minister Chou En-lai and the Communist Party General Secretary, Deng Xiaoping. They introduced new policies, abandoning many of those of the Great Leap.

Industry

Thousands of factories were closed down. Other factories were grouped together and technicians and professional advisers and managers were sent in. People were encouraged to set up their own businesses. Bonuses were given for increased output.

Agriculture

Millions of peasants were returned from manufacturing to farming. To encourage peasants to produce more food, private garden plots were returned.

Communes

These were reduced in size to about one-third of their original size.

Mao was angry at these changes. He felt that the new policies were creating new forms of social inequality.

- By bringing back private plots, the government was creating a new class of rich peasants.

- The payment of bonuses resulted in a new privileged class of workers.

- To make matters worse, government officials were beginning to behave like a privileged ruling class.

Questions

1   Is Source **A** useful to an historian studying the Great Leap Forward?
2   What, according to Mao in Source **B**, were the aims of the communes?
3   Why else did Mao decide on the Great Leap Forward?
4   Describe the organisation and work of a commune.
5   What differences are there between Sources **F** and **G** in their views of the situation in China in 1961?
6   Why do you think their views are so different?
7   What changes were brought in by Liu and the other two leaders? How did Mao react to these changes?

THE CULTURAL REVOLUTION 1966–69

In 1962 Mao came out of semi-retirement to launch the 'Socialist Education Movement'. This was a campaign to get the people back on the right path to Communism. However, Mao could do little while Liu and his supporters held most positions of power. Mao, therefore, turned to the army for help. Soldiers were ordered to study Mao's thoughts contained in the 'Little Red Book of Quotations from Chairman Mao' and spread his ideas throughout China. He told them to rid the country of the 'Four Olds' – Old ideas, Old culture, Old customs and Old ways of life. By 1965 Mao had enough support to launch a new super-campaign known as the Cultural Revolution.

SOURCE A

Oath taken by the Red Guards

We vow to apply sentence by sentence each of Chairman Mao's orders, even if we do not at first understand them.

Features of the Cultural Revolution

In 1966 attacks against Mao's opponents grew louder. At first the attacks were aimed at unnamed enemies of Communism. Later the attacks were centred on Liu and his followers.

In June 1966 schools and universities were closed down. The students joined the groups of Red Guards from the army which were springing up. Between August and November 1966, millions of students were brought to Peking by the army for a series of mass rallies. At a rally of one million young people in Peking, Mao called upon them to be 'Red Guards', seeking out 'revisionists' everywhere.

The Red Guards and students were ordered to rid the Communist Party of the enemies of Mao's policies. Opponents were humiliated, tortured, or executed and many party officials, including Liu, were removed from office. Huge posters with the names and 'crimes' of teachers and party bosses appeared on the streets. The Guards even called for a change in the traffic-light system – red should mean 'go' and not 'stop'!

Red Guards reading the thoughts of Chairman Mao

A Chinese official describes the Cultural Revolution

You can't imagine how exciting it all was. Every morning, you came to your office. You could hardly wait to get there to see what was new, to see what the new posters said. You never knew when you yourself might be attacked. It was a continuous fever. Everyone was swept up in it. It was a wonderful experience. It was the great experience of my life. Now I know what life in China means.

By 1967 China was on the verge of civil war. Red Guards were fighting with peasants and workers.

INDUSTRY

Factories were reorganised to give power to the workers. Prizes and bonuses for town workers were abolished. Instead special importance was placed on teamwork. Technicians were dismissed and production fell. Transport ground to a halt.

SOURCE D

Beijing Revolutionary Committee, 1967

Red Guards have caused work stoppages in the factories and the countryside by persuading workers and peasants that it is more important to intervene elsewhere than it is to work.

EDUCATION AND CULTURE

This was seriously disrupted. Students refused to sit examinations as they showed up inequalities between them. All books, plays and films had to be about workers or peasants, or stories with a Communist message. Many artists were humiliated and suffered at the hands of the Red Guards.

SOURCE E

Ken Ling, *From Schoolboy to Little General*, 1972

I saw rows of teachers with black ink poured over their heads and faces. They all wore dunces' caps. Hanging from their necks were buckets filled with rocks.

COUNTRYSIDE

Students and graduates were sent to work alongside peasants in the countryside.

Medical care did improve as thousands of 'barefoot doctors' (see p. 605) were trained. An effort was also made to provide every peasant with primary schooling.

Results of the Cultural Revolution

GOVERNMENT

Opponents were killed or sent into exile. Deng Xiaoping, the General Secretary of the Communist Party, was removed from his post. Probably as many as a million people died as a result of the Revolution. Revolutionary committees, dominated by the army, were set up to run the country. One of the goals of the Cultural Revolution was to give the masses more self-government. Yet in fact 95% of party officials were given their jobs back. However, they were now regularly sent out to work in the fields and factories to keep in touch with the people.

SOURCE F

A cartoon showing Liu Shao-chi and his wife on a visit to Indonesia

Indonesia

It is not certain how the Cultural Revolution ended. It seems likely that the army moved in to restore order. In 1969 Lin Piao was named as Mao's successor. Two years later Lin Piao tried to organise a complete take-over of government. He disappeared together with several military leaders.

In January 1976, Mao's lifelong friend and likely successor, Premier Chou En-lai, died of cancer. After a brief struggle, Hua Kuo-feng, a moderate, was appointed Premier. Then in September 1976 Mao died. His widow, Chiang Ching, with the help of three other leading Communists, tried to seize power. This attempt by the so-called 'Gang of Four' failed and they were arrested. In October Hua was appointed successor to Mao as Party Chairman.

Activities

1   Using the following table draw up a balance sheet to show Mao's achievements and failures.

Achievements	Failures

You should consider the following:

- Early leadership of the Communist Party.

- The Long March and the war against Japan.

- The successful revolution in 1949.

- Changes brought in 1949–58.

- The Great Leap Forward and its effects.

- The Cultural Revolution and its effects.

Overall, do you think Mao's leadership benefited China? Explain your answer.

2   Write a wall-poster for display during the Cultural Revolution. It is to attack the boss of your factory for the way it is being run without paying enough attention to the ideas of Chairman Mao.

Questions

1   Why did Mao decide on the Cultural Revolution?
2   Explain the following:
   a   the Red Guards.
   b   the Little Red Book.
3   Describe the events of the Cultural Revolution.
4   What can you learn about the Revolution from Source **C**? Is the writer of Source **C** for or against the Cultural Revolution? Give reasons for your answer.
5   What effects did the Cultural Revolution have on education, industry and agriculture?
6   What point is the cartoonist trying to make in Source **F**?
7   What view does Source **G** have of Mao? Why do you think it has this view?

SOURCE B

Extract from a speech by Deng in 1986

The main job of socialism is to increase production, steadily improve the life of the people and keep making society richer.

CHINA UNDER DENG, 1977–90

By the middle of 1977 Deng Xiaoping had emerged as the real leader of China. He brought in further changes.

Industry and agriculture

Deng saw that China needed to increase production and modernise industry to support its huge population which was close to 1 billion (1000 million). To encourage peasants and workers to produce more, new incentives were introduced such as piecework, overtime, bonus payments and profit-sharing. All of these were very different from Mao's methods. Prices paid by the state to peasants for grain and other food was raised. Peasants were allowed to grow more cash crops and sell their surplus at market value.

People were free to own their own small businesses. To satisfy demand, record numbers of consumer goods, such as bicycles, watches and sewing machines, were produced. Foreigners were encouraged to visit China and invest their money, even from the old enemy, the USA.

Private trade was encouraged. By 1983 China had 44,000 markets where farmers could sell their produce privately. The income of agricultural workers tripled between 1977 and 1983. Nevertheless there were problems:

- A television set cost two years' wages and a bicycle a month's pay in the mid-1980s.

- Unemployment, according to Western estimates, stood at 12% in 1983.

- Modernisation brought Western-style problems of a rising crime rate and football hooliganism.

Education

Deng also reversed the educational reforms of the Cultural Revolution. Under Mao, students were admitted to university if they had a good political record. Deng restored tough examinations for university places. Success in academic subjects once again became essential. Special key schools for the best students were set up to provide China with the skills needed to prosper. The time spent on political education and manual work was cut.

Birth control

Deng was determined to reduce the rate of population growth. In 1979 he introduced the 'one-child' family policy. During the Great Leap Forward, a birth control campaign was introduced which urged late marriage and birth control. During the Cultural Revolution the campaign was abandoned and the birth rate began to rise again. It was estimated that by the year 2000 China's population would be 1.282 billion.

The 'one-child' policy was launched with massive publicity. It has been effective in towns and cities where it is easier for the authorities to police it and issue 'single-child family' certificates. Not so successful in rural areas where it has been more difficult to enforce. The birth rate has slowed down, although recent predictions are that China's population will still reach 1.5 billion by the year 2025.

The policy has not been popular:

- It has encouraged late and compulsory abortion.

- In China only sons are supposed to continue the family line. The birth of a daughter has been greeted with disappointment. There is even evidence of discrimination against girls, including withholding food and health care.

Communist control

At first it appeared that Deng would move China closer to democracy. In 1979 elections were introduced at county and urban levels for the party congresses. The National People's Congress, set up in 1954 but given little power, was now allowed to change laws. Deng himself refused to become Chairman of the Party and insisted he preferred the idea of 'collective' leadership.

Deng, however, exercised tight control over the Chinese Communist Party. Mao's widow, Chiang Ching, was too important a figure to execute and she was sentenced to house arrest. Eventually in 1980 the 'Gang of Four' was put on trial. Chiang was accused of a host of crimes – including decadent Western activities such as watching *The Sound of Music* and playing poker. Deng described her as 'a very, very evil woman. She is so evil that anything you can say about her can't be evil enough'. All were found guilty and given long prison sentences.

In 1979 a small movement began to emerge demanding greater democracy. Members pasted posters on a wall on Chang'an Avenue, the main east–west street of Beijing (formerly Peking). This became known as 'democracy wall'. The posters demanded free speech and a parliament. At first Deng appeared to welcome this movement. In 1981, however, members were arrested and the movement crushed.

In 1986 unrest spread to students of the University of Science and Technology at Hefei in Anhui province. They were against Japanese investment in China and organised protest marches and demonstrations. These spread to the universities of Shanghai, Beijing and other cities. In 1987 Hu Yaobang, the Party Chairman, was dismissed by Deng for not acting firmly against these protests. It seemed to some that Hu sympathised with the student protests. In the following year Deng abolished price controls. Prices rose. There were riots and Deng brought back price controls.

Tiananmen Square, 1989

Deng's determination to keep control and crush all opposition was shown in 1989 at Tiananmen Square.

In April 1989 Hu Yaobang died. His funeral, which was held on 22 April, led to a massive demonstration in Beijing. In the weeks that followed Tiananmen Square was the scene for daily rallies which demanded democratic reforms. The students occupied the square for several weeks, in spite of being ordered to leave.

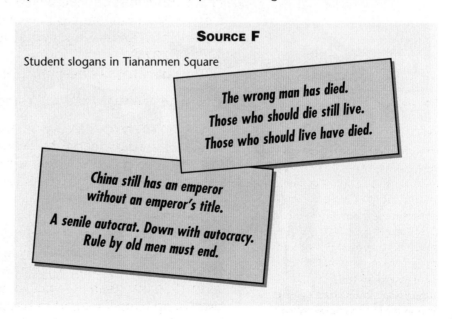

SOURCE F

Student slogans in Tiananmen Square

The wrong man has died.
Those who should die still live.
Those who should live have died.

China still has an emperor without an emperor's title.
A senile autocrat. Down with autocracy.
Rule by old men must end.

When the Soviet leader Mikhail Gorbachev visited China in the middle of May 1989 his official reception had to be shifted to the airport to avoid passing through Tiananmen Square where over a thousand students were on hunger strike. This seemed to show the weakness of China's leaders. The leaders hesitated for so long in acting against the students because:

- They had to be certain of the loyalty of the People's Liberation Army.

- There were many foreign journalists in Beijing. Force might have a bad effect on opinion abroad and reduce investment in China.

China's leaders, however, made sure that they had the loyalty of the People's Liberation Army. Nevertheless the first troops to arrive in Beijing seemed unwilling to use force. Deng now decided on force to remove the students. On the evening of 3 June troops broke down the barricades erected by the protestors and opened fire. Many of the casualties were shot in the streets around Tiananmen Square rather than in the square itself. By the early hours of 4 June all resistance had been crushed and the evidence that a massacre had occurred removed.

Source H

Fathers and Higgins, *Tiananmen,* 1989. The two authors were British journalists working in Beijing in 1989.

As bodies crumpled to the ground, the crowd behind them scattered. The army delivered a finale of machine gun fire from armoured troop carriers. Then, for a moment, the avenue was still: a hundred yard length of corpses, abandoned bicycles and terrified survivors. That first drama would repeat itself many times during the day.

Source G

Devastation in Chang'an Avenue, next to Tiananmen Square, 4 June 1989

The Chinese authorities later disclosed that 23 students had been killed accidentally. The figures were probably between 400 and 800. Later thousands more were arrested and imprisoned. At the Fourteenth Party Congress, held in October 1992, the dictatorship of the Communist Party was confirmed. No criticism or opposition was to be permitted.

Why was the massacre carried out?

There are several possible explanations:

- The Chinese government insisted that the students had foreign support and were trying to undo the Communist revolution.

- Deng certainly would not tolerate any opposition and saw the student movement as a genuine threat to his leadership.

- There was a power struggle to see who would take over once Deng retired or died. This was between Zhao Ziyang and Li Peng. Li Peng encouraged force against the students, believing this would win him the support of Deng.

SOURCE I

Army proclamation in Tiananmen Square, 2 am, 4 June 1989

A serious rebellion against the Revolution has broken out in the capital. The People's Liberation Army has been restrained for some days. However the rebellion must now be firmly counter-attacked.

Activity

You are a television reporter who witnesses the events of 3–4 June in Tiananmen Square. Write out your broadcast to the British people, describing what took place.

Questions

1   What do Sources **B** and **C** show about the effects of Deng's policies on the Chinese people?
2   According to Source **D**, what incentives were given to encourage one-child families? Why was there opposition to this policy?
3   What does Source **F** reveal about student attitudes to the Chinese leaders in 1989?
4   How useful is Source **G** to an historian studying the Tiananmen Square massacre?
5   Is the reason mentioned in Source **I** the real reason for the massacre?

CHINA'S RELATIONS WITH OTHER COUNTRIES

Four main ideas have influenced China's foreign affairs, especially since 1949.

1   China has a hatred of foreigners, especially Europeans and Americans. This dates from the time when foreigners ruled large parts of China under the emperors. They sympathise with countries wishing to fight for independence.

2   China is a poor peasant country and often allies with the poorer Third World countries of Africa and Asia.

3   The Chinese Communists achieved their victory in 1949 with little or no Russian or other foreign help. They therefore came to regard Russia as a friend, but an equal friend. This was not how Russia saw the situation, and they soon became enemies.

4   The USA was totally opposed to Communist China from the very start. They had supported Chiang Kai-shek and regarded the Communist victory as yet another advance for world Communism. During the years of the Cold War, China was almost completely cut off from contact with all other nations, except for fellow-Communists.

Relations with Russia

At first the two Communist nations were allies and Russia helped China's First Five-Year Plan. However, a split began to develop for several reasons. Mao did not like the Russian leader, Khrushchev. He seemed to be betraying Marx and Lenin in two ways:

- First by suggesting that Russia and the capitalist West should co-exist – that is, live together without hostility (p. 255).

- Second by giving privileges to Party members and experts so that they lost contact with the people.

Russia saw China as a junior partner and Mao found that the advice given to him in the 1920s was of no use at all. He had worked out his own form of Communism, based on the peasants. Mao saw himself as the true successor of Marx and Lenin. Mao was also annoyed at Russian refusal to help China develop an atomic bomb and to assist during their brief border war with India in 1962.

In 1960, the split became open and the Russians left China. The two sides drew further apart over the years. Mao disapproved of the Soviet invasion of Czechoslovakia in 1968. In addition there were frequent border clashes. Russia had been one of the countries making 'unequal' treaties' with China in the past. In 1969, shots were fired between soldiers on each side.

SOURCE A

An American view of relations between China and the USSR, 1979

Relations with the USA

The USA was hostile to Communist China from the very beginning. To the USA, the success of Mao in China was part of the worldwide advance of Communism in the years after the Second World War. The USA and its allies kept China out of the United Nations and completely isolated.

AMERICAN VIEW

To the USA, China was part of international Communism, a steadily advancing threat. The actions of China in Korea, Vietnam and Tibet seemed to confirm this. When the Chinese exploded a test nuclear bomb in 1964, the danger seemed all the greater.

CHINESE VIEW

The Chinese, however, saw things differently. The Americans were helping their old enemy, Chiang Kai-shek. They felt threatened by the huge American forces. The Chinese army was large, but poorly armed and not really capable of a foreign war. They feared a US nuclear attack. Their only defence seemed to be to develop their own nuclear weapons. American activity on China's borders in Korea and Vietnam seriously worried China's leaders.

SOURCE B

Statement from Richard Nixon in the Kennedy–Nixon Presidential TV debates, 1960

What do the Chinese Communists want? They don't want just Quemoy and Matsu. They don't just want Formosa [Taiwan]. They want the world.

With US support, China's seat at the United Nations was occupied by Chiang Kai-shek's Taiwan. Several times it was proposed that China should be admitted to the UN, but each time the USA and its allies voted against it. Eventually, however, in 1971, a majority of nations voted for the admission of China and the expulsion of Taiwan. This marked the end of China's isolation and the beginning of its move into a normal position among the nations.

Relations between the USA and China improved greatly in the 1970s. Following the experience of Vietnam, the USA began to change its foreign policy. It no longer seemed possible to fight Communism everywhere. President Nixon and his Secretary of State, Dr Kissinger, came to realise that the world contained several brands of Communism.

In 1972 Nixon visited China and met Mao. The new-found friendship increased as trade began to develop between China and Western countries. In 1971 Nixon had lifted the ban on trade with China. Within two years US–China trade had increased from a few million dollars to $500 million.

SOURCE C

Meeting between Mao and Nixon in Peking, February 1972

SOURCE D

The Times of India, February 1972

It all began at least ten years ago with the split between China and the Soviet Union. The more intelligent Americans began to realise that China was not a real threat to their vital interests. Two further developments took place before an American president could think about visiting China. As a result of the war in Vietnam the American people have lost the will and desire to serve as the world's policeman. At the same time, through two purges, one at the time of the Cultural Revolution and one last summer, Chairman Mao has got rid of those colleagues who want close relations with the USSR.

The Chinese were keen on closer relations with the USA:

• American trade and investment would help to build up Chinese industry.

• The USA would be a useful ally against Russia.

SOURCE E

An American cartoon at the time of President Nixon's visit to China in 1972

China's borders

Communist China has claimed all the territory traditionally ruled by the emperors. This has led to frequent border clashes with China's neighbours.

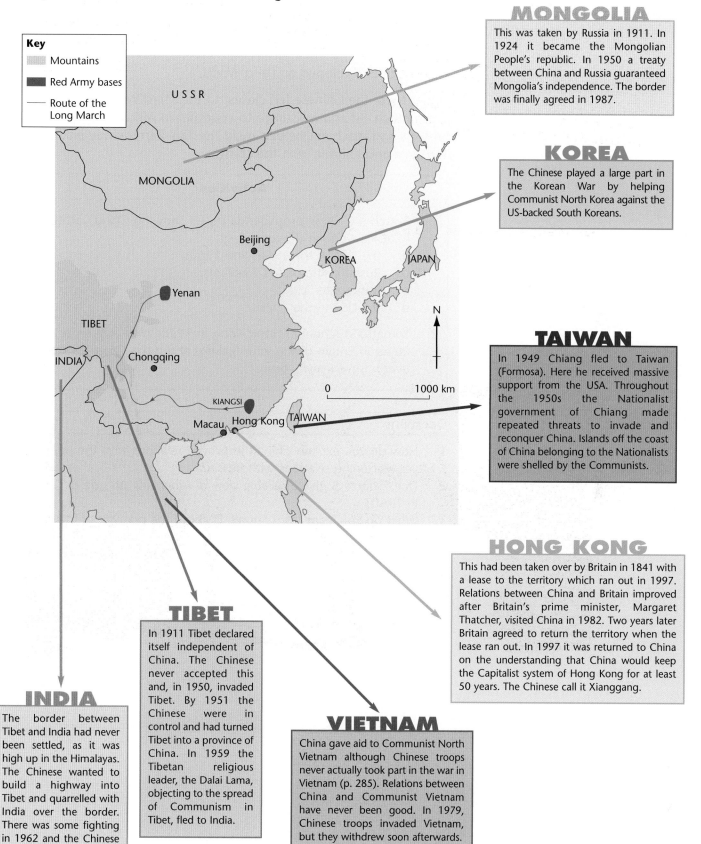

Key
- Mountains
- Red Army bases
- Route of the Long March

MONGOLIA
This was taken by Russia in 1911. In 1924 it became the Mongolian People's republic. In 1950 a treaty between China and Russia guaranteed Mongolia's independence. The border was finally agreed in 1987.

KOREA
The Chinese played a large part in the Korean War by helping Communist North Korea against the US-backed South Koreans.

TAIWAN
In 1949 Chiang fled to Taiwan (Formosa). Here he received massive support from the USA. Throughout the 1950s the Nationalist government of Chiang made repeated threats to invade and reconquer China. Islands off the coast of China belonging to the Nationalists were shelled by the Communists.

HONG KONG
This had been taken over by Britain in 1841 with a lease to the territory which ran out in 1997. Relations between China and Britain improved after Britain's prime minister, Margaret Thatcher, visited China in 1982. Two years later Britain agreed to return the territory when the lease ran out. In 1997 it was returned to China on the understanding that China would keep the Capitalist system of Hong Kong for at least 50 years. The Chinese call it Xianggang.

INDIA
The border between Tibet and India had never been settled, as it was high up in the Himalayas. The Chinese wanted to build a highway into Tibet and quarrelled with India over the border. There was some fighting in 1962 and the Chinese advanced slightly.

TIBET
In 1911 Tibet declared itself independent of China. The Chinese never accepted this and, in 1950, invaded Tibet. By 1951 the Chinese were in control and had turned Tibet into a province of China. In 1959 the Tibetan religious leader, the Dalai Lama, objecting to the spread of Communism in Tibet, fled to India.

VIETNAM
China gave aid to Communist North Vietnam although Chinese troops never actually took part in the war in Vietnam (p. 285). Relations between China and Communist Vietnam have never been good. In 1979, Chinese troops invaded Vietnam, but they withdrew soon afterwards.

Relations with the rest of the world

Chinese foreign policy divides the world into three groups:

- The superpowers – the USA and Russia.

- The developed nations of Europe, and other similar countries such as Canada and Australia.

- The underdeveloped or Third World.

Under Mao, the Chinese felt closest to the Third World. China has given much aid and assistance to countries in Africa. Chinese workers and machines helped build the Tan–Zam railway linking Tanzania and Zambia with the coast.

Activities

1   Sketch a Chinese propaganda poster showing China's attitude to at least one of the following:
    a   the USA in the 1950s and 1960s.
    b   Russia in the period 1949–60.
    c   Russia after 1960.
    d   the USA in the 1970s.

2   You attend school in Hong Kong in 1990. Write a letter to a friend in Britain giving your feelings about the Chinese take-over in seven years' time.

Questions

1   How do you explain China's improved relations with the USA and yet worsening relations with Russia?
2   Does Source **B** give a reliable view of America's attitude to China in 1960?
3   What do you learn from Source **D** about the reasons for improved relations between China and the USA?
4   What points are the cartoonists trying to make in Sources **A** and **E**?
5   Explain China's relations with the following:
    a   Tibet.
    b   Hong Kong.
    c   India.

Summary and revision

CHINA 1900–11

This section includes:

- The people of China, especially the plight of the peasants.

- How China was ruled – the emperor and the Mandarins.

- Foreign influence in China and the reaction of the Chinese.

- Causes, events and results of the Boxer Rebellion 1900.

- Causes of 1911 and influence of Sun Yat-sen.

- Events of the 'Double Tenth' and the new republic.

Revision questions

1   Why were many Chinese peasants unhappy in 1900?
2   What were the Mandarins and the Manchu dynasty?
3   Why did most Chinese resent foreign influence?
4   Describe the Boxer Rebellion?
5   Who was Sun Yat-sen and what part did he play in the revolution of 1911?
6   What happened on the 'Double Tenth'?

CHINA 1911–28

In this section, you need to include:

- The rule of Yuan Shi-kai.

- The impact of the First World War.

- The rule of the warlords.

- The May 4th Movement and its importance.

- The emergence of the Kuomintang and Chiang Kai-shek.

- The Civil War and reasons for the success of the Kuomintang.

Revision questions

1   Why did Sun not become president of the new republic?
2   Who was Yuan Shi-kai? Did he allow democracy?
3   What impact did the First World War have on China?
4   Explain the importance of the following:
    a   the May 4th Movement.
    b   the Kuomintang.
    c   the warlords.
5   What part did Chiang Kai-shek play in the Civil War of the 1920s? Why did he turn on the Communists?
6   Account for the victory of the Kuomintang in the Civil War.

Mao Tse Tung and the rise of Communism 1920–49

This section includes:

- Mao and the setting up of the Communist Party.

- Reorganising the Communists 1927–34.

- The Long March and its importance.

- China under the Kuomintang – why was Chiang unpopular?

- War with Japan and its importance for the Communists and the Kuomintang.

- Reasons for Communist victory 1945–49.

Revision questions

1   Why did Mao become involved in Communism?
2   How did he change the aims and organisation of the Party in the late 1920s and early 1930s? Why did this cause opposition?
3   Account for the popularity of the Communists in the 1930s and the unpopularity of Chiang and the Kuomintang.
4   Describe the Long March. Why was it so important in the development of the Communist Party?
5   Explain the war against Japan and Communist tactics. Were they successful?
6   In the struggle to get control of China, 1945–9, Mao and the Communists were eventually successful. Explain why.

China under Mao 1949–76

For this section, you need to understand:

- Problems faced by Mao in 1949.

- Changes in government, industry, agriculture, education, health and the position of women.

- Reasons for the Great Leap Forward and its impact.

- Reasons for the Cultural Revolution and its effects on China.

Revision questions

1   Explain the government established by Mao. How did it ensure control and remove opposition?
2   How did the following change in the first ten years of Communist rule:
    a   industry?
    b   agriculture?
    c   the position of women?
3   Why did Mao decide on the Great Leap Forward?
4   Describe its main features.
5   Was it a success? Explain your answer.
6   What effects did it have on Mao's position?
7   Why did Mao decide on the Cultural Revolution?
8   What impact did it have on China?

CHINA UNDER DENG 1977–90

This section contains the following:

- Changes in policy under Deng in industry, agriculture and education.

- Birth control and its effects.

- Political control and the emergence of student opposition.

- The causes, events and results of Tiananmen Square.

Revision questions

1 What were Deng's aims?
2 How did he change policies in industry and agriculture?
3 Why did China decide to limit family size? Was this popular?
4 Who were the 'Gang of Four'? Explain their trial in 1980.
5 Why did student unrest emerge in the 1980s?
6 Explain the events at Tiananmen Square. What effects did these have on world opinion?

CHINA'S RELATIONS WITH OTHER COUNTRIES

In this section, you will need to understand:

- Factors which influenced China's foreign policy.

- Relations with Russia – friendship and then hostility.

- Relations with the USA – hostility and then friendship.

- China and her neighbours – various disputes.

- China and the Third World.

Revision questions

1 Why did relations with Russia change from friendship to hostility?
2 Explain the rivalry between China and the USA 1949–72.
3 Why did the two countries become more friendly in the 1970s?
4 Explain China's relations with the following neighbouring countries:
   a Tibet.
   b India.
   c Korea.
   d Vietnam.
   e Hong Kong.
5 What is meant by the 'Third World'? Why is China close to countries of the Third World?

Index

Page numbers in italic refer to definitions/explanations